UNRAVELED

Six years after its enactment, Obamacare remains one of the most controversial, divisive, and enduring political issues in America. In this much-anticipated follow-up to his critically acclaimed *Unprecedented: The Constitutional Challenge to Obamacare* (2013), Professor Blackman argues that, to implement the law, President Obama has broken promises about cancelled insurance policies, exceeded the traditional bounds of executive power, and infringed on religious liberty. At the same time, conservative opponents have stopped at nothing to unravel Obamacare, including a three-week government shutdown, four Supreme Court cases, and fifty repeal votes. This legal thriller provides the definitive account of the battle to stop Obamacare from being "woven into the fabric of America." *Unraveled* is essential reading to understand the future of the Affordable Care Act in our gridlocked government in 2016, and beyond.

Josh Blackman is a constitutional law professor at the South Texas College of Law, Houston. He is the author of *Unprecedented: The Constitutional Challenge to Obamacare* (2013). Professor Blackman regularly provides public commentary on constitutional matters, and his work has appeared in the *New York Times*, *Wall Street Journal*, *Washington Post*, *USA Today*, *L.A. Times*, and other national publications.

Unraveled

OBAMACARE, RELIGIOUS LIBERTY, AND EXECUTIVE POWER

JOSH BLACKMAN

CAMBRIDGE
UNIVERSITY PRESS

One Liberty Plaza, 20th Floor, New York, NY 10006, USA

Cambridge University Press is part of the University of Cambridge.

It furthers the University's mission by disseminating knowledge in the pursuit of education, learning, and research at the highest international levels of excellence.

www.cambridge.org
Information on this title: www.cambridge.org/9781107169012

© Josh Blackman 2016

First published 2016

Printed in the United States of America by Sheridan Books, Inc. in 2016

A catalogue record for this publication is available from the British Library.

ISBN 978-1-107-16901-2 Hardback

For my parents, Iris and Jaimie,
who are my inspiration and motivation

"It seems so cynical to want to take coverage away from millions of people; to take care away from people who need it the most; to punish millions with higher costs of care and unravel what's now been woven into the fabric of America. And that kind of cynicism flies in the face of our history ... So five years in, what we are talking about it is no longer just a law. It's no longer just a theory. This isn't even just about the Affordable Care Act or Obamacare ... This is now part of the fabric of how we care for one another."

– President Barack Obama

"Congress passed the Affordable Care Act to improve health insurance markets, not to destroy them. If at all possible, we must interpret the Act in a way that is consistent with the former, and avoids the latter."

– Chief Justice John G. Roberts, Jr.

"Under all the usual rules of interpretation, in short, the Government should lose this case. But normal rules of interpretation seem always to yield to the overriding principle of the present Court: The Affordable Care Act must be saved ... We should start calling this law SCOTUScare."

– Justice Antonin Scalia

Contents

About the Author

Josh Blackman is Associate Professor of Law at the South Texas College of Law in Houston, where he specializes in constitutional law, the Supreme Court, and the intersection of law and technology. He authored the critically acclaimed *Unprecedented: The Constitutional Challenge to Obamacare* (2013).

Blackman has published three dozen law review articles, and his commentary has appeared in the *New York Times*, the *Wall Street Journal*, the *Washington Post*, *USA Today*, the *L.A. Times*, and other national publications. He is President of the Harlan Institute, the founder of FantasySCOTUS – the Internet's premier Supreme Court Fantasy League – and blogs at JoshBlackman.com. Josh serves as an adjunct scholar at the Cato Institute, and was selected by *Forbes Magazine* for the "30 Under 30" in Law and Policy.

Author's Note

By fate or design, my young career has tracked the trajectory of the Affordable Care Act. In September 2009, when I served as a law clerk after graduating from law school, I launched a blog to focus on constitutional and other legal issues. On my fourth day of blogging, I covered this new bill called Obamacare, and discussed whether the individual mandate could force someone to buy insurance. In November 2009, I was by chance present at a meeting where the legal strategy to challenge the individual mandate was hatched. In March 2010, I was unceremoniously asked to cut short my visit to the new Capitol Visitor Center; President Obama was about to enter, and give a final rallying call to House Democrats to vote for the Affordable Care Act (ACA). I emerged from the building to thousands of Tea Parties chantings "Kill the Bill."

After constitutional challenges to Obamacare were filed, my best friends and colleagues served as the attorneys and scholars developing the groundwork to attack the individual mandate. Throughout 2010 and 2011 while clerking, I continued to blog from a distance, based on closely following the case and on insights I gained from key players. In November 2011, shortly after the Supreme Court accepted review of the ACA cases, I was hired as a law professor at the South Texas College of Law in Houston. It was around that time that I decided to write a book about the legal challenges to Obamacare. I didn't quite know how the case would be resolved, but I knew there was an important story to be preserved for history.

Leading up to the Supreme Court's June 2012 decision in *NFIB v. Sebelius*, I assembled the chronology of how the challenge began and how it wound its way through the courts. The only uncertainty was how the book would end. To expedite the publishing process, I wrote two alternate endings: one in which the Supreme Court upheld the mandate on a 5–4 vote, with Justice Kennedy casting the decisive vote, and another in which the Court invalidated the mandate on a 5–4 vote, also with Justice Kennedy casting the decisive vote. Needless to say, neither happened, and I had to write the final ending, with the chief justice saving the law. In September 2013, I published my first book, *Unprecedented: The Constitutional Challenge to Obamacare*. The inexplicable and unexpected ending of *NFIB v. Sebelius* injected a strong political element into the legal thriller, and made the case unlike any other in modern times. But it also left the story of Obamacare unfinished.

Until 2013, I largely remained an interested observer, the *Rosencrantz and Guildenstern* of Obamacare – there at all the right moments, talking to all the key actors, but not doing anything of actual importance. But since 2013, I have become an active participant. I have submitted amicus briefs supporting the challengers in two Supreme Court cases: *King v. Burwell* (2015) and *Zubik v. Burwell* (2016). The briefs were filed on behalf of the Cato Institute, a libertarian think tank, where I am an adjunct scholar (an unpaid position). I have lectured nationwide, and authored more than two dozen articles about Obamacare. Details of these speeches and publications can be found at JoshBlackman.com/blog/c-v/. My impact on the Obamacare saga became clear when I mailed copies of *Unprecedented* to each of the nine justices. One wrote back, "I read your blog often." During my interview with a senior Justice Department attorney about *King v. Burwell*, he told me that he had read my blogging on the case, but was not persuaded. I am no longer just an interested observer.

I offer these disclosures not as a humblebrag, but to provide readers with the appropriate basis to assess my writing. With *Unraveled*, I attempted to bring the same neutral tone that I brought to *Unprecedented*, but I concede that my predispositions on *Hobby Lobby*, *King*, and *Zubik* were far stronger than with *NFIB v. Sebelius*. Despite my criticism of the ACA's legality and implementation, I have remained largely agnostic on the underlying questions of public health policy, and do not offer suggestions for future reform.

The most difficult aspect of writing a book that chronicles the ACA from 2013 through 2016 is coverage: what to cover, what not to cover, and when to cover it. Inherently, this is a very subjective decision. The inclusion of certain topics, exclusion of others, and presentation in a specific order are all essential to telling this compelling story. My goal was to use a bird's-eye view for most of this period, and to swoop down to a ground-level perspective for the major events. The choice of where to stay at a 30,000-foot perspective, and where to go granular, was an editorial decision I made.

It was impossible to tell the story purely chronologically, because political actors and judges alike do not always do things in sequences that make sense. To that end, sometimes the book will discuss an event with a date that does not fit in with the current timeframe. Additionally, the format of Supreme Court oral arguments – where each attorney is asked questions separately for thirty minutes – is not easy to follow along. My goal in discussing court cases is to blend the arguments together to create a faithful narrative that flows, rather than leaving it to the readers to pick out what was important from both sides. (This is the intractable task of the dedicated journalists who follow the Court every day.) All of the quotations, however, are reproduced from the transcripts, with slight editing for continuity and comprehensibility.

Finally, this book contains information from private conversations I had with attorneys for the challengers, government officials, and other Court watchers on "background." That means that I could not attribute specific quotations to them. These remarks have been reconstructed, from memory or notes, in as close-to-accurate form as I could without betraying confidences. I corroborated any accounts by cross-referencing their claims with others familiar with the situation.

I sincerely hope you enjoy reading this story as much as I enjoyed writing it.

Josh Blackman
Houston, Texas
July 2016

Prologue

During his first State of the Union address in February 2009, President Obama announced that "health care reform cannot wait, it must not wait, and it will not wait another year." At that instant in time, no one could have anticipated how the Affordable Care Act would fundamentally transform our polity. Eight years later, Obamacare remains one of the most controversial, divisive, and enduring political issues in America. I do not use *Obamacare* as a pejorative, but as a descriptor of the Affordable Care Act's divisive political valence. The partisan battle around health care reform, separate from the law's costs and benefits – and there are both – has taken on a life of its own. All three branches of government, and the body politic itself, have balkanized over Obamacare.

To its supporters, the Affordable Care Act (ACA) has expanded access to health insurance for twenty million Americans, moving the United States closer to universal coverage. To its opponents, the law amounts to an unconstitutional federal takeover of health care that accelerates us along the road to socialized medicine. Conservatives have stopped at nothing to destroy Obamacare, including a three-week government shutdown, four Supreme Court cases, and fifty-plus repeal votes. To defend the law, the White House injected new fissures into the already fragmented relationship between church and state, and pushed the bounds of executive power to suspend the law's onerous mandates. As its challengers fought to unravel Obamacare, the president derided those who would "unravel what has now been woven into the fabric of America."

Unraveled chronicles the story of how Obamacare has rippled throughout, and forever altered, our nation's political, cultural, and legal fault lines. This saga unfolds in eight parts.

PART I: THE PROMISE OF OBAMACARE
(JANUARY 20, 2009–JUNE 28, 2012)

From Obamacare's inception, the president sought to avoid the paradox of Hillarycare, the Clintons' ill-fated effort to reform health care two decades earlier. Americans overwhelmingly favored health care reform but simultaneously favored their own coverage. To change the health care system for some, the law had to change the health care system for all. This dilemma was resolved through an unkeepable promise: "If you like your health care plan, you can keep your health care plan." With this assurance in place, the president championed the law to the American people, extolling its guarantees, subsidization, and expansion of coverage.

Conceived as a compromise – it was based on a proposal from the conservative Heritage Foundation – the ACA nonetheless disappointed both sides of the aisle. Democrats vigorously advocated for a plan that would go further to ensure universal coverage. Republicans fiercely opposed the plan that went too far centralizing our health care system. In the end, recognizing the historical potential for the law, progressives rallied around the ACA. The bill was narrowly approved in the Senate, with sixty Democrats overcoming a unified Republican filibuster. The bill cleared the House of Representatives on a straight party-line vote. No other major social legislation had ever been enacted without some bipartisan support.

From its birth, Obamacare was mired in lawfare. Minutes after the triumphant president signed the bill, twenty-six states challenged the constitutionality of the law's individual mandate. This two-year legal battle culminated in the Supreme Court's decision upholding the ACA. But with its first judicial approval, the realities of health care reform would now meet the realities of political gridlock.

PART II: CONSCIENCE AND CONTRACEPTION
(JUNE 29, 2012–MAY 1, 2013)

During the legislative debates over the Affordable Care Act, pro-life Democrats at first resisted the bill, fearing that it would fund abortions. To assuage these concerns, on the eve of the House of Representative's vote, President Obama issued an executive order that reaffirmed long-standing prohibitions on federal payments for abortions. But this "signing statement on steroids" completely missed what would become the Affordable Care Act's major cultural clash. The Women's Health Amendment required employer-sponsored insurance to provide "preventive care" for women, without any copayments. Its sponsor refused to define in the amendment what "preventive care" entailed, but insisted that it would not include "abortion services." With that assurance, pro-life Democrats supported the Women's Health Amendment, and it became part of the ACA.

The Department of Health and Human Services (HHS) later determined that the Women's Health Amendment required employers to pay for the full range of FDA-approved contraceptives. This included emergency contraceptives, such as Plan B, which some religions view as abortifacients. The ACA did not have *any* conscience clause that would exclude religious employers from the contraceptive mandate. As a result, the Obama administration turned to executive action to issue a series of workarounds to the mandate – none of which fully relieved faith-based objections.

Initially, only houses of worship were exempted from the mandate. Religious charities that helped those outside the faith – such as the Little Sisters of the Poor, an order of nuns that cares for the elderly – were still required to pay for the contraception. The Conference of Bishops wrote that "even Jesus would not qualify" because he served people of different beliefs. After widespread outrage, the administration created a second accommodation. Insurance companies would now pay for contraceptive coverage under the auspices of the nonprofit's plan. The nonprofits objected to this workaround, which they said "hijacked" their plans. The lawfulness of this accommodation would not be considered by the Supreme Court until 2016. First, the federal courts would have to decide whether for-profit corporations could even exercise religion. Leading the charge against the mandate was Hobby Lobby, a national chain of craft stores, whose "faith was woven into their business." Their case would wind up before the Supreme Court in 2014.

PART III: SHUTDOWN (MAY 21, 2013–SEPTEMBER 30, 2013)

After President Obama defeated former governor Mitt Romney – whose "Romneycare" served as a basis for Obamacare – the White House began the process of implementing the ACA. But many in the White House worried about the administration's readiness for the challenge. The president's top advisers urged him to appoint a "health reform 'czar'" who could oversee the massive undertaking of establishing a federal exchange. The marketplace would allow people to purchase subsidized policies online. Those warnings went unheeded, and the management structure to build HealthCare.gov was undisciplined, unaccountable, and unprepared. President Obama promised that the website would make getting covered as easy as ordering "a TV on Amazon." It was more like a "train wreck."

Perhaps the only saving grace for Obamacare in its early days was that on the same day the exchange opened, the federal government closed. In a final effort to halt Obamacare before it went into effect, conservatives urged Congress to block any budget that funded the health care law. This movement culminated in Senator Ted Cruz's twenty-one-hour speech on the Senate floor, urging Americans to #MakeDCListen. Though not a filibuster – it could not delay a scheduled funding vote – Cruz's advocacy rallied the Republican-controlled House to defund Obamacare. The president and Senate Democrats refused to negotiate on any aspects of the ACA, and House Republicans refused to fund the law. With no budget in place, the shutdown began on October 1. Ultimately, after three weeks of park closures and federal furloughs, Republicans capitulated. Obamacare was fully funded, and the shutdown ended. Now, all eyes turned back to HealthCare.gov.

PART IV: OBAMACARE UNRAVELS
(OCTOBER 1, 2013–DECEMBER 30, 2013)

The period from October 1 through December 30 was a roller-coaster ride for Obamacare. When HealthCare.gov launched on October 1, 2013, the web site completely crashed, and only six people were able to register that day. Soon the president realized that the federal exchange, which he later called a "well-documented disaster," jeopardized the entire health care law. Now all eyes turned to the so-called "tech surge." This small group of Silicon Valley engineers was charged with salvaging the federal exchange, and the health care reform itself. Slowly but steadily the website improved, but the next crisis emerged.

During the fall of 2013, millions of Americans received insurance cancellation notices because their policies were no longer compliant with the ACA's mandates. The Obama administration had issued regulations making it even harder to grandfather old plans. After widespread outrage, the president apologized to those who relied on his promise that they could keep the policies they like. "I am sorry that they are finding themselves in this situation," he said. Politifact rated Obama's oft-repeated assurance the "lie of the year." To salvage the rollout, the president took a series of executive actions to delay, suspend, and modify the ACA's mandates. In a short span of time, the White House put the employer mandate on hold, waived the individual mandate, and grandfathered old plans that were not compliant with the ACA. Each of these short-term measures threatened the long-term viability of the exchanges. These actions also tested the bounds of executive power, and were challenged in court.

Despite the awful launch, and political fallout from the cancellations, the federal exchange had a remarkable turnaround. By the end of December 2013, more than one million customers had enrolled on the marketplace. After the final deadline in April 2014, the ranks swelled to eight million enrollees – an inconceivable number only two months earlier. There was a new reality: the ACA had an unmistakable impact on millions of Americans through its expansion of Medicaid, guarantee of coverage for all, and subsidized policies on the insurance exchanges. Republicans who sought to repeal the law now confronted the burden of taking away coverage from those who liked Obamacare, and wanted to keep it.

PART V: RELIGIOUS LIBERTY (DECEMBER 31, 2013–JULY 21, 2014)

When the Affordable Care Act would go live on January 1, 2014, so too would the contraceptive mandate. By that time, most of the religious nonprofits had already received temporary court orders, putting the mandate on hold. But not the Little Sisters of the Poor. On New Year's Eve, the order of nuns filed a last-minute appeal with the Supreme Court. Hours before she dropped the ball in Times Square, Justice Sotomayor answered their prayer for relief. The contraceptive mandate would be put on hold for the nonprofit as their case was appealed. But for-profit corporations, such as Hobby Lobby, would have their day in Court much sooner.

On the heels of the *Citizens United* decision, which recognized that corporations have rights of free speech, Hobby Lobby urged the Court to protect the corporation's right of free exercise. The craft store argued that the ACA imposed a substantial burden on its religious identity by mandating payment for certain contraceptives. The Obama administration countered that a corporation cannot exercise religion, and even if it could, paying for someone else's birth control doesn't burden faith. Granting an exemption to these employers, the government contended, would harm female employees, and deny them the ACA's benefits.

In a 5–4 decision, the Court ruled for Hobby Lobby, finding that certain closely-held corporations could establish a religious identity. However, Justice Kennedy's concurring opinion left open the possibility that the burden on female employees could trump the religious objection. Justice Ruth Bader Ginsburg, a.k.a. "The Notorious RBG," wrote a fierce dissent that made her a social media sensation. She later suggested that her five male colleagues in the majority suffered from a "blind spot." The question of conscience and contraception would come back to the Court two years later. But first, the justices would have to wrangle with the federal exchanges.

PART VI: NUCLEAR FALLOUT (JULY 22, 2014–
NOVEMBER 21, 2014)

To counter rising health care costs, the Affordable Care Act allowed states to sell federally subsidized insurance policies through online exchanges. If a state declined to establish an exchange – it could not be forced to act – the federal HealthCare.gov would operate as a backup exchange. The Obama administration treated the federal exchange as equivalent to the state exchange, so the same level of subsidies would be available on HealthCare.gov to reduce premiums. But then a benefits lawyer from South Carolina named Tom Christina read the 3,000-page law. To his surprise, he observed that subsidies were limited to customers "enrolled in through an Exchange *established by the State*." In December 2010, Christina presented his findings that the subsidies were available only on the state exchanges, and not on the federal exchange.

ACA opponents recognized the significance of Christina's finding and opened a new two-front attack on the ACA. First, states were urged not to establish exchanges. Second, legal challenges were filed to halt the payments of subsidies in the three-dozen states that did not establish exchanges. The effect of this "second wave" was the same: render the federal exchange, without subsidies, inoperable. If successful, Obamacare would unravel. On July 22, 2014, two federal courts of appeal divided on whether HealthCare.gov could provide subsidized insurance. Shortly after the circuit split formed, the Supreme Court accepted review of its third Obamacare case in four years.

PART VII: SUBSIDIZING OBAMACARE
(NOVEMBER 22, 2014–JUNE 26, 2015)

King v. Burwell would decide whether the Affordable Care Act permits the payment of subsidies on the federal exchanges. Although this case turned on fairly mundane principles of statutory interpretation, the import of the case was critical. If the Court ruled that federal exchange could not provide subsidies, ACA policies in those states would be unaffordable. Ultimately, the burden would fall to the legislative branch to provide the payments. During oral arguments, Justice Scalia asked Solicitor General Donald Verrilli whether Congress could so amend the ACA. He answered, sarcastically, "This Congress?" President Obama insisted he would only sign a one-sentence bill that provided the subsidies, and do nothing else. Republicans saw *King v. Burwell* as a "mulligan," an opportunity to build a "bridge away from Obamacare." A compromise in our gridlocked government seemed unlikely.

After oral arguments in March 2015, once again all eyes turned to Chief Justice Roberts. Three years earlier, the chief had voted to save the Affordable Care Act's individual mandate. As he did three years earlier, President Obama spoke publicly about the pending case. "It seems so cynical to want to take coverage away from millions of people," the president said. He could not understand why anyone would want to *"unravel* what's now been woven into the fabric of America."

The chief justice would agree. His majority opinion for six justices ruled that subsidies could be paid on the federal exchange. "Congress passed the Affordable Care Act to improve health insurance markets, not to destroy them," Roberts wrote. "If at all possible, we must interpret the Act in a way that is consistent with the former, and avoids the latter." In a blistering dissent – the last he would read from the bench – Justice Scalia charged that "the normal rules of interpretation seem always to yield to the overriding principle of the present Court: The Affordable Care Act must be saved." Nino quipped, "We should start calling this law SCOTUScare." Shortly after his victory, President Obama declared, "Five years in, this is no longer about a law ... This is not about the Affordable Care Act as legislation, or Obamacare as a political football. This is health care in America." The battle was not over. Not by a long shot.

PART VIII: THE NUNS (JUNE 26, 2015–MAY 16, 2016)

On July 16, 2015, the face of the Republican Party was forever altered – and he arrived on a gilded escalator in midtown Manhattan. Although all of the GOP presidential candidates promised to repeal and replace Obamacare, Donald J. Trump had been a long-time champion of universal health care. No longer. He promised to "repeal and replace [Obamacare] with something terrific." On the Democratic side, former secretary of state Hillary Clinton and Senator Bernie Sanders debated about the future direction of the ACA. Sanders proposed universal coverage through Medicaid for all. Clinton countered that his proposal was "naïve" and pledged to improve the ACA. Soon, the Supreme Court and the presidential election would collide.

On February 13, 2016, Justice Antonin Scalia passed away suddenly and unexpectedly at the age of seventy-nine. Within hours of his death, President Obama promised to fulfill his "constitutional responsibilities to nominate a successor in due time." Republicans countered that no hearings would be held, regardless of the nominee, until after the election. The Court was down to eight justices for its fourth Obamacare case in five years.

On March 23, 2016 – the ACA's sixth anniversary – the Supreme Court would hear the appeal of the Little Sisters of the Poor and other religious nonprofits. They sought to be exempted from the contraceptive mandate, arguing that the government's accommodation still made them complicit in sin. The government countered that under the accommodation, the insurance companies – and not the nonprofits – paid for the contraceptives. This work-around, the Obama administration explained, did not impose a substantial burden on their free exercise, and it was the only way to "seamlessly" provide female employees with contraceptive coverage.

The justices were called on to resolve this conflict between traditional values of conscience and modern access to contraception. They couldn't. In an unprecedented order, eight justices proposed yet another accommodation – which satisfied neither side – and asked the lower courts to consider it. The short-handed Court, unable to reach a decision, instead punted the case to return when the bench was full. The gridlock between Congress and the president had spilled over into the judiciary.

* * *

The ACA has endured attacks from all directions. During its first act, from 2009 to 2012, the law survived the primary constitutional challenge to its mandate. During its second act, from 2012 to 2016, Obamacare limped through its implementation, and was wounded by several court defeats, but endured. For its third act, in 2017 and beyond, Obamacare must stand on its own. That will prove to be its most formidable challenge. The future of the Affordable Care Act is yet unwritten. This book offers an early attempt to study its past.

PART I

The Promise of Obamacare
(January 20, 2009–June 28, 2012)

1

"If You Like Your Insurance, You Can Keep Your Insurance"

1.1. "HARRY AND LOUISE"

The story of Obamacare begins with Hillarycare. Shortly after his inauguration, Clinton established the Task Force on National Health Care Reform, which would be chaired by First Lady Hillary Rodham Clinton.[1] With a nod to President Franklin Roosevelt's blitz of progressive reform, the Task Force's mission was to "prepare health care reform legislation to be submitted to Congress within 100 days of our taking office."[2] Mrs. Clinton set out to develop a plan to provide universal health care for all Americans. Thomas Friedman wrote in the *New York Times* that it was "the most powerful official post ever assigned to a First Lady."[3] In a preview of the health care lawfare to come, the First Lady's participation in the Task Force's closed-door meetings was temporarily enjoined by a federal court – a decision that was later reversed on appeal.[4]

---

[1] Adam Clymer et al., *The Health Care Debate: What Went Wrong? How the Health Care Campaign Collapsed – A Special Report; For Health Care, Times was a Killer*, N.Y. TIMES (Aug. 28, 1994), nyti.ms/1QNAC7l.

[2] William J. Clinton, Remarks and an Exchange with Reporters on Health Care Reform (Jan. 25, 1993), perma.cc/E4H7-736Y.

[3] Thomas L. Friedman, *Hillary Clinton to Head Panel on Health Care*, N.Y. TIMES (Jan. 25, 1993), nyti.ms/1QNAJj7.

[4] On March 10, 1993, U.S. District Judge Royce Lamberth granted a preliminary injunction to halt the Task Force's meetings, finding that because Clinton was not a government employee, the Task Force could not convene behind closed-doors. Four months later, the D.C. Circuit Court of Appeals reversed and ruled that the First Lady was considered a government official and therefore the Task Force did not have to comply with the federal open meetings law. Ass'n of Am. Physicians & Surgeons, Inc. v. Clinton, 813 F. Supp. 82, 83 (D.D.C.) *rev'd*, 997 F.2d 898 (D.C. Cir. 1993). Four years later, long after the Health Security Act was defeated, Judge Lamberth once again ruled against the Task Force, criticizing it for "[a]cting dishonestly." The D.C. Circuit, again, reversed the judgment. Ass'n of Am. Physicians & Surgeons, Inc. v. Clinton, 989 F. Supp. 8, 15 (D.D.C. 1997) *rev'd*, 187 F.3d 655, 656 (D.C. Cir. 1999).

In September 1993, Mrs. Clinton asked Congress to join her and the president to "give the American people the health security they deserve," so that "every American will receive a health security card guaranteeing a comprehensive package of benefits that can never be taken away under any circumstance."[5] Under the proposed *Health Security Act*, all citizens would be required to enroll in a health plan.[6] Those with low incomes would pay nothing to enter these plans. The cornerstone of the Act was a requirement for employers to provide health insurance for their employees – a precursor to the so-called employer mandate. Dubbed by critics as *Hillarycare*, this proposal would be Clinton's first, but not last, attempt at reforming the American health care system. During her 2008 and 2016 campaigns for the presidency, she would often boast of the "scars from that experience."[7]

The immediate reaction to the plan was mixed. A poll conducted by *Time* in September 1993 found that the public was conflicted: 20% reported that the plan would make their families better off, 21% said it would make them worse off, and 57% felt they would be unaffected.[8] The tepid support would soon be replaced by broad opposition.

That month, the Health Insurance Association of America – the health insurance lobbying group – launched a $20 million advertising campaign to attack Hillarycare. The group aired a series of commercials depicting a husband and wife, named Harry and Louise, sitting at a kitchen table. As they pored over the details of the thousand-page bill, they worried about its impact on their finances and coverage.[9]

In one commercial, the phrase, "Sometime in the future" flashed across a black background, as slow piano music played. Louise, looking at a stack of bills, worries, "This was covered under our old plan." Harry answers, "Oh yeah, that was a good one, wasn't it?" A narrator intones, "Things are changing and not all for the better. The government may force us to pick from a few health care plans designed by government bureaucrats." Louise explains, "Having a choice we don't like is no choice at all." Harry begins, "They choose," and

---

5   Adam Clymer, *CLINTON'S HEALTH PLAN; Hillary Clinton, on Capitol Hill, Wins Raves, if Not a Health Plan*, N.Y. TIMES (Sept. 28, 1993), nyti.ms/1W3vohD.

6   Health Security Act, H.R. 3600, 103rd Cong. (1994), perma.cc/CGC4-8TJN.

7   Mark Leibovich, *Clinton Proudly Talks of Scars While Keeping Her Guard Up*, N.Y. TIMES (Dec. 9, 2007), nyti.ms/1Tqf2rm; *see also* Mark Leibovich, *Re-Re-Re-Reintroducing Hillary Clinton*, N.Y. TIMES MAG. (Jul. 15, 2015), nyti.ms/1rqYQQ9.

8   *Pulling It Together: What Will Health Care Reform Do for Me?*, KAISER FAMILY FOUNDATION (Feb. 24, 2009), perma.cc/C8KA-46TL.

9   *"Harry and Louise" Health Care Ads (Clinton Administration)*, YOUTUBE (Aug. 26, 2014), youtu.be/Cd_xPNT1Fh8.

Louise finishes her thought, "We lose." The narrator returned, "If we let the government choose, we lose."[10]

New rounds of commercials reinforced the same theme that the Health Security Act would limit choice and force the couple to lose their existing coverage. In one spot, Louise worries about "rationing" and "long waits for health care."[11] In another spot, Louise tells her co-worker that "Congress may load a bunch of new taxes for their health-care plan, *including* a tax on plans they think are too expensive."[12] (This proposal would return as the Affordable Care Act's unpopular "Cadillac Tax," which at the urging of candidate Hillary Clinton, was delayed until 2020.) In another commercial, Louise laments, "The government caps how much the country can spend on all health care and says: 'That's it!' There's got to be a better way." The messaging was clear: Americans wanted to keep their plans and did not want government to control the availability of options.

The year long advertising campaign was seen as a " 'catalyst' " in "grabb[ing] control of the debate" over health care reform.[13] In less than a year, surveys showed that Americans who thought the law would make them worse off jumped from 21% to 37%.[14] "People feared the Clinton proposal might force them out of their current health care arrangements," The Kaiser Family Foundation observed.[15] "That was undoubtedly a factor in undermining the plan." The commercials were so effective that President Clinton recorded a Democratic National Committee–sponsored response.[16] "Many of you still have doubts about reform and I sure can understand why," Clinton related.[17] "I see the same TV ads you do." The president observed, "Never in the history of the Republic has so much money been spent to defeat an idea."[18]

During the January 1994 State of the Union address, the White House sought to assuage fears that Americans would lose their choice of doctors. An early draft of President Clinton's address offered this assurance: "You'll pick the health plan and the doctor of your choice."[19] However, that wasn't quite right. White

---

[10]   *Id.*

[11]   PAUL RUTHERFORD, ENDLESS PROPAGANDA: THE ADVERTISING OF PUBLIC GOODS 247 (2000).

[12]   *Id.*

[13]   *Id.* at 248.

[14]   *Pulling It Together, supra* note 8.

[15]   *Id.*

[16]   RUTHERFORD, *supra* note 11, at 249.

[17]   *Id.*

[18]   *Id.*

[19]   *In a Memo from 1994, An Aide to Bill Clinton Warns About Over-promising on Health Care Reform,* WALL ST. J. (Feb. 28, 2014), perma.cc/6CMY-L5T3.

House aide Todd Stern wrote a memo urging the president to drop this promise, as it was impossible to keep:

> This sounds great and I know that it's just what people want to hear. But can we get away with it? Isn't the whole thrust of our health plan to steer people toward cheaper, HMO-style providers? It's one thing to say we'll preserve your option to *pick the doctor of your choice* (recognizing that this will cost more), it's quite another to appear to promise the nation that everyone will get to *pick the doctor of his or her choice*. And that's exactly what this line does. I am very worried about getting skewered for over-promising here on something we know full well we won't deliver.[20]

The White House chose not to overpromise and underdeliver. The line about the "doctor of your choice" didn't make it into the final speech. Instead, President Clinton explained that under his plan, Americans would have the "freedom to choose a plan and the right to choose your own doctor."[21] Being *free to choose your own doctor*, at whatever cost, is very different than picking and keeping the *doctor of your choice*. This exact same choice would be described quite differently by the Obama administration in 2009.

Facing massive resistance from Senate Republicans – and rising public opposition – the Health Security Act withered. In August 1994, Senate Majority Leader George Mitchell realized that he lacked the votes to pass the bill, and he could not stop a GOP-led filibuster. Ironically, Mitchell had declined President Clinton's offer to appoint him to replace the retiring Justice Harry Blackmun, in order to ensure the passage of the Health Security Act.[22] Instead, Clinton picked Stephen G. Breyer. Though not the President's first or second choice – Interior Secretary Bruce Babbitt and Eighth Circuit Judge Richard S. Arnold were – Breyer was, in the words of White House counsel Lloyd Cutler, "the one with the fewest problems."[23]

---

[20] *Id.*

[21] *1994 State of the Union Address*, Wash. Post (Jan. 25, 1994), perma.cc/B8RF-ZJ7T.

[22] Alex Altman, *Middle East Envoy George Mitchell*, Time (Jan. 22, 2009), ti.me/297s0dd.

[23] Gwen Ifill, *The Supreme Court; President Chooses Breyer, as Appeals Judge in Boston, for Blackmun's Court Seat*, N.Y. Times (May 14, 1994), nyti.ms/1SGhOfV. At the time, not everyone was as enthused with Breyer. Tom Perrelli, who would later serve as Deputy Attorney General for President Obama wrote, "Nothing in Judge Breyer's opinions suggests that he would be a great Supreme Court justice." Colby Itkowitz et al., *The Most Interesting Tidbits from the Clinton Document Dump (Part 50)*, Wash. Post (Jun. 6, 2014), perma.cc/29XE-DCSK. Ian Gershengorn, who became Obama's Acting Solicitor General, wrote, "There is very little heart and soul in Judge Breyer's opinions. Quite clearly, he is a rather cold fish." Ed Whelan, *Deputy Solicitor General: Breyer Is a Rather Cold Fish*, Nat'l Rev. (Jun. 9, 2014), perma.cc/3FAY-UL4T. A decade later, both Gershengorn and Perrelli would reunite to defend the Affordable Care Act in the lower courts. Josh Blackman Unprecedented: The Constitutional Challenge to Obamacare 64, 74, 80, 81, 99, 101 (2013).

By September 1994, Hillarycare was officially dead. Partly as a result of opposition to the Health Security Act, Republicans took the House of Representatives for the first time in four decades.[24] Evan Thomas wrote in *Newsweek*, "The 1994 mid-term election became a 'referendum on big government' – Hillary Clinton had launched a massive health-care reform plan that wound up strangled by its own red tape."[25] The Republicans now had control of both the House and the Senate, ending the Clinton administration's hope of bringing about health care reform. That goal would have to wait another fifteen years.

1.2. "PARADOX"

NetRoots Nation is an annual confab for liberal political activists and pundits, founded by *The Daily Kos*. The third annual convention in July 2008 was marked by for optimism. After eight years of a Republican presidency, Senator Barack Obama was on the verge of securing the Democratic nomination, and hoped to be a transformational president who could effect great change. The groundwork was already being laid to accomplish what had failed so many times before – national health care reform. On the morning of July 19, the conference hosted a discussion on "How the NetRoots Can Lead on Healthcare Reform." One of the panelists was twenty-four-year-old wunderkind Ezra Klein. Klein had already brandished his policy expertise as a blogger at *The American Prospect* and would go on to write at the *Washington Post's WonkBlog* and later became the editor-in-chief of *Vox*. As a testament to his rising influence, from 2009 through 2014, Klein would be invited to visit the White House more than two dozen times to meet with senior administration officials who wanted to discreetly disseminate information to the public.[26] GQ would name him one of the fifty most powerful people in Washington, D.C.[27]

But back in July 2008, Klein was still just a blogger, who told grassroots activists what needed to be done to succeed where others had failed. "I want to make one other point," he noted, "because I have the beautiful luxury of not working for an organization, thus I don't have to be diplomatic."[28] Klein explained there was a major "problem with health reform in this country"

---

[24] Andrew Glass, *Congress Runs into Republican Revolution Nov. 8, 1994*, POLITICO (Nov. 8, 2007), perma.cc/T6WG-7L8U.

[25] Evan Thomas, *Decline and Fall*, NEWSWEEK (Nov. 11, 2006), bit.ly/1Ky4S4B.

[26] Charlie Spiering, *'Vox King' Ezra Klein Visited the White House 27 Times*, BREITBART (May 9, 2014), perma.cc/S5PB-CGTY.

[27] Washington Post Editors, *2011: By the Numbers: A Memo to Post Staff from Managing Editor Raju Narisetti*, WASH. POST (Jan. 2, 2012), perma.cc/VKT7-SY2H.

[28] *Ezra Klein: The Deceptive Strategy Underlying Obamacare*, YOUTUBE (Jun. 25, 2009), youtu.be/FElipqE_Dl4.

based on public opinion.[29] The overwhelming majority of people "want to reform health care," but at the same time the overwhelming majority of people "are happy with what they have."[30]

Every year since 2001, *Gallup* has surveyed Americans on how they would rate the quality of their personal health care. Consistently, year after year, more than 80% of respondents rated it as good or excellent.[31] A February 2007 poll by *CBS News* found that 85% of people were satisfied with the quality of their own health insurance.[32] A September 2009 Quinnipiac University poll found that 88% of respondents were satisfied with their coverage.[33] A June 2009 survey by *ABC News* yielded an 81% satisfaction rate.[34] Similarly, an August 2009 survey by the Kaiser Family Foundation found that 91% of the insured Americans rated their coverage as excellent or good.[35] Among the insured, 67% were very satisfied with their choice of doctors, 66% were very satisfied with the quality of care, and 82% were at least somewhat satisfied with the amount they paid. Overwhelmingly, people who had insurance liked it.[36]

Yet, despite the fact that the insured were happy with their coverage, they recognized that the health care system did not serve all Americans. For example, 59% of the respondents in the CBS survey were very dissatisfied with the cost of insurance for the country as whole.[37] Further, 90% said the U.S. health care system needed fundamental change. The CBS pollsters observed a contradiction: "Americans think the U.S. health care system needs major fixing, though they are generally satisfied with the quality (but not the cost) of their own health care."[38]

Klein explained to the Netroots Nation attendees that in 1994 there were 35 million uninsured people, and in 2009 there were 47 million uninsured.[39]

---

[29] *Id.*

[30] *Id.*

[31] Frank Newport, *Americans' Views of Healthcare Quality, Cost, and Coverage*, GALLUP (Nov. 25, 2013), perma.cc/VF9D-8ZP9.

[32] Press Release, *CBS News Poll & The New York Times*, U.S Healthcare Politics (Mar. 1, 2007), perma.cc/PF73-DQEQ.

[33] Louis Jacobson, *Will Says That 95 Person of People with Health Insurance Are Satisfied with It*, POLITIFACT (Mar. 10, 2010), perma.cc/MQT6-XPF3.

[34] *Id.*

[35] *Data Note: Americans' Satisfaction with Insurance Converge*, KAISER FAMILY FOUND., Sep. 2009, perma.cc/4BPZ-V7UK.

[36] *Id.*

[37] *CBS News Poll, supra* note 32.

[38] *Id.*

[39] Angie Drobnic Holan, *Number of Those without Health Insurance about 46 Million*, POLITIFACT (Aug. 18, 2009), perma.cc/JT3Y-FU34.

That translates to 85% of Americans, or 250 million in total, having health insurance they were content with.[40]

Klein referred to this tension as "a paradox."[41] The problem was that the overwhelming majority of Americans were insured, and satisfied with their coverage. This was the root of the "Harry & Louise" campaign's success in 1994. Americans did not have much of an incentive to support reform that would alter the status quo, even if it would help several million of the neediest and sickest Americans gain access to insurance.

This paradox was well understood in the White House. In 2015, President Obama recalled that "pollsters" showed him surveys suggesting that "85 percent of folks at any given time had health care and so they weren't necessarily incentivized to support" reform.[42] His staff was worried that pushing for reform "could scare the heck out of them ... even if they weren't entirely satisfied with the existing system, [because] somehow it would be terrible to change it."[43] Advisers gave the president "warning signs about how tough this was," and that it would be "bad politics."[44]

"Time and again," Klein warned back in 2008, "well-meaning good people have gone to folks, and said 'you're scared about losing your health care, [so] here's what I'm going to do. I'm going to take it from you and build something new.' And every time we've done that we have had the hell kicked out of us."[45] Because of this paradox, a dozen "reform battles have gone nowhere," the blogger lamented.[46] "Every trend we hate, [has] continued."[47] Supporters of health care reform needed a new game plan. "At some point," Klein said, "you have to win. Not everything, but you have to put winning first."[48] This time, a different strategy was necessary.

---

[40] Jacobson, *supra* note 33.

[41] *Klein, supra* note at 28.

[42] President Barack Obama, Joint Press Conference by President Obama, President Calderon of Mexico, and Prime Minister Harper of Canada (Apr. 2, 2012), *in* Off. of Press Sec'y, perma.cc/G3HS-B79C

[43] *Klein, supra* note 28.

[44] *Id.*

[45] *Id.*

[46] *Id.*

[47] *Id.*

[48] Klein continued, "Yes, I would like to sign the insurance companies out of business with my pen. It would be sweet, but it has never happened in the history of this country that we've sent a multi-billion dollar industry employing tens of thousands of people in every district in America out in one shot." *Ezra Klein, supra* note 28. Klein finished with what he described as a necessary "sneaky strategy," which is "to put in place something that over time, [where] the natural incentive in its own market is to move it to single payer." *Id.*

1.3. "TRILEMMA"

Klein would later describe the compromises over health care reform in terms of a *trilemma*: A balance between (1) affordability, (2) comprehensiveness, and (3) accessibility.[49] It is not feasible for insurers to offer policies that are afford-able, comprehensive, *and* accessible. A balance of the three must be achieved.

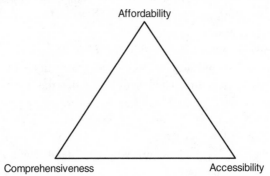

Before the enactment of the Affordable Care Act, in order to keep prices on the individual market low – so that people would be able to afford them – insurers had two approaches: Offer limited coverage and/or who were expensive to insure, such as those with pre-existing conditions. Under the former option, insurers sold policies that provided stingy coverage, lifetime limits on expenses, and high out-of-pocket costs. These risky plans, which may not provide adequate coverage in the event of a serious health crisis, were priced low to make them more attractive. For the latter option, by denying coverage to sick people – who account for a disproportionate share of medical costs – premiums for the majority of consumers could be kept low. Thus, *affordable* insurance would be *uncomprehensive* and/or *inaccessible*. In contrast, for customers who wanted better plans, the price tag would be higher. Thus, *comprehensive* and *accessible* insurance would not be *affordable*. Or worse, for people with preexisting conditions, insurance may not be *accessible* at all. (Some states had already prohibited underwriting policies based on a person's health status, or created special high-risk pools for these individuals.)

The Affordable Care Act would radically recalculate this trigonometry. The law mandated that all insurance must be both *comprehensive* (mandating "minimum essential coverage") and *accessible* (people with pre-existing conditions were guaranteed issuance of policies). The consequence of making insurance more comprehensive and more accessible was

---

[49] Ezra Klein, *The Health-Care Trilemma: How Obamacare Is Changing Insurance Premiums*, WASH. POST (Oct. 29, 2013), perma.cc/G8XU-EYEX.

predictable: Less-comprehensive policies, which are invariably cheaper, would no longer be valid. Klein wrote that under the trilemma, "every change has winners and losers. Put bluntly, the Affordable Care Act's changes are raising insurance premiums for some people who did well under the old system and lowering them for many of the people who were locked out or discriminated against."[50]

For President Obama, the paradox raised a dilemma: how to sell the American people on a transformational change in health care without scaring them away because of the necessary sacrifice. The marketing pitch for health care reform, which sought to eliminate any concerns about altering the status quo, was reduced to one sentence: "If you like your health care plan, you can keep your health care plan."

1.4. "NO ONE WILL TAKE IT AWAY"

On September 9, 2009, President Obama addressed a joint session of Congress to explain the details of the pending health reform bill that would become the Patient Protection and Affordable Care Act of 2010. He addressed all aspects of the trilemma.

First, Obama highlighted how the ACA would mandate that all plans must offer *comprehensive* coverage. Insurance companies, he said, "will no longer be able to place some arbitrary cap on the amount of coverage you can receive in a given year or in a lifetime."[51] The ACA will "place a limit on how much you can be charged for out-of-pocket expenses, because in the United States of America, no one should go broke because they get sick."[52] Under the law, Obama said, "insurance companies will be required to cover, with no extra charge, routine check-ups and preventive care, like mammograms and colonoscopies because there's no reason we shouldn't be catching diseases like breast cancer and colon cancer before they get worse."[53] He added, "That makes sense, it saves money, and it saves lives."[54] This requirement to cover

[50] *Id.*
[51] President Barack Obama, *Remarks by the President to a Joint Session of Congress on Health Care* (Sept. 9, 2009), perma.cc/A9S5-KU2M.
[52] *Id.*
[53] *Id.*
[54] *Id.* The former claim sounds plausible, but it is false. Congressional Budget Office (CBO) Director Douglas Elmendorf explained in a letter to Congress, "The evidence suggests that for most preventive services, expanded utilization leads to higher, not lower, medical spending overall." Letter from Douglas Elmendorf, CBO Director, to Nathan Deal, Subcommittee on Health, U.S. House of Representatives (Aug. 7, 2009), perma.cc/D8BX-5D42. Although a single test may be cheap for an individual, in the aggregate testing becomes quite expensive. *Politifact* rated the president's statement concerning saving money through expanding

preventive care would give rise to the so-called *contraceptive mandate* and two Supreme Court cases.

Second, the president highlighted how the law would make insurance more *affordable* for those who did not have it, or could not otherwise afford the more comprehensive policies. For "the tens of millions of Americans who don't currently have health insurance," the president continued, the law "will finally offer you quality, affordable choices."[55] The uninsured will be able to "shop for health insurance at competitive prices" on "a new insurance exchange."[56] The president noted that the exchange "will take effect in four years, which will give us time to do it right." Alas, the exchange would not quite be ready on time in October 2013.[57] And "for those individuals and small businesses who still can't afford the lower-priced insurance available in the exchange," Obama noted, "we'll provide tax credits, the size of which will be based on your need."[58] The president's speech assiduously avoided any comment about how the law would affect the cost of premiums. (I do not focus on oft-repeated promise that his plan would "bring down premiums by $2,500 for the typical family,"[59] because this pledge was made on the campaign trail in 2008 before the specifics of the health care reform were drafted.[60])

Third, the president promised that insurance would be *accessible* to all, for "it will be against the law for insurance companies to deny you coverage because of a pre-existing condition."[61] Under the Affordable Care Act, he said, "for insurance companies to drop your coverage when you get sick or water it down when you need it the most."[62] By far, this was one of the most popular aspects of the ACA, if not *the most* popular provision. A September 2009 Kaiser survey found that 80% of respondents supported this ban – that included 88% of Democrats and 67% of Republicans.[63]

---

preventive care as *false*. Catherine Richert, *Obama Says Preventive Care Saves Money. It Doesn't*, Politifact (Sep. 9, 2009), perma.cc/6GTJ-CLTS.

[55] *President's Remarks, supra* note 51.

[56] *Id.* The president repeatedly spoke of a singular "exchange" rather than exchanges in all fifty states. At the time, as we will discuss in Chapter 2, the House of Representatives' bill to create a single federal exchange was expected to prevail. However, the Senate bill, which allowed each state to establish its own exchange, would become law.

[57] *See infra* Chapters 11–12.

[58] *President's Remarks, supra* note 51.

[59] Kevin Sack, *Health Plan from Obama Spurs Debate*, N.Y. TIMES (Jul. 23, 2008), nyti.ms/1NiBfv3.

[60] J.B. Wogan, *No Cut in Premiums for Typical Family*, POLITIFACT (Aug. 31, 2012), perma.cc/PJ7W-XWPU.

[61] *President's Remarks, supra* note 51.

[62] *Id.*

[63] *Public Opinion on Health Care Issues*, KAISER FAMILY FOUND. (Sept. 2009), perma.cc/QDV2-UY94.

Among those supporters, however, only 56% still favored the provision if it resulted in higher premiums; 36% would oppose it.[64] Supporters almost certainly did not realize that requiring insurers to cover sick people would necessarily shift the cost onto everyone else.

Yet, there was a tension among these three planks that was understood implicitly by Harry and Louise fifteen years earlier. People insured who previously were able to get by with cheap insurance, or none at all, would now be forced to pay more to subsidize the costs of more accessible and more comprehensive insurance for poorer and sicker Americans. At its heart, the ACA was a form of redistribution. MIT economics professor Jonathan Gruber – who features prominently in Chapter 24– stated the issue bluntly: "Americans want a fair and fixed insurance market.... You cannot have that without some redistribution away from a small number of people."[65]

But the American people did not understand that this was how the law would operate. President Obama's long-time strategist David Axelrod conceded this critical contradiction of selling Obamacare. "We've created a sense that everyone can expect to win," Axelrod observed, where "nobody has to sacrifice."[66] In February 2009, the Kaiser Family Foundation surveyed whether people would be willing to sacrifice their own health insurance policies in order to achieve national health care reform.[67] The majority answered *no*: 56% of respondents said "if policymakers made the right changes, they could reform the health care system without changing the existing health care arrangements of people like yourself." This is impossible. In contrast, only 37% acknowledged "making any real reforms to the health care system will probably require people like yourself to change your existing health care arrangements."

The Obama administration understood this dynamic, but was not forthright about how the law would alter the landscape. William M. Daley, who advised the Obama-Biden Transition project, and later served as the President's chief of staff in 2011, explained, "Redistribution is a loaded word that conjures up all sorts of unfairness in people's minds."[68] Daley feared that Republicans would wield it "as a hammer" against Democrats, adding, "it's a word that, in the political world, you just don't use."[69] Journalist Steven Brill wrote in his book BITTER PILL, "Obamacare was a massive income redistribution program providing health insurance to those who could not pay for

---

[64] *Id.*

[65] John Harwood, *Don't Dare Call the Health Law 'Redistribution'*, N.Y. TIMES (Nov. 23, 2013), http://nyti.ms/24iT4BL.

[66] *Id.*

[67] *Public Opinion, supra* note 63.

[68] Harwood, *supra* note 65.

[69] *Id.*

it – something Democrats in a different time might have been proud, rather than afraid, to acknowledge."[70] The *New York Times* observed that the theme of redistribution had "been hidden away to make the Affordable Care Act more palatable to the public and less a target for Republicans," even though "the redistribution of wealth has always been a central feature of the law."[71] At bottom, the American people were rationally self-interested on the question of health care reform, and did not support change if it meant altering the coverage they were happy with. And more importantly, they were led to believe that the ACA would not affect their coverage. This misconception was assisted by the White House's misinformation.

Instead of admitting the inconvenient truth, the president repeatedly misled the public about the cornerstone of the law. Obama told Congress and the American people in September 2009, "If you are among the hundreds of millions of Americans who already have health insurance ... nothing in this plan will require you or your employer to change the coverage or the doctor you have."[72] There was booming applause in the chamber. "Let me repeat this: Nothing in our plan requires you to change what you have," the president exclaimed.[73] This is a promise the president made at least three dozen times between October 2008 and October 2013.[74] The clearest statement was in a high-profile speech to the American Medical Association in June 2009: "If you like your health care plan, you'll be able to keep your health care plan, period. No one will take it away, no matter what."[75]

In 1994, an adviser prevailed on President Clinton to alter his promise in the State of the Union because he was "worried about getting skewered for over-promising here on something we know full well we won't deliver."[76] In 2009, Obama had no such reservations in misleading Congress and the American people. Only four years later, and after four million policies were cancelled because of the ACA's mandates, would the extent of this deception become clear. *Politifact* would shame the pledge as the "Lie of the Year."[77] In

[70] STEVEN BRILL, AMERICA'S BITTER PILL: MONEY, POLITICS, BACKROOM DEALS, AND THE FIGHT TO FIX OUR BROKEN HEALTHCARE SYSTEM 214 (Random House Trade Paperback ed. 2015).

[71] Harwood, *supra* note 65.

[72] *President's Remarks, supra* note 51.

[73] *Id.*

[74] Obama: 'If You Like Your Health Care Plan, You'll be Able to Keep Your Health Care Plan,' POLITIFACT (Dec. 12, 2013), perma.cc/6P3F-BCL6; *see also 36 Times Obama Said You Could Keep Your Health Care Plan,* YOUTUBE (Nov. 5, 2013), bit.ly/1UkDLzt.

[75] President Barack Obama, Remarks by the President to the Annual Conference of the American Medical Association (Jun. 15, 2009), perma.cc/9BN4-BDGW.

[76] *Memo from 1994, supra* note 19.

[77] Angie Drobnic Holan, *Lie of the Year: 'If You Like Your Health Care Plan, You Can Keep It',* POLITIFACT (Dec. 12, 2013), perma.cc/E3YD-9FFF.

2013, the best Obama could muster was this half-hearted apology: "I am sorry that they are finding themselves in this situation based on assurances they got from me."[78]

This promise was how Obama dodged the paradox that defeated all presidents before him. This promise, which was essential to securing the necessary votes in the House and Senate, could not be kept – and the administration knew it. This promise was relied on by millions of Americans, who would find out the truth. Without this promise the Affordable Care Act would have never been enacted.

1.5. "THAT GREAT UNFINISHED BUSINESS OF OUR SOCIETY"

Toward the end of his speech to Congress, the president noted that he often receives letters from those "counting on us to succeed."[79] He paused for a moment, biting his lip. "I received one of those letters a few days ago. It was from our beloved friend and colleague, Ted Kennedy. He had written it back in May, shortly after he was told that his illness was terminal. He asked that it be delivered upon his death."[80]

The camera panned to the teary-eyed Vicki Kennedy, whose husband had passed away only six months shy of the enactment of the ACA.[81] In the letter, the lifetime champion of universal health care wrote Obama, "while I will not be there when it happens, you will be the President who at long last signs into law the health care reform that is the *great unfinished business of our society*."[82] Kennedy predicted, accurately, "there will be struggles," but "as we moved forward in these months, I learned that you will not yield to calls to retreat – that you will stay with the cause until it is won."[83] (The liberal lion of the Senate could never have fathomed that a Republican would fill his vacant seat in January 2010, nearly derailing the ACA.) Kennedy closed, "while I will not see the victory, I was able to look forward and know that we will – yes we will – fulfill the promise of health care in America as a right and not a privilege."[84]

---

[78] Chuck Todd, *Exclusive: Obama Personally Apologizes for Americans Losing Health Coverage*, NBC NEWS (Nov. 7, 2013), perma.cc/7WC4-KX93.

[79] *President's remarks, supra* note 51.

[80] *Id.*

[81] *President Obama: Address to Congress on Health Care Insurance Reform*, YOUTUBE (Sep. 10, 2009), bit.ly/20omm6o.

[82] Letter from Sen. Edward M. Kennedy to President Barack Obama (May 12, 2009), perma.cc/BBG5-QHK3.

[83] *Id.*

[84] *Id.*

The president drew inspiration from Kennedy's resolve. "I understand that the politically safe move would be to kick the can further down the road," Obama said, or "to defer reform one more year, or one more election, or one more term."[85] But that is "not what the moment calls for. That's not what we came here to do."[86] With optimism, the president extolled, "I still believe we can replace acrimony with civility, and gridlock with progress. I still believe we can do great things, and that here and now we will meet history's test."[87]

Half the chamber rose in a standing ovation. The other half sat quietly. Over the next eight years, rather than uniting America in a common cause, the battle over the ACA would institutionalize acrimony and gridlock in ways that no one, not even the President, could have foreseen.

[85] *Address to Congress, supra* note 81.
[86] *Id.*
[87] *Id.*

2

Federal and State Exchanges

2.1. "FINEST HOUR"

During the fall of 2009, the most contentious battles over the Affordable Care Act concerned the individual mandate, the Medicaid expansion, and whether there would be funding for abortions. A far more mundane yet foundational element of the law remained far outside the spotlight. The health care reform was premised on the so-called *three-legged stool*: three interlocking and interwoven elements would be used to expand access to affordable health insurance for millions of Americans. First, the law imposed on insurance companies requirements known as "community rating" and "guaranteed issue," which prohibited them from denying coverage to people with preexisting health conditions. This reform created two problems that were to be resolved by the other legs. Second, because these nondiscrimination provisions would cause insurance premiums to rise – covering sicker people with greater needs will shift costs to healthy customers – the government would provide subsidies to offset the cost and ensure policies remained affordable. Third, the individual mandate was created to require people to buy insurance *before* they became sick, rather than free-riding and waiting to buy a policy when they needed it. Guaranteed issue, subsidies, and the individual mandate were the three legs of the stool that were designed to prop up the health care reform.

The different versions of the bill that were being drafted in the House of Representatives and the Senate agreed that Americans should be able to purchase subsidized insurance policies on the individual market. There was a disagreement, however, on whether there would be one federal exchange, or if states would establish their own exchanges, or a combination of both.

As a threshold matter, Congress could not require, or "commandeer" the states to establish an exchange against their wishes. That would conflict with a 1997 Supreme Court decision holding that Congress could not force local sheriffs to conduct background checks under the Brady Handgun Violence Prevention Act.[1] In other words, the federal government could not mandate unwilling states to act. Democrats also worried that even if states wanted to build exchanges, they might do so poorly and prevent Americans from having access to affordable health insurance. Two Senate committees, along with the House of Representatives, followed different tracks to resolve this problem.

The House bill established a single federal exchange, where people could purchase policies subsidized by federal tax credits. The more progressive House did not trust the states – in particular, those red states opposed to the law – to create and manage the exchanges. The Senate took a different approach. Rather than creating a single federal exchange, the proposal from the Finance Committee gave states the option of establishing an exchange, but if they failed to do so, residents could fall back on federal exchanges established within the states.

Christopher E. Condeluci, a staff lawyer for the Republicans on the Finance Committee, told *The New York Times* in 2015 that in October 2009 they expected "five or ten [states] at the most" would not establish an exchange.[2] Indeed, in April 2010, President Obama predicted that "by 2014, *each* state will set up what we're calling a health insurance exchange."[3] That was unduly optimistic. Only 16 states and the District of Columbia established their own exchanges, leaving the federal marketplace to handle customers in all other states.[4]

At the time, what proved to be one of the most important provisions of the Finance Committee bill received barely any attention at all. The provision stated that subsidies would be available only for policies "which were enrolled in through an Exchange established by the State."[5] With slight alterations, this provision would ultimately be merged into the final version of the ACA that passed the Senate on December 24, 2009. Throughout the committee and floor debates, there was no legislative history concerning the "established

---

[1]   Printz v. U.S., 521 U.S. 898 (1997). *See also* N.Y. v. U.S., 505 U.S. 144 (1992).
[2]   Robert Pear, *Four Words that Imperil Health Care Law Were all a Mistake, Writers Now Say*, N.Y. TIMES (May 25, 2015), nyti.ms/1ZygUHb.
[3]   President Barack Obama, Remarks by the President on Health Insurance Reform in Portland, Maine (Apr. 1, 2010), perma.cc/A7FJ-FJ2P.
[4]   Ezra Klein & Sarah Kliff, *Obama's Last Campaign: Inside the White House Plan to Sell Obamacare*, WASH. POST (Jul. 17, 2013), perma.cc/E59S-C9QU.
[5]   Bill Summary & Status, 111th Congress, S. 1796, Thomas, Library of Congress, perma.cc/3LD9-HYH4; America's Healthy Future Act of 2009 § 36B(b)(2)(A)(i), S. 1796, 111th Cong. (2009), 1.usa.gov/1SXLZRC.

by the state" provision, indicating whether members of the Senate did, or did not, want to withhold tax credits from states that did not establish exchanges.

But then again, Senator Max Baucus (D-MT), who chaired the committee, admitted that he didn't even read the entire bill. "I don't think you want me to waste my time to read every page of the healthcare bill," Baucus said in 2010.[6] "You know why? It's statutory language … We hire experts" for that.[7] But Senate Majority Leader Harry Reid (D-NV) boasted "Of course I read it."[8] He admitted that he "didn't sit down on a Friday evening and read it" in one sitting. "This legislation was drafted over a period of months and months. I could pass a test on it, I knew the law pretty well."[9]

Estimates made by the Congressional Budget Office (CBO) in November 2009 were premised on the assumption that subsidies would be available in all states – there was no indication that they considered whether subsidies would be available on federal exchanges. CBO Director Douglas W. Elmendorf recounted: "To the best of our recollection, the possibility that those subsidies would only be available in states that created their own exchanges did not arise during the discussions CBO staff had with a wide range of congressional staff."[10]

While the legislation was being compiled in Senator Reid's office, he could have adopted a competing provision from the Health, Education, Labor, and Pensions (HELP) Committee. The proposal from the HELP Committee, which was closer to the House of Representative's bill, provided that a state with a federal exchange "shall be deemed to be a participating state."[11] This approach made clear that there was no legal distinction between states that did and did not establish their own exchanges. But Reid ignored the bill from the committee long chaired by Senator Kennedy. Instead, he adopted the language from Senator Baucus' Finance Committee bill, which contained the "established by the state" language.

Robert Greenawalt, who served as a tax adviser to Senator Reid, could "not recall any discussion of a distinction between federal and state exchanges for the purpose of subsidies."[12] He added, "In merging two bills that were so big, it's possible that something got left out. It would have been accidental."[13] Chris

[6] Jordan Fabian, *Key Senate Democrat Suggests That He Didn't Read Entire Healthcare Reform Bill*, THE HILL (Aug. 25, 2010) perma.cc/P2PC-CQ3J.

[7] *Id.*

[8] Alexander Bolton, *Reid: More Funding Needed to Prevent Obamacare from Becoming 'Train Wreck'*, THE HILL (May 1, 2013), perma.cc/LPS7-NPV2.

[9] *Id.*

[10] Pear, *supra* note 3.

[11] *Id.*

[12] *Id.*

[13] *Id.*

Condeluci, the Republican staffer on the Finance Committee, lamented the way the bill was drafted: "At the end of the day, this should have never happened, and is a product of the rushed way the law was passed."[14]

How the phrase "established by the state" emerged from Reid's office is at once clear yet shrouded in mystery. In BITTER PILL, Steven Brill describes Section 36B as a "drafting mistake" that was "the result of a last-minute change as the Senate bill was being passed early in the morning on Christmas Eve."[15] Brill adds, "someone had mistakenly cut and pasted language from a provision in an earlier draft that referred only to state exchanges and used it in one place, though not elsewhere, as a boilerplate reference to the exchanges in one of the clauses describing how the subsidies would work."[16]

That is an only partial explanation of what we know happened. At a minimum, Reid's office decided to adapt Section 36B from the Finance Committee bill, rather than the HELP bill. Russ Sullivan, the Democratic staff director for the Finance Committee, told the *New York Times* that the provision was "a holdover from what we had in the Finance Committee."[17] That much is undisputed. But it is not the case that this phrase was errantly copied and pasted in "one place." The phrase "established by the state" appears seven times in the bill.[18] Furthermore, language surrounding the phrase was edited, as cross-references were added to the new Section 1311, in order to reflect the organization of the merged bill. But no efforts were made to remove the "established by the state" provision.

Over the next five years, Case Western law professor Jonathan Adler would team up with Cato Institute scholar Michael Cannon to become the leading proponents of the position that Section 36B was designed to limit subsidies to state exchanges. "It's really amazing, Adler told me, "about what occurred in Harry Reid's office." The key provision "was written somewhat pretty well but somewhat roughly," the professor said. "In Harry Reid's office it becomes tighter and more consistent and cleaner. There are plenty of parts of the ACA that are anything but tight or clean. Somebody spent some time going through that section." Alder said he could never figure out who did it – it may have been "some kind of drafting Mandarin that just focuses on making language internally consistent." But

---

[14] Sarah Kliff, *The People Who Wrote Obamacare Think the New Supreme Court Case is Ridiculous*, VOX (Nov. 7, 2014), perma.cc/339Y-6LRY.
[15] STEVEN BRILL, AMERICA'S BITTER PILL: MONEY, POLITICS, BACKROOM DEALS, AND THE FIGHT TO FIX OUR BROKEN HEALTHCARE SYSTEM 191–192 (Random House Trade Paperback ed. 2015).
[16] *Id.*
[17] Pear, *supra* note 3.
[18] Jonathan H. Adler & Michael F. Cannon, *Taxation without Representation: The Illegal IRS Rule to Expand Tax Credits under the PPACA*, 23 HEALTH MATRIX 145–146 (2013).

Adler is doubtful, because when someone changes cross-references to other sections of the U.S. Code, "you've actually got to know what it's talking about to know what that means."

University of Michigan law professor Nicholas Bagley – who became a leading ACA advocate and good-natured foil to Adler and Cannon – discounted the mystique within Senator Reid's office. "If you imagine you're a staffer in Harry Reid's office," he noted, "all you're trying to do is to get this statute to reflect accurately what the members of Congress wanted you to do, and you don't want to mess anything up." Bagley argued that Congress wanted the subsidies to be available regardless of whether a state established an exchange. Congress, he told me, does not hide critical "instructions in the sub-sub-sub-provision of the Internal Revenue code." But as the Senate voted during a rare Christmas Eve roll call, it may not have mattered much what bill actually said.[19] "No one thought this would be the final law," Cannon told me. "That exercise in Harry Reid's office was not an exercise in crafting a perfect health care law." The oft-stated goal was to pass something that would garner sixty votes and then allow the House time to work on it. Ultimately, any differences would be worked out in a conference committee between the two chambers.[20]

In 2015, Michael Carvin would argue against the federal subsidies before the Supreme Court in *King v. Burwell*. In his usual brash manner, Carvin told me that the Democrats "didn't give a crap what was in the bill. They cared about one thing. Get to sixty. Anybody who has ever worked on the Hill for a minute will tell you that they will work it out in the conference." Generally, the House and Senate will appoint a joint committee to iron out differences between the two bills. A Senate staffer involved in drafting the ACA confirmed Carvin's suspicion in a conversation with *Talking Points Memo*. "It's definitely inartfully drafted," the aide conceded, and "we meant to clean it up in conference."[21]

---

[19] The last time the Senate had met on Christmas Eve was in 1895. JOSH BLACKMAN, UNPRECEDENTED: THE CONSTITUTIONAL CHALLENGE TO OBAMACARE 58 (2013). District Court Judge Henry Hudson, who would invalidate the ACA in 2010, noted the "haste with which the final version of the 2,700-page bill was rushed to the floor for a Christmas Eve vote." Virginia ex rel. Cuccinelli v. Sebelius, 728 F. Supp. 2d 768, 789 (E.D. Va. 2010), *vacated*, 656 F.3d 253 (4th Cir. 2011).

[20] EZEKIEL EMANUEL, REINVENTING AMERICAN HEALTH CARE: HOW THE AFFORDABLE CARE ACT WILL IMPROVE OUR TERRIBLY COMPLEX, BLATANTLY UNJUST, OUTRAGEOUSLY EXPENSIVE, GROSSLY INEFFICIENT, ERROR PRONE SYSTEM 283 (2014). ("In the process of enacting the ACA Phil Schiliro, the White House director of legislative affairs, constantly and wisely emphasized that getting something passed by both houses of Congress was the most important imperative. After that, he promised, substantive policy issues, including issues that would affect implementation, would be addressed in conference.")

[21] Dylan Scott, *Obamacare Drafter's Dismiss GOP's Last Ditch Legal Attack on the Law*, TALKING POINTS MEMO (Feb. 12, 2014), perma.cc/4ACJ-KQEM.

New York Times reporter Adam Nagourney visited the majority leader's office on December 23, 2009.[22] Senator Reid was eager to brag about his leadership. "He rose from his chair, walked over to his desk and picked up a clip from *Politico*, a collection of laudatory quotations highlighted in yellow by Reid's staff," Nagourney recounted. "Every one of these ... they all say the same thing," Reid boasted. "I'm not tall, dark and handsome," he demurred before reading from a clipping, but "'behind the scenes, his genius really comes to the floor. He's a virtuoso, a legislative technician. Whatever else can be said of health care reform, it's Reid's *finest hour.*'" The reporter noted that "[t]his need for validation was startling, if understandable."

On December 24, 2009, when the ACA finally came for a vote in the Senate, Reid inadvertently voted "no" and, after some laughter, quickly changed his vote.[23] The bill had passed the Senate with exactly sixty votes – just enough to overcome a Republican filibuster. Adler and Cannon observed, "Supporters opted for an imperfect bill – that is, a bill that did not accomplish all they may have set out to do, but for which they had the votes – over no bill at all."[24] But in an unexpected twist, the much-anticipated conference would *never* take place.

2.2. "FORTY-FIRST VOTE"

Senator Kennedy, who for decades championed universal health care, died in August 2009. Months earlier, as the ailing Kennedy was dying of brain cancer, and the Senate's sixtieth vote was in jeopardy, Reid, the "legislative technician" took precautionary measures. Massachusetts law provided that Kennedy's seat would remain vacant *until* a special election was held a few months later. The Nevadan urged Massachusetts Governor Deval Patrick, a Democrat, to change it.[25] Reid explained that unless Kennedy's seat was filled immediately by a gubernatorial appointment, it would deny the Democrats a filibuster-proof majority. Kennedy personally made a similar request to the governor in a letter shortly before his death.[26] In September 2009, the Massachusetts legislature approved a bill to allow Governor Patrick

[22] Adam Nagourney, *Reid Faces Battles in Washington and at Home*, N.Y. TIMES MAG. (Jan. 12, 2010), perma.cc/WPR9-9GEC.

[23] UNPRECEDENTED, *supra* note 21, at 59.

[24] Adler & Cannon, *supra* note 20, at 126.

[25] MARK LEIBOVICH, THIS TOWN: TWO PARTIES AND A FUNERAL – PLUS PLENTY OF VALET PARKING! – IN AMERICA'S GUILDED CAPITAL 81 (2013).

[26] Abby Goodnough & Katie Zezima, *Kennedy Asks to Alter Laws on his Successor*, N.Y. TIMES (Aug. 20, 2009), nyti.ms/1NiE13h.

to appoint a temporary successor for Kennedy, with a special election to be held 160 days later.

Ironically, five years earlier, the Democratic-controlled legislature had changed the law to block then-governor Mitt Romney, a Republican, from potentially appointing a replacement for then presidential candidate Senator John Kerry, a Democrat. *Politifact* gave the Bay State a "resounding full flop," as both actions only served to advance the "Democratic Party's interest."[27] Even more ironically, Kennedy himself supported the now-repealed special election bill in 2004 to hamstring Romney.[28] All politics, even national politics, is local. With the new law, Governor Patrick promptly appointed Democrat Paul G. Kirk, Jr. as interim senator, with a special election to be held on January 19, 2010. Kirk would be the sixtieth Democrat to vote for the ACA on Christmas Eve, 2009.

Then the unthinkable happened. Scott Brown, a Massachusetts Republican, rode the Tea Party wave to victory and was elected to the Senate on the promise of being the "forty-first vote" against Obamacare. Let's put this in perspective. In Massachusetts, one of the most liberal states in the Union – a state where Republican governor Mitt Romney had imposed an individual health insurance mandate five years earlier – a Republican opposing the same policy beat a Democrat to replace the liberal lion of the Senate. This staggering feat was a sign of the times and a testament to the surging opposition to Obamacare. However, to add another level of irony, Scott Brown had voted for Romneycare in 2006 as a state senator. Now he claimed, as Romney would on the campaign trail, that he opposed the individual mandate being imposed nationwide by the federal government. "Everyone is entitled to some form of insurance," Brown reasoned, "but why do we need a one-size-fits-all?"[29]

With Brown's surprise victory, the road to the ACA took a sharp detour. Former Senate majority leader Tom Daschle (D-SD), who served as a close adviser to the White House, wrote that on election night, "the health care reform effort seemed to collapse. Obama and the Democrats in Congress had been on the verge of making history, and they were closing in on the finish line. Now, the finish line had vanished."[30] Massachusetts, the home of the

---

[27] Louis Jacobson, *Massachusetts Legislature Flip-Flops on Governor's Senatorial Appointment Power*, POLITIFACT (Sept. 24, 2009), perma.cc/KD5D-HMQR. To continue the trend, in 2016, Reid sought to block Governor Charlie Baker, a Republican, from temporarily filling the seat of Senator Elizabeth Warren, a Democrat, who was rumored to be Hillary Clinton's Vice Presidential selection.

[28] Pam Belluck, *Massachusetts Politicians Fight over a Kerry Victory*, N.Y. TIMES (Jun. 25, 2004), nyti.ms/1UsGUQE.

[29] TOM DASCHLE & DAVID NATHER, GETTING IT DONE: OBAMA AND CONGRESS FINALLY BROKE THE STALEMATE TO MAKE WAY FOR HEALTH CARE REFORM 233 (2010).

[30] *Id.*

original Tea Party in 1773, had nearly empowered the modern Tea Party to dump Obamacare into the Potomac. Now, the Republicans would be able to filibuster the bill if there was another Senate vote. "The talks suddenly took on a greater sense of urgency," Daschle recalled.[31]

Although Senator Reid and his colleagues did not intend the Christmas Eve roll call to be the final vote they would take, the bill could not return to the Senate floor. If they tried, the forty-one vote GOP caucus would kill it with a filibuster. The much-ballyhooed conference was now out of the question. "I'm looking at the possibility of losing my sixtieth vote," President Obama told top House and Senate Democrats.[32] "Can't you work this out," the commander in chief implored his caucus. Steven Brill recounted that at a January 22 dinner, Justice Antonin Scalia was seated next to Ezekiel Emanuel, who was the brother of White House Chief of Staff Rahm Emanuel, and an adviser on the pending health care reform.[33] "Scalia kidded Emanuel about the apparent collapse of Obamacare," Brill wrote. "Zeke offered to bet him that they would get Obama's reform package through, somehow."[34] The gregarious justice would have been wise to decline the odds. Obamacare would not be stopped so easily.

Speaker Nancy Pelosi (D-CA) devised a parliamentary strategy to salvage the process: The House would vote on the Senate bill, and then a separate reconciliation bill, in such a way as to avoid sending it back for a full Senate vote. Through the reconciliation process, the reconciliation bill could pass the Senate with only fifty-one, rather than sixty votes. Critically, there would be no conference. Because of Brown's election, and the loss of a filibuster-proof majority, the *New York Times* observed, "a back-room conference, where changes could be considered in private, never happened."[35] The House would pass the Senate bill, along with a separate act containing a number of "fixes" that remedied the problems House Democrats had with the Senate bill. Notably, House Democrats made seven changes to Section 36B and five changes to the related Section 1401, which affected the subsidies. They even modified the provision to note that U.S. territories, such as Guam and American Samoa, would be treated the same as states. But no changes were made to the pivotal provision limiting subsidies to "exchanges established by the state."

Fifty-one health policy experts, including MIT economist Jonathan Gruber, wrote a letter urging the Democrats to "pass the Senate Bill" in its present

[31] *Id.*
[32] DASCHLE & NATHER, *supra* note 31, at 233.
[33] BRILL, *supra* note 17, at 195.
[34] *Id.*
[35] Jonathan Weisman & Robert Pear, *Partisan Gridlock Thwarts Effort to Alter Health Law*, N.Y. TIMES (May 26, 2013), nyti.ms/1Y3j2C4.

form. The professors explained that "these bills are imperfect. Yet they represent a huge step forward."[36] The letter stressed that "[w]hile the House and Senate bills differ on specific points, they are built on the same framework and common elements," including "offering affordability credits to those who cannot afford health insurance."[37] Notably, the House and Senate bills differed about how subsidized insurance policies would be sold – the former relied on a single federal exchange, and the latter allowed states to create their own exchanges with a federal fallback. The signatories urged, "Differences between the House and Senate bill can be negotiated through the reconciliation process."[38] (The tax credit provisions were not modified during reconciliation.)

The House passed the bill on March 21, 2010, 219–212. Zero Republicans voted aye, and thirty-four Democrats voted nay. In 2015, Chief Justice John Roberts lamented the "unfortunate reality" that "Congress wrote key parts of the Act behind closed doors, rather than through 'the traditional legislative process.'"[39] Combined with the reconciliation process, "which limited opportunities for debate and amendment," the chief justice wrote, "the Act does not reflect the type of care and deliberation that one might expect of such significant legislation."[40] He noted during his announcement of the opinion – known as the *hand down* – that "several features of the Act's passage contributed to the unfortunate reality of its, to be charitable, imprecision."[41] The phrase "imprecision" did not make it into Roberts's written opinion, which was joined by five other justices.

On March 23, 2010, the president signed the ACA into law. Within minutes of the ink of the president's signature drying, Florida and Virginia filed suits challenging the ACA's individual mandate. This litigation ushered in a two-year legal battle that culminated in the Supreme Court's decision upholding the individual mandate in *NFIB v. Sebelius*.[42] After the House and Senate voted on the reconciliation bill, the president signed that bill into law.[43] Through this stratagem, a House–Senate conference was

---

[36] Letter to Senators Reid, Baucus, and Harkin (January 26, 2010), bit.ly/29kB2WY.

[37] *Id.*

[38] *Id.*

[39] King v. Burwell, 135 S. Ct. 2480, 2492 (2015).

[40] *Id.*

[41] Opinion Announcement of *King v. Burwell* at 7:35 (June 25, 2015), http//oyez.org/cases/2014/14-114.

[42] *See* UNPRECEDENTED, *supra* note 21.

[43] There were hundreds of pages of changes made through reconciliation, but relevant changes to Section 36B. Phil Schiliro, who served as President Obama's director of legislative affairs, recalled this issue "never came up" during reconciliation. Phil Schiliro, *The Straightforward*

avoided, and the Senate did not need to revisit the ACA where it could be filibustered. Critically, Section 36B not materially altered. The "bill that they cobbled together back in Harry Reid's office just to get 60 votes by hook or by crook," Michael Cannon told me, "all of a sudden became the only thing that could pass. Whether that stuff in there made sense or not, that stuff ultimately became the law." And apparently no one would notice the text of Section 36B, until a South Carolina lawyer took the time to do what Congress would not – read the entire bill.

2.3.   TOM CHRISTINA'S "DISCOVERY"

During oral arguments in *NFIB v. Sebelius*, Justice Scalia joked that forcing his law clerks to read the entire 2,700-page ACA would be cruel and unusual punishment. "What happened to the Eighth Amendment?" he sarcastically quipped.[44] For Tom Christina, diving into the ACA was his job. The fifty-nine-year-old bearded and bespectacled Harvard Law School graduate worked at the Greensville, South Carolina office of Ogletree Deakins. As Christina told me during an interview, he was retained to do some "legislative work" on the ACA, so he began reviewing it even before it was enacted in March 2010. As an employee benefits lawyer, he explained that his "role at the firm was to be the person keeping up with the statute."[45] Six months into his research, in September 2010, Christina was "reading through the statute and noticed the literal language of Section 36B."

He walked me through his thought process. Pay close attention – this complicated statutory framework will be on the exam. First, he started with Section 36B, which stated that subsidies would be available for insurance plans "which were enrolled in through an Exchange established by the State under [Section] 1311." Second, he flipped to Section 1311 to "see what the requirements were and what the methodology was for establishing an exchange." Section 1311(d)(1) stated, "An Exchange shall be a governmental agency or nonprofit entity that is *established by a State*." Christina thought to himself that the subsidies would be available only if the exchange was established by the state. Third, he turned to Section 1321, which defined the federal fallback exchange. If the Secretary of Health and Human Services determines that a state has not established an exchange, then "the Secretary shall (directly or through agreement with a not-for-profit entity) establish and operate such

---

Explanation for "Established by the State" in the Affordable Care Act, HUFF. POST (Apr. 25, 2015), perma.cc/3G4S-4APY.

[44] *Justices: Don't Make Us Read the Law,* POLITICO (Mar. 8, 2012), perma.cc/PLQ3-UWZD.

[45] Stephanie Armour, *The Lawyer Who Helped Spark This Week's Affordable Care Act Rulings,* WALL ST. J. (July 24, 2014), on.wsj.com/1PlF29g.

Exchange within the State." Christina focused "very hard on the concept of what an electing state was because that implied in [his] mind that there were such things as non-electing states" that were treated differently. It became immediately obvious to Christina that there was no provision in the ACA that would offer subsidies for policies on the federal exchange operating in non-electing states.

At the time, Christina theorized that Congressional Democrats drafted Section 36B deliberately. "They understood the scope and the revolutionary nature of the act," he told me, "so they in effect required the states to affirmatively endorse a major portion of the act by establishing a state-based exchange." Recall, it would violate principles of federalism for Congress to commandeer the states to force them to establish exchanges. To avoid red-state dissent, Christina noted, Congress "threatened the loss of subsidies to the citizenry if a state didn't cooperate." Five years later during oral argument at the Supreme Court, Justice Elena Kagan subtly credited Christina, explaining, it "took a year and a half for anybody to even notice this language." Actually it took Christina six months, and his discovery held the potential to unravel Obamacare. But Christina did not act alone.

2.4. "DRIVE A STAKE THROUGH ITS HEART"

Tom Christina and Michael S. Greve are a study in contrasts. The legal wonks knew each other from their service as trustees of the Telluride Association, a nonprofit organization that provides educational programs to students. Christina is an unassuming employee benefits lawyer from South Carolina, while Greve is a no-holds-barred constitutional crusader. Where Christina is reserved, Greve is brash. But they did agree on one thing – they hated Obamacare. More importantly, they agreed that the then-pending challenges to the ACA's constitutionality were unlikely to succeed. After a September 2010 event at the Heritage Foundation – a conservative think tank – Christina and Greve began to talk about finding "some alternative theory" to halt Obamacare "that would appeal to Justice Kennedy as well as four other justices." Greve, a scholar at the free-market American Enterprise Institute, and his AEI colleague Thomas P. Miller planned an event to discuss different ways of challenging the ACA. In addition to the organizers and Christina, the think tank invited James F. Blumstein, a law professor at Vanderbilt Law School.[46]

---

[46] *Who's in Charge? More Legal Challenges to the Patient Protection and Affordable Care Act*, AMERICAN ENTERPRISE INSTITUTE (Dec. 6, 2010), perma.cc/725N-Y8T2.

Christina's sixteen-slide PowerPoint presentation was titled "What to Look for Beyond the Individual Mandate (And How to Look for It)."[47] He began by expressing skepticism over the current legal challenges to the individual mandate. A slide titled "a pessimist's search" noted that the minimum criterion for any successful challenge is that the "theory must appeal to Justice Kennedy," the Court's perennial swing vote. Further, that "relief [must be] certain to stop further implementation." A "bonus" would be that there is "room to advance liberty." In slide 11, Christina dropped the bomb: "there is no tax credit for a citizen of a state with an Exchange established by HHS under Section 1321." Christina recalled of his AEI presentation: "I don't think anyone quite recognized the full significance of what we were saying at the time." Those in attendance did not leave, asking, "Well, wait a minute. Wouldn't this mean that the system of subsidies would cease to work as intended to work?" The benefits lawyer recalled that the reaction was limited to "polite interest."

While Christina's presentation nearly changed the fate of the ACA, it would be Michael Greve's firebrand keynote, imploring the death of Obamacare, that would be immortalized:

> This bastard has to be killed as a matter of political hygiene. I do not care how this is done, whether it's dismembered, whether we drive a stake through its heart, whether we tar and feather it and drive it out of town, whether we strangle it. I don't care who does it, whether it's some court some place, or the United States Congress. Any which way, any dollar spent on that goal is worth spending, any brief filed toward that end is worth filing, any speech or panel contribution toward that end is of service to the United States.[48]

Of Greve's comments, Christina told me, "if he had to do it over, it might not have been quite so colorful." Miller referred to Greve's comment as "unfortunate" because of "how that language tends to echo." Greve was "undecided" whether he would be speaking until right before the event, and the response was "off the cuff" and "ad lib." Greve told me he said exactly what he meant. Miller agreed – Greve "meant that seriously."

In 2014, a video of Greve's battle cry was surfaced by the Constitutional Accountability Center – a progressive legal advocacy group – and later repeated in Linda Greenhouse's column in the *New York Times*. Greenhouse, who acknowledged that Greve's "rhetorical excess ... is part of his charm,"

---

[47] Presentation (Dec. 6, 2012), bit.ly/1XCklrq.
[48] Joey Meyer, *The Tale of a Political Attack in Search of a Legal Theory*, THE CONSTITUTIONAL ACCOUNTABILITY CENTER (Aug. 11, 2014), perma.cc/3DGL-W6TN.

explained that "as origin stories go, this makes for a good one."[49] Sheryl Gay Stolberg aptly described the oncoming legal onslaught on the front page of the *Times* in 2015:

> The subsidy lawsuits grew out of three years of work by conservative and libertarian theorists at Washington-based research organizations like the Cato Institute, the American Enterprise Institute and the Competitive Enterprise Institute. The cases are part of a multifaceted legal assault on the Affordable Care Act that began with the Supreme Court challenge to the law and shows no signs of abating.[50]

And so began the second wave of challenges.

[49] Linda Greenhouse, *By Any Means Necessary*, N.Y. TIMES (Aug. 20, 2014), nyti.ms/1r5oK9i.
[50] Sheryl Gay Stolberg, *A New Wave of Challenges to Health Law*, N.Y. TIMES (Dec. 2, 2013), nyti.ms/23wi3yp.

3

Life and Religious Liberty

3.1. "LET'S HONOR THE CONSCIENCE OF THOSE
WHO DISAGREE WITH ABORTION"

In May 2009, President Obama received an unexpected invitation to deliver the commencement address at Notre Dame University, the preeminent Catholic institution of higher learning. This invitation was viewed as controversial on two fronts. First, as the *Washington Post* reported, "Since becoming president, and before that for nearly two years on the campaign trail, Obama has sought to skirt the emotional anger that surrounds the debate over abortion. But his decision to speak to graduating Notre Dame students made that approach impossible."[1] And second, Notre Dame was roundly criticized for conferring an honorary degree on a president who believes in protecting a right to abortion. More than seventy Catholic bishops openly criticized the university's president, Rev. John I. Henkins. During the commencement, Father Jenkins offered a subtle rejoinder to his critics, stressing the university's mission "to foster dialogue with all people of good will, regardless of faith, background or perspective."[2] He added, "President Obama has come to Notre Dame, though he knows well that we are fully supportive of the Church's teaching on the sanctity of human life."[3]

A number of demonstrators were arrested at the commencement, including Norma McCorvey.[4] Better known as *Jane Roe*, the pseudonymic plaintiff in *Roe v. Wade* became a pro-life activist in the decades after

---

[1] Michael D. Shear, *Cheers, Protests at Notre Dame*, WASH. POST (May 18, 2009), perma.cc/DM8J-WYVS.

[2] Reverend John I. Jenkins, Remarks at the 164th Commencement at the University of Notre Dame (May 17, 2009), perma.cc/B4C9-S5WE.

[3] *Id.*

[4] *Obama Calls for 'Common Ground' on Abortion at Notre Dame*, CNN (May 18, 2009), perma.cc/YTR7-DVKZ.

the landmark 1973 abortion decision.[5] A few moments into the president's address, one protester screamed out "Abortion is murder! Stop killing the children!" Amid boos from the audience and chants of "Yes, we can!" – the president's campaign slogan – Obama calmed down the crowd: "We're not going to shy away from things that are uncomfortable sometimes."[6] His speech made clear that even though he did not agree with the Church's teachings on abortions, he was committed to a "fair-minded" debate:

> That's when we begin to say, 'Maybe we won't agree on abortion, but we can still agree that this heart-wrenching decision for any woman is not made casually, it has both moral and spiritual dimensions. So let us work together to reduce the number of women seeking abortions, let's reduce unintended pregnancies. Let's make adoption more available. Let's provide care and support for women who do carry their children to term. Let's honor the conscience of those who disagree with abortion, and draft a *sensible conscience clause*, and make sure that all of our health care policies are grounded not only in sound science, but also in clear ethics, as well as respect for the equality of women. Those are things we can do.[7]

Obama's reference to the "sensible conscience clause" alluded to the brewing debate over health care reform and abortion. In 1976 – three years after *Roe* was decided – Congress enacted what became known as the *Hyde Amendment*. Named after Representative Henry Hyde (R-IL), the rider prohibited spending federal money on abortions. In 1980, the Supreme Court ruled in *Harris v. McRae* that states were not constitutionally required to fund medically necessary abortions where federal funding was unavailable due to the Hyde Amendment.[8] Although the 5–4 decision did not challenge a woman's constitutional right to an abortion, the Court recognized that there was not "a constitutional entitlement to the financial resources to avail herself of the full range of protected choices."[9] The Hyde Amendment would be modified over the years, and has been added to every federal budget since its introduction. In its present form, federal funds cannot be used for abortions except where the mother's life is endangered or in cases of rape or incest. Despite this long-standing legislative compromise, the battle over how to draft a "sensible conscience clause" nearly derailed the Affordable Care Act before it began.

---

5   *Testimony of Norma McCorvey*, Before the Subcommittee on the Constitution of the Senate Judiciary Committee (Jun. 23, 2005), bit.ly/1pXiaTH.
6   Barack Obama, Address at the University of Notre Dame (May 17, 2009), perma.cc/U3KY-DLGR.
7   *Id.* (emphasis added).
8   Harris v. McRae, 448 U.S. 297, 326 (1980).
9   *Id.* at 316.

3.2. "YOU LIE!"

During the summer of 2009, as the debates over Obamacare's individual mandate stirred Tea Party rallies throughout the country, the spotlight in Washington shined on whether the new law would fund abortions. Family Research Council, a conservative advocacy group, aired a commercial meant to evoke the famous "Harry and Louise" campaign from two decades earlier that halted Hillarycare. The spot featured a husband and his wife discussing Obamacare over the kitchen table. "They won't pay for my surgery," the husband said, "but we're forced to pay for abortions."[10] The narrator intoned, "Our greatest generation, denied care. Our future generation, denied life. Call your senator. Stop the government takeover of health care."[11]

The president sought to dispel the campaign's message, which threatened to kill the legislative process, but at the same time not alienate pro-choice supporters. On July 21, the president remarked, "I'm pro-choice, but I think we also have the tradition in this town, historically, of not financing abortions as part of government-funded health care."[12] But this did little to alleviate pro-life concerns. Journalist Jonathan Alter reported that Cardinal Sean O'Malley of Boston lobbied the president during Senator Kennedy's funeral service on August 29.[13] He told the president that "the Catholic bishops were eager to back the bill but couldn't support anything that would open the way to abortions." Obama, Alter wrote, listened patiently, but "had no idea how actively the Church was about to flex its muscles."

On September 9, the president addressed a Joint Session of Congress to address concerns about the pending health care reform.[14] "There are also those who claim that our reform efforts would insure illegal immigrants," Obama said. "This, too, is false. The reforms I'm proposing would not apply to those who are here illegally."[15] In one of the more dramatic moments of the entire Obamacare campaign, Representative Joe Wilson (R-SC) screamed out "You Lie!"[16] A chorus of boos cascaded, reflecting the rancor of the congressional debate over health care. Moments later, Obama steadfastly denied that the law

[10] Viveca Novak, *Surgery for Seniors vs. Abortions?*, FACTCHECK (Jul. 31, 2009), perma.cc/BMM9-ERNB.
[11] *Id.*
[12] Stephanie Condon, *Obama: Abortion Funding Not Main Focus of Health Reform*, CBSNEWS (Jul. 21, 2009), perma.cc/5HR2-3TZ2.
[13] JONATHAN ALTER, THE PROMISE: PRESIDENT OBAMA, YEAR ONE 408 (2010).
[14] Remarks by the President to a Joint Session of Congress on Health Care, OFF. OF PRESS SEC. (Sept. 9, 2009), perma.cc/E46B-QHUV. We already discussed this speech in Chapter 2.
[15] *Id.*
[16] *GOP Rep. to Obama: 'You Lie!'*, YOUTUBE (Sep. 9, 2009), bit.ly/1PsWKK4.

would in any way affect abortions: "And one more misunderstanding I want to clear up – under our plan, no federal dollars will be used to fund abortions, and federal conscience laws will remain in place."[17]

However, the president had not yet convinced Democratic members of the Pro-Life Caucus, whose support he needed to cross the pivotal 216-vote threshold. This group was led by Representative Bart Stupak (D-MI). In November 2009, Stupak introduced an amendment to the House bill, providing that no funds "may be used to pay for any abortion" except in cases where a physician certifies that the "woman [is] in danger of death unless an abortion is performed ... or unless the pregnancy is the result of an act of rape or incest."[18] The U.S. Conference of Catholic Bishops supported the amendment and sent out a message to be "announced at all Masses": "Please support the Stupak Amendment that addresses essential pro-life concerns."[19] They added: "If these serious concerns are not addressed, the final bill should be opposed."[20]

Opponents of the Stupak proposal charged that it went much further than the Hyde Amendment. Cecile Richards, president of Planned Parenthood, stated that the amendment "would result in the elimination of abortion coverage in the new insurance market created under health care reform."[21] Specifically, subsidized individual policies – what the overwhelming majority of exchange customers would buy – could not cover abortions. Customers would have to pay for a separate, unsubsidized abortion rider. As more Americans were shifted to the exchange – that is, their old plans were no longer valid – NARAL warned, "it is possible that ultimately insurance coverage for abortion services will become a thing of the past."[22]

The *New York Times* reported that House Speaker Nancy Pelosi (D-CA) was unsuccessful in persuading pro-life Democrats to drop their support for the Stupak Amendment. "To save the health care bill," the *Times* reported, "she had to give in to abortion opponents in her party and allow them to propose tight restrictions barring any insurance plan that is purchased with

---

[17] *Joint Session, supra* note 14.
[18] D. Brad Wright, *The Facts on Abortion and Health Reform*, Huff. Post (Mar. 18, 2010), perma.cc/U4DT-3ZFZ.
[19] David M. Herszenhorn & Jackie Homes, *Abortion Was at Heart of Wrangling*, N.Y. Times (Nov. 7, 2009), perma.cc/ATC4-DSS9.
[20] *Id.*
[21] Press Release, Cecile Richards, president, Planned Parenthood Fed'n of Am., *Rep. Bart Stupak's Amendment Restricting Women's Health Care Access* (May 14, 2014), perma.cc/6RAA-9QXB.
[22] NARAL Pro-Choice Am. Found, *The Stupak-Pitts Amendment Goes Far Beyond Current Law, Imposes Unprecedented Restrictions on Abortion Coverage for Millions of Women* 4 (2009), bit.ly/29JReAP.

government subsidies from covering abortions."[23] After Pelosi allowed the amendment to come up for a vote, it passed 240-194, with 64 Democrats crossing the aisle to vote "Aye."[24]

Despite its bipartisan support in the House, President Obama opposed the amendment. "I laid out a very simple principle, which is this is a health care bill, not an abortion bill," he said.[25] "And we're not looking to change what is the principle that has been in place for a very long time, which is federal dollars are not used to subsidize abortions." House Minority Leader John Boehner (R-OH) faulted the president's opposition to the Stupak Amendment. "He is troubled that the bill contains a bipartisan amendment prohibiting federal funds for abortion," Boehner said, "an amendment reflecting the views held by most Americans and a bipartisan majority of legislators in the House."[26]

3.3. "THE CORNHUSKER KICKBACK"

On the other side of Capitol Hill, Senate Majority Leader Harry Reid did not include the Stupak Amendment in the Senate bill. Instead, he included language that mirrored a proposal by Representative Lois Capps (D-CA) that would have simply extended the restrictions imposed by the Hyde Amendment.[27] But this approach proved problematic. With no margin for error, Reid needed all sixty members of his caucus to support the bill. The fate of the ACA in the Senate would come down to the vote of Ben Nelson, a moderate pro-life Democrat from Nebraska. Nelson was "very pleased that the Stupak amendment passed in the House."[28] If the Senate version "doesn't make it clear that [the ACA] does not fund abortion with government money," he told *Fox News*, "you can be sure I will vote against the bill."[29]

Much to Reid's dismay, on December 1, Nelson announced that he was working on an "abortion amendment [that is] as identical to Stupak as it can be."[30] Nelson suggested that he might join the Republican filibuster if the bill

---

[23] Herszenhorm, *supra* note 19.

[24] *House Vote – 884 Restricts Federal Funding for Abortion*, N.Y. TIMES (Nov. 7, 2009), nyti.ms/1Z4tnOc.

[25] Transcript of ABC News Exclusive Interview with President Barack Obama, ABCNEWS (Nov. 9, 2009), perma.cc/MFD2-KVSQ.

[26] Trish Turner et al., *Abortion Haggling Looms over Health Care Debate in Senate*, FOXNEWS (Nov. 10, 2009), perma.cc/VN64-4EWZ.

[27] Dorinda C. Bordlee, *Saturday Night Fights*, NAT'L. REV. (Nov. 20, 2009), perma.cc/9NYX-WZ7Y.

[28] Turner, *supra* note 26.

[29] *Id.*

[30] Patrick O'Connor, *Ben Nelson to Offer Stupak-like Amendment*, POLITICO (Dec. 1, 2009), perma.cc/GWR6-3332.

was not changed. "Faced with a decision about whether or not to move a bill that is bad," he said, "I won't vote to move it. For sure."[31] The entire legislative process hinged on securing Nelson's vote to get over the sixty-vote threshold. The *Washington Post* reported that Senator Charles E. Schumer (D-NY) "put his head in his hands" and asked his majority leader, "What are we going to do?"[32]

With little time to spare, the Democratic caucus was able move past this impasse. On Friday, December 18, Schumer spent thirteen hours in Reid's office, eight of which focused on abortion funding, as they engaged in "shuttle negotiation[s]" between the Democratic leadership and Nelson.[33] The rest of the time focused on negotiating the costs of the Medicaid expansion. It was during the other five hours that the so-called *Cornhusker Kickback* was negotiated. Under this deal, Nebraska, and only Nebraska, would *permanently* receive full funding for Obamacare's Medicaid expansion. The other 49 states would receive full funding only for the first three years, and partial funding thereafter. Senator Saxby Chambliss (R-GA) observed, "It's pretty obvious that votes have been bought" to secure Nelson's support.[34] Senator Amy Klobuchar (D-MN) didn't disagree. "People fight for their own states. That's the nature of a democracy."[35] Senator Jay Rockefeller (D-WV) lamented the sweetheart deal. "We all walked around with our heads bowed down."[36]

Nelson would steadfastly deny that his vote was secured by the *Kickback*. He told Nebraska Public Radio, "It didn't exist and the people who characterized it that way knew it didn't exist. There wasn't something in there simply for Nebraska. There was something for all the states."[37] *Politico* reported, "while most insiders were focused on [the abortion deal], Nelson was quietly ensuring that his state would never have to pay for the Medicaid expansion being written into the bill – an agreement that had been in the works for weeks."[38] Nebraska Governor Dave Heineman thanked Nelson in a letter for the $100 million in additional funding the Cornhusker State received. He wrote that

---

[31] Jonathan Karl, *Democrat Ben Nelson Draws a Line in the Sand on Health Care*, ABCNews (Nov. 11, 2009), perma.cc/Z8FV-GYYP.

[32] Paul Kane, *To Sway Nelson, a Hard-Won Compromise on Abortion Issue*, Wash. Post (Dec. 20, 2009), perma.cc/8R4A-3B8J.

[33] *Id.*

[34] Trish Turner, *Nelson Accused of Selling Vote on Health Bill for Nebraska Pay-off*, FoxNews (Dec. 20, 2009), perma.cc/U85W-PZQ3.

[35] *Id.*

[36] Josh Blackman, Unprecedented: The Constitutional Challenge to Obamacare 54–55 (2013).

[37] Brent Martin, *Sen. Nelson Denies "Cornhusker Kickback" Ended His Political Career*, Neb. Radio Network (Jan. 2, 2013), perma.cc/8P4S-N5LB.

[38] Chris Frates, *Payoffs for States Get Reid to 60*, Politico (Dec. 19, 2009), perma.cc/VJX7-8DX7.

Nebraska "cannot afford an unfunded mandate and uncontrolled spending of this magnitude."[39] Florida, South Carolina, and other states were initially drawn to challenge the constitutionality of Obamacare's Medicaid expansion, because they alleged that the unequal levels of funding violated the Equal Protection Clause.[40] This aspect of the case was quickly replaced by the challenge to the individual mandate.

Reid saw no problem with the giveaways to Nebraska, alongside special treatments for other states with moderate Democratic Senators. There was the so-called *Louisiana Purchase*, to assuage Mary Landrieu and the *Florida Flim Flam*, for the benefit of Bill Nelson.[41] "You'll find a number of states that are treated differently than other states," Reid acknowledged.[42] "That's what legislating is all about. It's compromise."

According to the *Washington Post*, by 9:30 PM the evening of December 18 – after the Medicaid funding was settled – "Nelson was ready to cut the deal, no matter what the antiabortion groups" did.[43] The compromise was settled with a handshake.[44] "We have a deal," Reid told Senator Barbara Boxer (D-CA).[45] "It was a moment I'll never forget," Boxer recalled.[46] She wasn't enthused about the arrangement, but was content to have "the status quo preserved, which is the Hyde [Amendment], because it's been an uneasy truce between the people who are pro-choice and the people who are anti-choice."[47] After signing on, Nelson gave Boxer a "big hug."[48]

Under the compromise, states could opt out of allowing plans to cover abortions on the exchanges, and enrollees in plans that covered abortions could pay for a separate rider, apart from the subsidized premiums. In contrast, under the Stupak Amendment, such funding would have been prohibited in all states. "I know this is hard for some of my colleagues to accept," Nelson explained. "And I appreciate their right to disagree. But I would not have voted for this bill without these provisions," the Nebraskan insisted.[49] The sixty-vote

---

[39] *Id.*

[40] UNPRECEDENTED, *supra* note 36, at 59–60, 64–65.

[41] Brian Montopoli, *Tallying the Health Care Bill's Giveaways*, ABCNEWS (Dec. 21, 2009), perma.cc/8792-9SXZ.

[42] *Id.*

[43] Kane, *supra* note 32.

[44] *Id.*

[45] *Id.*

[46] *Id.*

[47] Karen Schuberg, *Boxer Says She Backs 'Hyde Idea' to Bar Federal Funds for Abortion, But Voted Against Hyde-like Language in Health Care Bill*, CNS NEWS (Dec. 15, 2009), perma.cc/ER2J-4JWC.

[48] Kane, *supra* note 32.

[49] *Id.*

bloc was solidified. Victorious, Reid called the president who was aboard Air Force One. "We did it, Mr. President."[50] During this tumultuous period, Reid could be forgiven for not paying any attention to Section 36B and the issue of subsidies on federal exchanges.

The Senate bill passed on Christmas Eve with the Nelson Amendment, and was headed to the House. As discussed in Chapter 2, the actual details of the bill didn't matter as much as reaching sixty votes. Most experts predicted that the House and Senate language on abortion would ultimately be resolved in a conference. Laurie Rubiner, Planned Parenthood's vice president of public policy, told *CBS News* that she was convinced that the Senate bill would prevail over the House language in conference committee.[51] "The Senate has always been a cooling-off place," Rubiner said.[52] "I don't see any reason to engage in brinksmanship at this point. This is about getting the best bill we can and making sure women aren't left worse off than they were before."[53]

All of these plans were uprooted after Scott Brown's election. Because of the forty-first Republican in the Senate, a conference became impossible, and House Democrats were forced to take the Senate bill as is. That included the language Reid offered to assuage Nelson's concerns about abortion. But there was another twist to this shift in tactics. The Democrats no longer needed Nelson's support for the sixtieth vote. With the reconciliation process, the magic number in the Senate was now 51. Two months later, President Obama would propose "[e]liminating the Nebraska ... provision" from the ACA that offered the Cornhusker state a 100% reimbursement rate.[54] The House agreed, and stripped the Kickback from the bill.[55] In an interview with *Politico*, Nelson joked that "those who didn't want me to be the 60th vote get their wish."[56]

Nelson would not run for re-election in 2012.[57] After he retired, he became the CEO of the National Association of Insurance Commissioners. Even out

---

[50] *Id.*
[51] Stephanie Condon, *Abortion Rights Groups Now Oppose House Health Care Bill*, CBS NEWS (Nov. 9, 2009), perma.cc/6HZ5-4QF4.
[52] *Id.*
[53] *Id.*
[54] White House Press Office, *The President's Proposal Puts American Families and Small Business Owners in Control of Their Own Health Care*, THE HILL (Feb. 22, 2010), perma.cc/MMQ6-VNHB.
[55] Jordan Fabian, *Obama's Healthcare Plan Mixes Ben Nelson's 'Cornhusker Kickback' Deal*, THE HILL (Jan. 22, 2010), perma.cc/RE6N-DFGM.
[56] Carrie Budoff Brown, *Nelson: National Exchange a Dealbreaker*, POLITICO (Jan. 25, 2010), perma.cc/W22R-ZTEB.
[57] Nelson deposited his papers and records from his time in the Senate at the libraries of the University of Nebraska-Lincoln. My attempt to research his files during the enactment of the ACA were unsuccessful, as Nelson restricted public access for ten years. I learned that the

of office, his role in the battle over the ACA was far from over. In the same interview with *Politico*, he also made a statement that would become instrumental to the litigation over the subsidies on the federal exchange. Nelson explained that a single "national exchange is unnecessary and I wouldn't support something that would start us down the road of federal regulation of insurance and a single-payer plan."[58] This sentence would later be cited, repeatedly, to prove that Nelson conditioned his support for the ACA on limiting subsidies to the state-established exchanges.

3.4. "CAST A LIFE-AFFIRMING 'YES' VOTE"

With the Senate bill secured, the process would soon move back to the House of Representatives. Conservative talk radio host Hugh Hewitt said that Nelson's compromise "launched the most important Congressional debate on abortion in three decades."[59] Stupak insisted that he and his caucus would not support the Senate bill. "We are going to hold firm," Stupak said, "and make sure" his restrictive language stays in the legislation.[60] "We will not vote for this bill if that language is not there. While I and many other pro-life Democratic House members wish to see health care coverage for all Americans, the proposed Senate language is unacceptable." The Susan B. Anthony List, a pro-life advocacy group, announced: "Let's pray that [Stupak] has continued strength not to compromise the lives of hundreds of thousands of unborn children!"[61]

However, support from religious groups began to splinter. *Network*, a National Catholic social justice group, published a letter speaking on behalf of 59,000 Catholic Sisters who supported the Affordable Care Act.[62] They urged Congress "to cast a life-affirming 'yes' vote." The Sisters explained, "While it is an imperfect measure, it is a crucial next step in realizing health care for all. It will invest in preventative care." Critically, "despite false claims to the contrary, the Senate bill will not provide taxpayer funding for elective abortions. It will uphold longstanding conscience protections." The Sisters wrote that this

---

Nebraska Historical Society, where Nelson's gubernatorial archives are housed, declined his request to store his Senatorial papers due to the unusually-lengthy restriction.

[58] Brown, *supra* note 56.

[59] Hugh Hewitt, *This Is the Most Important Abortion Debate in Congress in 30 Years, So Where's Bart Stupak?* (Dec. 22, 2009), perma.cc/876Z-CQM7.

[60] Steven Ertelt, *Bart Stupak Says He Will "Hold Firm" on Banning Abortion Funding in Health Care*, LifeNews (Dec. 21, 2009), perma.cc/H62X-VFY4.

[61] *Stupak: Nelson Compromise Is "Unacceptable,"* SBAList (Dec. 21, 2009), perma.cc/4SBM-HDUQ.

[62] Letter from Catholic Sisters in Support of Healthcare Reform Bill, Network (2010), perma.cc/5YUA-DFUT.

"is the REAL pro-life stance, and we as Catholics are all for it." Missing from the signatories were any representatives of the Little Sisters of the Poor, an order of nuns who would challenge the ACA's contraceptive mandate in federal court. Joining the nuns was the influential Catholic Health Association, a national organization of more than 1,200 Catholic health care sponsors and facilities, led by Sister Carol Keehan.

This broad coalition of support worked. On March 21, Representative Jim Cooper, a pro-life Democrat from Tennessee, announced his support for the bill. "I woke up this Sunday morning, said my prayers, and finally decided that I will vote YES on health care reform," Cooper said on the floor of the House.[63] He cited the support of the "the Catholic Health Association, Catholics United, and groups representing 59,000 Catholic Sisters [that] support the legislation." In June 2015, President Obama praised the Association and Sister Carol. "We would not have gotten the Affordable Care Act done had it not been for her," Obama said.[64] "I want to thank the entire Catholic Health Association for the incredible work you do. And it's true, I just love nuns, generally. I'm just saying."

Not all Catholics would agree. On March 23, 2010, the U.S. Conference of Catholic Bishops criticized the law "for whatever good [it] achieves or intends" because "there is compelling evidence that it would expand the role of the federal government in funding and facilitating abortion and plans that cover abortion."[65] The Bishops warned that the ACA "appropriates billions of dollars in new funding without explicitly prohibiting the use of these funds for abortion, and it provides federal subsidies for health plans covering elective abortions." The letter praised "the principled actions of the pro-life Members of Congress from both parties, in the House and the Senate, who have worked courageously to create legislation that respects" life. And in a not-too-subtle rejoinder to the Sisters, the letter closed: "As bishops of the Catholic Church, we speak in the name of the Church and for the Catholic faith itself."

The debate over Obamacare created a schism among American Catholics. The *New York Times* reported that "in breaking publicly with Roman Catholic bishops over the health care bill, a group of nuns has once again exposed the long-running rift between liberal and conservative

[63] Press Release, Jim Cooper, Cooper's Floor Statement on Health Reform (Mar. 20, 2010), perma.cc/U4WT-9NBY.

[64] Terence P. Jeffrey, *Obama: Without Catholic Nun We Would Not Have Gotten Obamacare Done*, CNSNews (Jun. 10, 2015), perma.cc/9KJM-SRMU.

[65] Press Release, United States Conference of Catholic Bishops, Universal Health Care Statement by Cardinal Francis George (Mar. 23, 2010), perma.cc/5CRN-U6DN.

theology in the Catholic Church."[66] Sister Simone Campbell of *Network* stopped short of criticizing the Bishops, but said that "some people could be motivated by a political loyalty that's outside of caring for the people who live at the margins of health care in society."[67] The letter from the Bishops countered, "The Catholic faith is not a partisan agenda, and we take this opportunity to recommit ourselves to working for health care which truly and fully safeguards the life, dignity, conscience and health of all, from the child in the womb to those in their last days on earth."[68] Father Frank Pavone of the organization Priests for Life – who would later sue the federal government over the contraceptive mandate – told *LifeNews* that "it is absurd to advocate social justice while risking the expansion of a holocaust. The right to life is at the heart of social justice. We can't pursue one by sacrificing the other."[69]

On March 19, Stupak dismissed the relevance of the Sisters' position on MSNBC's *Hardball*: "With all due respect to the nuns, when I deal or am working on right-to-life issues, we don't call the nuns."[70] He added in another interview that when "drafting right to life language," he calls on "leading bishops, Focus on the Family, and The National Right to Life Committee."[71] Sister Regina McKillip, a Dominican nun, scolded Stupak for his remarks. "We have a number of nuns in his district," she said, "and they've been calling him."[72] Stupak said that "all the phones are unplugged at [his] house," because his wife was "tired of the obscene calls and threats" (presumably not from the nuns).[73] Hearing people say "they're going to spit on you and all this," is "like a living hell." Until the eleventh hour, Stupak's vote was still in flux. Conservative columnist Tim Carney called Stupak "perhaps the single most important rank-and-file House member in passing the bill."[74]

---

[66] Helene Cooper, *Nuns Back Bill Amid Broad Rift over Whether It Limits Abortion Enough*, N.Y. TIMES (Mar. 19, 2010), nyti.ms/1OciHaC.

[67] *Id.*

[68] George, *supra* note 65.

[69] Steven Ertelt, *Pro-Life Advocates Dismiss Catholic Nuns' Letter Backing Pro-Abortion Health Care*, LIFENEWS (Mar. 16, 2010), perma.cc/R7AU-WMNR.

[70] Cooper, *supra* note 66.

[71] Ertelt, *supra* note 69.

[72] Cooper, *supra* note 66.

[73] Jeffrey Young & Bob Cusack, *Stupak: Health Fight Has Been 'Living Hell'*, THE HILL (Mar. 18, 2010), perma.cc/5HXS-S9JQ.

[74] Timothy P. Carney, *Reforming Your Way to Riches: Stupak Gets His Big K St. Payday*, WASH. EXAM'R (Apr. 11, 2011), perma.cc/3EFR-EHHT.

3.5. "SIGNING STATEMENT ON STEROIDS!"

To reach the necessary 216 votes to pass the Senate version of the ACA, Speaker Pelosi needed to wrangle the support of the pro-life caucus. However, she could not make any substantive changes to the ACA because that would disrupt the fragile reconciliation process and allow Republicans to kill the bill. Former Senate Majority Leader Tom Daschle (D-SD) recalled that the Democrats feared that if her caucus were not secure, Republicans would offer the Stupak Amendment language as a poison pill on a "motion to recommit." If Pelosi did not have enough support, the ACA would be dead in its tracks.[75]

To resolve this crisis, President Obama turned to what would become the new modus operandi of the ACA: use executive action to alter a health care law that the legislative process could not. On the suggestion of Chief of Staff Rahm Emanuel, the president offered Stupak and his colleagues an executive order. It clarified that the ACA would not provide subsidies for exchange-purchased policies that covered abortions. An executive order is only a temporary statement of the president's policies and can be revoked unilaterally at any point. It does not bind future presidents, or even the current president for that matter.

According to journalist Jonathan Alter, White House Counsel, Bob Bauer "banged out the new language on his computer on Sunday morning and brought it to the Oval Office."[76] When he saw it, "the President knew ... he had clinched the deal."[77] On March 21 at 3:00 PM, mere hours before the final vote, Obama called Stupak and told him, "We have a deal."[78] Executive Order 13535 provided: "The Act maintains current Hyde Amendment restrictions governing abortion policy and extends those restrictions to the newly created health insurance exchanges."[79] The president signed it "behind closed doors" without any fanfare.[80] Stupak later recalled that "president Obama assured me this [executive order] was an 'iron-clad agreement.'"[81] With that assurance, Stupak's caucus would support the bill. The votes were secured. "We're

75 Tom Daschle, Getting It Done: How Obama and Congress Finally Broke the Stalemate to Make Way for Health Care Reform 256 (2010).

76 Alter, *supra* note 13, at 433.

77 Id.

78 Daschle, *supra* note 75, at 256.

79 Press Release, Office of Press Secretary, Executive Order 13535 – Patient Protection and Affordable Care Act's Consistency with Longstanding Restrictions on the Use of Federal Funds for Abortion (Mar. 24, 2010), perma.cc/63DD-99VK.

80 Mimi Hall, *Both Sides of Abortion Issue Quick to Dismiss*, USA Today (Mar. 25, 2010), perma.cc/6AVP-V2RX.

81 David Lindsay, *Whole Life Democrats*, David Lindsay (Sept. 24, 2012), perma.cc/HT3A-X9LB.

feeling good," announced House Majority Whip James Clyburn, "with room to spare."[82] Pelosi celebrated, "We're very pleased that we have more votes for the bill."[83]

In one of the rare areas of overlap between pro-life and pro-choice groups, everyone agreed the executive order was meaningless. National Right to Life Committee dubbed it a "transparent political fig leaf."[84] Planned Parenthood called it a "symbolic gesture."[85] The executive order would not accomplish the primary goal of the Stupak Amendment – prohibiting insurance policies that cover abortions to be subsidized with federal money on the health care exchanges. Representative Jean Schmidt (R-OH) said that the executive order from the president "is not worth the paper it is printed on."[86] She pointed out that "it is not the law of the land. It can be rescinded in the blink of an eye by that jot of the president's pen." She was right.

Making the point far more eloquently was Harvard law professor Laurence Tribe, who two decades earlier taught constitutional law to a young Barack Obama. The day of the final House vote, Tribe was e-mailing back and forth with then–Solicitor General, and future Justice Elena Kagan. At 11:39 AM, Tribe had emailed Kagan, the former Dean of the Harvard Law School: "fingers and toes crossed today!"[87] Kagan replied, with gusto, "I hear they have the votes, Larry!!" She continued, "Simply Amazing." Tribe replied to Kagan, expressing incredulity that the ACA was about to be passed "with the Stupak group accepting the magic of what amounts to a *signing statement on steroids!*" Tribe stated the obvious, and what any first-year constitutional law student would know – that the order was legally impotent. At 5:06 PM, as the vote was about to proceed in the house, Tribe e-mailed Kagan again, "So health care is basically done! Remarkable." Two years later, Justice Kagan would look back at the "brokered compromise[s]" and "complex parliamentary shenanigans" that took place "across the street" as the bill traversed the legislative gauntlet.[88]

As the vote began in the House at 9:45 PM, an exhausted Speaker Pelosi urged everyone "to complete the great unfinished business of our society and

---

[82] Dana Bash et al., *Health Care Latest: Obama Says House Made "The Right Vote,"* CNN (Mar. 21, 2010), perma.cc/P43Q-ABHL.

[83] *Id.*

[84] Hall, *supra* note 80.

[85] *Id.*

[86] UNPRECEDENTED, *supra* note 36, at 75.

[87] Terence P. Jeffrey, *Kagan to Tribe on Day Obamacare Passed: 'I Hear They Have the Votes, Larry!! Simply Amazing',* CNSNews (Nov. 10, 2011), perma.cc/L65L-J6BD.

[88] Oral Argument at 37:50–38:07, NFIB v. Sebelius, 132 S. Ct. 2566 (2012), *Oyez*, bit.ly/1P4cXjn.

pass health insurance reform for all Americans that is a right and not a privilege."[89] The pivotal 216th vote was cast at 10:45 PM. The bill passed with 220 votes by 11:30 PM. Thirty-nine Democrats crossed the aisle to vote against the law. Not a single Republican voted for it. With the same gavel used during the passage of Medicaid, Pelosi closed the session and declared victory.

The president and vice president watched the final vote from the Roosevelt Room in the West Wing. "As the 216th vote registered on the screen," Tom Daschle recalled, "Obama, with a look of immense satisfaction and relief, turned to Biden and applauded."[90] As the loquacious vice president would mutter into a hot mic at the signing ceremony the next day, this was "a big fucking deal."[91]

At a press conference with other pro-life representatives, Stupak said he "stood on principle," because "there will be no public funding for abortion in this legislation."[92] Years later, he recalled that the "Executive Order also reaffirmed the 'conscience clause' which states that no person or institution can be forced to accept, provide or comply with health care policies or medical procedures contrary to their religious and moral beliefs."[93] Almost immediately, the Michigander received the Beltway version of an excommunication. He was heckled on the floor of the House by Representative Randy Neugebauer (R-MO), who called him a "baby killer."[94] The Susan B. Anthony List revoked Stupak's "Defender of Life" award.[95] A few months later, the embattled

[89] Pelosi: 'Today, We Have the Opportunity to Complete the Great Unfinished Business of Our Society and Pass Health Insurance Reform for All Americans*, PR NEWSWIRE (Mar. 22, 2010), perma.cc/XJV2-5UHT.

[90] UNPRECEDENTED, *supra* note 36, at 77.

[91] John Dickerson, *WTF Did Biden Just Say?*, SLATE (Mar. 23, 2010), perma.cc/FT7P-SNU8.

[92] Brian Montopoli, *Stupak to Vote Yes on Health Care Bill*, CBSNEWS (Mar. 21, 2010), perma.cc/C26B-8LWM.

[93] Lindsay, *supra* note 84.

[94] Jake Sherman, *Neugebauer: I Yelled 'Baby Killer'*, POLITICO (Mar. 22, 2010), perma.cc/YJ4D-RXBC.

[95] SBA would target several members of Congress in the upcoming midterm election, including Ohio Democrat Steve Driehaus, for their support of the ACA. Sarah Kliff, *The Hyde Amendment at 35: A New Abortion Divide*, WASH. POST (Oct. 2, 2011), perma.cc/HU7R-CZ9Q. The organization sought to put up a billboard that read "'Shame on Steve Driehaus! Driehaus voted FOR taxpayer-funded abortion.'" Dahlia Lithwick, *What's Scarier Than Truthiness in Politics?*, SLATE (Apr. 22, 2014), perma.cc/EDV8-P7PA. A few weeks before the election, the Ohio Elections Commission found that the advertisement was likely false, which made SBA potentially liable to a criminal prosecution. SBA challenged the Ohio "false statements" act in federal court. *See Susan B. Anthony List v. Driehaus*, 805 F. Supp. 2d 412 (S.D. Ohio 2011). Four years later, SBA would win a unanimous victory before the Supreme Court, which found that group was injured by the Commission's actions. *See Susan B. Anthony List v. Driehaus*, 134 S. Ct. 2334 (2014). SBA would be represented by Michael Carvin – the same lawyer who challenged the individual mandate in 2012 and the tax subsidies rule in 2015.

representative would announce his retirement from Congress. He stepped down in January 2011 and became a lobbyist a few months later.[96] But Stupak had played his role in history.

3.6. "ALERT, ALERT, ALERT"

Largely forgotten amidst L'Affaire Stupak were four words in the ACA – no, not "established by the state," but "preventive care and screenings." At the time, with the debate over life and religious liberty raging, this critical issue barely made a blip on the legislative radar. On December 1, 2009, as the Senate was considering amendments to the bill, Senator Barbara Mikulski (D-MD) took to the floor to address the blip:

> I must say: Alert, alert, alert. We have just been informed that a shrill advocacy group is spreading lies about [the Women's Health Amendment]. They are saying that because it is [about] prevention, it includes abortion services. There are no abortion services included in the Mikulski amendment. It is screening for diseases that are the biggest killers for women – the silent killers of women. *It also provides family planning – but family planning as recognized by other acts.* Please, no more lies. Let's get off of it and save lives.[97]

Mikulski's *Women's Health Amendment* originated in July 2009 before the HELP Committee. The provision would have mandated that all employers provide insurance policies that cover certain "preventive care and screenings." The bill was silent as to what those services were. NARAL, Planned Parenthood, and the National Organization for Women submitted a letter in support of Mikulski's Amendment.[98] The pro-choice groups highlighted that the provision would cover "family planning counseling and services, which help improve birth spacing."

Senator Orrin Hatch (R-UT), fearful that the provision could be expanded to cover abortions, asked if Mikulski would "be willing to put some language in [the bill about] not including abortion services."[99] Mikulski declined to change the statute, denying that it would cover abortions.[100] Senator Bob

---

[96] Erich Licthblau, *Stupak Signs On as a Lobbyist*, N.Y. TIMES (Apr. 11, 2011), perma.cc/ZQ8H-93A5.

[97] *Sen. Mikluski Floor Statement on Women's Healthcare Amendment*, C-SPAN (Dec. 1, 2009), cs.pn/21rtc1c (emphasis added).

[98] Letter from NARAL et al., to Barbara Mikulski, Senator, American Academy of Nursing (Jul. 8, 2009), bit.ly/29mByp3.

[99] Steven Ertelt, *Bob Casey Claims No Abortion Funding in Senate Health Care Bill, Draws Rebuke*, LIFENEWS (Sept. 3, 2009), perma.cc/VTQ5-FPKB.

[100] Susan Ferrechio, *Senate Health Bill Would Mandate Abortion Coverage*, WASH. EXAM'R (Jul. 8, 2009), perma.cc/4ND4-2XUV.

Casey (D-PA) voted against the amendment, explaining, "the way it is written is too broad."[101] He added, "The way it is written could be interpreted down the road to include something like abortion."[102] Coincidentally, the pro-life Democrat's father was the governor of Pennsylvania and the defender of the Commonwealth's abortion legislation in the Supreme Court's landmark 1991 decision of *Planned Parenthood v. Casey*. The Amendment passed through the HELP committee on a 12-11 vote.

Mikulski introduced the Women's Health Amendment on the Senate floor on November 30. Under the Amendment, new employer-provided insurance plans would be required to include coverage without cost sharing – that is, without any additional co-pays – "with respect to women, such *additional preventive care and screenings*."[103] Like with the HELP Committee bill, the Amendment did not define what those "preventive care and screenings" were. Rather, the amendment said, "comprehensive guidelines supported by the Health Resources and Services Administration," a unit of the Department of Health and Human Services (HHS), would resolve the question.[104] Congress would not have to approve the recommendations. Mikulski explained, "We want to end the punitive practices of the private insurance companies in their gender discrimination. We, the women of the Senate, are concerned that even being a woman is being viewed by the insurance companies as a pre-existing condition."[105] The remainder of her floor statement, and that of many other supporters on December 1 and 3, focused on mammograms, breast cancer, heart disease, diabetes, and ailments that can be detected with early screenings.

However, the concerns about abortions continued. *LifeNews* warned that Senator Mikulski's amendment "would essentially define abortion as preventative [sic] care and could result in mandates to private insurance plans that they define abortion as such and provide coverage of it."[106] The story quoted from a letter sent by the National Right to Life Committee, urging opposition to the Mikulski Amendment.[107] "If Congress were to grant any Executive Branch entity sweeping authority to define services that private health plans

---

[101] *Senate Approval of Mikulski Amendment Further Opens Health Care Bill to Massive Federal Funding of Abortion*, PR NEWSWIRE (Dec. 3, 2009), perma.cc/5FDF-MZKT.

[102] *Id.*

[103] 155 CONG. REC. S12,015 (2009), perma.cc/NV5W-XKT8.

[104] 45 C.F.R. § 147.130(a)(1)(iii).

[105] 155 CONG. REC. S12,026 (2009), perma.cc/X3QP-A67M.

[106] Steve Ertelt, *Senate Health Care Bill Amendment Would Define Abortion as Preventative Care*, LIFENEWS (Dec. 1, 2009), perma.cc/9TRT-DBFD.

[107] Letter from Douglas Johnson, Legislative Director & Susan T. Muskett, Senior Legislative Counsel, National Right to Life Committee, to Members of the U.S. Senate (Nov. 30, 2009), bit.ly/29lnHoF.

must cover, merely by declaring a given service to constitute 'preventive care,' then that authority could be employed in the future to require all health plans to cover abortions."[108] NRLC cited a 2009 publication by the National Abortion Federation referring to abortion care as a "comprehensive primary *preventive* health care."[109] The pro-life group urged a modification to the Mikulski Amendment to "explicitly remove abortion from the universe of services that could be defined as mandated 'preventive care.'"[110]

During a colloquy, Casey asked Mikulski if she would clarify that "abortion has never been defined as a preventive service and there is neither the legislative intent nor the language in this amendment to cover abortion as a preventive service or to mandate abortion coverage in any way."[111] Mikulski agreed, and stated:

> This amendment does not cover abortion. Abortion has never been defined as a preventive service. This amendment is strictly concerned with ensuring that women get the kind of preventive screenings and treatments they may need to prevent diseases particular to women such as breast cancer and cervical cancer. There is neither legislative intent nor legislative language that would cover abortion under this amendment, nor would abortion coverage be mandated in any way by the Secretary of Health and Human Services.[112]

Senator Brownback (R-KS) was not persuaded. "I have trouble, however, because I believe a future bureaucracy could interpret it differently."[113] Because it was up to Health Resource and Services Administration (HRSA), virtually anything could be covered by *preventive care*. Brownback asked to change the wording of the statute to expressly prohibit the classification of abortion as "preventive care." The future governor of Kansas explained, "But, as we all know as legislators, it is one thing to say something on the Senate floor, and it is one thing to have a colloquy, but it is far different to have it written in the base law."[114] Mikulski once again refused any alterations. The amendment passed by a vote of 61–39, with several female Republicans crossing the aisle to make up for several male Democratic defectors. Senator Lisa Murkowski (R-AK) proposed an amendment that would expressly prohibit HHS from classifying abortion as "preventive care," but it was defeated by a vote of 41–59.

[108] Steven Ertelt, *Planned Parenthood Launches Campaign to Fund Birth Control via ObamaCare*, LifeNews (Oct. 14, 2010), perma.cc/TA8N-A5QS.
[109] Johnson & Muskett, *supra* note 107, at 2.
[110] *Id.*
[111] 155 Cong. Rec. S12,274 (2009), perma.cc/TQ52-T7MA.
[112] *Id.*
[113] *Id.*
[114] *Id.*

While the Republicans were intent on asking about abortion services, perhaps they were not asking the right questions. Instead of asking about "abortions" alone, the senators should have been more specific – what did Senator Mikulski mean when she said "family planning" would be covered? The Food and Drug Administration has approved twenty methods of contraception. As the government would explain to the Supreme Court in 2014, four of these methods – two types of intrauterine devices (IUDs) and the emergency contraceptives commonly known as *Plan B* and *Ella* – "can function by preventing the implantation of a fertilized egg."[115] Many pro-life groups refer to these methods as "abortifacients" because they may be used to terminate a pregnancy.

However, as Justice Samuel Alito recognized in the *Hobby Lobby* decision, although people who "believe that life begins at conception regard these four methods as causing abortions ... federal regulations, which define pregnancy as beginning at implantation, do not so classify them."[116] Thus, under federal law, preventing the implantation of a fertilized egg would *not* be considered an abortion. Indeed, these forms of birth control have long been paid for by federal funds under Title X of the Public Health Service Act of 1970. The Hyde Amendment does not prohibit funding for these pre-implantation forms of birth control. The Office of Population Affairs boasts that providing contraceptive care through "Title X family planning centers help to avert an estimated 1.2 million unintended pregnancies."[117]

The senators who spoke in support of the Women's Health Amendment were very deliberate to use the congressional term of art "family planning" to refer to the scope of "preventive services" that would be included. For example, Senator Boxer said that the Amendment would cover "annual women's health screenings, and *family planning services*."[118] Senator Al Franken (D-MN) explained that under the Milkulski "amendment, the Health Resources and Services Administration will be able to include other important services at no cost, such as the well woman visit, prenatal care, and *family planning*."[119] Senator Patty Murray (D-WA) pointed out that the amendment will provide at no additional cost access to *"family planning services* [and] mammograms,

[115] Joint Appendix at 10a, Burwell v. Hobby Lobby, 134 S. Ct. 2751 (2014) (No.13–354); *see also* Brief for Petitioners at 9 n.4, Burwell v. Hobby Lobby, 134 S. Ct. 2751 (2014) (No.13–354).

[116] Burwell v. Hobby Lobby, 134 S. Ct. 2751, 2763 n.7 (2014) (citing Prescription Drug Products; Certain Combined Oral Contraceptives for Use as Postcoital Emergency Contraception, 62 Fed. Reg. 8611 (notice Feb. 25, 1997); 45 C.F.R. § 46.202(f) (2013) ("Pregnancy encompasses the period of time from implantation until delivery.")).

[117] Office of Population Affairs, *Title X: The National Family Planning Program*, U.S. Dep't of Health and Human Servs (2014), perma.cc/8U4K-3A7M.

[118] 155 Cong. Rec. S12,025 (2009), perma.cc/VKB2-GA9H.

[119] 155 Cong. Rec. S12,271 (2009), perma.cc/JY2A-5DCT.

which we have all talked about so many times, to make sure they maintain their health."[120] On December 8 – five days after the amendment passed – Senator Dick Durbin (D-IL) said, "[T]he *family planning* aspect of our health care reform will actually net fewer abortions in America."[121] Even Senator Nelson, who voted against the Mikulski Amendment because it did not explicitly exclude abortion services, acknowledged that he "strongly support[ed] the underlying goal of furthering preventive care for women ... [including] *family planning*."[122] Had the Republican senators asked about whether all employers would be mandated to pay for contraceptives that could prevent the implantation of a fertilized egg, rather than simply asking about "abortions," they would have received a very different answer.

After the vote on Mikulski's proposal, the *New York Times* reported that "the Senate approved an amendment to its health care legislation that would require insurance companies to offer free mammograms and other preventive services to women."[123] There was no mention of emergency contraception. The *Catholic Exchange* reported that "[p]ro-life leaders opposed the amendment over concerns that it provides authority that could be used to mandate abortion coverage in private insurance plans."[124] There was no mention of contraception. In their statement, the *National Organization for Women* was silent about *family planning*, and praised the provision because it would cover "mammograms and cervical cancer screenings."[125] Outside the congressional record, I could not find a single contemporaneous record to a mandate for "family planning," let alone an employer mandate to pay for contraception.

Had there been any discussion that this provision would be used to force employers, including religious nonprofits, to cover contraceptives that can prevent the implantation of a fertilized egg, there would have been an uproar. Such a bill was unlikely to have secured the vote of Senator Nelson and others in the fragile sixty-member caucus.

It is not clear that anyone in the House understood the Amendment would operate in this broad fashion. Representative Stupak explained that the "[t]he

[120] 155 CONG. REC. S12,274 (2009), perma.cc/JY2A-5DCT.
[121] 155 CONG. REC. S12,671 (2009), perma.cc/7AZK-6Q5W.
[122] 155 CONG. REC. S12,277 (2009), perma.cc/JY2A-5DCT.
[123] David M. Herszenhorn & Robert Pear, *Senate Passes Women's Health Amendment*, N.Y. TIMES (Dec. 3, 2009), perma.cc/B8D4-G3FQ.
[124] John J. Miller, *Senate Passes Amendment That Could Mandate Abortion Coverage in Insurance Plans*, CATHOLIC EXCH. (Dec. 4, 2009), perma.cc/X4PZ-SG4Q
[125] Press Release, National Organization for Women, Terry O'Neill, president, Senator Mikulski's Health Amendment Is an Important Improvement to the Senate Health Care Reform Bill (Dec. 1, 2009), perma.cc/Z53C-5ZMP.

principal tenet of [his the pro-life] Caucus members is their belief that the *fertilized embryo is a human life* and that any man-made disturbance of the embryo is a form of abortion."[126] FDA-approved contraceptives may have the effect of "preventing the implantation of a fertilized egg."[127] Under no circumstance could the pro-life caucus have supported a mandate that was contrary to their mission statement – even with the president's executive order, which would have no impact on the mandate. I could not locate a single contemporaneous statements from Stupak or anyone else in the House suggesting that they realized the "preventive care" mandate could be used to force religious employers to cover such contraceptive methods that his caucus opposed.

In contrast, the House took specific actions to create a very elaborate "religious conscience exemption" to excuse people from the individual mandate.[128] Certain "religious sect[s] or divisions" as well as members of a "health care sharing ministry" did not have to pay the individual mandate's penalty. The House recognized that forcing someone to buy insurance might conflict with his or her religious scruples. But there was *no* conscience exemption drafted for religious employers to pay for and cover contraceptives that that they consider abortifacients. The Women's Health Amendment did not even have a carve-out for houses of worship, let alone religious non-profits. All qualified employers were bound. (Exemptions and accommodations to the mandate, created through executive action, would be the subject of two Supreme Court cases.) Certainly the requirement to buy insurance – which has a lengthy series of exemptions – would pale in comparison with the requirement for nonprofit religious employers to pay for emergency contraceptives they deem sinful.

This is the proverbial *dog that didn't bark*, a legal principle derived from Sir Arthur Conan Doyle's classic story "Silver Blaze."[129] In the story, an officer from Scotland Yard is investigating a night-time robbery of a racehorse. He asks Detective Sherlock Holmes, "Is there any other point to which you would wish to draw my attention?" Holmes replies, "To the curious incident of the dog in the night-time." The officer is confused. "The dog did nothing in the night-time." Holmes deduces, "That was the curious incident ... Obviously the midnight visitor was someone whom the dog knew well." The dog that did not bark was the clue.

---

[126] Brief of Democrats for Life of America & Bart Stupak as Amici Curiae Supporting Respondents at 1, Burwell v. Hobby Lobby, 134 S. Ct. 2751 (2014) (No. 13–354).
[127] Joint Appendix, *supra note* 115.
[128] 26 U.S.C. § 5000A(d)(2) (2015).
[129] ARTHUR CONAN DOYLE, THE ADVENTURES OF SHERLOCK HOLMES, IN 4 STRAND MAG. 645, 656–57 (1892), bit.ly/1SVzKlr.

That no one objected to a mandate requiring all employers – with no exceptions for any religious groups – to provide contraceptives was itself the "curious incident." This issue is even more extreme than the Hyde Amendment
debate, as the issue was not about federal funding for abortions, but forcing
religious organizations to *pay directly* for these contraceptives. Amid the
debates over the individual mandate, funding for abortion, and the issue of
state-run exchanges, this pivotal detail went entirely unnoticed.

PART II

Conscience and Contraception
(June 29, 2012–May 1, 2013)

4

The Contraceptive Mandate

4.1. "THE FULL RANGE OF CONTRACEPTIVE METHODS"

On November 16, 2010 – less than a month before the first court would invalidate the Affordable Care Act's individual mandate – the Obama administration began to implement the contraceptive mandate. Through the Women's Health Amendment, Congress gave the Department of Health and Human Services (HHS) the discretion to determine what sorts of "preventive care and screenings" employers should be required to cover. HHS in turn funded the Institute of Medicine (IOM) to "conduct a review of effective preventive services to ensure women's health and well-being."[1]

IOM is not a governmental organization but "an arm of the National Academy of Sciences, an organization Congress established 'for the explicit purpose of furnishing advice to the Government.'"[2] Over the next six months, a committee of sixteen members met five times – including three open meetings – to "develop a set of recommendations" for HHS.[3] IOM would advise HHS on what should be covered by the Mikulski Amendment under the umbrella of "preventive care and screenings."

The research culminated in a 250-page report released on July 19, 2011. IOM offered recommendations on everything from mammograms to cervical cancer screenings to breastfeeding. But their most controversial recommendation concerned family planning: "The committee recommends for consideration as a preventive service for women: the full range of Food and Drug

---

[1] INST. OF MED., CLINICAL PREVENTIVE SERVICES FOR WOMEN: CLOSING THE GAPS 1 (2011), bit.ly/1rtIRko. I was unable to locate out how much funding HHS provided IOM for the report.

[2] Burwell v. Hobby Lobby Stores, Inc., 134 S. Ct. 2751, 2787 (2014) (Ginsburg, J., dissenting) (citing Public Citizen v. Department of Justice, 491 U.S. 440, 460, n. 11 (1989)).

[3] IOM, supra note 1, at 2, 3. Importantly, "[t]he cost-effectiveness of screenings or services could not be a factor for the committee to consider in its analyses leading to its recommendations."

Administration–approved contraceptive methods, sterilization procedures, and patient education and counseling for women with reproductive capacity." That would include emergency contraceptives such as *Plan B* and *Ella*.

The report noted that "[c]ontraception and contraceptive counseling are not currently in the array of preventive services available to women under the ACA."[4] This omission was deliberate. Senator Mikulski did not specify what "preventive care" was, and refused to add any sort of clarifying amendments. Professor Mark Rienzi, who teaches at Catholic University, told me "I think a lot of the health care law was written to be a blank check for the administrative state to do whatever it wants." The attorney, who would litigate this issue with the Becket Fund for Religious Liberty, quipped "There are people on the left who looked at the law and said, 'Great, the agencies can fill stuff in.'" Fittingly, a staff member from Senator Mikulski's office kicked off the IOM's inaugural meeting at the DuPont Hotel, and presented their charge to begin the process of filling stuff in.[5]

The IOM arrived at this conclusion, in part, based on a study of how insurance policies nationwide covered contraception. The report found that "85% of large employers and 62% of small employers offered coverage of FDA-approved contraceptives."[6] Additionally, the federal government provided contraceptives through its Federal Employee Health Benefits Program for civil servants, as well as through Medicaid and Medicare. Looking to the states, the IOM cited a Guttmacher Institute report indicating that "[t]wenty-eight states now have regulations requiring private insurers to cover contraceptives."[7]

However, what the IOM neglected to mention – but the Guttmacher Institute did – was that of those twenty-eight states, eighteen exempted religious employers.[8] This included progressive states such as California, Connecticut, Maryland, Massachusetts, New Jersey, and New York. The other states did not expressly exempt religious employers, but through arrangements such as church plans and self-insurance, objecting organizations were able to avoid the mandates.[9] In other words, both nonprofit and for-profit religious employers, in every state where a mandate existed were able to bypass it.

It should not have come as a surprise that IOM did not recognize that the majority of states with contraceptive mandates specifically granted exemptions

[4] *Id.* at 109.
[5] INST. OF MED., *Agenda: Meeting 1. Committee on Preventative Services for Women* (Nov. 16, 2010), perma.cc/PFM6-JL25.
[6] *Id.*
[7] *Id.* at 108.
[8] *Insurance Coverage of Contraceptives*, GUTTMACHER INST. (June 1, 2011), bit.ly/1SQKkez.
[9] *See* COLO. REV. STAT. § 10-16-104 (2010); GA. CODE ANN. § 33-24-59.6 (2005); ILL. REV. STAT. ch. 215 § 5/356z.4, § 125/5-3 and § 165/10; IOWA CODE § 514C.19; NEV. REV. STAT, § 689A. 0417, § 689B.0377, § 695.B1918, and § 695C.1695 (1999); N.H. REV. STAT. ANN. §§

for religious employers. In fairness, this was beyond the scope of their expertise. The members of the panel focused solely on public health issues, not
legal or ethical problems. The words "religion," "faith," "conscience," and
other similar phrases do not appear anywhere in the 250-page report.

Critics of the mandate, however, allege an alternate explanation. Wheaton
College, a Christian school in Illinois, faulted IOM for not inviting to its meeting any "religious groups or other groups that oppose government-mandated
coverage of contraception, sterilization, abortion."[10] IOM did invite representatives from the National Woman's Law Center, Planned Parenthood, and the
National Women's Health Network to speak at the kick-off confab.[11] *LifeNews*
reported that IOM refused to grant time to the Family Research Council and
the U.S. Conference of Catholic Bishops to speak.[12] Representatives from these
pro-life groups were only able to speak during the general public comment
portion towards the end of the meeting.

The IOM report was not unanimous. Dr. Anthony Lo Sasso, selected as
one of the sixteen committee members, dissented. "The view of this dissent," he wrote, "is that the committee process for evaluation of the evidence
lacked transparency and was largely subject to the preferences of the committee's composition." The professor from the University of Illinois wrote that
"Troublingly, the process tended to result in a mix of objective and subjective
determinations filtered through a lens of advocacy."[13] The other fifteen authors
of the report responded to the dissent, stating that "no other member shares
the opinion that report recommendations were not soundly evidence based."[14]

On July 19, 2011, IOM released its report. Less than two weeks later – a
lightning pace for a federal bureaucracy to digest the 250-page tome – HHS
announced that it was "supporting the IOM's recommendations on preventive services" in their entirety.[15] That included the requirement that employers
cover "[a]ll Food and Drug Administration approved contraceptive methods,
sterilization procedures, and patient education and counseling for all women

---

415:18-i, 420-A:17-c, 420-B:8-gg (1999); VT. STAT. ANN. TIT. 8 § 4099c (1999); WASH. REV.
  CODE § 48.41.110 (2007), WIS. STAT. § 609.805 and § 632.895 (17) (2009). We will discuss the
  intricacies of church, insured, and self-insured plans in Chapter 32.
[10] Complaint, Wheaton College v. Sebelius, 1:12-cv-1169 at 12 (D.D.C. Jul. 18, 2012),
  bit.ly/1TtdNb4.
[11] *Agenda*, supra note 5.
[12] Steven Ertelt, *Panel Told: Don't Put More Abortion, Birth Control Funding in ObamaCare*,
  LIFENEWS, (Nov. 16, 2010), perma.cc/XFG2-RUZS.
[13] *IOM*, supra note 1, at 232.
[14] *IOM*, supra note 1, at 235.
[15] *Women's Preventive Services: Required Health Plan Coverage Guidelines*, HEALTH RESOURCES
  AND SERVICES ADMINISTRATION (Aug. 2, 2011), perma.cc/PD8Y-Z25B.

with reproductive capacity."[16] The next step was to convert the IOM recommendations into binding regulations.

In almost all situations, when federal agencies propose new regulations, they must give the public a window of sixty days to formally submit comments. The goal of the "notice and comment" period is to ensure that the people who will be affected by the rule can voice their opinion *before* it goes into effect. The agency is required by law to consider those comments when it revises the *proposed* rule, and publishes the *final* rule after the sixty-day window.

However, this review period would be bypassed for the contraceptive mandate. The Obama administration found such a delay was "impracticable, unnecessary, [and] contrary to the public interest."[17] The new regulations were to take effect one year later on August 1, 2012. HHS determined that if an additional sixty-day review period were granted, it would not take effect until October 1, 2012. As a result, 1.5 million young adults who would begin college in August 2012 "could not benefit from the new prevention coverage ... until the 2013–14 school year."[18] A delay, the agencies determined, "could result in adverse health consequences that may not otherwise have occurred."[19]

In 2011, the only universities that did not already cover contraceptives were those with religious objections.[20] Indeed, many Christian universities such as Georgetown University and Boston College already covered them. The import of this expedited treatment was directed solely at putting the onus on the small number of religious universities that did not offer contraceptive policies to their students, as well as religious charities that had no students.[21] This urgency was contrived, however, as the Obama administration ultimately delayed the mandate for religious universities until January 2014. The courts would postpone it even further.

4.2. "MINISTERIAL EXCEPTION"

Under the Women's Health Amendment, *all* qualified employers with more than fifty employees are covered by the mandate. Unlike the *individual* mandate – which had several exemptions for religious objectors – Congress did

---

[16]   *Id.*
[17]   76 Fed. Reg. 149, bit.ly/26QJrsM.
[18]   *Id.*
[19]   *Id.*
[20]   Igor Volsky, *Many Catholic Universities, Hospitals Already Cover Contraception in Their Health Insurance Plans*, THINK PROGRESS (Feb. 7, 2012), perma.cc/8AG7-GY7V.
[21]   Valerie Schmalz, *Grading Catholic college's health insurance plans*, OUR SUNDAY VISITOR (May 13, 2009), perma.cc/VWT7-CYBR (noting that based on an "unscientific survey," there were "some bright spots in employee health care among the 245 degree-granting American Catholic colleges").

not include any conscience clause for the *employer* mandate. The statute itself said nothing about requiring any employers to cover contraceptives – it only spoke of "preventive care and screenings" for women. As a result, it is not surprising that Congress did not see the need to create any religious exemptions. However, once HHS adopted IOM's recommendation and determined that *all* FDA-approved contraceptives were covered, the Obama administration had to do something about religious employers. As written, the Mikulski amendment would have required that churches, mosques, and synagogues all pay for contraceptives for their employees. Subjecting houses of worship to severe fines was a bridge too far for the Obama administration. In August 2011, HHS proposed the first of many executive actions intended to balance religious liberty and contraceptive coverage. To keep track of them – and there will be many – let's call the initial offering *Exemption 1.0*.

In a press release, HHS announced that the administration will "allow religious institutions that offer insurance to their employees the choice of whether or not to cover contraception services."[22] A footnote on HHS's website – a precursor of what Chapter 13 calls *government by blog post* – explained that a religious employer was "*exempt* from the requirement to cover contraceptive services," so long as it "(1) has the inculcation of religious values as its purpose; (2) primarily employs persons who share its religious tenets; (3) primarily serves persons who share its religious tenets; and (4) is a nonprofit organization."[23] The first and fourth factors were easy enough to satisfy. The second and third elements would prove to be the most controversial. Consider a Catholic Church that manages a soup kitchen. The church hires non-Catholic employees and does not check baptismal certificates of homeless people seeking help. According to *Exemption 1.0*, the Church would not be deemed a "religious employer" because it does not primarily serve and hire people of the same faith. Thus, it would not qualify for the exemption.

The administration explained that it sought to "balance the extension of any coverage of contraceptive services under the HRSA Guidelines to as many women as possible, while respecting the unique relationship between *certain religious employers* and their *employees in certain religious positions*."[24] That is, the government sought to protect those institutions where *both* the employer and employee were of the same faith. The exemption was limited to these

---

[22] *Affordable Care Act Ensures Women Receive Preventative Services at No Additional Cost*, HHS (Aug. 1, 2011), perma.cc/YV7N-C55Z.

[23] HRSA, *Women's Preventive Services: Required Health Plan Coverage Guidelines*, U.S. DEPARTMENT OF HEALTH AND HUMAN SERVICES, perma.cc/5TQN-SMHV.

[24] *Group Health Plans and Health Insurance Issuers Relating to Coverage of Preventive Services*, 76 Fed. Reg. 46621, 46623 (Aug. 3, 2011), bit.ly/1SJnZzL (emphasis added).

congregations because it "respects the *unique* relationship between a *house of worship* and its *employees in ministerial positions*," the government explained.

The focus on "employees in ministerial positions" reflected the Obama administration's broader position on religious liberty. On August 2, 2011 – the day after HHS announced *Exemption 1.0* – the United States would file its brief with the Supreme Court in the case of *Hosanna–Tabor Evangelical Lutheran Church and School v. Equal Employment Opportunity Commission.*[25] Cheryl Perich, a "called" teacher at a Lutheran Church's school, had received theological training and was referred to as "Minister of Religion, Commissioned."[26] After Perich developed narcolepsy and became unable to work, the Church threatened to fire her. The teacher countered that she would sue the Church for a violation of the Americans with Disabilities Act. Perich was ultimately fired, and sued the Church for unlawful retaliation. Hosanna–Tabor defended against her claim based on the "ministerial exception" to the anti-discrimination law.[27] The Lutheran Church argued that the First Amendment's free exercise clause prohibits courts from intervening in disputes concerning the "employment relationship between a religious institution and one of its ministers."[28] Rather, the Church wrote, "Perich was a minister, and she had been fired for a religious reason – namely, that her threat to sue the Church violated the Synod's belief that Christians should resolve their disputes internally."[29]

Despite the fact that "the Courts of Appeals ha[d] uniformly recognized the existence of a 'ministerial exception,' grounded in the First Amendment," the Obama administration did not recognize it.[30] Deputy Solicitor General Leondra R. Kruger – who would be appointed by Governor Jerry Brown to the California Supreme Court in 2015[31] – explained to the Justices that because the Church

---

[25] Brief for the Federal Respondent, *Hosanna-Tabor v. EEOC*, 10-553, Supreme Court of the United States, bit.ly/26QRDJC.

[26] Hosanna–Tabor v. EEOC, 132 S.Ct. 694, 699 (2012).

[27] *See generally* Ilya Shapiro & David Gans, Religious Liberties for Corporations? Hobby Lobby, the Affordable Care Act, and the Constitution (2014) at 26–29.

[28] *Hosanna–Tabor*, 132 S.Ct. at 701.

[29] *Id.*

[30] *Id.* at 705. Ms. Perich also rejected the existence of the "ministerial exception" as applied to secular teachers at a religious school. *See* Brief for Respondent Cheryl Perich at 20, 26, *Hosanna–Tabor v. EEOC*, 10-553, Supreme Court of the United States, bit.ly/1W5I59C ("It bears emphasis at the threshold, however, that Hosanna-Tabor starts in the wrong place in assuming the existence of a 'ministerial exception' and proceeding to examine its scope. *The ADA, like other employment discrimination laws, contains no 'ministerial exception.'*) (emphasis added). Serving as counsel of record for Ms. Perich was Sri Srinivasan, then a partner at the D.C. law firm of O'Melveny & Myers. Now a judge on the D.C. Circuit Court of Appeals, Srinivasan was considered by President Obama on the "short list" to fill Justice Scalia's seat. *See infra* Chapter 30.

[31] David Siders, *Gov. Jerry Brown Names Obama Administration Lawyer to California Supreme Court*, The Sacramento Bee (Nov. 24, 2014), perma.cc/367W-YPYY.

"decided to open its doors to the public to provide" education to children of different faiths, Hosanna-Tabor lost autonomy over its instructors.[32]

During oral arguments, Justice Scalia was incredulous that a church's decision of who would "teach theology ... has to be subject to State control." Kruger countered that the government's interest in allowing employees to "report civil wrongs to civil authorities" without fear of retaliation "is an interest that we think overrides the burden on the association's religious message." In response to a question from the chief justice, Kruger added that the Church's "sincere religious belief was not sufficient to warrant an exemption from generally applicable ... laws."

Justice Kagan, who the year before worked for the Obama administration as Kruger's boss, asked the most devastating question of the day: "Do you believe, Ms. Kruger, that a church has a right that's grounded in the Free Exercise Clause and/or the Establishment Clause to institutional autonomy with respect to its employees?" Kruger responded, "We don't see that line of church autonomy principles in the Religion Clause jurisprudence as such." In English, that means "No." Kagan, agreeing with Scalia, responded incredulously, "I too find that *amazing*, that you think that neither the Free Exercise Clause nor the Establishment Clause has anything to say about a church's relationship with its own employees." The Supreme Court would *unanimously* reject the government's position and recognize that the "ministerial exception" is compelled by the First Amendment.

A careful study of the government's position in *Hosanna-Tabor* elucidates the reasoning behind *Exemption 1.0*. The Lutheran school was open to the public, and admitted students of all faiths. From the government's perspective, Hosanna–Tabor lacked adequate religiosity to warrant an exemption from the anti-discrimination law because it does not "primarily serve persons who share its religious tenets." The government's defense of the exemption – that it "respects the unique relationship between a house of worship and its *employees in ministerial positions*" - mirrors their position in *Hosanna–Tabor*. Faith was protected so long as it formed the bond between a minister and his flock.

The Obama administration would advance a similar position before the Supreme Court in 2015 during *Obergefell v. Hodges*, the same-sex marriage case. Chief Justice Roberts asked Solicitor General Donald Verrilli whether "a religious school that has married housing [would] be required to afford such housing to same-sex couples?" The school no doubt hires professors and admits students of different faiths. Would the First Amendment protect this

---

[32] Federal Respondent, *supra* note 25.

institution, which does not "primarily serve[] persons who share its religious
tenets"? Verrilli attempted to dodge the question, until Justice Alito put the
question differently, citing the 1983 decision in *Bob Jones University v. United
States*. In that case, the Court held that "a college was not entitled to tax-
exempt status if it opposed interracial dating," even if the objection was based
on religious beliefs. Alito asked the solicitor general if "the same [principle
would] apply to a university if it opposed same-sex marriage?" Verrilli's answer
was consistent with the Obama administration's position on religious liberty:
"You know, I don't think I can answer that question without knowing more
specifics, but it's certainly going to be an issue. I don't deny that. I don't deny
that, Justice Alito. It is going to be an issue."

4.3. "EVEN JESUS WOULD NOT QUALIFY"

The fallout from *Exemption 1.0*'s blinkered conception of religious accomo-
dations would be swift. The *Times* quoted one administration official who
said, "All *hell* broke loose."[33] An apt choice of words. The U.S. Conference
of Catholic Bishops faulted the exemption because it was "so narrow as to
exclude most Catholic social service agencies and healthcare providers."[34]
"For example," the Bishops pointed out, "under the new rule our institutions
would be free to act in accord with Catholic teaching on life and procreation
only if they were to stop hiring and serving non-Catholics." The Bishops submitted an official comment to HHS, where they explained that "even the ministry of Jesus and the early Christian Church would not qualify as 'religious'"
under *Exemption 1.0* "because they did not confine their ministry to their co-
religionists or engage only in a preaching ministry."[35]

Catholic University of America president John Garvey added that the
exemption is "too narrow to include Catholic universities, which observe
norms of academic freedom and teach chemical thermodynamics, aero-
space engineering, musical theater, Mandarin Chinese and the Victorian
novel along with theology."[36] Even liberal supporters of the president balked.
MSNBC host Chris Matthews said the rule was "frightening."[37] E. J. Dionne

---

[33] Helene Cooper, *Rule Shift on Birth Control Is Concession to Obama Allies*, N.Y. TIMES (Feb.
10, 2012), perma.cc/EGN5-YBGA.

[34] *HHS Mandate for Contraceptive and Abortifacient Drugs Violates Conscience Right*, UNITED
STATES CONFERENCE OF CATHOLIC BISHOPS (Aug. 1, 2011), perma.cc/4WLW-3RGQ.

[35] U.S. Conference of Catholic Bishops, *Comment to Interim Final Rules on Preventive Services*
at 19 (Aug. 31, 2011), bit.ly/1SM6P00.

[36] John Garvey, *HHS's Birth-Control Rules Intrude on Catholic Values*, WASH. POST (Sept. 30,
2011), perma.cc/GJR4-L9J8.

[37] *Cooper, supra* note 33.

wrote in the *Washington Post* that the president had "utterly botched" the issue.[38]

Among the biggest critics of the ACA's contraception mandate was the member of Congress most responsible for the law's religious compromise: Bart Stupak. Now a lobbyist, Stupak wrote that he was "perplexed and disappointed with the recent mandate put forth by HHS requiring faith-based employers to provide contraceptive coverage in their health care plans" in light of his "iron-clad agreement" with the president.[39] The executive order, Stupak recalled, required that "no person or institution can be forced to accept, provide or comply with health care policies or medical procedures contrary to their religious and moral beliefs." And that is exactly what he saw the mandate as doing. Stupak wrote that "[n]o individual or organization should be forced by government to set aside deeply held religious convictions, abdicate moral beliefs, or deny one's own conscience. Yet, the recent HHS rule requires faith based employers to abandon principles and provide contraception coverage for all employees." In an instant, the impotence of President Obama's "signing statement on steroids" became perfectly clear.

The Associated Press reported that Democrats were "deeply divided over President Barack Obama's new rule that religious schools and hospitals must provide insurance for free birth control to their employees."[40] However, efforts to halt the contraceptive mandate in Congress were unsuccessful. Senator Roy Blunt (R-MO) proposed an amendment that would have let employers refuse to cover contraceptives based on their "religious belief and moral conviction."[41] On March 1, it was voted down 51–48 – far short of the 61-vote bloc that approved the Women's Health Amendment. Joining the Republicans in support of the amendment were pro-life Democratic senators Bob Casey, Joe Manchin, and, of course, Ben Nelson. House Minority Leader John Boehner (R-OH) was disappointed by the vote. "Our government for 220 years has respected the religious views of the American people and for all of this time there's been an exception for those churches and other groups to protect the religious beliefs that they believe in. And that's being violated here."

---

[38] *Id.*

[39] David Lindsay, *Whole Life Democrats* (Sept. 24, 2012), perma.cc/U6SS-N4DF.

[40] Donna Cassata, *Obama Birth Control Policy Divides Democrats*, Associated Press (Feb. 9, 2012), perma.cc/R8G3-QGDC.

[41] Matt Negrin, *Senate Blocks Blunt's Repeal of Contraception Mandate*, ABC News (Mar. 1, 2012), abcn.ws/1Ol7zdA.

Democrats portrayed the vote as part of the *war on women*. Speaker Nancy Pelosi lampooned the bill: "The Republicans are kicking off Women's History Month by bringing the Blunt amendment to the floor in the United States Senate." She added, "as a Catholic, I support the right of a woman to make that decision," and "that 90 percent of Catholic women of childbearing age use birth control."[42] Senator Schumer added, "The closeness of this vote" – including several Democrats – "shows how high the stakes are for women in this country." Two years later, during oral arguments in *Hobby Lobby v. Burwell*, Justice Ginsburg would cite this vote to argue that Congress did not intend to provide an exemption for "secular employers and insurance providers."

Over the next few months, more than 100,000 comments were submitted to HHS concerning the contraceptive mandate.[43] One of the most pointed critiques came from Notre Dame University president Father Jenkins. He recalled how President Obama had promised in his commencement address to work toward a "sensible conscience clause."[44] Father Jenkins urged the president to "broaden the proposed definition of 'religious employer' to ensure conscience protections that will allow this university to continue its work as 'a Catholic academic community of higher learning.'" Under the current rule, Jenkins explained, the university would be required to offer coverage for "pills that act after fertilization to induce abortions." This would "compel Notre Dame to either pay for contraception and sterilization in violation of the Church's moral teaching, or to discontinue our employee and student health care plans in violation of the Church's social teaching. It is an impossible position."

Toward the end, Jenkins spoke directly to Obama: "May I suggest that this is not the kind of 'sensible' approach that the President had in mind when he spoke here." And, with a healthy dose of Catholic guilt, Jenkins chided Kathleen Sebelius, the Secretary of Health and Human Services (HHS): "Of course, Madam Secretary, as the daughter of a distinguished Notre Dame alumnus and faculty member, you are no stranger to our mission."[45] The prayers from the bishops and Father Jenkins would go unanswered.

---

[42] John Parkinson, *Women's Health vs. Religious Freedom: House Leaders Debate Birth Control Mandate*, ABC NEWS (Mar. 1, 2012), abcn.ws/1OtXcly.

[43] Sarah Kliff, *Congress Picks up the Birth Control Battle*, WASH. POST (Nov. 2, 2011), perma.cc/GT65-Y4X4.

[44] Letter from John L. Jenkins to Kathleen Sebelius (Sep. 28, 2011), perma.cc/5G6Z-U2XK.

[45] Sebelius's father was Notre Dame Law Professor John J. Gilligan. Michael R. Garvey, *In Memoriam: Former Ohio Governor and ND Law Professor Emeritus John J. Gilligan*, NOTRE DAME NEWS (Aug. 28, 2013), perma.cc/4T9D-PJ4R.

4.4. "WE HAVE A YEAR TO FIGURE OUT HOW TO VIOLATE OUR CONSCIENCES"

In February, HHS announced that the interim rule that had been proposed in August would be "finalize[d], without change."[46] Despite the outrage, the narrow conscience clause would remain the same. By outward accounts, the Obama administration was holding strong on its position. At a hearing the following month, Senator Hatch asked Secretary Sebelius if anyone at HHS had "conduct[ed] or request[ed] any analysis of the constitutional or statutory religious freedom issues" when crafting the exemption.[47] She dodged the question. Hatch asked, "Did you ask the Justice Department?" She replied, "I did not."

Internally, the process was far more divided than Sebelius let on. Initially, Vice President Biden, former chief of staff William Daley, and deputy national security adviser Denis McDonough implored the president to grant a broader exemption.[48] Biden warned the President that "allies would be furious" with such a narrow provision. However, according to the *New York Times*, "in difficult internal negotiations, a group of advisers had bested" Biden, "and sold the president on a stricter rule." Sebelius said the rule "strikes the appropriate balance between respecting religious freedom and increasing access to important preventive services."[49] But groups like the Little Sisters of the Poor that employed and helped people outside the faith would not be exempted.

To offer some solace to these religious organizations, the White House announced what would be the first of many delays of the Affordable Care Act's mandates. Religious employers that objected to the contraceptive mandate and did not currently cover contraceptives would be given an additional year to comply – until August 1, 2013. (So much for bypassing the "notice and comment" period to ensure that students at religious universities would get contraceptive coverage by August 2012). Sebelius explained that "[t]his additional year will allow these organizations more time and flexibility to adapt to this new rule."[50]

---

[46] Group Health Plans and Health Insurance Issuers Relating to Coverage of Preventive Services, 77 Fed. Reg. 8725, 8729 (Feb. 15, 2012), perma.cc/F5ET-WZLL.

[47] Kathryn Jean Lopez, *What We Learned Today in the Senate about the HHS Mandate*, NAT'L REVIEW (Feb. 15, 2012), perma.cc/9J32-XRAH.

[48] Helene Cooper, *Rule Shift on Birth Control Is Concession to Obama Allies*, N.Y. TIMES (Feb. 10, 2012), perma.cc/EGN5-YBGA

[49] Robert Pear, *Obama Reaffirms Insurers Must Cover Contraception*, N.Y. TIMES (Jan. 20, 2012), perma.cc/W5MF-WWHV.

[50] Rich Daily, *Religious Employers Get Reprieve on Birth Control Rule*, MOD. HEALTHCARE (Jan. 20, 2012), perma.cc/KBH4-4N8G.

The so-called *safe harbor* for religious employers that did not qualify for the exemption would be formalized in a guidance bulletin released on February 10.[51] Critically the safe harbor did not waive the mandate. Rather, the government would simply *"not take any enforcement action* against an employer"* who follows the rules.[52] This would be the first of many exercises of executive action where the Obama administration promised not to prosecute violations of the Affordable Care Act's mandates.

The one-year delay was viewed as tone-deaf. "In effect," Archbishop Timothy M. Dolan explained, "the president is saying we have a year to figure out how to violate our consciences."[53] Dolan, the president of the Conference of Bishops, had spoken with President Obama in November and thought they had an understanding over the mandate.[54] "The sentiments of hope that stemmed from reassurances that I thought I received in November," Dolan lamented, "were apparently misplaced."[55] In an interview with James Taranto in *The Wall Street Journal,* Dolan relayed a call he received from the President in January "to say that the mandates remain in place and that there would be no substantive change, and that the only thing that he could offer me was that we would have until August."[56] Obama stressed, "We're more or less giving you this time to find out how you're going to be able to comply." Dolan replied, "Well, sir, we don't need the [extra time]. I can tell you now we're unable to comply."

But as it turned out, HHS was not too eager to even enforce the mandate against religious organizations that did not qualify for the safe harbor. Wheaton College, a Christian school in Illinois was "dismayed to discover" that "due to an oversight," it was "inadvertently" covering *Plan B* and *Ella* – both emergency contraceptives – after February 2012.[57] Wheaton filed suit in July 2012, seeking to immediately halt the contraceptive mandate because it was not eligible for the safe harbor.

[51] *Guidance on the Temporary Enforcement Safe Harbor for Certain Employers*, DEP'T OF HEALTH & HUM. SERVS. (Feb. 10, 2012), bit.ly/1SJWRAy.

[52] *Id.*

[53] Sr. Mary Ann Walsh, *U.S. Bishops Vow to Fight HHS Edict*, UNITED STATES CONFERENCE OF CATHOLIC BISHOPS (Jan. 20, 2012), perma.cc/64M2-HHR9.

[54] *Statement on Meeting between Archbishop Dolan and President Obama*, UNITED STATES CONFERENCE OF CATHOLIC BISHOPS (Nov. 14, 2011), perma.cc/BFK3-F249.

[55] Robert Pear, *Obama Reaffirms Insurers Must Cover Contraception*, N.Y. TIMES (Jan. 20, 2012), perma.cc/W5MF-WWHV.

[56] James Taranto, *When the Archbishop Met the President*, WALL ST. J. (Mar. 31, 2012), on.wsj.com/1OtYGMF.

[57] Joint Appendix, Wheaton College v. Sebelius at JA166 (12-5273) (D.C. Cir. Oct. 5, 2012), bit.ly/1SXJNGN.

Less than month after the case was filed, rather than defending the mandate in court, HHS vastly expanded the safe harbor in such a way that Wheaton would qualify for it. An HHS administrator explained that even though Wheaton covered the emergency contraceptives after February 10, because it "took some action prior to February 10 to exclude coverage for emergency contraceptives … because of its religious beliefs," Wheaton College was eligible for the safe harbor.[58] These were not at all the terms of the original safe harbor. A month later, HHS released new "guidance" that "[was] not changing the February 10 policy; it [was] only clarifying" that "group health plans that took some action to try to exclude or limit contraceptive coverage that was not successful as of February 10, 2012, are not for that reason precluded from eligibility for the safe harbor."[59]

This was not a mere clarification, but was a significant change in the policy. Practically speaking, after the controversial announcement of the mandate by the Obama administration in August 2011, virtually *every* religious nonprofit took some steps to "exclude or limit contraceptive coverage." These actions, unbeknownst to the organizations, would now provide a blanket qualification for the safe harbor until 2013. As a result, they couldn't challenge the mandate in court, because it did not yet apply to them. Wheaton College was "grateful for this" change, but still wanted to contest the mandate in court.[60] The court disagreed and promptly dismissed the case on August 24, 2011, finding it was not yet ripe for review.[61]

The government may have had ulterior motives with the ever-expanding safe harbor. One of the attorneys for Wheaton College speculated that the government was making "deliberate litigation decisions" to keep the religious non-profits cases away from the courts. Rather, he told me, "they had decided that they want to face the businesses first," like the for-profit Hobby Lobby. He added that the "government didn't want its first case [before the Supreme Court] to be forcing monks from Belmont Abbey College to provide contraception." The attorney cited the fact that HHS promptly expanded the scope of the safe harbor less than a month after Wheaton College filed its complaint, even though it clearly would not have complied under the initial policy. In

---

[58] Michael Hash Decl., 1–4, Wheaton College v. Sebelius, 1:12-cv-01169-ESH, Document 17-2 (D.D.C. Aug. 10, 2012), bit.ly/1rRzVWz.

[59] *Guidance on the Temporary Enforcement Safe Harbor* at n.1, Dep't of Health & Hum. Servs. (Aug. 15, 2012), bit.ly/1Tt6hgn.

[60] *Opposition to Motion to Dismiss*,Wheaton Coll. v. Sebelius, 1:12-cv-1169 (D.D.C. Aug. 16, 2012), bit.ly/1Uxeoxk.

[61] Wheaton Coll. v. Sebelius, 887 F. Supp. 2d 102, 104 (D.D.C. 2012), *vacated* 2013 WL 5994617 (D.D.C. Aug. 19, 2013).

other words, the government didn't expect a Christian university to inadvertently cover Plan B – that discovery required a broadening of the safe harbor.

In June 2013, the Obama administration would once again extend the safe harbor, postponing the mandate until January 1, 2014.[62] So much for the urgent need to provide contraceptive coverage for students at a small number of Christian colleges by August 2012. On December 31, 2013 – the eve of the enforcement of the mandate – the Little Sisters of the Poor would receive a last-minute order from Justice Sotomayor, effectively postponing the mandate for three more years. In July 2014, after the safe harbor expired, a divided Supreme Court would grant Wheaton College emergency relief from the contraceptive mandate. Perhaps as designed by the government, the legality of the nonprofit accommodation would not be considered by the Supreme Court until March 2016 – two years after it ruled in favor of the for-profit Hobby Lobby.

4.5. "AS A CHRISTIAN, I CHERISH THIS RIGHT"

On February 10, President Obama held a press conference to announce a new direction.[63] He rejected the effort to "treat this as another political wedge." Rather, his government would now strike the right balance: "Religious liberty will be protected, and a law that requires free preventive care will not discriminate against women." Obama stressed that "[a]s we move to implement this rule we've been mindful that there's another principle at stake here, and that's the principle of religious liberty, an inalienable right that is enshrined in our Constitution."[64] Reading from his notes, the president said: "As a citizen and as a Christian, I cherish this right."[65] The *New York Times* reported that the president's about-face was spurred by Sister Keehan of the Catholic Health Association. She told him "he had made a really bad decision."[66]

Over the next two years, the administration would develop two tracks to safeguard religious liberty under the mandate. First, *Exemption 1.0* was upgraded to *Exemption 2.0*. Now, Houses of worship would be exempted from the mandate, regardless of whether they "primarily employ persons who share its religious tenets" or "primarily serve persons who share its religious tenets." As a result, the Church that runs a soup kitchen – whose staff and diners are

---

[62] 78 Fed. Reg. at 39870.
[63] The White House Office of the Press Secretary, *Remarks by the President on Preventive Care*, THE WHITE HOUSE (Feb. 10, 2012), perma.cc/J3NJ-GC35.
[64] *Id.*
[65] *White House Press Conference*, YOUTUBE (Feb. 10, 2012) at 2:10, youtu.be/ILpq_OECZn4.
[66] Cooper, *supra* note 33.

not "primarily" Catholic – would qualify, so long as it is recognized as a house of worship under the Internal Revenue Code.[67]

In an about-face, the government acknowledged that non-profits should not be denied an exemption because "they provide charitable social services to persons of different religious faiths or employ persons of different religious faiths when running a parochial school."[68] Somewhat implausibly, in light of the debate over the previous six months, the administration stated that "this was never the Departments' intention in connection with" *Exemption 1.0*.[69] The government would later explain to the Supreme Court that the exemption was granted to take into account "the special solicitude that churches receive under our Constitution under the First Amendment."[70] However, the United States never stated that the First Amendment compelled the exemption. This is consistent with its position in *Hosanna–Tabor*.

Notwithstanding the expanded exemption, other religious employers that did not qualify as houses of worship would still be bound by the mandate. Religious orders that do not focus on "exclusively religious activities" were out of luck.[71] For example, the Little Sisters of the Poor, an order of nuns who care for the elderly of all faiths would not be protected by *Exemption 2.0*. Instead, they would fall into the Obama Administration's lower-tier of religious protections. I will refer to this provision as *Accommodation 1.0*. While the *exemptions* excused houses of worship from the mandate altogether – so its employees would not receive contraceptive coverage – the *accommodations* required insurers, and not the religious employers, to pay for employees' contraceptive coverage. As the president explained at the press conference,

> If a woman's employer is a charity or a hospital that has a religious objection to providing contraceptive services as part of their health plan, but is not exempted, the insurance company — not the hospital, not the charity — will be required to reach out and offer the woman contraceptive care free of charge, without co-pays and without hassles. The result will be that religious organizations won't have to pay for these services, and no religious institution will have to provide these services directly. Let me repeat: These employers will not have to pay for, or provide, contraceptive services. But women who work at these institutions will have access to free contraceptive services.[72]

[67] 78 Fed. Reg. 8456.
[68] 78 Fed. Reg. 8461.
[69] *Id.*
[70] Tr. of Oral Arg. at 56–58, Burwell v. Hobby Lobby Stores, Inc., 134 S.Ct. 2751 (2014) (No. 05-493).
[71] 78 Fed. Reg. 8461.
[72] Remarks by the President on Preventive Care (Feb. 10, 2012), perma.cc/K5F4-DGMK.

Five days later, the administration announced that it would require insurance companies to issue policies without contraception coverage to certain religious nonprofits "and simultaneously to offer contraceptive coverage directly to the employer's plan participants (and their beneficiaries) who desire it, with no cost-sharing."[73]

On June 28, 2013, the Obama administration released *Accommodation 2.0*.[74] Under this accommodation, eligible organizations would not have to pay the cost of contraceptives for their employees. Rather, their insurer would pick up the tab. An organization qualifies for the accommodation if it (1) opposes providing contraceptive coverage, (2) is a nonprofit, (3) "holds itself out as a religious organization," and (4) "self-certif[ies]" to its insurer that it qualifies for the accommodation. Once the employer "provides a copy" of the self-certification form to its insurer, the insurer provides the contraceptive coverage.

The religious nonprofits were required to self-certify using *Employee Benefits Security Administration (EBSA) Form 700*.[75] The two-page form looks like countless other bureaucratic applications published by the Department of Labor. The government estimated it would take about fifty minutes to complete its five parts.[76]

1. Name of the objecting organization	
2. Name and title of the individual who is authorized to make, and makes, this certification on behalf of the organization	
3. Mailing and email addresses and phone number for the individual listed above	
4. I certify that, on account of religious objections, the organization opposes providing coverage for some or all of any contraceptive services that would otherwise be required to be covered; the organization is organized and operates as a nonprofit entity; and the organization holds itself out as a religious organization. Signature of the individual listed above Date	
5. The organization or its plan must provide a copy of this certification to the plan's health insurance issuer (for insured health plans) or a third party administrator (for self-insured health plans) in order for the plan to be accommodated with respect to the contraceptive coverage requirement. … This certification is an instrument under which the plan is operated.	

[73] 77 Fed. Reg. 8725, 8727. The rulemaking was announced in March 2012. 77 Fed. Reg. at 16502–03. It was finalized in February 2013. 78 Fed. Reg. 8456.
[74] 78 Fed. Reg. 39870, 39874 (July 2, 2013).
[75] EBSA Form 700, bit.ly/24nAtEK.
[76] 78 Fed. Reg. 39,890.

The form asks for the name and contact information of the employer. No problem there. But the last two requirements – certifying the objection, and providing a copy to the insurer – would prove to be controversial.

One of the biggest supporters of the new proposal was Sister Carol Keehan.[77] She was "very pleased with the White House's announcement that a resolution has been reached that protects the religious liberty and conscience rights of Catholic institutions." Sister Keehan noted the "difference" among Catholic institutions "has at times been uncomfortable." It would soon get more uncomfortable.

Over the next four years, nonexempt religious institutions– including the Little Sisters of the Poor, Priests for Life, and the University of Notre Dame – would storm the federal courts with wave after wave of lawsuits challenging the accommodations to the mandate. Additionally, religious for-profit employers would receive neither an exemption nor an accommodation. Companies like Hobby Lobby would be subjected to the mandate without an accommodation. They too would challenge the Obama administration in federal court – and they would win.

---

[77] *Catholic Health Association Is Very Pleased with Today's White House Resolution that Protects Religious Liberty and Conscience Rights*, CATHOLIC HEALTH ASSOC. OF THE U.S. (Feb. 10, 2012), bit.ly/232PuIN.

5

Election Slowdown

5.1. "ASSUMPTION THAT PASSAGE = EXECUTION"

During a January 2016 Twitter chat, President Obama was asked, "What is your greatest memory while being president?"[1] @POTUS replied: "the night aca passed; standing on truman balcony with all staff whod made it happen, knowing we'd helped millions."[2] (Capitalization, punctuation, and grammar are not essential on Twitter.) That momentous evening six years earlier was Sunday, March 21, 2010, hours after the Affordable Care Act cleared the House. White House photographer Pete Souza captured the moment: The triumphant president walked onto the balcony facing the South Lawn, as champagne-filled flutes were raised.[3] Souza noted that Obama had "invited everyone in the White House that had helped – both senior aides and support staff – but was the last one at the party because he had been making congratulatory calls to members of Congress." Amidst the jubilation, the president turned to business and said that everyone "needed to get started on carrying out the law the very next morning."[4]

Even with the White House's esprit de corps, some were not convinced that the administration was ready for the challenge. One of the champagne-toasting celebrants told journalist Steven Brill that he was "slightly troubled" by the president's philosophy on the balcony. Despite his sense of urgency, Obama "seemed more focused on the work ahead involving getting people to sign up on the exchanges, rather than on executing all the steps that had to be completed – the regulations, the software, the rules for the insurance

---

[1] Abi Cucumber (@nialler4th_lee) (Jan. 14, 2016), bit.ly/1Y7csum.
[2] Barack Obama (@POTUS) (Jan. 14, 2016), bit.ly/1W6qVIX.
[3] Pete Souza, FLICKR (Mar. 22, 2010), http://bit.ly/1QRTgen.
[4] Amy Goldstein and Juliet Eilperin, *HealthCare.gov: How Political Fear Was Pitted against Technical Needs*, WASH. POST (Nov. 2, 2013), perma.cc/E5FT-JARS.

companies – to get people to the stage where they could sign up."[5] That evening the staffer made an ominous entry in his journal: "Assumption that passage = execution, which is worrisome." That sentiment soon spread.

Two months later, Harvard professor David Cutler, who served as the Obama campaign's senior health advisor,[6] sounded the alarm to express his "concern about the way the way the Administration is implementing" the ACA.[7] Cutler sent the urgent four-page memo to Larry Summers, former Harvard University president and the director of the White House's National Economic Council. Cutler expressed his "concern[] that the personnel and processes [the Administration had] in place are not up to the task, and that health reform will be unsuccessful as a result." He worried that the team did not "have the capability to carry" out Obama's vision.[8]

The memo identified four specific "problem areas." First, the staff at the Centers for Medicare and Medicaid Services (CMS), which is responsible for a "good deal [of] reform implementation," is "not up to the task." At CMS, "there is no experience running a health care organization [and] the desire to move rapidly is lacking." CMS was responsible for administering federal health programs, not establishing a national health care exchange from scratch. Cutler concluded, "I have very little confidence that the Administration will make the right decisions about the direction and pace of delivery system reform."

Second, the letter expressed concern about "set[ing] up and run[ing] insurance exchanges." Because of the vigorous opposition to the ACA, unless the administration could "find a way to work with hesitant states" to facilitate the exchanges, "reform will blow up." *Hesitant* was a euphemism for hatred: two dozen red states sought, at all costs, to stop Obamacare. Cutler observed, "I have seen no indication that HHS even realizes this [problem], let alone is acting on it."

Third, HHS has failed to "explain" the new health care law to the insurance industry, and "show them how to respond to it." He added, "You can't change the culture by piling new responsibilities onto a broken system." This lack of communication with the health care community troubled Cutler, as the problem "does not appear to be on HHS's radar screen" at all.

5 STEVEN BRILL, AMERICA'S BITTER PILL: MONEY, POLITICS, BACKROOM DEALS, AND THE FIGHT TO FIX OUR BROKEN HEALTHCARE SYSTEM 194–195 (Random House Trade Paperback ed. 2015).
6 David M. Cutler, *Biography*, perma.cc/SR3Q-DJM3.
7 Letter from David Cutler to Larry Summers (May 11, 2010), bit.ly/1SLqSA8.
8 *Id.*

Fourth, and most critically, the Harvard professor wrote that the process within the Obama administration was "broken." Specifically, Cutler charged that Jeanne Lambrew, who was heading the White House's implementation of the ACA, "is known for her knowledge of Congress, her commitment to the poor, and her mistrust of insurance companies." She is not known for "operational ability, knowledge of delivery systems, or facilitating widespread change." On a personal note, Cutler added that "Jeanne and people like her cannot get along with other people in the Administration," which "means that the opportunities for collaborative engagement are limited, areas of great importance are not addressed, and valuable problem solving time is wasted on internal fights."

Cutler's letter closed on an ominous note: "I strongly encourage you to make changes now, before you are too late to get the outcomes we need." These four problems – inadequate staff, no relationship with the "hesitant" states, lack of communication with providers, and poor leadership – would plague the implementation of the ACA. In November 2013, Ezra Klein would look back on "the memo [as] prophetic."[9]

Larry Summers, along with Peter Orszag, head of the Office of Management and Budget, agreed with Cutler's dire warnings. According to the *Washington Post*, after the memo was circulated, "a tug of war played out inside the White House."[10] The economics team, along with adviser Zeke Emanuel, "lobbied for the president to appoint an outside health reform 'czar' with expertise in business, insurance and technology."[11] In December 2009, even before the bill passed the Senate, Emanuel warned Summers and Orszag "how difficult implementation was going to be" and urged them to "look[] to the private sector for leadership."[12] Emanuel's memo warned that "implementation of a complex piece of legislation in a very short timeframe poses significant challenges, and will become a dominant public policy issue."[13] Ironically, they "highlighted the necessity of sticking with the House's plan to have one national online exchange rather than risk the chaos of operating fifty-one exchanges, one for each state and the District of Columbia, as was called for by the Senate bill."[14] The

[9] Ezra Klein, *The Memo That Could Have Saved Obamacare*, WASH. POST (Nov. 4, 2013), perma.cc/B5U5-CEQM.
[10] Goldstein, *supra* note 4.
[11] *Id.*
[12] Brill, *supra* note 5 at 180.
[13] *Id.* at 181.
[14] *Id.*

latter approach substantially increased the complexity of the implementation. However, due to the need to pass the Senate bill after Scott Brown's election, the Obama administration would be forced to deal with many exchanges.

The President's policy aides, who guided the ACA through Congress, disagreed with the economists' assessment. Nancy-Ann DeParle developed her own implementation plan, where she would manage the program as the Director of White House Office of Health Reform. Jeanne Lambrew would be the head of the Office of Health Reform at HHS and "would supervise day-to-day implementation."[15] DeParle insisted "they could handle the job."[16] Further, in light of frequent Republican attacks on President Obama's *czars*, some worried that "appointing a health implementation czar would potentially open the administration to even more criticism."[17]

Emanuel pleaded with his brother, the Chief of Staff, to intervene with the president to fix the process. Rahm replied that he "didn't want to have to deal with this 'bureaucratic crap' now."[18] Ultimately the wonks lost the tug of war. The president selected DeParle to be in charge. "If you were to design a person in the lab to implement health care," Obama said, "it would be Nancy-Ann."[19] In a move that would "surprise many of her colleagues,"[20] DeParle would leave the White House in 2013 to become a partner in a private equity firm, months before HealthCare.gov imploded.[21] President Obama would later express regret for the poorly structured management structure, which was fragmented and stove piped between the White House, HHS, and CMS. He told Steven Brill, "In hindsight, there should have been one central person in charge, a CEO of the Marketplace."[22]

5.2. "NO NEED TO RUSH ANYTHING"

From the moment it was enacted, the Affordable Care Act was besieged by legal and political challenges. Before the ink of the president's signature had

---

[15] *Id.* at 184.

[16] Goldstein, *supra* note 4.

[17] EZEKIEL EMANUEL, REINVENTING AMERICAN HEALTH CARE 248 (2014). For a discussion of President Obama's czars, *see* DAVID E. BERNSTEIN, LAWLESS: THE OBAMA ADMINISTRATION'S UNPRECEDENTED ASSAULT ON THE CONSTITUTION AND THE RULE OF LAW 65-80 (2015).

[18] Brill, *supra* note 5 at 184.

[19] Goldstein, *supra* note 4.

[20] Brill, *supra* note 5 at 301.

[21] Brendan Williams, *ObamaCare's Revolving Door*, THE HILL (July 27, 2015), perma.cc/6V96-9HR7.

[22] Brill, *supra* note 5 at 301.

even dried, twenty-six states brought a lawsuit challenging the constitutionality of the law's individual mandate and Medicaid expansion. In the 2010 midterm election, Republicans gained control of the House of Representatives, defeating many vulnerable Democrats who had supported the Affordable Care Act. As their first order of business, the House Republicans voted to repeal Obamacare. Over the next five years, the House would vote to repeal the ACA more than fifty times – knowing full well that the bill was dead on arrival in the Democratic-controlled Senate, and would never make it past the president's veto pen. Nationally, the ACA remained unpopular, never breaking a 50% favorability rating. Deeming it illegitimate, in light of the manner in which it was enacted, many Republicans refused to call it a law, still referring to it as a *bill*.[23]

Because the ACA remained the most significant political football in America, the president approached the implementation of the law with trepidation, hesitant to do anything that could strengthen the law's unpopularity. The *Washington Post* reported that due to "the White House's political sensitivity to Republican hatred of the law … the president's aides ordered that some work be slowed down or remain secret for fear of feeding the opposition."[24] Specifically, the Obama administration "systematically delayed enacting a series of rules" concerning the ACA in order "to prevent them from becoming points of contention before the 2012 election."[25] Several current and former officials told the *Post* that the regulators "were instructed to hold off submitting proposals to the White House for up to a year" concerning "crucial elements of the Affordable Care Act … to ensure that they would not be issued *before* voters went to the polls."[26] Many of these regulations were ultimately released "just *after* Obama's reelection."[27] The "motives behind many of the delays," the *Post* concluded, "were clearly political."

Stephen Brill revealed a similar strategy at CMS. According to two officials, the agency was told in January 2012 "by their superiors that the already-slow rule-making process had to be slowed still more." There was no hurry, so "they could take their time sending drafts to the White House for approval … because the White House was only going to stall before sending whatever the

---

[23] Sam Baker, *GOP Lawmakers Bridle at Calling Affordable Care Act the Law*, THE HILL (Sept. 29, 2013), perma.cc/TY2W-QN87.

[24] Goldstein, *supra* note 4.

[25] Juliet Eilperin, *White House Delayed Enacting Rules Ahead of 2014 Election to Avoid Controversy*, WASH. POST (Dec. 14, 2013), perma.cc/CZQ5-7WMB.

[26] *Id.*

[27] Goldstein, *supra* note 4.

rule was over to [the Office of Management and Budget], which would stall even more."[28]

Brill recalled that a White House staffer told him "that there was no need to rush anything out the door" during the spring of 2012, rationalizing that "the person in charge of Obamacare is [Chief Justice] John Roberts."[29] Had the ACA been invalidated by the Supreme Court in June 2012, all of the implementation would have been for naught. Clearly, Brill concluded, "[t]hey did not want to make any waves before the election."[30] House Republicans took a similar wait-and-see approach. Representative Todd Tiahrt (R-KS) suggested to Speaker John Boehner that the House should vote to defund portions of the ACA in 2012, but "there just wasn't the appetite for it at the time."[31] Tiahrt recalled that the leadership "thought we don't need to worry about it because the Supreme Court will strike it down."[32]

The deliberate bottleneck extended to the influential Office of Information and Regulatory Affairs (OIRA).[33] Headed by former Harvard law professor and polymath Cass Sunstein,[34] OIRA oversaw the finalization of federal regulations. In a seventy-four-page report, the Administrative Conference of the United States – an independent agency that consults on regulatory issues – concluded that "OIRA reviews took longer in 2011 and 2012 because of concerns about the agencies issuing costly or controversial rules prior to the November 2012 election."[35] For hot-button issues that could affect the electorate, "such rules were not to be issued unless deemed absolutely necessary (e.g., a judicial deadline) or if it could be shown they were not controversial (e.g., clear net benefits)."[36]

This policy was "not in writing," but after meetings with White House officials, the preapproval process was imposed for all "sensitive rules."[37] While previous administrations were cognizant of controversial rulemaking in election years, the Administrative Conference observed that "political sensitivities

---

[28] *Brill, supra* note 5 at 241.

[29] *Id.*

[30] *Id.*

[31] Sheryl Gay Stolberg and Mike McIntyre, *A Federal Budget Crisis Months in the Planning*, N.Y. TIMES (Oct. 5, 2013), perma.cc/BV83-4VHP.

[32] *Id.*

[33] John M. Broder, *Powerful Shaper of U.S. Rules Quits, With Critics in Wake*, N.Y. TIMES (Aug. 3, 2012), http://nyti.ms/1Slz8t.

[34] *Id.*

[35] Curtis W. Copeland, *Length of Rule Reviews by OIRA* at 42, ADMINISTRATIVE CONFERENCE OF THE UNITED STATES (Dec. 2, 2013), bit.ly/1OdBNNG.

[36] *Id.*

[37] *Id.*

about rulemaking reached new heights during 2012."[38] Certain "rules that had been completely uncontroversial in the past were delayed for weeks at OIRA."[39] Sunstein explained that politics is "not a significant part of OIRA's own role," but candidly acknowledged that political issues "might be taken into account by other offices" within the White House.[40] As a result of these delays, a CMS official told Brill, "We literally fell a year behind." To avoid losing political points, the White House risked the success of the ACA by slow-walking its implementation.

Beyond the regulatory slowdown, as Cutler noted in his memo, it soon became clear that CMS was not up to the logistical challenge. Shifting the responsibility from under Sebelius to CMS "fragmented" the endeavor, the *Post* observed.[41] The policy staff was separated from the technical staff. Todd Park, who was appointed Chief Technology Officer of HHS and planned to oversee the development of HealthCare.gov, did not even supervise the CMS employees who were responsible for implementing the website. This led to a breakdown in communication between those trying to design the exchanges and those trying to tiptoe around the political minefields.

For example, in the spring of 2011, CMS staff members tried to persuade the White House to publish "concepts of operation" diagrams to explain to the states how the federal exchanges would operate. This was the sort of technical communication with the states that Cutler explained was pivotal to the law's success. However, the *Post* revealed that the administration refused to publish them because "the diagrams were complex."[42] Aides feared that the GOP would mock the complicated diagrams, as Senator Bob Dole (R-KS) did two decades earlier to attack HillaryCare's intricate charts. The ghosts of HillaryCare's past continued to haunt health care reform in the new millennium.

Ultimately, "the White House quashed the diagrams, telling CMS, instead, to praise early work on those state exchanges that matched the hidden federal thinking."[43] The toxic political climate forced the White House to make the implementation process even less transparent – and in doing so, made it more difficult to build functional exchanges. Despite the president's urgency on the Truman Balcony, many of the biggest setbacks of the ACA would be self-inflicted wounds.

---

[38] *Id.*

[39] *Id.*

[40] Cass Sunstein, *The Office of Information and Regulatory Affairs: Myths and Realities*, 126 HARV. L. REV. 1838, 1873–1874 (2013).

[41] Goldstein, *supra* note 4.

[42] *Id.*

[43] *Id.*

5.3. "UNPRECEDENTED"

In March 2012, the Supreme Court heard oral arguments in *NFIB v. Sebelius*, which considered the constitutionality of Obamacare's individual mandate and Medicaid expansion. The first claim considered whether Congress had the authority to compel individuals to purchase health insurance, or whether the law merely imposed a tax for failing to carry insurance. The second question asked if the ACA coerced states by threatening to withhold 100% of a state's Medicaid budget if the state did not expand the number of people covered under Medicaid. As I discussed in Parts VI–IX of my 2013 book, UNPRECEDENTED: THE CONSTITUTIONAL CHALLENGE TO OBAMACARE, the battle over the ACA in the spring of 2012 was as much political as it was legal.

Shortly after the case was argued, prominent Democrats, from President Obama to Senator Patrick Leahy, urged the Supreme Court to uphold the ACA and stressed that the Court should not step into the political fray of striking it down. On Monday, April 2, 2012, five days after the arguments – and three days after the Court's all-important conference when the votes were cast – President Obama offered some off-the-cuff comments to the press about the case. He said that it would be "unprecedented" for unelected justices to overturn an act of Congress enacted with popular support.

> Ultimately, I'm confident that the Supreme Court will not take what would be an unprecedented, extraordinary step of overturning a law that was passed by a strong majority of a democratically elected Congress. And I'd just remind conservative commentators that for years what we've heard is, the biggest problem on the bench was judicial activism or a lack of judicial restraint – that an unelected group of people would somehow overturn a duly constituted and passed law. Well, this is a good example. And I'm pretty confident that this Court will recognize that and not take that step.

We will return to the President's comments to the Supreme Court in Chapter 27 during the lead-up to *King v. Burwell*.

Liberals were not alone in opining on the pending case. Prominent conservatives, from Senator Mitch McConnell to conservative columnist George F. Will, returned fire at what they perceived as liberal preemptive attacks. They urged the chief justice to show some resolve. Under the headline "Liberals Put the Squeeze to Justice Roberts" in his syndicated column, Will claimed that progressives were "waging an embarrassingly obvious campaign, hoping [Roberts] will buckle beneath the pressure of their disapproval and declare Obamacare constitutional." Will charged that the Democrats "hope to secure [victory] by causing Roberts to worry about his reputation and that of his institution." These "clumsy attempts to bend the chief justice," Will wrote, "are apt to reveal his spine of steel." We would later learn that the chief justice's vote was in flux and that he changed his mind in favor of finding that the ACA was constitutional. However, many in Washington knew this fact much earlier and acted in their interests.[44]

The ACA's first day of reckoning came on June 28, 2012. It was a day that will live in legal infamy, as Hollywood could not have scripted a more dramatic conclusion to this perfect constitutional storm. At 10:06 AM, chief justice Roberts announced that he had written the opinion in *NFIB v. Sebelius*. Years earlier, Roberts had likened the role of a judge to that of an umpire – simply calling balls and strikes. In this case, the chief justice hurled a wicked constitutional curveball. With no cameras inside the Court, reporters outside scrambled to figure out the 193-page opinion. CNN and Fox News would initially report that the Court struck down the individual mandate. President Obama, watching these reports in the White House, was "crestfallen."[45] But the networks were wrong.

In a shocking surprise, the chief justice had voted to uphold the ACA by characterizing the penalty enforcing the individual mandate as a tax. Justices Scalia, Kennedy, Thomas, and Alito jointly dissented and would have jettisoned the entire ACA. This decision stunned almost everyone who anticipated that Justice Kennedy would be the pivotal swing vote – but not Solicitor General Donald Verrilli, who had realized that "the Chief Justice could be the fifth, and not the sixth, vote." The ACA, in the words of Justice Ginsburg, survived "largely unscathed." But the fight over Obamacare was far from over. The Supreme Court's decision in *NFIB v. Sebelius* was only the first battle in a much larger, prolonged campaign.

5.4. "ELECT A NEW PRESIDENT"

Within an hour of the decision, the triumphant President addressed the press. "Earlier today, the Supreme Court upheld the constitutionality of the Affordable Care Act," he said. "Whatever the politics, today's decision was a victory for people all over this country whose lives will be more secure because of this law and the Supreme Court's decision to uphold it." The President knew that the ACA – the defining aspect of his first term – was now

---

[44] JOSH BLACKMAN, UNPRECEDENTED, 229–233 (2013).

[45] Glenn Thrush, *CNN, Fox Fool Obama on SCOTUS*, POLITICO (June 28, 2012), perma.cc/Y6ZH-CPAK.

secured. Implementing the law in his second term would be a different story altogether.

Beaming, Obama said, "Today I'm as confident as ever that when we look back five years from now, or ten years from now, or twenty years from now, we'll be better off because we had the courage to pass this law and keep moving forward." Rahm Emanuel, the president's former chief of staff, put it succinctly: "The president had the courage to bend the needle of history and did something presidents have tried to do for sixty years."

Secretary of State Hillary Clinton, who two decades earlier had attempted to reform health care as First Lady, was ebullient. "You know, I haven't had the chance to read the decision," she said. "I literally just heard as we landed that the Supreme Court has upheld the health care law. Obviously I want to get into the details, but I'm very pleased ... There will be a lot of work to do to get it implemented and understand what the opinion says, but obviously I was quite excited to hear the results."

If Democrats were triumphant, Republicans were despondent. They determined to use the decision to galvanize support for the election. Reince Priebus, chairman of the Republican National Committee, set the tone. "Today's Supreme Court decision sets the stakes for the November election. Now the only way to save the country from Obamacare's budget-busting government takeover of health care is to elect a new president." John Boehner, Speaker of the House, echoed that sentiment: "Today's ruling underscores the urgency of repealing this harmful law in its entirety ... Republicans stand ready to work with a president who will listen to the people and will not repeat the mistakes that gave our country Obamacare." Senate Minority Leader McConnell looked forward to November: "Today's decision makes one thing clear: Congress must act to repeal this misguided law."

Republican Mitt Romney, who at that point was the presumptive nominee, gave a speech on Capitol Hill, faulting the Supreme Court's decision: "As you might imagine, I disagree with the Supreme Court's decision, and I agree with the dissent." Standing before a sign that read REPEAL & REPLACE OBAMACARE, he continued the theme. "If we want to get rid of Obamacare," Romney said, "we have to replace President Obama. What the court did not do on its last day of session, I will do on my first day [as President]. I will act to repeal Obamacare."

Easier said than done. With respect to health care, Mitt Romney's strongest opponent was Mitt Romney. After years of dancing around the issue, and perhaps hoping the Supreme Court would solve the problem for him,

Mitt Romney was finally forced to confront the fact that he was the "godfather" of Obamacare.[46] As governor of Massachusetts, and with the support of
Senator Edward Kennedy, Romney enacted health care reform that shared
many similarities with the ACA. Critically, the law included the same three-
legged stool as Obamacare: an individual mandate, subsidies for people who
could not afford polices, as well as prohibitions on discriminating against
people with preexisting conditions. It was aptly dubbed *Romneycare*. MIT
Economist Jonathan Gruber, who was an architect of both Romneycare and
Obamacare made the comparison succinctly: "They're the same fucking
bill."[47]

At the October 2012 debate in Denver, a triumphant Obama responded
to a Romney attack on Obamacare by saying, "I have become fond of this
term 'Obamacare.'" Romney repeated his qualified pledge to repeal it. The
president pounced on the "irony" that "we've seen this model work really well
in Massachusetts, because Governor Romney did a good thing, working with
Democrats in the state to set up what is essentially the identical model and as
a consequence people are covered there." Obama continued, rubbing it in:
"This was a bipartisan idea. In fact, it was a Republican idea. And Governor
Romney at the beginning of this debate wrote [that] Massachusetts could be
a model for the nation."

At the next debate in Hempstead, New York, Obama continued to mock
Romney's desire to "repeal Obamacare ... despite the fact that it's the same
health care plan that he passed in Massachusetts and is working well."
Notwithstanding his initial promise to repeal Obamacare, Romney soon
backed away from this position. On *Meet the Press*, Romney said, "I'm not
getting rid of all of health care reform," emphasizing that there were "a number of things that I like in health care reform that I'm going to put in place."[48]

By the final debate, Obamacare was mentioned only once. Romney could
not gain any traction on the issue. Former Senator Rick Santorum, who
surprised many with his success during the Republican primaries, labeled
Mitt Romney "the worst candidate to go against Barack Obama on the most
important issue of the day."[49] Eventually Romney's history caught up with

[46] Jon Ward, *Mitt Romney: "If I'm the Godfather of this thing, then it gives me the right to kill it."*
HUFFPOST POLITICS (Mar. 27, 2012), perma.cc/BD9Z-NEPJ.
[47] Avik Roy, *Gruber: Romney Is "Lying"; Romneycare and Obamacare Are "The Same F***ing
Bill,"* FORBES (Nov. 16, 2011), onforb.es/1QRVme1.
[48] Grace-Marie Turner, *Calm Down, Obamacare Foes*, NAT'L REV. (Sept. 10, 2012),
perma.cc/KAK2-CYUZ.
[49] CNN Political Unit, *On Supreme Court Steps, Santorum Lumps Romney with Obama on
Health Care*, CNN (Mar. 26, 2012), perma.cc/UBP9-UVCN.

him. Instead of being rewarded for reaching across the aisle and cooperating with Ted Kennedy to reform health care, Romney was mocked not only by the president but also by his own party. The Republican nominee for president had to forfeit the most divisive political issue of 2012.

However, one topic was conspicuously absent from the presidential debates: The Supreme Court. There was nary a mention of the justices, other than a question about abortion during the vice presidential debate. There were no attacks on the chief justice and no questions about the Court's legitimacy. It was exactly as John Roberts would have wanted it. However, any celebration at One First Street was premature. It would take another four years for the issue of the Supreme Court to trickle into the presidential campaign. The chief justice's vote in *NFIB v. Sebelius* in 2012, and his subsequent vote in *King v. Burwell* in 2015, would soon become a campaign issue and alter the calculus of replacing Justice Scalia.

5.5. "SHORT-TERM POLITICAL GAIN"

After Chief Justice Roberts saved Obamacare, Steven Brill observed that most industry players "assumed they would start seeing the necessary regulations and other preparations [for the ACA] flowing out from Washington with firehose velocity." But with November three months away, the White House was still playing it safe. "Through the summer of 2012, nothing happened," Brill observed, because "there was a presidential election looming." He observed that "the Obama political team didn't want to pollute the news cycles with anything that could prompt an Obamacare story." A senior CMS official told Brill, "We were told by the White House to do nothing, not even circulate drafts of regs, because they might leak out if lobbyists got ahold of them."

As a result of these deliberate delays, pivotal rules setting the standards for insurance coverage under the exchanges were set further back.[50] For example, the all-important regulations concerning "essential health benefits" were held up. Health insurance policies that did not meet this minimum threshold would not be valid under the ACA's strict grandfathering requirements. The rules were not proposed until late November 2012, after the election.[51] They were not finalized until February 2013, only eight months before the launch of HealthCare.gov.[52]

---

[50] Goldstein, *supra* note 4.
[51] Timothy Jost, *Implementing Health Reform: Essential Health Benefits, Actuarial Value, and Accreditation*, HEALTH AFFAIRS BLOG (Nov. 21, 2012), bit.ly/1WHnNm7.
[52] Timothy Jost, *Implementing Health Reform: The Essential Health Benefits Rule*, HEALTH AFFAIRS BLOG (Feb. 20, 2013), bit.ly/1SXME2n.

It is not clear why this process took so long. As Professor Timothy Jost observed, despite receiving nearly 6,000 public comments, "the final rule [made] virtually no changes of significance [from] the proposed rule."[53] In other words, the delay was not to account for revisions. But the slow-down carried a significant cost. According to Richard Foster, who served as Medicare's chief actuary for two decades, these delays were "a singularly bad decision. It's the president's most significant domestic policy achievement."[54] Tragically, Foster added, the administration was risking a failed implementation "for a short-term political gain." Perhaps the reason why this provision was delayed so long was that it established the "minimum essential coverage" criteria for policies under the ACA. As a result, millions of noncompliant policies that did not meet the threshold would be cancelled during the fall of 2013.

5.6. "THE MOST IMPORTANT THING"

On November 6, 2012, after weeks of conjectures about skewed polls and undecided voters in Ohio flocking to Romney,[55] the election went exactly as polling analyst Nate Silver predicted.[56] On Election Day, the race was over by 11:15 PM. The only thing standing between Barack Obama and his second term of office was Chief Justice John Roberts and the oath of office.

President Barack Obama shares a record with President Franklin D. Roosevelt as the only two presidents to receive the oath of office four times. Prior to the enactment of the 22nd Amendment, Roosevelt was elected, and inaugurated four times. President Obama was limited to two terms. During his first inauguration on January 20, 2009, Obama and Roberts flubbed the oath. The two started to speak over one another in an embarrassing moment to begin a new presidency. Jeffrey Toobin reported that Roberts had e-mailed the designated staffers an annotated oath card, marking the spots where he would pause to allow the president to repeat.[57] Apparently, the card never made it to Team Obama.[58] As a precaution – to

---

[53] *Id.*

[54] Goldstein, *supra* note 4.

[55] Eric Benson, *Unskewed Polls Founder Dean Chambers Takes Stock of Obama's Win*, DAILY INTELLIGENCER (Nov. 9, 2012), perma.cc/7A5H-9HAQ.

[56] Chris Taylor, *Triumph of the Nerds: Nate Silver Wins in 50 States*, MASHABLE (Nov. 7, 2012), perma.cc/6HH3-4TEM.

[57] JEFFREY TOOBIN, THE OATH 6-7 (2013).

[58] Nina Totenberg, *The Presidential Oath: Not Always Perfect, But It Gets the Job Done*, NPR (Jan. 20, 2013), perma.cc/UC83-CCV4.

prevent any legal challenges to the legality of Obama's office – the following day the chief justice administered the oath a second time during a private ceremony.[59]

In 2013, they would have to do it twice, again. The Twentieth Amendment provides that the president's term begins on January 20. That year, January 20 fell on Sunday, a day on which the public inauguration would not be scheduled. As a result, there would be two oaths: the first in a private ceremony at the White House on Sunday, January 20, and the second at the public inauguration in front of the Capitol on Monday, January 21.

When asked if he was worried about the chief justice flubbing the oath again, the president's press secretary said, "Given health care, I don't care if he speaks in tongues."[60] On Sunday, the third oath was successfully delivered. The pool reporter noted that "the two men seemed warm, but formal, with no hint of animosity."[61] Obama smiled and said, "Thank you, Chief Justice. Thank you so much." No doubt Obama had every reason to be very thankful to the chief justice.

The next day, more than one million people crowded onto the National Mall to catch the inauguration. On this frigid day in Washington, D.C., all nine justices attended. Justice Scalia donned a traditional skullcap fashioned after a hat worn by Sir Thomas More.[62] Behind the burly Scalia, the diminutive Justice Ginsburg could barely be seen underneath her huge fur hat. Justice Alito wore a hip pair of sunglasses.

Roberts and Obama met again, face to face, in front of the American people. The chief justice brought notes and delivered the oath flawlessly. This time it was the President who stumbled. The *Associated Press* reported that "Obama stammered briefly over [the word] 'states' as he repeated back the words 'the office of president of the United States.'"[63] But it was close enough. Roberts shook his hand and said, "Congratulations, Mr. President." The President's

[59] *Obama Retakes Oath of Office after Roberts' Mistake*, CNN (Jan. 22, 2009), perma.cc/ KBX7-YEWE.
[60] Adam Liptak, *For President and Chief Justice, Another Chance To Get It Right*, N.Y. TIMES (Jan. 19, 2013), nyti.ms/1ONTWDW.
[61] Steven T. Dennis, *Obama Sworn In for Second Term*, ROLL CALL (Jan. 20, 2013), perma.cc/7ZW5-VUDY.
[62] Josh Blackman, *Scalia the Originalist: His Skullcap Is a Replica of the One Sir Thomas More Wore*, JOSH BLACKMAN'S BLOG (Jan. 21, 2013), perma.cc/B9RN-EL5B.
[63] *Obama Stumbles on "States" during Swearing in*, ASSOCIATED PRESS (Jan. 21, 2013), perma.cc/ZX6P-HBD7.

first term was dedicated to enacting the Affordable Care Act. His second term would be tested by its implementation.

The previous month, President Obama told a dozen senior officials, including Kathleen Sebelius, that the ACA was "the most important thing" in his presidency.[64] "We've got to do it right."[65] But the urgency the president preached on the Truman Balcony three years before would not materialize – until it was almost too late.

[64] Goldstein, *supra* note 4.
[65] *Id.*

6

Faith in the Courts

6.1. RESTORING RELIGIOUS FREEDOM

Through the First Amendment, the Framers crafted two approaches to protecting religious freedom from governmental burdens: "Congress shall make
no law [1] respecting an *establishment of religion,* or [2] prohibiting the *free
exercise* thereof."[1] The former is the establishment clause, and the latter is the
free exercise clause. Neither clause had much of an impact on constitutional
case law until the mid-twentieth century, when the Warren Court began to
interpret them to place limitations on the power of the government to burden
religion.

One of the key cases during this era was the 1963 decision of *Sherbert v.
Verner,* which involved a classic clash between the state and a minority faith.[2]
Sherbert was a member of the Seventh-Day Adventist Church.[3] Unable to
find a job that would allow her to rest on Saturday, her Sabbath, she applied
for unemployment compensation from the state. South Carolina determined that the only day of rest that could excuse someone from working
would be Sunday, the traditional Sabbath for almost all Christian denomi-
nations. Because Sherbert was unwilling to accept work on Saturday, she
was denied unemployment benefits. The sabbatarian appealed her case to
the Supreme Court, and won a decisive victory for religious freedom.

Writing for the Court, Justice William Brennan found that South Carolina's
policy "forces [Sherbert] to choose between following the precepts of her religion and forfeiting benefits, on the one hand, and abandoning one of the
precepts of her religion in order to accept work, on the other hand."[4] Such a

---

[1] U.S. Const. am. 1.
[2] Sherbert v. Verner, 374 U.S. 398 (1963).
[3] *Id.* at 399.
[4] *Id.* at 404.

dilemma violates the First Amendments' free exercise clause. "Any incidental burden on the free exercise of appellant's religion," Brennan wrote, must be "justified by a 'compelling state interest in the regulation of a subject within the State's constitutional power to regulate.'"[5] There was no such interest present in this case, as the state did not have a sufficient reason to trump Sherbert's belief that Saturday was the proper day of rest. If the state granted one day of rest on Sunday, Sherbert could be also be accommodated with one day of rest on Saturday.

Justice John Marshall Harlan II dissented. He countered that South Carolina's policy was "uniformly applied," irrespective of religious beliefs. It did not target sabbatarians, even if it had a negative impact on their exercise. As a result, Harlan wrote, there was no violation of the First Amendment. Rather, the Court's holding requires the Constitution to be read to "compel [the Justices] to carve out an exception – and to provide benefits – for those whose unavailability is due to their religious convictions."[6]

Over this dissent, the rule of *Sherbert* would largely prevail for nearly three decades, though not without criticism. As UCLA Law Professor Eugene Volokh noted, the conservative wing of the Court, led by Chief Justice William Rehnquist, "had been championing a retreat from the 'liberal' Free Exercise Clause view for years."[7] Judges, critics argued, should not be in the business of excusing people from the law due to their religious beliefs.

The critics prevailed in the 1990 decision of *Employment Division v. Smith*. During his Native American religious ceremonies, Alfred Smith ingested peyote, an illegal hallucinogen. Smith was terminated by his employer due to the peyote ritual.[8] The state of Oregon denied Smith's application for unemployment benefits because he was terminated for acting contrary to law – using an illegal controlled substance. Smith challenged the denial of benefits as a violation of the First Amendment's Free Exercise Clause.[9] Like Sherbert three decades earlier, Smith claimed that he was forced with the choice of violating his beliefs to receive benefits or following his beliefs and being denied benefits. These facts are somewhat similar to those of *Sherbert*, but the outcome would be very different.

[5] *Id.* (quoting NAACP v. Button, 371 U. S. 415, 438).
[6] *Id.* at 420.
[7] Eugene Volokh, *Many Liberals (Sensible) Retreat from the Old Justice Brennan/ACLU Position on Religious Exemptions*, Volokh Conspiracy, WASH. POST (Apr. 1, 2015), perma.cc/MF3T-EEC9
[8] Employment Division v. Smith, 494 U.S. 872 (1990).
[9] *Id.*

In a controversial 5-4 decision by Justice Scalia, the Supreme Court held that the Free Exercise Clause did not afford Smith a religious accommodation because his peyote use was illegal. The Oregon policy was known as a *law of general applicability*, in that it applied evenly to all faiths.[10] Denying unemployment compensation for someone who used illegal controlled substances was not targeted directly at criminalizing the Native American sacrament. In contrast, Sherbert's sabbatarianism was perfectly lawful.

Justice Scalia determined that the Constitution did not allow courts to be in the business of exempting people, like Smith the Native American, from generally applicable laws based on their religious beliefs. If that were true, he asked, how should the diverse "religious preference[s]" of our "cosmopolitan nation" be protected?[11] Scalia answered, "[v]alues that are protected against government interference through enshrinement in the Bill of Rights are not thereby banished from the political process."[12] In other words, democracy can provide special safeguards for religious beliefs. In the final paragraph of the Court's opinion, Scalia concedes the shortcomings of his conclusion: "It may fairly be said that leaving accommodation to the political process will place at a relative disadvantage those *religious practices that are not widely engaged in*."[13] But that was not enough to rule for Mr. Smith. The First Amendment, Scalia explained, "does not require this" result.[14]

Three decades after *Sherbert*, Justice Brennan found his opinion discarded by *Smith*, and joined Justice O'Connor's dissent. The dissent would have retained *Sherbert*, for free exercise is not a collective right, subject to the democratic process, but an "*individual* religious liberty."[15] Professor Michael Stokes Paulsen laments that the majority, all "judicial conservatives," engaged in an "utterly unforced error," as the Justices who would otherwise "support a broad construction of First Amendment freedoms" failed to "embrace the overriding value of religious liberty."[16] The job of "defend[ing the] Free Exercise clause as a substantive freedom fell to the three dissenting liberals."[17]

---

[10] *Id.*
[11] *Id.* (quoting Braunfeld v. Brown, 366 U. S., at 606). *See also* Town of Greece v. Galloway, 134 S.Ct. 1811, 1849, (2014) (Kagan, J., dissenting) ("[T]he American community is today, as it long has been, a rich mosaic of religious faiths.").
[12] *Smith*, 494 U.S. at 890.
[13] *Id. See also* Burwell v. Hobby Lobby Stores, 134 S.Ct. 2751, 2787 (2014) (Kennedy, J., concurring).
[14] *Smith*, 494 U.S. at 888–89.
[15] *Id.* at 891 (emphasis added).
[16] Michael Stokes Paulsen, *Justice Scalia's Worst Opinion*, PUBLIC DISCOURSE (Apr. 17, 2015), perma.cc/P22R-6E2F.
[17] *Id.*

Justice Scalia's decision in *Smith* resulted in a massive political backlash that lead to the enactment of the *Religious Freedom Restoration Act* (RFRA, pronounced Riff-Rah). In 1993, then-Representative Charles Schumer of New York introduced RFRA in the House of Representatives.[18] Its counterpart bill in the Senate was co-sponsored by Senator Edward Kennedy. RFRA was backed by the "ACLU joined with a broad coalition of religious and civil liberties groups, including People for the American Way [and] the National Association of Evangelicals."[19] The bill enjoyed such wide-ranging bipartisan support that it passed the House on a voice vote, passed the Senate by a vote of 97-3, and was promptly signed into law by President Clinton. (Imagine such a significant law passing today with this kind of vote!)

The law provides that the "Government shall not substantially burden a person's exercise of religion" unless it "is in furtherance of a compelling governmental interest" and "is the least restrictive means of furthering that compelling governmental interest." In 2014, the Supreme Court would grapple with RFRA, and determine whether the contraceptive mandate imposed a "substantial burden" on the free exercise of the plaintiffs; and if it did, whether that was the "least restrictive" way of achieving the government's "compelling" interest in providing female employees with cost-free contraception.

6.2. "VIOLATE THEIR OBLIGATIONS AND VOWS"

Religious non-profits, such as the Little Sisters of the Poor, were not exempted from the contraceptive mandate. Rather, under *Accommodation 2.0*, the insurer, not the employer, would pay for the cost of contraceptive coverage. However, the Little Sisters claimed that the accommodation violated their rights under RFRA. They argued that the act of filling out Employee Benefits Security Administration Form 700 and delivering it to their insurers triggers the provisioning of contraceptives. Signing the form, they argue, creates a contractual relationship with an insurer, the sole purpose of which is to authorize the insurer to do that which they deem sinful. In other words, completing the form allows the government to hijack their insurance plans.

Consider the position of Mother Loraine Marie Claire Maguire, the Provincial Superior of the Little Sisters of the Poor. She explained that she could not "[s]ign the self-certification form that on its face authorizes another organization to deliver contraceptives, sterilization, and abortifacients to the Little Sisters' employees and other beneficiaries." The Little Sisters argued

---

[18] Chuck Schumer on RFRA, C-SPAN (May 11, 1993), perma.cc/T83C-4JTZ.
[19] *The ACLU and Freedom of Religion and Belief*, ACLU, bit.ly/1ZdiJ81.

in court that their "religious convictions equally forbid them from contracting with an insurance company that will provide free coverage for, or access to, contraception." On a deeper level, however, contracting with the insurer would "violate their commitment to Christian witness by being seen to participate in the government's program. Doing so would not only directly violate their obligations and vows, but also would risk leading others astray." This runs contrary to the Catholic doctrine of *scandal*.[20]

Failing to sign the form had a steep financial cost. If an employer-sponsored health care plan did not cover contraceptives by January 1, 2014, it would result in a fine of $100 per employee per day.[21] The employers could drop their health insurance plans altogether, which would subject them to a $2,000 per worker annual fine under the employer mandate. But this was no solace for the Little Sisters, who told the court that they should not be forced to deny their staff health insurance. "Catholic faith compels them to promote the spiritual and physical well-being of their employees by providing them with health benefits within the construct of Catholic beliefs," they explained. Dropping insurance coverage would violate those beliefs.

Finally, the Little Sisters countered that there were other ways the government could expand access to contraception, including "directly provid[ing] contraceptive services" on the new health insurance exchanges. The accommodation to the contraceptive mandate, they argued, is not the "least restrictive means of furthering" the government's interest. If the government has such a strong desire that women have access to birth control, it can do so with means less burdensome to conscience.

The government countered that there was not a substantial burden on the employer's free exercise. The Little Sisters would not have to pay for the contraceptives, and the act of signing the form merely notifies the insurer that they are now required to provide the coverage. Delivery of the form in no way triggers the provisioning of contraceptives – rather, that process occurs by operation of federal regulations. The form merely notifies the insurer to avail themselves of the federal reimbursement program. The non-profits are not required to provide, participate in, contract, or arrange for the provisioning of contraceptives, the government argued. In its regulations, the Obama administration maintained that to the extent there is any burden on free exercise, it is only "minimal," and not "substantial."[22]

---

[20] *Catechism of the Catholic Church*, THE VATICAN, perma.cc/3EBN-TPMK.
[21] 26 U.S.C. § 4980D(b) & (e)(1). In Chapter 32, we will discuss how the Little Sisters' "church plan" made it impossible for the government to actually fine them.
[22] 78 Fed. Reg. 39887.

Over the next three years, nearly 200 federal judges would wrestle with how to balance the government's power to provide seamless access to contraceptives and the bedrock principles of religious liberty. In total, fifty for-profit corporations, thirty-seven universities, forty religious charities, and fifteen dioceses challenged the contraceptive mandate.[23] Several prominent public interest law firms that focus on faith in the courts filed the bulk of the cases. Alliance Defending Freedom, formerly the Alliance Defense Fund, led the way with twenty suits.[24] Noel Francisco of the Jones Day Law Firm (the same firm Michael Carvin practices at) filed eighteen suits, primarily on behalf of dioceses around the country.[25] The Thomas More Law Center in Michigan filed thirteen

---

[23] *HHS Mandate Information Central*, The Becket Fund for Religious Liberty, bit.ly/1rUM1y7.

[24] Louisiana Coll. v. Sebelius, 38 F. Supp. 3d 766 (W.D. La. 2014); Geneva Coll. v. Sebelius, 988 F. Supp. 2d 511, 514 (W.D. Pa. 2013) *rev'd sub nom.* Geneva Coll. v. Sec'y U.S. Dep't of Health & Human Servs., 778 F.3d 422 (3d Cir. 2015); Newland v. Sebelius, 881 F. Supp. 2d 1287 (D. Colo. 2012) *aff'd*, 542 F. App'x 706 (10th Cir. 2013); Grace Sch. v. Sebelius, 988 F. Supp. 2d 935, 940 (N.D. Ind. 2013) *rev'd and remanded sub nom.* Grace Sch. v. Burwell, 801 F.3d 788 (7th Cir. 2015); Tyndale House Publishers, Inc. v. Sebelius, 904 F. Supp. 2d 106 (D.D.C. 2012); Grote Indus., LLC v. Sebelius, 914 F. Supp. 2d 943 (S.D. Ind. 2012); Conestoga Wood Specialties Corp. v. Sec'y of U.S. Dep't of Health & Human Servs, 724 F.3d 377 (3d Cir. 2013) *rev'd and remanded*, Burwell v. Hobby Lobby Stores, Inc., 134 S. Ct. 2751, 189 L. Ed. 2d 675 (2014) and *rev'd sub nom*; Conestoga Wood Specialties Corp. v. Sec'y of U.S. Dep't of Health & Human Servs; No. 13–1144, 2014 WL 4467879 (3d Cir. Aug. 5, 2014); Sioux Chief Mfg. Co., Inc. v. Sylvia Burwell, No. 13-0036-CV-W-ODS, (W.D. MO. Nov. 12, 2014); Briscoe v. Sebelius, No. 1:13-cv-00285-WYD-BNB (D. Colo. 2015); Armstrong v. Sebelius, No. 13-CV-00563-RBJ, 2013 WL 5213640 (D. Colo. Sept. 17, 2013); Bindon v. Sebelius, No. 1:13-cv-1207-EGS (D.D.C. 2013); Midwest Fastener Corp. v. Burwell, No. 13-01337 (ESH) (D.D.C. 2014); S. Nazarene Univ. v. Sebelius, No. CIV-13-1015-F, 2013 WL 6804265 (W.D. Okla. Dec. 23, 2013) *rev'd sub nom*; Little Sisters of the Poor Home for the Aged, Denver, Colo. v. Burwell, 794 F.3d 1151 (10th Cir. 2015); Randy Reed Automotive v. Burwell, No. 13-6117-CV-SJ-ODS (W.D. MO. 2014); Dordt Coll. v. Sebelius, 22 F. Supp. 3d 934, 938 (N.D. Iowa 2014) *aff'd sub nom*; Dordt Coll. v. Burwell, 801 F.3d 946 (8th Cir. 2015); Ave Maria Univ. v. Sebelius, No. 2:12-CV-88-FTM-99SPC, 2012 WL 3128015 (M.D. Fla. July 31, 2012); Fellowship of Catholic University Students v. Burwell, No. 1:13-cv-03263-MSK-KMT (D. Co. 2015); Dobson v. Sebelius, 38 F. Supp. 3d 1245, 1249 (D. Colo. 2014); Mar. for Life v. Burwell, No. 14-CV-1149 (RJL), 2015 WL 5139099 (D.D.C. Aug. 31, 2015).

[25] Roman Catholic Archbishop of Washington v. Sebelius, 19 F. Supp. 3d 48, 59 (D.D.C. 2013) *aff'd in part, vacated in part sub nom*; Priests For Life v. U.S. Dep't of Health & Human Servs., 772 F.3d 229 (D.C. Cir. 2014); Roman Catholic Archdiocese of New York v. Sebelius, 987 F. Supp. 2d 232, 236 (E.D.N.Y. 2013) *rev'd sub nom*; Catholic Health Care Sys. v. Burwell, 796 F.3d 207 (2d Cir. 2015); Zubik v. Sebelius, 983 F. Supp. 2d 576, 580 (W.D. Pa. 2013) *overruled by* Geneva Coll. v. Sec'y U.S. Dep't of Health & Human Serv's 778 F.3d 422, 430 (3d Cir.) *cert. granted in part sub nom*; Zubik v. Burwell, 136 S. Ct. 444 (2015) and *cert. granted sub nom*; Geneva Coll. v. Burwell, 136 S. Ct. 445 (2015); Geneva Coll. v. Sec'y U.S. Dep't of Health & Human Servs, 778 F.3d 422, 429 (3d Cir.) *cert. granted in part sub nom*; Zubik v. Burwell, 136 S. Ct. 444 (2015) and *cert. granted sub nom*; Geneva Coll. v. Burwell, 136 S. Ct. 445 (2015); Roman Catholic Diocese of Dallas v. Sebelius, 927 F. Supp. 2d 406 (N.D. Tex.

cases.[26] The Becket Fund for Religious Liberty brought nine cases, including the very first challenge in November 2011 on behalf of Belmont Abbey College.[27] Mark Rienzi, one of the lawyers for the Becket Fund, told me that in 2011 and 2012, religious employers were pleading for help. "Our phone was ringing off the hook. I can't begin to count the number of calls we received." The American

2013); Roman Catholic Diocese of Fort Worth v. Sebelius, No. 4:12–CV–314–Y (N.D.Tex. Jan. 31, 2013); Franciscan Univ. of Steubenville v. Sebelius, No. 2:12-CV-440, 2013 WL 1189854 (S.D. Ohio Mar. 22, 2013); Catholic Diocese of Biloxi, Inc. v. Sebelius, No. 1:12CV158-HSO-RHW, 2012 WL 6831407 (S.D. Miss. Dec. 20, 2012); Univ. of Notre Dame v. Sebelius, 743 F.3d 547, 549 (7th Cir. 2014) *cert. granted, judgment vacated sub nom*; Univ. of Notre Dame v. Burwell, 135 S. Ct. 1528, 191 L. Ed. 2d 557 (2015); Diocese of Fort Wayne-S. Bend, Inc. v. Sebelius, 988 F. Supp. 2d 958 (N.D. Ind. 2013); Archdiocese of St. Louis v. Sebelius, 920 F. Supp. 2d 1018 (E.D. Mo. 2013); Conlon v. Sebelius, 923 F. Supp. 2d 1126, 1128 (N.D. Ill. 2013); Catholic Diocese of Peoria v. Sebelius, No. 12–1276, 2013 WL 74240 (C.D. Ill. Jan. 4, 2013); Catholic Diocese of Nashville v. Sebelius, No. 3-12-0934, 2012 WL 5879796 (M.D. Tenn. Nov. 21, 2012); Roman Catholic Archdiocese of Atlanta v. Sebelius, No. 1:12-CV-03489-WSD, 2014 WL 1256373 (N.D. Ga. Mar. 26, 2014) *on reconsideration in part*, No. 1:12-CV-03489-WSD, 2014 WL 2441742 (N.D. Ga. May 30, 2014); Rev. Wenski v. Sebelius, No. 12-23820-Civ-Graham/Goodman, (S. D. FLA., 2013); Michigan Catholic Conference & Catholic Family Servs. v. Burwell, 755 F.3d 372, 378 (6th Cir. 2014) *cert. granted, judgment vacated sub nom*; Michigan Catholic Conference v. Burwell, 135 S. Ct. 1914 (2015); Catholic Diocese of Beaumont v. Sebelius, 10 F. Supp. 3d 725 (E.D. Tex. 2014) *rev'd sub nom*; E. Texas Baptist Univ. v. Burwell, 793 F.3d 449 (5th Cir. 2015) *cert. granted*, 136 S. Ct. 444 (2015).

[26] Legatus v. Sebelius, 901 F. Supp. 2d 980 (E.D. Mich. 2012); Autocam Corp. v. Sebelius, 730 F.3d 618, 624 (6th Cir. 2013) *cert. granted, judgment vacated sub nom*; Autocam Corp. v. Burwell, 134 S. Ct. 2901 (2014) *abrogated by* Burwell v. Hobby Lobby Stores, Inc., 134 S. Ct. 2751 (2014); Monaghan v. Sebelius, 931 F. Supp. 2d 794, 798 (E.D. Mich. 2013); Beckwith Elec. Co. v. Sebelius, 960 F. Supp. 2d 1328 (M.D. Fla. 2013); Eden Foods, Inc. v. Sebelius, 733 F.3d 626 (6th Cir. 2013) *cert. granted, judgment vacated sub nom*; Eden Foods, Inc. v. Burwell, 134 S. Ct. 2902 (2014); Mersino Mgmt. Co. v. Sebelius, No. 13-CV-11296, 2013 WL 3546702 (E.D. Mich. July 11, 2013) *rev'd and remanded sub nom*; Mersino Mgmt. Co. v. Burwell, No. 13–1944, 2015 WL 9850709 (6th Cir. Jan. 28, 2015); M&N Plastics v. Burwell, No. 5:13-cv-14754 (E.D. Mich., 2014); Willis Law v. Sebelius, No. 13-01124 (CKK) (D.D.C. 2013); Wieland v. U.S. Dep't of Health & Human Servs., 793 F.3d 949 (8th Cir. 2015); Mersino Management Co. v. Burwell, No. 13-cv-11296 (E.D. Mich., 2015); Barron Indus. v. Sebelius, No. 1:13-cv-1330 (D.D.C. Sept. 25, 2013); Williams v. Burwell, No. 1:13-cv-01699, (D.D.C. 2014); Ave Maria Found. v. Sebelius, 991 F. Supp. 2d 957 (E.D. Mich. 2014).

[27] Wheaton Coll. v. Sebelius, 703 F.3d 551 (D.C. Cir. 2012); Colorado Christian Univ. v. Sebelius, No. 11-CV-03350-CMA-BNB, 2013 WL 93188 (D. Colo. Jan. 7, 2013); Eternal Word Television Network, Inc. v. Sebelius, 935 F. Supp. 2d 1196 (N.D. Ala. 2013); Ave Maria Found. v. Sebelius, 991 F. Supp. 2d 957 (E.D. Mich. 2014); Wheaton Coll. v. Sebelius, 887 F. Supp. 2d 102 (D.D.C. 2012) *vacated*, No. CV 12–1169 (ESH), 2013 WL 5994617 (D.D.C. Aug. 19, 2013); Hobby Lobby Stores, Inc. v. Sebelius, 870 F. Supp. 2d 1278 (W.D. Okla. 2012) *rev'd and remanded*, 723 F.3d 1114 (10th Cir. 2013) *aff'd sub nom*; Burwell v. Hobby Lobby Stores, Inc., 134 S. Ct. 2751 (2014); E. Texas Baptist Univ. v. Sebelius, 988 F. Supp. 2d 743(S.D. Tex. 2013) *rev'd sub nom*; E. Texas Baptist Univ. v. Burwell, 793 F.3d 449 (5th Cir. 2015); Little Sisters of the Poor Home for the Aged v. Sebelius, 6 F. Supp. 3d 1225(D. Colo. 2013) *aff'd sub nom*; Little Sisters of the Poor Home for the Aged, Denver, Colo. v. Burwell, 794 F.3d 1151 (10th Cir. 2015); Reaching Souls Int'l, Inc. v. Sebelius, No. CIV-13-1092-D, 2013 WL 6804259 (W.D. Okla. Dec. 20, 2013) *rev'd*

Center for Law & Justice, led by Jay Sekulow, brought eight cases.[28] The Liberty Institute, now known as the First Liberty Institute, filed seven challenges.[29] Finally, the American Freedom Law Center brought two cases.[30]

The nonprofit challenges would not reach the Supreme Court until 2016. Between 2012 and 2014, perhaps as the Obama administration intended, the main focus was on the challenges by for-profit employers.

6.3. "FAITH IS WOVEN INTO THEIR BUSINESS"

Hobby Lobby Stores, Inc. was founded by David Green in 1970. Green grew the small picture frame company into one of the nation's largest arts-and-crafts chains. Today, the company has 514 stores in 41 states, with more than 13,000 employees. Hobby Lobby is not publicly traded, but is owned through trusts by members of the Green family – all devout Christians. The Greens explain that "faith is woven into their business. It is reflected in what they sell, in how they advertise, in how they treat employees, in how much they give to charity, and in the one day of the week when their stores are closed." If you've ever run out of yarn on a Sunday, Hobby Lobby would not be of any help. As explained in the company's statement of purpose, they are committed to "[h]onoring the Lord in all we do by operating the company in a manner

---

    sub nom; Little Sisters of the Poor Home for the Aged, Denver, Colo. v. Burwell, 794 F.3d 1151 (10th Cir. 2015).

[28] O'Brien v. U.S. Dep't of Health & Human Servs., 894 F. Supp. 2d 1149 (E.D. Mo. 2012) *rev'd in part, vacated in part*, 766 F.3d 862 (8th Cir. 2014); Korte v. U.S. Dep't of Health & Human Servs., 912 F. Supp. 2d 735 (S.D. Ill. 2012) *rev'd and remanded sub nom*; Korte v. Sebelius, 735 F.3d 654 (7th Cir. 2013); Am. Pulverizer Co. v. U.S. Dep't of Health & Human Servs., No. 12-3459-CV-S-RED, 2012 WL 6951316 (W.D. Mo. Dec. 20, 2012); Gilardi v. Sebelius, 926 F. Supp. 2d 273 (D.D.C.) *aff'd in part, rev'd in part sub nom*; Gilardi v. U.S. Dep't of Health & Human Servs., 733 F.3d 1208 (D.C. Cir. 2013) *cert. granted, judgment vacated sub nom*; Gilardi v. Dep't of Health & Human Servs., 134 S. Ct. 2902 (2014); Lindsay v. Burwell, No. 1:13-cv-01210 (N.D. Ill., 2014); Bick Holding Inc. v. Sebelius, No. 4:13-cv-00462-AGF (E.D. MO., 2013); Hartenbower v. Burwell, No. 1:13-CV-02253 (N.D. Ill., 2014); The C.W. Zumbiel Co. v. U.S. Dept. of Health and Services, No. 13–1611 (RBW) (D.D.C. 2014).

[29] Criswell v. Sebelius, No. 3:12-CV-4409-N (N.D. Tex. 2013); American Family Association v. Sebelius, No. 1:13-CV-00032-SA-DAS (N.D. Miss. 2013); Holland v. Burwell, No. 2:13-cv-15487 (S.D.W.V. 2013); Hastings Automotive v. Sebelius, No. 14-cv-265 (PAM/HB) (D.MT. 2014); Valley Forge Christian College v. Burwell, No. 2:14-cv-4622-AB (D. Penn. 2014); Christian and Missionary Alliance Foundation v. Burwell, No: 2:14-cv-580-FtM-29CM (M.D. Fl., 2015); Insight for Living Ministries v. Burwell, No. 4:14-cv-675 (E.D. Tex., 2014).

[30] Priests for Life v. United States Dep't of Health & Human Servs., 7 F. Supp. 3d 88 (D.D.C. 2013) *aff'd sub nom*; Priests for Life v. U.S. Dep't of Health & Human Servs., 772 F.3d 229 (D.D.C. Cir. 2014); Johnson v. Burwell, No. 13-00609, (D.D.C., 2014).

consistent with Biblical principles." That means forgoing profits by keeping the store closed on the Sabbath. The family view their business as a "ministry."

Long before the Affordable Care Act, the Greens provided their employees with what they described as "excellent health insurance through a [self-insured] plan." In 2012, a lawyer from the Becket Fund called Hobby Lobby to ask whether they would be willing to challenge the contraceptive mandate in court.[31] After receiving the call, David Green ordered a "review of the company's health plans" and found that Hobby Lobby had "inadvertently included" Plan B and Ella.[32] Green "immediately excluded them," explaining that they "cannot in good conscience knowingly offer coverage for abortion-causing drugs or devices."[33] Many critics would later charge the Greens with hypocrisy excluding these drugs after the mandate was announced.[34] Hobby Lobby signed on with Becket to challenge the mandate.

Recall that under *Exemption 2.0*, houses of worship were permanently excused from the mandate. In contrast, under *Accommodation 2.0* – working in tandem with the indefinite safe harbor and several court orders – religious nonprofit employers would not face the contraceptive mandate through 2013. However, religious for-profit employers faced far different stakes: they were not eligible for an exemption, accommodation, or safe harbor. Rather, they would be required to provide contraceptive coverage on January 1, 2013, or face ruinous fines. For example, Hobby Lobby would have to pay $1.3 million each day it did not provide contraceptive coverage for its employees.[35] Failing to provide insurance altogether would trigger $26 million in fines annually under the employer mandate.

In September 2012, Hobby Lobby tried to halt the mandate by seeking a preliminary injunction. The Greens argued that the mandate substantially burdened the corporation's rights of free exercise under RFRA and the First Amendment. They asked the federal court to put the mandate on hold before the December 31 deadline. Hobby Lobby explained that the mandate compels it "to provide employees with insurance coverage they believe implicates them in an immoral practice" and "pressures them by exacting a steep price for maintaining their beliefs." They viewed this dilemma as "a Hobson's

[31] Janet Adamy, *Are Firms Entitled to Religious Protections?*, WALL ST. J. (Mar. 21, 2014), on.wsj.com/1SArZTV.

[32] Motion for Preliminary Injunction, Hobby Lobby v. Sebelius at 3, 5:12-cv-01000 (W.D.OK. Sept. 12, 2012), bit.ly/1X9bglC.

[33] *Id.*

[34] Katie Sanders, *Did Hobby Lobby Once Provide the Birth Control Coverage It Sued the Obama Administration Over?*, PUNDITFACT (July 1, 2014), perma.cc/2KVR-KVY9.

[35] Anugrah Kumar, *Hobby Lobby Delays Obamacare Fines for Now; Avoids $18.2 Million Penalty*, FAITH NEWS NETWORK (Jan. 14, 2013), perma.cc/Q8LU-AK3B.

choice – an illusory choice where the only realistically possible course of action trenches on an adherent's sincerely held religious belief."

The government agreed that the Greens' beliefs were sincerely held, but vigorously rejected the notion that the corporation itself could exercise religious beliefs. "To hold otherwise," the Justice Department told the court, "would permit for-profit, secular corporations and their owners to become laws unto themselves." (This was the crux of Justice Scalia's opinion in *Employment Division v. Smith*.) Although the Green family members may be affected indirectly, the contraceptive mandate itself operates only on the corporation, not its individual officers. As a result, the government argued, the Greens could not raise religious defenses through the corporate veil: "A corporation and its owners are wholly separate entities, and the Court should not permit the Greens to eliminate that legal separation to impose their personal religious beliefs on the corporate entity or its employees."

Finally, even if there was a burden, the government argued that the mandate was "narrowly tailored to serve two compelling governmental interests: improving the health of women and children, and equalizing the provision of recommended preventive care for women and men." Beyond this case, where the Greens were sympathetic plaintiffs, the government warned that there are "an infinite variety of alleged religious beliefs [where] such companies and their owners could claim countless exemptions from" laws "designed to protect against unfair discrimination in the workplace."

The district court agreed with the government and found that the Hobby Lobby corporation could not, "separate and apart from the actions or belief systems of their individual owners or employees, exercise religion. They do not pray, worship, observe sacraments or take other religiously-motivated actions separate and apart from the intention and direction of their individual actors. Religious exercise is, by its nature, one of those 'purely personal' rights."[36] As a result, the court denied the preliminary injunction on November 19, barely a month away from the December 31 deadline.

The next morning, Hobby Lobby asked the Tenth Circuit Court of Appeals in Denver to put the contraceptive mandate on hold while the case was being litigated – a process that could take more than a year. On December 20, 2013, only eleven days before the deadline, a two-judge panel of the Tenth Circuit refused to put the mandate on hold. The Tenth Circuit's decision was an outlier. Eight other federal courts, including the Seventh and Eighth Circuit Courts of Appeals, enjoined the mandate pending appeal.[37] Other than Hobby

---

[36] Burwell v. Hobby Lobby Stores, Inc., 134 S. Ct. 2751, 2762 (2014).

[37] Korte v. Sebelius, 2012 WL 6757353 (7th Cir. Dec. 28, 2012) (granting injunction pending appeal); O'Brien v. U.S. Dept. of Health & Human Svcs., No. 12–3357 (8th Cir. Nov. 28, 2012)

Lobby, only two other for-profit corporations were denied an injunction before January 1: Autocam, a Michigan manufacturing company; and Grote Industries, a family-run auto lighting company based in Indiana.[38]

6.4. "EXTRAORDINARY RELIEF"

Three days before Christmas, Hobby Lobby filed an emergency application with Justice Sonia Sotomayor. (Each justice is assigned to supervise emergency appeals from each of the thirteen regions, or Circuits. Sotomayor is the Circuit Justice for the Tenth Circuit). "In just ten days," their attorneys implored, the contraceptive mandate "will expose [Hobby Lobby] to draconian fines unless they abandon their religious convictions and provide insurance coverage for abortion-inducing drugs." An injunction from the Court is "necessary to prevent immediate and irreparable harm to [Hobby Lobby] during the appellate process, including any further review by this Court." Simply stated, as this case is appealed through the system, and ultimately to the Supreme Court itself, the mandate should temporarily be put on hold.

Over Christmas, Hobby Lobby got coal in its stockings. On December 26, Justice Sotomayor denied the injunction in a four-page *in chambers* opinion, without first referring it to the other eight Justices. She observed that the Court "has not previously addressed similar RFRA or free exercise claims brought by closely held for-profit corporations ... alleging that the mandatory provision of certain employee benefits substantially burdens their exercise of religion." As a result, Hobby Lobby does "not satisfy the demanding standard for the extraordinary relief they seek." After the defeat, CEO David Green explained, "We simply cannot abandon our religious beliefs to comply with this mandate. We're Christians, and we run our business on Christian principles."[39] Mark Rienzi, one of the lawyers for Hobby

---

(granting "[a]ppellants' motion for stay pending appeal," without further comment); Sharpe Holdings, Inc. v. U.S. Dept. of Health & Human Svcs., 2012 WL 6738489 (E.D. Mo. Dec. 31, 2012) (granting motion for temporary restraining order); Monaghan v. Sebelius, 2012 WL 6738476 (E.D. Mich. Dec. 30, 2012) (same); American Pulverizer Co. v. U.S. Dept. of Health & Human Svcs., No. 12-3459-CV-S-RED, slip op. (W.D. Mo. Dec. 20, 2012) (granting preliminary injunction); Tyndale House Publishers, Inc. v. Sebelius, 2012 WL 5817323 (D.D.C. Nov. 16, 2012) (same); Legatus v. Sebelius, 2012 WL 5359630 (E.D. Mich. Oct. 31, 2012) (same); and Newland v. Sebelius, 2012 WL 3069154 (D. Colo. July 27, 2012) (same).

[38] Autocam Corp. v. Sebelius, No. 12–2673, slip op. (6th Cir. Dec. 28, 2012) (denying preliminary injunction pending appeal); Hobby Lobby Stores, Inc. v. Sebelius, No. 12–6294, slip op. (10th Cir. Dec. 20, 2012) (same); Grote Indus., LLC v. Sebelius, 2012 WL 6725905 (S.D. Ind. Dec. 27, 2012) (denying motion for preliminary injunction).

[39] Anugrah Kumar, *Hobby Lobby Delays Obamacare Fines for Now; Avoids $18.2 Million Penalty*, FAITH NEWS NETWORK (Jan. 14, 2013), perma.cc/Q8LU-AK3B.

Lobby, told me that they had a "very bad Christmas. We felt the weight of the obligation to protect these people and we failed."

The contraceptive mandate would officially go into effect on January 1, 2013. However, to the surprise of everyone, Hobby Lobby found a loophole. On January 10, Hobby Lobby's general counsel Peter Dobelbower released a statement: "Hobby Lobby discovered a way to shift the plan year for its employee health insurance, thus postponing the effective date of the mandate for several months."[40] While Hobby Lobby's new health insurance plan was scheduled to begin on January 1, 2013, the company changed that date, so the mandate would not kick in right away. Exactly how they did is, or how long the delay would last, was unclear at the time. One of Hobby Lobby's attorneys told me that after Justice Sotomayor's order, "they had massive 'What are we going to do?' meetings" and came up with this solution. *NewsOK* reported, "A representative for Hobby Lobby declined to elaborate on how long the company will have before its new plan year will start [and] when the federal mandate on emergency contraceptives coverage would kick in."[41]

The store would later offer more details in its brief to the Tenth Circuit. They explained that the Employee Retirement Income Security Act (ERISA) allowed them to make a "retroactive modification to their plan year. Accordingly, [Hobby Lobby's] plan year has now changed so that the mandate will not take effect against them until July 1, 2013." However it worked, Hobby Lobby was able to postpone the millions in fines until the Supreme Court was able to resolve the case.[42] (The Supreme Court's term coincidentally concludes during the last week in June.) However, Hobby Lobby's clock was ticking. Without emergency relief from the Supreme Court, the Greens turned back to the Tenth Circuit.

In virtually every instance, federal appeals courts hear arguments in panels of three judges. The losing party then has the option of asking all of the judges on the court of appeals to hear the case together, or *en banc*. However, Hobby Lobby was short on time – changing the plan year only bought six more months. In a crafty gambit, the craft store petitioned to skip the initial three-judge panel and proceed directly to the full *en banc*

---

[40] THE BECKET FUND, Statement Regarding Hobby Lobby (Jan. 10, 2013) perma.cc/AVX3-L9DE.

[41] Brianna Bailey, *Hobby Lobby Shifts Health Plan to Avoid Potential Penalties in Contraception Case*, NewsOK (Jan. 10, 2013), perma.cc/4HWG-8QD8.

[42] Eric Marrapodi, *Hobby Lobby Finds Way around $1.3-Million-a-Day Obamacare Hit – for Now*, CNN Belief Blog (Jan. 11, 2013), perma.cc/W3EG-W3YX.

court.[43] Hobby Lobby told the court that it should hear the case "en banc in the first instance" because there were already several other virtually identical controversies pending on the same issue. Further, the Tenth Circuit's denial of a stay in December was "out of step with the majority of courts that have correctly granted injunctive relief to similarly-situated business owners." The plaintiffs insisted that this was an "extraordinary situation where initial en banc hearing is needed to secure the uniformity of this Court's decisions – and their consistency with other circuits – on a question of national importance."

Initial *en banc* proceedings are extremely rare – I could only locate about two dozen during the last three decades across all thirteen federal circuits. For example, in the constitutional challenge to the Affordable Care Act two years earlier, Florida attempted a similar bypass to go straight from the district court to the full Eleventh Circuit.[44] Even with a case of such magnitude, the court denied that request.

Miraculously, Hobby Lobby's prayer for relief was answered on, of all days, Good Friday. On Friday, March 29, the Tenth Circuit announced that it would hear the case right away *en banc*.[45] A two-page order explained that "a poll was called and a majority of the available active judges in regular service have voted to grant initial en banc hearing." The case would be argued on May 23 before all eight judges. Barely one month later on June 27 – three days before Hobby Lobby would be subjected to the contraceptive mandate – the craft store's prayers continued to be answered. The eight judges on the panel fractured in many different ways, yielding a complicated 168-page opinion. But the end-result was clear: five judges agreed that Hobby Lobby was likely to succeed on its RFRA claims, and would be irreparably harmed by the imposition of the contraceptive mandate.[46] The mandate would once again be put on hold.

The solicitor general filed a petition for certiorari with the U.S. Supreme Court, which was granted two months later on November 26, 2013. The Green family's Thanksgiving in 2013 was much better than their Christmas in 2012. The Supreme Court would soon hear its second major Obamacare case in three years.

[43] Pl.'s En banc pet., 1–15, Hobby Lobby v. Sebelius, 12-6924 (10th Cir. Jan 10, 2013), bit.ly/1qoKIf4.
[44] JOSH BLACKMAN, UNPRECEDENTED: THE CONSTITUTIONAL CHALLENGE TO OBAMACARE 132 (2013).
[45] Order Granting En Banc Petition, Hobby Lobby v. Sebelius, 12-6924 (10th Cir. Mar. 29, 2013), bit.ly/hT1G4Ll.
[46] Hobby Lobby Stores, Inc. v. Sebelius, 723 F.3d 1114 (10th Cir. 2013).

PART III

Shutdown (May 2, 2013–September 30, 2013)

7

Exchanges "Established by the State"

7.1. "EQUIVALENT"

In January 2011, a reporter for Bloomberg BNA wrote an article titled "Opponents of New Federal Health Care Law Wage Constitutional War in Courts." In the piece he discussed several possible legal challenges to the including those presented at the American Enterprise Institute the previous month. Citing Tom Christina's presentation, the journalist noted in an anodyne fashion that "the individual income tax credit under Section 36B available for citizens of states that have established their own exchanges is not available to citizens of states with HHS exchanges." There was no elaboration or indication of what that would portend.

The article was read by Emily McMahon, who then served as Acting Assistant Secretary at the Treasury Department. McMahon would later testify before Congress that after reading the article, she "was the one who first [in the government who] became aware that some individuals were suggesting as a possible interpretation of the relevant provisions that the credit would not be available in a Federal exchange."[1] In English, that means that before Christina's presentation, no one in the Treasury Department was aware that Section 36B – which limited subsidies to plans enrolled in through an "exchange established by the state" – could be interpreted to limit subsidies to an exchange established by the state.

Even if McMahon had not heard that others were making this argument, she should have been aware that this could be a "possible interpretation" of the statute. Indeed, the IRS had already assembled a "36B Working Group" in "late summer of 2010" to develop regulations concerning the ACA's subsidies.[2]

---

[1] *Oversight of IRS' Legal Basis for Expanding Obamacare's Taxes and Subsidies: Hearing before the Subcommittee on Energy Policy, Health Care, and Entitlements*, 113th Cong. at 80 (2013), bit.ly/1rX2z8E.

[2] *Administration Conducted Inadequate Review of Key Issues Prior to Expanding Health Law's Taxes and Subsidies House of Representatives*, Committee on Oversight and Government Reform at 15 (2014), bit.ly/1TLiH5H.

As revealed in a report by the House Republican's Oversight Committee, all interviewed IRS and Treasury employees acknowledged that there "was an early consensus that these tax credits would be available in all exchanges."[3] At that time, the working group "did not consider the availability of tax credits in federal exchanges as a central issue during the rulemaking process and they spent relatively little time on it." Tom Christina said it was "flattering" if the IRS discovered the subsidies issue only after reading about his presentation.

However, Christina's discovery altered Treasury's thinking. Nicholas Bagley, the Michigan law professor, told me that "once it was brought to the IRS's attention," the government "recognized that there was a potential problem in the statute." Before the *Bloomberg* article in January 2011, the "early draft" of the IRS's regulations "included the language 'exchange established by the State' in the section entitled 'Eligibility for the Premium Tax Credit.'"[4] They copied the language verbatim from the statute. However, "[b]etween March 10, 2011 and March 15, 2011 – after McMahon's epiphany – the explicit reference to 'exchange established by the State' was removed" from the draft regulation.[5]

Very soon these initial drafts, the issue was elevated from career civil servants to the "larger departmental group, which included [politically appointed] senior IRS and Treasury officials."[6] At a March 25, 2011 meeting, the IRS Chief Counsel's Office distributed a four-sentence-long memorandum to explain a new rule the Treasury Department would propose to interpret Section 36B:

> Section 1321(c)(1) of the PPACA provides that if a state fails to establish an exchange, the Secretary of HHS will, directly or through a nonprofit, establish and operate "such" exchange within the state and implement the other exchange requirement. This language indicates that when HHS established an exchange, it do [sic] so as the surrogate of the state, and that *Congress viewed an exchange established by HHS as the equivalent of an exchange a state establishes directly. Thus*, the phrase "established by a state" *may be interpreted* to refer to an exchange established to operate in a state. Accordingly, all exchanges established within a state under PPACA, including those HHS must establish on the state's behalf, are exchanges established by the state under section 1311 of the PPACA.[7]

---

3 *Id.* at 16.
4 *Id.* at 17.
5 *Id.*
6 *Id.*
7 *Id.* (emphasis added).

The Treasury regulation assumed that Congress viewed the state exchanges – which would be the vehicles for subsidies – as the "equivalent" to the federal exchanges established by HHS. In other words, "established by a state under Section 1311" is best understood to mean an exchange "established by the state *or the federal government.*" There were no differences between the two types. Briefings provided by the IRS and Treasury personnel to the House Oversight Committee revealed that "this one-paragraph analysis is the only written analysis produced by Treasury and IRS regarding the availability of premium subsidies in federal exchanges before the proposed rule was issued."[8] Then again, this report must be taken with a grain of salt. Bagley noted that it was a "politically motivated report by a Republican Congress that detested the Affordable Care Act. The report itself contains a lot of evidence that these questions were taken seriously." (In this chapter, I tried to excerpt only documentary records, rather than conclusions of the Committee.)

On August 17, 2011, the Treasury Department published a notice on page 50,934 of Volume 76 of the Federal Register. A section titled "explanation of provisions," announced: "The proposed regulations provide that a taxpayer is eligible for the credit for a taxable year if the taxpayer ... is enrolled in one or more qualified health plans through an Exchange established under section 1311 *or 1321 of the Affordable Care Act.*" Recall that Section 36B provides subsidies if a taxpayer "is enrolled in one or more qualified health plans through an Exchange established under section 1311 of the Affordable Care Act." There is no mention of Section 1321, which is what provides the authority for HHS to establish a federal exchange.

During the rulemaking process, numerous commenters argued that the IRS lacked the authority to provide subsidized insurance policies in states with federal exchanges.[9] Senator Orin Hatch told the Secretary of the Treasury the regulations are "inconsistent with the relevant statutory language" and would "exceed your regulatory authority, violating the separation of powers."[10] Twenty-four members of Congress echoed those comments to the IRS Commissioner, pointing out that the "proposed rule's language [is] inconsistent with PPACA's statutory text."[11] Michael Carvin, the lawyer who would argue this case before the Supreme Court, told me the rulemaking process "was emblematic of the way that the Obama administration and the IRS did stuff. 'What's the best policy? I don't need any stinking language. Congress couldn't have meant that.

[8] *Id.* (emphasis added).
[9] *Id.* at 20.
[10] Letter from Orrin G. Hatch, to Timothy F. Geithner (Dec. 1, 2011), perma.cc/6B6B-8VTC.
[11] Letter from Phil Roe to Douglas H. Schuman (Nov. 4, 2011), bit.ly/1rX9ezL.

So I will pretend they didn't say it.'" Tom Christina, after reading the analysis in the Federal Register, thought, "wow, this is not going to impress the courts."

7.2. "MY JAW DROPPED"

Law professor Jonathan Adler is a nationally renowned expert in administrative law at Case Western Reserve University in Cleveland. His background in regulatory matters gave him a knack for reading through complicated regulatory statutes to figure out how they tick. The voluminous Affordable Care Act was fecund ground for the scholar. Adler was invited to write a paper for the University of Kansas's *Journal of Law & Public Policy* about how federalism would work under the ACA. The goal of his article was to study how the federal government and the states would work together to implement the new health care law. "I read the statute, unfortunately," Adler told me.

While traversing the 3,000-page bill, he focused on Section 36B. It struck him that states were given an awful choice – either build an exchange so your residents can get subsidies, or refuse to build an exchange and your residents would be unable to afford the unsubsidized insurance. Adler viewed this dilemma as extremely problematic under principles of "cooperative federalism," where the federal government could not coerce states to act by threatening to withhold huge amounts of money. By that point Adler had already seen the video of Christina's presentation, but he told me that he likely would have noticed the provisions even if Christina had not. "I assume so because I went through the statute," he said.

At his Kansas presentation in the spring of 2011, Adler recalled explaining that "if the state doesn't create an exchange, its citizens would lose their tax credits." There were many insurance experts in the room, including Sandy Praeger, the Kansas Insurance Commissioner, but no one asked any questions. "There was nothing particularly controversial about the suggestion that you wouldn't get tax credits." Adler noted that, "at the time the idea that the state might say 'no' wasn't really on the table." The professor did not think much of the research and doubted anyone could use it as a basis for a legal challenge.

On August 17, 2011, the same day that the IRS released the proposed regulation, Adler sent a note about it to Michael F. Cannon, the Director of Health Policy Studies at the libertarian Cato Institute. With a shaved head, angled jaw, and Sumerian amagi tattoo on his forearm,[12] Cannon's eyes exude passion

---

[12] The "amagi" symbol, written in Sumerian cuneiform, is believed to be the first written representation of the concept of liberty. It is a popular tattoo in libertarian circles, and is the symbol

for his major goal in life – destroying Obamacare to improve health care through markets. Cannon stated the issue bluntly: "After the ACA was enacted and after the president signed it, a lot of people – me included – decided that we weren't going to take this lying down, and we were going to try to block it and ultimately either get the Supreme Court to overturn it or Congress to repeal it."[13] Adler quips about Cannon. "Michael wakes up in the morning and says, 'How can I kill Obamacare?' I mean read the signature on his e-mail." All of Michael's e-mails end with "Tyrannis delenda est," meaning "tyranny must be destroyed."[14] It is a variant of *Carthago Delenda Est*, a phrase aptly attributed to Cato the Elder, as a battle cry for the Romans to destroy Carthage during the Punic Wars. Cannon told me his goal is to repeal the Affordable Care Act "root and branch."

Adler's e-mail to Cannon casually mentioned that "if a state doesn't create an exchange, it won't get tax credits either." Cannon recalled, "My jaw dropped." His eyes widened with the opportunity to devastate the Affordable Care Act. Cannon replied, "Oh my god, you have no idea what this means." He later told me, "I do not think Adler recognized the significance." Adler admitted as much: Cannon "had to explain to me why this was a big deal." *Newsweek* reported that this e-mail bolstered a case that "could unravel a significant portion of" Obamacare.[15]

Before this propitious e-mail, Cannon was urging governors nationwide not to establish Obamacare exchanges. His barnstorming message to the states was simple: resist all facets of the law. As the *New Republic* framed it, "Cannon spent a lot of time traveling around the country during the past few years – with visits to more than a dozen states and calls to far more – explaining to state officials opposed to the law that, if they simply refused to set up exchanges of their own and thereby shunted their citizens onto the federal exchange, they would greatly raise the odds of the law's total collapse if and when the courts agreed with him that the federal exchange couldn't award subsidies."[16] "When I was going to the states," Cannon said, "I got the sense that there were a lot of state officials who knew they wanted to stop this law and didn't know how.

---

of the Liberty Fund. Online Library of Liberty, *Amagi Symbol: Liberty Fund's Logo* (Apr. 10, 2014), perma.cc/CM8Z-8R9A.

[13] Sheryl Gay Stolberg, *A New Wave of Challenges to Health Law*, N.Y. TIMES (Dec. 2, 2013), nyti.ms/23wi3yp.

[14] Eric Stirgus, *Experts Say Federal Law Trumps State Law on 'Obamacare Exchange' Claim*, POLITIFACT GEORGIA (Nov. 28, 2012), perma.cc/K47R-CT3A.

[15] Pema Levy, *The Case That Could Topple Obamacare*, NEWSWEEK (Dec. 17, 2013), perma.cc/CZ9R-QUYF.

[16] Alec Macgillis, *Obamacare's Single Most Relentless Antagonist*, NEW REPUBLIC (Nov. 12, 2013), perma.cc/6KJG-S3ZZ.

When people like me would go to the states and say they were better off not creating the exchanges, it gave them the information they needed."[17]

But armed with this new information, Cannon had a new argument for recalcitrant states: "Oh my God, you could stop the entire thing!" If states refused to establish exchanges, then no subsidized policies would be available. In Cannon's view, "people would face the full cost of the regulations and they will demand that the law be repealed." A May 2012 *YouTube* video features Cannon looking directly at the camera: "These exchanges are new government bureaucracies through which the health care [law] will force Americans to purchase health insurance. But the health care law doesn't actually require states to establish exchanges, and without these exchanges, the whole law falls apart."[18] He urges, "what states should be doing is refusing to establish exchanges, no matter how the Supreme Court rules." But then comes the key: "Every employer in the state, including the state government itself, will be able to challenge that unconstitutional overreach in court, but *only* if the state does not create an exchange." The states would then "be in a position to drive a stake through the heart of this very bad law." Obamacare delenda est.

With this new pitch, Cannon notched several victories. In 2012, he was able to dissuade Maine Governor Paul LePage from establishing an exchange. "I made lots of arguments to the governor and this is one of them," Cannon told me. "I said, by blocking the state exchanges you can force Congress to reopen, or get rid of, this very bad law."[19] Jonathan Cohn of the *New Republic* feted Cannon: "[N]o single individual has done more to make the case for state resistance to Obamacare than Cannon."[20]

Public records revealed that the Cato Institute and the American Legislative Exchange Council urged the Maine governor to resist signing an executive order that would have established an exchange. "That's one of the things I was reminding them," Cannon said. "You don't have to do this. Don't just do something, stand there!" Cannon's initial message was simple – the federal government can't require you to do it, so you shouldn't. But once Cannon added the subsidies issue, he now had a far more powerful cudgel. Maine Representative Sharon Treat explained the pitch: "Now, they're advancing the idea of don't do anything, because we don't want to

---

[17] *Id.*

[18] *States Should Flatly Reject ObamaCare Exchanges,* YouTube (May 31, 2012), youtu.be/lAbmzAMZnJw.

[19] Steven Mistler, *Outspoken Critic of Obamacare Helped to Turn LePage against State Exchange,* Portland Press Herald (Nov. 23, 2014), perma.cc/2QAX-3XJ7.

[20] Jonathan Cohn, *The Legal Crusade to Undermine Obamacare – and Rewrite History,* New Republic (Dec. 4, 2012), perma.cc/K3E9-LUB8.

help President Obama." The message spread to New Hampshire and New Jersey. Cannon praised Governor Chris Christie, "He has used the most powerful tool available to states to block Obamacare, and so he has done the best thing for the state's residents. Cannon's persistence laid the groundwork for future lawsuits. Before you "have the ability to make a legal challenge," Tom Miller of the American Enterprise Institute told me, "you try to work it on the political front."

In addition to pitching the states, Cannon told anyone who would listen that the IRS was violating the law and unlawfully implementing Obamacare. Cannon started calling reporters and saying, "They are violating the law here, they cannot do this." Adler and Cannon set out to develop the legal theories for why the IRS rule was unlawful, culminating in an influential article published in 2012 in *Health Matrix*.

7.3. "SECOND WAVE"

While Adler was researching and Cannon was barnstorming, Tom Christina and his colleagues at the American Enterprise Institute and the Competitive Enterprise Institute were gearing up for litigation. The South Carolina lawyer realized that the implications of Section 36B went far beyond the availability of the subsidies. It soon clicked in his head that without the subsidies, the ACA's "employer mandate" would not operate. Obamacare gave companies with more than fifty employees a choice: provide qualified health insurance to their employees or pay a penalty. Christina recalled that without subsidies, "it occurred to me that the employer mandate penalty would not necessarily apply to employers in the States that have not established their own exchanges." If no subsidies were available, the employer mandate's penalty might not be triggered for people who were unable to afford insurance. Thus, if there were no subsidies on the exchanges, then there may not be penalties for the employers. Tom Miller told me, "[T]he key element that we were targeting was the employer mandate." Further, because millions of policies sold on the exchanges would no longer be subsidized, people who could no longer afford insurance could become exempt from the law's individual mandate penalty.

Knocking out the subsidies could cripple both the individual and employer mandates in states that refused to establish exchanges. "The significance of section 36B dawned on me," Christina told me. He admitted that "it wasn't like lightning struck. It was a gradual process. But I knew this was a significant enough issue that it would end up in the courts."[21] Adler credits Vanderbilt law professor Jim Blumstein, "who was the first person to say someone could sue because this is connected to the employer mandate and then therefore an employer might be able to sue."

More importantly, the lawyers understood that this challenge might serve as a backup if the pending case against the constitutionality of the individual mandate failed. Christina saw this suit as part of a "second wave" of litigation. He added that the federalism-styled case may "have appealed to Justice Kennedy" because it would allow the states to "opt out of the employer mandate."

Turning the argument into a lawsuit is yet another origin story. Tom Miller described himself in the early stages as a "solo operator," who supervised this project without any official involvement from AEI. He "never had to burn up any funds or resources." In hindsight, Miller admits that in 2011 he "wasn't interested in capturing headlines. I was trying to think what would be a way to make a case successful. Usually, you don't do that by claiming a lot of attention until you're ready to go." Before anyone could sue, two things had to happen. First, the IRS had to issue the final rule – the proposed rule published in August 2011 was not yet permanent. "You couldn't sue on a hypothetical," Miller explained. Second, and far more daunting, they had to find plaintiffs to challenge the rule.

Christina was retained to begin drafting a complaint challenging the IRS rule, and finished it in April 2012, shortly after oral arguments in *NFIB v. Sebelius*. The case was premised on finding a state government agency that also employed workers. That way, the same plaintiff could challenge the subsidies both in terms of a violation of the principles of federalism and as an employer that would be subject to the employer mandate penalty. Up to this point, Christina was working *on spec*. In early May, Miller realized they needed to fund the litigation. He contacted Michael Greve, the chairman of the Competitive Enterprise Institute. He asked, "We need to get a go-ahead. Can CEI handle this?" Greve, who was enthusiastic and highly supportive, successfully obtained the approval of the CEI Board. After that, all systems were go. From that point on, Miller described the case as a "CEI operation." Christina and Miller began working with Sam Kazman, who was general counsel of CEI.

Kazman told me that there were two motivations for getting involved. First, it could "knock out a good chunk of Obamacare," but "he was never convinced it would spell the end of Obamacare." Second, and "more importantly," CEI wanted to vindicate the "rule of law." If the statute could be "stretched to

[21] Stephanie Armour, *The Lawyer Who Helped Spark This Week's Affordable Care Act Rulings*, WALL ST. J. (July 24, 2013), on.wsj.com/1PlF29g.

mean something contrary to what it says, the checks and balances go out the window."

In May 2012, the IRS published its final rule providing that subsidies would be available in *all* states "regardless of whether the Exchange is established and operated by a State ... or by HHS."[22] At that point Christina had already completed the second draft of his complaint, but the case was still on the down-low. Christina told me at this juncture they could not make it public "until the individual mandate case was taken care of." From the perspective of atmospherics, Miller explained that if everyone is "putting all their investments in 'we're going to win'" the individual mandate case in the Supreme Court, people do not want to start backing Plan B. "You couldn't bring this until the individual mandate case was decided." Cannon agreed – hold onto the case until *NFIB v. Sebelius* was decided. If they "strike the whole thing down," he said, "no one is going to care about this." The suit should have been filed, Christina told me "immediately after what I anticipated would be an unfavorable decision in the *NFIB*." Why? Because "if the mandate had been struck down, I think Congress would have been forced to go back to the drawing board and really that's all that I ever really wanted."

On June 28, 2012, the day *NFIB v. Sebelius* was decided, CEI moved the "second wave" of litigation into swift action with a strategy conference call.

7.4. "THE EASIEST CASE I'VE EVER SEEN"

Michael Carvin was one of the two lawyers who argued before the Supreme Court that the ACA's individual mandate was unconstitutional. Carvin, a partner at the Jones Day Law firm, developed a reputation as one of the top conservative litigators. Tom Goldstein, appellate attorney and publisher of the influential SCOTUSBlog, said, "Carvin is a genius and the truest of true believers. When he has a case he bleeds the client's blood, and the justices know that. He is the hard right's best advocate."

In June 2012, Carvin was crushed by the Chief Justice's vote to uphold the Affordable Care Act. The brash attorney never quite got over the defeat, though he considered it a moral victory: "The operation was a success, but the patient died," he often repeated.[23] Even as that defeat set in, Carvin told me that he had "heard about the subsidies case in the air." Yaakov Roth, an associate at Jones Day, recalled that there were discussions of Section 36B at

---

[22] 26 C.F.R. § 1.36B-2 (2012); 45 C.F.R. § 155.20 (2012).
[23] Sheryl Gay Stolberg, *A Lawyer Taking Aim at the Health Care Act Gets a Supreme Court Rematch*, N.Y. Times (Mar. 4, 2015), nyti.ms/1OSwkOq.

the *NFIB* "non-victory party". Roth joked "that it was originally planned as a victory party to thank all the people who worked on the case," but the chief justice's decision changed the mood. At the event, Roth remembered chatting with others, "Oh did you hear about this regulation?" Carvin was already thinking about the next round of challenges to the ACA.

The strength of the case was made clear to Carvin over a lunch with Obamacare's grand inquisitor. At the meeting, Carvin told Michael Cannon, "show me the language." He did. Carvin replied, "this is the easiest case I've ever seen in my entire life." Cannon recalled that Carvin "was already sold on the idea before I even met with him. But he did not let me know that." (Coincidentally, Cannon was connected to Carvin through his Jones Day partner Noel Francisco, who would argue the contraceptive mandate case before the Supreme Court in 2016.)

In October 2012, Carvin asked Roth to write a memo analyzing a potential legal challenge. Carvin sent the memo to the National Federation of Independent Business (NFIB), who had been his client in the first challenge to the individual mandate. However, NFIB was tired of litigation, and more pressingly, many of its members wanted the subsidies to be available in states without exchanges. Jonathan Adler, the Case Western law professor, told me that "they taken their swing and were not eager to do this again." Roth determined that the case was not only feasible but had a high chance of success. Rather than focusing on state employers – which was Tom Christina's initial strategy – Jones Day decided it would be more feasible to focus on individual plaintiffs who could challenge the IRS rule.

The day *NFIB* was decided, Miller and Christina were on a strategy conference call with Sam Kazman at the Competitive Enterprise Institute to discuss how to proceed with the "second wave" of litigation. They officially reached out to Mike Carvin. At that point Carvin said, "Sure, I'm interested," and "got involved with the case." Kazman told me that Carvin was the "first person" they called. He had been lead counsel for CEI in a constitutional challenge to how members of the Public Company Accounting Oversight Board could be removed from office.[24] Kazman was "tremendously impressed with his work at every stage of that litigation," and was impressed with how he had performed in the first challenge to Obamacare. Michael Greve beamed that "CEI and Mike Carvin have jointly menaced the administrative state on earlier occasions."[25] Carvin offered to work for a "flat rate" for work through the

---

[24] Free Enterprise Fund v. Public Company Accounting Oversight Board, 561 U.S. 477 (2010).
[25] Michael S. Greve, *Halbig and Obamacare: What We Have Learned (Part I)*, LIBRARY OF LAW AND LIBERTY (Aug. 5, 2014), perma.cc/WD7R-SARW.

court of appeals and an additional fee if the Supreme Court took the case. From the outset, they had contemplated a fee structure all the way to the top. Kazman told me the rate was "not only fair, but discounted." Carvin's usual rate is $975 per hour.[26] CEI was prepared to go the distance with this case.

7.5. BOOMER SOONER!

Oklahoma Attorney General Scott Pruitt was elected to office in November 2010 on a Tea Party wave of support. With eyes on combatting federal overreach in the Sooner State, Pruitt appointed Patrick Wyrick as his solicitor general and constitutional adviser. At the time, Florida's constitutional challenge to the ACA's was already on its way to the Supreme Court. Oklahoma's previous attorney general, a Democrat, did not join that challenge.

Before Pruitt had even assumed office, Wyrick urged him to file a new lawsuit challenging the constitutionality of Obamacare. At face value, this move did not make sense. Florida's case was hurdling toward the Supreme Court, and would likely be resolved within eighteen months. But Wyrick had an insight. He was certain that in the aftermath of the Supreme Court's decision, there would be additional issues that could pop up. The odds are that the case won't amount to anything, he told the attorney general, but there is a chance this case may be meaningful. This gives Oklahoma options rather than being a tag-along, nominal party in the Florida litigation. By having a lawsuit already filed, ready to go in the district court, Oklahoma would be the first at bat to challenge other aspects of the law. The attorney general agreed, and on January 21, 2011 – ten days after he assumed office! – the case of *Pruitt v. Sebelius* was filed in federal district court in Muskogee, Oklahoma. The case plodded along until November 23 of that year, when Judge Ronald A. White put the case on hold pending a ruling by the U.S. Supreme Court – exactly as Wyrick had anticipated. Tom Christina recognized that Oklahoma had a special "opportunity." Their case had "been parked to the side" and "frozen" while the Supreme Court resolved the bigger issue. As a result, "they were already in court," ready to be the first to challenge the IRS rule.

Once *NFIB* was decided, Judge White granted Oklahoma's motion to amend its complaint – it would be due two months later on September 19. Amending a complaint is a procedure that would allow the parties to bring

[26] Stolberg, *supra* note 23.

forward any new claims in light of the Court's decision in *NFIB*. This is generally a formality, and no doubt Judge White expected the case to go away because the Justices upheld the mandate. Oklahoma had other plans. Tom Miller told me that no one in Muskogee had any idea what was coming. He thought the case would quickly go away in light of *NFIB*, but "he caught a different train."

In July, Pruitt asked Wyrick to investigate which claims could be added to the pending suit. Wyrick remembered reading several months earlier a post about the IRS Rule by Professor Jonathan Adler on the *Volokh Conspiracy*, a popular legal blog. He thought, this was a very strong argument on the merits. Wyrick e-mailed Attorney General Pruitt that evening and said, I think I found our claim. Pruitt encouraged him to pursue the case. A few days later, Adler received an e-mail out of the blue from Wyrick, asking to talk about the tax credit issue. The two spoke on the phone, though Adler was doubtful the rule could be challenged in court. After more research, Wyrick disagreed with Adler, and determined that the state would have what is known as *standing* to bring the suit. Tom Miller agreed that Oklahoma was "both an employer and a state government – a dual thing."

During July 2012, CEI General Counsel Sam Kazman put Tom Christina in touch with Wyrick, who advised Oklahoma on drafting the amended complaint. While the brief was being put together, Oklahoma shopped the case around to other hard-core Republican states that they expected would be interested in joining it. However, no one wanted anything to do with it. I was told the other states had ACA fatigue on the heels of the loss. Texas Solicitor General Jonathan Mitchell was not interested, Tom Miller told me, noting that "they were in the middle of their voting rights case." Florida Attorney General Pam Bondi, who had just suffered a defeat in the first Obamacare case, was not warm to receive it. Other state attorneys general declined, cited budget constraints.

There was still some concern whether the state would have standing to file the suit. Miller and Christina, along with Grace Marie Turner of the free-market Galen Institute, "scrambled" and spent several weeks in September trying to find possible plaintiffs for the Oklahoma case. One of the attorneys involved told me that Oklahoma had a surprisingly difficult time locating plaintiffs that would put their name on a lawsuit where it looks like their are trying to avoid giving insurance to their employees.

On the last possible day before the deadline, Oklahoma decided to go it alone. Wyrick's insight in January proved accurate. *Boomer Sooner!* Oklahoma would win the race to the court. The amended complaint was field on September 19, 2012, officially launching the "second wave" of challenges to the Affordable Care Act. Tom Miller and Michael Cannon had not been in touch until the complaint was filed in Oklahoma. That day, Cannon e-mailed Miller: "You've been busy, haven't you?" Cannon did not know the suit was coming.

Cannon was not the only person whose ears perked up with the Oklahoma suit. The solicitor general's office first became aware of the challenge to the subsidies after *NFIB* was decided, but as soon as the case got filed, that's when the so-called *10th Justice* paid close attention. Although district court litigation is handled by the Civil Division of the Department of Justice, Solicitor General's office, I learned, was keeping an eye on the case. As the case progresses, the system in the S.G. gets more and more engaged.

"Oklahoma [was] in a unique position," Attorney General Pruitt told the press, because it had "the only active lawsuit against the Affordable Care Act to hold the federal government accountable in how it implements the law. Now that the Supreme Court has deemed the ACA a tax, and therefore constitutional, the federal government must follow the law and proper procedures, and that is not being done."[27] But Pruitt faced an immediate political roadblock. By November 14, it became known that Oklahoma Governor Mary Fallin changed her mind and was considering establishing an exchange. This would have killed the case before the court even ruled on it. Pruitt took action.

On the evening of November 15, Justice Samuel Alito was speaking at the Federalist Society's 30th Anniversary Gala Dinner at the Marriott Wardman Park in Washington, D.C. The Federalist Society for Law & Public Policy is the nation's most influential conservative and libertarian legal organization. Named after the seminal Federalist Papers, the group boasts among its members three Supreme Court justices, dozens of lower court judges, and 40,000 attorneys nationwide. Its members have also had an influential effect on Obamacare. During the Federalist Society's 2009 convention, the constitutional challenge to the individual mandate was hatched in the grand hallway of the Mayflower Hotel.[28]

Wyrick, who attended the dinner that evening, learned about Governor Fallin's change of heart. He was dealing with this matter on his phone, as e-mails went back and forth. Wyrick had to get up and leave the dinner and go back to his hotel room to write a letter to Governor Fallin from Attorney General Pruitt. Their goal was to lay out the implications of the Governor's

---

[27] *AG Pruitt Revises Health-care Suit, Aims to Block Affordable Care Act Taxes, Subsidies,* TULSA WORLD (Sept. 20, 2012), perma.cc/7AH7-ZUU4.

[28] By chance, I was present at that initial meeting, which I dubbed *The Mayflower Compact.* JOSH BLACKMAN, UNPRECEDENTED: THE CONSTITUTIONAL CHALLENGE TO OBAMACARE 40-44 (2013).

decision to set up an exchange in light of Oklahoma's lawsuit. The letter, later released through Freedom of Information Act requests, stated the issue succinctly: "The lawsuit is predicated, of course, on the fact that the State is not implementing a state-established exchange. If the state does implement an exchange, I will have to dismiss the lawsuit."[29]

An attorney from the Oklahoma attorney general's office described the purpose of the communiqué: It's your decision to make, but we want you to know the legal implications of your decision. The office was very careful to stress that this was a policy decision for the Governor to make, and did not tell the Governor what was good policy. Pruitt sent the letter the next morning. That afternoon, Gov. Fallin's chief of staff would email a colleague that the letter was "political and purely self-serving." Tom Miller told me that Pruitt spent "a lot of political capital" to stop the exchange. Three days later, Fallin announced that she would not establish an exchange. The lawsuit could proceed.

7.6. HALBIG IS IT

By November 2012, CEI and Michael Carvin were preparing their own challenge to the IRS rule. After the case was handed over to CEI, Christina had "minimal involvement" and consulted on a few issues with Carvin, who had been his colleague at the Justice Department during the Reagan Administration. Further, Christina explained that he did not interact much with Adler and Cannon – he "didn't want it ever to appear that their work was being colored by a litigation strategy or advice from me. That was the right decision because they were clearly completely independent and there was a great value for academic independence." Christina would largely recede back to the cozy confines of his South Carolina office – until the case was on the doorsteps of the Supreme Court. Similarly, Cannon remarked that he "provided support when CEI asked for stuff. I probably called them more than they called me." But for the most part Cannon and Adler "kept [their] distance" from Jones Day. Unlike Christina, however, Cannon would maintain a persistent influence on the public battle over Section 36B.

Rather than relying on employers for purposes of standing, Carvin and CEI decided to focus on finding individual employees who fell into a very specific income band. As Carvin explained it, they needed people in the gray area – "poor enough to be eligible for subsidies but rich enough that the subsidies

[29] Sam Stein, *The Lawsuit That Could Take Down Obamacare Has a Paper-Trail Problem*, HUFFPOST POLITICS (Mar. 25, 2015), perma.cc/G8PM-7CFN.

would put them into the individual mandate bucket. So you can't get a really rich person because they're not eligible for the subsidies. You can't get a really poor person because even the really poor people might have to spend more than 80 percent even with the subsidies." And if "they're really poor, then they're eligible for Medicaid." The task of finding the plaintiffs fell to CEI general counsel Sam Kazman, and Carvin's associates, Jonathan Berry and Yaakov Roth.

On February 23, 2013, an e-mail from Roth fell into my inbox, asking me if any of my friends would be interested in serving as a plaintiff in the next challenge to Obamacare. (Roth is a close personal friend, and in 2010 we cofounded *The Harlan Institute*, an educational nonprofit.) He wrote:

> The ideal profile for this plaintiff would be a self-employed individual (or one who is not eligible for insurance through his employer) making between $20K–$40K per year, or someone married with a household income of up to $55K, or someone with a wife and two kids and an income between $35K–$85K. Ideally, if there is a spouse, that person is also not eligible for employer-provided insurance. The person would live in one of the 26 States that will not be operating their own insurance exchanges – Alabama, Alaska, Arizona, Florida, Georgia, Indiana, Kansas, Louisiana, Maine, Mississippi, Missouri, Montana, Nebraska, New Jersey, North Carolina, North Dakota, Ohio, Oklahoma, Pennsylvania, South Carolina, South Dakota, Tennessee, Texas, Virginia, Wisconsin, or Wyoming. The person would not have or want health insurance.

I e-mailed a few friends but was unable to find anyone who fell into the sweet spot. The next day, Roth e-mailed me back: "Any luck with plaintiffs? Carvin is bugging me!" Miller explained that finding plaintiffs was a tough task because the "regulations hadn't been written yet, so you were guessing as to what the subsidy structure would look like. You're somewhat shooting in the dark." Carvin added, "We had a rough guesstimate as to how much the unsubsidized premium would be and the subsidies." The accuracy of these estimates would come back to haunt the plaintiffs two years later as the case was argued before the Supreme Court.

Fortunately, Carvin had more resources at hand. CEI "did a survey of our own supporters to see who might be interested," I learned, and "put out emails to likeminded groups" including the Tea Party group FreedomWorks. Ultimately, they were able to identify four plaintiffs: Jacqueline Halbig of Virginia, David Klemencic of West Virginia, Carrie Lowery of Tennessee, and Sarah Rumpf of Texas.

Carvin stressed that the income wasn't everything: "The important part for them was to be sufficiently opposed to the individual mandate so that they want to get involved in a controversial case like this." Klemencic, who owned a carpet store in West Virginia, previously served as a plaintiff in the 2012 constitutional challenge to the individual mandate. Back for more, Klemencic believed in the case wholeheartedly. He told the *New York Times*, "If I'm forced into some sort of program where it's subsidized by the government, I won't go see a doctor."[30]

CEI's suit was filed in federal court in the District of Columbia. Tom Miller told me that Carvin is "more comfortable with things closer to home." Indeed, the offices of Jones Day are three blocks away from the courtroom of Judge Richard W. Roberts, who was assigned the case on May 2, 2013. But that was about as close as Carvin would get to Roberts's bench. (Though it is fitting that the case began, and ended, before judges named Roberts). Carvin argued in his briefs that because the IRS rule would take effect on January 1, 2014 – the date the Obamacare subsidies would start being paid – the court should rule in an expeditious manner well in advance of the new year. Over the next four months, Carvin and the government filed a bevy of dueling motions, the former trying to rush the case and the latter trying to stall. Despite the pressing nature of the case, Judge Roberts did not rule on a single motion. Carvin lambasted the court for sitting on the case: "My point is, he literally did nothing. He didn't even hold a status conference, or rule on the government's requests for extensions." One of the lawyers for the plaintiffs told me that Judge Roberts had a reputation as the slowest judge in D.C. on everything.

Carvin took matters into his own hands. On September 10, he filed a motion for a preliminary injunction and requested expedited hearing within twenty-one days, noting that the IRS rule would go into effect in less than three months. Carvin had to make the "practical point. We knew once that the money had started flowing out of the Treasury, the government would argue, 'Oh, it's too late now to unscramble the omelette.' We thought quite reasonably of course that it was better from everyone's perspective to get this resolved before the money started flowing in, not just our perspective, from the taxpayer's perspective and from the government's perspective."

Then Carvin rolled the dice. He submitted a "suggestion of reassignment," asking the court to transfer the case to another judge. This move was risky, as Judge Roberts may have resented the suggestion that he was unfit for the case. Carvin, however, had legitimate grounds for

---

[30] *Stolberg, supra* note 23.

the reassignment. Two months earlier, Judge Roberts was elevated to become Chief Judge of the district, which entailed significant administrative duties. When Roberts was named Chief Judge, Carvin told me, that "gave us the excuse" to file a motion to transfer it to another judge. "Plaintiffs understand that, in light of those [additional] duties, the Court has been unable to rule on any of the various motions, substantive or procedural, that have been filed since this action was initiated in early May 2013." Therefore, the lawyers respectfully suggested, "that the Court consider reassigning this case to another judge with a smaller docket of pending matters and without the further responsibilities of serving as Chief Judge."

The overworked Roberts finally found a motion he wanted to rule on. Three days later, *Halbig v. Sebelius* was reassigned to Judge Paul L. Friedman, who promptly scheduled oral arguments for October 22, 2013. Miller explained that "what Carvin did to accelerate this was pretty important." The district court "wasn't doing squat."

Back in Oklahoma, Solicitor General Wyrick was unable to expedite his case like Carvin did, ironically enough, due to the Obama administration's delay of the employer mandate. (We will discuss these delays during 2013 in Chapter 13.) Oklahoma's suit was premised on the state being an employer. Due to the delay, the employer mandate would not kick in until 2015. Therefore, Wyrick could not tell the district court to expedite the case. There was no urgency. Judge White ultimately ruled in favor of Oklahoma, but its victory in *Pruitt v. Sebelius* did not come till September 30, 2014 – by that point, the Supreme Court had already agreed to hear CEI's case.

7.7. "SPEED BUMP"

Carvin, however, was not content to let the entire case hinge on how the D.C. court would rule. Long before the case was reassigned, CEI began searching for a new set of plaintiffs to file an identical suit in Virginia. Like the *Halbig* plaintiffs, Carvin told me, the new plaintiffs "were generally already affiliated with conservative organizations in one way or another." David M. King, who would serve as lead plaintiff in what would become *King v. Burwell*, dubbed the president a "narcissist."[31] Mr. King, proud of his

[31] Robert Pear, *Obama Reaffirms Insurers Must Cover Contraception*, N.Y. TIMES (Jan. 20, 2012), perma.cc/W5MF-WWHV.

role in the case, said, "I listen to everybody bitch and moan and cry about Obamacare. We did something about it."

There were several purposes for filing the parallel suit in Virginia. First, the federal district court in Richmond is known as the *Rocket Docket*. Carvin was more concerned with speed than the result. "I don't really care" how they rule. "I just want them to rule fast," he recounted. He reminded me, "I was much less interested in securing a victory than I was in securing an opinion quickly" so the case could be appealed to the Supreme Court as soon as possible. The Virginia case was, in Tom Miller's words, "a backstop in case we can't get anything moving in D.C." Carvin chose to file the case in Richmond rather than in nearby Alexandria, hoping to draw Judge Henry Hudson. In 2010, Hudson ruled against the constitutionality of the individual mandate. No such luck – the case was assigned to Judge James R. Spencer.

Second, and more importantly, CEI was already looking ahead to the Supreme Court. The Supreme Court is more likely to accept a case for review if the issue has divided the federal courts of appeals. This is known in as a *circuit split*. By litigating parallel cases in D.C. and Virginia, Carvin speculated that if one rules in his favor and the other rules against him, that would make the likelihood of Supreme Court review much greater. This stratagem proved to be prescient, as this is precisely what happened on July 22, 2014 – each court went in a different direction on the same day. After the case was reassigned and expedited, both cases moved at an uncharacteristically brisk pace.

Carvin said the proceedings in D.C. "went like butter because Judge Friedman did his job, moved things along very quickly because he intuitively and expressly understood that he was just the first stop in a long journey." During oral arguments, Carvin recalled that Friedman told everyone, "Look, I'm just the speed bump. You guys want to get out." In contrast, Carvin recalled that Judge Spencer in Virginia did not seem to "invest very much in the case"; he was signaling, "I'm punching the clock so let's move it along."

Judge Friedman was the first to decide. On January 15, 2014, six weeks after the case was argued, the court ruled in favor of the government. "On its face, the plain language ... viewed in isolation, appears to support plaintiffs' interpretation," Judge Friedman began. "Why would Congress have inserted the phrase 'established by the State' if it intended to refer to Exchanges created by a state or by HHS?" However, he countered, the government also has a "plausible and persuasive answer" – "even where a state does not actually establish an Exchange, the federal government can create 'an Exchange established by the State' on behalf of that state."

The court found that "each side provides a credible construction of the language." No longer limited *just* to the text of the relevant provision, Judge Friedman concluded that "the statutory structure, and the statutory purpose make clear that Congress intended to make premium tax credits available on both state-run and federally-facilitated Exchanges." The court rejected the argument that Congress intended to withhold subsidies from states that did not establish exchanges.[32] In short, "The Court finds that the plain text of the statute, the statutory structure, and the statutory purpose make clear that Congress intended to make premium tax credits available on both state-run and federally-facilitated Exchanges."

One month later, Judge Spencer in Virginia ruled against King. "In light of the applicable legislative history of the ACA and the above discussion of the anomalous consequences of Plaintiffs' reading of the ACA, Defendants at the very least have presented a reasonable interpretation of HHS's regulations and, thus, section 36B." Carvin described the latter opinion as "very similar to Judge Friedman's decision." With that, the challengers were off to the races. Judge Spencer's decision was appealed to the Fourth Circuit Court of Appeals, also in Richmond. Judge Friedman's decision was appealed to the D.C. Circuit Court of Appeals, which promptly ordered expedited briefing and oral arguments. The latter case would be heard on March 25, 2014 – the same day the Supreme Court held arguments a few blocks away in *Hobby Lobby*.

---

[32] *Transcript of Motions Hearing*, Halbig v. Sebelius at 8-18, 1:13-cv-623 (D.D.C. Dec. 3, 2013), bit.ly/1YaQerl.

8

Tea Party Summer

8.1. "BLUEPRINT TO DEFUNDING OBAMACARE"

On Valentine's Day 2013, several weeks after the inauguration, Barack and Michelle Obama had a romantic dinner at Minibar, Jose Andres's super-exclusive restaurant in Penn Quarter. At the time, it was the "hardest reservation to snag in all of D.C."[1] The conservative *White House Dossier* estimated that the meal for two cost more than $900. "Each bite," the blog quipped, "probably costs about $10."[2] Earlier that day at an event in Decatur, Georgia, the president joked, "I can't imagine a more romantic way to spend Valentine's Day than with all of you, with all the press here. Actually, Michelle says 'hello.' She made me promise to get back in time for our date tonight. That's important."[3] Several years later on an episode of *The Ellen DeGeneres Show*, the president would send a fitting Valentine to his wife: "Because I love you so much, I Obama*care* about you more than you even know."[4]

Not everyone was showing the president love that day. On February 14, 2013, less than eight months remained until the federal health care exchange would open, and ten months until federal subsidies for insurance would become available. That morning, a group of prominent conservative activists announced the final plan to stop Obamacare before it began: the aptly named *Blueprint to Defunding Obamacare*.[5] If the law was not halted before

[1]   Maura Judkis, *Obama Picks Minibar for Romantic Valentine's Day Dinner*, WASH. POST (Feb. 15, 2013), perma.cc/HS7R-6JFV.
[2]   Keith Koffl, *Middle Class Warrior's $900 Valentine's Day Dinner*, WHITE HOUSE DOSSIER (Feb. 14, 2013), perma.cc/ALH7-3QVA.
[3]   Devin Dwyer, *Love at the White House: Obamas' Valentine's Date, Daughter Dating?*, ABCNEWS (Feb. 14, 2013), perma.cc/G3NP-6QKB.
[4]   Paige Lavender, *Obama Sends a Valentine's Day Message to His Wife with a Little Help from Ellen*, HUFFPOST POLITICS (Feb. 21, 2016), perma.cc/KLS4-3H56.
[5]   Matt Kibbe, *Coalition Letter: Congress Must Honor Sequester Savings and Defund Obamacare before It Is Too Late*, FREEDOMWORKS (Feb. 14, 2013), perma.cc/S6FP-VXA8.

the exchanges open and subsidies begin, the *Blueprint* conceded, it "all but ensur[es] that these new entitlements will become a permanent fixture of life in America. The window of opportunity to stop the implementation of these massive new subsidies is closing." Jenny Beth Martin, president of the Tea Party Patriots, acknowledged, "If we don't . . . stop spending on the law, the law may become completely cemented."[6]

Recognizing that the Affordable Care Act could not be repealed while President Obama was still in office, the plan instead sought to use the budgetary process to defund the implementation of the law. In recent years, the president and Congress had been unable to agree on a budget. Instead, Republicans and Democrats voted to enact a series of short-term continuing resolutions (CRs) that would fund the federal government for a limited period of time. The current CR was set to expire on March 27, 2013. The *Blueprint* seized on this deadline and called on "Conservatives not [to] approve a CR unless it defunds Obamacare." The time to strike was now.

The defund consortium was led by the Constitution Action Project, a group founded by former Attorney General Edwin Meese III, who served under President Reagan. The group's mission was "to facilitate conservative leaders working together on behalf of common goals."[7] Meese explained that stopping Obamacare was of the utmost urgency to the group. "I think people realized that with the imminent beginning of Obamacare," he observed, "this was a critical time to make every effort to stop something."[8] Defunding the law, the former attorney general concluded, was "a logical strategy."

The *Blueprint* was signed by the leaders of nearly fifty conservative organizations, including Meese, Chris Chocola of the Club for Growth, Matt Kibbe of FreedomWorks, and Mike Needham of Heritage Action for America. Needham told *The New York Times*, "We felt very strongly at the start of this year that the House needed to use the power of the purse."[9] He added, "At least at Heritage Action, we felt very strongly from the start that this was a fight that we were going to pick."

The game plan to cripple Obamacare had four fronts. First, to prevent the remainder of the law from going into effect, the memo called for an appropriation rider that would prohibit funding "the implementation of Obamacare,

---

[6] Catalina Camia, *Tea Party Push to Block 'Obamacare' Funding Divides GOP*, USA TODAY (Aug. 27, 2013), perma.cc/K9Q4-VPKZ/.

[7] Press Release, Heritage Action for American, Conservation Leaders Respond to Attacks on Conservatives on Capitol Hill and Paul Teller (Dec. 13, 2013), perma.cc/3CZ8-F2JE.

[8] Sheryl Gay Stolberg & Mike McIntire, *A Federal Budget Crisis Months in the Planning*, N.Y. TIMES (Oct. 5, 2013), nyti.ms/29rNZN9.

[9] *Id.*

covering salaries, rulemaking, enforcement, etc." If there were no appropriations, the president would be prohibited from taking any steps to put the law further into effect. (At the time, many provisions of the ACA had already been implemented.) Second, the *Blueprint* sought to defund the HHS contraceptive mandate because it "attacks the religious values and principles of countless Americans." (In March 2012, a bill that would have granted broad conscience exemptions to the contraceptive mandate was defeated.[10])

Third, the strategy called for an appropriations rider to "eliminate the refundable tax credits for premiums and the cost sharing subsidies that are essentially used to support insurance purchased in the Obamacare exchanges, which starts January 1, 2014." This approach would have accomplished in one fell swoop what the *Halbig* litigation sought to achieve in states that did not establish exchanges: eliminate the subsidies that defray the cost of Obamacare premiums. If the tax credits were unavailable, insurance would become unaffordable in light of the ACA's strict requirements for "minimum essential coverage." As a result, millions would be exempted from the individual mandate, and their employers would no longer be subject to the employer mandate. This would drive a stake through the heart of the law. Recall that Michael Cannon of the Cato Institute had already persuaded several states not to build exchanges, because the absence of subsidies would eliminate these mandates. This element of the strategy would halt the subsidies – and thus the mandates – nationwide.

Fourth, the *Blueprint* called for an appropriations rider to "eliminate the enhanced match funding for the Medicaid expansion, which takes effect January 1, 2014." Medicaid is a federally funded program whereby states administer health care for low-income people. Under the Affordable Care Act, states that opted to expand Medicaid to cover its residents at 138% of the poverty line would be reimbursed by the federal government at the rate of 100% in 2014, with the rates decreasing each year until dropping to 90% in 2020.[11] In 2009 – before the ACA was enacted – Arizona Governor Jan Brewer notified HHS that her state would not expand Medicaid.[12] HHS threatened Brewer that if she refused to participate, Arizona would lose its *entire* $8 billion Medicaid budget. In *NFIB v. Sebelius*, seven justices would rely on this letter to rule that the all-or-nothing expansion was unconstitutionally coercive on the states. Critically, Chief Justice Roberts, joined by Justices Breyer and

---

[10] See *supra* Chapter 4.

[11] Glenn Kessler, *Rubio's Claim that Medicaid Expansion Funds Will 'Go Away'*, WASH. POST (Jan 14, 2014), perma.cc/R9V3-GPUK.

[12] JOSH BLACKMAN, UNPRECEDENTED: THE CONSTITUTIONAL CHALLENGE TO OBAMACARE 203–204 (2013).

Kagan, saved the expansion by rewriting it to grant states the choice of opting into the new Medicaid program. States that declined the new funding could keep their old funding. (Justices Scalia, Kennedy, Thomas, and Alito would have invalidated the expansion in its entirety, even for willing states).

Under the Supreme Court's modified Medicaid expansion – what Justice Scalia would later refer to as "SCOTUSCare" – states now had a choice. However, by March 2013, only twenty-seven states, plus the District of Columbia, supported the expansion. The remainder of states did not, many out of vigorous opposition to Obamacare. There was a cost for low-income residents in refusenik states. Ezra Klein observed that these "Republican governors are saying no to billions of dollars in Medicaid money ... That cuts them off from much-needed funds and cuts their poorest constituents off from free health insurance."[13] All to "take a stand against Obamacare!"[14]

Two prominent states run by Republican governors opted to expand. Ironically, Governor Brewer – who four years earlier refused to participate – acquiesced, even in the face of opposition by the Arizona legislature.[15] Ohio Governor John Kasich also expanded Medicaid, explaining that Buckeye taxpayers were already sending money to Washington. "It's our money," he said, "let's bring it home."[16] (Kasich would come under criticism for the Medicaid expansion during his run for the presidency in 2016).[17] The *Blueprint's* goal on this front was to keep the number of states that expanded Medicaid as low as possible to prevent further entrenchment and reliance on the ACA. In hindsight, even with the availability of matching funds, the expansion has proceeded very slowly. By 2016, only five more governors expanded Medicaid, bringing the total to thirty-two states plus the District of Columbia.

---

[13] Ezra Klein, *The GOP's Kamikaze Mission to Stop Obamacare*, WASH. POST (Aug. 2, 2013), perma.cc/6389-LEVQ.

[14] *Id.*

[15] Josh Blackman, *Obamacare Comes Full Circle in Arizona*, VOLOKH CONSPIRACY (Sept. 12, 2013), perma.cc/JDX6-2NZF. The Goldwater Institute challenged the expansion, arguing that it violated the Arizona Constitution. Kyle Cheney, *Medicaid Expansion Ballot Fails*, POLITICO (Sept. 12, 2013), perma.cc/455N-3NYV. The Arizona Constitution requires a two-thirds majority to pass a new tax increase. The suit alleged that the vote to expand Medicaid included a new tax, which was not backed by a two-thirds majority. In a fitting dose of déjà vu, supporters of the expansion said it was a "fee," not a tax. In 2015, a Maricopa County superior court judge upheld the program. Mary Jo Pitzi, *Judge: Arizona Medicaid Expansion was Constitutional*, AZCENTRAL (Aug. 27, 2015), perma.cc/E42D-UK3F.

[16] Rebecca Adams & John Reichard, *Sebelius Praises Kasich Backing of Medicaid Expansion*, COMMONWEALTH FUND (Feb. 4, 2013), bit.ly/1T9L6nY.

[17] *See infra* Chapter 29.

The *Blueprint*, however, was entirely silent on *how* these four appropriation riders would pass the House and Senate and overcome a presidential veto. This aspect of the strategy would emerge over the next eight months.

8.2. "LAST OPPORTUNITY"

Senators Mike Lee (R-UT) and Ted Cruz (R-TX) share a lot in common.[18] Both were distinguished attorneys who clerked on the U.S. Supreme Court (Lee with Alito, and Cruz with Rehnquist). Both were freshman senators from conservative states, who were ushered into office by a wave of Tea Party support. And most importantly, both saw 2013 CR as the last opportunity to stop the Affordable Care Act. The deadline for the March 2013 that was identified by the *Blueprint* came and went, and no action was taken. During the spring of 2013, Cruz and Lee asked their Republican colleagues, "What are we going to do to stop Obamacare from kicking in?"[19] They received the same answer: "nothing." Cruz recalled in his autobiography that "[r]isk aversion dominated their thinking; a fight was risky, and could imperil reelection." The duo found the Republican apathy "unacceptable," so they devised an "alternative strategy." Following the path laid out in the *Blueprint*, they would use the budgetary process to fund everything in the federal government – except Obamacare.

The timing of the stratagem seemed fortuitous. The current CR would expire on September 30, 2013. The federal health exchange was scheduled to launch the very next day, on October 1, 2013. If Lee and Cruz were successful, it would be a literal eleventh-hour stoppage of the ACA. Lee explained, "September 30, when the continuing resolution [to fund the government] expires ... will be our last opportunity to defund Obamacare."[20] (Little did Cruz or Lee know at the time that the failed launch of HealthCare.gov would prevent the exchanges from being functional until December 2013.)

In September 2013, when the defunding strategy collided with the government shutdown, Cruz would get the most credit – or blame, depending whom you ask. But Lee was the primary mover in the summer of 2013. *Time* wrote that "Mike Lee is – and Cruz is not – the understated, policy-oriented leader behind the Defund Obamacare movement."[21] L. Brent Bozell III, the founder of the Media Research Center, said that "Mike Lee is the intellectual

---

[18]   For purposes of full disclosure, I informally advised Senator Cruz's presidential campaign.

[19]   TED CRUZ, A TIME FOR TRUTH: REIGNITING THE PROMISE OF AMERICA AT 4086 (Kindle ed. 2015).

[20]   Becket Adams, *GOP Senator Says Coalition to Block and Defund Obamacare Is Growing, Names Names,* YAHOO! NEWS THE BLAZE (Jul. 22, 2013), perma.cc/Z32T-YRJS.

[21]   Alex Rogers, *Utah Senator Mike Lee: The Man behind the Shutdown Curtain,* TIME (Oct. 22, 2013), perma.cc/2H98-TKFG.

powerhouse of this entire movement."[22] During his twenty-one-hour filibuster, Cruz lauded his colleague: "In my judgment there is no Senator in this body, Republican or Democrat who is more principled, who is more dedicated, who is more fearless and willing to fight for the principles that make this Nation great than is Senator Mike Lee."[23]

On July 17, Lee hosted several Republican senators, along with leaders from conservative grassroots organizations, for an after-hours meeting to put the strategy in motion.[24] Joining Lee and Cruz were Senators Mike Enzi (R-WY), Jeff Flake (R-AZ), Jim Inhofe (R-OK), Ron Johnson (R-WI), Jim Risch (R-WI), Pat Toomey (R-PA), and Marco Rubio (R-PA).[25] The following week, twelve senators sent a letter to Senate Majority Leader Harry Reid, announcing that they "will not support any continuing resolution or appropriations legislation that funds further implementation or enforcement of Obamacare."[26] Joining Cruz and Lee on the letter were several attendees at the after-hours meeting – Enzi, Inhofe, Risch, and Rubio – plus new additions: Rand Paul (R-KY), David Vitter (R-LA), John Thune (R-SD), Deb Fischer (R-NE), and Chuck Grassley (R-IA).[27]

The dozen senators wrote that "the only way to avert disaster is to fully repeal Obamacare and start over with a more sensible, practical approach to reforming our healthcare system." Lee told talk radio host Glenn Beck that their goal was to "fund government, not ObamaCare."[28] The strategy was not to shut down the government. However, as health care analyst Avik Roy observed on *Forbes*, the proposal "risk[s] a government shutdown if Lee's objectives are not achieved."[29]

A similar movement was afoot in the House of Representatives. On August 21, first-term Representative Mark Meadows (R-NC) sent a letter to Speaker John Boehner on behalf of eighty members of Congress, "encouraging [the House] to defund Obamacare through the appropriations process."[30] Meadows's letter

---

[22] *Id.*

[23] *Sen. Ted Cruz's Marathon Speech against Obamacare on Sept. 24*, WASH. POST (Sept. 25, 2013), perma.cc/HQ4X-EPAT. Chapter 10 will explain why it wasn't actually a filibuster.

[24] *Rogers, supra* note 21.

[25] *Id.*

[26] Press Release, Mike Lee U.S. Senator for Utah, Senators Call for Defunding of ObamaCare in Upcoming CR (Jul. 25, 2013), perma.cc/R628-W9XR.

[27] For purposes of full disclosure, before advising Sen. Cruz's presidential campaign, I advised Sen. Rand Paul's presidential campaign as a member of his Law Professor Advisory Committee.

[28] Wilson, *Senator Mike Lee: "Tell Them to Fund the Government, Not Obamacare,"* GLENN BECK (Jul. 25, 2013), perma.cc/A3JF-KVGW.

[29] Avik Roy, *GOP Divides on Whether to Shut Down the Government over Obamacare Funding,* FORBES (Jul. 29, 2013), perma.cc/LPY8-7EFN.

[30] *U.S. Rep. Mark Meadows Sends Letter to Boehner. Cantor Encouraging House Leadership to Defund Obamacare,* HCPRESS (Aug. 22, 2013), perma.cc/X3XJ-2PWX.

quoted James Madison in *Federalist No.* 58, extoling Congress's power to check the president through its "power over the purse." This essential limit on executive power, *Publius* observed, is "the most complete and effectual weapon with which any constitution can arm the immediate representatives of the people." Meadows, although a freshman member of Congress, was able to unite a sizeable coalition. "They've been hugely influential," said David Wasserman of the nonpartisan Cook Political Report. "When else in our history has a freshman member of Congress from North Carolina been able to round up a gang of 80 that's essentially ground the government to a halt?"[31]

The import of these letters was that 25% of the Senate GOP Caucus and 30% of the House GOP Caucus were on record that they would not vote for an appropriations bill if it funded the ACA. In an editorial, Senator Rubio wrote that Congress should pass a spending bill "that keeps the government open, but doesn't waste any more money on ObamaCare."[32] The future presidential candidate predicted "the president and his allies – and even some Republicans – will accuse us of threatening to shut down the government." And that is precisely what happened.

As summer turned to fall, and the specter of a government shutdown became real, the limited support began to fade. Almost all of the signatories of the Lee letter would eventually retreat from the strategy. Fox News Channel host Sean Hannity asked Senator Paul if the Republicans would have the "courage" to defund Obamacare. Paul laughed out loud and said, "Frankly, probably not."[33] Conservative columnist Erick Erickson expressed his frustration at what he saw as Republican cowardice. "When confronted with the challenge of opposing continuing funding of the government if that funding goes to Obamacare," Erickson wrote, "their testicular fortitude runs down their leg and out the door."[34]

With Cruz and Lee's proposal in place, the next step was to take the message to the American people and urge them to exert pressure on Congress to support the defunding campaign. Leading that effort would be the junior senator from Texas.

[31] *Stolberg, supra* note 8.
[32] Sen. Marco Rubio, *America, It's Not too Late to Stop ObamaCare*, FoxNews (Jul. 25, 2013), perma.cc/ERK4-F4H6.
[33] Sahil Kapur, *Conservatives Concede Defeat in Obamacare Shutdown Fight*, Talking Points Memo (Jul. 30, 2013), perma.cc/6RUZ-HFGL.
[34] Erick Erickson, *The Sad Joke from John Cornyn's Office*, RedState (Jul. 28, 2013), perma.cc/6MG3-BR22.

8.3. "GRASSROOTS TSUNAMI"

The camera pans to a rustic red barn.[35] In the background, Ted Cruz's voice booms, "It is driving up the cost of health insurance." The shot cuts to the inside of the barn, which is filled with rows of empty chairs facing a dais draped with American flags. "The wheels are coming off, and it is destroying our health care system," Cruz continues. "It is destroying our economy." The scene changes to a time-lapse shot of hundreds entering the barn. Cruz, still off camera, implores the audience, "Between now and September 30th, we have to see a grassroots tsunami. Millions of people standing up, and saying Obamacare isn't working."

The first-term senator chuckled and said, "There is nothing that scares elected officials more than hearing from their constituents." The shot changes to Cruz standing in front of a packed auditorium, with a banner in the background that reads: "Heritage Action: Defund Obamacare." Cruz tells the rapt crowd, "Liberty is never safer then when politicians are terrified." The audience erupts in applause, as Cruz tells "millions of Americans to hold our elected officials accountable." With rolled-up sleeves and a grin on his face, the former constitutional litigator extols the virtue that "sovereignty doesn't rest with a bunch of politicians in Washington. Under our Constitution, Sovereignty is with 'We the people.'" This *YouTube* video was watched by thousands,[36] but Cruz's message would impact millions.

In the tradition of tent revivals from days gone by, Cruz embarked on a "Defund Obamacare Tour," traveling the country to stir up a "grassroots tsunami." In an August 2013 interview with *CNN*, Cruz conceded that "we do not have the votes right now" to stop the ACA.[37] However, he saw a "new paradigm in politics" that makes "politicians in both parties very uncomfortable."[38] At an event in Dallas, nearly 1,000 turned out to see Cruz.[39] "You're here because now is the single best time we have to defund Obamacare," the senator said.[40] "This is a fight we can win."[41]

Supporting Cruz's barnstorming tour was Heritage Action for America, an influential conservative advocacy organization. Joining the Texas senator

---

[35] Heritage Action for America, *Defund Obamacare Town Hall*, YouTube (Aug. 25, 2013), bit.ly/1LcUlMv.

[36] *Id.*

[37] Paul Steinhauser, *Defund Obamacare Supporters Target Top Republicans*, CNN (Aug. 27, 2013), perma.cc/9YT3-5FAP.

[38] *Id.*

[39] Stolberg, *supra* note 8.

[40] *Id.*

[41] *Id.*

on stage were Jim DeMint, president of the Heritage Foundation, and Mike Needham, CEO of Heritage Action. Needham implored the crowd:

> The time to fight is now. On October 1, sign ups start. On January 1, the subsidies start flowing. Now is the time to fight, and all of you working with Heritage Action can make this happen. We can make it stop. We're the ones who go to the polls. We're the ones who go to Town Halls. We are the ones who can preserve liberty if we do exactly what we are doing today. We are here to save this country for future generations.

After Needham concluded, DeMint took the stage. "Our ideas are worth standing up for, they're worth fighting for. Since when do Americans not fight for what they know is right, because they're afraid we might lose?" DeMint joined Heritage in 2013 after retiring as senator from South Carolina. The *New York Times* reported that since DeMint's arrival, the venerable think tank had "become more of a political organization feeding off the rising populism of the Tea Party movement."[42] DeMint was unabashed about Heritage's new direction: "Politics follows the culture. The conservative movement has been derelict in not putting together an organized movement across this country."[43] Perhaps the prime example of this shift was Heritage's zealous advocacy to defund Obamacare, even as other Republicans balked at the strategy.

DeMint stated that he considered using the appropriations process to defund Obamacare since the law's passage. Throughout all of the funding battles in 2012, "there was discussion of 'O.K., we're not going to fight the Obamacare fight, we'll do it next time.' The conservatives who ran in 2010 promising to repeal it kept hearing, 'This is not the right time to fight this battle.'"[44] Now was that time, DeMint concluded. *Time* observed that Heritage had a "three-pronged strategy to twist arms on Capitol Hill: lobbying members on hot-button issues, ranking them publicly on how they vote, and getting word out far and wide when lawmakers buck the conservative line."[45] The goal of the tour was to get the word out and encourage attendees to hold their representatives' feet to the fire to defund Obamacare.

As Heritage barnstormed the country, the Senate Conservatives Fund PAC blanketed cable news with commercials featuring Lee and Cruz urging people

---

[42] Molly Ball, *The Fall of the Heritage Foundation and the Death of Republican Ideas*, ATLANTIC (Sept. 25, 2013), perma.cc/HPJ7-NJEN.

[43] Jennifer Steinhauer & Jonathan Weisman, *In the DeMint Era at Heritage, a Shift from Policy to Politics*, N.Y. TIMES (Feb. 23, 2014), nyti.ms/29IFaAY.

[44] Stolberg, *supra* note 8.

[45] Zeke J. Miller, *Hidden Hand: How Heritage Action Drove DC to Shut Down*, TIME (Sept. 30, 2013), ti.me/1PLmqji.

to support the defunding of the ACA.[46] "On October 1, millions of Americans will have to begin enrolling in Obamacare," Lee explained in one video. Predicting the chaos of the cancelled policies, Lee noted, "Many could lose their doctors and be forced to pay higher premiums and higher taxes. Obamacare's unaffordable and it's unfair." Offering hope, Lee said, "Republicans in Congress can stop Obamacare. They can simply refuse to fund it. I'm working to lead this effort but I need your help. Please tell Congress 'don't fund Obamacare.'" Cruz's commercial took a sharper tone.[47] "There's bipartisan agreement that Obamacare isn't working," he began. "The Constitution gives Congress the power of the purse. And we need Congress to stand up and defund Obamacare now." Calling for action, the Texas senator said, "Please join me so we can get America back on track." The narrator intones, "Tell Congress to defund Obamacare now," and visit DontFundIt.com.

8.4. "DUMBEST IDEA I'VE EVER HEARD OF"

The most vociferous opposition to the defund strategy came not from the Democrats, but from the Republicans. In his autobiography Cruz recalled the reaction in July when he and Lee told the GOP caucus about their plan: it was "immediate, visceral, and virtually unanimous. 'Absolutely not!' 'A terrible idea!'" Cruz wrote that his colleagues "openly laughed at the idea, telling Mike and me that we just didn't understand how Washington works."[48] As the pair spread the message to the American people, the fissure among conservatives broke into the open.

Senator Richard Burr (R-NC) said the strategy was "the dumbest idea I've ever heard of. Listen, as long as Barack Obama is president the Affordable Care Act is gonna be law."[49] In agreement was Senator John McCain (R-AZ), who had previously referred to Cruz as a "wacko bird" for his unwillingness to follow traditional Senate procedures.[50] "It is a suicide note," the 2008 GOP presidential candidate said. Referring to the Republicans' bitter losses after the 1996 shutdown, McCain said, "I was here the last time we saw this movie."[51]

---

[46] *Mike Lee: Don't Fund Obamacare*, YouTube (Aug. 6, 2013), bit.ly/23TVGDu.
[47] *Don't Fund Obamacare – Ted Cruz*, YouTube (Aug. 10, 2013) bit.ly/1LcX2ok.
[48] CRUZ, *supra* note 19, at 4107.
[49] Daniel Strauss, *Burr: Shutdown over Defunding ObamaCare 'Dumbest Idea' Ever*, THE HILL (Jul, 26, 2013), bit.ly/1SFcRFi.
[50] Jon Ward, *John McCain: Getting Back to Maverick, an Eye on Retirement*, HUFF. POST (Jan. 23, 2014), huff.to/20H5CB0.
[51] *Senate Republicans Fumbling to Find Strategy on Obamacare*, NATIONAL JOURNAL, bit.ly/1nZiW2q.

Senator Tom Coburn (R-OK), known for his unflagging efforts to root out government waste, rejected the proposal out of hand. "It's not an achievable strategy. It's creating the false impression that you can do something when you can't. And it's dishonest."[52] Coburn added that he would "love to defund it. I'd be leading the charge if I thought this would work. But it will not work." The senior senator from Oklahoma asked rhetorically, "The president is never going to sign a bill defunding Obamacare. Do you think he's going to cave?" There is no other strategy, the Coburn concluded, because "we lost the [election]."[53]

All of the previous efforts at stopping the ACA had failed. In 2010, Republicans were unable to stop the enactment of the ACA, even after the election of Scott Brown eliminated the Democrats' filibuster-proof majority. In June 2012, Chief Justice Roberts rejected the constitutional challenge to the individual mandate and upheld the ACA. Mitt Romney's defeat in November 2012 ensured that President Obama would be at the helm for the implementation of the ACA. Why would this effort be any different, Coburn asked?

The Republican leadership dismissed the strategy. House Speaker John Boehner explained, "The American people do not want the president's health-care bill, and they don't want the government to shut down."[54] Boehner had enraged many conservatives in November 2012 by referring to Obamacare as "the law of the land."[55] Senate Minority Leader Mitch McConnell played it a little closer to the vest, insisting that "our main goal going into the year-end discussion is to not walk away from the bipartisan agreement that we made two years ago to reduce spending" through the sequestration.[56] But he would not directly address Cruz's strategy. John Cornyn, the second-ranked Senate Republican, called the idea unreasonable. "I don't think that any reasonable person thinks there's anything to be gained by a government shutdown," the senior senator from Texas explained.[57]

Byron York aptly summarized the opposition in the *Washington Examiner*: "Even though Republicans don't have the votes to defund

---

[52] Byron York, *Tom Coburn: Campaign to Defund Obamacare 'Dishonest' Hype*, Wash. Exam'r (Jul. 26, 2013), washex.am/20SpAWo.

[53] *Id.*

[54] Sam Baker, *GOP Lawmakers Bridle at Calling Affordable Care Act the Law*, The Hill (Sept. 29, 2013), bit.ly/1K8VkCg.

[55] David Nather, *Boehner: Obamacare Is Law of Land*, Politico (Nov. 8, 2012), politi.co/1PiaiER.

[56] Chris Good, *Conservative Senators: Defund Obamacare or Shut Down Government*, ABC News (Jul. 24, 2013), abcn.ws/1XfoazW.

[57] J. Scott Applewhite, *House Republicans Push New Plan to Defund 'Obamacare' Without Causing Default*, N. Y. Daily News (Sept. 18, 2013), nydn.us/1PLomsa.

Obamacare, they do have the power, if they choose, to bring the government to a halt."[58] And many senators predicted that this would be the only possible outcome of the defund strategy. From the liberal perspective, Ezra Klein described the defund strategy as a "kamikaze mission to stop Obamacare."[59] He noted that the "current crop of Republican strategies ask conservative congressmen to hurt their constituents and their political prospects, conservative governors to hurt their states, and conservative activists to hurt themselves."[60]

Senator Lee basked in the shunning from his own party. "I understand that there are some in the Washington establishment ... who aren't happy with me over this," Lee said on *Fox News Sunday*.[61] "In this instance, I'm going to take that as a compliment, an indication that I'm doing something right." On September 23, 2013, from the floor of the U.S. Senate, Cruz would #MakeDCListen.

---

[58] York, *supra* note 52.
[59] Klein, *supra* note 13.
[60] *Id.*
[61] Ian Tuttle, *Mike Lee: We Must Defund Obamacare*, NAT'L REV. (Jul. 28, 2013), bit.ly/1PyreF4.

9

"Train Wreck"

9.1. "THE SAME WAY YOU SHOP FOR A PLANE TICKET ON KAYAK"

The Affordable Care Act's new online marketplaces, known as exchanges, were cornerstones of the law. They would allow consumers to easily purchase an insurance policy online. President Obama described the exchange as a "website where you can compare and purchase affordable health insurance plans, side-by-side."[1] It would work "the same way you shop for a plane ticket on Kayak" or "for a TV on Amazon," Obama predicted. Customers can "enter some basic information," and they will "be presented with a list of quality, affordable plans that are available in [their] area, with clear descriptions of what each plan covers, and what it will cost." Based on the customer's income and other information, the website would calculate the amount of subsidies available, and how much they would offset the premiums. With these options, customers would be able to sign up for health insurance policies from the provider of their choice.

As discussed in Chapter 2, during the enactment of the ACA, the Senate and House adopted competing approaches to the exchanges. The Senate bill allowed each state to establish its own exchange. However, if a state failed to establish its own exchange, HHS would provide a fallback federal marketplace. At the time, Democrats assumed that virtually every state would establish its own exchange. President Obama predicted, "By 2014, *each* state will set up what we're calling a health insurance exchange."[2]

The House approach was far more skeptical. It called for a single federal exchange in which people in all states would be able to participate. Many in the House did not trust conservative governors to take the adequate steps to build a

---

[1] Remarks by the President on the Affordable Care Act (Sept. 26, 2013), perma.cc/WW9T-9SZS.
[2] Remarks by the President on Health Insurance Reform in Portland, Maine (Apr. 1, 2010), perma.cc/A7FJ-FJ2P.

functional exchange, citing experiences with state administration of Medicaid. In hindsight, this caution was prescient. However, because of the election of Senator Scott Brown, the House Democrats were forced to adopt the Senate bill, which allowed for states to establish their own exchanges in the first instance. Throughout 2012 and 2013, states were invited to submit proposals to build their own marketplaces. Contrary to the president's optimistic forecast, by 2014 only sixteen states opted to establish their own exchanges. As a result, the federal government became responsible for developing a fallback federal exchange in the remaining states.

The president's first important decision, which was discussed in Chapter 5, was to place the development of the exchanges within the Centers for Medicare and Medicaid Services (CMS). Recall that in 2010, Harvard professor David Cutler wrote a memo to the Obama administration warning that CMS was "not up to the task" because they did not have "experience running a health care organization."[3] In hindsight, Cutler was exactly right. A September 2011 internal progress report found that CMS did not have enough employees "to manage the multiple activities and contractors happening concurrently."[4] This was deemed a "major risk" to the whole project.[5] But behind the risky decision was a financial necessity.

The ACA did not provide any funding for the federal exchange. According to *Politico*, Congress appropriated to HHS "essentially unlimited sums for helping states create their own exchanges," but provided absolutely no money to establish its own exchange.[6] This made sense at the time because the working assumption was that all states would establish their own exchanges. Since its enactment, Republicans would not appropriate any additional funding. HHS Secretary Kathleen Sebelius "simply could not scrounge together enough money to keep a group of people developing the exchanges working directly under her."[7]

As a result, according to an HHS adviser, the government had to "get creative about the financing."[8] Sebelius would personally solicit funds to promote Obamacare outreach from private organizations, including the Robert Wood Johnson Foundation and H&R Block.[9]

---

[3] Letter from David Cutler to Larry Summers (May 11, 2010), bit.ly/1SLqSA8.

[4] Robert Pear, Sharon LaFraniere & Ian Austen, *From the State, Signs of Trouble at Health Portal*, N.Y. TIMES (Oct. 12, 2013), nyti.ms/1q2VktU.

[5] *Id.*

[6] J. Lester Feder, *HHS Exchange May Require Creativity*, POLITICO (Aug. 16, 2011), perma.cc/PUL7-2NKJ.

[7] *Id.*

[8] *Id.*

[9] Sarah Kliff, *How to Think about the Latest ObamaCare Delay*, WASH. POST (Nov. 22, 2013), perma.cc/7G96-QZQG.

But HHS could not host a bake sale to fund all of HealthCare.gov: It would cost hundreds of millions of dollars. While Secretary Sebelius had severe cash flow problems, the Centers for Medicaid and Medicare Services did not. According to the *Washington Post*, the "political rationale for the move" to CMS was that it "would be better insulated from the efforts of House Republicans, who were looking for ways to undermine the law."[10] Its budget was secure, and would not be slashed by Congress – even (as we will see in Chapter 11) during a government shutdown.

9.2. "THIRD-WORLD EXPERIENCE"

Though fiscally sound, moving the project to CMS came at a cost. Shifting the responsibility away from Sebelius and the White House "fragmented" the endeavor, as the policy staff was separated from the technical staff.[11] Leading the charge at CMS was Henry Chao, the deputy information officer, who was a two-decade veteran with the agency.[12] The *New York Times* reported that at all times, Chao "had to consult with senior department officials and the White House, and was unable to make many decisions on his own." One official, who faulted the White House's strict oversight, told the *Times* that "Nothing was decided without a conversation there."[13]

Soon, CMS's inadequacy became apparent. Originally, the agency planned to finish the exchanges "at least six months before" HealthCare.gov launched on October 1, 2013.[14] This would afford adequate time for testing. To that end, the government signed a $94 million deal with CGI Federal in December 2011. However, because the government did not issue specifications to CGI for another year, the contractor could not start writing code until the spring of 2013 – months before the launch date. A 2014 Government Accountability Office (GAO) report revealed that due to the delays, CMS postponed the readiness testing for the exchange from March to

---

[10] Amy Goldstein & Juliet Eilperin, *HealthCare.gov: How Political Fear Was Pitted against Technical Needs*, WASH. POST (Nov. 2, 2013), perma.cc/E5FT-JARS.

[11] *Id.*

[12] Jason Miller, *Former HealthCare.gov IT Program Manager Chao Retires from CMS* (May 1, 2015), perma.cc/A8XD-3RHB.

[13] Eric Lipton, Ian Austen & Sharon LaFraniere, *Tension and Flaws before Health Website Crash*, N.Y. TIMES (Nov. 22, 2013), perma.cc/6XDT-ZH35.

[14] U. S. Gov't accountability office, GAO-14-694, Healthcare.Gov: Ineffective Planning and Oversight Practices Underscore the Need for Improved Contract Management (2014), bit.ly/24AZDMy.

September, "just weeks before the launch."[15] This "compressed time frame" allowed "little time for any unexpected problems to be addressed despite the significant challenges the project faced."[16]

Further, CMS proved unable to properly oversee its two primary contractors: CGI, which was hired to develop the exchange; and QSSI, another contractor that connected federal, state, and private networks. The GAO report revealed that much of the confusion was due to the fact that the contractors received directions based on "ad hoc decisions made by multiple program staff," and "it was not always clear which CMS officials were responsible for reviewing and accepting contractor deliverables."[17] Documents revealed that there were "repeated questions about who was responsible for reviewing the deliverables."

The *Wall Street Journal* concluded that the root of the problem was a "disjointed bureaucracy," as "no single leader oversaw implementation of the health law's signature online marketplace – a complex software project that would have been difficult under the best circumstances."[18] In light of this balkanization of responsibility and oversight, the *Washington Post* observed that "no one at the CMS or elsewhere at Department of Health and Human Services, of which the agency is a part, had the job of managing the project full time."[19]

Henry Chao's inability to oversee the massive endeavor was illustrated in a series of e-mails he sent in 2013. On July 8, a CGI contractor warned that the exchange's financial management system, which handles payments, "appears to be way off track and getting worse."[20] He worried that "our entire build is in jeopardy." Rather than acknowledge the problem and attempt to fix it, Chao asked several contractors to "get [him] a response on this to refute" the whistleblower's claim.

Denial ultimately gave way to an uncomfortable acceptance. In another e-mail, Chao wrote, "We are in bad shape. Perhaps worse than ever before and we are not even touching the hard stuff yet."[21] The CMS veteran wrote to several colleagues, "I just need to feel more confident they

15 *Id.*
16 *Id.*
17 *Id.*
18 Christopher Weaver & Louise Radnofsky, *Federal Health Site Stymied by Lack of Direction*, WALL ST. J. (Oct. 28, 2013), on.wsj.com/26YTb4a.
19 Amy Goldstein & Juliet Eilperin, *HealthCare.gov Contractor had High Confidence but Low Success*, WASH. POST (Nov. 23, 2013), perma.cc/JFA7-DKRL.
20 Email from Mark Calem, to Henry Chao (Jul. 9, 2013), bit.ly/1T4mcHF.
21 Amy Goldstein & Julie Eilperin, *CMS Demanded Results Too Late to Meet Obamacare Deadline*, FISCAL TIMES (Nov. 24, 2013), perma.cc/NJP5-9DMJ.

are not going to crash the plane at takeoff, regardless of the price."[22] Or, in his most infamous message, Chao wrote, "Let's just make sure it's not a third-world experience."[23]

9.3. "A MATERIALLY HIGH RISK OF SYSTEM INSTABILITY"

In March 2013, McKinsey, the international business consulting firm, gave CMS a fourteen-slide presentation warning of critical problems with HealthCare.gov.[24] First, the requirements were constantly "evolving." With less than 180 days till launch, the design was "still presumed to be open." Second, due to the compressed deadlines, there was "insufficient time and scope [for] end-to-end testing." Recognizing the fractured nature of the managerial structure, McKinsey urged CMS to "name a single implementation leader" who can "manage [the] critical path" ahead. That person would need "specific support from HHS and the White House to successfully operationalize the marketplaces." If these steps were not taken, the consultants concluded that there was a "a materially high risk of system instability." In April, McKinsey briefed Secretary Sebelius and CMS Administrator Marilyn Tavenner.[25] The briefing had no outward effect on Sebelius, who continued to testify before Congress that everything was proceeding according to plan.

During a hearing on April 17, Senator Max Baucus (D-MT) told Sebelius, "I just see a huge train wreck coming down. You and I have discussed this many times, and I don't see any results yet."[26] Baucus – whose Finance Committee Bill was the blueprint for the ACA – was concerned that people did not understand how the law works, and that HHS was not working hard enough to raise awareness. The senator added, despairingly, "I'm very concerned that not enough is being done so far – very concerned." Sebelius, who only responded in platitudes, frustrated Baucus. "You need data. Do you have any data? You've never given me data," the Senator bemoaned. "You only give me concepts, frankly." On May 1, Senate Majority Leader Harry Reid seconded Senator Max Baucus's admonition. "Max said unless we implement

---

[22]   Gautham Nagesh, *Health Website Problems Weren't Flagged in Time*, WALL ST. J. (Dec. 2, 2013), on.wsj.com/1q2W1Dw.

[23]   Philip Klein, *Obamacare Official: "Let's Just Make Sure It's Not a Third-World Experience*, WASH. EXAM'R (Mar. 22, 20130), perma.cc/H98U-54HA.

[24]   CENTS. FOR MEDICARE & MEDICAID SERVS., Red Team Discussion Document (2013), bit.ly/1SSWQa4.

[25]   John Whitesides, *The Painful Path to Obamacare Deadline*, REUTERS (Dec. 24, 2013), perma.cc/7L79-XYP7.

[26]   Sam Baker, *Baucus Warns of 'Huge Train Wreck' Enacting ObamaCare Provisions*, THE HILL (Apr. 17, 2013), perma.cc/ATV7-NQXG.

this properly it's going to be a train wreck, and I agree with him."[27] What Sebelius did not mention was that by the spring of 2013, HHS estimated that the federal exchange would be only 65% complete by October 1.[28]

The McKinsey analysis went all the way to the top. White House logs show two McKinsey consultants arrived at 1600 Pennsylvania Avenue on April 8. White House Press Secretary Jay Carney acknowledged that the president was briefed on McKinsey's findings.[29] However, beyond the McKinsey report, there is no evidence that the president, or any of his staffers, were aware of the impending crash.

This is all the more striking in light of the focus Obama put on the web site within his administration, starting with his speech on the Truman Balcony the evening the ACA passed the House. The *Washington Post* observed that the president "emphasized the exchange's central importance during regular staff meetings to monitor progress." Denis McDonough, White House Chief of Staff, said the president would end each meeting by saying, "I want to remind the team that this only works if the technology works."[30] In a July 2013 interview with the *New York Times*, the president was asked what he was "going to be doing to build support" in light of the ACA's declining popularity.[31] Obama answered, "We're going to implement it."

After the botched launch of HealthCare.gov, Ezra Klein wrote in hindsight that the president and his staff were "blindsided."[32] CMS officials "deep in the process knew that HealthCare.gov wasn't ready for primetime. But those frustrations were hidden from top-level managers." Klein observed: "Somewhere along the chain the information was spun, softened, or just plain buried." As a result, the White House "didn't know the truth about its own top initiative – and so they were unprepared for the disastrous launch. They didn't even know they needed to be lowering expectations." Steven Brill offered a more critical assessment: "When it came to Obama and his direct reports, this seemed to be more about aloof, incompetent management than a cover-up, though the Republicans would try to make the latter charge stick."[33]

[27] Alex Bolton, *Reid: More Funding Needed to Prevent ObamaCare from Becoming a 'Train Wreck'*, THE HILL (May 1, 2013), perma.cc/8GKK-ZU8P.

[28] Robert Pear, *Work to Bolster Health Website is Raising Cost, Officials Say*, N.Y. TIMES (Jul. 31, 2014), nyti.ms/29xVVyU.

[29] Justin Sink, *Obama Was Aware of Report on Healthcare Website's Problems*, THE HILL (Nov. 19, 2013), perma.cc/NB9R-T87E.

[30] Steven Brill, *Obama's Trauma Team*, TIME (Mar. 10, 2014), bit.ly/1Rk4cpO.

[31] *Interview with President Obama*, N.Y. TIMES (Jul. 27, 2013), nyti.ms/29BUK1U.

[32] Ezra Klein & Evan Soltas, *Wonkbook: Can Obama Fix Obamacare?*, WASH. POST (Oct. 21, 2013), perma.cc/M53L-DF4F.

[33] STEVEN BRILL, AMERICA'S BITTER PILL: MONEY, POLITICS, BACKROOM DEALS, AND THE FIGHT TO FIX OUR BROKEN HEALTHCARE SYSTEM 373 (Random House Paperback Trade ed. 2015).

9.4. "BOUNDARY CONDITION OF OCTOBER 1 AS THE LAUNCH DATE"

Compounding the federal health care exchange's technological difficulties was a stark political reality: delaying the launch of the website to finish it was impossible. The Affordable Care Act was silent about when enrollment for the health care exchanges must open up. The only date certain was that the individual mandate and the tax subsidies on the exchange would begin on January 1, 2014. By late 2010, the Obama administration decided that the exchanges would open up on October 1, 2013. Steven Brill observed, "There could be no delay. In [the White House's] view the Republicans would be merciless in their attacks on the administration's competence if they let the deadline slip."[34] The *New York Times* reported that "there was so much of a political push to get it ready on time, that concerns for the technology seem to have been pushed aside."[35]

Had this been any other project, the deadline would have postponed. Kevin Walsh, managing director for health eligibility systems at Xerox, explained in late September that "[i]f this wasn't such a date-driven project, I think a lot of people would be having discussions about slipping the date." However, instead, the government chose to "slip out some of the functionality because the go live [date] is so important."[36] Aetna CEO Mark Bertolini was asked if he would have delayed the launch. "I would have, if I'd been in their seat," he replied. But, he added, "the politics got in the way of a good business decision."[37] The *Washington Post* quoted a White House official who said, "You're basically trying to build a complicated building in a war zone, because the Republicans are lobbing bombs at us."[38]

The March 2013 McKinsey report revealed that "extending the go-live date should not be part" of any mitigation strategy, as CMS "worked with a boundary condition of October 1 as the launch date."[39] According to *The New York Times*, Henry Chao was told that "failure was not an option," nor was "rolling out the system in stages or on a smaller scale."[40] The White House "feared that any backtracking would further embolden Republican critics who were trying to repeal the health care law."[41]

---

[34] *Id.* at 275.

[35] Pear, *supra* note 4.

[36] Sarah Kliff, *A Guide to Freaking Out About the Newest Obamacare Glitch*, WASH. POST (Sept. 20, 2013), perma.cc/GY3L-FXLD.

[37] Dan Mangan, *'So Much Wrong': Aetna CEO Blasts Obamacare Tech Debacle*, CNBC (Oct. 14, 2013), perma.cc/8A3H-M3DD.

[38] Goldstein, *supra* note 10.

[39] Red Team, *supra* note 24.

[40] Pear, *supra* note 4.

[41] *Id.*

In May, President Obama commiserated with the hundreds of federal employees working on the exchange: "I know it's hard, it's a lot of work," he told them.[42] "It's very rare in the annals of American history where we have to set up something this quick. And let's face it, it's not as if the political environment has always been friendly in terms of getting this stuff done." On September 5, several White House officials visited CMS for a demonstration of how HealthCare.gov would operate. The *Washington Post* reported that CMS staffers "worried that it would fail right in front of the president's aides."[43] Perhaps even more troubling, "a few secretly rooted for it to fail so that perhaps the White House would wait to open the exchange until it was ready." Alas, the simplified demonstration succeeded.

9.5. "WE ARE ON SCHEDULE"

As the summer of 2013 rolled on – and Ted Cruz barnstormed the country urging Americans to oppose Obamacare – the last-ditch efforts to get HealthCare.gov ready for its debut failed. The *Washington Post* noted that over the summer of 2013, "[m]ajor insurers, state health-care officials and Democratic allies repeatedly warned the Obama administration that the new federal health-insurance exchange had significant problems."[44] One analyst from Deloitte said the development process was "pretty much a black box. They tell us, 'It's freakishly on schedule.' They use those exact words. But only the people who work in this can tell you if it's actually running on time."[45] A senior executive from Xerox, who was working with several states on implementing their exchanges, said, "Everybody is having sleepless nights given the magnitude of the effort and the short amount of time. It's like building a bridge from both ends and hoping, in the end, they connect."[46] Aetna CEO Mark Bertolini – a steadfast ACA supporter – explained on CNBC's *Squawk Box*, "We were pretty nervous as we got further along. As they started missing deadlines, we were pretty convinced it was going to be a difficult launch."[47]

With the launch date drawing near, it became clear that CMS could not certify that HealthCare.gov would be ready on time. In mid-September, the *Wall Street Journal* pointed out that the "government's software [could not]

---

[42] Ezra Klein & Sarah Kliff, *Obama's Last Campaign: Inside the White House Plan to Sell Obamacare*, WASH. POST (Jul. 17, 2013), perma.cc/A8X4-8SAM.

[43] Goldstein, *supra* note 10.

[44] Juliet Eilperin, Amy Goldstein & Sandhya Somashekhar, *Many Remain Locked Out of Federal Health-care Web Site*, WASH. POST (Oct. 8, 2013), perma.cc/CK6S-UJ82.

[45] Klein, *supra* note 42.

[46] *Id.*

[47] Mangan, *supra* note 37.

reliably determine how much people need to pay for coverage."[48] One senior health insurance executive told the *Journal*, "There's a blanket acknowledgment that rates are being calculated incorrectly."

According to a *Washington Post* investigation, a "pre-flight checklist" compiled a week before HealthCare.gov's launch showed that "41 of 91 separate functions that CGI [Federal] was responsible for finishing by the launch were still not working," including five that were deemed "critical."[49] Even those features that "CGI had expressed high confidence" in would not be ready by the launch date. As late as August 17, 2013 – six weeks before launch date – CGI Federal sent an e-mail to a dozen CMS employees indicating that the exchange was only 55% complete.[50] Days before the launch, system tests were "not good and not consistent at all," an HHS official told *Reuters*. The system was designed to handle 10,000 simultaneous users; it crashed with only 500.[51]

Further, the site could not meet all of the requisite federal security accreditation standards. On August 2, the CMS inspector general released a report, concluding that the federal government was months behind in security testing for HealthCare.gov.[52] One security expert told *Reuters* that "they've removed their margin for error," which includes the threat of identity theft.[53] *CBS News* revealed that the "final, required top-to-bottom security tests never got done" prior to launch.[54] In a report CGI sent to CMS on September 6, the contractors warned that there were "open risks" and "open issues" that needed to be resolved before the launch.[55] Further, the remaining time was "not adequate to complete full functional, system, and integration testing activities." They noted that there was a "near certainty" that the impact would be "severe."[56]

[48] Christopher Weaver, Timothy W. Martin & Jennifer Corbett Dooren, *Pricing Glitch Afflicts Rollout of Online Health Exchanges*, WALL ST. J. (Sept. 19, 2013), on.wsj.com/24B0KMc.

[49] *Low Success*, *supra* note 19.

[50] Email from Shabnam Shahmohammad, to Tyrone Thompson (Aug. 17, 2013, 4:45 PM), bit.ly/1rZbMNO.

[51] Whitesides, *supra* note 25.

[52] Sharon Begley, *Obamacare Months Behind in Testing IT Data Security: Government*, REUTERS (Aug. 6, 2013), perma.cc/XBZ8-KUPK.

[53] *Id.*

[54] Sharyl Attkisson, *Healthcare.gov Ducked Final Security Requirements Before Launch*, CBS NEWS (Nov. 4, 2013), perma.cc/8EE8-HN9A.

[55] HOUSE OVERSIGHT & GOV'T REFORM COMM., CGI Monthly Project Status Report (2013), bit.ly/1Yc7bBQ.

[56] Juliet Eilperin, *CGI Warned of HealthCare.gov Problems a Month Before Launch, Documents Show*, WASH. POST (Oct. 29, 2013), perma.cc/B7HN-ACEX.

A September 3 memo found two high-risk issues with the exchange, warning that "the threat and risk potential (to the system) is limitless."[57] A September 27 memo to CMS Administrator Marilyn Tavenner indicated that due to insufficient testing, there was "a level of uncertainty that can be deemed as a high risk."[58] Teresa Fryer, who served as the Chief Information Security Officer for CMS, recommended that the so-called "Authority to Operate" be denied in light of the serious warnings. This was the certification that would allow HealthCare.gov to go live. However, Fryer was "overruled by her supervisors."[59]

Notwithstanding these concerns, Tavenner approved the security certification on September 27 – two days after Senator Cruz's filibuster concluded. *CBS News* reported that Tavenner's staff prepared an "unusual 'risk acknowledgement' saying that the agency's mitigation plan for rigorous monitoring and ongoing tests did 'not reduce the (security) risk to the ... system itself going into operation on October 1, 2013.'" In other words, they launched it knowing that there would be significant vulnerabilities to the system, risking customer's personal information. The Government Accountability Office concluded in a 2014 report that HealthCare.gov was launched "without the required verification that it met performance requirements."[60]

Tavenner's boss, Kathleen Sebelius, was oblivious to these problems. "I was not aware of this," she testified before Congress, "and I did not have these discussions with the White House because I wasn't aware of them."[61] Likewise, Henry Chao was never copied on these memos, and claimed he was cut out of the loop on the project he was supposed to be managing. "I just want to say that I haven't seen this before," he testified during a hearing.[62]

Yet to the public, the Obama administration continued to present a unified message of confidence. CMS spokesman Brian Cook insisted, "We are on schedule and will be ready for the Marketplaces to open on

---

[57] Sharyl Attkisson, *Memo Warned of "Limitless" Security Risks for Healthcare.gov*, CBS News (Nov. 11, 2013), perma.cc/Q86P-MZSY.

[58] Jack Gillum & Ricardo Alonso-Zaldivar, *Gov't Document: Health Site Posed a Security Risk*, Associated Press (Oct. 30, 2013), perma.cc/6RK2-HRVQ.

[59] Sharyl Attkisson, *High Security Risk Found After HealthCare.gov Launch*, CBS News (Dec. 20, 2013), perma.cc/823M-EJMG.

[60] GAO, *supra* note 14.

[61] Sharyl Attkisson, *Departing Obamacare Security Official Didn't Sign Off on Site Launch*, CBS News (Nov. 6, 2013), perma.cc/KRV9-FRAF.

[62] Robert Pear, *Official at Health Site Says He Didn't Know of Potential Risk*, N.Y. Times (Nov. 11, 2013), nyti.ms/1SQVi3R.

October 1."[63] Senator Baucus walked back his "train wreck" comment: "I think the train is doing a little better," he said. "There's been no crash. I don't think it's derailed. We're still chugging along here."[64] Senate Republican Leader Mitch McConnell disagreed. He said that Obamacare would be "an albatross around the neck of every Democrat who voted for it. This thing can't possibly work," he added. "It will be a huge disaster in 2014."[65]

[63] Sarah Kliff, *Uh-oh: Obamacare Security Testing Is Months Behind, Report Says*, WASH. POST (Aug. 6, 2013), perma.cc/3MEY-QT6U.
[64] Klein, *supra* note 42.
[65] Ricardo Alonso-Zaldivar, *Republicans: Obamacare is Key to 2014*, HUFF. POST (May 26, 2013), perma.cc/63GK-REM5.

10

Filibuster

10.1. "IT'S TIME FOR US TO SAY NO"

The battle over defunding Obamacare would be waged during the final ten days of September 2013. Building on the momentum of Cruz's summer campaign, on September 20, the House of Representatives approved a continuing resolution that funded most of the government until December 2013. Critically, however, it eliminated *all* future funding for the Affordable Care Act.[1] The CR passed by a 230–189 vote, with two Democrats crossing over to vote "yes."

After the vote, the triumphant Republican Caucus assembled in the Rayburn Room, just off the House floor. Standing in front of a lectern adorned with the hashtag #SenateMustAct, Speaker John Boehner announced, "It's time for us to say no. It's time to stop this before it causes any more damage to American families and American businesses." Flanked by 200 Republicans, Boehner sent a message to the Senate: "The American people don't want the government shut down, and they don't want ObamaCare. The House has listened to the American people. Now it's time for the United States Senate to listen to them as well." Originally the House speaker opposed the strategy, but realized the overwhelming majority of his caucus supported it, so he acquiesced. The *Washington Post* reported that the "summer onslaught" led by Cruz forced Boehner into a series of "capitulations," leading to the September 20 vote.[2] The *Post* noted that on October 2, President Obama asked Boehner, "John, what happened?"[3] Boehner replied, "I got overrun, that's what happened."

[1] Pete Kasperowicz & Russell Berman, *House Votes to Fund Government Through Mid-December, Defund Obamacare*, THE HILL (Sept. 20, 2013), perma.cc/FA5Y-9M5L.

[2] Lori Montgomery, Paul Kane & Rosalind S. Helderman, *House GOP Pushes U.S. to Edge of Shutdown*, WASH. POST (Sept. 29, 2013), perma.cc/PU22-E8SD.

[3] Manu Raju, John Bresnahan, Jake Sherman, Carrie Budoff Brown, *Anatomy of a Shutdown*, POLITICO (Oct. 18, 2013), perma.cc/H28A-UQE5.

Who led the stampede? "Lucifer in the flesh."[4] Boehner's resentment for Cruz boiled over in April 2016. He blamed the Freshman Senator for forcing him to lose control of his caucus, which ultimately led to the shutdown. "I have Democrat friends and Republican friends," the Ohioan said. "I get along with almost everyone, but I have never worked with a more miserable son of a bitch in my life." Cruz shot back that during the shutdown he and Senator Lee offered to meet with the Speaker. Cruz was informed that Boehner declined, saying, "I have no interest in talking to him. What possibly could be accomplished by having a conversation? No I will not meet."[5] In September 2015, Boehner resigned as Speaker, amidst wide-ranging unpopularity in the House.

Democrats quickly responded that the CR had zero chance of passing Senate Majority Leader Reid's gavel or President Obama's veto pen. Funding would expire at midnight on September 30, resulting in a government shutdown. "Republican attempts to take an entire law hostage," Reid said, "simply to appease the Tea Party anarchists are outrageous, irresponsible and futile."[6] House Minority Leader Nancy Pelosi charged that "what is brought to the floor today is without a doubt a measure designed to shut down government."[7]

That evening, President Obama called Speaker Boehner and told him that he would not compromise. According to the *Washington Post*, Obama explained that "the American people have worked too long and too hard to dig the nation out of the worst economic downturn since the Great Depression and the last thing that they and the nation's economy needs is another politically motivated, self-inflicted wound."[8]

Having passed the House of Representatives, the CR to fund the government – minus the ACA – was sent to the Senate. A vote to consider the House CR, known in parliamentary parlance as a motion to invoke cloture, was scheduled for Wednesday, September 25, at 1:00 PM. But first, the junior senator from Texas would speak.

---

4   Ada Statler-Throckmorton, *John Boehner Talks Election, Time in Office*, STANFORD DAILY (Apr. 28, 2016), perma.cc/5LJF-XLZH.
5   Nolan D. McCaskil, *Cruz: Boehner's 'Inner Trump' Came Out*, POLITICO (Apr. 28, 2016), perma.cc/T9TE-WC7V.
6   Lori Montgomery & Philip Rucker, *House Passes GOP Spending Plan that Defunds Obamacare*, WASH. POST (Sept. 20, 2013), perma.cc/3QKB-8FRY.
7   *Pelosi Floor Speech in Opposition to the House GOP Continuing Resolution* (Sept. 20, 2013), perma.cc/WRQ8-WJES.
8   Montgomery, *supra* note 6.

10.2. #MakeDCListen

At 2:41 PM on Tuesday, September 24, Ted Cruz took to the floor of the Senate.[9]

> I rise today in opposition to ObamaCare. I rise today in an effort to speak for 26 million Texans and for 300 million Americans. All across this country Americans are suffering because of ObamaCare. ObamaCare isn't working. Yet fundamentally there are politicians in this body who are not listening to the people. They are not listening to the concerns of their constituents, they are not listening to the jobs lost or the people forced into part-time work, to the people losing their health insurance, to the people who are struggling. A great many Texans, a great many Americans feel they don't have a voice. I hope to play some very small part in helping provide that voice for them. I intend to speak in opposition to ObamaCare, I intend to speak in support of defunding ObamaCare, until I am no longer able to stand, to do everything I can to help Americans stand together and recognize this grand experiment three-and-a-half years ago is, quite simply, not working. It is time, quite simply, to make D.C. listen. That is a point I intend to make over and over, because it is fundamentally what we are trying to do. We are trying to gather the American people to make D.C. listen.

Over the next twenty-one hours, Cruz would indeed speak "over and over" again about how the ACA was not working, how it was costing jobs, and how it was making millions of Americans worse off. The theme of his oration, as summed up in his Twitter hashtag, was #MakeDCListen. He repeated the mantra three dozen times. He called on the American people "who have something [to] say" to "tweet with the hashtag #MakeDCListen." Cruz would later read dozens of tweets from the lectern. Senator Jeff Sessions (R-AL) told Cruz that "that during the course of this afternoon, the hashtag #MakeDCListen has been trending No. 1 because the American people are frustrated."

Less than an hour after his talkathon concluded, the next day Cruz made a rare guest appearance on the *Rush Limbaugh Show* to explain his goal.[10] The conservative talk radio icon told Cruz, "So many people are so happy that there finally is some leadership. They're so happy that, finally, somebody is doing in Washington what they were elected to do, what they said they were going to do." Cruz replied that "in many ways the central issue that we were trying to focus on in the filibuster was not the continuing resolution. It wasn't even Obamacare, as horrific as it is for the economy." Rather, "the central issue

9 All twenty-one hours and nineteen minutes of the speech can be found at cs.pn/1QU9weR.
10 *Senator Cruz Continues the Filibuster on EIB*, RUSH LIMBAUGH SHOW (Sept. 25, 2013), perma.cc/EC9J-3XDQ/.

is the long-standing problem we have had with Washington not listening to the American people with Democrats and Republicans." In Washington, there is "very little willingness to actually stand up and fight on behalf of the American people."[11]

Although Cruz's twenty-one-hour oration was the fourth-longest in Senate history – Strom Thurmond's twenty-four-hour stand still holds the record – it was not actually a filibuster.[12] As Reid pointed out before Cruz began speaking, "There will be no filibuster today. Filibusters are to stop people from voting, and we are going to vote tomorrow. Under the rules, no one can stop that. We are going to vote tomorrow regardless of what anyone says or does today." As a result, Cruz would have to stop talking at noon the following day to allow for the cloture vote scheduled for an hour later.

It has become conventional wisdom that Cruz's speech forced the government shutdown. For example, before Cruz began speaking, Republican Senate Minority Leader Mitch McConnell said, "I just do not happen to think filibustering a bill that defunds ObamaCare is the best route to defunding ObamaCare. All it does is shut down the government and keep ObamaCare funded. And none of us want that. That would be the results of filibustering." Cruz did not, and indeed could not, delay the vote that Reid had already scheduled. Senator Dick Durbin (D-IL) correctly pointed out "the object [of the filibuster] is to *slow down* the business of the Senate."[13] Ultimately, the Senate voted exactly when Reid planned they would – not a minute later, although because of Cruz's actions, not a minute earlier.

What forced the government shutdown was that the House CR defunded Obamacare, and the Senate CR funded Obamacare. As a result of this discrepancy, there was no unified funding bill that passed both chambers for the President to sign. Thus, funding ran out on October 1. Without a doubt, Cruz's last stand strengthened the resolve of House Republicans, but – to the dismay of Speaker Boehner – they had already taken their own stand five days earlier in voting to defund the ACA. Even if Cruz had not held the floor for

---

[11] After Senator Cruz suspended his presidential campaign, *The Wall Street Journal* editorial board wrote that the Texan's strategy to defund Obamacare "raised Mr. Cruz's profile among conservatives, but one price was to stigmatize all other GOP candidates as 'establishment,' even conservative Governors. Another was to set the stage for Mr. Trump, who co-opted the rebellion." *A Cruz Postmortem: How the Texan Made Trump Possible and Sunk His Own Candidacy*, WALL ST. J. (May 4, 2016), on.wsj.com/1QUio5D.

[12] Josh Voorhees, *Where Ted Cruz's Fake Filibuster Would Rank If It Were a Real Filibuster*, SLATE (Sept. 25, 2013), perma.cc/YL3Y-BHFG.

[13] Senator Dick Durbin, Floor Speech on Obamacare (Sept. 24, 2013), perma.cc/LE8N-A9HG (emphasis added).

twenty-one hours, the exact same sequence of events would have likely played out over the next five days.

10.3. "WILL THE SENATOR YIELD FOR A QUESTION?"

In order to maintain the floor, senators must continue to talk and stand. If they sit down, or stop talking, they lose the floor. However, other senators are allowed to ask questions of the filibustering member. The *Congressional Research Service* observed that "the peculiar advantage of this tactic is that it sometimes takes Senators quite some time to ask their question ... [so the] participating Senators can extend the debate through an exchange of what sometimes are long questions followed by short answers."[14] And it gives the filibusterer a break.

During Cruz's twenty-one-hour oration, several supportive senators asked the Texan questions – and in the process gave him a brief respite. First up was Cruz's partner in the defunding effort, Senator Mike Lee. In his autobiography, Cruz recounted that moments before his talkathon began, he prayed with Lee in his "'hideaway' office wedged into a dome in the Capitol Building."[15] They "bowed [their] heads, read from the Book of Psalms, and asked for the Lord's guidance." One hour into the filibuster, Lee took to the floor, and asked, "Will the Senator yield for a question?" Cruz replied, "I am happy to yield for a question without yielding the floor." By not yielding the floor, Cruz made clear that he wasn't finished talking. Lee expressed his astonishment on the length of the 2,700-page health care law, which no senator could have conceivably read before voting on it. Senator Max Baucus (D-MT), who chaired the finance committee, admitted that not even he read the entire bill. "I don't think you want me to waste my time to read every page of the healthcare bill," Baucus admitted in 2010.[16]

Since it was enacted, Lee continued, the law "has expanded ... to include within its penumbra 20,000 pages of regulatory text." The son of Ronald Reagan's Solicitor General Rex Lee, and former Supreme Court clerk, said the ACA "reminds me of something James Madison wrote ... in Federalist No. 62." He said, "if I may paraphrase him, *it will be of little benefit to the American people that their laws may be written by individuals of their own*

---

[14] RICHARD S. BETH & VALERIE HEITSHUSEN, *Cong. Research Serv., Filibusters and Cloture in the Senate* 6 (2014), bit.ly/27oCy8r.

[15] TED CRUZ, A TIME FOR TRUTH: REIGNITING THE PROMISE OF AMERICA 3926 (Kindle Ed. 2015).

[16] Jordan Fabian, *Key Senate Democrat Suggests that He Didn't Read Entire Healthcare Reform Bill*, THE HILL (Aug. 25, 2010), perma.cc/P2PC-CQ3J.

choosing if those laws are so voluminous and complex that they can't reasonably be read and understood by the American people." Cruz replied, "Let me note there are many reasons why I love the Senator from Utah. But very near the top of the list is the fact that when he 'paraphrases' the *Federalist Papers*, it is darn near a word-for-word, verbatim quote." (Madison's actual quotation was only a few words off: "It will be of little avail to the people, that the laws are made by men of their own choice, if the laws be so voluminous that they cannot be read, or so incoherent that they cannot be understood.")[17]

Later, Senator Marco Rubio (R-FL) praised Cruz for putting a focus on "this opportunity that we have to stop ObamaCare because of the impact this is having on real people." The junior senator from Florida added, "At the end of the day, that is what we are fighting for. We are not fighting against ObamaCare, and we are fighting for these people." Cruz extolled the virtues of his soon-to-be opponent in the presidential campaign: "Senator Rubio is inspiring. Senator Marco Rubio is a critical national leader. I don't know if there is anyone more effective, more articulate, or a more persuasive voice for conservative principles than my friend Marco Rubio."

Cruz was also asked questions by other Republican senators, including Jeff Sessions, David Vitter, Pat Roberts, Mike Enzi, Jim Risch, Chuck Grassley, Jim Inhofe, and Rand Paul. It would be the last questioner that would stir up the most controversy.

10.4. #STANDWITHRAND

In May 2013, Senator Rand Paul of Kentucky launched an impromptu thirteen-hour filibuster on the danger posed to U.S. citizens by government drone strikes.[18] As Cruz recounted during his own oration later that year, "[W]hen Senator Paul began that filibuster, many Members of this body viewed what he was doing as curious, if not quixotic." But as Paul continued to speak, and the hashtag #StandWithRand trended, Cruz observed, "[W]e saw something incredible happen during that time, which is the American people got engaged, got involved, began speaking out, and it transformed the debate." The Texan took a lesson from Rand's stand: "If you want Washington to listen, the only way that will happen is if it comes from the American people."

---

[17] THE FEDERALIST NO. 62.

[18] Philip Ewing, *Rand Paul Pulls Plug on Nearly 13-Hour Filibuster*, POLITICO (Mar. 6, 2013), perma.cc/PV97-DNZD.

Three hours into the filibuster, Paul rose to give Cruz some helpful advice: "Make sure the Senator had comfortable shoes on [and] make sure he is getting enough to eat, but try not to eat on television." What ended Paul's filibuster was not the Senate calendar, but his bladder. Unlike Cruz, who was bounded by a scheduled vote, Paul could have gone the distance. Alas, he stopped in hour thirteen. "I would try to go another 12 hours and try to break Strom Thurmond's record, but there are some limits to filibustering and I am going to have to go take care of one of those here."[19] Heeding Paul's advice, Cruz had "only one small glass of water" so he "simply did not need to go."[20]

Paul asked Cruz whether it was his intention to "shut down the government" or "is it the President's intention to shut down the government," or as the deadline draws near, was this "a good time for dialog because no one ever seems to talk at any other time." Cruz replied, "[T]he question Senator Rand Paul asked was an excellent question. Let me be absolutely clear. We should not shut down the government. I sincerely hope Senator Reid and President Obama do not choose to force a government shutdown simply to force ObamaCare on the American people." Paul continued with a series of follow-up questions. "Will [you] work with the President and will [you] work with the majority leader ... to find a compromise?" Paul, who supported Cruz and Lee's efforts since the outset, later admitted that "the whole battle" of "shutting down the government" was "a dumb idea."[21]

Cruz answered he would not vote for "something that is a middle ground." He would not "vote for something less than defunding ObamaCare" because he "committed publicly over and over to the American people that I will not vote for a continuing resolution that funds one penny of ObamaCare." Cruz would later criticize Paul, and wrote that his questions "seemed deliberately designed to undermine our efforts," and that he "marveled that Rand had decided not to be with us in this fight."[22] Paul did not understand the criticism, and recalled that Cruz "sent me a really nice, handwritten congratulatory note thanking me for my help."[23] Despite this disagreement, two days later, Paul would join Lee and Cruz to block Reid's cloture motion to fund Obamacare.

---

[19] *Id.*

[20] Cruz, *supra* note 15 at 3945.

[21] Charles Krauthammer, *Rand Paul on Shutdown: "Even Though It Appeared I Was Participating in It, It Was a Dumb Idea*, REAL CLEAR POLITICS (Nov. 18, 2013), perma.cc/W3HB-8DZQ.

[22] Cruz, *supra* note 15 at 3957.

[23] Manu Raju, *GOP Senators Challenge Cruz Book Claims*, POLITICO (Jul. 14, 2015), perma.cc/CS7C-MWJ6.

10.5. "GREEN EGGS AND HAM"

At 8:00 PM, about two hours into the filibuster, Cruz took off his senator hat and put on his daddy hat. He smiled and said his daughters, Caroline (five years old) and Catherine (two years old), were "both at home getting ready to go to bed" and "they are both watching C-SPAN." Cruz, looking right at the camera, said "[I]f you will forgive me, I want to take the opportunity to read two bedtime stories to my girls." He recounted in his autobiography that "the delighted girls, in their pink PJs, got right up next to the television and giggled with glee." Caroline, who was then "kindergarten-aged … thought [that] was 'kind of cool.'"

First, Cruz read from *Proverbs*, King Solomon's Wise Words. One of them was particularly apt for the moment: "You will say the wrong thing if you talk too much, so be sensible and watch what you say." He joked, "That is not an encouraging Proverb for someone in the midst of a filibuster."

Second, Cruz read his daughters their favorite story, *Green Eggs and Ham*. The premise of the Dr. Seuss classic is that Sam-I-Am pesters another to eat a meal of green eggs and ham. The other character steadfastly refuses, repeating, "I do not like them, Sam-I-Am." Finally, after much argument, he tries green eggs and ham and says, "I do so like green eggs and ham. Thank you. Thank you, Sam-I-Am." Cruz used the story as a parable for Obamacare.

> Three years ago President Obama and Senate Democrats told the American people, 'Just try ObamaCare. Just try it.' There were an awful lot of Republicans who were very skeptical of it, I think for good reasons, but very skeptical. But the difference with *Green Eggs and Ham* is when Americans tried it, they discovered they did not like green eggs and ham and they did not like ObamaCare either. They did not like ObamaCare in a box, with a fox, in a house, or with a mouse.

Hours later, Senator Charles Schumer (D-NY) would draw a different lesson from the story. "Anyone who knows that book," Schumer said, "knows the moral … is to try something before you condemn it. You might actually like it." In the book, the main character "resisted eating green eggs and ham. Maybe if he were a Senator, he would speak on the floor for 21 hours," Schumer quipped. "But then when he tasted green eggs and ham, he actually liked them. Maybe as the President's health care bill goes into effect, Senator Cruz may actually find that he and his constituents actually like it." In December 2015, Cruz released a Dr. Seuss-themed campaign commercial for "How Obamacare Stole Christmas."

10.6. "THIS CHAMBER HAS REVERBERATED WITH A MARATHON OF SPEAKING"

Cruz would continue to speak throughout the late hours of the night and into the early morning, receiving questions from Democratic Senators Dick

Durbin and Tim Kaine. At 11:35 AM – with only twenty-five minutes left before he would have to cede the floor – Senator Reid invited Cruz to engage in a colloquy. (In Senate parlance, this is a back-and-forth exchange.) Cruz, with his tie loosened and voice hoarse, said, "With the reservation that I do not lose the right to the floor, I am pleased to engage in a colloquy with the majority leader." Reid once again reminded everyone that "this is not a filibuster," and "we are going to have a vote about 1 o'clock today," regardless of how long the Texan talked.

Reid predicted (accurately) that the House of Representatives "may not accept what we send them," and "may want to send us something back." At that point Cruz interrupted Reid: "I have decided to not yield my right to the floor. I was amenable to a colloquy. The majority leader is giving a speech." A stunned Reid replied, "If I could ask for a unanimous consent agreement with my friend." Once again, Cruz objected: "I cannot be asked to consent to an unnamed consent agreement" if "the majority is going to cut off and muzzle us in another twenty-four minutes." Cruz explained, "I will yield time to [Reid] for a question when the majority leader is prepared to yield to the American people." Reid left the chamber, and Senators Sessions, Lee, and Risch asked questions, offering a brief respite to the exhausted Texan.

At 11:56 AM, with time ticking away, Cruz began to wind down. He asked for "unanimous consent that the cloture vote at 1 PM be vitiated and that at the conclusion of my remarks the motion to proceed to the resolution be agreed to." In other words, he asked for the Senate to be able to vote on the House CR and not proceed to fund Obamacare. Senator Pat Leahy (D-VT), sitting as president pro tempore, asked, "Is there objection?" Senator Reid, to the surprise of no one, objected: "At 1 PM the Senate will speak, and we will follow the rules of the Senate."

At 11:58 AM, Cruz concluded: "Well then, it appears I have the floor for another 90 seconds or so. The only path, if we are to oppose ObamaCare, is to stand together and oppose cloture." The final sixteen words of his twenty-one-hour #MakeDCListen oration were directed at those least likely to listen: "I ask my friends on the Democratic side of the aisle to listen to this plea." Cruz was finished, and walked out of the chamber as dozens of microphones and cameras were thrust into his face.

Against protocol, rounds of applause boomed throughout the chamber. Senator Leahy spoke over the clapping: "[T]he hour of 12 noon having arrived, the Senate having been in continuous session since convening yesterday, the Senate will suspend for a prayer." The chaplain of the Senate, Dr. Barry C. Black, offered this fitting invocation. "Eternal God, our refuge and strength, may the fact that this Chamber has reverberated with a marathon of speaking help us to remember to direct our thoughts and words toward Your throne in continuous prayer for our Nation. During this challenging season, give our Senators the wisdom to make full and complete their commitment to serve the American people. We pray in Your great Name. Amen."

10.7. "ELECTIONS HAVE CONSEQUENCES"

After the prayer, Senator Reid took the floor. "We all admire the Senator from Texas for his wanting to talk," the Nevadan said. "With all due respect, I am not sure we learned anything new. It has been interesting to watch, but, for lack of a better way of describing this, it has been a big waste of time." Reid continued, "the American people know that every hour that he has spoken or speaks pushes us another hour closer to a Republican government shutdown."

The Democratic leader stressed that it was not just his own party that opposed Cruz's plan. "I know the majority of my Republican colleagues," he said, "recognize this strategy for the foolishness it is, and I am glad to see them speak up." Leading the charge from the right was Senator John McCain, the Republican presidential candidate in 2008. Earlier that day, Reid had asked Cruz to cede time for McCain to speak, to which Cruz objected. Now, Reid specifically gave McCain time from the Democrats' allotment. "He can use whatever time he needs from us," Reid said.

McCain rose, and recalled that "we fought as hard as we could [to stop the enactment of Obamacare] in a fair and honest manner, and we lost. One of the reasons we lost was because we were in the minority." The Arizonan was proud of the GOP effort to stop Obamacare, remembering it as "one of the most hard-fought and fair debates that has taken place on the floor of the Senate in the time I have been here." But they lost. With the Democrats in control of the presidency and both branches of Congress, "the majority almost always governs and passes legislation." And after the 2012 election where "ObamaCare was a major issue in the campaign," the Republicans lost. "The people spoke," McCain said, "much to my dismay," and "reelected the President of United States." In a theme repeated throughout the shutdown debate, the Arizonan explained "that elections have consequences and those elections were clear in a significant majority." Because of the election, "the majority of the American people supported the President of the United States and renewed his stewardship of this country. I don't like it. It was not something that I wanted the outcome to be, but I think all of us should respect the outcome of elections which reflects the will of the people."

Several other Republicans also criticized Cruz. Senator Tom Coburn (R-OK) said Cruz's motives were "pure" but his tactics were "tremendously erroneous." Cruz's senior colleague from Texas, John Cornyn, explained that he was "committed to defunding ObamaCare. But I also believe that we ought to avoid a Government shutdown." If the Senate follows Cruz's strategy, Cornyn said, "It may well prompt the government shutdown, which I think benefits no one, and it could possibly damage our economy."

Many conservative pundits agreed with McCain, Coburn, and Cornyn. Columnist Charles Krauthammer explained, "[I]f I thought this would work, I would support it. But I don't fancy suicide. It has a tendency to be fatal."[24] *National Review* editor Byron York tweeted, "I believe GOP's last chance to stop Obamacare before implementation was 2012 election."[25] A CNBC poll reflected that the public opposed defunding Obamacare 44% to 38%, and opposed shutting down the government 59% to 19%.[26]

Senate Minority Leader Mitch McConnell was far cagier than his colleagues. "I wish to start by acknowledging the work of my colleague, the junior the Senator from Texas, who held the floor for nearly a day speaking passionately about an issue that unites every single Republican, ObamaCare," he said. Without directly doubting Cruz's strategy, McConnell looked ahead to the vote later this week to defund Obamacare. "All we need is five Democrats to show enough courage to stand against their party and with the American people on this vote. That is enough to pass the bill – enough to keep the government open and to keep ObamaCare funding out of it – before this train collides with reality." In closing, McConnell urged his "Democratic colleagues to join us, the members of my conference who are already united in our opposition to ObamaCare." This plea would not succeed – and McConnell knew it. One week later, the Kentuckian would say of Cruz's strategy, "It was not a smart play. It had no chance of success."[27]

10.8. "COME AND TAKE IT"

One of the more poignant critiques came from Tennessee Republican Lamar Alexander, who turned to Texas history to explain his disagreement with Cruz's stand. There were "two famous Tennesseans, patriotic, brave men, both of

---

[24] Charles Krauthammer, *Charles Krauthammer: How Fractured Is the GOP?*, WASH. POST (Aug. 1, 2013), perma.cc/AE57-PKAP.

[25] @ByronYork, Twitter (Sept. 22, 2013), bit.ly/1rz24Rl.

[26] Steve Liesman, *Most Americans Against Defunding Obamacare: Survey*, CNBC (Sept. 23, 2013), perma.cc/35UT-DD5G.

[27] *Anatomy of a Shutdown, supra* note 3.

whom went to Texas," Alexander said. "They had the same goal in mind, the independence of Texas, but they had different tactics." First, there was Davy Crocket, who ignored all warnings, and risked his life at the famous last stand. "He went to the Alamo anyway," Alexander said, "and he did get killed, but we remember him for his bravery and we remember the Alamo."

The second patriot, General Sam Houston, "took a different tack." When faced with a possible defeat, he "withdrew with his men to San Jacinto," Texas. Alexander recalled that Houston "was heavily criticized by some people in Texas at that time for withdrawing," and "some said it was a retreat." But Houston's rested army was able to surprise and defeat General Santa Anna at the Battle of San Jacinto, which won the war for the Republic of Texas. Alexander regaled, "[T]oday we celebrate both men. We think of them both as patriots, as great Americans." But whose strategy should the Senate adopt? Alexander said he was in "Sam Houston's camp," because "sometimes in a long battle, patience is a valuable tactic."

Without saying a word, Cruz responded that he was on Team Crocket. In October 1835 – five months before the Battle of the Alamo – the Mexican army demanded that the Texians in the city of Gonzales surrender their cannon. They refused, and instead raised a white banner depicting a cannon and a star, with the caption, "COME AND TAKE IT." It was a paraphrase of *Molon Labe*, which translates as "come and take them," the Spartan's defiant cry at the Battle of Thermopylae. When Mexico attacked, the small militia – with the aid of the legendary cannon – managed to hold off General Santa Anna's army. Fittingly, after this first victory of the Texas revolution at Gonzales, the cannon was dispatched to the Alamo, where it could provide Davy Crocket's last line of defense.[28]

To Alexander's point, without the revolutionaries starting the war at the Battle of Gonzales, and risking their lives at the Alamo, Sam Houston would have never had a chance at San Jacinto. Three-score years earlier, without the Battle of Bunker Hill, there would never have been victory at Yorktown. In a tribute to this revolutionary history, during his filibuster Cruz wore a "COME AND TAKE IT" lapel pin.[29] But it may as well have been a coonskin cap.

---

[28] The cannon never made it to the Alamo, and was reportedly buried in a peach orchard outside of Gonzales. After a massive flood in 1936, a bronze cannon was discovered amid the washed-away soil. There is some dispute about whether that was in fact the original cannon, but the unearthed munition sits proudly in a museum in Gonzales. (The docent assured me on my visit that it was authentic!) *Gonzales Come and Take It Cannon*, TX STATE HISTORICAL ASS'N, perma.cc/95TN-S28V.

[29] *Ted Cruz Rocks a 'Come and Take It' Flag Pin on the Senate Floor*, TWITCHY (Sept. 25, 2013), perma.cc/8G5V-2CYG.

10.9. "PUSHING THE GOVERNMENT TOWARD SHUTDOWN"

At 12:55 PM on Wednesday, September 25, the Senate voted 100–0 to invoke cloture and begin debating the House bill.[30] This unanimous vote was no surprise. The day before, Cruz predicted the "vote to pass overwhelmingly, if not unanimously." This was by no means an endorsement of the House CR – which defunded Obamacare – but was the parliamentary process that allowed the Senate to vote on an amended CR. Over the next two days, senators could speak for or against the House bill. However, in order to end debate on the House bill, Senate Democrats needed sixty votes. If all of the Senate Republicans voted as a bloc, they could have prevented the Democrats from proceeding to amend the House bill. Had that happened, Senate Democrats would have been unable to strip out the provision defunding Obamacare. Unless a compromise was reached, no bill could have been sent to the president's desk, and funding for the government would have run out on September 30.

This, in effect, was the plan that Senators Cruz and Lee advanced throughout the summer. In his autobiography Cruz said he was "never Pollyannaish about what was possible about this plan."[31] Even if a veto could not be overcome to repeal the law in its entirety, "there were a lot of middle outcomes, where, if we united Republicans and put enough heat on red-state Democrats, Obama might feel enough political pressure to agree to some sort of compromise."[32] In other words, the Republicans might be able to extract some concessions if the Senate could not pass any CR and the president feared a shutdown. Something was better than nothing, Cruz thought.

However, if Republicans joined the Democrats, the Senate could then promptly strip out the provision that would defund Obamacare with a simple majority vote. Cruz explained during his filibuster, "[O]nce cloture is invoked, the rules of the Senate allow the majority leader to introduce the amendment to fund ObamaCare and then to have it pass with just fifty-one votes."

On September 27, at 12:29 PM – almost forty-eight hours after Cruz finished his speech – the Senate voted 79–19 to invoke cloture on the House CR and end debate.[33] Moments before the roll call, Senator Lee explained that "everyone knows that the vote we're about to take – cloture on the

---

[30] *U.S. Senate Roll Call Votes 113th Congress – 1st Session*, U.S. SENATE (Sept. 25, 2013), perma.cc/MS64-K4MJ.

[31] Cruz, *supra* note 15 at 4102.

[32] *Id.* at 4106.

[33] *U.S. Senate Roll Call Votes 113th Congress – 1st Session*, U.S. SENATE (Sept. 27, 2015), perma.cc/E2LJ-RXWD.

House-passed continued resolution – is essentially a vote to allow Democrats to gut the House bill. That's why every Senate Democrat is supporting it."[34] Twenty-five Republicans joined with fifty-four Democrats to vote "yea." In the end, nineteen Republicans – including Cruz, Lee, Paul, and Rubio – voted "nay."[35]

With debate on the House bill halted, Senate Democrats were immediately able to amend the House bill and propose a "clean" CR that funded the government in its entirety, including Obamacare. Only one hour later, at 1:31 PM, the Senate voted 54-44 for the "clean" CR.[36] This vote was straight down party lines, with fifty-four Democrats voting "aye" and forty-four Republicans voting "nay" (two Republicans were not present). Considering only the latter vote, it would appear that Republicans were unified in supporting the House bill to defund Obamacare. But in light of the earlier vote – which most analysts overlooked – twenty-five of those Republicans supported the parliamentary proceeding to allow the funding of Obamacare. In other words, if forty-four Republicans who voted against the latter proposal had also voted against the earlier proposal, the House bill could not have been amended. The latter vote is what Senator Cruz referred to as a "show vote" that Republicans can brag about back home, without taking a consequential stand.

After the vote, a triumphant Harry Reid had a message for the House: "This is it. Time is gone. They need to accept what we just passed."[37] President Obama had a similar message: "The House Republicans are so concerned with appeasing the Tea Party that they've threatened a government shutdown or worse unless I gut or repeal the Affordable Care Act. I said this yesterday; let me repeat it: That's not going to happen."[38]

After the Senate vote, the House was now faced with a choice. They could either approve the clean CR, which would go to the president for his signature, or pass a modified CR and send it back to the Senate. The House chose Door #2. Early in the morning of Saturday, September 29, the House GOP Caucus held a closed-door meeting. Conservatives pushed Speaker Boehner to support a CR that funded the government through December, but (1) delayed Obamacare for one year, (2) allowed employers to opt out of

---

[34] Alexander Bolton & Ramsey Cox, *Senate Defies Cruz, Strips Language Defunding ObamaCare*, THE HILL (Sept. 27, 2013), perma.cc/47YG-Z48A.

[35] *Id.*

[36] *U.S. Senate Roll Call Votes 113th Congress – 1st Session*, U.S. SENATE (Sept. 27, 2015), perma.cc/8DGE-NE3D.

[37] Stephen Dinan, *Senate Defeats Cruz Filibuster, Passes Bill that Funds Obamacare*, WASH. TIMES (Sept. 27, 2013), perma.cc/CRU5-AV3R.

[38] President Barack Obama, Statement by the President (Sept. 27, 2013), perma.cc/GXZ4-WLXN.

the contraceptive mandate, and (3) repealed the ACA's 2.3% tax on medical devices.[39]

At first, Boehner opposed the strategy. The Ohio Republican wanted to negotiate over Obamacare during the debt celling fight that would emerge on October 18. The plan was to fund the government but attach a one-year delay of the ACA to the debt ceiling bill. In early September, House Republican Whip Kevin McCarthy said that the debt ceiling fight is "the 'perfect' venue for an Obamacare battle."[40] However, conservative pressure was too strong. *National Review* reported that "chants of 'Vote! Vote! Vote!' echoed through the room."[41] Representative Matt Salmon (R-AZ) recalled, "People went bonkers."

Boehner capitulated and agreed to bring the new CR for a vote. After a full day of debate, at 12:16 AM on September 29, the House approved the CR that delayed Obamacare. The final vote was 231–192, with two Democrats crossing the aisle.[42] House Majority Leader Eric Cantor said, "We will do everything we can to protect Americans against the harmful effects of Obamacare. This bill does that. We're united in the House as Republicans." Cantor added, "Now it's up to the Senate Democrats to answer."[43]

The House CR was dead on arrival in the Senate. Reid said, "[T]o be absolutely clear, the Senate will reject both the one-year delay of the Affordable Care Act and the repeal of the medical device tax. After weeks of futile political games from Republicans, we are still at square one."[44] More pressingly, President Obama issued a veto threat for the House CR: "By including extraneous measures that have no place in a government funding bill and that the President and Senate already made clear are unacceptable, House Republicans are pushing the Government toward shutdown."

The House GOP leadership rejected the notion that their bill – which would fund the entire government, save Obamacare – would force a shutdown. "We will do our job and send this bill over," House GOP leaders said

[39] Pete Kasperowicz, *GOP Spending Bill Includes Language Targeting Birth Control Mandate*, THE HILL (Sept. 28, 2013), perma.cc/BFF2-Y2C3.

[40] Jonathan Strong, *House Leaders to Delay CR Vote*, NAT'L REV. (Sept. 11, 2013), perma.cc/JK24-YU88.

[41] Robert Costa & Jonathan Strong, *Battling Opponents on Both Sides of the Aisle, Boehner Struggles to Avert Shutdown*, NAT'L REV. (Sept. 30, 2013), perma.cc/4Q63-ARR6.

[42] *Final Vote Results for Roll Call 498*, U.S. HOUSE OF REPRESENTATIVES (Sept. 29, 2013), perma.cc/DUG2-Y5LX.

[43] Lori Montgomery, Paul Kane, Rosalind S. Helderman, *House GOP Pushes U.S. to Edge of Shutdown*, WASH. POST (Sept. 2013), perma.cc/U6JA-KLVC.

[44] *House Votes to Keep Government Open, Delay Obamacare by 1 Year*, FoxNEWS (Sept. 29, 2013), perma.cc/YWV9-AURW.

in a statement, "and then it's up to the Senate to pass it and stop a government shutdown."[45] Representative Phil Gingrey (R-GA) was asked what would happen after the Senate rejects the House CR. "It comes back to us, I guess," he replied. "We really didn't talk about exactly what the plan would be then."[46]

The final action would come down to the wire on September 30. At 2:03 PM, after only twenty-five minutes of debate, the Senate voted 54–46 for a clean CR that eliminated the Obamacare delay.[47] At 5:00 PM, President Obama scolded the House Republicans. "One faction of one party in one house of Congress in one branch of government doesn't get to shut down the entire government just to refight the results of an election. You don't get to extract a ransom for doing your job, for doing what you're supposed to be doing anyway, or just because there's a law there that you don't like."[48] Boehner summed up a ten-minute conversation he had with the president that night: "I'm not going to negotiate. I'm not going to negotiate."[49]

National Review reported that by Sunday evening, "pangs of fear were replacing those good spirits for many in the GOP. With a shutdown imminent, Boehner and his allies were scrambling to craft another eleventh-hour plan."[50] At 8:40 PM, the House voted 228–201 for a CR that delayed the individual mandate by one year.[51] Only twenty-six minutes later, at 9:06 PM, the Senate voted 54–46 (the same vote as earlier that day) to table, and thus reject, the House CR.[52]

That evening, Sylvia Matthews Burwell, head of the Office of Management and Budget – and future HHS Secretary – ordered federal agencies to "execute plans for an orderly shutdown due to the absence of appropriations."[53] At 11:45 PM, the literal eleventh hour, the House proposed a resolution that would request a conference with the Senate to negotiate over the budget. Reid rejected the proposal. "We will not negotiate with a gun to our head," he said.[54] The clock struck midnight.

[45] Susan Davis, *House GOP Votes to Delay Obamacare for One More Year*, USA Today (Sept. 29, 2013), perma.cc/GDY9-2VYG.

[46] *Edge of Shutdown*, *supra* note 43.

[47] Jonathan Weisman & Jeremy W. Peters, *Government Shuts Down Budget Impasse*, N.Y. Times (Sept. 30, 2013), perma.cc/5J9W-LSYG; *U.S. Senate Roll Call Votes 113th Congress – 1st Session*, U.S. Senate (Sept. 30, 2015, 2:03 PM), perma.cc/F6A8-QMYK.

[48] *President's Statement*, *supra* note 38.

[49] Weisman, *supra* note 47.

[50] Costa, *supra* note 41.

[51] *House Vote 504 – Passes Spending Bill with Individual Coverage Mandate Delay*, N.Y. Times (Sept. 30, 2013), nyti.ms/29zbohq.

[52] *U.S. Senate Roll Call Votes 113th Congress – 1st Session*, U.S. Senate (Sept. 30, 2015), perma.cc/E2LJ-RXWD.

[53] Weisman, *supra* note 47.

[54] Davis, *supra* note 45.

The notion of a government shutdown is something of a misnomer, because many services deemed "essential" remained funded.[55] National parks closed, but post offices remained open. Discretionary spending ceased, but "mandatory" spending such as Social Security and Medicaid checks continued. Ironically enough, one aspect of the federal government would continue unabated during the shutdown: Obamacare.

During his floor statement, Senator Cornyn noted the "ultimate irony" of the defunding strategy: "If we are to shut down the government because we refuse to pass a continuing resolution to keep the government operating, ObamaCare still gets funded." Senator Kelly Ayotte (R-NH) would later tell *Time*, "[T]he fact that the exchanges opened with the government shut down demonstrates on its face that [the defund strategy] was not going to succeed."[56] In July 2013, the Congressional Research Service predicted "that substantial ACA implementation might continue during a lapse in annual appropriations that resulted in a temporary government shutdown."[57] Unless Obamacare was repealed in its entirety, the law appropriated the funding the administration needed.

Specifically, the shutdown would not affect the individual mandate, nor would it halt the subsidies paid out on the exchange, because they are "permanently appropriated outside of the annual appropriations process."[58] Further, following HHS's 2012 "shutdown contingency plan," all "ACA implementation activities at [the Centers for Medicaid and Medicare Services] would continue because of the mandatory funding provided" by the law.[59] That includes the operation and "establishment of exchanges."[60] As discussed in Chapter 9, Secretary Sebelius deliberately assigned the implementation of HealthCare.gov to CMS because its mandatory funding was safe from Republicans and could not be defunded.[61] However fiscally prescient this decision was, the following morning it would prove to be a strategic blunder.

---

[55] Brad Plumer, *Absolutely Everything You Need to Know About How the Government Shutdown Will Work*, WASH. POST (Sept. 30, 2013), perma.cc/2PDB-TXCG.

[56] Jessica Taylor, *GOP Senator: Heritage in Danger of Not Amounting to 'Anything Anymore'*, MSNBC (Oct. 21, 2013), perma.cc/L6RH-AFGR.

[57] CONG. RESEARCH SERV., 7-5700, *Potential Effects of a Government Shutdown on Implementation of the Patient Protection and Affordable Care Act* (2013), bit.ly/1TMLF5m.

[58] *Id.* at 9.

[59] *Id.* at 5.

[60] DEP'T OF HEALTH & HUMAN SERVS, *Contingency Staffing Plan for Operations in the Absence of Enacted Annual Appropriation* (2008), bit.ly/1NlXbWa.

[61] Amy Goldstein & Juliet Eilperin, *HealthCare.gov: How Political Fear Was Pitted against Technical Needs*, WASH. POST (Nov. 2, 2013), perma.cc/E5FT-JARS.

10.10. "THE LAUNCH WILL BE TOTALLY ANTI-CLIMACTIC"

As September 30 drew to a close and October 1 began, most eyes in Washington were focused on the impending government shutdown. But October 1 would also mark the opening of the Affordable Care Act's state and federal exchanges, which would allow people to purchase subsidized insurance. Shortly after Senator Cruz finished his filibuster, Senator Max Baucus, who had previously warned that the implementation of the ACA was a "train wreck," looked forward. "We are full steam ahead on implementing the Affordable Care Act. In six days, the health exchanges will open for business and the Affordable Care Act kicks in."

On the eve of the launch of HealthCare.gov, Secretary Sebelius predicted, "We're about to make some history."[62] She added that tomorrow "is not the end of anything; it is the beginning." In an interview three months earlier, Sebelius was asked what was going to happen on the launch day. She replied, "I'm sure there will be operational challenges in the opening of the markets, but I think we're trying to build in redundancies and be able to respond very rapidly. And we see October 1 as the beginning of the campaign that lasts for six months."[63] Pressed, she conceded that the deadlines are "very tight," but "all systems are a go for the first of October."[64]

White House Deputy Senior Adviser David Simas downplayed the October 1 launch date, noting that the entire month would be "light for enrollment": "Some people will sign up. November will be a little better. December, when people can sign up and know they get coverage in a week or two weeks, will be better than the previous month."[65] Gary Cohen, a senior HHS official, explained that "we may encounter some bumps when open enrollment begins but we'll solve them."[66] Marilyn Tavenner, the CMS administrator, was similarly confident. Tom Scully, a former Medicare administration and longtime colleague of Tavenner, who "talked to Marilyn a lot before the rollout," said she "seemed pretty confident it would work."[67]

---

[62] Wynton Hall, *Sec. Sebelius: 'We're About to Make Some History'*, BREITBART (Sept. 30, 2013), perma.cc/W2VX-F8P6.

[63] Sandhya Somasshekhar, *Exclusive: Kathleen Sebelius on Obamacare's 'Very Tight' Deadlines*, WASH. POST (Jul. 26, 2013), perma.cc/RL5L-WZZZ.

[64] *Id.*

[65] Sarah Kliff, *How the White House Thinks About the Obamacare's Launch*, WASH. POST (Sept. 28, 2013), perma.cc/L3DZ-JYNL.

[66] Christopher Weaver, et al., *Pricing Glitch Afflicts Rollout of Online Health Exchanges*, WALL ST. J, (Sept. 19, 2013), on.wsj.com/24B0KMc.

[67] Sarah Kliff, *Medicare Chief Marilyn Tavenner to Testify Before Congress about HealthCare. gov*, WASH. POST (Oct. 28, 2013), perma.cc/DZE4-M567.

Denis McDonough, the White House Chief of Staff, told one friend the day before the launch, "[W]hen we turn it on tomorrow morning, we're gonna knock your socks off."[68]

Many pundits predicted that the launch would be a smashing success. *Slate* blogger Matthew Yglesias set out his position starkly: "I wanted to once again take the opportunity to lay down a marker and say once again that Obamacare implementation is going to be a huge political success."[69] He added, "[C]onservatives are certainly fooling themselves if they're expecting a backlash driven by problems around implementation ... Snafus will be real enough, but broadly speaking, the rollout is going to be a huge success."[70] *New York Times* columnist Paul Krugman wrote that a successful Obamacare would be "the right's worst nightmare."[71] Jonathan Cohn wrote in the *New Republic* that "Republicans and conservative intellectuals keep seizing on setbacks – some real, some imagined – and predicting that Obamacare will be a catastrophe. They are almost certainly wrong."[72] Sarah Kliff concluded at *Wonkblog* that the "launch will be totally anti-climactic."[73]

[68] David Martosko, *Revealed: How Obama Considered SCRAPPING Healthcare.gov Website Just 16 Days After Its Disastrous Launch*, DAILY MAIL (Feb. 27, 2014), perma.cc/S6DA-368S.

[69] Matthew Yglesias, *Obamacare's Going to Be Great*, SLATE (Jul. 17, 2013), perma.cc/XY9P-JZLA.

[70] Matthew Yglesias, *Obamacare Skeptics Are Deluding Themselves*, SLATE (Jul. 16, 2013), perma.cc/7UGA-X5S3.

[71] Paul Krugman, *Obamacare Is the Right's Worst Nightmare*, N.Y. TIMES (Jul. 17, 2013), perma.cc/5LR8-VPDT.

[72] Jonathan Cohn, *The Obamacare Train Still Hasn't Wrecked*, NEW REPUBLIC (Jul. 18, 2013), perma.cc/3Y47-3VH3.

[73] Sarah Kliff, *Obamacare's Launch Will Be Totally Anti-Climactic*, WASH. POST (Sept. 30, 2013), perma.cc/M5TE-4ZRZ.

PART IV

Obamacare Unravels
(October 1, 2013–December 30, 2013)

11

Lights Out

11.1. "6 ENROLLMENTS"

At 12:01 AM on October 1, 2013, the federal government closed. In a cosmic coincidence, at the exact same moment, HealthCare.gov opened for business. Or at least it was supposed to. One of the first visitors was Jon Tucci of West Virginia, who stayed up till midnight to sign up. The site, however, would not load. "I've applied for a lot of things," Tucci said, "and there are always glitches. But this was totally disappointing."[1] Following several attempts, the registered Democrat and Obama supporter called it a night. After getting some shuteye, he tried again at 6:00 AM. Still no luck. Tucci called the customer service number. After forty-five minutes on hold, the agent read from a script, put him on hold, and disconnected the call. "I'm just really frustrated," Tucci explained. His experience was not a fluke. On the first day, the site was inaccessible.

In the early hours of the launch, the White House announced that HealthCare.gov was flooded with nearly five million visits. The malfunction, the administration claimed, was the "product of overwhelming traffic."[2] The homepage of HealthCare.gov was soon replaced with a graphic that read "We have a lot of visitors on the site right now. Please stay on this page."

The next day, Sarah Kliff wrote at *Wonkblog* that "Obamacare's biggest problem right now isn't glitches. It's traffic."[3] She added, "I don't tend to think these initial glitches will have a significant impact on the law's success." Indeed, some speculated that Obamacare opponents may be deliberately

---

[1] Sarah Kliff, *Signing up for Obamacare: 'This Was Totally Disappointing.'*, WASH. POST (Oct. 1, 2013), perma.cc/2SPH-R558.

[2] Sarah Kliff, *Obamacare's Biggest Problem Right Now Isn't Glitches. It's Traffic.*, WASH. POST (Oct. 2, 2013), perma.cc/LTM3-P8VF.

[3] *Id.*

sabotaging the site by flooding it with traffic, in what is known as a distributed denial of service (DDoS) attack. Brian Beutler of the liberal *Salon* speculated that the "early stories about problems with healthcare.gov and other exchange sites around the country don't suggest sabotage … yet."[4]

Secretary Sebelius called for patience: "We're building a complicated piece of technology, and hopefully you'll give us the same slack you give Apple."[5] The president offered a similar message. "Consider that just a couple of weeks ago," Obama explained, "Apple rolled out a new mobile operating system, and within days, they found a glitch, so they fixed it." The government should at least get as much slack as a Steve Jobs–inspired gadget. "I don't remember anybody suggesting Apple should stop selling iPhones or iPads or threatening to shut down the company if they didn't," Obama added.[6] Not everyone was persuaded. ACA pundit, Ezra Klein retorted, "If Apple launched a major new product that functioned as badly as Obamacare's online insurance market-place, the tech world would be calling for [CEO] Tim Cook's head."[7]

After two nerve-wracking days without any verified signups, under a graphic of a unicorn leaping in front of rainbow, Klein's Wonkblog reported that they have "been on a hunt for this mythical creature," but have not found any.[8] Later that day, the Obamacare poster child emerged – and he was straight out of central casting. Twenty-one-year-old Chad Henderson of Georgia claimed that he was able to successfully enroll on HealthCare.gov.[9] Henderson, who supported President Obama, claimed that his decision to sign up after mid-night was to help the law succeed: "I've read a few articles about how young people are very critical to the law's success," he said. "I really just wanted to do my part to help out with the entire process." Signing up, he recalled, took about three hours. After creating an account, "it was pretty smooth sailing," Henderson said.

---

[4] Brian Beutler, *How Republican Idiocy Backfired – and Is Helping Obamacare*, SALON (Oct. 2, 2013), perma.cc/8RUQ-9464.

[5] Matthew Yglesias, *Sebelius: "Give Us the Same Slack You Give Apple*," SLATE (Oct. 1, 2013), perma.cc/Z3SZ-H933.

[6] Ian Schwartz, *Obama Likens Obamacare to Apple's iPhone: "I Don't Remember Anybody Suggesting Apple Should Stop Selling iPhones*," REAL CLEAR POLITICS (Oct. 1, 2013), perma.cc/E3PA-7WJT.

[7] Ezra Klein & Evan Soltas, *Wonkbook: Obamacare's Web Site Is Really Bad*, WASH. POST (Oct. 4, 2013), perma.cc/EXC2-BUE4.

[8] Sarah Kliff, *The White House Says People Have Bought Obamacare. We Haven't Met Them Quite Yet*, WASH. POST (Oct. 3, 2013), perma.cc/R9AD-7S3W.

[9] Sarah Kliff, *Meet Chad Henderson, the Obamacare Enrollee Tons of Reporters Are Calling*, WASH. POST (Oct. 3, 2013), perma.cc/JMP3-NHB4.

His signup went viral. The DNC outreach group Organizing for Action (formerly Obama for America) retweeted Henderson's account as an ACA success story.[10] Alas, it was too good to be true.[11] Chad's father, Bill, told Peter Suderman of the libertarian *Reason Magazine* that his son did not actually enroll in a plan on HealthCare.gov. Chad soon confessed that he chose which plan he wanted to buy but did not actually purchase it yet.[12] The slacktivist insisted that he had not "misled anyone."[13]

It soon became apparent that the problem was not a deluge of traffic, or a lack of capacity. Even when customers were able to access the site, they could not sign up. A person who worked on the exchange told the *New York Times*, "They kept looking, looking, looking, but there wasn't anybody moving through the system."[14] Internally, the administration entered panic mode. On October 1, a senior adviser at the Centers for Medicare and Medicaid Services (CMS) sent her staff an e-mail with a subject line celebrating "2 enrollments!" – one in North Carolina and one in Ohio.[15] Notes from the CMS "War Room" morning meeting on October 2 revealed that there were "6 enrollments ... spread across 5 issuers."[16] On the first day, only six people nationwide signed up.[17]

After October 1, the President convened meetings almost every day, but they could not compile "actionable intel" about the cause of the failures.[18] One senior White House adviser who attended recalled that "those meetings drove the President crazy. Nobody could even tell us if the system was up as we were sitting there, except by taking out laptops and trying to go on it."[19] Meetings at CMS's war room in Baltimore were described as a trip to a "war zone."

A senior Obama adviser told Steven Brill that they could blame traffic only for so long. "For the fourth day in a row" they were saying it was "volume

---

[10] @obamacare, Twitter (Oct. 1, 2013, 5:56 PM), bit.ly/2717fu5.

[11] Kyle Cheney, *ACA Enrollee Gets 5 Minutes of Fame*, POLITICO (Oct. 4, 2013), perma.cc/JV3U-RQ4D.

[12] Sarah Kliff, *Is Obamacare's Celebrity Enrollee Actually Signed Up?*, WASH. POST (Oct. 4, 2013), perma.cc/2ZC3-TQ5A.

[13] *Id.*

[14] Sheryl Gay Stolberg & Michael D. Shear, *Inside the Race to Rescue a Health Care Site, and Obama*, N.Y. TIMES (Nov. 20, 2013), nyti.ms/1TMT3gR.

[15] *Healthcare.gov Rollout Stats – 90*, JUDICIAL WATCH (May 19, 2014), perma.cc/KGJ4-JWA8.

[16] *CCIIO-Wide War Room Notes 10.2.13 AM*, Oversight & Gov't Reform, bit.ly/1TMT4la.

[17] Sarah Kliff, *Obamacare's Launch Looked Even Worse from the Inside*, WASH. POST (Oct. 31, 2013), perma.cc/GX7X-6X3U.

[18] Steven Brill, *TIME: Obama Considered 'Scrapping' ObamaCare Site and 'Starting Over' After Disastrous Launch*, FOXNATION (Feb. 28, 2014), perma.cc/72RB-YLYJ.

[19] *Id.*

and it'll get better in a day or two."[20] That excuse was "not going to work next week," they realized. It definitely "wasn't going to work if and when the government shutdown drama ended and the crashed web site became the country's top story."[21] During an uncomfortable press conference on October 3, White House Press Secretary Jay Carney announced that people had been able to sign up, but would not give a number. "We don't have the data," Carney said.[22] Had he revealed that six people signed up nationwide, it would have been an embarrassment. Four days later, the White House revealed that enrollment numbers would not be released until November, at the earliest.[23]

11.2. 1-800-FUCKYO

Despite the failed launch of the site, the Obama administration continued its marketing campaign. To reach millenials – an essential demographic – Sebelius appeared on *The Daily Show with Jon Stewart*. It did not go well. Stewart skewered Sebelius and HealthCare.gov. At one point, the host pulled out a laptop, and said, "We're going to do a challenge. I'm going to try and download every movie ever made and you are going to try to sign up for Obamacare – and we'll see which happens first."[24] Sebelius could only muster an uncomfortable laugh. "How many people have signed up?" Stewart asked. "I can't tell you because I don't know," she replied. As the studio audience laughed, the host frowned. "The Democrats are as good as the Republicans at doing a shutdown," Stewart said. A White House political adviser told Steven Brill that the interview "was like watching one of those fights where the ref takes too long to step in and the guy gets carried out on a stretcher."

Late-night comedians had a field day with the launch. Jay Leno joked on *The Tonight Show*, "A friend of mine was given six months by his doctor. Not to live, to sign up for Obamacare." Jimmy Kimmel piled on: "If you are in need of health care, you have two options: you can wait for them to get the

---

[20] STEVEN BRILL, AMERICA'S BITTER PILL: MONEY, POLITICS, BACKROOM DEALS, AND THE FIGHT TO FIX OUR BROKEN HEALTHCARE SYSTEM 349 (Random House Trade Paperback ed. 2015).

[21] *Id.*

[22] Sarah Kliff, et al., *'A Trickle, Not a Wave:' What Insurers Are Seeing in Obamacare Enrollment*, WASH. POST (Oct. 3, 2013), perma.cc/KX7F-V6CJ.

[23] Jake Tapper, *Obama Administration: No Obamacare Enrollment Numbers Until November at Earliest, Volume Is Problem on Website*, CNN (Oct. 7, 2013), perma.cc/L2BD-5CWD.

[24] Lucy McCalmont, *Sebelius Gets the Stewart Treatment*, POLITICO (Oct. 8, 2015), perma.cc/W4HD-GXZ2.

site fixed, or you can enroll in medical school and graduate, and then just take care of yourself, which will probably be faster."

The Saturday Night Live sketch about HealthCare.gov was closer to truth than satire.[25] Kate McKinnon, portraying Kathleen Sebelius, explained that the site was "overloaded from traffic," but "unfortunately it was designed only to handle *six* users at a time."[26] Ironically, that was the exact number of people who signed up on the first day. And in one of the more subtle digs at President Obama, the Sebelius character encouraged customers to visit *Kayak*, "where you can purchase airline tickets to Canada and buy cheaper prescription drugs." Conan O'Brien joked that the toll-free number for Obamacare was "1-800-We Didn't Think This Through." Once again, the truth was stranger than fiction: HealthCare.gov's toll-free number (800-318-2596) spells 1-800-FUCKYO.[27]

Perhaps the most enduring image on HealthCare.gov was the smiling woman prominently featured on the homepage. Dubbed the "enigmatic Mona Lisa of health care," the anonymous model was mocked and ridiculed.[28] Stephen Colbert called her the "vaguely ethnic smiling woman."[29] Conservative blogger David Burge tweeted that she is the "most despised face on the planet."[30] On October 27, HHS took down her photograph and replaced it with a generic graphic offering advice of how to sign up.[31] But who was she?

On November 13, the face of Obamacare came forward. A Marylander named Adriana appeared on *Good Morning America*. The saga began innocuously enough. She responded to an e-mail from HHS, which offered to take free head shots in exchange for using them on the new health care exchange. Adriana was never paid for the photographs. A spokesperson from HHS explained that the individuals who were photographed "understood

---

[25] *Obamacare Website Tips*, Saturday Night Live (Oct. 26, 2013), bit.ly/1VN69yf.

[26] Kirsten Acuna, *Here's the 'SNL' Skit that Correctly Predicted How Few Users Would Sign Up for Obamacare*, Bus. Insider (Nov. 1, 2013), perma.cc/8CRM-K8UR.

[27] Duane Patterson, *Obamacare's National Hotline? 1-800-F...You*, Hot Air (Oct. 2, 2013), perma.cc/J4W4-VFC8.

[28] Mark Memmott, *HealthCare.gov's Mystery Lady Says She's Been Cyberbullied*, NPR (Nov. 13, 2013), perma.cc/CKH2-4VWL.

[29] Katla McGlynn, *Heartbroken Colbert Seeks 'Vaguely Ethnic' Woman Missing from Obamacare Website*, Huffpost Comedy (Oct. 29, 2013), perma.cc/S43U-5KZW.

[30] Tara Brady, *Obamacare Girl Vanishes! Mysterious Woman Who Was the Face of New Scheme Is Suddenly Taken Down as the Hunt for Her Goes Wild*, Daily Mail (Oct. 27, 2013), perma.cc/PF28-DEXL.

[31] Sarah Kliff, *Goodbye, HealthCare.gov Lady. We Barely Knew You*, Wash. Post (Oct. 27, 2013), perma.cc/2LZQ-8FC6.

how their images would be used."[32] During the interview, Adriana explained how she was the victim of cyberbullying.[33] "I'm here to stand up for myself," she said, "and defend myself and let people know the truth." Contrary to some rumors, the Colombian was a lawful permanent resident, and was thus eligible for Obamacare. However, she did not attempt to sign up on HealthCare.gov.[34]

11.3. "IT'S AWFUL, JUST AWFUL"

As Obamacare's first week progressed, there were a few glimmers of hope. By the fourth day, some "marathon shoppers" who repeatedly checked the site were able to purchase a policy.[35] Carl Bidelman, a sixty-three-year-old from San Francisco, enjoyed a beer in triumph: "I had to take a moment and celebrate finally getting this done."[36] Additionally, several of the state exchanges functioned as designed. Shortly after its launch, Robyn J. Sckrebes in Minnesota managed to sign up for insurance in about two hours using the state-run exchange. She said the policy was "affordable" and "good coverage," but perhaps most importantly, the "web site of the Minnesota exchange was pretty simple to use, pretty straightforward."[37] Other states also reported early successes. After the first week, 28,000 applications were completed in California, and 40,000 signed up in New York.[38]

Perhaps the gold standard of all the exchanges was in Kentucky. Governor Steve Beshear, a Democrat, sought to separate President Obama – who was very unpopular in the Commonwealth – from the health care law: "My message to Kentuckians is simply this. You don't have to like the president; you don't have to like me. Because this isn't about him, and it's not about me. It's about you, your family and your children. So do yourself a favor. Find what you can get for yourself. You're going to like what you find."[39] Early on, Brandon Hardy of Louisville managed to sign

[32] Brill, *supra* note 20 at 273.

[33] Abd Phillip, *Exclusive: Obamacare's Mystery Woman Says She Fell Victim to Cyberbullies*, ABC News (Nov. 13, 2013), bit.ly/1Ohh8Ik.

[34] Joe Coscarelli, *Everything We Now Know about Adriana, the Obamacare Woman*, N.Y. Mag. (Nov. 13, 2013), nym.ag/25GNUOo.

[35] Sarah Kliff, *For Some Shoppers, Buying Obamacare Is Turning into a Marathon*, Wash. Post (Oct. 4, 2013), perma.cc/9AUW-LMALl.

[36] *Id.*

[37] Robert Pear & Abby Goodnough, *Uninsured Find More Success Via Health Exchanges Run by States*, N.Y. Times (Oct. 8, 2013), nyti.ms/1VN6qRG.

[38] Juliet Eilperin, et al., *Many Remain Locked Out of Federal Health-care Web Site*, Wash. Post (Oct. 8, 2013), perma.cc/Y8VH-7F65.

[39] Trip Gabriel, *A Governor's Last Campaign: To Prove Health Law Works*, N.Y. Times (Oct. 19, 2013), nyti.ms/1ryXEuc.

up on *Kynect* in less than forty-five minutes.[40] After three weeks, 11,000 people had signed up in the only southern state to establish its own exchange.

This success was not mirrored by the federal exchange, which would soon become the most pressing issue facing the administration. As early as October 4, Ezra Klein observed that "according to a number of designers ... the site is badly coded."[41] On October 5, *Reuters* interviewed five technology experts who asserted that "flaws in system architecture, not traffic alone, contributed to the problems."[42] The following day, *The Wall Street Journal* reported that the site "appeared to be built on a sloppy software foundation."[43] By the middle of October, one insurance executive told the *New York Times*, "These are not glitches. The extent of the problems is pretty enormous. At the end of our calls, people say, 'It's awful, just awful.'"[44] Aetna CEO Mark Bertolini – an ACA advocate – appeared frustrated on CNBC's *Squawk Box*. "There's so much wrong, you just don't know what's broken until you get a lot more of it fixed."[45]

On October 15, President Obama met in the Oval Office with Vice President Biden, Chief of Staff Denis McDonough, HHS Secretary Kathleen Sebelius, and CMS Chief Marilyn Tavenner. *The New York Times* reported that for "90 excruciating minutes, a furious and frustrated president peppered his team with questions, drilling into the arcane minutiae of web design as he struggled to understand the scope of a crisis that suddenly threatened his presidency."[46] Fortunately for the president, attention was still focused on the shutdown. "With eyes glued on the shutdown this week," pundit Matthew Yglesias wrote at *Slate*, "HHS will have the chance to do fixes and anyone who can't log on today will just come back next week."[47]

11.4. "FURLOUGHED"

On the morning of October 1, as the Obama administration slowly began to realize that the federal health exchange was inoperable, 800,000 federal

[40] Pear, *supra* note 37.
[41] *Really Bad*, *supra* note 7.
[42] Sharon Begley, *Analysis: IT Experts Question Architecture of Obamacare Website*, Reuters (Oct. 5, 2013), perma.cc/L27Y-AUES.
[43] Christopher Weaver, et al., *Software, Design Defects Cripple Health-Care Website: Government Acknowledges Problems It Needs to Fix Design and Software Problems*, WALL ST. J. (Oct. 6, 2013), on.wsj.com/24Cnb3V.
[44] Stolberg, *supra* note 14.
[45] Ezra Klein, *Aetna CEO on Obamacare: 'There's so Much Wrong, You Just Don't Know What's Broken Until You Get a Lot More of It Fixed'*, WASH. POST (Oct. 15, 2013), perma.cc/5LE7-2RZ6.
[46] Stolberg, *supra* note 14.
[47] Yglesias, *supra* note 5.

employees stayed in their pajamas. They were furloughed, and on indefinite unpaid leave.[48] Roughly 1.3 million active military personnel would remain on the job but would not receive a paycheck.[49] Sixteen thousand FBI agents, deemed "essential" to protecting the country, would remain on the payroll. The same treatment extended to State Department employees, as well as Health and Human Services civil servants who worked on Medicare and Medicaid services. The U.S. Postal Service would stay open because it receives a permanent appropriation. Ultimately, all federal employees would receive back pay following the conclusion of the shutdown. In a rare bipartisan consensus, this bill passed the House 407–0. "This is not their fault and they should not suffer as a result," said Representative Elijah Cummings (D-MD).[50]

Meanwhile, members of Congress continued to receive their salary during the shutdown.[51] The annual congressional salary of $174,000 had been written into permanent law, and was unaffected by the shutdown.[52] Senator Barbara Boxer (D-CA) announced that she would sponsor a bill to block congressional salaries during the shutdown.[53] But such a provision would run afoul of the somewhat obscure Twenty-Seventh Amendment, which states: "No law, varying the compensation for the services of the Senators and Representatives, shall take effect, until an election of Representatives shall have intervened."[54] In other words, any change in congressional pay must take effect after the next election. The provision prevents Congress from increasing – or in this case decreasing – its own pay until the voters have a say.

The Supreme Court stayed open and was fully funded; judicial salaries are guaranteed by Article III of the Constitution. "The Judges, both of the supreme and inferior Courts, shall hold their Offices during good Behaviour,

---

[48] Michael S. Schmidt, et al., *Federal Agencies Lay Out Contingency Plans for Possible Shutdown*, N.Y. Times (Sept. 28, 2013), nyti.ms/29AnpDd.

[49] *Id.*

[50] Associated Press, *Federal Workers Will Get Back Pay after Shutdown, Congress and President Say*, PennLive (Oct. 5, 2013), perma.cc/S2QS-GCXM.

[51] Brad Plumer, *Congress Gets Paid during a Shutdown, While Staffers Don't. Here's Why*, Wash. Post (Oct. 1, 2013), perma.cc/H6GJ-LNWS.

[52] 95 Stat. 958 (Public Law 97-51 Oct.1, 1981), perma.cc/3D7A-DFHA.

[53] Alexis Levinson, *Obama, House Republicans Run Out Clock in Shutdown Staring Match*, Daily Caller (Sept. 30, 2013), perma.cc/A6K7-NVTG.

[54] This amendment was originally drafted by Representative James Madison in 1789, and was sent to the states for ratification. While today we like to think of the Second Amendment as the right to keep and bear arms, the original proposed Second Amendment that was sent to the states was this provision on congressional pay. The First Amendment had nothing to do with free speech or religion, but concerned the size of congressional districts. Neither of these two original amendments were ratified in 1791, while the *proposed* amendments 3 through 12

and shall, at stated Times, receive for their Services, a Compensation, which shall not be diminished during their Continuance in Office."[55] Justice Scalia explained it was not his business if the government shut down: "I have a deal with the Congress. I leave them alone. They leave me alone."[56]

11.5. "THE GERMANS COULDN'T STOP THEM"

Beyond the furloughed civil servants, the most visible effect of the government shutdown was the closure of all 401 national parks.[57] At 6:00 PM on September 30 – as House Republicans frantically tried to make a last-minute deal – the National Park Services erected barricades along the national mall at the World War II, Vietnam Veterans, Lincoln, and other memorials.[58] By the dawn's early light, hundreds of World War II veterans arrived in Washington, D.C. aboard the *Honor Flight*. This nonprofit organization transports veterans of foreign wars to visit the memorials dedicated in their honor. On the morning of October 1, a delegation from Mississippi arrived at the open-air World War II memorial, only to find that it was barricaded and closed to the public.

A sign warned, "Because of the federal government shutdown, all national parks are closed." A Park Services spokeswoman explained that "while the government is shut down, all of [these] events have to be canceled, including" the Honor Flight.[59] The concern was that trash and debris would pile up, and there were no personnel to remove it. "Without staff or funding to ensure the safety of visitors," she said, "the memorials on the National Mall – just like Yellowstone and the Grand Canyon – are closed."

The barriers posed no obstacle for the greatest generation. The octogenarians and their escorts pushed aside the barricades. "We just opened the gates," recalled Representative Steven Palazzo (R-MS), as we "allowed 91 World War II veterans to come see their monument that was erected in their honor."[60] One of the sponsors cheered the delegation. "The Japanese couldn't stop

---

became the *ratified* amendments 1 through 10. After a two-century gap, the second proposed amendment was ratified as the Twenty-seventh Amendment in 1992.

[55] U.S. CONST. art. III, § 1.

[56] Josh Blackman, *The Framers Made the Appointment Process Explicitly Political*, NAT'L REV. (Feb. 15, 2016), perma.cc/7S5J-DP5W.

[57] *The Government Shutdown and Your National Parks: What You Need to Know*, Nat'l Park Found., perma.cc/5RM8-7AZG.

[58] Mila Mimica, *Government Shutdown Closes National Mall, Monuments*, NBC WASH. (Oct. 1, 2013), perma.cc/Q6QX-UHB7.

[59] *Id.*

[60] Matthew Stabley, *Congressmen Move Barrier at World War II Memorial to Let Veterans See Their Monument*, NBC WASH. (Oct. 1, 2013), perma.cc/YGJ3-ZYV5.

them. The Germans couldn't stop them. Apparently, a little gate couldn't stop our veterans either."[61] Later that evening, one of the veterans arrived back home in Mississippi, holding a strip of yellow caution tape as a memento.[62]

As the shutdown progressed, the barricades at the World War II memorial became a political flashpoint. During another Honor Flight visit, Representative Randy Neugebauer (R-TX) confronted a Park Service officer who was blocking entry to the memorial. "How do you look at them," he asked, and "deny them access?"[63] The officer replied, "It is difficult. I'm sorry sir." Neugebauer charged back, "The Park Service should be ashamed of themselves." She replied, "I'm not ashamed."

An onlooker, who said he was a thirty-year federal employee, joined the fray. "This woman is doing her job, just like me. [But] I'm out of work." Neugebauer retorted that the reason she was out of a job was "because Mr. Reid decided to shut down the government." The civil servant charged back, "No, it's because the government won't do its job and pass a budget." Another spectator exclaimed, "The House did its job; it passed appropriations. The Senate hasn't." As the debate continued, Neugebauer walked away. Three years earlier, the Texas Republican made headlines when he shouted "baby killer" at Bart Stupak, as the pro-life Democrat explained why he was satisfied with President Obama's executive order protecting religious liberty.[64]

Soon, the Park Service announced a constitutional compromise: "The Honor Flights are being granted access to the WWII memorial to conduct *First Amendment activities* in accordance with National Park Service regulations applicable to the National Mall and Memorial Parks."[65] A paper sign clipped to the barricades in front of Memorial stated, "Because of the federal government shutdown, this National Park Service area is closed, except for 1st Amendment activities."[66] The veterans, exercising their First Amendment rights, were allowed entrance to the barricaded memorials.

---

[61] *Veterans Granted Access to Closed World War II Memorial*, NBC Wash. (Oct. 1, 2013), perma.cc/NYE9-9W6Q.

[62] *Id.*

[63] Mark Segraves, *Congressman Confronts Park Ranger Over Closed WWII Memorial*, NBC Wash. (Oct. 4, 2013), perma.cc/8SX4-8WAM.

[64] Mark Memmott, *Update: 'Baby Killer' Shouter Was Rep. Randy Neugebauer, R-Texas*, NPR (Mar. 22, 2010), perma.cc/8STJ-GAW6.

[65] Nicole Rossoll, Anneta Konstantinides, Matthew Larotonda & Jack Date, *World War II Veterans Prove Unstoppable, Entering Memorial*, ABC News (Oct. 2, 2013), bit.ly/29wWOVo (emphasis added).

[66] *WWII Memorial Closed "Except for 1st Amendment Activities*, Josh Blackman's Blog (Oct. 2, 2013), perma.cc/66Y7-CZ8R.

However, all other parks remained closed – even if states were willing to fund the attractions. Arizona Governor Jan Brewer offered to use state funds to keep the Grand Canyon open. The Obama administration rejected this offer.[67] The mayor of nearby Tusayan charged, "The administration just wanted the American people to feel the pain of the shutdown in a very visible way."[68]

The Park Service not only closed the entrance to Mt. Rushmore in South Dakota but also used yellow traffic cones to block the roadside viewing areas outside the park. "I just don't know what they're trying to accomplish," the South Dakota Secretary of Tourism said.[69] "They won't even let you pull off on the side of the [public] road."[70] The White House also rebuffed efforts by House Republicans to fund the World War II Memorial and Mount Rushmore during the shutdown.[71] The editors of *National Review* referred to the closure of the national parks as "act of political theater, a gross and possibly illegal abuse of political power ... and a wanton subjugation of responsible governance to the political interests of President Obama and his party."[72] *The Atlantic* observed that the "National Park Service closures have become the most visible face of the shutdown."

Initially, the White House refused to accept any piecemeal funding solution and insisted on funding the entire government at once or nothing at all. By October 10 – after much public pressure – the administration reached an agreement to allow states to temporarily fund national parks. Through a payment of $61,000 a day, New York governor Andrew Cuomo arranged to reopen the Statue of Liberty and Ellis Island in New York Harbor.[73]

---

[67] *Government Shutdown: Arizona Gov. Jan Brewer Rejected in Offer to Reopen Grand Canyon*, ABC 15 Arizona (Oct. 3, 2013), perma.cc/U72Z-NZ37.

[68] Aamer Madhani, *GOP Asks: Why Were National Parks Shut Down, Anyway?*, USA Today (Oct. 16, 2013), perma.cc/BMD3-6BC9.

[69] The Editors, *Vindictive Shutdown Theater*, NAT'L REV. (Oct. 7, 2013), perma.cc/7TDB-GN2P.

[70] *Id.*

[71] Garance Franke-Ruta, *How the National Parks Became the Biggest Battleground in the Shutdown*, ATLANTIC (Oct. 11, 2013), perma.cc/6N5T-RQQL.

[72] *Vindictive Shutdown*, *supra* note 69. Two scholars proposed that Congress should amend federal appropriation law so that during a government shutdown, the public is inconvenienced as little as possible. For example, spending is reduced, but national parks stay open and federal employees are not furloughed. John O. McGinnis & Michael B. Rappaport, *How to End the Government Shutdown Option*, WALL ST. J. (Dec. 29, 2014), on.wsj.com/1Ttc318.

[73] Michael Virtanen, *Statue of Liberty to Reopen Amid Government Shutdown as Feds, State Reach Agreement*, ASSOCIATED PRESS (Oct. 12, 2013), perma.cc/4ARL-UYW5. In New Jersey v. New York, the Supreme Court held that Ellis Island was closer to the Jersey Shore, and thus belonged to the Garden State. 523 U.S. 767 (1998).

(That is roughly the cost of two nights at the Four Seasons Penthouse in Manhattan.)[74]

NBC News interviewed several of the Honor Flight veterans and asked what they thought of the shutdown situation. "It is absurd," one replied. "There is no compromise. It's ridiculous."[75] Another added that "fighting the bureaucracy of Congress" is tougher than fighting the Axis powers.[76] The memorials became a microcosm for the maelstrom that was Washington, D.C.

11.6. "WILL NOT NEGOTIATE"

Before the shutdown began, President Obama insisted that he would not negotiate over the budget. On October 5, President Obama told the Associated Press, "We know that there are enough members in the House of Representatives – Democrats and Republicans – who are prepared to vote to reopen the government. The only thing that is keeping that from happening is Speaker Boehner has made a decision that he is going to hold out to see if he can get additional concessions from us."[77] Boehner described a meeting at the White House with Reid, Pelosi, and McConnell. The president "reiterated one more time tonight," Boehner related, "that he will not negotiate."[78] President Obama told Republicans that "there is one way out."[79] Fund the government. In his autobiography, Senator Cruz describes "one of the most bizarre meetings" he attended at the White House. The president entered the room, and said, "I just want you to know I will not negotiate. I will not compromise. I will not give in on anything. The government will remain shut down until you agree to everything I want."[80]

As each day elapsed – with federal employees furloughed and parks closed – pressure began to mount on Republicans. *The Wall Street Journal* quoted an unnamed senior administration official who said the White House was not concerned with the government shutdown. "We are winning … It doesn't really matter to us" how long the shutdown lasts "because what matters is

---

[74] Emily H. Bratcher, *World's Most Expensive Hotel Rooms*, U.S. NEWS & WORLD REPORT (Dec. 8, 2010), bit.ly/1UHwb5w.

[75] Stabley, *supra* note 60.

[76] *Id.*

[77] *Back Pay, supra* note 50.

[78] Carol E. Lee & Peter Nicholas, *White House's Hard Line on Shutdown, Debt Ceiling Has Risks Attached*, WALL ST. J. (Oct. 4, 2013), on.wsj.com/24yY8lw.

[79] *Id.*

[80] TED CRUZ, A TIME FOR TRUTH: REIGNITING THE PROMISE OF AMERICA 4213 (Kindle Ed. 2015).

the end result." A furious Boehner replied to the comment: "This isn't some damn game."[81]

Within the Senate GOP Caucus, the ire increased toward Senator Cruz. *Politico* reported that in a closed-door meeting, one unnamed Republican senator told the Texan, "The president gets up every day and reads the newspaper and thanks God that Ted Cruz is in the United States Senate."[82] Senator John Boozman (R-AR) reportedly "tore apart Cruz" and said "he was making GOP senators seem like they were for Obamacare when they had fought so hard to torpedo it." Perversely, during the shutdown, as the web site imploded, the popularity of the law increased. The percentage of Americans who thought Obamacare was a "good idea" increased from 31% in September to 38% in October.[83] Ezra Klein would later write that Congress's "decision to shut down the government on the exact day the health-care law launched was a miracle for the White House."[84] Klein mused that if Ted Cruz "didn't exist, Democrats would have to invent him."[85]

The polls reflected that the president's position was getting stronger. A *CBS News* Poll on October 4 showed that 44% of respondents blamed the shutdown on Congressional Republicans, while 35% blamed President Obama and the Democrats.[86] One week later, an *NBC/WSJ* poll found that the public blamed the GOP for the shutdown by a 53% to 31% margin over the president and the Democrats.[87] This was "a wider margin of blame for the GOP than the party received during the poll during the last shutdown in 1995–96."[88] Also setting an all-time low, only 24% of respondents had a favorable opinion of the Republican Party. Perhaps most importantly, respondents favored a Democratic-controlled Congress for the 2014 elections by eight points, 47% to 39% – up from three points the month before. These numbers would turn out to be ephemeral. In 2014, Republicans *expanded* their advantage in the House, and took the Senate with a net gain of nine seats.

---

[81] *Back Pay, supra* note 50.

[82] Manu Raju, et al., *Anatomy of a Shutdown*, POLITICO (Oct. 18, 2013), perma.cc/H28A-UQE5.

[83] Mark Murray, *NBC/WSJ Poll: Shutdown Debate Damages GOP*, NBC NEWS (Oct. 10, 2013), perma.cc/TNN8-CU28.

[84] Ezra Klein, *Five Thoughts on the Obamacare Disaster*, WASH. POST (Oct. 14, 2013), perma.cc/H9YL-

[85] Ezra Klein, *If Cruz Didn't Exist, Democrats Would Have to Invent Him*, WASH. POST (Oct. 16, 2013). perma.cc/5W2K-PST9.

[86] Murray, *supra* note 83.

[87] *Id.*

[88] *Id.*

11.7. "THE BYSTANDER PRESIDENT"

As President Obama held the stronger hand in the negotiations over the shutdown, he realized his administration had effectively folded on the design of HealthCare.gov. The White House needed to turn the implementation around as soon as possible. "Nobody's madder than me about the website not working as well as it should," Obama said, "which means it's going to get fixed."[89] "We failed at ... launch," he later told Steven Brill.[90] During the presidential campaign, Obama recalled, he "could simply say, 'who are the best folks out there, let's get them around a table, let's figure out what we're doing and we're just going to continue to improve it and refine it and work on our goals.'"[91] This did not work within the massive federal bureaucracy.[92]

President Obama later subjected himself to "some Monday morning quarterbacking."[93] He conceded that "the federal government has not been good at this stuff in the past" and "two years ago" his administration "might have done more to make sure that we were breaking the mold on how we were going to be setting this up."[94] The contrite president admitted, "But that doesn't help us now." The *Washington Post* observed that "the cool and cerebral chief executive, whose reliance on smart people and rational analysis has been at the foundation of his often-insulated governing style, has been forced to admit that he and his team vastly underestimated the challenge of implementing the Affordable Care Act."[95]

Sebelius took complete responsibility. "Hold me accountable for the debacle," she testified before Congress. "I'm responsible."[96] Sebelius added, "I was not informed directly that the Web site would not be working the way it was supposed to. Had I been informed, I wouldn't be going out saying, 'boy, this is going to be great.'"[97] Representative Fred Upton (R-MI) charged that "either

[89] Greg Botelho, *HHS Chief: President Didn't Know of Obamacare Website Beforehand*, CNN (Oct. 23, 2013), perma.cc/5BYK-8WRQ.
[90] Brill, *supra* note 20 at 386.
[91] President Barack Obama, Statement by the President on the Affordable Care Act (Nov. 14, 2013), perma.cc/94RH-JYC4.
[92] *Transcript: President Obama's Nov. 14 News Conference on the Affordable Care Act*, WASH. POST (Nov. 14, 2013), perma.cc/SZN8-CXD7.
[93] *Id.*
[94] *Id.*
[95] Dan Balz, *For Obama, the Last Campaign May Be the Most Difficult*, WASH. POST (Nov. 14, 2013), perma.cc/B5HZ-JS6Z.
[96] Sarah Kliff, et al, *Sebelius on Health-care Law Rollout: Hold Me Accountable for the Debacle. I'm Responsible.*, WASH. POST (Oct. 30, 2013), perma.cc/7T43-SFSG.
[97] Kevin Bogardus & Jonathan Easley, *Before O-Care Debacle, Sebelius Made Many Trips to White House*, THE HILL (Feb. 13, 2014), perma.cc/44A3-C7R6.

those officials did not know how bad the situation was, or they did not disclose it."[98] On October 30, after three hours of Sebelius testifying before the House Energy and Commerce Committee, HealthCare.gov crashed on the computer in the hearing room. "Please try again later," the screen displayed. Sebelius would later explain on *Meet the Press* that this moment was her "lowest point," and was a "pretty dismal time."[99]

Senator Baucus (D-MT) heaped blame onto the White House: "It has been disappointing to see members of the administration say they didn't see the problems coming."[100] In December 2013, Baucus revealed that he had a "flash of anger" over the botched rollout, and blamed Sebelius for delivering only "platitudes. The more I asked the more concerned I became."[101] On day fourteen, Ezra Klein acknowledged the launch was a "failure" of "stunning ... magnitude," and not "trouble" or a "glitch."[102] He queried whether "anybody [is] going to be held accountable? Is anybody going to be fired? Will anyone new be brought in to run the cleanup effort? Does the Obama administration know what went wrong, and are there real plans to find out?"[103]

Did Sebelius know when the president first learned "there was a problem?" "No, sir," she told CNN's Dr. Sanjay Gupta.[104] Sebelius insisted that the president did not know about any of the problems before October 1.[105] White House Press Secretary Jay Carney told reporters, "While we knew that there would be some glitches, and actually said publicly that we expected some problems, we did not know until the problems manifested themselves after the launch that they would be as significant as they turned out to be."[106] Neither Carney nor Sebelius addressed McKinsey's briefing to the president in March 2013, which warned of "a materially high risk of system instability."[107]

---

[98] *The Obamacare Finger-Pointing Chart*, NAT'L J., perma.cc/J6EN-PEGL.

[99] Josh Blackman, *Sebelius on her "Low Point,"* Josh Blackman's Blog (Apr. 13, 2014), perma.cc/L54E-STH2.

[100] Chuck Todd, *Exclusive: Obama Personally Apologizes for Americans Losing Health Coverage*, NBC NEWS (Nov. 7, 2013), perma.cc/EQR2-5RN3.

[101] Sheryl Gay Stolberg, *Baucus, Conflicted Architect of Health Overhaul, Is Obama's Pick for China*, N.Y. TIMES (Dec. 18, 2013), nyti.ms/29rGdYI.

[102] *Five Thoughts, supra* note 84.

[103] *Id.*

[104] Botelho, *supra* note 89.

[105] *Id.*

[106] Jay Carney, Press Secretary, Press Briefing by Press Secretary Jay Carney (Oct. 23, 2013), perma.cc/4SSJ-3228.

[107] John Whitesides, *The Painful Path to Obamacare Deadline*, Reuters (Dec. 24, 2013), perma.cc/6893-ZPRY; Justin Sink, *Obama Was Aware of Report on Healthcare Website's Problems*, THE HILL (Nov. 19, 2013), perma.cc/2TDS-YM32.

The *Washington Post* highlighted how the President's inattention to details "has left him knowing too little at times about issues that matter the most to his legacy ... Obama's broad-stroke view of government and the insular West Wing he runs seem more like liabilities than benefits, raising questions about how much information Obama wants and how he receives it."[108] In a detailed exposé, based on interviews with dozens of administration officials, the *New York Times* observed that the "most perilous moments in Mr. Obama's presidency ... reveals an insular White House that did not initially appreciate the magnitude of its self-inflicted wounds, and sought help from trusted insiders as it scrambled to protect Mr. Obama's image."[109] Citing the web site launch and other instances where the president claimed he was unaware of issues within his own administration, the GOP dubbed Obama *the Bystander President.* "Scandal after scandal, Obama sings the same tune: he is always the last to know."[110]

Obama only offered a subtle defense of his HHS Secretary: "Kathleen Sebelius doesn't write code," the president explained. "She wasn't our IT person."[111] But she was not out of the woods. *The New York Times* observed that the next four months would form Sebelius's "slow-motion resignation," where she "largely stay[ed] out of the national limelight but crisscross[ed] the country in a furious effort to enroll people in health insurance."[112] Calls on her to step down immediately were unlikely to succeed because the president would have been unable to timely appoint a replacement in the face of fierce Republican opposition.[113]

At a tense White House meeting on October 15 – the day before the shutdown would end – President Obama directed his aides to tell the public "yes, the web site is screwed up."[114] The White House Director of Communications explained that once the government reopened, all of the attention would turn to the website: "We knew that we were a little bit on borrowed time."[115]

---

[108] Evan Soltas, *Wonkbook: The End of 'If You Like Your Plan, You Can Keep It'*, WASH. POST (Oct. 30, 2013), perma.cc/23Q2-K23A.

[109] Stolberg, *supra* note 14.

[110] *The Bystander President*, GOP (Oct. 28, 2013), perma.cc/9X5Y-6GSA.

[111] Todd, *supra* note 100.

[112] Michael D. Shear, Jackie Calmes & Robert Pear, *Sebelius's Slow-Motion Resignation From the Cabinet*, N.Y. TIMES (Apr. 11, 2014), nyti.ms/1Wfbj6S.

[113] David Hawkings, *Sebelius' Tenure as Obamacare Overseer Hangs with Vulnerable Democrats*, ROLL CALL (Oct. 23, 2013), perma.cc/7C6R-ZTWL.

[114] Stolberg, *supra* note 14.

[115] *Id.*

11.8. "ECONOMIC SHUTDOWN AROUND THE WORLD"

Beyond the ongoing government shutdown, Republicans faced another impending deadline. The Treasury Department calculated that on October 17, the United States would reach its congressionally capped credit limit. Breaching the so-called *debt ceiling* would force the federal government to reprioritize its spending and default on certain debts. President Obama warned that breaching the debt ceiling "would be far more dangerous than a government shutdown. It would effectively be an economic shutdown, with impacts not just here, but around the world."[116] Repeating his refrain from the shutdown fights, Obama insisted, "There will be no negotiations over this."[117]

Over the past five decades, each president and Congress have made some budgetary concessions before increasing the debt ceiling.[118] Speaker Boehner recalled that "during the Clinton administration, there were three fights over the debt limit." More recently, before raising the debt ceiling in 2011, President Obama agreed to automatic spending reductions – known as *the sequester* – as a compromise with Republicans. Boehner said the House would not "raise the debt limit without a serious conversation about dealing with problems that are driving the debt up. It would be irresponsible of me to do this." But on this occasion, President Obama drew a line in the sand and refused to provide any concessions.

During the early days of the shutdown, House Republicans passed a series of mini-spending bills that would have funded the National Institutes of Health, the National Park Services, the Food and Drug Administration, and other specific federal programs. The Democratic-controlled Senate refused to consider any piecemeal funding bills. One House bill would have restored pay for "essential" federal workers. It drew a veto threat from President Obama because it "does nothing to solve the immediate, pressing obligations the Congress has to open the Government and pay its bills."[119] The only vote the president wanted was a "straight up or down vote on" the *clean* Senate bill "to reopen the Government [and] bring all the Nation's dedicated civil servants back to work."

---

[116] Lori Montgomery, Paul Kane & Rosalind S. Helderman, *House GOP Pushes U.S. to Edge of Shutdown*, WASH. POST (Sept. 29, 2013), perma.cc/Z4M8-MS2T.

[117] Lee, *supra* note 78.

[118] Kevin Bohn, *Debt Ceiling Hikes Included Policy Ideas in the Past*, CNN – Political Ticker (Oct. 7, 2013), perma.cc/RK5Q-M7J9.

[119] Presidential Statement of Administration Policy in Disapproval of H.J. Res. 89 & H.R. 3273 (Oct. 8, 2013), bit.ly/1SSXcRv.

On October 10, with only a week before reaching the debt ceiling, Speaker Boehner proposed a six-week extension of the debt limit. Senate Majority Leader Reid promptly rejected the proposal, and insisted that Democrats would not negotiate. On October 12, Senator Susan Collins (R-ME) proposed a deal that would end the shutdown, lift the debt ceiling, and delay the Affordable Care Act's medical device tax. Senator Reid rejected it, countering with a bill to raise the debt limit through the end of 2014, without any concessions. Senate Republicans voted together to deny cloture on the bill.[120]

Three days later, House Republicans proposed a bill that would fund the government through December 2013, extend the debt ceiling through February 2014, and eliminate health care subsidies for members of Congress.[121] This last GOP effort to extract any meaningful concessions did not garner enough support for a majority vote, let alone enough to invoke cloture.

The shutdown would come to a head on October 16 at 8:15 PM. By a vote of 81–18, the Senate approved a *clean* bill to fund the government through January 15 and extend the debt ceiling through February 7.[122] Among the eighteen voting "nay" were Senators Cruz, Lee, Paul, and Rubio. The final Senate bill made no concessions for Republicans other than improving income verification for Obamacare enrollees. Rather than auditing every applicant, however, all the compromise required was that HHS must submit a report to Congress that explains the procedures to verify eligibility for subsidies.[123] This measure, designed to prevent fraud, was effectively "meaningless."[124] In his autobiography Senator Cruz wrote that "the Republican Senate leadership agreed to fund Obamacare in exchange for ... nothing."[125]

Less than two hours later, at 10:15 PM, the House voted to approve the Senate bill 285–144, with eighty-seven Republicans crossing the aisle to vote "yes."[126] After announcing the deal, House Speaker John Boehner said, "We'll live to fight another day."[127] At 12:30 AM on October 17, President Obama

---

[120] *Senate Vote 216 – S.1569: On Cloture on the Motion to Proceeds S. 1569*, N.Y. Times (Oct. 12, 2013), nyti.ms/1Nm7w4n.

[121] John Welsman, *House Republicans Look to Vote on New Bill*, N.Y. Times (Oct. 15, 2013), perma.cc/7XDB-HAW2.

[122] *Senate Vote 219 – Approves Budget Compromise*, N.Y. Times (Oct. 16, 2013), nyti.ms/1Tt6i3y.

[123] Sarah Kliff, *The GOP's Income Verification 'Concession' is Meaningless*, Wash. Post (Oct. 17, 2013), perma.cc/D8FJ-KWTA.

[124] *Id.*

[125] Cruz, *supra* note 80 at 4219.

[126] *House Vote 550 – Passes Senate Budget Compromise*, N.Y. Times (Oct. 16, 2013), nyti.ms/24z18yp.

[127] Ben Jacobs, *House Republicans Throw in the Towel*, Daily Beast (Oct. 16, 2013), perma.cc/UC79.

signed the bill into law, ending the shutdown and raising the debt ceiling. With the federal government reopened and the debt ceiling raised, all eyes turned to HealthCare.gov.

11.9. "MOST PAINFUL PRESS BRIEFING WE'VE EVER SEEN"

On the afternoon of October 17, White House Secretary Jay Carney faced the press corps to discuss the status of Obamacare.[128] One question after another highlighted errors plaguing the site. "A question on Obamacare," Brianna Keilar of CNN asked. "My colleague created a login and a user name on HealthCare.gov on October 9. She's still unable to use the web site." Carney, talking over the question, replied, "There are certainly issues with the web site and people have been working 24/7, around the clock to resolve them and make the consumer experience better." Keiler shot back, "So when is it done?" Carney answered that we were only "seventeen days into a 182-day period." Keilar inquired further: "Who is held accountable for the failure of" the website? Carney dodged the question: "The people who are responsible for making it work are hard at work fixing the problems."

Ed Henry of *Fox News* pressed, "Short of somebody being fired, what kind of accountability will there be?" Carney answered, "What I can tell you is the accountability the President seeks today is the accountability that comes from those who are working on implementation." And the same line of questioning continued. Steven Brill reported that one senior Obama aide called it "probably the most painful press briefing we've ever seen ... It was like one of those scenes out of *The West Wing* where everyone's yelling at him."[129]

Just as the shutdown was resolved, and the administration was getting a handle on the website, the next major crisis emerged – the cancellation of millions of health insurance policies, in direct conflict with the president's promise that people can keep the policies they like.

---

[128] Jay Carney, Press Secretary, Press Briefing by Press Secretary Jay Carney (Oct 17, 2013), perma.cc/CC4J-9FVH.

[129] Brill, *supra* note 20 at 353.

12

Cancelled

12.1. "TECH SURGE"

Two weeks after the launch of HealthCare.gov, President Obama had to decide whether the exchange could be fixed, or if it should be scrapped to start over.[1] The White House soon tapped Jeffrey Zients to lead the initial assessment effort. The veteran business consultant, previously nominated to lead the Office of Management and Budget, had a reputation as a problem solver who could get things done. After a preliminary review, Zients determined that HealthCare.gov was "fixable," and there was no need to start from square one.[2] He acknowledged that "it will take a lot of work, and there are a lot of problems that need to be addressed."[3] After putting together a prioritized list of items to fix – known as a *punch list* – Zients promised to "punch them out one by one."[4]

On October 20, the HHS blog announced what would become known as the "tech surge."[5] The post explained, "Our team is bringing in some of the best and brightest from both inside and outside government to scrub in with the team and help improve HealthCare.gov." Zients, who was already on board at that point, would be directing the surge. Joining Zients was Michael Dickerson, a site reliability engineer from Google, who wanted to "actually mak[e] a difference."[6] The president would later praise the

[1] Steven Brill, *Obama's Trauma Team*, TIME (Mar. 10, 2014), bit.ly/1Rk4cpO.
[2] Dominic Rushe, *Obama Appoints Jeffrey Zients to Fix Healthcare Website*, GUARDIAN (Oct. 25, 2013), perma.cc/9VX4-7GZW.
[3] *Id.*
[4] *Id.*
[5] HHS.gov, *Doing Better: Making Improvements to HealthCare.gov* (Oct. 20, 2013), perma.cc/AD57-2WAT.
[6] Sheryl Gay Stolberg and Michael D. Shear, *Inside the Race to Rescue a Health Care Site, and Obama*, N.Y. TIMES (Nov. 30, 2013), nyti.ms/1MERH2E.

"folks at Google and Facebook and Twitter and all these amazing firms who really wanted to find some way to engage in public service."[7] While the announcement of the surge brought to mind an army of engineers storming the Potomac in barges, there were only about six engineers who took leave to work on the site. One of the geeks admitted, "Surge was probably an overstatement."[8] These half-dozen coders would accomplish in a month what hundreds of contractors and hundreds of millions of dollars failed to achieve in a year.

The following day – three weeks after the launch of HealthCare.gov – the president spoke to the nation from the Rose Garden.[9] Obama was introduced by Janice Baker, who was the first person in Delaware to enroll through the marketplace. In a thirty-minute address, the president admitted that the website "hasn't worked as smoothly as it was supposed to work." Ezra Klein called this an "understatement."[10] Obama admitted, "Nobody is madder than me about the fact that the Web site isn't working as well as it should, which means it's going to get fixed." To fix the problems, the president said, "experts from some of America's top private-sector tech companies ... [are] offering to send help." Obama officially referred to this Silicon Valley influx as the "tech surge." He was confident that "we will get all the problems fixed."

The new approach was a significant change. Amy Goldstein wrote in the *Washington Post* that the president's remarks "represent a slight strategic shift for an administration that has repeatedly refused to say publicly exactly what is wrong with the site or what is being done to fix it."[11] Not everyone was impressed by the new direction. On *The Daily Show*, host Jon Stewart lampooned the notion of the tech surge. "A surge?" the comic asked.[12] "Your website is so fucked up, we have to use the same strategy that we used to salvage the Iraq war?"

---

7   Robert Safian, *President Obama: The Fast Company Interview*, FAST COMPANY (June 15, 2015), perma.cc/FSP7-3NJH.

8   *Stolberg, supra* note 6.

9   *Remarks by the President on the Affordable Care Act*, WHITE HOUSE (Oct. 21, 2013), perma.cc/2H4L-ZHMF.

10 Ezra Klein, *Obama's Speech Underplayed Obamacare's Problems. But It Doesn't Matter*, WASH. POST (Oct. 21, 2013), perma.cc/6FP7-6NFJ.

11 Amy Goldstein, *Healthcare.gov's Glitches Prompt Obama to Call in More Computer Experts*, WASH. POST (Oct. 20, 2013), perma.cc/6WDK-R7LT.

12 Peter Weber, *Watch the Daily Show Get in on the ObamaCare-bashing*, WEEK (Oct. 22, 2013), perma.cc/F4B5-MSNY.

12.2. "MILLIONS OF AMERICANS ARE CONTENT WITH THEIR HEALTH CARE COVERAGE"

Chapter 1 introduced the paradox of health care reform. When President Obama was elected, roughly 80% of Americans wanted to reform the health care system, but the same percentage of Americans were happy with their existing coverage. Herein lies the paradox: Americans would support reform for everyone else only if they were assured they could keep the health insurance they like. Of course, these dual promises are impossible to reconcile. HillaryCare's downfall in 1994, as illustrated by the "Harry and Louise" ads, was caused by a valid fear that health insurance policies would be cancelled.

President Obama acknowledged the paradox in his speech at the American Medical Association's annual conference in June 2009 – nine months before the enactment of the ACA.[13] "I know that there are millions of Americans who are content with their health care coverage," Obama said, and "they like their plan and, most importantly, they value their relationship with their doctor." Addressing the auditorium filled with thousands of doctors – a necessary constituency to support the law – he stressed, "They trust you." In order to sell the ACA, the president understood that he had to protect that relationship.

Because of that important bond, "no matter how we reform health care," Obama said, "we will keep this promise to the American people: If you like your doctor, you will be able to keep your doctor, period." The auditorium boomed with applause.[14] "If you like your health care plan, you'll be able to keep your health care plan, period." The applause rang out again. "No one will take it away, no matter what." This was the central guarantee that assuaged concerns and paved the way for health care reform. Without this essential promise, ObamaCare would have likely suffered the same demise as HillaryCare two decades earlier.

Throughout late 2009 and early 2010, as the Affordable Care Act (ACA) was being debated, the president repeated this promise nearly verbatim on two-dozen occasions. During his weekly address on June 6, he stated the message succinctly: "If you like the doctor you have, you can keep your doctor, too. The only change you'll see are falling costs as our reforms take hold."[15] Five days later at a town hall in Green Bay, Wisconsin, he said it again. "No matter how we reform health care, I intend to keep this promise: If you like

---

[13] *Remarks by the President to the Annual Conference of the American Medical Association,* WHITE HOUSE (Jun. 15, 2009), perma.cc/N8JV-TUQT.

[14] *Obama Health Care Law Violates Constitution, Conscience & His Own Promises,* YOUTUBE (Feb. 16, 2012), bit.ly/21Ga5Rf.

[15] *Weekly Address: President Obama Outlines Goals for Health Care Reform,* WHITE HOUSE (Jun. 5, 2009), perma.cc/2ZEU-8S4R.

your health care plan, you'll be able to keep your health care plan."[16] At a press conference on June 23, Obama said, "If you like your plan and you like your doctor, you won't have to do a thing. You keep your plan. You keep your doctor."[17] From the Rose Garden on July 15, the president promised, "If you like your doctor or health care provider, you can keep them."[18]

At a July 16 rally in New Jersey for Governor Jon Corzine, the president repeated, "If you've got health insurance, you like your doctor, you like your plan, you can keep your doctor, you can keep your plan. Nobody is talking about taking that away from you."[19] During his weekly address on July 18, the president explained that "under our proposals ... if you like your current insurance, you keep that insurance. Period, end of story."[20] Again from the Rose Garden on July 21, Obama said, "Let me repeat that: If you like your plan, you'll be able to keep it."[21] In Shaker Heights, Ohio, on July 23, the president promised that the ACA will give "you the option to keep your coverage if you're happy with it."[22] At a July 29 town hall in Raleigh, North Carolina, the president said "I have been as clear as I can be. Under the reform I've proposed, if you like your doctor, you keep your doctor ... These folks need to stop scaring everybody. Nobody is talking about you [being forced] ... to change your plans."[23]

One week later during his weekly address, he reiterated that "under the reforms we seek, if you like your doctor, you can keep your doctor."[24] In a discussion on the ACA at a town hall meeting in Portsmouth, New Hampshire, on August 11, the president told the crowd, "Under the reform we're proposing, if you like your doctor, you can keep your doctor."[25] Three days later at a town

---

16   *A Town Hall, and a Health Care Model, in Green Bay*, WHITE HOUSE (Jun. 11, 2009), perma.cc/QJ5X-EBH6.

17   *Press Conference by the President, 6-23-09*, WHITE HOUSE (Jun. 23, 2009), perma.cc/XLF3-332T.

18   *Remarks by the President on Health Care Reform*, WHITE HOUSE (Mar. 3, 2010), perma.cc/7TSP-7GKQ.

19   *Remarks by the President at Rally for Governor Jon Corzine*, WHITE HOUSE (Jul. 16, 2009), perma.cc/JCT5-GF84.

20   *Weekly Address: President Obama Says Health Care Reform Cannot Wait*, WHITE HOUSE (Jul. 17, 2009), perma.cc/C2F3-AGBX.

21   *Remarks by the President on Health Care and the Senate Vote on F-22 Funding*, WHITE HOUSE (Jul. 21, 2009), perma.cc/ZTH7-BY8P.

22   *Remarks by the President at Health Care Reform Town Hall*, WHITE HOUSE (Jul. 23, 2009), perma.cc/ZUP7-GT2D.

23   *Remarks by the President at Town Hall in Raleigh, North Carolina*, WHITE HOUSE (Jul. 29, 2009), perma.cc/39DA-AWAH.

24   *Weekly Address: President Obama Calls Health Insurance Reform Key*, WHITE HOUSE (Aug. 8, 2009), perma.cc/TRL6-AQB6.

25   *Remarks by the President at Town Hall on Health Insurance Reform in Portsmouth, New Hampshire*, WHITE HOUSE (Aug. 11, 2009), perma.cc/Z4FJ-S7EE.

hall in Montana – the home state of Senator Max Baucus – Obama assured the crowd that "this is not some government takeover. If you like your doctor, you can keep seeing your doctor. This is important."[26]

As August progressed, beyond simply making the promise, the president shifted to correcting what he viewed as misinformation being spread by the Tea Party and other conservative groups. On August 15, the president assured the American people, "No matter what you've heard, if you like your doctor or health care plan, you can keep it."[27] Later that day at a town hall in Colorado, he warned that "somehow folks aren't listening" to him, and reassured the crowd that "if you like your health care plan, you keep your health care plan."[28] At an August 20 event for his outreach group, Organizing for America, Obama said, "No matter what you've heard, if you like your doctor, you can keep your doctor under the reform proposals that we've put forward."[29] Two days later, during his weekly address, the president debunked "phony claims" about the bill that are "meant to divide us," and repeated that, "under the reform we seek, if you like your doctor, you can keep your doctor."[30]

During the period from September 2009 through February 2010 – as the ACA narrowly passed the Senate and was sent to the House – the president did not make a single statement about people being able to keep their plans. He returned to this message in March 2010 for the final three-week push to secure the votes in the House of Representatives. During this period, he made the promise seven times.

On March 3, Obama said, "If you like your doctor, you can keep your doctor. Because I can tell you that as the father of two young girls, I wouldn't want any plan that interferes with the relationship between a family and their doctor."[31] During his weekly address on March 6, he said, "What won't change when this bill is signed is this: If you like the insurance plan you have now, you can keep it ... Because nothing should get in the way of the relationship between a family and their doctor."[32] In two separate events in Missouri on

[26] *Remarks by the President in Town Hall on Health Care, Belgrade, Montana*, WHITE HOUSE (Aug. 14, 2009), perma.cc/37PN-RSMJ.

[27] *Weekly Address: President Obama Says Health Reform Will Put Patients' Interests Ahead of Insurance Company Profits*, WHITE HOUSE (Aug. 15, 2009), perma.cc/C7XK-SA6J.

[28] *Remarks by the President in Town Hall on Health Care Grand Junction Colorado*, WHITE HOUSE (Aug. 15, 2009), perma.cc/2R3A-FB9U.

[29] *Remarks by the President at the Organizing for America National Health Care Forum*, WHITE HOUSE (Aug. 20, 2009), perma.cc/6R6A-GJSL.

[30] *Weekly Address: President Obama Debunks "Phony Claims" about Health Reform; Emphasizes Consumer Protections*, WHITE HOUSE (Aug. 22, 2009), perma.cc/W8E4-DF8M.

[31] *Excerpts from the President's Remarks on Health Insurance Reform Today*, WHITE HOUSE (Mar. 3, 2010), perma.cc/Z2CY-GWSV.

[32] *Weekly Address: Health Reform Will Benefit American Families and Businesses This Year*, WHITE HOUSE (Mar. 6, 2010), perma.cc/3Y28-HDGR.

March 10, he repeated verbatim, "If you like your plan, you can keep your plan. If you like your doctor, you can keep your doctor."[33] He said much the same in Strongsville, Ohio, on the ides of March: "If you like your plan, you can keep your plan."[34] On March 19, three days before the ACA passed the House of Representatives, Obama repeated his promise, and added, "I don't believe we should give government or the insurance companies more control over health care in America. I think it's time to give you, the American people, more control over your health."[35]

On March 25, 2010 – three days after the ACA was signed into law – a triumphant President Obama appeared at a rally at the University of Iowa to chants of *Yes we can!* "You like your plan?" he asked the cheering crowd. "You'll be keeping your plan. No one is taking that away from you." Obama joked that in the future when Americans are "sitting in a doctor's office," reading old copies of *People* magazine, they will say, "Hey, this is the same doctor, same plan. It wasn't Armageddon."[36] A week later in Portland, Maine, Obama charged that his critics will "see that if Americans like their doctor, they will keep their doctor. And if you like your insurance plan, you will keep it. No one will be able to take that away from you. It hasn't happened yet. It won't happen in the future."[37] It would happen in the fall of 2013.

12.3. "GRANDFATHER CLAUSE"

One of the three pillars of the Affordable Care Act is the individual mandate. This provision required most Americans who earn above a certain income threshold to "maintain minimum essential coverage" after January 1, 2014.[38] In other words, their health insurance had to meet certain minimum thresholds established by the federal government, such as coverage for a wide range of medical services and no maximum lifetime limits. Failure to keep a policy

[33] *Remarks by the President on Health Insurance Reform in St. Charles, MO*, WHITE HOUSE (Mar. 10, 2010), perma.cc/QCT7-2YSM; *Remarks by the President at a Fundraising Dinner for Senator Claire McCaskill*, WHITE HOUSE (Mar. 10, 2010), perma.cc/NRD5-ZN2V.

[34] *Remarks by the President on Health Care Reform in Strongsville, Ohio*, WHITE HOUSE (Mar. 15, 2010), perma.cc/T4HJ-BR6W.

[35] *Remarks by the President on Health Insurance Reform in Fairfax, Virginia*, WHITE HOUSE (Mar. 19, 2010), perma.cc/66BY-WCUZ.

[36] *Remarks by the President on Health Insurance Reform, University of Iowa Field House, Iowa City, Iowa*, WHITE HOUSE (Mar. 25, 2010), perma.cc/73EU-BGEY.

[37] *Remarks by the President on Health Insurance Reform in Portland, Maine*, WHITE HOUSE (Apr. 1, 2010), perma.cc/ZY8L-H6T4.

[38] 26 U.S.C. § 5000A(a).

that meets all of these requirements would result in the payment of a penalty.[39]

In *NFIB v. Sebelius*, Chief Justice Roberts upheld the individual mandate, and its resulting penalty, as a constitutional tax.[40] The purpose of the individual mandate was twofold. First, it would incentivize millions of people to enter the insurance markets, in order to subsidize the high cost of caring for older and sicker people. Faced with the choice of paying the penalty, or paying for insurance, the government hoped younger and healthier people would choose the latter option. Second, it would ensure that Americans who already had insurance would receive a minimum level of coverage, and hopefully avert future, more serious medical problems. For example, cheap plans with sparse coverage, or a cap on how much the policy would pay, could leave people with extreme medical problems in financial ruin.

Purchasing substandard plans that did not meet this threshold would still subject a person to the individual mandate's penalty. As a result, insurance companies would abandon these thrifty policies for new customers. Shortly after the law was enacted, the question arose of what to do with customers who wanted to buy these thrifty plans before 2014. After some pressure from insurance companies, the administration agreed to a transition period that allowed noncompliant plans to continue to be sold through the end of 2013. This was something of a compromise. Jeanne Lambrew, whom President Obama put in charge of ACA implementation, wanted to eliminate these threadbare policies immediately. At a staff meeting Lambrew lambasted an insurance company that she "hate[d]" because it offered inexpensive, but stingy plans.[41] "They're bottom feeders," she said.[42] "But I guess we need them to stay in business until 2014."[43] Starting January 1, 2014, however, buying new plans that did not guarantee "minimum essential coverage" would still subject customers to the individual mandate's penalty.

The most significant debate, subject to vigorous "internal fights" within the White House, concerned how many of these inadequate plans that were purchased *before* 2014 would be grandfathered.[44] The Affordable Care Act left it to the executive branch to define what changes would result in a plan losing its

---

[39] 42 U.S.C. §§ 300gg–300gg-6, 300gg-8, 18011, 18011(1).

[40] For an extended discussion of the Court's holding in NFIB v. Sebelius, see JOSH BLACKMAN, UNPRECEDENTED: THE CONSTITUTIONAL CHALLENGE TO OBAMACARE 235-266 (2013).

[41] STEVEN BRILL, AMERICA'S BITTER PILL: MONEY, POLITICS, BACKROOM DEALS, AND THE FIGHT TO FIX OUR BROKEN HEALTHCARE SYSTEM 207 (Random House Trade Paperback ed. 2015).

[42] *Id.*

[43] *Id.*

[44] *Id.* at 146.

grandfathered status.[45] Lambrew did not want any of the incompatible policies to be grandfathered after the exchanges opened for business in 2014. According to Steven Brill, at one meeting she explained that "she hated the insurance companies," and "especially hated the insurers who sold those skimpy, often useless policies."[46] On day one, she said, "consumers needed to be protected. Period."[47] If a policy did not meet the standards for minimum essential coverage, Lambrew argued, it should be eliminated right away. Such an approach would be flatly inconsistent with the president's unqualified guarantee about keeping the policies people liked.

Senior advisers Larry Summers and Peter Orszag urged the president's communication team to qualify his "keep your insurance" promise to make clear that plans that were not good enough would be canceled.[48] But they refused. A former administration official told *The Wall Street Journal*, "You try to talk about health care in broad, intelligible points that cut through, and you inevitably lose some accuracy when you do that."[49] The official quipped that it "isn't a salable point" to promise "if you like your plan, you can probably keep it."[50]

The Obama administration quietly announced the strict grandfathering policy on page 34,552 of the June 17, 2010 edition of the *Federal Register* in an entry titled "Interim Final Rules for Group Health Plans and Health Insurance Coverage Relating to Status as a Grandfathered Health Plan under the Patient Protection and Affordable Care Act."[51] You are forgiven if you did not notice it at the time.

These regulations defined the grandfathering policy very narrowly, such that even the smallest changes – such as altering the amount of deductibles, the required copay, or the scope of benefits – would result in a loss of the grandfather status.[52] Philip Klein reported in the *Washington Examiner* that if an insurer made a fairly minor change to a policy – such as changing the amount enrollees must pay toward their own medical expenses from 10% to 11%, or

---

[45]   42 U.S.C. § 18011.

[46]   Brill, *supra* note 41 at 146.

[47]   *Id.*

[48]   *Id.* at 367.

[49]   Colleen McCain Nelson, *Peter Nicholas and Carol E. Lee, Aides Debated Obama Health-Care Coverage Promise*, WALL ST. J. (Nov. 2, 2013), on.wsj.com/1SpDfoA.

[50]   *Id.*

[51]   75 Fed. Reg. 34,538, 34,553 (June 17, 2010), perma.cc/YV5Q-DPF8. The implementing regulations are found in 29 CFR 2590.715-1251, perma.cc/62KW-DX93.

[52]   Lisa Myers and Hannah Rappleye, *Obama Admin. Knew Millions Could Not Keep Their Health Insurance*, NBC NEWS (Oct. 28, 2013), perma.cc/L4H3-HSNH.

adjusting the annual deductible or out-of-pocket limit – it could no longer be renewed.[53]

In the *Federal Register*, the government conservatively estimated that by the end of 2013, "66 percent of small employer plans and 45 percent of large employer plans will relinquish their grandfather status." Their high-end estimate predicted that 80% of small employer plans and 64% of large employer plans would lose their grandfather status. *NBC News* would later report that the White House knew that "50 to 75 percent of the 14 million consumers who buy their insurance individually" would receive cancellation notices "because their existing policies don't meet the standards mandated by the new health care law."[54]

The insurance companies were outraged by the new regulations. Karen Ignani, president of America's Health Insurance Plans, told the White House that the cancellations would "cause chaos" when people were cut off from their old plans toward the end of 2013.[55] Ignani, who had been the chief lobbyist to push for the enactment of the ACA, accurately predicted the controversies that would erupt in the October 2013 as cancellation notices were mailed to millions of Americans. An insurance executive told Steven Brill that "those regulations were written when the Obama people were riding high. They had all been having fun bashing the insurance companies, especially Lambrew. She thought those regs were a compromise. If it was up to her, she'd have killed all those plans in 2010, not 2014."

The White House deemed these cancellations a worthwhile sacrifice. After Ignani's complaints, Lambrew told Valerie Jarrett, senior advisor to the President, about the forecasted cancellations. But she assured Jarrett that "it was not a real issue – that the insurance people always complained about consumer-friendly regulations."[56] MIT economist Jonathan Gruber would later defend the narrow grandfathering provision, which he called a "deliberate policy decision."[57] He explained: "We've decided as a society that we don't want people to have insurance plans that expose them to more than six thousand dollars in out-of-pocket expenses."[58]

---

[53] Philip Klein, *6 Ways a Health Care Plan Can Lose Its 'Grandfathered' Status under Obamacare*, WASH. EXAM'R (Oct. 20, 2013), perma.cc/94NR-BYFA.
[54] Myers, *supra* note 52.
[55] Brill, *supra* note 41 at 206.
[56] *Id.* at 367.
[57] Ryan Lizza, *Obamacare's Three Per Cent*, NEW YORKER (Oct. 30, 2013), perma.cc/8QXX-2ZGQ.
[58] *Id.*

A White House communications official carped that Lambrew, "and the others who worked for her, had tin ears."[59] He added that they "weren't sensitive to the larger political arena where this was going to be played out."[60] That insensitivity put the White House in an "unforgivably bad, horribly stupid" situation that they "walked into … right after the website failure."[61]

Even after publishing the notice that millions would lose their policies, the Obama administration continued to repeat the unqualified promise. In a June 14, 2010 blog post, Secretary Sebelius wrote: "The bottom line is that under the Affordable Care Act, if you like your doctor and plan, you can keep them."[62] On June 28, 2012, hours after the Supreme Court upheld the ACA's individual mandate, a triumphant President Obama reassured everyone, "If you're one of the more than 250 million Americans who already have health insurance, you will keep your health insurance – this law will only make it more secure and more affordable."[63]

On the campaign trail, President Obama continued to extol the ACA's guarantee. At a July 16 event in the swing state of Pennsylvania, the once-again candidate assured the crowd, "If you have health insurance, the only thing that changes for you is you're more secure because insurance companies can't drop you when you get sick." A week later at a campaign event in Virginia Beach, Obama said, "If you already have health care, the only thing this bill does is make sure that it's even more secure and insurance companies can't jerk you around." During the first presidential debate in Denver on October 3, Obama challenged Mitt Romney's attack on the ACA: "If you've got health insurance, it doesn't mean a government takeover. You keep your own insurance. You keep your own doctor. But it does say insurance companies can't jerk you around."[64]

Robert Laszewski, a health care consultant, explained that as the president was repeating the promise, his administration "knew half the people in [the individual] market outright couldn't keep what they had and then they wrote the rules so that others couldn't make it either."[65] Less than a year later, the president's central promise would quickly unravel.

---

[59] Brill, *supra* note 41 at 367.

[60] *Id.* at 367-68.

[61] *Id.* at 368.

[62] Kathleen Sebelius, *Keeping the Plan You Like*, WHITE HOUSE (June 14, 2010), perma.cc/9JZT-C7BN.

[63] Remarks by the President on the Supreme Court Ruling on the Affordable Care Act, WHITE HOUSE (June 28, 2012), perma.cc/8VK6-WB7X.

[64] *Commission on Presidential Debates*, DEBATE TRANSCRIPT (Oct. 3, 2012), bit.ly/2a7QoOx.

[65] Myers, *supra* note 52.

12.4. "OBAMA LIED, MY HEALTH PLAN DIED"

In September 2013, conservative pundit Michelle Malkin received a notification from BlueCross BlueShield that her family's insurance would be canceled due to "changes from health care reform (also called the Affordable Care Act or ACA)."[66] The letter informed her that "[t]o meet the requirements of the new laws, your current plan can no longer be continued beyond your 2014 renewal date." Malkin's column captured what would become the new front in the war against Obamacare: "Obama lied, my health plan died."[67]

As September turned to October, and HealthCare.gov sputtered along, an unknown number of Americans began to receive cancellation letters similar to Malkin's.[68] On September 20, Representative Cory Gardner (R-CO) – who would be elected to the Senate in 2014 – tweeted, "Pres. said if u like ur healthcare u can keep it. I opted out of federal health care. My family's individual plan has been cancelled."[69] Gardner told Malkin that he declined the subsidized plan for members of Congress "because I wanted to be in the same boat as my constituents. And now that boat is sinking!" During a hearing with Secretary Sebelius, Gardner brandished his cancellation letter, which he held up as proof of the president's dishonesty.

Sebelius countered that these were not true cancellation notices, as everyone who received a letter was guaranteed to be able to find another policy. Before the ACA, she said, people were "on their own. They could be locked out, priced out, dumped out. And that happened each and every day. So this will finally provide the kind of protections that we all enjoy in our health care plans."[70]

The exact number of canceled policies remains unclear. A spokesman from America's Health Plan – the insurance industry's lobby – could not offer a precise number of how many letters were mailed.[71] Florida's BlueCross BlueShield projected that 300,000 customers would be affected.[72] In California, BlueShield and Kaiser Permanente withdrew a combined 280,000 policies from the market.

---

[66] Michelle Malkin, *Obama Lied, My Health Died*, MICHELLEMALKIN.COM (Sept. 25, 2013), perma.cc/6768-SRQ7.

[67] *Id.*

[68] Lori Ziganto, *Hey, Know What You Get To Keep With Obamacare? Cancellation Notices*, TWITCHY (Sept. 22, 2013), perma.cc/8PH7-RZGW.

[69] @SenCoryGardner, (Sept. 20, 2013, 10:36 a.m.), bit.ly/24zteta.

[70] David Firestone, *The Uproar over Insurance 'Cancellation' Letters*, N.Y. TIMES (Oct. 30, 2013), perma.cc/QH7U-MV8A.

[71] Myers, *supra* note 52.

[72] Alex Nussbaum, *Health Policies Canceled in Latest Hurdle for Obamacare*, BLOOMBERG (Oct. 30, 2013), perma.cc/KS3H-D3WD.

HighMark Health Services in Pittsburgh told 40,000 customers that their old plans would not be renewed. In the District of Columbia, Maryland, and Virginia, 70,000 customers of CareFirst had to find new policies.

In early November, the Associated Press estimated that the number was around 3.5 million Americans, but data was unavailable in half the states.[73] By December 26, the AP revised its estimate upward to 4.7 million Americans based on available data from thirty states.[74] The other twenty states did not offer the information, or were not keeping track of cancellations. A survey conducted by the Urban Institute in December 2013 – which did not analyze numbers from insurers – estimated that 2.6 million people had their policies canceled.[75] This range is consistent with the forecast the Obama administration made in its June 2010 regulation, narrowing the grandfathering clause.

On September 26, 2013 – a week after Gardner and Malkin received their cancellation notices – President Obama made what would turn out to be the final repetition of his guarantee. At an event in Largo, Maryland, Obama said that if you are one of the "85 percent of Americans [who] already have health insurance," then "it's reasonable that you might worry whether health care reform is going to create changes that are a problem for you." This was especially true "when you're bombarded with all sorts of fear-mongering." On the eve of the government shutdown, the president sought to assuage these fears: "So the first thing you need to know is this: if you already have health care, you don't have to do anything."[76]

12.5. "WE SHOULD HAVE KNOWN THIS WAS COMING"

As the cancellation notices streamed into mailboxes nationwide, once again Obama was "blindsided."[77] Steven Brill reported that the president had never been briefed on the grandfathering policy. According to a White House adviser, President Obama was "truly furious" and told everyone "this was a problem we brought on ourselves. We should have known this was coming."[78]

[73] Ricardo Alonso-zaldiva, *At Least 3.5 Million Americans Have Now Had Their Health Insurance Policies Canceled Thanks to Obamacare*, A.P. (Nov. 3, 2013), perma.cc/4QCR-2E27.
[74] *Policy Notification and Current Status, by State*, YAHOO FINANCE (Dec. 26, 2013), bit.ly/29W5J8n.
[75] Lisa Clemens-Cope and Nathaniel Anderson, *How Many Nongroup Policies Were Canceled? Estimates from December 2013*, HEALTH AFFAIRS BLOG (Mar. 3, 2014), bit.ly/29w2sIr.
[76] *Remarks by the President on the Affordable Care Act*, WHITE HOUSE (Sept. 26, 2013), perma.cc/8VH7-7XKN.
[77] Brill, *supra* note 41 at 367.
[78] *Id.* at 368.

Denis McDonough asked Lambrew about the cancellation crisis. She told them "it was not a big deal, that people would understand."[79] McDonough pressed the health care wonk for an estimate of how many policies would be canceled. She replied that she did not know an accurate number, because no one knew how many individual health insurance plans were in existence, let alone how many would be subject to the grandfathering requirements. McDonough soon discovered the estimate that Lambrew and Sebelius had published in the *Federal Register* three years earlier.

The White House entered into damage control mode, attempting to deflect the blame. Press Secretary Jay Carney was asked if the president misled people. He answered, "No," because people could keep the "grandfathered" policies. But "no health care reform" could maintain all plans as "grandfathered ... [as that] would undermine the basic premise of providing minimum benefits for the American people."[80] Others in the administration took a different approach. On the evening of October 28, senior advisor Valerie Jarrett threw the insurance industry under the bus. She tweeted, "FACT. Nothing in #Obamacare forces people out of their health plans. No change is required unless insurance companies change existing plans."[81] The *New York Times* reported that the tweet "touched a nerve," because the White House used the insurance companies as a "scapegoat."[82] One executive recalled thinking, "Here it comes – we knew it would happen."

12.6. "YOU COULD KEEP IT IF IT HASN'T CHANGED SINCE THE LAW WAS PASSED"

By the end of October, according to the *New York Times*, "the sense of crisis and damage control inside the White House peaked ... as the president's top aides began to fully grasp the breadth of the political challenges they faced."[83] On October 30, the president appeared in Boston at Faneuil Hall, where seven years earlier then-governor Mitt Romney signed RomneyCare into law. In this Revolutionary-era meeting place, Obama revised his promise: "For the *vast majority* of people who have health insurance that works, you can keep it," he explained. "If you had one of these substandard plans before the Affordable Care Act became law and you really liked that plan, you're able

---

[79] *Id.*
[80] Aaron Blake, *Carney: Obama Didn't Mislead on Keeping Insurance Plans*, Wash. Post (Oct. 29, 2013), perma.cc/J7N7-M9HA.
[81] Stolberg, *supra* note 6.
[82] *Id.*
[83] *Id.*

to keep it." However, "if insurers decided to downgrade or cancel these sub-standard plans, what we said under the law is you've got to replace them with quality, comprehensive coverage." In other words, if a policy was changed, it would no longer be grandfathered, and a customer could not keep it, no matter how much they liked it.

Acknowledging the growing unrest, Obama noted that "if you're getting one of those [cancellation] letters, just shop around in the new marketplace," and you'll "get a better deal." Further, echoing Sebelius's sentiments, the president contended that these cancellation notices were not actually that big of a deal. "Nobody is losing their right to health care coverage. And no insurance company will ever be able to deny you coverage, or drop you as a customer altogether. Those days are over."

On November 4, the president spoke to a group of ACA coalition partners three blocks from the White House at the St. Regis Hotel.[84] Obama further refined his long-standing promise: "Now, if you have or had one of these plans before the Affordable Care Act came into law and you really like that plan, what we said was you could keep it *if it hasn't changed since the law was passed.*" The last part was new. He added, "So we wrote into the Affordable Care Act you're grandfathered in on that plan" if it hasn't changed. At a December 2013 press conference, Obama claimed that "original intent of the grandfather clause that was in the law" was to help people "who get caught in that transition."[85] He added, "Obviously, the problem was [the grandfather clause] didn't catch enough people." Yet, Lambrew's parsimonious grandfather clause – of which the president was entirely unaware – made it even harder for plans to maintain their grandfather status.[86] Ultimately, the president would concede that enrollees "might have to switch doctors," but he said the trade-off is worth it because they are ultimately "saving money."[87] That wasn't the same as "if you like your doctor, you can keep your doctor."

Analysts quickly pointed out that the promise was never meant to be kept. Columnist Jonathan Chait acknowledged that the "promise that felt like a mere oversimplification at the time, and may eventually feel like one in retrospect, currently feels like a lie."[88] At *Wonkblog*, Sarah Kliff wrote the

[84] *Remarks by the President to ACA Coalition Partners and Supporters*, WHITE HOUSE (Nov. 3, 2013), perma.cc/F5T5-LN6V.
[85] *Press Conference by the President*, WHITE HOUSE (Dec. 20, 2013), perma.cc/RR9R-U8GF.
[86] *See* 45 C.F.R. § 147.140(g) (2010).
[87] Duentz, *Obama: You 'Might Have to Switch Doctors,'* TRUTH REVOLT (Mar. 14, 2014), perma.cc/Q7G2-5RXN.
[88] Jonathan Chait, *If You Like Your Plan, You Can Keep It. Well, Not Exactly*, DAILY INTELLIGENCER (Oct. 29, 2013), perma.cc/KS43-RXSA.

president's assurance was "a weird promise to make when one of the key goals of the health-care law is to change individual market insurance coverage."[89] MIT economist Jonathan Gruber was asked about the president's promise. He replied, "As a society [we have to] be able to accept that" those policies should be canceled to improve the overall marketplace.[90] "Don't get me wrong," Gruber said, the cancellations are a "shame, but no law in the history of America makes everyone better off."[91] Columnist Josh Barro agreed with the rationale behind not grandfathering old plans: "One of the key reasons that America needed health care reform is that a lot of existing health plans were bad. There are a lot of health plans that Americans shouldn't be able to keep."[92]

In the court of popular opinion, the widespread cancellation of policies rendered the original promise a lie. The *Washington Post* fact checker gave Obama "Four Pinocchios."[93] *Politifact* dubbed the president's promise the "Lie of the Year."[94] Reviewing each of the thirty-seven instances in which the president or someone from his administration made the promise, *Politifact* wrote that they never "offered the caveat that it only applies to plans that hadn't changed after the law's passage."[95] Moreover, seven of the promises came after Lambrew's regulations made clear that millions of policies would *not* be grandfathered.

The administration attempted to shield itself from criticisms of dishonesty by citing a brief disclaimer made by Kathleen Sebelius at a June 14, 2010 press conference.[96] Citing the president's promise, Sebelius answered a reporter's question about grandfathering and said, "If you have a plan that you like, you keep it."[97] She paused briefly. "But," Sebelius cautioned, "if indeed insurers or employers decide to make dramatic shifts, to the detriment of employees, huge cost shifts, huge increases in deductibles, slashing benefits, whatever, they then no longer qualify for the grandfather status, because that's really a change in the plan, and that isn't a plan that most people like very much."[98]

[89] Sarah Kliff, *This Is Why Obamacare Is Canceling Some People's Insurance Plans*, WASH. POST (Oct. 29, 2013), perma.cc/92FC-E6Y9,

[90] Lizza, *supra* note 57.

[91] *Id.*

[92] Josh Barro, *If You Like Your Health Plan. You Probably Shouldn't Be Able to Keep It*, BUSINESS INSIDER (Oct. 21, 2013), perma.cc/B9U3-Z5JH.

[93] Glenn Kessler, *Obama's Pledge that 'No One Will Take Away' Your Health Plan*, WASH. POST (Oct. 30, 2013), perma.cc/VMT8-3G2S.

[94] Louis Jacobson, *Barack Obama Says That What He'd Said Was You Could Keep Your Plan 'If It Hasn't Changed Since the Law Passed*,' Politifact (Nov. 6, 2013), perma.cc/8WDK-RUBE.

[95] *Id.*

[96] *Id.*

[97] *Health Reform: Grandfathering Your Current Insurance Plan*, YOUTUBE (Jun. 14, 2010), bit.ly/21GeSlM. A transcript of the press conference is available at Health Reform: *Grandfathering Your Current Insurance Plan (06/14/2010 Press Conference)*, perma.cc/Y6SJ-L23C.

[98] Jacobson, *supra* note 94.

The comment was picked up by the *Washington Post*, which quoted Senator McConnell as charging that the regulation "flatly contradicts the president's repeated promises."[99] Secretary Sebelius offered this tepid response: the president "wanted to make sure as much as possible that if people had plans that they liked they got to keep them and balance that with, you know, some overall protection for consumers."[100]

This was the *only* contemporaneous discussion that the White House could point to where the administration warned people about the potential cancellation of policies that lost their grandfather status. In light of the dozens of times that Obama and Sebelius insisted that people can keep their policies, *Politifact* concluded that Sebelius's "one mention of the extent to which grandfathered plans might be doomed strikes us as the equivalent of the fine print on a television commercial running in heavy rotation."

12.7. "I AM SORRY THAT THEY ARE FINDING THEMSELVES IN THIS SITUATION"

On November 7, the president sat down for an interview with Chuck Todd on *NBC News*. The future *Meet the Press* anchor asked Obama about the canceled policies.[101] At first, he deflected the question, explaining that people could keep their "subpar plans," but due to "churn in the markets," a "small amount of the population" will get cancellation letters. Todd asked directly, "Do you feel like you owe these folks an apology for misleading them? Even if you didn't intentionally do it?" In a very disjointed response for the characteristically articulate orator, Obama stumbled around an apology:

> You know – I regret very much that – what we intended to do, which is to make sure that everybody is moving into better plans because they want 'em, as opposed to because they're forced into it. That, you know, we weren't as clear as we needed to be – in terms of the changes that were taking place. And I want to do everything we can to make sure that people are finding themselves in a good position – a better position than they were before this law happened ... So – the majority of folks will end up being better off, of course, because the website's not working right. They don't necessarily know it right. But it – even though it's a small percentage of folks who may be disadvantaged, you know, it means a lot to them. And it's scary to them. *And*

---

99 David S. Hilzenrath and N.C. Aizenman, *New Health-Care Rules Could Add Costs, and Benefits, to Some Insurance Plans*, WASH. POST (Jun. 15, 2010), perma.cc/JC2K-KEED.
100 *Id.*
101 Sarah Kliff, *Video: Watch Obama (Kinda, Sorta), Apologize to Americans Losing Their Health Plans*, WASH. POST (Nov. 7, 2013), perma.cc/3V7F-QLT9.

I am sorry that they – you know, are finding themselves in this situation, based on assurances they got from me. We've got to work hard to make sure that – they know – we hear 'em and that we're going to do everything we can – to deal with folks who find themselves – in a tough position as a consequence of this.

Sarah Kliff wrote that the president did not actually apologize for the cancellations: "Eliminating certain health plans from the market – ones that the White House thinks are too skimpy – is a feature, not a bug, of the Affordable Care Act."[102] Ezra Klein added, "The answer is a bit of a dodge. People aren't finding themselves in this situation based on the president's promises. They're finding themselves in this situation based on his policy. And Obama isn't apologizing for the policy."[103]

The following month, the president stated his apology more coherently: "There is no doubt that the way I put that forward unequivocally ended up not being accurate," he said.[104] "It was not because of my intention not to deliver on that commitment and that promise. We put a grandfather clause into the law, but it was insufficient." Again, the president showed no awareness of the scope of Lambrew's restrictive grandfather clause.

The cancellations, combined with the botched launch of HealthCare.gov, seriously impacted President Obama's public standing. A November 20 *CBS News* poll found that in the span of one month, the ACA's favorability dropped twelve points and President Obama's approval rate dropped eleven points.[105] Obama's disapproval rating climbed to 57%, the highest level of his presidency. A December 2013 Pew Research Poll found that the percentage of respondents who viewed Obama as "not trustworthy" had risen fifteen points over the course of the year, from 30% to 45%.[106] In September, 38% of respondents said the ACA's effect had been "mostly negative." By December, that number jumped to 49%. The cancellations largely reversed any popularity gains made during the government shutdown.

Perhaps the clearest illustration of this shift was how the White House described the ACA. Since it was upheld by the Supreme Court, the president was fond of touting his eponymous law. At an event in San Antonio in July 2012,

---

[102] *Id.*

[103] Ezra Klein, *Wonkbook: Obama Shouldn't Apologize for Blowing Up the Terrible Individual Market*, Wash. Post (Nov. 8, 2013), perma.cc/Q8AV-2AJX.

[104] *Statement by the President on the Affordable Care Act*, White House (Nov. 14, 2013), perma. cc/B59F-8AP9.

[105] Sarah Dutton, et al, *Poll: Obamacare Support, Obama Approval Sink to New Lows*, CBS News (Nov. 20, 2013), perma.cc/YW3S-NS9T.

[106] *Obama Job Rating Regains Some Ground, But 2013 Has Taken a Toll*, Pew Research Center (Dec. 10, 2013), perma.cc/8UD4-62KA.

the president said, "The Affordable Health Care Act – otherwise known as Obamacare – was the right thing to do. And you know what, they're right, I do care."[107] At an October 2012 campaign event in Iowa, the president beamed, "We passed Obamacare – yes, I like the term – we passed it because I do care, and I want to put these choices in your hands where they belong."[108] On the eve of the launch of HealthCare.gov on September 29, 2013, he joked that "once it's working really well, I guarantee you they will not call it ObamaCare."[109] In early October 2013, his political organization Organizing for America promoted on social media the meme, "I Like Obamacare." The group's Facebook page declared: "Obamacare: Signed. Sealed. Delivering …"[110]

However, by November 2013, the president changed his marketing plan. *Politico* reported that all references to Obamacare had been scrubbed from HealthCare.gov, and that leading Democrats no longer used the term.[111] In December, *CBS* reporter Mark Knoller noted that the last time the president had used the phrase *Obamacare* was in a November 4 speech: "It works. Obamacare is working for people," Obama said at the time.[112] Since then, Knoller observed, the president avoided using *Obamacare* in his speeches.[113] *Politico* added that "White House talking points distributed to Democrats … refer to the Affordable Care Act in suggested sound bites, not Obamacare."[114]

Indeed, merely associating the ACA with Obama decreased the health care reform's popularity. A November 2013 *Gallup* poll revealed that when asking about the law, "mentioning the Affordable Care Act yields the highest support (45%), while only mentioning Obamacare yields the lowest support (38%).[115] During an episode of *Jimmy Kimmel Live*, people on the streets of Hollywood were asked whether they prefer "Obamacare" or the "Affordable Care Act."[116]

[107] *Remarks by the President at Campaign Event in San Antonio, TX*, WHITE HOUSE (July 17, 2012), perma.cc/6CTX-Y4X2.

[108] *Remarks by the President at a Campaign Event in Mt. Vernon, IA*, WHITE HOUSE (Oct. 17, 2012), perma.cc/2PZU-HN3E.

[109] Sam Baker, *GOP Lawmakers Bridle at Calling Affordable Care Act the law*, THE HILL (Sept. 9, 2013), perma.cc/MKH9-TLJ7.

[110] Josh Blackman, *Should We Not Call It "Obamacare" Anymore?*, JOSH BLACKMAN'S BLOG (Oct. 3, 2013), perma.cc/M5UA-MBHK.

[111] Reid J. Epstein, *Taking 'Obama' Out of Health Care*, POLITICO (Nov. 19, 2013), perma.cc/3AB9-HLDA.

[112] @MarkKnoller (Dec. 2, 2013, 3:06 p.m.), Tweet, bit.ly/21Gfx6y.

[113] @MarkKnoller (Dec. 2, 2013, 3:05 p.m.), Tweet, bit.ly/29HMBcD.

[114] Epstein, *supra* note 111.

[115] Mark Blumenthal, Ariel Edwards-Levy, *HUFFPOLLSTER: Few Outside Washington Have Strong Opinions on Filibuster*, HUFF. POST (Nov. 21, 2013), perma.cc/EFZ3-GX7E.

[116] Jimmy Kimmel Live, *Six of One – Obamacare vs. The Affordable Care Act*, YOUTUBE (Oct. 1, 2013), bit.ly/1UGivHp.

By a large margin, they chose the ACA. A *Fox News* poll found that among Republicans, the "Affordable Care Act" polled eight points better than "Obamacare."[117] *National Public Radio* issued a memorandum urging its reporters to shift away from calling it Obamacare, which "seems to be straddling somewhere between being a politically-charged term and an accepted part of the vernacular."[118]

By the end of October, Republicans knew that the website would eventually be fixed, so GOP strategists decided they should "go heavy on the broken promise."[119] In *The Wall Street Journal*, Louise Radnofsky wrote that the GOP now "trained their fire" on the president's promise that people could keep their policies. "The issue, while long known in health-policy circles," she added, "pushed its way to the national stage as more people around the country received cancellation notices."[120] *CQ Roll Call* reported on a leaked Republican guide, titled "House Republican Playbook: Because of Obamacare … I Lost My Insurance."[121] The manual focused on how to best "communicate in your district about the disastrous Obamacare rollout," focusing on the president's promise of keeping your policy. On social media, Republicans publicized the letters of countless Americans whose policies were canceled as proof the president lied.

Obama would call the failures of the website and the cancellation as "two fumbles … on a big game," but he stressed that "the game's not over."[122] In response to rising pressure to do something about these crises, the president would soon turn to the power of executive action in an attempt to save the law.

---

[117] Ezra Klein, *This Obamacare Video Will Make You Sad. For America*, WASH. POST (Oct. 1, 2013), perma.cc/2USJ-47J3.

[118] Andrew Beaujon, *NPR Will Use the Term 'Obamacare' Less*, POYNTER (Oct. 3, 2013), perma.cc/AS8W-DFGJ.

[119] Stolberg, *supra* note 6.

[120] Evan Soltas, *Wonkbook: The End of 'If you like your plan, you can keep it'*, WASH. POST (Oct. 30, 2013), wapo.st/25zbKv2.

[121] Matt Fuller, *GOP Playbook Looks to Capitalize on Obamacare Woes*, ROLL CALL (Nov. 8, 2013), perma.cc/5QBS-RAHT.

[122] *Full Transcript of Obama's News Conference on Health Care*, N.Y. TIMES (Nov. 14, 2013), nyti.ms/1RsDgEo.

13

Government by Blog Post

13.1. "PEN AND PHONE"

In the 2010 midterm elections, Democrats lost their majority in the House of Representatives, and lost their filibuster-proof majority in the Senate, due in large part to the rising unpopularity of Obamacare and the growing strength of the Tea Party. During the final six years of his administration, President Obama was largely unable to advance his agenda through the legislative process. Faced with Republican opposition at every step, Obama increasingly turned to executive power to take action where Congress would not. By 2011, the mantra of his presidency became "We can't wait." Charlie Savage reported that the president coined this slogan at a meeting to "more aggressively use executive power to govern in the face of Congressional obstructionism."[1] When Congress would not legislate to the president's satisfaction, he would act alone. In a White House blog post fittingly titled "We Can't Wait," the administration listed all of the president's executive actions, stressing that he "is not letting congressional gridlock slow our economic growth."[2] By my count, Obama has repeated this phrase at least a dozen times to justify taking executive action where Congress would not pass the bill he wanted.[3]

If "We Can't Wait" was President Obama's mantra, the "Pen and Phone" became his method. In 2014 a cabinet meeting he explained, "We're not just going to be *waiting* for legislation in order to make sure that we're providing Americans the kind of help they need. I've got a pen and I've got a phone."[4] Specifically, he

---

[1] Charlie Savage, *Shift on Executive Power Lets Obama Bypass Rivals*, N.Y. TIMES (Apr. 22, 2012), nyti.ms/1SgzZnC.

[2] *We Can't Wait*, WHITEHOUSE.GOV (Oct. 24, 2011), perma.cc/R34T-HMPH.

[3] Josh Blackman, *Government by Blog Post*, 11 FIU L.REV. 389 (2016); See also Josh Blackman, *Gridlock*, 130 HARV. L.REV. __ (2016).

[4] *Obama on Executive Actions: 'I've Got a Pen and I've Got a Phone'*, CBS DC (Jan. 14, 2014), perma.cc/BCH6-4D4Z.

said, "I can use that pen to sign executive orders and take executive actions and administrative actions that move the ball forward" to "advance a mission that ... unifies all Americans."[5] To accomplish this mission, the president insisted that his cabinet "use all the tools available to us, not just legislation." The president's chief of staff John Podesta put it bluntly: "The upshot: Congressional gridlock does not mean the federal government stands still."[6]

The Obama approach to governance was crystallized in a November 2014 *Saturday Night Live* parody of *Schoolhouse Rock!* – "How a bill does not become a law."[7] A character dressed as a Bill, stands on the steps of Capitol Hill, and sings to a boy how he would become a law. "Well first I go to the House, and they vote on me. But then I need from the Senate a majority. And if I pass the legislative test, then I wind up on the president's desk." An actor playing President Obama appears, and shoves the Bill down the steps. The boy shouts, "President Obama, what's the big idea? That bill was trying to become a law." The smirking president tells the boy, "There's actually an even easier way to get things done around here, and it's called an executive order." Another character, dressed as an Executive Order, appears. "I'm an executive order," he sings, "and I pretty much just happen." The boy asks, "Don't you have to go through Congress at some point?" The Executive Order, cigarette in hand, dismisses the boy. "Oh that's adorable, you still think that's how government works." The Bill, gasping for air, climbs back up the steps and sings, "we look at the midterm elections, and people clearly don't want this" executive order. "We're going to take you to Court, and we're going to shut down Congress." Obama shoves the Bill down the steps one last time.

During the implementation of the Affordable Care Act, President Obama repeatedly turned to this all-too-familiar pattern of executive action. (Note that executive action, an umbrella term that includes memoranda and other informal guidance documents from administrative agencies, is far broader than actual executive orders signed by the president).[8] First, the ACA made

---

[5] Rebecca Kaplan, *Obama: I Will Use My Pen and Phone to Take on Congress*, CBSNEWS (Jan. 14, 2014), perma.cc/9VVW-F8LF.

[6] *Id.*

[7] Saturday Night Live, *How a Bill Does Not Become a Law*, NBC.com (Dec. 20, 2014), bit.ly/21GEWx7

[8] Gregory Korte, *Obama Issues "Executive Orders by Another Name,"* USA TODAY (Dec. 17, 2014), perma.cc/BUU6-7DKD (President Obama had "already signed 33% more presidential memoranda in less than six years than Bush did in eight. He's also issued 45% more than the last Democratic president, Bill Clinton, who assertively used memoranda to signal what kinds of regulations he wanted federal agencies to adopt. Obama is not the first president to use memoranda to accomplish policy aims. But at this point in his presidency, he's the first to use them more often than executive orders.")

certain groups worse off. Second, as a result, Congress was pressured to modify the law to alleviate Obamacare's burdens. However, Democrats feared that Republicans would seize the opportunity to unravel other portions of the law. This halted any possible bipartisan support for legislative amendments. Third, in the face of this gridlock, President Obama turned to executive action to unilaterally alter the ACA's onerous mandates. During the summer and fall of 2013, the Obama administration unilaterally delayed and suspended the individual and employer mandates, as well as modified provisions affecting benefits for Congressional employees.

Each of these executive actions – announced through formal notice-and-comment rulemaking or informal social media blogging – came as a complete surprise. Each change, focused only on near-team survival, posed long-term risks to the sustainability of the health care reform. Each modification relied on tenuous readings of the ACA and dubious assertions of executive authority to accomplish ends entirely at odds with what Congress designed. Each action was contested in court by states and private parties. However, because the executive actions had the effect of lifting burdens rather than imposing any injuries, the government vigorously contested that no one had standing to bring suit – and the courts almost uniformly agreed. As a result, the ultimate legality of these moves was not decided by judges, but by the president, who acted alone to salvage his signature law during desperate times.

One of the more disconcerting aspects of the law's implementation, beyond the numerous delays and waivers, has been the cavalier approach by which the government announced these changes. More often than not, the explanation of a modification would come in a social media update on the HHS blog (often on a Friday afternoon). For example, Sarah Kliff observed, "on the Friday following the Fourth of July, [the administration] quietly released a 606-page regulation that delayed requirements for the marketplaces to verify workers' incomes and employment status."[9] One benefits lawyer lamented that this process "is how HHS often breaks controversial regulatory news."[10] It soon became a painful pastime of ferreting through these massive document dumps and attempting to find the actual basis for the rule previously announced in the blog post. And invariably, the policy, as stated in the blog post, did not quite match up to what was in the rule. This was no longer a government of law, but a government by blog post.[11]

[9] Ezra Klein and Sarah Kliff, *Obama's Last Campaign: Inside the White House Plan to Sell Obamacare*, WASH. POST (July 17, 2013), perma.cc/QYT8-VXWD.

[10] *Id.*

[11] Josh Blackman, *Obamacare and Government by Blog Post*, LIBERTY LAW SITE (Mar. 10, 2014), perma.cc/KP28-FEJR. *See also Government by Blog Post, supra* note 3.

13.2. "BUSINESSES CAME TO US"

Although the Affordable Care Act's exchanges opened on October 1, 2013, the crucial date imposed by Congress was actually January 1, 2014. On this day there would be three major milestones. First, the individual mandate would kick in, penalizing people who were uninsured, or who had insurance that did not meet the requirements of "minimum essential coverage." Second, for the new year, the ACA's employer mandate required businesses with more than fifty employees to provide their full-time workers with a qualified health insurance plan, or alternatively pay a penalty.[12] Third, policies purchased on the ACA exchanges – subsidized by federal tax credits – would begin.

Congress directed these three interlocking mechanisms to go into effect simultaneously on January 1, 2014, so that all Americans would benefit from the comprehensive health care reform at once. Or at least that was the plan. After millions of cancelled plans, difficulties of signing up online, and opposition from the business community, President Obama would alter each of these mandates in ways Congress never intended. (Additionally, Justice Sotomayor's New Year's Eve injunction, discussed in Chapter 15, would put the contraceptive mandate on hold for the Little Sisters of the Poor).

The first crack in the ACA's armor formed in July 2013, months before HealthCare.gov launched. Since its inception, businesses lobbied the White House to delay or modify the employer mandate in order to avoid the added cost of insuring their employees.[13] Specifically, businesses warned that they would drop workers from full time to part time – less than thirty hours per week – in order to avoid the ACA penalty. Neil Trautwein, Vice President of the National Retail Federation, explained that if the mandate went into effect, employers would start cutting hours: "If you set a hard 30-hour limit for eligibility," he said, "you encourage employers to cut where they can. You're not going to cut willy-nilly, but potentially you increase your part-time workforce."[14]

Their rent-seeking worked. President Obama would later explain that "businesses came to us and said, listen, we were supportive of providing health insurance to employees, in fact, we provide health insurance to our

---

[12] 26 U.S.C. § 4980H(a)-(c).
[13] Robb Mandelbaum, *The Employer Mandate Has Been Delayed. Will It Be Rewritten?*, N.Y. TIMES Blog (July 3, 2013), perma.cc/73X5-EEKH.
[14] Sarah Kliff, *The Politics of Delaying Obamacare*, WASH. POST (July 2, 2013), perma.cc/CRU6-7HGT.

employees; we understand you want to get at the bad actors here, but are there ways to provide us some administrative relief?"[15] And he did just that. On July 2, Mark Mazur, the assistant secretary for tax policy, took to social media to update the ACA's status.

In a blog post titled "Continuing to Implement the ACA in a Careful, Thoughtful Manner," the Obama administration nonchalantly announced the suspension of the employer mandate.[16] The ACA provides that the employer mandate "shall apply to months beginning after December 31, 2013." That is, it goes into effect on January 1, 2014. However, Mazur blogged that the government "will provide an additional year before the ACA mandatory employer and insurer reporting requirements begin."

To justify this "transitional" policy, the blog post cited the "complexity of the requirements and the need for more time to implement them effectively." Although Mazur's announcement was framed in terms of relaxing the ACA's onerous reporting demands – over which the HHS secretary does have significant discretion – the real impact of this delay was to prevent the government from being able to penalize noncompliant employers. The post mentions, almost as a side note, that "we recognize that this transition relief will make it impractical to determine which employers owe shared responsibility payments [i.e., penalties]… Accordingly, we are extending this transition relief to [them]." In other words, because employers were not obligated to report to the government how many uninsured workers they had, the government had no method to calculate the penalties. With the click of a mouse – without so much as a tweet of advance notice to affected parties – the employer mandate would be suspended for *all* employers, regardless of their size, in 2014.

Shortly after the blog post went viral, the IRS released a notice regarding "transition relief," announcing that the employer mandate's penalty will not be "assessed for 2014."[17] Mark Iwry, Deputy Assistant Secretary at Treasury, defended the delay by explaining that the agency has done this a dozen times before, without any Congressional objection: "On a number of prior occasions across administrations," he said, "this authority has been used to postpone the application of new legislation when the immediate application would have subjected taxpayers to unreasonable administrative burdens or costs."[18]

[15] *Interview with President Obama*, N.Y. TIMES (July 27 2013), nyti.ms/29KeaDO.
[16] *Continuing to Implement the ACA in a Careful, Thoughtful Manner*, U.S. DEPT. OF TREASURY BLOG (July 2, 2013), perma.cc/E88D-DJA8.
[17] IRS Notice 2013-45, 2013-31 I.R.B. 116, at 3 (July 9, 2013), bit.ly/1XdAEgm.
[18] Sarah Kliff, *The White House Keeps Changing Obamacare. Is That Legal?*, WASH. POST (Aug. 7, 2013), perma.cc/9BHZ-XJWE.

Critics saw different motivations for the change, beyond administrative convenience. Sarah Kliff noted that aside from the "complexity of the [reporting] requirements," some "observers saw a political motivation as well."[19] Michigan law professor Nicholas Bagley, generally supportive of the ACA, was skeptical about the purported reason for the delay: "Affording transitional relief for a law that was enacted four years ago raised the question of, shouldn't you have had your ducks in a row when you knew this was coming down the pike?"[20] The business community, which stood to benefit from this largess, was pleased. "I think this is less about readiness and more about the fact that they're trying to be flexible in their implementation," said Rhett Buttle, vice president at the Small Business Majority. "It does seem like an olive branch" to the business community, he said.[21]

13.3. "LET'S MAKE A TECHNICAL CHANGE OF THE LAW"

The decision to delay the employer mandate came as a surprise to virtually everyone outside of the White House. The *Washington Post* reported that thirty minutes before the Treasury Department published the blog post, the administration informed the Democratic leadership in the Senate and House.[22] This last-minute notice was deemed a slight, because only a week earlier on June 24, Jeanne Lambrew offered no indication that the mandate was in flux. The *Post*, quoting an anonymous White House official, attributed the secrecy to GOP opposition to Obamacare: "It's very hard for a staffer to talk to a member of Congress about a decision that's not made yet." This delay was also the first major hint that something was awry with the ACA. Sarah Kliff wrote on *WonkBlog* that the delay of the employer mandate, along with the earlier delay of the launch of the small business insurance marketplaces, "could draw criticism that the administration will not be able to put into effect its signature legislative accomplishment on schedule."[23]

Reportedly, the White House even kept the Treasury Department out of the loop until the very end. A March 2014 letter by House Oversight Committee Chairman Darrell Issa (R-CA) charged that "the White House Chief of Staff

---

[19] Sarah Kliff, *The Politics of Delaying Obamacare*, WASH. POST (July 2, 2013), perma.cc/CRU6-7HGT.

[20] *Keeps Changing, supra* note 18.

[21] *Politics of Delay, supra* note 19.

[22] Amy Goldstein and Juliet Eilperin, *HealthCare.gov: How Political Fear Was Pitted against Technical Needs*, WASH. POST, (Nov. 2, 2013), perma.cc/E5FT-JARS.

[23] Sarah Kliff, *White House Delays Employer Mandate Requirement Until 2015*, WASH. POST (July 2, 2013), perma.cc/3BVW-47QG.

knew about the employer mandate delay *prior* to the head of the [Treasury] department implementing the program."[24] Issa noted that this approach raised "serious questions about whether the White House directed the delay of the employer mandate for political reasons." The Californian explained that Mark Mazur, the blog post's author, could not recall if any lawyers within Treasury discussed if they had the legal authority to delay the mandate.

The president attempted to justify the delay by faulting the Republicans, whom he deemed unwilling to make a minor change to the law. "In a normal political environment," Obama explained, "it would have been easier for me to simply call up the Speaker and say … 'let's make a technical change of the law.'" In a different time, the president suggested, "that would be the normal thing that I would prefer to do." For example, in 1936, President Roosevelt's implementation of Social Security had to be delayed because the government could not figure out how to create 26 million unique numbers.[25] President Johnson signed Medicare into law on July 30, 1965, and it was scheduled to go into effect on July 1, 1966 – a day the *New York Times* dubbed "M-Day."[26] The enrollment effort successfully enrolled 93% of eligible seniors by 1966 – in some cases forest rangers tracked down hermits in the woods.[27] But that was not enough time. President Johnson was able to persuade Congress to delay the rollout by two months in order to get more people to register.[28] In 2013, however, President Obama said we were "not in a normal atmosphere around here when it comes to, quote-unquote, 'Obamacare.'"[29] However, this was not accurate – there in fact was bipartisan support to delay the employer mandate.

On July 17, two weeks after the Treasury Department published its blog post, the House of Representatives passed the *Authority for Mandate Delay Act*.[30] The two-page bill would have delayed the implementation of the employer mandate until 2015.[31] That is *precisely* what the blog post announced, except

---

[24] Jonathan Easley, *Issa questions Treasury's Authority to Delay ObamaCare Employer Mandate*, THE HILL (Mar. 20, 2014), perma.cc/2EXC-3S4B (emphasis added).

[25] STEVEN BRILL, AMERICA'S BITTER PILL: MONEY, POLITICS, BACKROOM DEALS, AND THE FIGHT TO FIX OUR BROKEN HEALTHCARE SYSTEM 314 (Random House Trade Paperback ed. 2015).

[26] Sarah Kliff, *When Medicare Launched, Nobody Had Any Clue Whether It Would Work*, WASH. POST (May 17, 2013), perma.cc/AW6A-6QW6.

[27] *Id.*

[28] Brill, *supra* note 25 at 315.

[29] *TRANSCRIPT: President Obama's August 9, 2013, News Conference at the White House*, WASH. POST (Aug. 9, 2013), perma.cc/9BRB-RS5E.

[30] Final Vote Results for Roll Call 361, bit.ly/29LCNgD.

[31] Authority for Mandate Delay Act, H. R. 2667, 113th Congress (2013), perma.cc/W37M-W5FG.

it had the backing of the legislative branch. It was enacted on a 264–161 vote, with 35 Democrats voting "yea."

In response to this bill, which would have unequivocally given him the legal authority to delay the mandate, the president issued a veto threat. The White House said it was "unnecessary."[32] Underlying this veto threat was a concern that Republicans could later add amendments to the bill, which would repeal other provisions of the law. Because of the president's executive action, the Democratic-controlled Senate – spared the need to take a tough vote – never even considered the bill.

With the employer mandate already delayed until January 2015, lobbying was enhanced to push it back even further. Harvard professor John McDonough, who advised Senator Ted Kennedy, explained that the initial delay is "not a freebie." "Politically, it won't get easier a year from now [to implement], it will get harder," he said. "You've given the employer community a sense of confidence that maybe they can kill this. If I were an employer, I would smell blood in the water."[33]

Once again, the rent-seeking worked. Seven months after the initial blog post, the Treasury Department postponed the full implementation of the employer mandate another year until 2016.[34] But in doing so, the executive branch did not merely delay the requirement. Instead, it modified the mandate in a fragmented manner, with novel standards that deviated from Congress' design. Under the statute, the mandate applied to *all* employers with more than 50 employees starting in 2014. Under the president's modified approach, different standards would apply based on the size of the workforce.

First, for businesses with 50 to 100 full-time employees, the penalty would not be assessed *at all* during 2015. For these companies, the employer mandate would be entirely delayed for two full years. According to the *Small Business Administration*, there are roughly 8 million people (7% of all workers in America) at companies in this range.[35] Second, the mandate would only be partially implemented for businesses with more than 100 employees. In 2015, these businesses would not be subjected to the penalty if they offered health insurance coverage for at least 70% of their

[32] Executive Office of the President, Statement of Administration Policy (July 16, 2013), bit.ly/24CW7kV.

[33] Sarah Kliff, *The Politics of Delaying Obamacare*, WASH. POST (July 2, 2013), perma.cc/CRU6-7HGT.

[34] *Shared Responsibility for Employers Regarding Health Coverage*, 79 Fed. Reg. 8544, 8574 (Feb. 12, 2014).

[35] Sarah Kliff, *The White House Is Relaxing the Employer Mandate Again*, WASH. POST (Feb. 10, 2014), perma.cc/LV2C-87FH.

workforce. Starting in 2016, an employer that offered coverage to 95% of its employees would not be subject to the penalty.

Absolutely none of this – not the bifurcation of employers, not the 70% transitional mandate, not the 95% final threshold – is in the ACA. The president suspended the employer mandate for 2014, partially waived it for 2015, and decided that in 2016 the mandate would not be fully implemented as Congress designed. The delay of the employer mandate would form the basis of a 2014 lawsuit brought by the U.S. House of Representatives, which we will discuss in Chapter 23.

13.4. "CONGRESS SHOULD LIVE UNDER THE SAME LAWS IT PASSES"

Influential corporations would not be the only beneficiaries of executive-action largess. In September 2009, when the ACA was being drafted, Senator Chuck Grassley (R-IA) proposed an amendment requiring members of Congress and their staff to use the newly-created exchanges. "The more that Congress experiences the laws we pass," Grassley said, "the better the laws are likely to be."[36] The veteran fiscal hawk added, "My interest in having Members of Congress participate in the exchange is consistent with my long-held view that Congress should live under the same laws it passes for the rest of the country." The amendment, which was merged into the final Senate bill, provided that the federal government could only offer members of Congress and their staff health insurance plans that were "created under" the ACA, or "through an Exchange established under" the new law.[37]

As a result of the amendment, unlike all other federal workers, members of Congress and their staffers would no longer be eligible for the generous Federal Employees Health Benefits Plan (FEHBP). Under FEHBP, the government pays approximately 75% of an employee's annual premium. This annual tax-free contribution of between $5,000 and $12,000 was *far* more generous than the income-adjusted subsidies available on HealthCare.gov. Indeed, many well-compensated congressional employees, or those with high household incomes, would be ineligible for any subsidies on the exchange. These well-to-do civil servants would be put in the same position as other Americans who had to pay the full cost of their insurance, without any governmental assistance.

---

[36] *Grassley Amendment Makes Congress Obtain Coverage from Health Care Plan Established in Reform Bill*, Grassley.Senate.gov (Sep. 30, 2009), perma.cc/P55Z-EHD5.

[37] Section 1312(d)(3)(D).

Recall that while the Senate was crafting its bill in 2009, the House of Representatives was working on a parallel track. In contrast with the Grassley amendment, the House bill would have allowed members and their staff to remain on FEHBP, with the full 75% government-sponsored contribution. This provision, which would have maintained the status quo, would not make it into the final bill. Due to the election of Senator Scott Brown in January 2010, and the urgent need to enact the Senate bill, the House was forced to accept Grassley's amendment without any debate. Representative Diana DeGette (D-CO), who voted for the ACA, explained, "We had to take the Senate version of the health care bill. This is not anything we spent time talking about here in the House."[38] Another House Democrat told the *New York Times*, "This was a stupid provision that never should have gotten into the law."[39] But it did.

The Grassley amendment was extremely unpopular on Capitol Hill. In May 2013, Senator Reid acknowledged that there was a "conflict" over how the ACA treats congressional staff. The Majority Leader said, "We're trying to work that out" with Speaker John Boehner.[40] *Politico* reported that during the summer of 2013, Boehner and Reid quietly collaborated to develop a "legislative fix" that would ensure that congressional benefits would not be disrupted.[41] The duo even personally lobbied President Obama at the White House, while using a cover story so as not to arouse suspicions.[42]

However, as the movement to repeal and replace Obamacare grew during July and August, the House GOP leadership abandoned any efforts to modify the ACA, short of total repeal. By September, a spokesman for Boehner explained, "We always made it clear that the House would not pass any legislative 'fix.'"[43] Republicans now viewed this as a wedge issue that could force Democrats to negotiate over the ACA, lest their staff lose their truly affordable care. The spokesman said that the Speaker "was always clear, however, that any 'fix' would be a Democratic 'fix.' His 'fix' is repealing" Obamacare."

Responding to this gridlock, *Politico* wrote that President Obama became "personally involved in the dispute." Senator Dick Durbin (D-IL) relayed,

[38] Robert Pear, *Wrinkle in Health Law Vexes Lawmakers' Aides*, N.Y. TIMES (July 29, 2013), nyti.ms/1PX5PEG.

[39] *Id.*

[40] Alexander Bolton, *Reid: More Funding Needed to Prevent ObamaCare from Becoming 'Train Wreck'*, THE HILL (May 1, 2013), perma.cc/LW3Y-5LWY.

[41] John Bresnahan, *Boehner's Fight for Hill Subsidies*, POLITICO (Oct. 1, 2013), perma.cc/V2L7-A6S7.

[42] *Id.*

[43] *Id.*

"The president is aware of it. His people are working on it."[44] But once again, there was the distinct risk that allowing legislative modifications to the statute could open the door for Republican amendments that would impact other aspects of the law. Like with the employer mandate, the president was not willing to take that chance. A more attractive option, as noted by Senator Barbara Mikulski (D-MD), was for the president to act unilaterally. She explained that Democrats were "looking at what we can do with it administratively."[45] Obama would do just that, and once again turn to the executive action to bypass a legislative impasse.

On September 30 – as the barricades were going up and HealthCare. gov was going down – the White House deployed a twofold strategy. First, the Office of Personnel Management (OPM) announced that members of Congress and their staff would be able to purchase health insurance on the District of Columbia's Small Business Health Options Program, known as the D.C. SHOP exchange.[46] The ACA authorized these new SHOP exchanges to offer a health insurance marketplace for workers at small businesses with fewer than fifty employees.[47] OPM determined that after a congressional employee enrolled on the District of Columbia's SHOP Exchange, the government could then provide the *same* 75% contribution that was offered under the FEHBP.[48] Thus, there would be no meaningful disruption in benefits for Hill staffers. However, there is a problem with this approach. In no sense of the English language can the House and Senate be considered a "business." They are also not "small."—Congress employs more than 20,000 workers.[49]

Second, to address this deficiency, the Centers for Medicare and Medicaid Services posted on its blog a new *Frequently Asked Question*.[50] "How will Members of Congress and Congressional staff access health insurance coverage through an Exchange?," the agency rhetorically asked. The answer: "CMS clarifies that offices of the Members of Congress, as qualified employers, are eligible to participate in a SHOP *regardless of the size.*"

[44] John Bresnahan, *Obama on Hill's ACA Mess: I'm on It*, POLITICO (July 31, 2013), perma.cc/L3U8-ZRYT.
[45] *Id.*
[46] 78 Fed. Reg. 60653, 60653–54 (Oct. 2, 2013).
[47] 42 U.S.C. § 18024(b)(2). 45 C.F.R. § 155.710(b).
[48] 5 C.F.R § 890.501(h).
[49] *Vital Statistics on Congress Chapter 5: Congressional Staff and Operating Expenses*, BROOKINGS INSTITUTION (July 11, 2013), bit.ly/1T5nDFI.
[50] CMS, *Members of Congress and Staff Accessing Coverage through Health Insurance Exchanges (Marketplaces)*, (Sep. 30, 2013), bit.ly/1q51qtL.

Because of this new FAQ – another exercise of government by blog post[51] – each congressional office was treated as a *separate* employer. Rather than viewing the entire Congressional workforce as a small business – which it was certainly not – CMS and OPM chopped up the Capitol into hundreds of distinct offices, each deemed its own small business – which they certainly were not. Even though the Speaker's office had more than fifty employees, OPM would still treat it as a small business, "regardless of the size," and despite the obvious fact that it wasn't an actually a business. To paraphrase Justice Scalia's dissent in *King v. Burwell*, "Words no longer have meaning" if Congress is a small business.

Further, once members of Congress and their employees were enrolled on the D.C. SHOP exchange, under the OPM rule, they would be eligible for the full 75% government-provided contribution. This is a benefit that no one else on the SHOP exchange would be eligible for. Notwithstanding the Grassley amendment, which expressly sought to put congressional employees on the *same* footing as Americans on the exchanges, now congressional employees would be in the *exact same* position as they were before the enactment of the ACA. The OPM fix was a blatant effort to bypass an unpopular law.

Senator Ron Johnson (R-WI) would challenge the legality of the OPM rule in 2014. The court dismissed the case because the senator – who actually benefited from the more generous benefits – was not injured, and thus lacked what is known as *standing*.[52] The Seventh Circuit Court of Appeals affirmed the dismissal of the case on standing grounds.[53]

13.5. "THE PRESIDENT SHOULD HONOR THE COMMITMENT" HE MADE

In October 2013, as HealthCare.gov sputtered along, a bipartisan consensus formed that the millions of people whose policies were canceled deserved relief. Senator Mary Landrieu (D-LA) introduced the *Keeping the Affordable*

---

[51] A sole FAQ by itself cannot be the source of legal authority. In a different case, a federal court ruled that CMS could not rely on a Frequently Asked Question on their blog as the basis to support their policy. The court found that because FAQ 33 was the "sole authority" for the government's decision, it has to be set aside as unlawful. Texas Children's Hosp. v. Burwell, 76 F. Supp. 3d 224, 238 (D.D.C. 2014).

[52] Johnson v. OPM, 1:14-CV-009 (E.D. Wisc. 2014), available at bit.ly/29F1ufw.

[53] Johnson v. U.S. Office of Pers. Mgmt., 783 F.3d 655 (7th Cir. 2015).

Care Act Promise Act.[54] The bill – whose title was a direct rebuke to the president's broken promise – would have grandfathered all active plans that were valid on December 31, 2013. "When we passed the Affordable Care Act," Landrieu explained, "we did so with the intention that 'if you liked your health plan, you could keep it.' A promise was made and this legislation will ensure that this promise is kept."[55] Under her proposal, the individual mandate – which required that millions of Americans purchase new, more comprehensive plans – would be temporarily suspended. The bill was supported by moderate Democrat Joe Manchin of West Virginia, and Republicans Susan Collins from Maine and Lisa Murkowski of Alaska.[56]

Senator Landrieu's bill posed two risks for the Obama administration. First, delaying the mandate could undermine the stability of the exchanges. If healthy people – no longer subject to the mandate's penalty – failed to purchase comprehensive health insurance, the exchanges would be skewed with older, sicker patients, driving costs up. The American Academy of Actuaries warned that "delaying the implementation of the ACA's individual mandate or extending the enrollment period for obtaining coverage could have negative consequences for health insurance coverage and costs."[57] This could result in an *adverse-selection death spiral*: as premiums continue to increase to cover sicker patients, the higher prices force healthier people to drop out of the market. The drafters of the ACA sought to avoid this spiral through the individual mandate, which penalized people for going uninsured.

The *New York Times* reported that Landrieu's "legislation and a similar bill written by a Republican House member set off alarms among [White House] policy aides, who feared that letting consumers keep old plans could further undermine the health care law."[58] In July, the House of Representatives passed the *Fairness for American Families Act*, which would have delayed the individual mandate for a year.[59] President Obama threatened to veto it, claiming

---

[54] Keeping the Affordable Care Act Promise Act, S. 1642, 113th Congress (2013), perma.cc/9LNP-XZ95.

[55] Ezra Klein, *Obamacare Is in Much More Trouble than It Was One Week Ago*, WASH. POST (Nov. 13, 2013), perma.cc/99QF-CQNU.

[56] Jackie Calmes and Jonathan Weisman, *Despite Fumbles, Obama Defends Health Care Law*, N.Y. TIMES (Nov. 6, 2013), nyti.ms/1TEJtP3.

[57] Jonathan Easely, *Actuaries: ACA Delays Would Cause Chaos*, THE HILL (Nov. 6, 2013), bit.ly/1qwKKMJ.

[58] Sheryl Gay Stolberg and Michael D. Shear, *Inside the Race to Rescue a Health Care Site, and Obama*, N.Y. TIMES (Nov. 30, 2013), nyti.ms/1MERH2E.

[59] Fairness for American Families Act, H.R. 2668, 113th Congress (2013), perma.cc/469L-S3Q4.

it would "raise health insurance premiums and increase the number of uninsured Americans." Representative Chris Van Hollen (D-MD) added that if there were a delay of the individual mandate, "premiums would jump much higher," which "would sabotage the entire purpose of the exchange."[60] In other words, delaying the the individual mandate could contribute to a death spiral.

Second, amending the law to delay the individual mandate created the risk that Republican amendments could be used to repeal other aspects of the ACA. Ezra Klein observed that "once Congress reopens Obamacare, no one knows where they stop. Landrieu's bill, for instance, will also have to pass the House – and they're going to want to attach provisions to it that Democrats won't much like."[61] Similar fears prevented the Democratic leadership from supporting legislative fixes for the employer mandate and for congressional employees' benefits.

As a result, pressure mounted on the president, once again, to take executive action to deal with the canceled plans. During Kathleen Sebelius's appearance on *The Daily Show*, host Jon Stewart pointed out that businesses already received an administrative reprieve from the employer mandate, but individuals with canceled policies were out of luck. "But would you say that's a legitimate criticism that an individual doesn't get to delay it, but a business does? Is that not legitimate?"[62] Sebelius replied that individuals are not actually required to buy insurance. But if they go uninsured, she added, "they pay a fine at the end of the year." (Barely a year after the Supreme Court upheld the individual mandate as a *tax*, and Sebelius still referred to it as a *fine*.).

Even the forty-second president joined the fray, urging the forty-fourth president to take action. Bill Clinton said that people should be allowed to keep their policies: "I personally believe, even if it takes a change in the law, that the president should honor the commitment the federal government made to those people and let them keep what they've got."[63] Obama

---

[60] Ezra Klein, *What Republicans Don't Understand About the Politics of Obamacare*, WASH. POST (Sep. 24, 2013), wapo.st/1SolrM7.

[61] *Much more trouble, supra* note 55.

[62] Lucy McCalmont, *Sebelius Gets the Stewart Treatment*, POLITICO (Oct. 8, 2013), perma.cc/38S2-9B6G.

[63] Jonathan Easley, *Clinton: Let People Keep Coverage*, THE HILL (Nov. 12, 2013), perma.cc/38SW-LJBZ.

had once called Clinton the "Secretary of Explaining Things," and the former president understood the risk of canceled policies all too well.[64] It was Harry and Louise's fear that they would have to change their coverage that doomed HillaryCare in 1994. Speaker John Boehner relished in Clinton's critique: "These comments signify a growing recognition that Americans were misled when they were promised that they could keep their coverage under President Obama's health care law. The entire health care law is a train wreck that needs to go."[65]

Hillary Clinton said nothing about the canceled policies.[66] On the campaign trail six years earlier, candidate Clinton's health care plan featured an individual mandate, which would have also resulted in the cancellation of inadequate plans. To assuage the fears that derailed her health care reform two decades earlier, during a 2007 event in Iowa, Clinton made an all-too-familiar promise: "You can keep the doctors you know and trust. You keep the insurance you have. If you have private insurance you like, nothing changes – you can keep that insurance."[67]

Ironically, during the 2008 campaign, candidate Obama attacked the individual mandate. He likened Clinton's plan to "solv[ing] homelessness by mandating that everyone buy a house."[68] However, once Obama secured the nomination, he copied Clinton's plan almost in its entirety – including the individual mandate. Neera Tanden, who had been Clinton's adviser, joined Obama's policy staff. She recalled that when she asked the first-term senator what he thought of a mandate, Obama replied, "I kind of think Hillary was right."[69] In the race for the White House in 2016, Clinton embraced the ACA as her own. During a February 2016 debate in Milwaukee, Clinton boasted, "You know, before it was called Obamacare, it was called Hillarycare."

---

[64] Jonathan Cohn, *Bill Clinton Is Wrong. This Is How Obamacare Works*, NEW REPUBLIC (Nov. 12, 2013), perma.cc/BTZ3-VT3U.

[65] Juliet Eilperin, *Bill Clinton Identifies 3 Big Problems with the Obamacare Rollout*, WASH. POST (Nov. 12, 2013), perma.cc/JMD6-7SC4.

[66] Josh Gerstein, *Obama's Critic-in-Chief Strikes Again*, POLITICO (Nov. 12, 2013), perma.cc/M7FA-LTX3.

[67] Rebecca Berg, *Hillary Clinton in 2007: 'If you have a plan you like, you keep it'*, WASH. EXAM'R (Nov. 14, 2013), perma.cc/Q83U-QA6V.

[68] David Ono, *Vote 08: Barack Obama Wins Illinois*, ABC 7 (Feb. 5, 2008), perma.cc/47ZU-HYZD.

[69] Scott Gottlieb, *The Clintonian Roots of Obamacare*, NTL. AFFAIRS (2015), perma.cc/TZ5B-J7SH.

13.6. "SABOTAGE THE HEALTH CARE LAW"

On November 5, President Obama and Vice President Biden met with six-teen Democratic senators at the White House to discuss the dueling crises of HealthCare.gov and the canceled policies. At the confab, Senator Landrieu and other vulnerable democrats who were up for reelection, dubbed the "2014ers," criticized the president for nearly two hours in the Roosevelt Room. Reportedly, Biden was willing to serve as the scapegoat. "Just attack us," he said.[70] "Blame us." *Politico* wrote that the vulnerable senators were given a "green light to bash the White House and call for certain legislative fixes. But they've been urged by senior administration officials not to insist on delaying" the individual mandate.[71] According to a readout from the meeting, Obama "emphasized that he shared the Senators' commitment to ensuring that Americans who want to enroll in health insurance through the Marketplaces are able to do so in time for insurance coverage to start as early as January 1st."[72] But he stopped short of endorsing a delay.

As the pressure mounted, in the House of Representatives both Speaker Boehner and Minority Leader Pelosi agreed that Congress should take legisla-tive action to deal with the canceled plans.[73] "I'm highly skeptical they can do this administratively," Boehner said, doubting that executive action could fix the situation.[74] Pelosi said, "I want to do both" – a statute and an administra-tive fix, for a "belt and suspenders" approach. On November 15, the House of Representatives passed the *Keep Your Health Plan Act of 2013* on a bipartisan vote, 261–157.[75] The one-page bill – similar to Senator Landrieu's proposal – would have allowed any plan that was valid in 2013 to be grandfathered into 2014.[76]

Thirty-nine Democrats crossed the aisle to vote "yea." A senior adviser to Representative Pelosi said the defectors were trying to "insulate" themselves from the unpopular cancellations.[77] The *Washington Post* observed that the "vote was a striking show of Democratic disunity and the largest Democratic

---

[70] Stolberg, *supra* note 58.

[71] Manu Raju and Seung Min Kim, *Dems Give W.H. Tight ACA Deadline*, POLITICO (Nov. 7, 2013), perma.cc/ER2D-SKB3.

[72] *Readout of the President's Meeting With Senators on the Affordable Care Act*, WHITE HOUSE (Nov. 6, 2013), perma.cc/EYZ8-4DTY.

[73] Aaron Blake and Paul Kane, *Boehner, Pelosi say Legislative Fix Needed for Obamacare*, WASH. POST (Nov. 14, 2013), perma.cc/9VZA-UHZP.

[74] *Id.*

[75] H.R. 3350 (113th): Keep Your Health Plan Act of 2013, perma.cc/5PM9-6TMZ.

[76] *Id.*

[77] Sean Sullivan, *Pelosi Downplays Obamacare Defections; Clyburn Says Dems 'Insulating' Themselves*, WASH. POST (Nov. 17, 2013), perma.cc/CM4P-XMTW.

defection on a major piece of legislation this year."[78] Fearing that the bill could pass the Senate – with the vulnerable 2014ers already backing a similar proposal from Senator Landrieu – the president issued a veto threat to the House bill.[79] Obama claimed that it would "allow[] insurers to continue to sell" inadequate plans, and would "sabotage the health care law."[80] But it was not the veto threat that prevented the Senate from taking action on the bill – it was the president's newly announced executive action.

13.7. OBAMACARE IS "NOT THE REASON WHY INSURERS HAVE TO CANCEL YOUR PLAN"

On November 14 – one hour before the House of Representatives voted on the Keep Your Health Plan Act – the president announced what would become known as the *administrative fix*.[81] In a speech in the White House press room, Obama recognized the difficulties posed by the canceled policies. "I completely get how upsetting this can be for a lot of Americans," he said, "particularly after assurances they heard from me that if they had a plan that they liked, they could keep it."[82] In response, the president "offer[ed] an idea that will help." HHS would "extend" the ACA's "grandfather clause" to "people whose plans have changed since the law took effect." The decree permitted – but did not require – "insurers [to] extend current plans that would otherwise be canceled into 2014." If an insurer elected to offer cancelled plans, customers "whose plans have been cancelled [can] choose to re-enroll in the same kind of plan." It would be up to state insurance commissioners and the individual insurance companies to decide whether to allow noncompliant policies to be sold. However, neither would be required to embrace the fix.

Ironically, this executive action mirrored the *Keep Your Health Plan Act* – the same bill that Obama threatened to veto earlier that day because it would "sabotage" the ACA. Now, Obama was unilaterally implementing virtually the same reform, without the virtue of congressional support. Even more ironically, *The Wall Street Journal* observed, "Mr. Obama is doing through executive fiat what Republicans shut down the government to get him to do."[83] One

---

[78] *Id.*

[79] Justin Sink, *White House Threatens Veto of Upton Bill*, THE HILL (Nov. 14, 2013), perma.cc/BW9H-R2V3.

[80] Statement of Administration Policy (Nov. 14, 2013), bit.ly/1TNcdn2.

[81] *Statement by the President on the Affordable Care Act*, WHITE HOUSE (Nov. 14, 2013), perma.cc/2YYC-LP2U.

[82] Politifact selected this assurance as 2013's "Lie of the Year." Angie D. Holan, *Lie of the Year: 'If You Like Your Health Care Plan, You Can Keep It,'* POLITIFACT (Dec. 12, 2013), perma.cc/74PB-PKDK.

[83] WALL ST. J., *Obama Repeals ObamaCare* (Dec. 22, 2013), on.wsj.com/1RHiX6h.

of the eleventh-hour attempts to avert a shutdown was a one-year delay of the individual mandate. President Obama refused to negotiate on this point – or any other for that matter – warning that such a delay would undermine the law. Yet, not even a month later, he did exactly that.

Shortly after the announcement, HHS memorialized the new policy in a letter, stating that noncompliant health plans "will not be considered to be out of compliance" in certain circumstances.[84] In other words, the very plans that were un-grandfathered because they did not provide "minimum essential coverage" would now be re-grandfathered. The administrative fix waived the requirements for millions; people who renewed old, thrifty plans were exempted from the individual mandate's penalty.

After the president finished answering questions from the press, his chief of staff Denis McDonough met with the fifty-five members of the Democratic Caucus.[85] *The New York Times* reported that White House officials "tried to calm the group and pleaded for time to try to repair the damage without any legislative interference, pledging to fix the federal Web site." Afterwards, McDonough and his staff crossed the Hill to meet with 200 House Democrats. In total, the urgent meetings ran nearly four hours. Ezra Klein observed that the executive action "makes it easier for the White House to stop congressional Democrats from signing onto something like Landrieu's" bill.[86]

The announcement of the administrative fix took the insurance industry by total surprise, once again. They were not prepared for the sudden "about-face" in light of the president's previous opposition to a delay.[87] "What we want to do is to be able to say to these folks," Obama said, is that "the Affordable Care Act is not going to be the reason why insurers have to cancel your plan."[88] As Sarah Kliff observed, the president "described this policy decision as one allowing the White House to shift the blame for cancellations from the [President] to the health plans."[89] In other words, it will be

---

[84] Letter from Gary Cohen, Dir., Ctr. for Consumer Info. & Ins. Oversight, HHS, to State Ins. Comm'rs (Nov. 14, 2013)

[85] Paul Kane and Jackie Kucinich, *Health-care Law's Problems Test Loyalty of Democrats in Congress*, WASH. POST (Nov. 14, 2013), perma.cc/7MXT-2DEM.

[86] Ezra Klein, *Everything You Need to Know about the Plans to "Fix" Obamacare*, WASH. POST (Nov. 14, 2013), perma.cc/2XCK-T7MK.

[87] Stolberg, *supra* note 58.

[88] *Statement by the President on the Affordable Care Act*, WHITE HOUSE (Nov. 14, 2013), perma.cc/7GBJ-UC77.

[89] Sarah Kliff, *Insurers Are Furious about the White House's New Obamacare Plan*, WASH. POST (Nov. 14, 2013), perma.cc/5QAV-3SZX.

the insurers fault if they do not re-grandfather the plans cancelled because of Obamacare.

The insurance companies were "furious" at the fix.[90] Karen Ignani, president of America's Health Insurance Plans, charged that the cancellations are a direct result of Obamacare. "The only reason consumers are getting notices about their current coverage changing," she said, "is because the ACA requires all policies to cover a broad range of benefits that go beyond what many people choose to purchase today."[91] The law was working exactly as Jeanne Lambrew and others in the Obama administration had designed. But now that people were being harmed by these decisions, the White House was improvising.

Ignani feared that "changing the rules after health plans have already met the requirements of the law could destabilize the market and result in higher premiums for consumers." She warned the administration that "additional steps must be taken to stabilize the marketplace and mitigate the adverse impact on consumers." After the announcement, an emergency meeting was convened between the president and health care executives to address what the *Washington Post* referred to as the "level of anxiety within the insurance industry about the administration's policy fix."[92] Robert Laszewski, an insurance industry consultant, wrote to his clients that day, "This [fix] puts the insurance companies who have successfully complied with the law in a hell of a mess."[93]

The administrative fix also took state insurance commissioners by surprise. They were now responsible for deciding whether to allow noncompliant plans to be sold in their states.[94] Washington state insurance commissioner Kreidler – who was an ACA supporter – immediately came out in opposition to the fix: "We will not be allowing insurance companies to extend their policies," he said.[95] "I believe this is in the best interest of the health insurance market in Washington." Kreidler explained that he found out about the fix while he was at the gym that morning. He was surprised that the president pursued executive action rather than a legislative amendment. "What I didn't expect

[90] *Id.*
[91] *Id.*
[92] Sarah Kliff, *How States Are Deciding Whether to Accept Obama's Cancellation 'Fix'*, WASH. POST (Nov. 15, 2013), perma.cc/PDU2-LH26.
[93] Sarah Kliff, *The White House's Obamacare Fix Is About to Make a Big Mess*, WASH. POST (Nov. 14, 2013), perma.cc/Q3YL-YTEK.
[94] Letter from Dept. of Health and Human Services to Insurance Commissioners (Nov. 14, 2013), bit.ly/24zUzLU.
[95] Sarah Kliff, *The Backlash to the Obamacare Fix Has Already Started*, WASH. POST (Nov. 14, 2013), perma.cc/A47M-N4NV.

or anticipate," he said, "was the fact the president would make this announcement" without any advance warning.[96]

After the president's announcement, Kreidler recalled, an e-mail was sent out with "big exclamation points" scheduling an "emergency meeting of insurance commissioners."[97] National Association of Insurance Commissioners president Jim Donelon told the *Washington Post*, "It only dropped in our laps yesterday morning."[98] A statement from NAIC said the fix "threatens to undermine the new market, and may lead to higher premiums and market disruptions in 2014 and beyond."[99] Kansas Insurance Commissioner Sandy Praeger, a rare ACA supporter in a red state, lamented, "It's just a big mess right now."[100] She added, "I don't know what to tell people."

William P. White, the District of Columbia's insurance commissioner, rejected the administrative fix.[101] "The action today undercuts the purpose of the exchanges," White said, "by creating exceptions that make it more difficult for them to operate."[102] The next day, D.C. Mayor Vincent Gray fired White, stating that he was not authorized to criticize the president's announcement. Council member Vincent Orange, who oversaw the District's insurance department, explained, "You can't have the commissioner out there taking on the president, and the mayor being on a different page."

The delay of the individual mandate did not go through what is known as notice-and-comment rulemaking. This process affords the public a sixty-day opportunity to comment on a regulation before it is published – and the agency is supposed to reply to objections. HHS announced that it had "good cause" to forego rulemaking. "There have been unforeseen barriers to enrollment on the exchanges." Waiting at least two months would not allow people to sign up before the December 31 deadline, they argued.[103] Michael Greve – who helped launch the legal challenge to the IRS rule – quipped,

---

[96] Sarah Kliff, *Wash. Insurance Regulator Supports Obamacare – and Rejected Obama's 'Fix'. Here's Why*, WASH. POST (Nov. 16, 2013), perma.cc/46CT-KG47

[97] *Id.*

[98] Sarah Kliff, *Obama's Meeting with Insurance Regulators Is Going to Be a Bit Awkward*, WASH. POST (Nov. 20, 2013), perma.cc/4WRJ-7CU6.

[99] Aaron C. Davis, *D.C. Insurance Commissioner Fired a Day after Questioning Obamacare Fix*, WASH. POST (Nov. 16, 2013), perma.cc/F2KF-LNW5.

[100] Juliet Eilperin and Amy Goldstein, *White House Relying More on Insurance Carriers to Help Fix HealthCare.gov*, WASH. POST (Nov. 9, 2013), perma.cc/ACS7-W6TR.

[101] Mike DeBonis, *D.C. Insurance Chief Is Undecided on Obamacare Exemptions*, WASH. POST (Nov. 14, 2013), perma.cc/XX37-NRPV.

[102] Davis, *supra* note 99.

[103] Michael S. Greve, *Obamacare's Unforeseen Barriers*, LIBRARY OF LAW AND LIBERTY (Dec. 16, 2013), perma.cc/R8Q6-5XE9.

"You don't say. The 'unforeseen barriers' are principally a result of HHS's own fantastic screw-up."[104] In July 2014, West Virginia would challenge the legality of the "administrative fix."

13.8. "OBAMACARE ITSELF IS THE HARDSHIP"

Even with the November administrative fix in place, many canceled plans would remain canceled. Half of the states rejected the administrative fix, and even in those states that embraced it, many insurers declined to reissue certain canceled plans. Those affected customers would now be forced to purchase new policies on the exchanges. There was a growing concern that it would be unfair to penalize people whose policies were canceled by the ACA and who were required to buy more expensive insurance, or could not sign up on HealthCare.gov.

On December 19 – with less than two weeks before the individual mandate would go into effect – a group of six vulnerable Senate Democrats wrote an urgent letter to Secretary Sebelius.[105] They requested "explicit clarity" on whether those who had canceled plans but could not buy new policies would be exempted from the mandate's penalty.[106] Senator Joe Manchin of West Virginia, one of the signatories of the letter, worried that if plans on the exchanges are "so much more expensive than what we anticipated, and if the coverage is not as good as what we've had, [then] you've got a complete meltdown at that time."[107] The law, he said, "falls of its own weight if basically the cost becomes more than we can absorb."

The very next day, Sebelius wrote back to the sextet, acknowledging that "too many [consumers] have found [that] their policies bec[a]me unaffordable."[108] In "half the states" that accepted the administrative fix, Sebelius wrote, the number of people with "canceled plans who do not have quality, affordable coverage for 2014 is clearly shrinking." Nonetheless, she noted, "despite all these efforts, there still may be a small number of consumers who are not able to renew their existing plans and are having difficulty finding an acceptable replacement in the Marketplace." Sebelius offered a "clarification" of the law. "Those with canceled plans who might be having difficulty paying for a" compliant plan should "qualify for [a] temporary hardship exemption," thereby excusing them "from the individual responsibility requirement." In English,

---

[104] *Id.*

[105] *Obama Repeals, supra* note 83.

[106] Letter from Senator Warner et al. to Secretary Sebelius (Dec. 19, 2013), bit.ly/1rzugno.

[107] Aaron Blake, *Manchin: Obamacare Could Suffer 'Complete Meltdown'*, WASH. POST (Dec. 22, 2013), perma.cc/JB2V-9G42.

[108] Letter from Secretary Sebelius to Senator Warner (Dec. 20, 2013), bit.ly/1TNcFSo.

that means if a person's policy was canceled, and he or she could not afford to buy a new one, then he or she would be excused from the individual mandate. Yuval Levin, a conservative commentator, referred to the letter from the senators as "bizarre kabuki theater." [109] He quipped, "If you think a regulatory change announced Thursday was made in response to a letter sent Wednesday, I've got a bridge over the East River to sell you."

In a memorandum issued the same day, HHS explained that anyone whose policy "will not be renewed," or whose new plan is "more expensive than" the canceled plan, "will be eligible for a hardship exemption."[110] These consumers were, in effect, excused from the individual mandate on a showing that their old policy was canceled, or that a new policy was more expensive. This would be true in virtually every single case – this was especially true because there was no verification process in place to validate these claims. Applicants were on the honor system.

Through her brief letter, Sebelius disrupted the intricate compromises the Obama administration reached years earlier to ensure that people would be required to purchase comprehensive plans. Steven Brill observed that "the hard line on grandfathering that Lambrew and the other Obama people had taken had now completely backfired."[111] Further, the hardship exemption was in no way restricted by financial need; a person only needed to show that their plan was canceled. Ezra Klein admitted that "this puts the administration on some very difficult-to-defend ground."[112] Those who had their policies canceled – regardless of their income – were exempted, but previously uninsured people were still subject to the penalty.

The legal basis for the hardship fix was sketched out by Professors Nicholas Bagley and Austin Frakt two months earlier, in an article aptly titled "Saving Obamacare without Congress."[113] First, the professors explained that the law allows for a "hardship exemption" for anyone who has "suffered a hardship with respect to the capability to obtain coverage under a qualified health plan." Second, they wrote, Secretary Sebelius can "grant a certification" for particular individuals attesting that "there is no affordable qualified health

[109] Yuval Levin, *Pounding on the Panic Button*, Nat'l. Rev. (Dec. 20, 2013), perma.cc/57K7-EHTU.
[110] CMS Memorandum, "Options Available for Consumers with Cancelled Policies," (Dec. 19, 2013), bit.ly/1s27wgm.
[111] Brill, *supra* note 25 at 380.
[112] Ezra Klein, *The Individual Mandate No Longer Applies to People Whose Plans Were Canceled*, Wash. Post (Dec. 19, 2013), perma.cc/NLY4-GW73.
[113] Nicholas Bagley, *Saving Obamacare Without Congress*, Bloomberg View (Oct. 21, 2013), perma.cc/GYB8-N55G.

plan available through the Exchange." As a result, if these two provisions are put together, the scholars explained, it could be a "hardship" if there was "no affordable qualified health plan available through the Exchange."

But there is an ironic quality to this reasoning. Congress created several categories of people who would be exempted from the individual mandate's penalty: "individuals who cannot afford coverage," "taxpayers with incomes below filing threshold," "member[s] of Indian tribes," and anyone who "suffered a hardship with respect to the capability to obtain coverage under a qualified plan."[114] Congress set a strict threshold for exemptions from the penalty due to inability to pay: those for whom the annual cost of coverage exceeds 8 percent of household income.[115] These are individuals with extremely low incomes, who would likely qualify for Medicaid.

HHS's blanket policy of exempting *anyone* whose insurance was "more expensive" than before, irrespective of annual income, is impossible to reconcile with the congressional scheme. This hardship "exemption" swallows the rule. Ezra Klein aptly summarized the change: "In other words, Obamacare itself is the hardship."[116] University of Houston Law professor Seth Chandler joked, "Surely, however, the existence of the ACA itself cannot be the human-caused event creating the hardship."[117] Through this administrative-law shell game, the executive swept away Congress's exemption design. The *Wall Street Journal* editorialized, "A tornado destroys the neighborhood or ObamaCare blows up the individual insurance market, what's the difference?"[118]

Once again the insurance industry was caught off guard by this distortion to the exchanges. Karen Ignani said, "This latest rule change could cause significant instability in the marketplace and lead to further confusion and disruption for consumers."[119] Analyst Avik Roy explained that the "insurers are at their wits' end, trying to make sense of what to do next."[120] MIT's Jonathan Gruber explained that this delay is "by itself not a huge problem," but he added that "more widespread cracks in the mandate could start to cause

[114] 26 USC § 5000A(e)(1)-(5).

[115] 26 U.S.C. § 5000A(e)(1)(A).

[116] *Delayed, supra* note 112.

[117] Seth Chandler, *Obama Administration Shocking Decision to Drop Individual Mandate – But Only for Some*, ACAdeathspirl.org (Dec. 19, 2013), perma.cc/A56Q-3F58.

[118] *Obama Repeals, supra* note 83.

[119] Jennifer Haberkorn and Carrie Budoff Brown, *White House Broadens Obamacare Exemptions*, POLITICO (Dec. 20, 2013), perma.cc/BHA3-WE22.

[120] Avik Roy, *Obamacare's Insurance Mandate, 'Unaffordable' Exchanges*, FORBES (Dec. 20, 2013), onforb.es/1VC1QnS.

enormous problems for insurers."[121] In March 2014, the Obama administration extended the hardship exemption until 2016 – right in time for the presidential election.[122] The individual mandate – the purported cornerstone of the law, without which it could not function – was modified, delayed, and suspended in 2014 and 2015.

[121] Dylan Scott, *Does New Obamacare Mandate Exemption Open a Pandora's Box?*, TALKING POINTS MEMO (Dec. 20, 2013), perma.cc/H7N6-J4YM.
[122] Jason Millman, *Will states go along with the latest Obamacare fix?*, WASH. POST (Mar. 7, 2014), perma.cc/4TD2-GM57.

14

Crashing into the Deadline

14.1. "OPERATE SMOOTHLY FOR THE VAST MAJORITY OF CONSUMERS"

By the end of October, the White House began to move past the failed launch of HealthCare.gov, which President Obama later referred to as a "well-documented disaster."[1] Jeffrey Zients, who was tapped to lead the tech surge, offered a new goal: "We are confident by the end of the month of November, HealthCare.gov will operate smoothly for the vast majority of consumers."[2] Zients promised that within a month, "most users will be able to navigate the marketplace from account creation, through the application, all the way to enrollment."[3] The administration defined this goal as an 80% success rate for customers, the first clear performance standard in the history of the site.[4] President Obama repeated this promise, predicting that by December, "the majority of people who use it will be able to see it operate the way it was supposed to."[5] Obama said that "it will be a lot better" but acknowledged "there will still be some problems."[6]

Questions lingered about whether this deadline was feasible. Henry Chao, the deputy information officer, told Congress seven weeks after the site

---

[1] Robert Safian, *What Are the Overarching Goals Here?*, FAST COMPANY (Jun. 15, 2015), perma.cc/4CRE-WE3C.
[2] Sarah Kliff, *Here's the Obama Administration's Plan to Fix HealthCare.gov*, WASH. POST (Oct. 25, 2013), perma.cc/GRY4-5QQ6.
[3] Juliet Eilperin, and Amy Goldstein, *HealthCare.gov Goal is for 80% of Users to Be Able to Enroll for Insurance*, WASH. POST (Nov. 16, 2013), perma.cc/4ELR-PCYC.
[4] Eilperin & Goldstein, *supra* note 3.
[5] Juliet Eilperin, Amy Goldstein, and Lena H. Sun, *Obama Announces Change to Address Health Insurance Cancellations*, WASH. POST (Nov. 14, 2013), perma.cc/FHJ6-HC59.
[6] Juliet Eilperin, *Obama: 'There Will Still Be Problems' after Nov. 30 with Health-care Site*, WASH. POST (Nov. 14, 2013), perma.cc/6X8M-HFUB.

launched that 30–40% of the project was still being developed.[7] The *New York Times* reported that as many as "five million lines of software code may need to be rewritten before the Web site runs properly."[8] Mark Bertolini, chief executive of Aetna, worried, "There's so much wrong, you just don't know what's broken until you get a lot more of it fixed."[9] One of the tech surgers gave journalist Steven Brill an assessment of the damages: "What were the tech problems? Were they beyond repair? Nothing I saw was beyond repair."[10]

Columnist Jonathan Chait quipped there are three possible perspectives of the December 1 deadline: "(1) They know what they're doing. (2) They have fooled themselves into thinking they know what they're doing, but don't. (3) Meteor."[11] A senior Obama administration official denied the final option: "No!!!" Bruce Willis and the drilling team from *Armageddon* could not be reached for comment. Mindful of the high stakes, HHS Secretary Kathleen Sebelius attempted to temper expectations. "The 30th of November is not a magic go, no-go date," she said. "It is a work of constant improvement." Sebelius admitted, however, that it was a "critical juncture" and a "pretty scary date."[12]

Zients, who earned his reputation as a turnaround specialist, quickly divided his engineers into four teams: technical, policy, communications, and operations.[13] Every Sunday, the groups were given specific goals to accomplish. Zients assigned responsibility for each task to a single person, who was required to evaluate its ongoing progress: green for finished, yellow for in-progress, and red for no-progress. Zients demanded emails every thirty minutes during upgrades to the site, so he was always on top of the situation. Each week, Zients personally briefed Obama and Sebelius.

The tech surge's agile and lean strategy accomplished what hundreds of millions of dollars and a bloated bureaucracy could not. Zients's team changed the rules of federal IT implementation to save HealthCare.gov. But that was

---

[7] Robert Pear, *Health Insurance Marketplace Is Still About 40 Percent Incomplete, Official Says*, N.Y. Times (Nov. 19, 2013), nyti.ms/1sMawoz.

[8] Ian Austen, Sharon LaFraniere & Robert Pear, *Contractors See Weeks of Work on Health Site*, N.Y. Times (Oct. 20, 2013), nyti.ms/1ZZq2kn.

[9] Michael D. Shear & Sheryl Gay Stolberg, *Inside the Race to Rescue a Health Care Site, and Obama*, N.Y. Times (Nov. 30, 2013), nyti.ms/1TMT3gR.

[10] Steven Brill, America's Bitter Pill at 359 (2016).

[11] Jonathan Chait, *White House Sets November Obamacare Deadline*, N.Y. Mag. (Oct. 25, 2013), perma.cc/ZQJ9-R6UG.

[12] *Obamacare Launch 'Terribly Flawed,'* A.P. (Apr. 13, 2014), perma.cc/9ULZ-J47W.

[13] Juliet Eilperin & Zachary A. Goldfarb, *Jeff Zients Helped Salvage HealthCare.gov. Now He'll Be Obama's Go-to Guy on Economy*, Wash. Post (Dec. 22, 2013), perma.cc/T37Q-2D8C.

not enough. At the same time, Senate Democrats changed the rules of judicial confirmation to save the Affordable Care Act itself.

14.2. "NUCLEAR OPTION"

Article II of the Constitution vests the president with the power to nominate officers and judges, "with the Advice and Consent of the Senate." Procedurally, the Constitution only requires a bare majority of senators to confirm the nominee. Practically speaking, however, the magic number is three-fifths. Under the Senate's long-standing rules, to end debate, sixty senators must vote to invoke cloture. Thus forty-one unified senators can block a floor vote, even if the nominee enjoys majority support. Generally, senators of both parties have supported cloture to allow a vote, even if the judicial nominee would not receive sixty votes. For example, in 1991, Clarence Thomas was confirmed to the Supreme Court by a narrow margin of 52-48.[14] The forty-eight opposition votes would have been more than enough to filibuster and block cloture. But Senate Democrats who opposed Thomas allowed a floor vote to proceed.

Over the past two decades, both parties bear responsibility for corroding this process. After the contested Florida recount and the Supreme Court's controversial decision in *Bush v. Gore,* many scholars contended that George W. Bush was not legitimately elected president. Bruce Ackerman, a law professor at Yale, charged that Bush lacked the authority to appoint new justices. "Forty senators should simply make it plain," he wrote, "that they will block all Supreme Court nominations until the next presidential election."[15] Law professors Laurence Tribe and Cass Sunstein, from Harvard and the University of Chicago, respectively, expanded this strategy to the lower courts. According to the *New York Times,* the duo advised Senate Democrats that Bush's nominees – even those who enjoyed majority support – should be filibustered to prevent a rightward shift of the judiciary. The scholars reportedly said "it was important for the Senate to change the ground rules," because "there was no obligation to confirm someone just because they are scholarly or erudite."[16] From 2001 to 2002, the Democrats controlled the Senate – thanks to Jim Jeffords of Vermont switching his party affiliation – and could simply refuse to schedule floor votes for Bush's contested nominees. However, when the Republicans took control of the Senate in 2003, the minority party

14 Supreme Court Nominations, present–1789, UNITED STATES SENATE, perma.cc/9B8G-T294. Justice Thomas's confirmation process will be discussed in Chapter 30.
15 Bruce Ackerman, *The Court Packs* Itself, AM. PROSPECT (Feb. 12, 2001), perma.cc/R6J5-EH8Q.
16 Neil A. Lewis, *Washington Talk: Democrats Readying for Judicial Fight,* N.Y. TIMES (May 1, 2001), nyti.ms/264BLoW.

filibustered Miguel Estrada, a nominee to the D.C. Circuit.[17] Forty-two Democrats – including Hillary Clinton and Harry Reid – united to deny cloture for Estrada. Even though fifty-five Senators voted yea – more than enough for confirmation – his floor vote was blocked.[18] Senate Democrats would repeat this process, and filibuster nine other Bush nominees to the circuit courts.[19]

In response to these filibusters, Senate Majority Leader Trent Lott (R-MS) considered invoking the so-called *nuclear option*.[20] This parliamentary rule change would have eliminated the sixty-vote threshold for judicial nominations – only a simple majority would be required. Democrats charged that this tactic was an affront to the Senate's long-standing tradition of promoting debate. Then-Senator Barack Obama wrote in his autobiography that the nuclear option "seemed to perfectly capture the loss of perspective that had come to characterize judicial confirmations."[21]

In 2005, to avert the rule change, a compromise was reached by the so-called *Gang of 14* (a group of seven Democrats and seven Republicans). Five of the seven filibustered nominees would receive floor votes, including Janice Rogers Brown for the D.C. Circuit of Appeals.[22] This appointment was among the most critical, because the D.C. Circuit is considered the second most important court after the Supreme Court. Because of its jurisdiction over federal agencies, the small court hears a large share of high-profile constitutional cases that test the bounds of the separation of powers. Chief Justice Roberts, who previously served on the D.C. Circuit, wrote that it has a "special responsibility to review legal challenges to the conduct of the national government."[23] The composition

---

[17] Tim O'Brien, *Democrats Begin Filibuster against Estrada*, CNN (Feb. 13, 2003), perma.cc/4EYB-G4L5.

[18] U.S. Senate Roll Call Votes, 108th Congress – 1st Session (Mar. 13, 2003), perma.cc/598S-JP7C.

[19] Richard S. Beth, *Cloture Attempts on Nominations: Data and Historical Development*, CONG. RES. SERV. (Jun. 26, 2013), bit.ly/1Yy7toZ. Between 2001 and 2005, ten of President Bush's circuit court nominees were not confirmed after Democrats blocked cloture: Miguel A. Estrada, Charles W. Pickering, Sr., William H. Pryor, Jr., Priscilla Richman Owen, Carolyn B. Kuhl, Janice Rogers Brown, William Gerry Myers III, David W. McKeague, Henry W. Saad, and Richard A. Griffin.

[20] William Safire, *Nuclear Options*, N.Y. TIMES (Mar. 20, 2005), nyti.ms/1WVeLn2.

[21] BARACK OBAMA, THE AUDACITY OF HOPE: THOUGHTS ON RECLAIMING AMERICA 82–83 (2006).

[22] Estrada, Pickering, and Kuhl had withdrawn after cloture on their votes was denied. The Gang of 14 reached deals to allow votes for Pryor, Owen, Brown, McKeague, and Griffin, who were confirmed. No deals were reached on Myers and Saad, who were never confirmed. *Senators Compromise on Filibusters*, CNN (May 24, 2005), perma.cc/5GYN-SCDA.

[23] John G. Roberts, Jr., *What Makes the D.C. Circuit Different? A Historical View*, 92 VA. L. REV. 375 (2006).

of this court would prove to be particularly critical with respect to the ACA. From 2010 through 2016, the D.C. Circuit would hear a case involving every major Obamacare challenge.[24] Judge Brown's decision in one of those cases in 2013 would make the nuclear option radiate once again.

14.3. "SWITCH THE MAJORITY"

After President Obama's election in 2008, the roles quickly reversed. Senate Republicans – now in the minority – filibustered three of President Obama's judicial nominees: Robert Bacharach, Goodwin Liu, and Caitlin Halligan.[25] Halligan was selected to fill the seat formerly occupied by John Roberts on the D.C. Circuit, which had been vacant since 2005.[26] In March 2013, her cloture vote failed by a razor-thin margin, 51-41, with eight abstentions.[27] Two months later, Republicans dropped their opposition to Obama's second selection for the D.C. Circuit, Sri Srinivasan, as part of a broader compromise with the Democrats. Srinivasan, who served in private practice and in the Solicitor's General Office, was confirmed by a vote of 97-0.[28]

In June 2013, President Obama announced three nominations to fill the remaining vacancies on the D.C. Circuit: Patricia Ann Millett, Cornelia T. L. Pillard, and Robert L. Wilkins.[29] White House Press Secretary Jay Carney explained that the trio was simultaneously nominated because the court "should be fully staffed."[30]

---

[24] Seven-Sky v. Holder, 661 F.3d 1 (D.C. Cir. 2011) (challenge to the individual mandate); Gilardi v. HHS, 733 F.3d 1208, 1210 (D.C. Cir. 2013) (challenge to contraception mandate); Halbig v. Burwell, 758 F.3d 390, 393 (D.C. Cir. 2014) (challenge to the IRS subsidies rule); Priests for Life v. HHS, 808 F.3d 1 (D.C. Cir. 2015) (challenge to accommodation to the contraception mandate); Sissel v. HHS, 799 F.3d 1035 (D.C. Cir. 2015) (origination clause challenge); West Virginia v. HHS, 15-5309, 2016 WL 3568089 (D.C. Cir. Jul. 1, 2016) (challenge to "administrative fix."). House of Representatives v. Burwell, the challenge to the government's payment of ACA cost-sharing subsidies to insurance companies, will be argued before the D.C. Circuit in late 2016. The latter three cases will be discussed in Chapter 22.

[25] Beth, *supra* note 19. Bacharach was ultimately confirmed in February 2013. Both Liu and Halligan withdrew their nominations after cloture was blocked.

[26] Paul Kane, *Judicial Nominee Goodwin Liu Blocked by Senate Republicans*, WASH. POST (May 19, 2011), perma.cc/5XL3-Q9PM; U.S. Senate Roll Call Votes, 112th Congress – 1st Session (Dec. 6, 2011), perma.cc/5A7Y-8H3K.

[27] U.S. Senate Roll Call Votes, 113th Congress – 1st Session (Mar. 6, 2013), perma.cc/T3AP-X4YH.

[28] Juliet Eilperin, *Sri Srinivasan Confirmed to Judicial Seat in Unanimous Senate Vote*, WASH. POST (May 23, 2013), perma.cc/WS8A-QMNP.

[29] *Remarks by the President on the Nominations to the U.S. Court of Appeals for the District of Columbia*, THE WHITE HOUSE (June 4, 2013), perma.cc/R32A-AFXV.

[30] Josh Gerstein, *Obama: Court Push Not about Politics*, POLITICO (June 4, 2013), perma.cc/5LC2-J3D6.

Senate Majority Leader Harry Reid offered a different explanation, in his usual blunt manner: "There's three vacancies, we need at least one more and that will switch the majority."[31] The composition on the eleven-member court was evenly divided: There were three Clinton appointees, four judges appointed by the Presidents Bush, one Obama nominee, and three vacancies. Senate Republicans filibustered the troika.[32] Reid, who a decade earlier filibustered Estrada and Brown's nominations to the D.C. Circuit, now castigated Republicans for doing the same. "There isn't a single legitimate objection to the qualifications of any of these nominees," he charged.[33] "Republicans simply don't want President Obama to make any appointments at all to this vital court."

In response, Democrats would take a page out of the GOP's old play-book. Fittingly, it was Obamacare that finally triggered the nuclear option. On November 1, 2003, the D.C. Circuit invalidated the ACA's contraceptive mandate. Writing the majority opinion was Judge Brown, who received a confirmation vote only after *The Gang of 14's* compromise. She concluded that the mandate "trammels the right of free exercise" of a for-profit grocery store owned by devout Catholics.[34] Reid still regretted that his fellow Democrats allowed Judge Brown and her colleagues onto the D.C. Circuit. "I don't think they deserve to be on any court," he lamented, "but we put them on there, and they have been terrible."[35] According to The *New York Times*, Judge Brown's decision "represented a turning point" for Senate Democrats.[36] At a closed-door meeting, Reid told his caucus, "These are the kinds of decisions we are going to have to live with," unless Democrats could confirm more Obama appointees.

The Nevadan began "speaking individually with members of his caucus to gauge whether there [was] enough support to change filibuster rules."[37] Democrats quickly lined up behind their leader. Senator Barbara Boxer (D-CA) explained she was "very open to changing the rules for

[31] Niels Lesniewski, *Reid Pushes to Flip Balance of D.C. Circuit Court, Hints at Another Filibuster Battle*, ROLL CALL (Aug. 9, 2013), perma.cc/L3WQ-EDCR.

[32] Memorandum from Richard S. Beth & Elizabeth Rybicki, *Nominations with Cloture Motions, 2009 to the Present*, CONG. RES. SERV. (Nov. 21, 2013), bit.ly/1WSGIvQ.

[33] Sahil Kapur, *Harry Reid's Full Speech Calling for Filibuster Reform*, TALKING POINTS MEMO (Nov. 21, 2013), perma.cc/79XE-HB7S.

[34] Gilardi v. HHS, 733 F.3d 1208, 1210 (D.C. Cir. 2013).

[35] Lesniewski, *supra* note 31.

[36] Jeremy W. Peters, *Abortion Cases in Court Helped Tilt Democrats against the Filibuster*, N.Y. TIMES (Nov. 29, 2013), nyti.ms/28PsDTO.

[37] Jeremy W. Peters, *Reid Preparing to Move for Limits on Filibuster*, N.Y. TIMES (Nov. 19, 2013), nyti.ms/1XywdxF.

nominees."[38] She said, "I was not before, because I felt we could work with them. But it's gotten to an extreme situation where really qualified people can't get an up-or-down vote." Also changing her position was Senator Dianne Feinstein (D-CA), who regretted "the usual politics," and the "unconscionable" strategy to block Obama's nominees. A decade earlier, both Californians had filibustered Estrada, Brown, and the others. The *Times* reported that fifty-two of the fifty-five-member Democratic caucus supported Reid's calculated political decision: "[T]hey had to risk a backlash in the Senate to head off what they saw as a far greater long-term threat to their priorities in the form of a judiciary tilted to the right." Even if the decision allowed a future Republican president to more easily confirm conservative judges, Democrats chose to act now to insulate President Obama's agenda from judicial scrutiny.

On November 23, 2013, through an intricate parliamentary procedure, Majority Leader Reid proposed a rule change to eliminate the filibuster for all executive and judicial officers other than Supreme Court justices.[39] This rule change only needed fifty-one votes to pass. Fifty-two democrats supported the rule, while all forty-five republicans and three democrats voted nay. With this new rule in place, only a simple majority was now necessary for a judicial nominee to be confirmed. Millett, Pillard, and Wilkins – no longer blocked by a GOP filibuster – were promptly confirmed to the D.C. Circuit. As we will discuss in Chapter 22, the nuclear judges would play an important role in halting Halbig's challenge to the IRS subsidies rule.

Republicans, who considered but abandoned the nuclear option a decade earlier, were now outraged. Senate Minority Leader Mitch McConnell (R-KY) warned the Democrats: "You'll regret this, and you may regret this a lot sooner than you think."[40] In 2016, many Republicans would cite this episode to justify their opposition to President Obama's replacement for Justice Scalia.

It is tempting, but unavailing to charge Republicans and Democrats with parliamentary hypocrisy. When in the majority, both parties favored the nuclear option. When in the minority, both parties opposed it. Commentator Michael Barone's evergreen observation is apt: "[I]n politics ... all procedural arguments are insincere."[41]

[38] Jennifer Bendery, *Key Senate Democrats Flip, Now Ready for Filibuster Reform Via 'Nuclear Option,'* HUFF. POST (Nov. 20, 2013), perma.cc/UD2Q-HHFK.
[39] Brad Plumer, *It's Official: The Senate Just Got Rid of Part of the Filibuster,* WASH. POST (Nov. 21, 2013), perma.cc/C2PU-X4L4.
[40] *Id.*
[41] Michael Barone, *Senate Lineup for 2010,* WASH. EXAMINER (May 5, 2009), perma.cc/D87N-V2LX.

14.4. "NIGHT AND DAY"

As the political clashes in Congress worsened, HealthCare.gov's status slowly but steadily improved. By November 11, the site loaded in less than one second, a stark improvement over the previous load time of eight seconds.[42] The exchange's "up time" increased from 42% to 95%.[43] When more than 50,000 users logged on at once, the site set up a queuing system and notified people to return when there was more capacity.[44] Nearly 400 bugs were removed from the "punch list," as Jeffrey Zients held twice-a-day meetings with leadership. Secretary Kathleen Sebelius praised his efforts. "We have some very specific things we know we need to complete by [November] 30th," she said, "and that punch list is getting knocked out every week."[45]

Soon, the public began to realize that things were getting better. The *Washington Post* reported that "consumer advocates say it is becoming easier for people to sign up for coverage."[46] *National Journal* explained that "the truth is, the system is getting stronger as it recovers from its disastrous launch."[47] *Politico* added that "for the first time in weeks, congressional Democrats are starting to breathe easier."[48]

On December 3, President Obama officially rebooted HealthCare.gov. Speaking alongside people who benefited from the ACA, the triumphant Chief Executive celebrated the now-functioning website.[49] "Our poor execution in the first couple months," Obama began, "clouded the fact that there are a whole bunch of people who stand to benefit." Now that the exchange is working, he explained, "we need to make sure that folks refocus on what's at stake here, which is the capacity for you or your families to be able to have the security of decent health insurance at a reasonable cost."[50]

[42] Sheryl Gay Stolberg, *Health Website Tests a Tycoon and Tinkerer*, N.Y. TIMES (Nov. 10, 2013), nyti.ms/23ksC6m.

[43] Sarah Kliff, *The White House Says It Met Its Obamacare Goal. There's Still More Work Ahead*, WASH. POST (Dec. 1, 2013), perma.cc/FX25-DMX7.

[44] Sarah Kliff, *HealthCare.gov Finally Works – for Some People*, WASH. POST (Dec. 2, 2013), perma.cc/3KCT-R5WM.

[45] Robert Pear, *Health Insurance Marketplace Is Still About 40 Percent Incomplete, Official Says*, N.Y. TIMES (Nov. 19, 2013), nyti.ms/1sMawoz.

[46] Amy Goldstein & Sandhya Somashekhar, *Obamacare Update: Consumers See Progress but Insurers Smell Trouble*, WASH. POST (Nov. 25, 2013), perma.cc/J994-XX54.

[47] Sam Baker, *How Will We Know the Obamacare Site Is Fixed?*, NAT'L J. (June 19, 2016), perma.cc/3PKH-DSS3.

[48] Seung Min Kim, *ACA Anger Fading among Hill Dems*, POLITICO (Dec. 3, 2013), perma.cc/758Y-WZA9.

[49] *Remarks by the President on the Affordable Care Act*, THE WHITE HOUSE (Dec. 3, 2013), perma.cc/JT5N-DUCW.

[50] Juliet Eilperin & Zachary A. Goldfarb, *Obama Embarks on New Health-care Push after Website Fixes, Urges Americans to Sign Up*, WASH. POST (Dec. 3, 2013), perma.cc/5ABQ-Q3E6.

Kathleen Sebelius wrote in *USA Today*: "[T]oday's user experience on HealthCare.gov is a dramatic improvement over where it was on Oct. 1. The site is running faster, it's responding quicker and it can handle larger amounts of traffic."[51] Jeffrey Zients praised the work of his tech surgers. "HealthCare.Gov on Dec. 1 is night and day from where it was on Oct. 1." He beamed, "While we still have work to do, we've made significant progress with HealthCare.gov working for the vast majority of consumers."[52]

He was right. More people signed up for Obamacare on the first two days of December than in all of October combined.[53] Even President Obama signed up for a bronze policy, although it was "largely symbolic." He would continue to receive his health care from the military.[54] *Huffington Post* reporter Jeffrey Young tweeted, "Obama is a health insurance company's favorite kind of customer: one who will never, ever file a claim!"[55] Alas, POTUS skimped, and did not get a gold or platinum plan.

President Obama predicted, "[T]wo years from now, when we look back, we're going to be able to say that even more people have health insurance who didn't have it before."[56] He explained, "[T]hat is part of the reason why I pushed so hard to get this law done in the first place." Obama closed his remarks by offering a warning to Republicans, who continued to attack the law. If "you still think this law is a bad idea then you've got to tell us specifically what you'd do differently to cut costs, cover more people, and make insurance more secure." With the Affordable Care Act settling into place, there was a new reality that the GOP would continue to resist: Any effort to repeal the law would result in people losing coverage they liked.

14.5. "DECEMBER DELUGE"

With the website now operational, the White House did everything in its power to ensure that as many people as possible could get covered by January 1. On December 12 – three days before the deadline – the administration

---

[51] Kathleen Sebelius, *Improvement Dramatic over Oct. 1*, USA TODAY (Dec. 1, 2013), perma.cc/E6KK-2VRG.

[52] Kliff, *supra* note 43.

[53] Sarah Kliff, *More Signed Up for Obamacare in First Two Days of December than in all of October*, WASH. POST (Dec. 4, 2013), perma.cc/6AXP-QY3J.

[54] Sarah Kliff, *Obama Will Be His Health Insurer's Very Favorite Enrollee*, WASH. POST (Dec. 23, 2013), perma.cc/Z9SD-DXXD.

[55] Jeffrey Young (@JeffYoung), TWITTER (Dec. 23, 2013), bit.ly/1Sd36bj.

[56] *President Obama's December 20 News Conference*, WASH. POST (Dec. 20, 2013), perma.cc/HY4X-X59L.

pushed the signup window back till December 23.[57] Additionally, HHS
nudged insurance companies to allow policies to go into effect on New Year's
Day, even if customers did not pay by December 31. HHS spokeswoman
Julie Bataille encouraged insurers to provide "retroactive coverage."[58] One
industry official told the *Washington Post*, "it seems like this is another effort
to put more of the onus on insurers."[59] It worked. Aetna agreed to accept
late payments through January 8. A week later, America's Health Insurance
Plans announced that its members would follow suit.[60] There would be more
delays.

On December 23, health care shoppers received an early Christmas present. Without any public announcement, the White House granted customers
another day to sign up.[61] The deadline was now 11:59 PM on December 24,
2013 – four years to the date since the Senate voted for the Affordable Care Act.
Once again, the insurance companies got coal in their stockings. An industry
official told *The Washington Post* that the "quiet deadline extension" was "yet
another last-minute change to the rules by shortening an already-tight time
period in which to process enrollments." This extension, he said, "makes it
even harder to ensure people who have selected a plan are able to have their
coverage begin in January."[62]

Reuters dubbed December 24 as the "moment of truth for Obamacare."[63]
If the exchange does not achieve the "right mix of young and old," the entire
law "risks eventually *unraveling*."[64] Not quite. With chestnuts roasting on the
open fire, and Santa on his way, there would be yet another extension. On
Christmas Eve, HHS quietly announced that customers who tried to enroll
in a plan but ran into "delays caused by heavy traffic to HealthCare.gov,
maintenance periods, or other issues with our systems" could sign up late and
still be covered on January 1.[65] But the government refused to call it a delay.

[57] Sarah Kliff, *Obamacare's Deadlines Are Changing. Again.* WASH. POST (Dec. 12, 2013),
      perma.cc/4SLW-ZL2L.
[58] *Id.*
[59] *Id.*
[60] Sarah Kliff, *Insurers Are Giving Obamacare Shoppers More Time to Pay,* WASH. POST (Dec.
      18, 2013), perma.cc/VGE5-YVPB.
[61] Juliet Eilperin & Amy Goldstein, *Obama Administration Quietly Extends Health-care
      Enrollment Deadline by a Day,* WASH. POST (Dec. 23, 2013), perma.cc/28GT-NQVP.
[62] Juliet Eilperin & Amy Goldstein, *Consumers Get One More Day to Sign Up for Health
      Insurance,* MIAMI HERALD (Dec. 23, 2013), perma.cc/95A6-KPTG.
[63] John Whitesides, *The Painful Path to Obamacare Deadline,* REUTERS (Dec. 24, 2013),
      perma.cc/4LEP-MP4V.
[64] *Id.*
[65] Joanne Kenen & Jason Millman, *Final ACA Deadline Not Quite Final,* POLITICO (Dec. 24,
      2013), perma.cc/6FKX-GP99.

@HealthCare.gov tweeted "Reports of extended deadline are incorrect."[66] There would be many more delays leading up to the March 2014 deadline, which we will discuss in Chapter 18.

What were the final results of the signup season? In light of the botched launch, the milestones were simply remarkable. Nearly one million people signed up in December, more than nine times the number of enrollees in October and November combined. HHS announced that nearly two million people had visited the site on December 23 alone.[67] *Wonkblog* called it the "December deluge."[68] The administration was still behind the pace of reaching their estimated goal of seven million signups by March. But "what seemed impossible in October," analyst Sarah Kliff observed, "suddenly became a lot more plausible."[69]

President Obama, who was vacationing in Hawaii, must have had a very, merry Christmas when he received a "detailed report" about the signups.[70] Having a far more difficult Christmas season were the Little Sisters of the Poor. The contraceptive mandate would to go into effect on January 1, and they were still praying for relief from Obamacare.

[66] HealthCare.gov (@HealthCare.gov), TWITTER (Dec. 24, 2013), bit.ly/1OxJdBd.
[67] Kenen & Millman, *supra* note 65.
[68] Sarah Kliff, *The December Deluge: 1.1 million Have Enrolled on HealthCare.gov*, WASH. POST (Dec. 29, 2013), perma.cc/874U-XZGC.
[69] Sarah Kliff, *Obamacare Just Might Net Its 7 Million Sign-Ups*, WASH. POST (Dec. 30, 2013), perma.cc/874U-XZGC.
[70] Ezra Klein & Evan Soltas, *Wonkbook: What Today's Obamacare Deadline Is Actually About*, WASH. POST (Dec. 24, 2013), perma.cc/2KVB-WJCA.

PART V

Religious Liberty (December 31, 2013–July 21, 2014)

15

New Year's Resolution

In September 2013, as a government shutdown loomed, and with only three months before the contraceptive mandate went into effect, the Little Sisters of the Poor finally challenged *Accommodation 2.0* in court. One of their attorneys told me that they were very late to file because the Little Sisters didn't want to have anything to do with litigation. But as New Year's Eve drew near, the order of nuns were left with no other options. Over the next three months their lawyers at the Becket Fund for Religious Liberty anxiously waited for a decision. "We kept calling, saying, 'hey we have an emergency coming up,'" the lawyer told me. "We needed an answer."

Finally, late in the afternoon on Friday, December 27, the district court ruled against the Little Sisters. Judge William J. Martínez did not question whether the mandate conflicts with their religious beliefs. However, Martínez did "analyze the challenged regulations to determine whether their implementation will cause the allegedly harmful act to in fact occur."[1] Despite the Little Sisters' objection to filling out the form, the court concluded that "nothing on the face of the Form expressly authorizes [providing] contraceptive care." Signing the form "does not authorize any organization to deliver contraceptive coverage to Little Sisters' employees," the court concluded. As a result, *Accommodation 2.0* does "not substantially burden Plaintiffs' religious beliefs," and the Little Sisters are not actually "required to buy into a scheme that substantially burdens their religious beliefs."

At that time, the overwhelming majority of courts had already granted interim relief to religious non-profits. One of the attorneys for the Little Sisters was shocked that the court ruled against them. "I would have thought that of

---

[1] Little Sisters of the Poor Home for the Aged v. Sebelius, 6 F. Supp. 3d 1225, 1239 (D. Colo. 2013).

all the clients in the country who were going to get relief from the lower courts, the one I don't need to worry about is the Little Sisters of the Poor, because who's really going to turn down Little Sisters of the Poor? They're so obviously religious that it's idiotic to not call them a religious employer."

After an all-nighter, the very next day the Becket Fund lawyers requested an emergency injunction from the Tenth Circuit Court of Appeals in Denver. The twenty-one-page brief explained: "By midnight on New Year's Eve, Mother Provincial Loraine Marie Maguire must decide whether the Little Sisters should adhere to their religious conviction that they cannot participate in the Mandate, or whether they should sacrifice that religious belief to spare their ministry from the government's crushing fines." This prayer for relief would also go unanswered.

Three days later, at noon on December 31, 2013 – as it had done a year earlier with *Hobby Lobby* – the Tenth Circuit denied the injunction. Judges Paul Joseph Kelly, Jr. and Carlos F. Lucero found that under the accommodation, "there is no enforceable obligation … for any of the Plaintiffs to provide any of the objectionable coverage." As a result, "an injunction pending appeal at this stage is not warranted."

Like the year before, the Tenth Circuit's refusal to put the mandate on hold was at odds with virtually all other federal courts to consider the issue. In seventeen out of nineteen cases, the courts had granted an injunction for the religious non-profits before the December 31 deadline. Leading up to New Year's Eve, only the Little Sisters and Notre Dame University were denied an injunction by the lower courts.[2]

In early December, Father Jenkins, who had invited Obama to speak at Notre Dame four years earlier, explained that succumbing to the mandate will lead us "down a path that ultimately will undermine those [religious] institutions."[3] However, with a decision that surprised many, Notre Dame acquiesced to the Seventh Circuit's order. A spokesperson for the university announced on December 31, "Having been denied a stay, Notre Dame is advising employees that pursuant to the Affordable Care Act, our third party administrator is required to notify plan participants of coverage provided under its contraceptives payment program."[4] Coverage of emergency contraceptives such as Plan B and Ella would soon become available through Notre Dame's insurance plan.

---

[2]   Order Denying Appellants' Emergency Motion for Injunction Pending Appeal, Notre Dame v. Sebelius, No. 13-01276 (7th Cir. 2013) (Posner, Flaum, Hamilton), bit.ly/1s3fBBz.

[3]   Paul Browne, *Notre Dame, on Religious Liberty Grounds, Sues from Relief from Federal Mandate*, NOTRE DAME NEWS (Dec. 3, 2013), perma.cc/G4LQ-4VYH.

[4]   *Notre Dame Issues Statement on Contraceptive Care Injunction Denial*, WNDU 16 (Dec. 31, 2013), perma.cc/R94M-N8N4.

Many criticized the university for not having a strong enough commitment to fight the mandate all the way. Father Bill Miscamble, a professor of history at Notre Dame, told the *National Catholic Register* that he was disappointed "with the tepid way in which Notre Dame has acquiesced with the Obamacare provisions and authorized its health-insurance administrator to implement the HHS mandate."[5] Notre Dame did not seek an injunction from the Supreme Court. I asked one of the attorneys for the Little Sisters why Notre Dame did not request emergency relief from the Justices. He replied, "I don't know, and you will never find out." Notre Dame continued to challenge the mandate in the lower courts, but by that point it had already complied with the accommodation.

Later that month, Pope Francis spoke about Notre Dame, saying, "[I]t is my hope that the University of Notre Dame will continue to offer unambiguous testimony to this aspect of its foundational Catholic identity, especially in the face of efforts, from whatever quarter, to dilute that indispensable witness.... And this is important: its identity, as it was intended from the beginning. To defend it, to preserve it and to advance it!" Notre Dame Professor Carter Snead saw the Pope's remarks as encouraging the university to continue its fight against the contraception mandate: "The Holy Father's words strike me as a timely and profound encouragement to Notre Dame in its continuing efforts to defend its religious liberty in court."[6] Patrick Deneen, also a Professor at Notre Dame, told *National Review* that "[o]n the same day that Pope Francis's statement was publicized, members of the university community were given notice that we would be receiving new health ID cards for 'women's preventive services.'"[7]

The Little Sisters of the Poor would not be so easily deterred. Mother Provincial Loraine joked with one of her attorneys, "Well, really, how many nuns can they put in jail?"

15.2. "SOTOMAYOR DROPS BALL ON OBAMACARE"

With less than twelve hours till the new year, the contraceptive mandate was barreling toward the Little Sisters like an oncoming train. Justice Sonia Sotomayor – who at that very moment was riding Amtrak to New York

[5] Joan Frawley Desmond, *Notre Dame Complies with Contraception Mandate*, Nat'l Catholic Reg. (Jan. 1, 2014), perma.cc/U5DL-YC59.
[6] Barbara Boland, *Pope Tells Notre Dame: Defend the Freedom of the Church*, CNSNews (Jan. 30, 2014), perma.cc/TYJ4-YBV3.
[7] Kathryn Jean Lopez, *Pope Francis Speaks to Notre Dame about Uncompromising Christian Witness and Religious Freedom*, Nat'l Rev. (Jan. 30, 2014), perma.cc/U6MW-WWV4.

City – would soon pull the emergency break. The Bronx native was invited to push the button to start the New Year's Eve ball drop. The president of the Times Square Alliance exclaimed, "Who better to join us in the crossroads of the world than one of New York's own?"[8] Sotomayor would receive notice of the Little Sisters' emergency petition around 5:00 PM while she was on the northbound train from Union Station to Penn Station. Fortunately, Amtrak's wireless Internet actually worked that evening.

The Little Sisters made their case: "Mother Loraine must make that decision by midnight tonight, unless relief is granted by this Court." There was a strong sense of déjà vu to this appeal. The Becket Fund represented both Hobby Lobby and the Little Sisters. And just like the year before, the attorneys were forced to frantically file a last-minute appeal with Circuit Justice Sotomayor on December 31. The year before, Sotomayor rebuffed Hobby Lobby. Fortunately, *should old acquaintance be forgot and never brought to mind*, this prayer for extraordinary relief was answered.

Before Justice Sotomayor released the Waterford Crystal Ball over the Crossroads of the World, she would first release an injunction halting the contraceptive mandate. Or, as *The Drudge Report* more colorfully captioned it, "Sotomayor Drops Ball on Obamacare."[9] At 10:00 PM, Mark Rienzi's phone rang. It was Danny Bickel, the Supreme Court's Emergency Applications clerk. Capital defense lawyers have dubbed Bickel "the death clerk" because he handles the eleventh-hour requests to stay executions.[10] But tonight, there was a far less somber call to make. Bickel told the Becket Fund attorney that the Court would soon issue an order, and he would send him a copy. Around 10:15 PM, as hundreds of thousands massed in Times Square, Sotomayor issued a one-paragraph order:

> IT IS ORDERED that [the government is] temporarily enjoined from enforcing against [the Little Sisters of the Poor] the contraceptive coverage requirements imposed by the Patient Protection and Affordable Care Act, and related regulations pending the receipt of a response and further order of the undersigned or of the Court. The response to the application is due Friday, January 3, 2014, by 10 AM.

Success! But this was an ephemeral victory, and the nuns' angst was not quite over. Sotomayor's December 31 order was only temporary. That evening, Mark

---

[8] Tony Mauro, *Sotomayor Will Count Down to New Year in Times Square*, BLT (Dec. 31, 2013), perma.cc/G7WX-ZLCL.

[9] Josh Blackman, *Sotomayor Drops Ball on Obamacare*, JOSH BLACKMAN'S BLOG (Jan. 1, 2014), perma.cc/9B8M-TZ9A.

[10] Adam Liptak, *To Beat the Execution Clock, the Justices Prepare Early*, N.Y. TIMES (Sept. 3, 2012), nyti.ms/1WgQvfd.

Rienzi called Mother Loraine, who had "been praying about what she was going to do tomorrow." He told her, "[W]e at least have life for a little while." As the nuns hailed Mary, Miley Cyrus twerked away 2013 in Times Square.[11] Fortunately, the *New York Times* observed, "Viewers should not expect to see Ms. Cyrus twerking near Justice Sotomayor."[12] The Justice had a private space to handle these more pressing matters.[13]

15.3. ACCOMMODATION 3.0

On Friday, the government submitted its reply, and urged the Court that the injunction should be denied. "Applicants claim a right to extraordinary relief," the solicitor general wrote, "even though compliance with the procedure they challenge will not result in anyone else's provision of the items and services to which applicants object." Recall that under *Accommodation 2.0*, the nuns, would not have to pay for the contraceptives. The Becket Fund lawyers replied that same day in a plea to keep the injunction in place:

> The temporary injunction issued Tuesday night saved Mother Provincial Loraine Marie Maguire from the choice of violating her faith by executing the government's required form, or exposing the Little Sisters' ministry to decimation by IRS penalties. She exercised her religion that night, and each day since, by acting in accordance with God's will as she understands it. The temporary injunction protected, and continues to protect, that religious exercise. That injunction should remain in place.

Twenty-one days of silence from the Court would follow. Then on January 24, the Justices issued a one-paragraph order:

> The application for an injunction having been submitted to Justice Sotomayor and by her referred to the Court, the Court orders: If the employer applicants inform the Secretary of Health and Human Services in writing that they are non-profit organizations that hold themselves out as religious

---

[11] *New Year's Eve 2013 Performers to Include Miley Cyrus and More*, CBS NEWS (Dec. 30, 2013), perma.cc/FR49-BZJ7.

[12] Emma G. Fitzsimmons, *Sotomayor Countdown to New Year in Times Square*, N.Y. TIMES (Dec. 29, 2013), perma.cc/A2R6-W9X3.

[13] And as if December 31, 2013 was not chaotic enough, that evening Sotomayor also received an emergency application for a stay from the governor of Utah, who was trying to put on hold a district court order permitting same-sex marriages in the Beehive State. In contrast with the relief for the Little Sisters, Sotomayor *only* called for a response from the challengers, but *did not* put the marriages on hold. Only six days later, and after hundreds of marriages were performed, did Sotomayor refer the petition to the entire Court, which put the lower court's judgment on hold with no recorded dissent. Josh Blackman & Howard M. Wasserman, *The Process of Marriage Equality*, 43 HASTINGS CONST. LAW Q. 289–290 (2016).

and have religious objections to providing coverage for contraceptive services, the respondents are enjoined from enforcing against the applicants
the challenged provisions of the Patient Protection and Affordable Care Act
and related regulations pending final disposition of the appeal by the United
States Court of Appeals for the Tenth Circuit. To meet the condition for
injunction pending appeal, applicants need not use the form prescribed
by the Government and need not send copies to third-party administrators.
The Court issues this order based on all of the circumstances of the case,
and this order should not be construed as an expression of the Court's views
on the merits.

Simply stated, if the Little Sisters notify the government in writing that they
"have a religious objection to providing coverage for contraceptive service,"
which they obviously do, they are exempted from the contraceptive mandate
altogether. I will refer to this approach as *Accommodation 3.0*, although in
effect it mirrors the exemption given to the houses of worship. Rather than
having to certify a religious objection, which would serve as notice for the
insurer to begin paying for contraceptive coverage, under *Accommodation 3.0*,
the employees of the Little Sister would not receive the coverage at all. There
was no need for the Little Sisters to use the form provided by the government.
Critically, however, the Justices stressed that "this order should not be construed as an expression of the Court's views on the merits." With that order,
the Little Sisters finally received the relief they needed.

There was no recorded dissent to the order, but that does not mean that all
of the Justices in fact agreed. For example, when the court refuses to halt an
execution, Justice Ginsburg has explained that the lack of dissent on a last-
minute appeal does not mean everyone concurs: "When a stay [of execution]
is denied," she observed, "it doesn't mean we are in fact unanimous."[14]

A senior DOJ official told me that they "were a little bit surprised" by the
claim of the Little Sisters of the Poor and other religious non-profits. In contrast with Hobby Lobby, where the position of the government was that there
was no RFRA claim at all, for the Little Sisters, there had been this evolution
of working to try to frame that accommodation that would work for religious
non-profits, or at least the vast majority of them. He added that there had
been a lot of discussions between the administration and representatives of
religious organizations to try to find some common ground, to find some way
to make it work. That resulted in these changes over time in the nature of
accommodation. That is, the upgrade from Accommodation 1.0 to 2.0. The

---

[14] Mark Sherman, No public opposition to Arizona execution from Supreme court, Assoc'd
Press (Aug. 4, 2014), perma.cc/3QR2-GCCL.

Justice Department, he explained, did think by the time we've gotten to the idea of the form, that it would be perceived that we had avoided a substantial burden on religion and come up with a system that really seemed fair and would work. He shrugged his shoulders, and said, "So I think we were a little surprised about the stay."

The Little Sisters' fight was far from over. The case would be sent back to the Tenth Circuit Court of Appeals for another round of litigation. But first, exactly two months later on March 25, 2014, the Supreme Court would hear oral arguments in *Sebelius v. Hobby Lobby Stores*.

15.4. "NO BOSSES IN MY BEDROOM"

The Supreme Court is one of the last places on earth where cameras are prohibited. The justices do not provide a live broadcast of proceedings. Once or twice a year, a same-day release of audio is available. The only way to witness the proceedings is to be physically present. The Supreme Court releases a small number of tickets for the general public, usually fifty, on the day of arguments. The only way to obtain a ticket is to wait on the sidewalk outside the Supreme Court before the crack of dawn.

For most cases, it is necessary to arrive the night before and camp out on the sidewalk. The most unsettling aspect of the SCOTUS campout (take it from my experiences) is the sprinklers. They turn on every morning around 2:00 AM and give all sleeping spectators a wet wake-up call. For the most part, social norms develop that allow people to make a run for Union Station (the only bathroom open at night), or buy some food or coffee at the nearby Au Bon Pain. However, the Supreme Court police will not enforce the line. If you leave, you may forfeit your spot. For high-profile cases, the wait is even longer. Before the Obamacare cases were argued in March 2012, a group of dedicated SCOTUS watchers endured the elements for ninety-two hours to secure one of the fifty coveted tickets. *Hobby Lobby* would be no exception.

By the dawn's early light on Wednesday, March 25, 2014, the masses began to assemble outside One First Street. The line waiters, ever-so-close to the elusive golden ticket, had been freezing for more than seventy-two hours during "an unseasonably cold day Monday, followed by a Tuesday morning snowstorm that had a bit more to it that forecasters had predicted."[15] By 6:00 a.m., the media began to set up cameras and microphones to broadcast live

---

[15] Mark Walsh, *ACA's Return Taxes to the High Court*, SCOTUSBLOG (Mar. 25, 2014), perma.cc/2CWW-5E4F.

from the Court. Standing in the shadow of the U.S. Capitol, which looms on the other side of First Street, demonstrators flooded the plaza.

Those supporting the contraception mandate had an impressive array of signs. A popular placard read, "Hey Supreme Court. No Bosses in my bedroom." The graphic depicted a silhouette of a man in a suit leering over a bed. Another handwritten sign read, "Keep your hobbies off my ovaries." Next to a picture of the Holy Bible was the caption, "This is not a healthcare plan." Above a picture of a "Craft Store" was the caption, "This is not a church. #FreedomFraud." And my personal favorite, "If men could get pregnant, birth control would be available from gumball machines and be bacon flavored."

One woman was dressed up like a pack of birth control pills. Another woman knitted a pink uterus, with fallopian tubes dangling on each side, like pigtails.[16] She held a sign that said "Hobby Lobby. This uterus is for you!" Presumably she did not buy the yarn at Hobby Lobby. As part of an online campaign dubbed the "snatchel project," women mailed a "fuzzy uterus" to Hobby Lobby's Oklahoma headquarters, with the tag, "Here's one of your very own, to control as you wish."[17]

I asked one of Hobby Lobby's attorneys if the Green family was prepared for the backlash it would receive for its position. He replied that the owners of the firm were "aware that they were getting themselves in a big public fight over an issue a big chunk of the public would be against them." When the suit was filed, they "didn't know that their one case would be the one that would go to the Supreme Court." But he stressed, "I don't know if they fully anticipated what would happen." Did the Greens have a Plan B if the Court ruled against them, I asked. The lawyers told me he did not "know if they had fully come to grips with exactly what they would do if the government tried to put them out of business." He added, "The fines would be so significant that they couldn't continue to live according to their faith." The attorney relayed a conversation with Hobby Lobby CEO David Green, who said, "Well, let's not worry about it. We're going to win." The attorney explained that the truth is that very prayerful people can do things in a way that other folks may not be able to.

Hobby Lobby's supporters on the Supreme Court plaza were just as passionate, but their shtick was not nearly as witty. The signs read, "I am pro-life generation," "Religious Freedom: Everyone's Business," "Stand up for Religious Freedom," and hashtag "#TeamLife." Six men clad in kilts – one

---

[16] Instructions for this craft project can be found at the aptly named crochet site, Ravelry. *Crocheted Uterus*, TinksWorld (Nov. 2011), perma.cc/QX49-62PL.

[17] Sarah Mink, *Eight New Lobbying Hobbies That Fight against Hobby Lobby*, bitchmedia (June 30, 2014), perma.cc/4AA2-35S2; *see also The Snatchel Project*, Gov. Free VJJ perma.cc/5MS2-JFF7.

playing *Amazing Grace* on bagpipes – held up a banner that read, "God's Law Comes first. Repeal Socialist Obamacare!" Another held a sign that read, "Obamacare mandate persecutes Catholics." Around 9:00 AM, people began to trickle into the Supreme Court.

15.5. "FIVE-TOOL PLAYER"

After the contraceptive mandate was announced in August 2011, nearly fifty lawsuits were filed by for-profit religious employers nationwide. However, the Supreme Court chose only two of these cases for review: Hobby Lobby Stores and Conestoga Wood Specialties. The latter was a furniture business owned by the Hahns, a Mennonite family in Pennsylvania. Conestoga was represented by Alliance Defending Freedom. Hobby Lobby was represented by the Becket Fund for Religious Liberty.

The Court granted a total of ninety minutes of argument time – more than the usual hour – but the justices did not divide the time among the two plaintiffs. Only one person would argue on behalf of both parties. That job fell to the lawyer that the *Washington Post* lauded as "the best advocate of his generation" – Paul Clement.[18] That *Post* article is framed prominently in the lobby of Clement's firm, Bancroft PLLC.

Clement has argued more than seventy-five cases before the Supreme Court, first as President George W. Bush's solicitor general, and later in private practice. National Public Radio reporter Nina Totenberg referred to him as the "legal wunderkind." Clement puts the justices at ease with his conversational delivery and thorough preparation. One of Clement's colleagues described him as a "five-tool player," using the baseball metaphor for a perfect all-around athlete. People know him for being outstanding at oral argument, the lawyer said, but he is also great at brief writing and managing a team. Clement, his colleague noted, is such a great strategist who can see the path through a case even at an early stage. He has the "uncanny ability to know where to zig and where to zag."

As to how Clement was chosen to argue this case, one of the lawyers involved in the process would only say that ultimately the decision was made that Paul would argue on behalf of everybody. He added, "Obviously this was the right call. He's the best." The Green Family retained Paul Clement, who split the table at the Court with lawyers from both the Becket Fund and Alliance Defending Freedom. Another attorney involved with the case told me that

---

[18] Michael Leahy, *Esteemed Lawyer Paul Clement's Next Challenge Is Arguing against Health-care Law*, WASH. POST (Mar. 11, 2012), perma.cc/4SRH-QTBT.

"ADF knows Paul, is comfortable with Paul, is comfortable with a lot of the other lawyers [at Bancroft], and the same is true for the Beckett Fund." They all had a good relationship because they shared the sense that this is going to be really important going forward in terms of matters that are held very deeply.

At 9:37 AM on that cold Wednesday morning, Clement and his associates entered the Court. A few minutes later, Solicitor General Donald B. Verrilli, Jr. walked into the Court. Wearing a morning coat and tails – the customary garb for the solicitor general – Verrilli looked even taller and more slender than usual. The soft-spoken attorney served as a key participant in the Obama administration's defense of all aspects of Obamacare, and through that process became a close confidante of the president himself. Verrilli had won a decisive victory in *NFIB v. Sebelius*, although his performance was largely – and, in my opinion, unjustifiably[19] – criticized.

Before arguments began, as is custom, Verrilli and Clement shook hands and exchanged small talk. For both attorneys, this case was a bit of déjà vu. Exactly two years ago to the date, the two faced off against each other on the constitutionality of Affordable Care Act. In that sense, it felt like a reunion. Indeed, even the justices felt like they had been there before. At one point during the case, Paul Clement referred to the payment for not providing insurance as a "penalty." Justice Sotomayor interjected, "It's not called a penalty. It's called a tax." To booming laughter, the chief justice agreed. "She's right about that." Clement, who had been on the losing end of that argument two years earlier, noted, "It has been treated for some purposes as a penalty. And I think for this purpose, it certainly feels punitive." Reporter Mark Walsh observed that "the four Justices who wrote the joint dissent on that issue – Antonin Scalia, Anthony M. Kennedy, Clarence Thomas, and Samuel A. Alito Jr. – did not appear to find it amusing."[20] Later in the argument, Justice Kennedy asked the solicitor general, "Does that mean the constitutionality of the whole Act has to be examined before we accept your view?" To laughter, Verrilli replied, "Well, I think it has been examined, Your Honor, to my recollection."

But at the same time, this was a different case. One of the attorneys for the Greens told me that he "always thought of Hobby Lobby as much more a religious liberty case than an Obamacare case. There was no sense in which it would take down the Act or really even open a huge wound in the ACA." Rather, he added, this case was about "making sure that the Religious Freedom Restoration Act (RFRA) wasn't tortured for the sake of some ACA related value."

---

[19] Josh Blackman, UNPRECEDENTED: THE CONSTITUTIONAL CHALLENGE TO OBAMACARE 188–194 (2013).

[20] *Walsh, supra* note 15.

Another one of the Greens' attorneys explained "that this was not the normal cause litigation where people file a suit because they don't like something. Maybe it affects them, or maybe it doesn't," he told me, "but they figure out a way to create a dispute that can get them to court to take down a thing they don't like." The challenge to the subsidies on the federal exchange, which if successful would blow a huge hole in the ACA, was very much this sort of *cause litigation*.

But that was not the case here. "The government was forcing something upon the Greens and they had a choice," the lawyer told me. "They could either say, 'Fine, we'll just take it and compromise our religious liberties and move on knowing that the government says we have to do it.' Or they can say, 'No. Our religious liberties matter more to us than the trouble of litigation.'" More importantly, all of the advocates realized that "we really need to work hard and we need to get along and we need to check our egos at the door because this case is a lot bigger than who gets to claim victory for this or whose name is first; it is about ensuring the protection of people's deepest held religious beliefs."

This case was about something far greater than Obamacare. The government agreed, in a way. A senior DOJ lawyer told me that in Hobby Lobby "we were really not thinking so much in Obamacare terms, as just trying to think about ourselves in the role of lawyers for the government trying to protect the operation of programs Congress has enacted, and the Executive Branch of government is administering." Secretary Sebelius, who attended arguments in *NFIB* two years earlier, did not even come to the Court for *Hobby Lobby*. *King v. Burwell* would be a very different case for the government.

At exactly 10:00 AM, all nine justices instantly appeared, as if by magic, from behind the majestic crimson curtains that drape the Supreme Court. They quickly took their seats. Chief Justice Roberts began, "We'll hear argument this morning in consolidated cases, *Sebelius v. Hobby Lobby Stores*; and *Conestoga Wood Specialties Corporation v. Sebelius*. Mr. Clement."

16

Substantial Burden

16.1. "WE THE CORPORATIONS"

To determine whether the contraceptive mandate violates the Religious Freedom Restoration Act (RFRA), the Court would have to answer four questions. First, is Hobby Lobby a "person" for purposes of the law? Second, if it is a "person," did the mandate "substantially burden" its "exercise of religion"? Third, is the requirement that employers provide cost-free contraceptive coverage, "in furtherance of a compelling governmental interest"? Finally, is the contraceptive mandate "the least restrictive means of furthering that compelling governmental interest," or can the government achieve that goal without substantially burdening religion?

The threshold issue for the Court was whether Hobby Lobby was, for purposes of RFRA at least, "a person." The issue of corporate personhood was fresh on the minds of the justices, and the country as a whole. In 2010, a sharply divided 5–4 Court decided *Citizens United v. FEC*. The Case held that the government could not prohibit a corporation from financing a movie critical of Hillary Clinton that would be broadcasted within thirty days of the election.[1]

The backlash to the decision took on a life of its own, as the mantra spread that corporations could not exercise constitutional rights. After the decision was announced, MSNBC pundit Keith Olbermann said that *Citizens United* "might actually have more dire implications than *Dred Scott*," the infamous 1857 opinion in which Chief Justice Roger Taney stated that African Americans had "no rights which the white man was bound to respect."

---

[1] Citizens United v. FEC, 558 U.S. 310 (2010). Coincidentally, Citizens United was the first case Solicitor Elena Kagan argued before the Supreme Court (or any appellate court for that matter), and the first case Justice Sotomayor voted on. They were both on the losing end. Robert Barnes, *Elena Kagan: '10th Justice' Has Deep Legal Knowledge but No Bench Experience*, WASH. POST (May 10, 2010), perma.cc/C4KA-G62Y.

A week after *Citizens United* was decided, President Obama openly criticized the justices who were sitting about fifty feet away from him during the 2010 State of the Union address. He breached the figurative and literal separation of powers. Obama said the decision "reversed a century of law that I believe will open the floodgates for special interests." In response to the president's barbs, Justice Alito cringed, shook his head no, and seemed to mouth, "Not true." That would be Justice Alito's last trip to the State of the Union, but it would not be corporate personhood's last trip to the Supreme Court.

Hobby Lobby served as a potent sequel to *Citizens United*. In *Citizens United*, corporations asserted a right to free speech. In *Hobby Lobby*, corporations claimed a right to free exercise of religion. This claim was viewed in many segments of society as unfathomable. A political cartoon published in 2014 summed up the argument well. It depicted the Constitution written on parchment. However, the preamble "We the People" was altered to say "We the Corporations." The letters used to spell out "Corporations" were cut from magazines using Hobby Lobby–branded scissors, and were glued ransom-note-style over the word "People." The caption read, "Crafty." This argument was also deemed unpersuasive by many in the legal academy. "For-profit corporations do not and should not have religious rights," said University of Miami law professor Caroline Mala Corbin.[2] "They have no soul, and they certainly don't have a relationship with God."

During oral arguments, Justice Sotomayor asked, "How does a corporation exercise religion?" With a pregnant pause for sarcasm, she alluded to *Citizens United*, "I mean, I know how it speaks and we have, according to our jurisprudence, 200 years of corporations speaking in its own interests. But where are the cases that show that a corporation exercises religion?" Solicitor General Verrilli said there were none. He told the justices, "In the entire history of this country, there is not a single case in which a for-profit corporation was granted an exemption on" religious grounds.

But that did not resolve the issue. Justice Scalia promptly shot back that there was also "not a single case in which [a corporation] was denied [an] exemption ... on the ground that it was a for-profit enterprise." Once again, an Obamacare mandate was *unprecedented* – there were not cases on either side of the scale. A senior DOJ official told me that the government recognized "fairly early on in the process that it was going to be a very hard sell to establish the propositions that for-profit corporations categorically could never bring RFRA claims."

[2] Richard Wolf, *Religious challenge to health care law hits high court*, USA Today (Mar. 20, 2014), perma.cc/7XZN-M2DH.

The "hard sell" became apparent after a series of questions posed by Justices Alito, Kennedy, and Breyer. Justice Alito noted that "Denmark recently prohibited kosher and halal slaughter methods because [the people] believe that they are inhumane." He asked, if Congress enacted the same law, could an incorporated kosher or halal butcher challenge it?[3] Verrilli tried to fight the hypothetical by explaining that it would be a different question if the law singled out Jewish or Muslim butchers. Justice Kennedy stressed that the "impetus for this [law] was humane treatment of animals, and there was no animus to religion at all." Eventually, the solicitor general answered, as he knew he had to: perhaps individual customers of the butcher shop could sue, but the incorporated butchers could not challenge the law.

Justice Breyer – who was uncharacteristically quiet, asking only four questions – became animated with this response. He interrupted the solicitor general midsentence. "Take five Jewish or Muslim butchers and what you're saying to them is if they choose to work under the corporate form ... you have to give up on ... the Free Exercise Clause [rights] that [they'd] otherwise have," Breyer queried. "Now, looked at that way," he said, speaking over Verrilli, "I don't think it matters whether they call themselves a corporation or whether they call themselves individuals." With this simple line of questions, the weakness of the proposition that the owners of a corporation cannot exercise religion through their corporations – in this case by exercising ritual slaughter of animals – was revealed.

Justice Kagan seemed similarly unpersuaded by the notion that a for-profit corporation could *never* bring a claim under RFRA. She responded to the solicitor general, "I'm not sure I understand ... that the claim is not cognizable at all." In other words, she thought that the incorporated kosher butcher could challenge the law in the first place; that was a totally separate question from whether the claim would succeed. One of Hobby Lobby's attorneys told me that it was obvious from their comments at argument that Justices Kagan and Breyer did not buy the government's argument. He added, "If they didn't have Kagan and Breyer, we knew they're not going to win on that." At a minimum, the lawyers were thrilled and felt very comfortable that we had won that piece.

The government recognized the risk of taking the absolutist position that no corporation, no matter how small, could ever bring a religious liberty claim. They understood that certain tightly knit businesses may have *bona fide*

---

[3] A month before oral arguments, I posed a very similar hypothetical about Poland prohibiting kosher slaughter out of concerns for preventing animal cruelty, and asked how such a law would fare if challenged by a corporation under RFRA. Josh Blackman, *Would a Ban on Kosher Slaughter Be Constitutional, and Valid under RFRA*, JOSH BLACKMAN'S BLOG (Feb. 27, 2014), perma.cc/9FAU-WNPR.

religious objections, so they were never particularly optimistic the government was going to be able to prevail on that issue. But it was an argument they had to make. I was told that after a lot of discussion in the Department they made a collective decision that opposing free exercise rights for corporations was the correct position for the government to take because otherwise the potential scope of the exemption would be overly broad.

During arguments, only Justices Ginsburg and Sotomayor openly doubted that Hobby Lobby could have standing to raise its religious beliefs in court. Sotomayor pressed Paul Clement, "How do we determine when a corporation has that belief? When the majority of shareholders agree?" The bigger challenge was how to limit the size of a "small" business. Hobby Lobby had more than 500 stores and 14,000 employees. Chief Justice Roberts, who leaned toward the challengers, offered one solution – "That's a question of State corporate law" – and noted that it can be limited to a "Chapter S Corporation that is closely held."

One of Hobby Lobby's attorneys explained that it was a "false dichotomy" to separate Hobby Lobby and the Green family, and their strategy was to make that point clear to the justices. Paul Clement countered that this was not a case of "people who are arrested in possession of large quantities of marijuana and they assert that they belong to the church of marijuana," or of a "large corporation" that defends against some claim based on religion "that's going to save them lots of money." The Greens have long and publicly held these beliefs. Clement added, "It is no accident that the claims that you have before you in these cases are brought by small closely held corporations that have firmly held religious beliefs." Exxon or Pepsi, as large publicly traded companies, could never develop enough consensus among their many shareholders to assert a single religious identity. In contrast, these family-owned businesses were sincere and united in their beliefs. To that extent, Justice Sotomayor agreed, and told Paul Clement, "You picked great plaintiffs." Members of the Green family, who were sitting in the gallery, smiled.[4]

16.2. "IF THIS THING VIOLATES YOUR RELIGION, YOU CAN DO ANOTHER THING"

Assuming that Hobby Lobby was a "person," the next question for the justices to resolve was whether the contraceptive mandate imposed a "substantial burden" on its "exercise of religion." Paul Clement laid out the stakes to the justices

---

[4] Mark Walsh, *ACA's Return Taxes to the High Court*, SCOTUSBLOG (Mar. 25, 2014), perma.cc/2CWW-5E4F.

in frank terms. On the one hand, Hobby Lobby could "pay a $475 million per year penalty" for providing insurance without contraceptive coverage. On the other hand, the company could "pay a $26 million per year" employer mandate penalty for dropping its insurance policy. But door number three, paying for contraceptive coverage, was not an option they would take.

The government rejected the notion that forcing Hobby Lobby to pay for someone else's contraception would be a substantial burden on its own free exercise. As a senior Obama administration official described the strategy, the government was not prepared to accept the mandate as a substantial burden on religion. "As an objective matter," he told me, the mandate is the type of thing "that the government does with everybody:" make employers pay for stuff that is for their employees, whether the employer likes it or not. Importantly, the mandate "doesn't require the employer to personally do anything or to forbear from doing anything." The Greens were not required to buy or use the contraception themselves. It cannot substantially burden their free exercise to pay for someone else to do so.

Justice Kagan told Paul Clement that dropping the health insurance coverage altogether and paying the $26 million penalty would more or less cancel each other out. As Justice Kennedy noted, it may be "a wash" on the bottom line. Kagan said the mandate is not forcing the Greens to do anything – it is giving them a choice. They can either provide contraceptive coverage or, "if this thing violates your religion, you can do another thing," which would be dropping its entire health insurance plan. The other option, Kagan noted, "is approximately the same price as the thing that you don't want to do." So where's the beef? Hobby Lobby, she suggested, may actually make more money by dropping insurance coverage, and at the same time avoid the contraceptive mandate.

Clement steadfastly resisted the notion that it would be a fiscal "wash." More importantly, the lower-court record was silent on this issue, and the justices could not base a ruling of this magnitude on back-of-the-envelope calculations. Further, he argued that dropping health insurance would put Hobby Lobby at a competitive disadvantage in the marketplace. Justice Scalia, for whom Clement clerked, chimed in and said, "Of course it wouldn't be the same price at the end of the day. If they deny health insurance, they're going to have to raise wages if they are going to get employees." Clement responded with alacrity to his old boss, "Absolutely, your Honor."

16.3. "WOMEN ARE QUITE DIRECTLY, TANGIBLY HARMED"

The government's stronger argument did not dwell on whether Hobby Lobby was negatively impacted. Rather, the solicitor general's strategy was to focus on how excusing Hobby Lobby from the mandate would impact female employees who would not receive contraceptive coverage. Verrilli told the justices, "When you are analyzing what is required under RFRA, the court must take account of the way in which the requested accommodation will affect the rights and interests of third parties." Verrilli cited the Supreme Court's 1982 decision in *United States v. Lee*. In that case, the Court held that an Amish employer could not be exempted from paying Social Security payroll taxes, even though he claimed it burdened his free exercise. A senior DOJ attorney summarized the holding pithily: "Well, the problem here is that if the Amish employer doesn't pay social security, then the Amish employees get screwed." By the same token, the government argued, if Hobby Lobby does not provide contraceptive coverage to its employees, then female Hobby Lobby employees "get screwed."

Justice Kagan agreed, and noted that in the Court's precedents, where "there was harm to identifiable third parties ... you could not get an accommodation for that kind of harm." With the ACA, "Congress has given a statutory entitlement to women," Kagan added, which "includes contraceptive coverage."[5] She continued, "when the employer says, 'no, I don't want to give that coverage,'" then "wom[e]n [are] quite directly, quite tangibly harmed." Justice Ginsburg agreed that "the accommodation must be measured so it doesn't override other significant interests." Justice Kennedy followed up, and asked how to "think about the position and the rights of the employees?" A RFRA accommodation, Kennedy reasoned, would "allow the employer to put the employee in a disadvantageous position." He added, "The employee may not agree with the religious beliefs of the employer." This is certainly true with a large portion of Hobby Lobby's 14,000 employees across the country. "Does the religious beliefs of the employer just trump?" Kennedy asked.

For the government, the issue of the third-party burden was a "big part of their argument." A DOJ attorney familiar with the solicitor general's strategy told me that his

> thinking evolved about how it helped the government's chance of winning. It became increasingly clear that their best, probably only hope of winning was to focus on the existence of third party harms. Because it would provide a means to articulate a quite important point. When you are making a decision about whether to grant a religious exemption from requirement of the law under RFRA, it has a direct cost to somebody else. That seemed to be a pretty powerful intuition, to think about the way RFRA will encompass the interest of

---

5   Not quite. HHS, and not Congress, made the decision to cover contraceptives. *See* Chapter 4. *See also* Josh Blackman, *Gridlock*, 130 HARV. L.REV. __ (2016).

third parties if you apply it in broader terms. This wasn't just about regulating the behavior of the employer.

Justice Kennedy's question validated this intuition.

Paul Clement rejected this argument as flatly wrong. "The government has an argument that somehow third-party interests" should be considered under RFRA, "where we bear the burden" of persuasion. He answered his own question: "We don't think that's right at all." Instead, Clement argued, any effects on third parties should be considered in the compelling interest and narrow tailoring part of the RFRA analysis, where the government bears the burden of persuasion. In other words, it was not Hobby Lobby's responsibility to justify why their free exercise might burden third parties. It was enough to say its rights were substantially burdened, and the government had to then make the case. More importantly, he stressed, "this is not about access to the contraception." Granting Hobby Lobby an accommodation would not criminalize birth control, or prevent employees from acquiring it by other means.

Rather, Clement stressed case was only "about *who is* going to pay for the government's preferred subsidy." In that context, he added, "there are ample alternative ways to address any burdens on third parties." With this pivot, Clement was moving to the third element of the RFRA inquiry: Was the contraceptive mandate "the least restrictive means of furthering" the governments compelling interest? Or could the government expand contraceptive coverage through different approaches without substantially burdening religious liberty?

Justice Alito followed Clement's lead: "Are there ways of accommodating the interests of the women who may want these particular drugs or devices without imposing a substantial burden on the employer who has the religious objection to it?" The lawyer caught the softball: "There are ample less restrictive alternatives, Your Honor." Clement turned the Obamacare exchange into a sword against the Obamacare mandate. "If the employer doesn't provide healthcare," he answered, "those employees [can] go on to the exchanges with a subsidy from the government." Why can't Hobby Lobby's employees "do the same thing?" Clement asked. The government could directly provide subsidized or even free contraceptives on HealthCare.gov, without burdening anyone's religion.

One of Hobby Lobby's attorneys told me that in a world before Obamacare, you might have needed the employers to provide birth control. But in an Obamacare world, that assumption is gone because of the exchanges. Justice Sotomayor interjected that this proposal was different. "You're asking the government to incur" the cost of covering the contraceptives, she said. A method that shifts a new burden onto the government, Sotomayor explained, could not be considered "least restrictive."

Clement countered that the federal government already offered to pay for contraceptive coverage for employees at religious non-profits such as the Little Sisters of the Poor. (Just two months earlier the Court had put *Accommodation 2.0* on hold for the nuns). "The whole debate," Clement explained, "is about how much complicity there has to be from the employer in order to trigger that coverage." He concluded, "Whatever the answer is for [the] Little Sisters of the Poor, presumably you can extend the same thing to my clients and there wouldn't be a problem with that." This argument demonstrates why the government would have wanted the for-profits to go to the Supreme Court first: any rule set for the Little Sisters would probably extend to Hobby Lobby. It would be easier to deny relief to Hobby Lobby first, and then later rule for the more sympathetic Little Sisters.

But this response begs the question. Would Hobby Lobby also object if offered *Accommodation 2.0* – to which the Little Sisters already objected? That is, would Hobby Lobby sign the form, which would then allow its insurer to pay for contraceptive coverage? Solicitor General Verrilli told the Court that Hobby Lobby has "studiously avoided arguing [that the Accommodation] is a less restrictive alternative," but "for the first time at the podium this morning [Hobby Lobby argued] that a less restrictive means would be to extend the accommodation that currently exists." Justice Sotomayor asked Paul Clement the question point blank: "Will your clients claim that filling out the form" burdens their free exercise? Clement would not answer the question. "We haven't been offered that accommodation, so we haven't had to decide what kind of objection, if any, we would make to that." One of Hobby Lobby's attorneys told me that they "never had a conversation" with the Greens about whether they would accept the accommodation.

Finally, in response to the solicitor general's charge that Hobby Lobby made the argument for the first time that morning, Paul Clement told the justices, "If you look at page 58 of our brief, the red brief, we specifically say that one of the least restrictive alternatives would be the most obvious least restrictive alternative; for the government to pay for their favorite contraception methods themselves." On page 58, the brief noted "Indeed the government has attempted something like that with respect to certain objecting employers," with a citation to *Accommodation 2.0*. At that moment, Clement earned his title as "best advocate of his generation," not just for his argument skills but for his assiduous preparation.

One of Clement's associates remembered that as "one of the most dramatic moments of the day." The import of his claim was that whatever the answer is for Little Sisters of the Poor, presumably the government could extend the same relief to Hobby Lobby. But just because the government gave an accommodation to the Little Sisters did not mean that the accommodation was lawful. To put this in terms of RFRA, that *a less* restrictive alternative exists does not mean that it is "*the least* restrictive means" possible to avoid a substantial burden on religious exercise. RFRA requires that whatever path the government chooses must impose the *smallest* burden on free exercise that would still allow it to achieve the government's interest. Two years later, Clement and Verrilli would be back at the Supreme Court, arguing about just this question – whether the accommodation for the Little Sisters is valid.

16.4. "GRANDFATHER CLAUSE"

The final question for the justices under the Religious Freedom Restoration Act, taken out of order, was the third – whether the contraceptive mandate served "a compelling governmental interest." That is, how significant was it for the federal government to ensure that women received cost-free access to contraception through their employer's health insurance plan?

Hobby Lobby vigorously argued that the government's interest in mandating employer-provided contraceptive care was *not* a compelling state interest of the highest order. (This was totally separate and apart from whether birth control was legal, or available by other means). Why? Because the government had already carved out so many exceptions to the mandate. Houses of worship were exempted altogether. For religious nonprofits, insurers would pick up the cost under the accommodation. The mandate did not even apply to employers with fewer than fifty employees. Their employees could gain access to subsidized contraceptive coverage on HealthCare.gov. If this was such an important interest, Hobby Lobby argued, why were so many women not covered by it?

But the biggest point of contention during oral arguments concerned the *grandfather clause*. Health insurance plans that were in existence before the mandate came into effect were grandfathered, and were not subject to the mandate unless they were changed. (Ironically, Hobby Lobby's plan lost its grandfather status after the Greens removed coverage of Plan B, which in turn made them subject to the mandate to cover Plan B). How could the government's interest be so *compelling*, Hobby Lobby argued, if thousands of grandfathered plans nationwide were exempted? One of the lawyers for Hobby Lobby told me that when the government has a compelling interest, you don't exempt over half of the people that it applies to. And if the interest is not compelling, under the RFRA analysis, Hobby Lobby would be entitled to a religious accommodation.

The government took that argument very seriously. A senior DOJ attorney acknowledged that "we didn't have an iron-clad answer on grandfathering and it was a liability for us." Chief Justice Roberts exploited this liability with a series of questions. Roberts asked the solicitor general, "Can you make a representation to us about how long the grandfathering is going to be in effect?" In other words, how long would the grandfathered plans – that are not subject to the mandate – stick around? Verrilli would not answer the question. "I can't give you a precise figure, [but] there's a clear downward trajectory." Ironically enough, the president's false promise that people can keep their plans provided the basis for the solicitor general's answer. Every year, more and more old, noncompliant plans would be cancelled. Invariably, as plans were changed, they would lose grandfather status and become subject to the Affordable Care Act's mandates. But Verrilli could not say that in Court. All he could say was that "[t]here's significant movement downward every year in the numbers." Paul Clement pounced on this concession, which he called "devastating." When the "government pursues compelling interest, it demands immediate compliance. It doesn't say, 'Get around to it whenever it's convenient.'"

But a senior DOJ attorney told me that the government had "a pretty good counter punch" to the grandfathering argument: Title VII of the Civil Rights Act of 1964, which prohibited workplace discrimination. Even five decades after its enactment, the solicitor general explained to the Court, "employers with 15 or fewer people are [still] not subject to that law, and that's 80 percent of the employers in the country." As a result, Verrilli continued, as many as "22 million people . . . are [still] not within the coverage" of the landmark discrimination law. He asked rhetorically, "No one would say that because the coverage is incomplete in that respect, that Title VII doesn't advance a compelling state interest." The DOJ attorney with whom I spoke told me it was going to be "hard to draw a principled distinction" between eliminating discrimination and expanding access to contraceptive coverage – they were both compelling, and implemented in an incomplete fashion.

Paul Clement had a response at the ready. "There's nothing inconsistent," he countered, in focusing on "the people who actually employ the most people and therefore can engage in the most discrimination." It makes sense to focus on larger employers, because that is where the discrimination is most likely to occur. However, Clement continued, it is "quite a different matter" for Congress to pass a variant of Title VII that said, "Hey, as long as you have a pre-existing discriminatory policy, you're allowed to keep it." The DOJ attorney I interviewed conceded that the government's grandfathering argument was not airtight. He admitted, "Maybe at the end of the day we would lose some votes on that."

16.5. VACCINES, BLOOD TRANSFUSIONS, AND SEX DISCRIMINATION

To this point, we have covered the four aspects of the RFRA analysis: (1) whether Hobby Lobby was a "person"; (2) whether the mandate "substantially burdens" Hobby Lobby's "exercise of religion"; (3) whether mandating employer-provided contraceptive coverage "is in furtherance of a compelling governmental interest"; and (4) whether the mandate is the "least restrictive means of furthering that compelling governmental interest." The remainder of the arguments in Court focused on the proverbial "slippery slope" argument: If the Court rules for or against Hobby Lobby, what other terrible things may happen?

Justice Sotomayor kicked off the parade of horribles roughly forty seconds and forty words into Paul Clement's opening statement. "Is your claim limited to sensitive materials like contraceptives," she asked, "or does it include items like blood transfusions or vaccines?" If an employer has a religious basis to object, Sotomayor continued, "[c]ould an employer preclude the use of those items as well?" (Jehovah's Witnesses object to blood transfusions and Christian Scientists object to vaccines). Later, Justice Kagan added, "there are many people who have religious objections to vaccinations. So suppose an employer refuses to fund vaccinations for her employees, what happens then?" These questions were expected, because the solicitor general's brief cited all of these examples.

Paul Clement had an answer at the ready. "I do think in the context of vaccinations, the government may have a stronger compelling interest than it does in this context because there are notions of herd immunity." Under the principle of herd or community immunity, when a certain percentage of a population is vaccinated, even those who are not vaccinated "get some protection because the spread of contagious disease is contained."[6]

Kagan volleyed right back, talking over Clement: "Blood transfusions? There are quite a number of medical treatments that different religious groups," such as Jehovah's Witnesses, "object to." Here, Clement's answer was not as sharp. "I think [each case] would have to be evaluated on its own and

---

[6]   *Community Immunity ("Herd Immunity")*, VACCINES.GOV, perma.cc/7KFZ-SJBR.

apply the compelling interest–least restrictive alternative test and the substantial burdens part of the test."

The junior justice recognized that there was an insufficient response to this question. "So one religious group could opt out of this," Kagan asked, "and another religious group could opt out of that and everything would be piecemeal." Clement conceded the point, and replied that this non-uniform approach was what Congress intended when it enacted the Religious Freedom Restoration Act in 1993. "Congress made a judgment that RFRA was going to apply to all manner of federal statutes," Clement said. This law, by necessity, would result in an uneven enforcement of laws that touch on questions of free exercise.

Sliding further down the slope, beyond excluding vaccines or blood transfusions, the justices pushed Clement on whether RFRA could be used as a defense against claims of discrimination. Justice Kagan asked what would happen when an employer has "a religious objection" to sex discrimination laws, to minimum wage laws, to family leave, or to child labor laws? Paul Clement's first line of defense was to argue that very few of these cases had been brought to date, and none were successful. Once again, Justice Alito provided Clement with the helpful question.

Alito asked, "In all the years since RFRA has been on the books, have any of these claims involving the minimum wage, for example, been brought and have they succeeded?" Clement responded, "Very few of these claims have been brought. Very few of them have succeeded." For example, the government's brief cited a 1985 Minnesota case where an employer defended against a gender discrimination claim by citing his religious beliefs.[7] One of the Hobby Lobby lawyers pithily described the case to me: "The owner of a health club said, 'We won't hire women without permission from their spouse or their father.' And the court said, 'No, you can't do that.'"

But past performance is not an indicator of future success. Justice Kagan predicted that if Hobby Lobby wins, "then you would see religious objectors come out of the woodwork with respect to all of these laws." Clement answered candidly. "Look, you've got to trust the courts. Just because free exercise claims are being brought doesn't mean that the courts can't separate the sheep from the goats." Simply because these claims can be made does not mean judges lack the competency to throw out the bad ones. A senior DOJ official praised Clement's response: "Paul always does a great job in argument and I thought he handled those questions extremely well."

---

[7] In re State v. Sports & Health Club, Inc., 370 N.W.2d 844, 847 (Minn. 1985).

16.6. "FORCED TO PAY FOR ABORTIONS"

The slippery slope also slides to the left. If the Court ruled *against* Hobby Lobby, what other laws could the government enact that infringe on religious liberty? During arguments, Justice Kennedy posed the pivotal question. "Under your view," the median justice asked, "could a for-profit corporation be forced to pay for abortions?" Verrilli attempted to duck the question by noting that "the law now is to the contrary," and that abortions could not be mandated. Kennedy countered, saying that if the laws were changed, "your reasoning would permit that." Verrilli tried to avoid answering directly, and said that "religious nonprofits" and a "church" could challenge an abortion mandate in court. Kennedy pushed back, "No, I'm talking about a for-profit corporation." Verrilli answered the question as he had to: "Under our theory the for-profit corporation wouldn't have an ability to sue" and the mandate would stand. But he added, "there is no law like that on the books." In other words, Congress could require for-profit corporations to cover abortion services, and under the government's theory, no one would be able to challenge it in court.

The chief justice interjected, "I'm sorry, I lost track of that." Roberts inquired, "There is no law on the books that does *what*?" Verrilli answered, "that requires for-profit corporations to provide abortions." Roberts asked quizzically, "Isn't that what we are talking about in terms of their religious beliefs? One of the religious beliefs [of the Greens] is that they have to pay for these four methods of contraception [including Plan B] that they believe provide abortions. I thought that's what we had before us." One of the attorneys for Hobby Lobby recalled this was a dramatic moment, and said "the transcript doesn't do justice to how that question was asked." Verrilli's only answer was to say that federal law does "not consider these particular forms of contraception to be abortion." As Senator Barbara Mikulski, the sponsor of the Woman's Health Amendment certainly knew in 2009, there is a difference between "family planning" and "abortion," regardless of how the Green Family or Bart Stupak understand Plan B.

During his rebuttal, Paul Clement rejected the government's theory if it would mean that a corporation could not legally challenge an abortion mandate. Under the government's view of the law, Clement explained, "if Congress changes its judgment and says that a for-profit medical provider has to provide an abortion, RFRA doesn't apply. That, with all due respect, cannot be what Congress had in mind when it passed RFRA."

One of the attorneys for Hobby Lobby observed that Verrilli had to admit that under his thinking about the case, the abortion mandate was unassailable in court. The DOJ attorney I spoke with acknowledged that the abortion question was "a hard question for us, obviously." Answering Justice Kennedy's question yes was a "consequence of our position." However, he insisted, "as a practical matter I don't think it is something the government would ever compel companies to cover abortion. That seemed pretty remote." Leaving the argument, things did not look good for the government.

16.7. "THE BEST WAY TO LOSE"

The hearing finished at 11:30 A.M. Quickly, those inside the Court walked outside into the snowy March morning.[8] David and Barbara Green, husband and wife, and cofounders, smiled as they approached the waiting microphones. Flanked by a dozen members of their family – who are also the owners of the company – Barbara read a prepared statement from a folded up piece of paper. "Our family started Hobby Lobby built on our faith and together as a family. We've kept that tradition for more than forty years. And we want to continue to live out our faith, and the way we do business. The choice the government has forced on us is unfair and not in keeping with the history of our great nation founded on religious freedom. We believe that Americans don't lose their religious freedoms when they open a family business. We were encouraged by today's arguments. We are thankful the Supreme Court took our case. We prayerfully await the Justices' decisions."

As the Greens were chauffeured to waiting cars, and a John Deere tractor pushed snow across the Supreme Court's plaza, Lori Windham from the Becket Fund stepped forward. "We were encouraged by the arguments today. The justices seemed deeply skeptical of the government's arguments that Americans who open a small family business give up their rights to religious freedom and can be subject to whatever the government mandates that they do. We are hopeful for a good decision later this term." After Windham spoke, the queue lengthened, and the scrum for the microphones began.

Marcia Greenberger, president of the National Women's Law Center, approached the microphone to "speak for the women whose health and future were at stake with respect to their access to contraceptive coverage." She said that her organization "heard from someone who was not heard from in the Court. A woman who was an employee of Hobby Lobby, and she spoke about the importance of contraceptives to her and her family." After Greenberger

---

[8] *Sebelius v. Hobby Lobby Stores Reaction*, C-SPAN (Mar. 25, 2014), cs.pn/24DVKqe.

finished speaking, Emily Hardman of the Becket Fund tried to regain the microphone, but she was pushed aside by Cecile Richards, president of Planned Parenthood. Richards smiled and told her, "We'll be very brief. We're already here." Ilyse Hogue, president of NARAL, repeated the slogan from the signs saying, "Our bodies are not our boss's business." Richards added, "what we saw today was the importance of having women on the Supreme Court. I believe this Court understood that women have the right to make their own decisions about their birth control, and it is not their boss's decision." When Richards finished, Hardman leaned in to get the microphone, but Louise Melling of the ACLU burst forward, and pushed her aside. "We were heartened to see the justices asking questions about women and the rights of third parties," Mellin said.

Third time was the charm: Hardman reclaimed the microphone and invited Paul Clement to make his statement. "We are gratified the Court heard these cases," Clement said. He sounded a note of optimism. "There are real concerns where the government takes the position that a kosher deli that was told that it would have to be open on a Saturday would have no basis to get into court and make that claim. That is a very difficult argument to sustain." A reporter asked Clement whether this decision would be "unprecedented" because it would eliminate a statutory benefit for women because of the religious beliefs of a for-profit corporation. He answered, "There was really no case on either side that says that for-profit corporations have religious exercise, and no cases that say they definitely don't. But the ramification of saying that a for-profit corporation, under no circumstances, can get into court, is untenable." As is his custom after all arguments, Clement refused to provide a prediction when asked, and offered his usual response with a wry smile: "The only sense I have from the questions is the Court took this case very seriously, as they do every one of their cases, and we eagerly await their decision."

Walking along First Street, the lawyers for Hobby Lobby felt confident. Clement always tells his colleagues "you can never ever know." One of his associates asked himself, "Would I rather be in the government's position, or our position?" He did not know if he was going to win but "felt like he would rather be in his position." Another colleague, citing Justice Kennedy's abortion question, added he "felt pretty good."

The government had a similar disposition. A senior DOJ attorney told me quite candidly, "We didn't think we were going to win." Rather, they were hoping for "the best way to lose:" That the Court rules against the government because the mandate was not "narrowly tailored" enough. Such a ruling would mean that the government could at least leave open the option of framing a parallel accommodation for employers like Hobby Lobby. However, if the Court found that there was "no compelling interest here," and mandating employer-provided contraceptive care was not important, "that would've been a really severe way to lose the case."

17

"Glitch"

Coincidentally, oral arguments in *Halbig v. Sebelius* were held on March 25, 2014 – the same day the Supreme Court would hear arguments in *Hobby Lobby v. Sebelius*. As the proceeding began, D.C. Circuit Judge Thomas B. Griffith joked, "So, I guess this is the group that couldn't get into First Street this morning."[1] The Supreme Court, located at One First Street NE, was about half a mile down Constitution Avenue. Joining Judge Griffith on the bench were Judges Harry T. Edwards and A. Raymond Randolph. Before the hearing even began, the plaintiffs viewed the random assignment as propitious. Michael Carvin, who represented the challengers, told me, "we got lucky" because "we got a good panel. Sometimes it's that roll of the dice that makes a difference."

Edwards served as the first African-American professor at the University of Michigan Law School, and later moved to Harvard Law School. After serving as the Chairman of the Board of Amtrak, he was appointed by President Carter to the D.C. Circuit in February 1980, serving as chief judge from 1994 to 2001.

Randolph clerked for the iconic Henry Friendly on the Second Circuit, and served as a deputy solicitor general from 1975 to 1977 under future judge – and almost justice – Robert Bork. Following a stint in private practice, President George H.W. Bush nominated Randolph to the D.C. Circuit in 1990. (Randolph was also my First Amendment Professor at the George Mason University School of Law in 2008).

---

[1] Transcript, Halbig v. Sebelius (D.C. Cir. Mar. 25, 2014), bit.ly/1SXkBhv.

The wild card was Judge Griffith. He "was a question," Carvin told me. Griffith served as the Senate's chief legal counsel from 1995 to 2005, offering him a keen insight into how business is actually done on Capitol Hill. President George W. Bush nominated Griffith in 2004, after the Democrats successfully waged a two-year filibuster against Miguel Estrada. Griffith was viewed as more of a moderate selection. The *Washington Post* endorsed Griffith's nomination, saying he was "widely respected by people in both parties" as a "sober lawyer with an open mind."[2] Mike Carvin had his strategy set. "My only goal in that argument was to talk to Judge Griffith. There was no point talking to Judge Edwards. I think his questions were nonsense. My implicit message is 'I'm going to go talk to a judge that I've actually got a shot at.'" Carvin would argue against Stuart F. Delery, who was the chief of the Civil Division at the Justice Department.

17.2. "IS IT OUR JOB TO FIX THE PROBLEM?"

Section 36B of the Affordable Care Act provides that subsidies are available for plans enrolled in "through an Exchange *established by the State* under Section 1311." As Tom Christina concluded nearly four years earlier, the text seems as plain as day – subsidies are available only if a state builds and operates the exchange. Delery had to convince the court that when read in context with the rest of the 3,000-page bill, Section 36B is best understood to provide subsidies even in states that did not establish an exchange. He told the court, "Congress intended a nationwide system to provide affordable healthcare." With a single question, Judge Griffith set the tenor of the entire arguments: "Who established the exchange in West Virginia?" "The secretary" of HHS, Delery replied. Judge Griffith stated the obvious, "West Virginia did not establish the exchange." Delery answered, as he must. "That's correct, Your Honor," but he added that, "the challenger's fundamental error is to focus on one phrase in one provision in isolation."

Judge Randolph rejected this argument. "It's not one phrase. I've heard that so many times. It appears seven times, not just once, do you disagree with that?" Delery answered, "It does appear several times, your Honor." Judge Randolph quickly replied, "Not several, I said seven. There's an absurdity principle, but I don't think there's a stupidity principle." He added, "If legislation is just stupid, I don't see that it's up to the court to save it."

The government's challenge was to reconcile a congressional goal of a "nationwide system" with language that seems to treat states exchanges

2 *Three Nominees*, WASH. POST (Mar. 17, 2005), bit.ly/1OiqTGc.

differently than the federal exchange. One possible way to explain Section 36B is that Congress simply made a mistake. After Tom Christina's discovery, some thought that Congress flubbed in drafting the statute. Case Western professor Jonathan Adler and Cato Institute scholar Michael Cannon adopted that theory in November 2011. In *The Wall Street Journal*, they wrote that Section 36B was "a major *glitch* that threatens [Obamacare's] basic functioning." Adler would tell me that they selected the word "glitch" because that was how the Affordable Care Act was being discussed in 2011, "as things were kind of messy and glitchy." He recalled Speaker Nancy Pelosi's (D-CA) infamous admonition that "we have to pass the [health care] bill so that you can find out what's in it."[3] Cannon told me that in 2011 he initially thought it was a "drafting error." Indeed, the House Oversight Committee report revealed that early internal e-mails within the Obama administration considered that "the language restricting tax credits to state-established exchanges may have been a 'drafting oversight.'" In 2015, Chief Justice Roberts would write: "The Affordable Care Act contains more than a few examples of inartful drafting."

During the course of the *Halbig* and *King* litigation, several senators stated that Section 36B was a "drafting error." Olympia J. Snowe, a former moderate Republican senator from Maine who served on the Finance Committee, could not "recall any distinction between federal and state exchanges," and suggested that the four words were "inadvertent language."[4] Jeff Bingaman, a former Democratic senator from New Mexico, called the provision a "drafting error" that "escaped everyone's attention, or it would have been deleted." *New York Times* reporter Robert Pear interviewed more than two dozen Democrats and Republicans who were involved in writing the ACA. He concluded that the language was "carelessly left in place as the legislation evolved."[5]

Perhaps counterintuitively, if Senators Snowe and Bingaman are correct, and Section 36B was indeed a "drafting error," the courts would be unable to fix it. To illustrate this principle, consider Paul Krugman's column in the *New York Times*, where he referred to Section 36B as an "obvious typo."[6] Krugman recounts that the deed for his childhood home was incomplete, and the boundaries excluded part of the yard. His father discovered this error

[3] Jonathan Capehart, *Pelosi Defends Her Infamous Health Care Remark*, WASH. POST (Jun. 20, 2012), perma.cc/BNN2-T8J3.

[4] Robert Pear, *Four Words That Imperil Health Care Law Were All a Mistake, Writers Now Say*, N.Y. TIMES (May 25, 2015), perma.cc/7VHC-87KK.

[5] *Id.*

[6] Paul Krugman, *Death by Typo the Latest Frivolous Attack on Obamacare*, N.Y. TIMES (Nov. 9, 2014), nyti.ms/1S3wQwJ.

with a "shock" long after buying the property. "Whoever wrote down the lot's description had somehow skipped a clause." But then the story takes a turn for the implausible. "And of course the town clerk fixed the language. After all, it would have been ludicrous and cruel to take away most of my parents' property on the basis of sloppy drafting, when the drafters' intention was perfectly clear." This tale is tall.

In property law, boundaries are demarcated by detailed surveys using precise measurements known as "metes and bounds." If your deed is incorrect, you cannot simply get the "town clerk" to "fix the language." An "incorrect" deed means you do not own the land you are on, regardless of the intent of the drafters. If the facts were as Krugman told them, the fault lies with his father, who failed to obtain a competent survey before he bought the lot, notwithstanding the "sloppy drafting." Similar principles apply to interpreting acts of Congress. As Justice Elena Kagan explained in a 2014 statutory interpretation case, the Supreme "Court has no roving license, in even ordinary cases of statutory interpretation, to disregard clear language simply on the view that ... Congress 'must have intended' something broader."[7] If the Obama administration had told the courts Section 36B was a woopsie, shrugged, and asked the judges to fix the statute to implement what Congress really meant, the government would have had no case. For this reason, the Justice Department wisely never adopted the "drafting error" argument. It had to be deliberate. So why would Congress intentionally draft Section 36B the way it did?

Carvin focused on this contradiction during oral arguments. "The Government can't offer any rational explanation of why the subsidy provision says precisely the opposite of what they contend is the rule. This is a very straight-forward statutory construction case where I think the plain language of the statute dictates the result." Judge Griffith, who seemed to agree, asked the DOJ lawyer rhetorically, if Congress "didn't legislate clearly enough, is it our job to fix the problem?"

17.3. "ben nelson cared"

However, even if the text was clear, Judge Griffith did not seem fully persuaded that Congress *intended* to withhold subsidies from states as an incentive for them to establish exchanges. The former chief legal officer of the Senate asked Carvin, "Is there anything in the legislative history, any floor statements, any committee reports that you can point us to that show that this was on the mind of Congress?" Carvin could point to nothing. Judge Edwards

[7] Michigan v. Bay Mills Indian Cmty, 134 S. Ct. 2024, 2026 (2014).

put the question far more forcefully: "As far as I can see no one understood what you're arguing now at the time this bill was passed. When I read that argument, to be very honest, it seems preposterous." Judge Edwards pushed the challenger's theory further and asked, "What advantage is there to a state to set up the exchange?"

Carvin, with a perturbed tone, shot back: So state officials can "get reelected. Do you want to go out and tell your citizens I have just denied you hundreds of billions of subsidies?" the *New York Times* described his style as a "blunt-talking and rumpled."[8] This approach was deliberate, Carvin told me: "Edwards yelled at me. So I yelled back. I don't normally have that kind of high volume exchange with federal judges. I've argued in front of Edwards I would say five, six times and I know two things about him. He's relentless and in my experience, if you don't give as good as you get, it goes on and on and on. So I somewhat consciously upped the volume, upped the reaction." The shouting match continued. Carvin explained during our interview, "I try to be aggressive but not disrespectful which, you know, you can draw a line. I try to make my points forcefully." Judge Edwards dismissed Carvin's efforts. "No, no, no, no, no! Your argument makes no sense. Who cares who sets up the exchange?"

Judge Randolph intervened: "Ben Nelson." Everyone in the court perked up, as one judge answered the other judge's question. Randolph repeated himself. "Ben Nelson cared." Randolph explained the theory: "Congress acted on the assumption that dangling this carrot in front of the Governors would lead to the states themselves setting up exchanges rather than the federal government."

Carvin followed the lead. The Senate "couldn't get to 60 [votes] unless Senator Ben Nelson" was satisfied that there would not be a single "federally run exchange," which was the proposal in the House of Representatives. Instead, Carvin explained, Nelson demanded that the Senate adhere to "basic principles of Federalism" so "the states are going to run those exchanges." Otherwise, Nelson would not "vote for it" and the ACA "doesn't get passed." Judge Griffith asked Carvin, "[Did] anyone make this point before Professors Adler and Cannon came up with it?" The answer was no.

Although Adler and Cannon initially believed that Section 36B was a "glitch," they ultimately arrived at the conclusion that the provision was deliberately designed to withhold subsidies from states that did not establish exchanges. Adler later explained that when he first researched Section 36B

---

[8] Sheryl Gay Stolberg, *A Lawyer Taking Aim at the Health Care Act Gets a Supreme Court Rematch*, N. Y. TIMES (Mar. 4, 2015), nyti.ms/1OSwkOq.

in early 2011, he assumed that Congress was "using the lure of tax credits to induce state cooperation."[9] He noted this could have been an application of what is known as *cooperative federalism,* in which the federal government attempts to nudge states in the right direction without coercing them. In this way there was an incentive for the states to take action. But, gradually, his conjecture turned into certainty.

During late 2011, Cannon asked his research assistant, Brittany La Couture, to locate "every mention of exchanges in the debate over the ACA." Cannon joked the experience was "emotionally scarring," though Adler added, "There were [far fewer] references that you would think." Indeed, the scholars were shocked at how little history there was about the exchanges. Cannon told me, contrary to his initial suspicions, "There was no discussion whatsoever about the status of subsidies on federal exchanges under the ACA." Rather than insisting that Section 36B was a "glitch," they now argued that it was deliberately designed as a means to encourage states to establish exchanges. That is, if a state government refused to establish an exchange, its residents would be punished by not having access to subsidized insurance. Congress could not force states to establish exchanges. That would amount to unconstitutional "commandeering" and would violate the Tenth Amendment and principles of federalism.[10] So instead of beating the states with a stick, Congress would dangle a very enticing carrot. The theory went that the availability of subsidized insurance policies would serve as an incentive for states to establish an exchange.

The biggest problem with Adler and Cannon's theory of the case, however, is that virtually everyone involved in the legislative process later insisted it was absolutely absurd. At *Vox,* Sarah Kliff wrote an article titled, "The people who wrote Obamacare think the new Supreme Court case is ridiculous."[11] Chris Condeluci, who served as counsel for the Republicans on the Senate Finance Committee, but wasn't involved in the drafting process, said "It was always intended that the federal fallback exchange would do everything that the statute told the states to do, which includes delivering the subsidies."[12] John McDonough, who worked for the Democrats on the Health, Education, Labor, and Pension (HELP) Committee, stated "There is not a scintilla of evidence that the Democratic lawmakers who designed the law intended to deny subsidies to any state, regardless of exchange status."

9 Jonathan H. Adler, *How "the Case That Could Topple Obamacare" Began,* WASH. POST (Jan. 22, 2014), perma.cc/DXA8-8U35.

10 *Printz v. United States,* 117 S. Ct. 2365, 2380 (1997). *New York v. United States,* 505 U.S. 144 (1992).

11 Sarah Kliff, *The People Who Wrote Obamacare Think the New Supreme Court Case Is Ridiculous,* VOX (Nov. 7, 2014), perma.cc/P5BJ-4QMW.

12 *Id.*

Topher Spiro, who was deputy staff director on the HELP Committee, said, "It's crazy to think of a mandate" that requires people to buy insurance "without subsidies" to make it more affordable. "It just doesn't make any sense."

Jonathan Cohn, writing in the *New Republic*, called Cannon's mission a "legal crusade to undermine Obamacare and rewrite history."[13] Cohn asked rhetorically, "Can one very determined libertarian and one very distorted version of history keep millions of people from getting health insurance?"[14] Speaking from his own experiences of covering health care reform since 2008, Cohn recalled that "[t]he idea that a state could deny its citizens insurance subsidies by choosing not to build an exchange is simply not an option the law's architects ever contemplated." Liz Fowler, who served as Senator Baucus's senior health care adviser, and later worked in the White House, emphatically rejected Cannon's theory. "Of course Congress did not intend to deny anyone in any state access to tax credits to which they are entitled," she said.[15] "That is not how the law is drafted."

Michael Cannon rejected these post-enactment statements from the interviewed staffers because they were "not involved in the process" of drafting Section 36B. Rather, the "people who wrote this provision have been utterly silent for almost four years," Cannon told me. A 2015 *New York Times* article by Robert Pear traces the origin of Section 36B to the keyboard of James W. Fransen, a nonpartisan professional drafter, who actually wrote the pivotal four words. However, the employees at the Legislative Council's Office, including Fransen, did not respond to requests from the press. (Fransen had recently retired after forty years of federal service and did not reply to my request for an interview).

Michael Carvin found "comical" all of the efforts to interview Senate staffers who were not involved with drafting Section 36B. "Legally it's irrelevant at every conceivable level." He deliberately planted questions with reporters, to inquire, "Why did you write the sentence that way?" They could never offer an answer. Carvin came up with two possible reasons why the sentence was drafted the way it was. First, "they are the stupidest people that have ever walked the face of the earth and shouldn't be allowed out in public." Second, "nobody paid any attention."

One of the more charitable critics of Adler and Cannon was Michigan law professor Nicholas Bagley. Bagley describes the disjointed manner in which the different Senate bills were compiled as a "version error." With multiple

---

[13] Jonathan Cohn, *The Legal Crusade to Undermine Obamacare – and Rewrite History*, NEW REPUBLIC (Dec. 4, 2012), perma.cc/K3E9-LUB8.
[14] *Id.*
[15] *Id.*

authors, it "made sense at one point in time, but doesn't make any sense once you rearrange the pieces," he told me. That is how "the language made it in there in the final bill." Bagley candidly conceded that the provision was not "felicitous" for the government, but countered that the language was due to "inattention and oversight" rather than any "subjective intent by Congress to exclude tax credits for states that didn't set up exchanges." The evidence is "overwhelming," Bagley told me, "that Congress didn't mean to withdraw tax credit from states that failed to establish their own exchanges."

Bagley analogized Adler and Cannon's role to the children's story, *Amelia Bedelia Helps Out.*[16] In the story, Amelia Bedelia is told to "weed the garden," so "the literal-minded but bighearted housekeeper … decides to plant a big row of really big weeds." When Amelia Bedelia is asked "why anyone would want more weeds," she replies "maybe vegetables get hot just like people," and "they need big weeds to shade them.'" In an interview, Bagley explained, "That's what I view Jonathan Adler's and Michael Cannon's contribution as. They are the ones who said, 'Hey, we can come up with a story about why Congress wanted to do this.'" However, the usually mild-mannered Bagley emphatically rejected this theory: "The idea that this is what Congress meant to do is a fiction."

The key contemporaneous proof that Adler and Cannon could find for this position were statements by Senator Ben Nelson. As a moderate Democrat, Nelson's support was essential to hold together the precarious sixty-vote bloc to defeat a Republican filibuster. Recall from Chapter 3 that Nelson's decision to walk away from the Stupak Amendment, concerning funding for abortions, ensured the passage of the Senate bill.

During the drafting of the ACA in the House, Democrats eliminated the need for any state exchanges, and created only a single federal exchange. In 2010, Nelson explained his vote was contingent on rejecting this approach. "The national exchange is unnecessary," Nelson said, "and I wouldn't support something that would start us down the road of federal regulation of insurance and a single-payer plan."[17] Nelson's support for the ACA was pivotal, as the bill passed the Senate on December 24, 2009 with *exactly* sixty votes. Adler and Cannon identified Nelson's position as evidence that the bill was designed to withhold subsidies from recalcitrant states, as a way to nudge them to establish exchanges. His preference was for 50 state-run exchanges. This is what Judge Randolph meant by "Ben Nelson cared."

[16]   Nicholas Bagley, *In Ruling on Obamacare Provision, Court Didn't Rewrite Law – It Read It*, L.A. Times (June 25, 2015), perma.cc/K9F7-7FLN.
[17]   Carrie Budoff Brown, *Nelson: National Exchange a Dealbreaker*, Politico (Jan. 25, 2010), perma.cc/6MLJ-82H7.

In January 2015, the Nebraskan finally spoke up. The retired Senator wrote a letter to Senator Bob Casey (D-PA) about his recollections concerning subsidies. "I *always* believed that tax credits should be available in all 50 states, regardless of who built the exchange." He added, "The *final law also reflects* that belief as well." The last part is key. He argued that the text of the bill – which was actually voted on – reflects those intensions. Contrary to what the other Senators told the *New York Times*, it was *not* a drafting error. (My efforts to review Senator Nelson's papers from 2009 at the University of Nebraska – Lincoln were unsuccessful, because they are under a 10-year restriction.)

Notwithstanding Nelson's letter, the challengers continued to argue that Section 36B was designed to incentivize states to establish exchanges. Statements made by a single Senator five years later, who was rationally self-interested in the ACA's success, did not hold much weight for Adler and Cannon. Cannon is a true believer that this is what Congress intended. He told me, "I am a hundred percent convinced that whoever wrote this intended to condition the subsidies on state cooperation." He explained, "Best guess is that Nelson and others wanted state-run exchanges, and some staffer or legislative counsel said, 'We'll just condition these subsidies on state cooperation because that's how we always do stuff.'" Bagley rejected this proposition. "Nelson didn't insist on the rule as his price for signing onto the Affordable Care Act. It's just false."

Back in the D.C. Circuit, Judge Edwards retorted sarcastically, "So this all comes down to Ben Nelson?" Delery, the government lawyer, dismissed the Cornhusker Conspiracy. "It's an after-the-fact account manufactured without evidence from the record at the time." Judge Edwards agreed. "There was no evidence at the time this bill was passed that this was the consequence."

The lack of legislative history, however, cuts in both directions. There were no statements in the legislative record saying that subsidies would be withheld from states that failed to establish exchanges, but there was also nothing in the record indicating that there would be subsidies available on the federal exchange. Adler told me, unequivocally, "To this day there is not a single contemporaneous statement by anybody saying there will be tax credits in federal exchanges under this bill."

Judge Griffith seemed at equipoise: "The legislative history is a wash, right? I mean, you parry and they thrust, and there doesn't seem to be any clear legislative history here showing that this was an item of great concern to Congress." But this did not end the issue. He challenged Delery: "Given the plain language 'established by the state' don't you have a special burden to show from legislative history that that doesn't mean what it appears to mean?" Carvin later told me that this question was the key to success. "I still win, because I've got the text. I don't need the legislative history to echo what we've got in the text. At an absolute minimum, they need some legislative history to undermine the text."

17.4. "IT'S A TYPICAL DRAFTING THING IN CONGRESS"

If the language was not a "glitch," and there was no history suggesting that the statute was designed to withhold subsidies from nonelecting states, how did the phrase "established by the state" wind up in Section 36B? Judge Randolph offered an explanation based on the antecedent bills that came out of the Senate Committees and similar bills enacted years earlier. "It's a typical drafting thing in Congress," he explained, "if you've already done it once [before] what you do is you take that provision and you copy it into the subsidy provision of the Affordable Care Act."

What became Section 36B in the Affordable Care Act originated from two different committee bills. First, the Finance Committee bill provided that the subsidies would only be available for policies "which were enrolled in through an Exchange established by the State."[18] The final Section 36B that merged together in Majority Leader Reid's office adopted this language, almost verbatim. Second, the HELP Committee bill provided more explicitly that if a state did not establish a "Gateway" (a form of an exchange) within four years after the law's enactment, "the residents of such State *shall not be eligible for credits* ... until such State becomes a participating State."[19] Under this approach, subsidies would not be available on the federal exchange because a state refused to establish an exchange.

As Michael Cannon gleefully reminded me, both Senators Snowe and Bingaman – who insisted that Section 36B was a "drafting error" – voted for committee bills that also conditioned the receipt of subsidies on states establishing exchanges. A beaming Cannon insisted, "Don't tell me that it's unheard of to condition tax credits on states implement[ing] exchanges." In particular, Senator Snowe was the *only* Republican who voted for the bill on the Finance Committee and did not raise any objections in 2009.

Senator Bingaman voted for the HELP Committee bill, which limited subsidies on the federal exchange. He insisted that the conditioning language "escaped everyone's attention."[20] Bingaman may not have read the bill,

---

[18] S. 1796, 111th Cong. HR 3590 (2009), perma.cc/Q5BH-YPWX; America's Healthy Future Act of 2009, S. 1796, 111th Cong. § 1205 (2009), 1.usa.gov/1UItqAc. *See also* 26 U.S.C. § 35(a), (e)(2).

[19] *See* Affordable Health Choices Act, S.1679, 111th Cong. § 3104(d) (2009), 1.usa.gov/1PDwYB0.

[20] Pear, *supra* note 4.

and he was not alone. Senator Max Baucus (D-MT), who chaired the Finance Committee, admitted quite candidly that he did not read the entire bill. "I don't think you want me to waste my time to read every page of the healthcare bill," Baucus said in 2010. "You know why? It's statutory language ... We hire experts."[21] Cannon told me that the senators "voted for that bill with clear language. It does not matter if they didn't read it. It did not matter if they wanted something else."

The senators were not alone in forgetting this legislative history. Emily McMahon, who developed the IRS rule at the Treasury Department, testified that her working group "did look very carefully at the legislative history."[22] Yet, she also testified "that she did not recall whether Treasury considered that Congress" could have used the subsidies as an incentive to create state exchanges.[23] Specifically, McMahon was "not prepared to discuss the antecedent bills" from the Finance and HELP committees and how they conditioned premium tax credits on state compliance.[24] Likewise, Cameron Arterton, who served as Deputy Tax Legislative Counsel for Treasury, "did not remember *ever* discussing the issue of whether the statute authorized premium subsidies in federal exchanges with other members of the working group developing the 36B rule."[25] Notwithstanding these omissions, on May 23, 2012, the Treasury Department published its final rule, concluding that "*the relevant legislative history* does not demonstrate that Congress intended to limit the premium tax credit to State Exchanges."[26]

But what was the relevance of proposals that were not enacted? In his opinion four months later, Judge Griffith would look to this history. The HELP Committee bill, he wrote, "certainly demonstrates that members of Congress at least considered the notion of using subsidies as an incentive to gain states' cooperation."[27] However, Judge Griffith concluded, "inferences from

[21] Jordan Fabian, *Key Senate Democrat Suggests That He Didn't Read Entire Healthcare Reform Bill*, THE HILL (Aug. 25, 2010), perma.cc/ZM9Z-ZYB6.
[22] *Oversight of IRS' Legal Basis for Expanding Obamacare's Taxes and Subsidies: Hearing Before the Subcommittee on Energy Policy, Health Care, and Entitlements*, 113th Cong. at 80 (2013), bit.ly/1rX2z8E.
[23] *Administration Conducted Inadequate Review of Key Issues Prior to Expanding Health Law's Taxes and Subsidies House of Representatives*, COMMITTEE ON OVERSIGHT AND GOVERNMENT REFORM at 32 (2014), bit.ly/1TLiH5H.
[24] *Id.* at 33.
[25] *Id.* at 21.
[26] Department of the Treasury, Internal Revenue Service, *Health Insurance Premium Tax Credit*, 77 Fed. Reg. 30,378 (May 23, 2012) (emphasis added).
[27] Halbig v. Burwell, 758 F.3d 390, 408 (D.C. Cir. 2014).

unenacted legislation are too uncertain to be a helpful guide to the intent behind a specific provision."

17.5. "GUT THE STATUTE"

Eleven times during the oral argument Judge Edwards charged that Michael Carvin's goal in invalidating the IRS rule was to "gut" the entire ACA. "No one assumed that if you choose not to create an exchange because you don't want to be bothered with it, you'll effectively *gut the statute*." Carvin interjected curtly, "Teriffic." Judge Edwards shot back, "Congress doesn't talk about something like that if that's what their purpose is, *gut the statute*." The Carter appointee, with a dollop of sarcasm, quipped, "Hello, where's that coming from?"

If the IRS rule was invalidated, the consequences could be devastating for the thirty-four states that did not elect to establish exchanges. First, 8 million Americans in those states would no longer be eligible for subsidized health insurance on HealthCare.gov.[28] By this point, the federal marketplace was already operational, and people had come to rely and depend on the subsidized insurance. Indeed, this became one of the most potent rallying cries of ACA supporters – if the court invalidated the IRS rule, Americans could lose their health insurance. Progressive pundit Ian Millhiser wrote at *Think Progress* an aptly titled piece: "8 Million People Will Lose Health Care if Supreme Court Decides to Gut Obamacare."[29] This, of course, presumed that the states would not be willing to establish exchanges in the face of the loss of subsidies, or that Congress could not amend the law to provide subsidies in all fifty states.

Second, another immediate consequence of the invalidation of the IRS rule is that the employer mandate would no longer be applicable to many businesses in states without exchanges. Recall that when Tom Christina and Tom Miller first fashioned this suit, their goal, in part, was to weaken the employer mandate either rather than "gut" the entire ACA. If employees were not eligible for subsidies, then their employers would be exempt from having to pay a penalty for not providing insurance. As a result, the workers would not get insurance from their job, and they would not be able to afford unsubsidized

[28] Linda J. Blumberg, et al., *The Implications of a Supreme Court Finding for the Plaintiff in King v. Burwell: 8.2 Millions More Uninsured and 35% Higher Premiums*, URBAN INSTITUTE (Jan. 8, 2015), perma.cc/9LMP-DTDX.
[29] Ian Millhiser, *Studies: 8 Million People Will Lose Health Care If Supreme Court Decided to Gut Obamacare*, THINKPROGRESS (Jan. 12, 2015), perma.cc/Y9N9-AEPF.

insurance on the federal exchange. Even fewer Americans would be in the health insurance market.

Third, since millions of Americans could no longer afford the unsubsidized price of health insurance, they would be exempted from the individual mandate's penalty. The penalty only kicks in if a person is uninsured *and* the cost of insurance is less than 8 percent of their household income. Without the subsidies, the price of insurance for millions of Americans would have exceeded the threshold, exempting them from the penalty. If enough young and healthy people opted not to purchase health insurance – no longer compelled to do so by the penalty – the risk pools would become concentrated with older and sicker customers. This could potentially trigger an adverse-selection death spiral, where rates continue to increase to cover the sicker risk pool, which in turn causes more customers to exit the market due to unaffordable premiums.

Judge Edwards stated the stakes quite succinctly: "Come on, let's put it on the table. What you're asking for is to destroy the individual mandate, which guts the statute. You admit that's what this case is about. There's nothing hidden about that, you kill the individual mandate, you gut the statute, and you get what you want."

Walking out of the courthouse, Carvin was not sure if he would get what he wanted. He knew "Judge Edwards was against us. I strongly suspected Judge Randolph was with us." As for Judge Griffith, "I thought he was leaning my way but believe me, I've gotten some very bitter experience. I never count my chickens before they hatch."

17.6. "I WAS SO DEAD"

Two months later, on May 14, 2014, the Fourth Circuit Court of Appeals would hear arguments in *King v. Sebelius*. Recall that the Competitive Enterprise Institute had filed a second case challenging the IRS rule in Richmond, Virginia, with the hope of getting another case to the Supreme Court on a quicker trajectory. Unlike in the D.C. Circuit, where the judges hearing the case are announced two months in advance, in Richmond, the composition of the panel is revealed the morning of the argument.

While Carvin was optimistic about the D.C. Circuit panel, he thought the Fourth Circuit judges were not going to be sympathetic. Presiding over the case was Judge Roger L. Gregory. He was initially recess-appointed by President Clinton in June 2000, and later nominated by George W. Bush as a goodwill gesture in 2001. Reginald J. Brown, who served as a special assistant to President Bush on appointing judges, said he wished "he could get back" that seat.[30] The second judge, Andre M. Davis, was also nominated by President Clinton in October 2000, but was not confirmed before the election. President Bush did not renominate Davis. Three months after taking office in April 2009, President Obama promptly nominated Davis to his long-awaited seat. Judge Davis had ruled in favor of the government in a 2011 challenge to the Affordable Care Act's individual mandate.[31] The third judge was Stephanie D. Thacker, who was nominated by President Obama. The Fourth Circuit, once considered one of the most conservative appellate courts in the Country, had been remade by the Obama administration, which nominated six of the fifteen judges.[32]

When Carvin saw the lineup, he turned to his associate Yaakov Roth. "Do you want to argue this?" he asked. "I could be signing Broadway show tunes with these judges. We've lost this case." Carvin told me that the arguments in Richmond were "not nearly as contentious" as those in D.C. "They would let me ramble on, and I had really good points to make, none of which they were listening to, but they weren't bothering to interrupt me."

As is tradition in the Fourth Circuit, after arguments, the judges leave the bench, and shake hands with the advocates. I asked Carvin if he had any glimmer of hope as the hearing concluded. "Nah," he replied. "I was so dead."

[30] Josh Blackman, *President Bush's Judiciary at Ten Years, and Looking Forward to 2017*, JOSH BLACKMAN'S BLOG (Sep. 28, 2015), perma.cc/D6Y3-J8SC.
[31] Liberty Univ., Inc. v. Geithner, 671 F.3d 391, 422 (4th Cir. 2011) (Davis, J., dissenting).
[32] Frank Green, *4th Circuit Shedding Conservative Reputation*, RICH. TIMES-DISP. (Nov. 19, 2012), perma.cc/22AM-ARXA.

18

Between Two Ferns

18.1. #GetCovered

The viability of the federal exchange hinged on attracting a diverse risk pool. MIT economist Jonathan Gruber, whom we will hear much more about in Chapter 24, explained that the only way to ensure that insurance companies can afford to cover all customers – regardless of their preexisting conditions – was to "bring everyone into the system" so they will "pay one fair price." Young and old, healthy and sick, would all diversify the risk pool. The White House announced that for the system to work, 2.7 million of the expected 7 million signups on the exchange (roughly 40%) would have to be under the age of thirty-five.[1]

Millennials, however, were least likely to pay for expensive and unwanted coverage.[2] A Kaiser Family Foundation survey in 2013 found that 27% of the 19–34 age group was uninsured, the highest rate of *any* demographic.[3] Before the ACA, millions of these so-called "young invincibles" were able to skate by with thrifty catastrophic insurance or no insurance at all. Starting in 2014, they would be required to purchase a comprehensive policy, or pay the individual mandate's penalty. The invincibles' premiums would then be used to subsidize the care of older and sicker patients. Professor Gruber explained that under Obamacare, the "genetic winners, the lottery winners who've been

---

[1] Ben Tracy, *Obamacare targets "Young Invincibles" Demographic*, CBS News (Aug. 15, 2013), perma.cc/SXR5-2JRY.

[2] According to *Time*, millennials are Americans born between 1980 and 2000. Joel Stein, *Millennials: The Me Me Me Generation*, Time (May 20, 2013), bit.ly/2av1xu5. Your author was born on the early side of that range, but does not associate with this demographic.

[3] Sarah Kliff, *Five Myths about 'Young Invincibles'*, Wash. Post (Nov. 26, 2013), perma.cc/44QQ-ZNRK.

paying an artificially low price because of this discrimination now will have to pay more in return."[4] It's like *Soylent Green* in reverse.

There was still concern about whether the mandate penalty would be a sufficient incentive for the youths to enroll. In May 2013, former White House adviser Ezekiel Emanuel warned that "insurance companies are spooked by [the] possibility" that the invincibles would not buy health insurance and instead pay the penalty.[5] A shortage of youths would make the risk pools less diverse, resulting in higher premiums, and thus fewer enrollments due to sticker shock. This adverse selection threatened to undermine the health care reform. To avoid this *death spiral*, team Obama, which had twice before turned out the youth vote, launched an advertising campaign microtargeting millennials.

The White House enlisted celebrities including Ellen DeGeneres, Katy Perry, Lady Gaga, Kerry Washington, John Legend, and others to tweet the hashtag #GetCovered to their 350 million followers.[6] Not everyone got the message right. Former *NSYNC star Lance Bass tweeted a selfie at 1600 Pennsylvania Avenue. "Entering the White House to meet w the President to discuss health reform. HealthCare.org."[7] He got the website wrong – it was HealthCare.gov. An hour later he deleted the tweet, and clarified "Brain fart!! It's healthcare.gov! I've been dealing w too many charities lately!"

One of the more memorable millennial-targeted advertisements was released by the Colorado Consumer Health Initiative. It depicted two frat-attired partiers holding up the legs of a third, while he did a keg-stand (a handstand on top of a beer keg) with the tap in his mouth. The commercial announced: "Brosurance. Keg stands are crazy. Not having health insurance is crazier. Don't tap into your beer money to cover those medical bills. We got it covered. Thanks Obamacare."[8]

Another advertisement featured the mothers of actor Jonah Hill and musicians Adam Levine, Jennifer Lopez, and Alicia Keys.[9] The message was

---

4 Ian Schwartz, *Obamacare Architect: Genetic "Lottery Winners" Have Been Paying an "Artificially Low Price,"* REAL CLEAR POLITICS (Nov. 13, 2013), bit.ly/2al4fmJ.

5 Ezekiel J. Emanuel, *Health-Care Exchanges Need the Young Invincibles*, WALL ST. J. (May 6, 2013), on.wsj.com/28Q7CBZ.

6 Zeke J. Miller, *All The President's Celebrities: How The White House Used Stars to Sell Obamacare*, TIME (Apr. 1, 2014), bit.ly/28PmCoA. Asawin Suebsaeng, *32 Celebrities Who Want to Sell You Obamacare – and 5 Who Don't*, MOTHER JONES (Oct. 25, 2013), perma.cc/CGW4-BX3J.

7 Tal Kopan, *Bass Visits W.H., Flubs Site Address*, POLITICO (Mar. 12, 2014), perma.cc/N4AS-HMYK.

8 Got Insurance?, DOYOUGOTINSURANCE.COM, bit.ly/1Ow7uHQ.

9 Dan Hirschhorn, *Jonah Hill's Mom Wants You to Get Obamacare*, TIME (Mar. 14, 2014), perma.cc/LPY6-KBDP.

simple: moms should encourage their kids to get covered. "Trust me, us moms put up with a lot," Hill's mother explained. "But one thing we should never have to put up with is our kid not having health care," she said. Levine's mother added, "Young people feel invincible, until something actually happens, they will continue to feel invincible. And unfortunately something will happen." Lopez's mom implored the kiddoes, "Please get covered." Keys's mom finished with a guilt trip: "Do it for your mom."

To reach a broader audience, President Obama personally invited basketball superstar LeBron James to record a public service announcement. The NBA MVP said, "Any way I can help the president, that's pretty cool."[10] In the video, James urged fans to visit HealthCare.gov, where they can "find an affordable plan as part of the health care law." He reminded everyone, "The deadline to enroll is March 31, so sign up now." *The Bleacher Report* called the twenty-nine-year-old icon the "ideal pitchman to the target audience." The White House boasted that "top athletes and celebrities, like LeBron, have enormous power to connect with their young fans about the importance of getting covered."[11]

One of the less successful campaigns urged parents to talk to their children about health care over the holidays. Shortly before Christmas, the president tweeted a picture of a bespectacled twenty-something sitting on a couch with string lights glowing in the background. He was wearing a red-and-black flannel onesie and holding a mug.[12] Obama asked, "How do you plan to spend the cold days of December?" The infographic provided the answer: "Wear pajamas. Drink hot chocolate. Talk about health insurance. #GetTalking." The millennial – later revealed to be Ethan Krupp, an employee of Obama's outreach group – was ridiculed on social media as *pajama boy*.[13]

National Review columnist Charles C.W. Cooke wrote that he was a "vaguely androgynous, student-glasses-wearing, Williamsburg hipster."[14] Conservative pundit Rich Lowry called pajama boy an "insufferable man child."[15] Lowry compared him to President Obama's 2012 internet cartoon about the *Life of Julia*, which depicted a girl who relied on government programs at each stage

---

[10] Ethan Skolnick, *Lebron James to Promote Affordable Care Act*, BLEACHER REPORT (Mar. 14, 2014), perma.cc/UM3P-G5W4.

[11] JulieAnn McKellogg, *Lebron James Joins the Celeb Cast of Healthcare.gov PSAs*, WASH. POST (Mar. 14, 2014), wapo.st/28UZfT1.

[12] Obama, Barack (@BarackObama). (Dec. 17, 2013,), bit.ly/1PA3b9g.

[13] Charlie Spiering, *Meet Ethan Krupp: Pajamacare Boy and Organizing for Action Employee*, WASH. EXAMINER (Dec. 19, 2013), perma.cc/U244-2XL2.

[14] Charles C.W. Cooke, *The New Face of Obamacare Is a Man in a Onesie. Of course.*, NATL. REV. (Dec. 18, 2013), perma.cc/QT6L-X56N.

[15] Rich Lowry, *Pajama Boy. An Insufferable Man-Child*, POLITICO (Dec. 18, 2013), perma.cc/KC73-Y5GD.

of her life.[16] "Neither is a symbol of self-reliant, responsible adulthood," Lowry explained. "And so both are ideal consumers of government." Krupp initially boasted on Twitter, "Hey I'm in this," before the embattled pitchman deleted his account.[17]

18.2. "young people think they're invincible"

Perhaps the most important social media campaign was President Obama's sit-down with Zach Galifianakis on *Between Two Ferns*. If you have no idea who Zach Galifianakis is, or have never heard of *Between Two Ferns*, then you are likely not part of the target demographic. Galifianakis, the scruffy-faced crass comedian who starred in *The Hangover* movies, hosts a mock public access program on the comedy site FunnyOrDie.com. Seated between two potted plants – hence the name of the show – Galifianakis asks his celebrity guests awkward, offensive, and hilarious questions. On March 11, 2014, the commander in chief sat down for an interview.[18]

After an awkward introduction – the host feigned trouble pronouncing Barack – Galifianakis bluntly asked the president about sending Ambassador Dennis Rodman to "North Ikea," being "the last black president," and whether his presidential library would be in Hawaii or his "home country of Kenya."[19] About halfway through the eight-minute exchange, Galifianakis inquired, "So do you go to any websites that are dot-coms, or dot-nets, or do you mainly just stick with dot-govs?" Obama replied, "Have you heard of HealthCare.gov?" Galifianakis sighed. "Here we go, okay, let's get this out of the way, what did you come here to plug?" The president asked, "Have you heard of the Affordable Care Act?" The host answered, "Oh yeah, I heard about that, that's the thing that doesn't work." Referencing Microsoft's failed MP3 player, he asked, "Why would you get the guy that created the Zune to make your website?"

Obama corrected him. "HealthCare.gov works great now and millions of Americans have already gotten health insurance plans." Next came the pitch. "Most young Americans right now are not covered and the truth is they can get coverage for what it costs to pay their cell phone bill." A visibly bored Galifianakis interjected: "Is this what they mean by drones?" Obama ignored

---

[16] Laura Bassett, *Life of Julia, Obama Campaign's New Online Tool, Touts Pro-Woman Policies*, Huff.Post (May 3, 2012), perma.cc/GF3P-ZMAF.

[17] Spiering, *supra* note 13.

[18] *Between Two Ferns with Zach Galifianakis: President Obama*, Funny or Die (Oct. 11, 2014), bit.ly/28RfMXp.

[19] James Crugnale, *Read Obama and Zach Galifianakis' Full Transcript of 'Between Two Ferns' Interview*, The Wrap (Mar. 11, 2014), perma.cc/F3Q3-TFSN.

him: "The point is that a lot of young people think they're invincible." "Did you say invisible?" the host asked. A perturbed Obama replied, "No, no, not invisible, invincible. Meaning that they don't think they can get hurt."

The president continued, "If they get that health insurance they can really make a big difference, and they've got until March 31st to sign up." Customers can sign up online, by phone, or in person, he explained. "The law means that insurers can't discriminate against you," Obama said, even "if you've got a preexisting condition." Galifianakis rolled up his sleeve and showed the president his forearm: "Yeah, but what about this, though?" With a perfect deadpan, Obama stared back at him: "That's disgusting." The host replied, "Spider bites. I got attacked by spiders." The disturbed commander in chief told him, "Zach, you need to get that checked right away, you need to get on HealthCare.gov, because that's one of the most disgusting things I've ever seen." Galifianakis, who was ready to tune out, asked, "Is your plug finally over?" Obama paused. "Uh, I suppose so."

Obama's appearance on *Between Two Ferns* was a viral sensation. The White House reported that after the video, there was a 40% spike in traffic to HealthCare.gov.[20] The leader of the free world scored 34 million views, followed closely by musician Justin Bieber's interview between two ferns, which was watched by 31 million.[21]

18.3. "THE AFFORDABLE CARE ACT IS HERE TO STAY"

On April 1, 2014 – the six-month anniversary of HealthCare.gov's launch – President Obama entered the Rose Garden to announce the final signup numbers.[22] "Last night, the first open-enrollment period under this law came to an end," he began. "Despite several lost weeks out of the gate because of problems with the website," the triumphant president beamed, "7.1 million Americans have now signed up for private insurance plans through these marketplaces." The crowd erupted in applause. Seven million, a target the *Associated Press* reported was once "thought to be out of reach by most experts," had now become a reality.[23]

[20] Aaron Blake, *'Between Two Ferns' Video Leads to 40 Percent More Visits to HealthCare.gov*, WASH. POST (Mar. 12, 2014), perma.cc/Z7N6-J6D5.

[21] *Between Two Ferns with Zach Galifianakis: Justin Bieber*, FUNNY OR DIE (Sept. 26, 2013), bit.ly/291141V.

[22] *President Obama's Remarks on the Affordable Care Act*, DAILY KOS (Apr. 1, 2014), perma.cc/RBT2-7ZXD.

[23] Nedra Pickler, *Obama: 7.1 Million Americans Have Signed Up for Health Care*, AP (Apr. 1, 2014), perma.cc/M2JV-HJJQ.

The Affordable Care Act, the president said, ensures "that all of us can count on the security of health care when we get sick." With his tongue in cheek, he continued, "that's what the Affordable Care Act, or *Obamacare*, is all about." Now that the health care reform was going well, the president was all too happy to use the nickname for his eponymous law. During an interview with basketball Hall of Famer Charles Barkley, Obama said he "like[d]" calling it Obamacare. "Five years from now," the president predicted, "when everybody's saying, 'Man, I'm sure glad we got healthcare,' there are going to be a whole bunch of people who don't call it Obamacare anymore because they don't want me to get the credit."[24]

Even after March 31 – despite Secretary Sebelius's promise that the deadline would not be extended – people could still sign up late.[25] HHS announced that consumers who began to apply for coverage online but did not finish by March 31 would have until mid-April to complete the process.[26] Applicants were on the honor system. The late-filers would only have to check a box indicating that they attempted to sign up before the deadline but could not finish on time. The government was banking on millennials to procrastinate and join at the very end. Secretary Sebelius noted that they learned from the Romneycare experience in Massachusetts "that young adults tend to sign up later in the process."[27] President Obama announced from the Rose Garden that "anybody who was stuck in line because of the huge surge in demand over the past few days can still go back and finish your enrollment." The extension worked. By April 10, the exchange reached 7.5 million enrollees.[28] One week later, the tally for 2014 was finalized: 8 million signups.[29]

Back in the Rose Garden, the president offered an ultimatum to Republicans still committed to eliminating the ACA: "I will always work with anyone who is willing to make this law work even better. But the debate over repealing this law is over. The Affordable Care Act is here to stay." He warned that "history is not kind to those who would deny Americans their basic economic security,"

[24] Daniel Halper, *Obama: Signing Up for Obamacare Is "Just Part of Growing Up"*, WEEKLY STANDARD (Feb. 17, 2014), perma.cc/JW7Y-4STG.

[25] Jonathan Easley, *Sebelius Says Mandate Won't Be Delayed*, THE HILL (Mar. 12, 2014), perma.cc/RU8G-ZL94.

[26] Amy Goldstein, *Obama Administration Will Allow More Time to Enroll in Health Care on Federal Marketplace*, WASH. POST (Mar. 25, 2014), perma.cc/WX2K-ZCMF.

[27] Jason Millman, *Obamacare Enrollment Drops Off in February*, WASH. POST (Mar. 11, 2014), perma.cc/487X-44UM.

[28] Sandhya Somashekhar, *Obamacare Enrollment reaches 7.5 million*, WASH. POST (Apr. 10, 2014), perma.cc/CLV9-EXB8.

[29] Jason Millman, *Here's how we got to 8 million Obamacare Signups*, WASH. POST (Apr. 17, 2014), perma.cc/BC55-U3W4.

and "nobody remembers well those who stand in the way of America's progress." Two months earlier during his State of the Union address, Obama blasted Republicans for their never-ending string of repeal votes. "If you have specific plans to cut costs, cover more people, and increase choice, tell America what you'd do differently," he said. "Let's see if the numbers add up. But let's not have another forty-something votes to repeal a law that's already helping millions of Americans. The first forty were plenty. We got it. We all owe it to the American people to say what we're for, not just what we're against."

In March 2014, the House cast its fiftieth vote to repeal the ACA.[30] Unlike the repeal votes in 2013 – before ACA policies went into effect – now there was a tangible cost. Brian Beutler observed in *Salon* that a vote to eliminate Obamacare now served as a "statement of intent to annul millions of people's healthcare benefits."[31] Senator Ron Johnson (R–WI), who was elected during the Tea Party surge of 2010, explained the paradigm shift. "It's no longer just a piece of paper that you can repeal and it goes away," he said. "There's something there. We have to recognize that reality. We have to deal with the people that are currently covered under Obamacare."[32] Health insurance analyst Robert Laszewski aptly observed, "Obamacare is not going to be repealed. The sooner Republicans come to understand that the better for them."[33] Though the party did not discard its promise to "repeal and replace" the law, internally the focus shifted. The GOP's spring 2014 legislative agenda quietly omittted any action on Obamacare.[34]

18.4. "OMG, HE'S HOT"

HHS Secretary Kathleen Sebelius did not join the president for his celebration in the Rose Garden on April 1. Barely a week later, she announced her long-anticipated resignation.[35] Although she was not forced out, the *New York Times* noted that "the frustration at the White House over her performance had become increasingly clear, as administration aides worried that the

---

[30] Sahil Kapur, *GOP House Votes to Delay Obamacare Mandate, Which Wouldn't Do Much Now*, TALKING POINTS MEMO (Mar. 5, 2014), perma.cc/66R9-SB3S.

[31] Brian Beutler, *GOP Finally Goes Too Far on Obamacare: Why the 50th Repeal Vote Is Not the Charm*, SALON (Mar. 3, 2014), perma.cc/8BCA-X3CD.

[32] Jonathan Weisman, *With Health Law Cemented, G.O.P. Debates Next Move*, N.Y. TIMES (Dec. 26, 2013), nyti.ms/28SjRoH.

[33] Robert Laszewski, *With the November Election Six Months Away Obamacare Is Up for Grabs*, HEALTH CARE POLICY AND MARKETPLACE REVIEW (May 13, 2014), perma.cc/8A29-Q28R.

[34] Sahil Kapur, *The GOP's Incredible Disappearing Question to Repeal Obamacare*, TALKING POINTS MEMO (May 14, 2014), perma.cc/6LZB-6YKK.

[35] Michael D. Shear, *Sebelius Resigns after Troubles Over Health Site*, N.Y. TIMES (Apr. 10, 2014), nyti.ms/28VdA1X.

crippling problems at HealthCare.gov ... would result in lasting damage to the president's legacy."[36] Even her departure was glitchy. While reading her farewell address, Sebelius became flustered.[37] "Unfortunately, a page is missing," she said. A fitting conclusion to her tenure, as HealthCare.gov was plagued with the infamous *404 error message*: page "not found."[38] Praising his Secretary, President Obama said she would "go down in history" for her work on the ACA.[39]

Sebelius, the former Kansas governor, was briefly buzzed about for a Senate run in the Sunflower State, but declined.[40] Marilyn Tavenner, who served as the administrator for the Center for Medicare and Medicaid Services, departed a year later.[41] She would replace Karen Ignani as the chief of America's Health Insurance Plans. Her new job was to lobby Congress about the health care reform she implemented.

Sebelius's replacement would be Sylvia Matthew Burwell, who headed the Office of Management and Budget. One of her first official acts was to continue HHS's defense of the contraceptive mandate in the case now styled *Burwell v. Hobby Lobby Stores*. Because of the Affordable Care Act, nearly eight million women gained insurance that guaranteed contraceptive coverage.[42] One of the more colorful campaigns raising awareness for this benefit was released by the Colorado Consumer Health Initiative (the same group that released the "Brosurance" spot).[43] The ad showed a smirking twenty-something guy with his arm around the waist of a smiling twenty-something girl. She is holding a pack of birth control pills, with her thumbs up. The headline read, "Let's get physical." Not much was left to the imagination. "OMG, he's hot! Let's hope he's as easy to get as this birth control. My health insurance covers the pill, which means all I have to worry about is getting him between the covers. Thanks Obamacare!" Three weeks after Burwell took office, the Supreme Court would decide if female employees at religious for-profit corporations would be covered between the covers.

---

[36] *Id.*

[37] Jonathan Easley, *Sebelius's Final Glitch*, THE HILL (Apr. 11, 2014), perma.cc/K7QA-CBR7.

[38] Tim Fisher, *How to Fix a 404 Not Found Error*, ABOUT TECH (Mar. 8, 2016), perma.cc/E879-XDWL.

[39] Justin Sink, *Obama: Sebelius Will 'Go Down in History,'* THE HILL (Apr. 11, 2014), perma.cc/H6AV-E8N2.

[40] Catalina Camia, *Report: Sebelius Not considering Senate Race*, USA TODAY (Apr. 18, 2014), perma.cc/68JU-GXED.

[41] Robert Pear, *Head of Obama's Health Care Rollout to Lobby for Insurers*, N.Y. TIMES (Jul. 15, 2015), nyti.ms/28Opyex.

[42] ASPA, *The Affordable Care Act Is Working*, HHS.GOV (Jun. 24, 2015), perma.cc/3XKZ-Y3NH.

[43] Got Insurance?, DOYOUGOTINSURANCE.COM, perma.cc/62EM-KKVR.

19

Corporate Prayer

19.1. "AN AFFRONT TO PERSONAL DIGNITY"

As is tradition, the justices leave their most controversial decisions for the last day of the term at the end of June. *Hobby Lobby* would be no exception, and would be handed down – in a proceeding known as the "hand down" – on June 30, 2014. The weather on that sunny Monday morning was much more hospitable for demonstrations than the snowy March day when the case was argued. Two camps of supporters congregated outside the Court. One side chanted, "Ho, Ho, Hey, Hey, birth control is here to stay!" The other side responded, "Hey, Hey, Ho, Ho, *Roe v. Wade* has got to go!" One side held signs that read "Keep your rosaries off my ovaries." The other side put pieces of red tape over their mouths, with "Life" written on it. Everyone waited in anticipation for the Court to announce the decision.

At 9:54 AM, Justice John Paul Stevens took his seat in the VIP section of the Court.[1] Stevens, appointed by President Ford as a moderate in 1975, would go on to lead the Court's liberal wing for more than three decades. When he retired in 2010, he held the record as the second-oldest justice and the third longest-serving justice.[2] On that final day of the term, Stevens knew that there were only two cases remaining, both of which looked to be likely victories for the conservative wing of the Court: *Harris v. Quinn* and *Burwell v. Hobby Lobby Stores*. The first case considered whether the First Amendment prohibited public-sector unions from collecting mandatory "agency fees" from employees who did not want to join the union. During oral arguments in *Quinn*, five justices seemed intent to rule against the labor unions.

---

[1] Mark Walsh, A *"View" from the Court: Justice Alito Has His Day in Finale*, SCOTUSBLOG (Jun. 30, 2014), perma.cc/3QPV-MCN6.

[2] Debra Cassens Weiss, *John Paul Stevens Second-Oldest Justice Ever*, ABA JOURNAL (Nov. 19, 2007), perma.cc/B7YH-DRNU.

At exactly 10:00 AM, the justices emerged from behind the vermillion curtains and took their seats. However, there were only eight on the bench. Justice Scalia was already abroad, teaching a class on "Perspectives on the U.S. Supreme Court" in Galway, Ireland.[3] The following week, two of the other justices would gallivant across the Atlantic: Kennedy to Salzburg, Austria, and the chief to London.[4] Stevens – who witnessed Babe Ruth's "called shot" in the 1932 World Series[5] – was not available to pinch hit for the absent Scalia.[6]

The chief justice began the session and announced, "Justice Alito has the opinions of the Court in our two remaining cases this morning." Alito would write the majority decisions in both *Harris* and *Hobby Lobby*. In the Court, reporter Mark Walsh recalled that the announcement was "greeted with some degree of surprise."[7] Many expected Alito to write the union case; he was the only justice who had not yet written an opinion from the January sitting, when *Harris* was argued, and the assignments are usually distributed equally. But many expected that Roberts, once again, would keep the Obamacare case for himself. The chief justice always assigns the opinion when he is in the majority – it is one of the few perks of being in the middle. The previous evening, a sullen photo of John Roberts splashed across *The Drudge Report*, with the headline, "Pill: Round two for Roberts and Obamacare."[8] Alas, Roberts would be quiet. However, it would be a busy day for the first justice from New Jersey since William Brennan.

As the demonstrators outside waited with baited breath for *Hobby Lobby*, Justice Alito spent fifteen minutes reading from his opinion in *Harris*. "Here is what is at stake in this case," he explained. "Compelling a person

---

3 *Chief Justice John Roberts Jr., Justice Antonin Scalia, Both Return to New England Law Boston International Study Programs*, N. ENGL. LAW BOSTON NEWS (Jul. 2, 2014), perma.cc/9DCS-6EXF.

4 *Summer Program in Salzburg*, MCGEORGE.EDU, perma.cc/63H8-2XEC.

5 Ed Sherman, *Did Babe Ruth's Called Shot Happen?*, CHI. TRIB. (Mar. 28, 2014), perma.cc/Y6QT-NHW3.

6 In 2010, Senator Patrick Leahy (D-VT) proposed a bill to permit retired justices to serve when one of the active justices recuses. Robert Barnes, *A Deep Bench of Substitute Justices Goes Unused*, WASH. POST (Aug. 9, 2010), perma.cc/DVK6-W6RB. That would have allowed Stevens, along with Justices David H. Souter and Sandra Day O'Connor, to be called on to serve. This option was especially appealing for Democrats, who would gladly swap a recused Justice Alito for one of these three. The proposal did not make it out of committee. In 2016, Justice Stevens announced that he endorsed this proposal while he was on the Court, but declined an opportunity to fill Justice Scalia's vacant seat. Cristian Farias, *Retired Justice John Paul Stevens Tells Senate to Get Moving on That Supreme Court Nominee*, HUFF. POST (May 5, 2016), perma.cc/83RL-UPEX.

7 Walsh, *supra* note 1.

8 Josh Blackman, *Chief Justice Roberts Leading the Drudge Report*, JOSH BLACKMAN'S BLOG (Jun. 29, 2014), perma.cc/74VX-PP8C.

to mouth words that are contrary to the person's beliefs is an affront to personal dignity." For this reason, the compelled payment "undermines the free marketplace of ideas on which our democratic form of government is based and it violates the First Amendment." However, progressives let out a brief sigh of relief because the Court stopped short of overruling *Abood v. Detroit Board of Education*, a 1976 case that allowed unions to withhold other types of fees from the paychecks of government workers. The Court would revisit that issue in the 2016 case of *Friedrichs v. California Teachers Association*, but with only eight justices, would deadlock 4–4. Most in the Court were far more concerned with Alito's next opinion.

19.2. "FREEDOM OF RELIGION"

At 10:15 AM, Alito offered a segue from *Harris* to *Hobby Lobby*. "The first decision that I summarized involved freedom of speech and freedom of association," he explained. "The opinion that I will now summarize," Alito continued, "involves freedom of religion." Reporter Mark Walsh observed that Alito, "on such an important day for his opinions, [was] more animated than usual, becoming even more so as he announces his second decision." As everyone inside the Court waited for Alito to reveal the holding, pandemonium would soon erupt outside.

The moment that Justice Alito began reading his statement – even before the opinion is published online – the Public Information Office in the basement of the Supreme Court hands out printed copies. This triggers the famous *Running of the Interns*. Interns for the news networks, wearing business attire and sneakers, stand by, waiting to receive the opinions. Once the opinions are in hand, the interns sprint a quarter-mile from inside the Court, out the door, down the stairs, and into the media scrum. The *Running* has become an annual tradition every June at the Supreme Court.[9]

The first to make it to the every June at the Supreme Court plaza that day was khaki-clad Jason Donner of Fox News. Host Shannon Bream tweeted, "Jason Donner once again smokes the competition at the Sup Ct on behalf of @foxnews."[10] Donner, however, was not an intern, so he was disqualified. The grand prize went to the pink-sneakered sprinter Leah of Fox Business Channel. The other networks took honorable mention. As the interns

---

[9] Benny Johnson, *The 2014 Running of the Interns*, BUZZFEEDNEWS (Jun. 30, 2014), perma.cc/2UWS-WG8M.

[10] @ShannonBream, TWITTER (Jun. 30, 2014, 9:56 AM), bit.ly/1XeXfJw.

hustled, the Hobby Lobby supporters chanted, "I believe that we will win." Their prayers would come true.

At 10:17 AM, Tom Goldstein, the publisher of SCOTUSBlog, reported: "Closely held corporations cannot be required to provide contraception coverage." Hobby Lobby prevailed. The message spread like wildfire on First Street, which erupted in celebrations. Kristan Hawkins, President of Students for Life, stood at a microphone of the pro-life rally. She ripped apart a piece of paper, exclaiming, "This was my losing speech."[11] Following the beat of a drum, chants of "Hobby Lobby Wins" boomed. Back in the Court, the environment was far more somber.

19.3. "CLOSELY HELD FOR-PROFIT CORPORATIONS"

In 2012, Chief Justice Roberts's Janus-faced hand down of *NFIB v. Sebelius* left many in the Court uncertain of the outcome; first, the mandate violated the commerce clause, but second, it could be saved as a tax. Justice Alito's framing of the case, however, cut right to the chase. Rather than focusing on the artificial corporate form, Alito began his statement with a discussion of the individuals who exercised their religion through their businesses. He named the Green and Hahn families, discussed their faith – "devout Christians" and "devout Mennonites" – and offered a brief sketch of their life stories. "The Hahns have religious beliefs and they are trying to live their lives in accordance with those beliefs. The same is true of the Greens."

With this background, Alito noted that "the family members and the businesses" alleged that the contraceptive mandate violated their "religious liberty" that RFRA protects. "Both the Hahns and the Greens," Alito explained, "believe that they have a religious obligation to run their businesses in accordance with the tenets of their faith." However, they "object to offering coverage for four methods of contraception that may operate after conception." The contraceptive mandate "require[s] them to do just that." He lingered on the word "that" for emphasis.

As a surprise to no one in the room, Alito first held that "the language of RFRA makes it clear that" the Court can hear the case of these "closely held for-profit corporations," many of which, he added, "are mom and pop operations," or "corner store[s]." These Main Street colloquialisms did not make it into the Court's majority opinion. Often during the hand down a Justice will add some rhetorical flourishes that the others in the

---

[11] *Supreme Court Ruling on Contraceptive Mandate Vigil*, C-SPAN (Jun. 30, 2014), cs.pn/21JyMfD.

majority opinion did not agree, which sometimes creates some resentment. "The owners of a closely held corporation," Alito concluded, "can exercise religion."

Refusing to allow these businesses to sue would put the owners "to a cruel choice." They could "give up the protection for religious liberty" by benefiting from the corporate form, or they "could give up the benefits of the corporate form" to preserve their religious liberty. Alito said the Court was "confident that [Congress] did not want religious believers with dissenting views to be turned into second class citizens" through this Catch-22. However, "HHS's [mandate] would do just that."

In the first surprise of the day, Justice Alito said that HHS's rejection of corporate personhood was "endorsed by [only] two of the dissenting justices." At the time, no one in the Court knew the vote breakdown, though experts predicted this would be a 5–4 decision. But with this remark, Alito made clear that two of the justices – Breyer and Kagan – did not go along with Ginsburg and Sotomayor on the question of corporate personhood. Breyer and Kagan would write a three-sentence dissenting opinion in which they noted that "we need not and do not decide whether either for-profit corporations or their owners may bring claims under" RFRA.

The government wasn't surprised they lost the votes of Justices Breyer and Kagan. "I think it's a hard question," a senior DOJ attorney told me, because "there are circumstances in which it is difficult to think of the owners of the corporation and the corporation as entirely separate entities." He recalled that both Justices Breyer and Kagan asked questions about that during oral arguments.

19.4. "COMPELLING INTEREST"

After resolving the threshold issue of whether corporations could exercise religion, the Court turned to whether the contraceptive mandate substantially burdened that freedom. If the Hahns and the Greens "comply with the HHS Mandate," Alito explained, "they believe they will be facilitating abortions and committing a grave wrong." This is true, even though, as the majority opinion clarified, "federal regulations, which define pregnancy as beginning at implantation," rather than at fertilization, "do not so classify [such contraceptives] ... as causing abortions."[12] The Hanhs and the Greens are

---

[12] Burwell v. Hobby Lobby Stores, Inc., 134 S. Ct. 2751, 2763 n. 7 (2014) ((citing 62 Fed. Reg. 8611 (Feb. 25, 1997)); 45 C.F.R. § 46.202(f) (2013) ("Pregnancy encompasses the period of time from implantation until delivery.").

faced with a choice between a $1.3 million daily fine and violating their conscience. "If these consequences do not amount to a substantial burden," Alito asked, "it is hard to see what would."

Finding that there was a substantial burden, the next inquiry for the Court was whether "the Government has a *compelling interest* in making sure that every woman whose employer is subject to the mandate is able to get every FDA approved contraceptive without any out of pocket expense." If the interest was not compelling, then under no circumstances could the substantial burden on free exercise be justified. On this question the five justices in the majority punted: "We assume for present purposes that this requirement is satisfied." Recall that the government determined that a finding that there was no compelling interest in providing employer-provided birth control "would've been a really severe way to lose the case." Instead, the manner in which the Court ruled was deemed by DOJ as "the best way to lose." The contraceptive mandate would live to fight another day.

As is often the case in 5–4 decisions on the Roberts Court, Justice Kennedy provided the decisive tie-breaking vote. And, as is his custom, Kennedy wrote separately to highlight certain grounds where he disagrees with the majority, and other grounds where he agrees with the dissent. His brief four-page concurring opinion in *Hobby Lobby* began, "It seems to me appropriate, in joining the Court's opinion, to add these few remarks." Critically, he addressed the question of whether a compelling interest was at stake.

In his usual cryptic manner, Kennedy wrote, "It is important to confirm that a premise of the Court's opinion is its assumption that the HHS regulation here at issue furthers a legitimate and compelling interest in the health of female employees." What did this mean? A senior DOJ official I spoke with said there were two different ways Justice Kennedy's opinion can be read. One, Kennedy was simply assuming for purposes of this decision that there was a "compelling interest," but determined that contraceptives could be covered in less burdensome ways. Or two, he was "pretty confident that this qualifies as a compelling interest," but it was not narrowly tailored. He told me, "I think it would be open to Justice Kennedy in the future to go either way based on what the concurring opinion said." Kennedy was likely anticipating the non-profit cases that were coming down the pike.

In any event, Justice Alito's decision not to resolve the question of whether the government had a compelling interest was probably necessitated by the need to assuage Justice Kennedy's concerns, and prevent him from breaking off and not joining the majority opinion.

19.5. "AN ALTERNATIVE"

Having shown that (1) a closely held for-profit corporation can exercise religion, (2) that the mandate imposed a substantial burden on that exercise, and (3) providing employer-provided contraceptive was arguably a compelling interest, the government had only one last line of defense: to prove that the mandate was "the least restrictive means" by which the compelling interest could be achieved. Here, the Little Sisters saved Hobby Lobby.

"HHS has already devised and implemented a system that seeks to respect the religious liberty of religious non-profit corporations" like the Little Sisters of the Poor, Alito noted, "while ensuring that the employees of these entities have precisely the same access to all FDA approved contraceptives." If *Accommodation* 2.0 works for non-profit groups like the Little Sisters, Alito asked why could it not "be made available when the owners of for-profit corporations have similar religious objections?"

The Court "concluded that this system constitutes *an alternative* that achieves all of the Government's aims while providing greater respect for religious liberty." I emphasized the phrase *an alternative*, because the Court did not hold that the accommodation offered to the religious non-profits was "the least restrictive means." In other words, that the government can achieve its compelling interest without the HHS mandate is evidenced by the fact that it gave the Little Sisters the accommodation; but that does not mean the accommodation itself is the most narrowly tailored approach to achieving its compelling interest. In his concurring opinion Justice Kennedy agreed that the government lost this case because "there is an existing, recognized, workable, and already-implemented framework to provide coverage," namely the accommodation offered to the non-profits. Kennedy wrote that the accommodation "is *less restrictive* than the means challenged by the plaintiffs in these cases." Like the majority, the concurring Justice did not say it is "the *least* restrictive alternative." While the distinction between an *alternative* and the *least restrictive alternative* may not seem significant, the careful phrasing would leave unresolved the very issue the Little Sisters would bring to the Supreme Court two years later – and Wheaton College would bring to the Court later that day.

Was the accommodation lawful? Justice Alito stopped short of ruling on the legality of the accommodation, writing, "We do not decide today whether an approach of this type complies with RFRA." That decision would be for another day. In her oral dissent Justice Ginsburg noted that the majority "hedges," and "declines to decide whether the [accommodation] complies with workers for purposes of all religious claims." In a footnote Justice

Ginsburg wrote that Little Sisters' case is "currently *sub judice*," Latin for "under consideration."

At 10:34 AM, Justice Alito finished reading his opinion. By that point he had been reading for more than thirty minutes, and everyone outside the Court already knew what happened. But the "Notorious RBG" was about to get started. Alito concluded, "Justice Ginsburg has filed a dissenting opinion."

19.6. "FIFTY YEARS FROM NOW"

A Supreme Court dissenting opinion does not carry the force of law. It serves a different purpose. As Chief Justice Charles Evans Hughes explained, the dissent is "an appeal to the brooding spirit of the law, to the intelligence of a future day, when a later decision may possibly correct the error into which the dissenting judge believes the Court to have been betrayed."[13] The reasoning of a dissent often stands the test of time, and may ultimately turn into a majority opinion. Justice Benjamin Cardozo wrote that a justice in dissent speaks "to the future," with his "voice pitched to a key that will carry throughout the years."[14] Justice Scalia enjoyed telling law school crowds that he wrote his dissents "for casebooks. There's no other reason to write them."[15] Scalia wanted generations of law students to study his dissents, with the sincere hope that one day his views will prevail. To make a lasting impression, a justice can read his or her dissent from the bench, after the majority opinion has been handed down. *New York Times* reporter Adam Liptak observed, "A few times a year, Supreme Court justices go out of their way to emphasize their unhappiness by reading a dissent from the bench out loud, supplementing the dry reason on the page with vivid tones of sarcasm, regret, anger and disdain."[16] Scalia was an expert at all-of-the-above tones.

Due to the right-leaning composition of the Court during Justice Ruth Bader Ginsburg's two-decade tenure, for controversial 5–4 decisions, more often than not she has been in dissent. And according to a 2010 study, Ginsburg is the champion of the oral dissent: she "holds the modern record," with more than 10% of her dissenting opinions being read from the bench.[17] Perhaps her most

---

[13] Andrew Lowy, *Reading a Dissent from the Supreme Court Bench*, CONSTITUTION DAILY (Jul. 18, 2014), perma.cc/ZWD6-QAZT.

[14] *Id.*

[15] Jerry de Jaager, *Justice Scalia Comes Home to the Law School*, RECORD (Spring 2012), perma.cc/A7T6-DXYB.

[16] Adam Liptak, *In a Polarized Court, Getting the Last Word*, N.Y. TIMES (Mar. 8, 2010), nyti.ms/2aDumY5.

[17] *Id.*

influential oral dissent came in the 2007 case of *Lilly Ledbetter v. Goodyear Tire*, which ruled against a female employee who did not timely report claims of pay discrimination.[18]

Ginsburg's dissent fired a warning across First Street. She said that after the Court's "parsimonious reading" of the employment law, the "ball is in Congress's court" to change it. Ginsburg's dissent galvanized public attention to the issue of pay discrimination. It also elevated Lilly Ledbetter as a spokesperson for gender equality. She even campaigned alongside candidate Barack Obama. And most importantly, Congress heeded Ginsburg's call. The first bill President Obama signed into law was the *Lilly Ledbetter Fair Pay Act*. A framed copy of the law, signed by the president, hangs on the wall in Ginsburg's chambers.[19] Obama wrote to her, "Thanks for helping create a more equal and just society." In an interview with Katie Couric, the Clinton nominee said that this is one of her proudest achievements, even though it did not take place in the Supreme Court.

Ginsburg would later explain that "50 years from now, people will not be able to understand *Hobby Lobby*."[20] The goal of her dissenting opinion was not just to issue a call to arms today but to speak to future generations and help them understand why she viewed the Court's decision as so flawed. When asked about her dissenting opinion, she would later explain, "We have a great tradition in our country of justices explaining why they disagree. Many of those dissents are now unquestionably the law of the land."

Ginsburg's dissent laid out the stakes in clear terms: "In a decision of startling breadth, the Court holds that commercial enterprises ... can opt out of any law ... they judge incompatible with their sincerely held religious beliefs. Persuaded that Congress enacted RFRA to serve a far less radical purpose, and mindful of the havoc the Court's judgment can introduce, I dissent."

19.7. "SPECIAL SOLICITUDE"

Despite her passion, Justice Ginsburg speaks very slowly. For example, an auctioneer spits out about 250 words per minute.[21] Most audiobooks are recorded

---

[18]   Ledbetter v. Goodyear Tire & Rubber Co., 550 U.S. 618 (2007).

[19]   Jeffrey Toobin, *Will Ginsburg's Ledbetter Play Work Twice?*, NEW YORKER (Jun. 24, 2013), bit.ly/2abd4vZ.

[20]   Jessica Weisberg, *Supreme Court Justice Ruth Bader Ginsburg: I'm Not Going Anywhere*, ELLE (Sept. 23, 2014), perma.cc/GG64-RMKV.

[21]   Timothy Noah, *The 1,000-Word Dash*, SLATE (Feb. 18, 2000), perma.cc/DL7U-M33M.

at 175 words per minute.[22] The average rate of speech is about 150 words per minute.[23] By way of comparison, Justice Alito delivered his 2,400-word *Hobby Lobby* majority opinion in a little over 17 minutes, at a below-average rate of 140 words per minute. In contrast, Justice Ginsburg's 1,500-word dissent took 14.5 minutes, for a plodding rate of 104 words per minute. Yet, the slow cadence – with deliberate pauses every few words – allows time for the message to sink in and resonate.

First, Ginsburg rejected the notion that for-profit corporations could exercise religion. The dispute, she explained, is "whether RFRA which speaks of a person's exercise of religion even applies to for profit corporations for they are not flesh and blood persons, they are artificial entities created by law." Ginsburg acknowledged that *some* corporations can exercise religion, because the First Amendment and RFRA "shield ... churches and other non-profit religion-based organizations" – all of which are incorporated. However, these special corporations have been treated with a "special solicitude" because they are "religious institutions." (During oral arguments, Solicitor General Verrilli repeated the phrase "special solicitude" three times. This distinction seemed to catch on with at least two justices.) For-profit corporations have not received such protections.

This different treatment makes sense, Ginsburg noted, because "religious organizations exist to foster the interest of persons subscribing to the same religious faith." That is "not so for profit corporations." Whereas religious institutions focus on a "community of believers in the same religion," the "workers who sustain the operations of for-profit corporations commonly are not drawn from one religious community." The employees of Hobby Lobby likely do not share the beliefs of the Green family.

Justice Ginsburg concluded, "Justice Sotomayor and I would hold that for-profit corporations should not be equated to non-profits existing to serve a religious community." She was quick to note, however, that "Justices Breyer and Kagan have not endorsed the Court's reasoning on this point. They simply would not decide the threshold question whether for-profit corporations or their owners can bring RFRA claims." But they also would not endorse Ginsburg's reasoning on this point. With a deliberate pause before she resumed, Ginsburg explained, "All four of us, however, agree in unison that RFRA gives Hobby Lobby and Conestoga no right to opt-out of contraceptive coverage."

---

[22] *Id.*
[23] *Tutorials – Voice Qualities*, Nat'l Ctr. for Voice & Speech, perma.cc/R2SJ-4K5T.

19.8. "CONTROL THEIR REPRODUCTIVE LIVES"

Unlike Justice Alito's majority opinion, which focused exclusively on the burden of the employers, Justice Ginsburg's dissent highlighted the strain a religious accommodation puts on the "employees who do not share their employer's religious beliefs." Not all of Hobby Lobby's employees agree with their bosses about the sinfulness of contraception, she explained, for "our cosmopolitan nation is made up of people of almost every conceivable religious preference." It should make no difference for female employees whether they work at Hobby Lobby or the "shop next door." Neither corporation should "deprive employees holding different beliefs of the employer-insured preventive care."

Ginsburg linked the availability of contraception to the broader goals of gender equality in our society, citing Justice Kennedy's landmark abortion decision in *Planned Parenthood v. Casey*: "The ability of women to participate equally in the economic and social life of the Nation has been facilitated by their ability to control their reproductive lives."[24] On this understanding, Ginsburg explained, Congress mandated through the ACA "coverage of preventive care responsive to women's needs."[25]

Justice Kennedy would agree on this front. In the penultimate paragraph of his concurring opinion, Kennedy wrote that the free exercise of religion cannot "unduly restrict *other persons*, such as employees, in protecting their own interests, interests the law deems compelling." In other words, the burden on third parties must be considered when deciding the scope of a person's free exercise right.

During oral arguments, Solicitor General Verrilli implored the Justices that "when you are analyzing what is required under RFRA, the Court must take account of the way in which the requested accommodation will affect the rights and interests of third parties." Justice Kennedy heeded this request, which the government considered a "big part of their argument," and indeed was "probably their only hope of winning." They did not win the case, but at least five justices recognized the impact on third parties within the RFRA analysis. In an interview the following month, Ginsburg was asked if she thought the symbol of the United States should be a pendulum, rather than an eagle, with

---

[24] Planned Parenthood v. Casey, 505 U.S. 833, 856 (1992). In this landmark abortion case, which was jointly authored by Justices O'Connor, Kennedy, and Souter, the Court did not overturn Roe v. Wade, nor did it uphold that decision in its entirety.

[25] Although, as discussed in Chapter 3, members of Congress avoided any reference to the sorts of contraceptives that would be considered "preventive care."

respect to protecting women's rights. She replied, "To be frank, it's one person who made the difference: Justice Kennedy."[26]

19.9. "STOPPING POINT"

The final portion of Justice Ginsburg's dissent charted the slippery slope following the majority opinion's reasoning. First, she rejected the Court's admonition that the government could simply pay for the contraceptives itself. The ACA, she notes, "requires coverage of preventive services through *existing employer-based systems* of health insurance, not through substitution of the Government as [the] payer." What if it "offends an employer's religious belief," Ginsburg asks "to pay the minimum wage or to accord women equal pay for substantially similar work." Couldn't the government simply accommodate, and pay the additional amount of money the employees lost? She asked rhetorically, "Where is the stopping point to [the] let-the-Government-pay solution?" Ginsburg noted as an aside that it is ultimately the "general public" who would foot the bill.

Second, Justice Ginsburg raised a series of hypotheticals that were brought up during oral argument. Would accommodations be required for "employers with religiously grounded objections to blood transfusions (Jehovah's Witnesses); antidepressants (Scientologists); medications derived from pigs (certain Muslims, Jews, and Hindus); and vaccinations (Christian Scientists)?" In his oral statement from the bench, Justice Alito responded that "cases involving other procedures or drugs," such as vaccines, "are likely to implicate different considerations such as preventing the spread of disease." He did not respond to the hypothetical Paul Clement also could not answer for months earlier: what about blood transfusions? In the published majority opinion, Alito stressed that there was "no evidence that insurance plans in existence prior to the enactment of ACA excluded coverage for such items." Since the enactment of the ACA, there have been no employers seeking religious exemptions for anything "other than the contraceptive mandate." That it has not happened before, Alito suggests, is a reason not to worry about it happening in the future.

Third, Ginsburg asked about an "employer whose religious faith teaches that it is sinful to employ a single woman without her father's consent or a married woman without her husband's consent." Would such an employer be exempted from "Title VII's ban on gender discrimination in employment,"

---

[26] Weisberg, *supra* note 20.

she asked. This scenario, Ginsburg notes, is "not hypothetical."[27] Indeed, it is based on a case cited by the solicitor general's brief from the Minnesota Supreme Court.[28] Although it is not hypothetical, it was also not successful. Justice Ginsburg omitted the fact that the court rejected this claim.

Justice Alito responded directly to this charge. "We do not hold that RFRA protects invidious discrimination that is said to be based on a religious belief," he said. "The Government has a compelling interest in providing an equal opportunity to participate in the workforce without regard to race," Alito explained, "and prohibitions on racial discrimination are precisely tailored to achieve that critical goal." That means that the *only* way of eradicating racial discrimination is to prohibit it in all instances, without any exceptions. A senior DOJ official I spoke with pointed out that Alito "didn't mention anything other race discrimination," omitting gender, sexual orientation, or gender identity.

In her oral dissent Ginsburg did not mention LGBT discrimination, but with the same-sex marriage cases already trickling up toward the Court, this was certainly on her mind. In the published dissent, Justice Ginsburg cited the case of *Elane Photography v. Willock*, in which a "for-profit photography business owned by a husband and wife refused to photograph a lesbian couple's commitment ceremony based on the religious beliefs of the company's owners."[29] The New Mexico Supreme Court ruled against the photographer, finding that the state RFRA could not be used as a defense in the discrimination claim.[30]

Ginsburg concluded her opinion by noting that "today's potentially sweeping decision minimizes the Government's compelling interest in uniform compliance with laws governing workplaces." Through RFRA, Congress maintained the "tradition in which one person's right to free exercise of her religion must be kept in harmony with the rights of her fellow citizens and with the common good." In one of the more memorable lines of her dissent, Ginsburg offered that "[y]our right to swing your arms ends just where the other man's nose begins."[31] Your liberty only extends so far so as not to harm

---

[27] In re State v. Sports & Health Club, Inc., 370 N.W.2d 844, 847 (Minn. 1985).

[28] *Id.*

[29] Elane Photography, LLC v. Willock, 309 P. 3d 53 (N.M. 2013). Elane Photograph was represented by Alliance Defending Freedom, co-counsel in *Hobby Lobby*. *See* Eugene Volokh & Ilya Shapiro, *Choosing What to Protect Is a Form of Speech*, WALL ST. J. (Mar. 17, 2014), bit.ly/1q2JLTt.

[30] For a discussion of how RFRA interacts with discrimination law, *see* Josh Blackman, *Is Indiana Protecting Discrimination?*, NAT'L REV. (Mar. 30, 2015), perma.cc/8274-77XK.

[31] This quote is often attributed to Harvard Law School Professor Zechariah Chafee, *Freedom of Speech in War Time*, 32 HARV. LAW REV. 932, 957 (1919), although variants of the quotation were used decades earlier, *Your Liberty to Swing Your Fist Ends Just Where My Nose Begins*, QUOTE INVESTIGATOR, perma.cc/2AG7-W4LV.

others. In the penultimate sentence of her opinion, Ginsburg closed, "The Court, I fear, has ventured into a minefield."

At 10:50 AM, nearly an hour after the session began, Ginsburg finished reading. Chief Justice Roberts closed the session. "I am authorized to announce that the Court has acted upon all cases submitted to the Court for decision this term." Pamela Talkin, the Court's Marshall, banged the gavel and announced, "The honorable Court is now adjourned to the time and place appointed by law." The Court would be in recess until the first Monday in October, which Congress has mandated as the start of the new term.

But the justices were not quite done for the summer. The day before, Wheaton College, a Christian college in Illinois, filed an emergency application with the Supreme Court to put the contraceptive mandate on hold. Seventy-two hours later, the issue of religious liberty would return to One First Street, as a divided Court clashed over the legality of the accommodation for religious non-profits.

20

Notorious RBG

20.1. "CONSTITUTIONAL LAWYER IN THE OVAL OFFICE"

Almost immediately after the decision in *Hobby Lobby* was announced, and long before Justice Ginsburg finished reading her dissent, politicians on both sides of the aisle mounted their virtual soap boxes.

Republicans tweeted their vindication. Speaker John Boehner gloated, "#HobbyLobby decision is another defeat for an administration that has repeatedly crossed constitutional lines." (The decision had nothing to do with the Constitution.) Senate Minority Leader Mitch McConnell exclaimed, "Today's Supreme Court decision makes clear that the Obama administration cannot trample on the religious freedoms that Americans hold dear." Senator Roy Blunt (R-MO) added, "Americans should not be forced to give up their business for their faith or give up their faith for their business."

Democrats tweeted their indignation. House Minority Leader Nancy Pelosi lamented, "SCOTUS took an outrageous step against women's rights, setting a dangerous precedent that permits corporations to choose which laws to obey." Senator Barbara Boxer (D-CA) tweeted, "Is #SCOTUS living in the 19th or 21st century? My colleagues & I are already working to remedy this injustice." Senate Majority Leader Harry Reid added, "If the Supreme Court will not protect women's access to health care, then Democrats will."

The White House expressed its resignation. The Justice Department did not expect to win, so this was not much of a surprise. That afternoon, Press Secretary Josh Earnest briefed the media on *Hobby Lobby*: "President Obama believes that women should make personal health care decisions for themselves rather than their bosses deciding for them."[1]

---

[1] Press Briefing by Press Secretary Josh Earnest, WHITE HOUSE (Jun. 30, 2014), perma.cc/8CS2-ZH45.

A reporter asked Earnest, "Does the constitutional lawyer who sits in the Oval Office agree with the Supreme Court that companies have freedom of religion?" Obama taught constitutional law at the University of Chicago Law School as a senior lecturer – a non-tenure-track adjunct – from 1996 to 2004.[2] Earnest replied, "The constitutional lawyer in the Oval Office disagrees with that conclusion from the Supreme Court ... [that] there are now a group of women who no longer have access to free contraceptive coverage simply because of some religious views that are held not by them, but by their bosses." Earnest added, "We believe that the owners of for-profit companies should not be allowed to assert their personal religious views to deny their employees federally mandated benefits."

Next, Earnest was asked what options the administration was considering to restore the coverage invalidated by the Court. He declined to answer. "I'm not in a position to do that right now," he said, but added that the president has called on Congress to "act to address the concerns of the women who are affected by this decision." Congress was fully equipped, in theory at least, to legislate another means to provide employees with contraceptive coverage that did not burden religious liberty. Of course, the prospects of amending Obamacare in the age of gridlock seemed bleak.

To that answer, a third reporter asked about the president's modus operandi: "In the era of the pen and the phone, why is the president calling on Congress to act so quickly?" The reporter added, "Why the focus on Congress right away?" The easiest solution, he suggested, was for the president simply to "apply the same regulatory fix that was used for nonprofits" for the for-profits. That is, give Hobby Lobby the same accommodation offered to the Little Sisters, so neither would have to pay for the contraceptives. Earnest replied, with his tongue in cheek: "[Are you] evincing some skepticism about Congress's ability to act quickly to solve commonsense problems?" He then answered his own question: "What I'll say is that as we assess the impact of this decision, we'll consider whether or not there is a range of other options that may be available that don't require legislative action."

Even a week after the decision, the White House was still weighing its options of how to offer contraceptives to women without violating the free exercise of their employers. As the *New York Times* explained, the president was "under such pressure that no one has been able to work out details of how the alternatives would be financed or administered."[3]

---

[2] Jodi Kantor, *Teaching Law, Testing Ideas, Obama Stood Slightly Apart*, N.Y. Times (Jul. 30, 2008), nyti.ms/1SYvJKR.

[3] Robert Pear & Adam Liptak, *Obama Weighs Steps to Cover Contraception*, N.Y. Times (Jul. 4, 2014), nyti.ms/1WikGm2.

20.2. "FIVE WHITE MEN"

It was not lost on the public that the five-member majority in *Hobby Lobby* were all men. Representative Nancy Pelosi charged that "we should be afraid of this Court [when] *five guys* ... start determining what contraceptions are legal." (*Hobby Lobby* said nothing about the *legality* of birth control). Senator Harry Reid expressed a similar sentiment: "The one thing we are going to do during this work period ... is to ensure that women's lives are not determined by virtue of *five white men*." (Reid's spokesperson later apologized for this "mistake," as Justice Thomas is not white).[4]

In the *Washington Post*, Ruth Marcus offered a "slightly crude" explanation for why the three female justices – Ginsburg, Sotomayor, and Kagan – were in dissent: they "have uteruses."[5] Having female reproductive organs, Marcus added, "is not a prerequisite for understanding the importance of access to birth control." Look at Stephen Breyer, who also dissented. (*Slate* columnist Dahlia Lithwick dubbed Breyer "the fourth feminist," because he was a "staunch defender of women's rights"[6]). But, Marcus stressed, being a woman "helps."

Even though several female judges on the lower courts ruled against the contraceptive mandate,[7] Marcus's sentiment echoed throughout the media. Indeed, it also resonated inside the Court, at least among its "notorious" media sensation.

20.3. "BLIND SPOT"

Americans are largely ignorant about who the Supreme Court justices are and what they do.[8] A 2012 survey revealed that nearly two-thirds of respondents could not name a single justice, and only 1% could name all nine justices.[9] Yet, in recent years, one justice's celebrity has soared – Ruth Bader Ginsburg.

---

4 Glenn Kessler, *Democrats on Hobby Lobby: 'Misspeaks,' 'Opinion' and Overheated Rhetoric*, WASH. POST (Jul. 14, 2014), perma.cc/8APS-594L.

5 Ruth Marcus, *Judging from Experience*, WASH. POST (Jul. 1, 2014), perma.cc/7H28-KAGW.

6 Dahlia Lithwick, *The Fourth Feminist*, SLATE (Aug. 11, 2014), perma.cc/BSL5-K92K.

7 *See*, e.g., *Korte v. Sebelius*, 735 F.3d 654 (7th Cir. 2013) (Sykes, J.); *Gilardi v. U.S. Dep't of Health and Human Services*, 733 F.3d 1208 (D.C. Cir. 2013) (Brown, J.); *Geneva College v. Sebelius*, 988 F. Supp.2d 511 (W.D.Pa. 2013) (Conti, J.).

8 *See* ILYA SOMIN, DEMOCRACY AND POLITICAL IGNORANCE: WHY SMALLER GOVERNMENT IS SMARTER 23–24 (2013).

9 Steve Eder, *Most Americans Can't Name a U.S. Supreme Court Justice, Survey Says*, WALL ST. J. (Aug. 20, 2012), on.wsj.com/1TNXyrv.

Her dissent in *Hobby Lobby* and her public persona promoting gender equality have sent her iconic status into the stratosphere.

During a July 2014 interview, Katie Couric asked Ginsburg, "Do you believe the five male justices truly understood the ramifications of their decision in *Hobby Lobby*"?[10] In a rebuke of her Y-chromosomed colleagues, Ginsburg replied, "I would have to say no." Still, she was "hopeful that if the Court has a *blind spot* today, its eyes will be opened tomorrow." The irony of paraphrasing the Gospel of John – which told of Jesus miraculously healing a blind person – to dismiss her colleague's "blind spot" about religious freedom was apparently lost on Ginsburg.[11] Couric pressed her further and asked if the five male justices "had a bit of a *blind spot*." Ginsburg replied, "In *Hobby Lobby*, yes. They had the same kind of *blind spot* the majority had in the *Lilly Ledbetter*" pay discrimination case. But, she hoped, the "justices continue to think and can change." This message reverberated throughout progressive circles.

Ginsburg, more often then her colleagues, often gives such interviews that appeal to liberal causes. Her candor has elevated her to an elite celebrity icon. The super-fandom began in earnest in 2013, when law student Shana Knizhnik started the "Notorious RBG" Tumblr. The title of the blog was a pun on the rapper Notorious B.I.G., with Ruth Bader Ginsburg's initials. (On the Court, the justices are referred to internally by their initials). Ginsburg told Couric, "I had to be told by my law clerk what this 'Notorious' is, and they explained it to me."

The blog began after Ginsburg dissented from the Court's 2013 decision in *Shelby County v. Holder*. Knizhnik was "appalled" at how the Court invalidated provisions of the Voting Rights Act, and saw Ginsburg's dissent as a "shining beacon, exemplifying the egalitarian and inclusive values I knew were embodied in the Constitution."[12] With her *Hobby Lobby* dissent one year later, Ginsburg was canonized as a patron saint of progressive causes.

On the blog, Knizhnik curated photographs, music videos, and other forms of "Ginsburgiana" lionizing RBG as a "supersignifier of liberal idealism."[13] *The New Republic* Basquiat-crowned Ginsburg as "the most popular woman

---

[10] *Ruth Bader Ginsburg on Hobby Lobby, Roe v. Wade, Retirement and Notorious R.B.G.*, Yahoo! News, yhoo.it/1rGldkz.

[11] John 9:25 (New International Version), perma.cc/XEH5-VHAG ("He replied, 'Whether he is a sinner or not, I don't know. One thing I do know. I was blind but now I see!'").

[12] Shana Knizhnik, *Notorious RBG: The Life and Times of Ruth Bader Ginsburg*, ACSBlog (Jan. 15, 2016), perma.cc/VKU6-BH5P.

[13] Jennifer Senior, *Review: 'Notorious RBG: The Life and Times of Ruth Bader Ginsburg'*, N.Y. Times (Oct. 25, 2015), nyti.ms/2aqwNLH.

on the internet."[14] One meme beamed, "You can't spell truth without Ruth." Another meme superimposed Beyoncé lyrics over a photograph of Ginsburg's pensive stare: "All them fives need to listen when a ten is talking."[15] T-shirts were sold that said "I ♥ RBG." Another said, "Fear the Frill," with a silhouette of Ginsburg wearing her customary frilly judicial collar. It is formally known as a jabot, but I've fondly dubbed it a *neck doily*.[16] In 2015, Knizhnik and MSNBC analyst Irin Carmon published NOTORIOUS RBG, a book the *New York Times* lauded as an "artisanal hagiography."[17]

Ginsburg's rockstar treatment outside the Court could not be denied. At the White House Hanukkah Party, President Obama welcomed Ruth Bader Ginsburg, who he noted is "also known as the Notorious RBG."[18] Ginsburg reciprocates the adoration, stating that the president's push for the Affordable Care Act was "brave."[19] And, at each State of the Union since 2009, shutters fly when Ginsburg embraces President Obama for their annual hug.[20] Nevertheless, she often dozes off during the address itself. In 2015, Ginsburg admitted that she was not "100 percent sober" during the State of the Union address, having had too much wine beforehand.[21] Afterwards, her granddaughter told her, "Bubbe, you were sleeping." Katie Couric asked Ginsburg if she was aware of how her dissent in *Hobby Lobby* "made you a bit of a rock star online." Ginsburg corrected her: "I think it started *before Hobby Lobby*."

However, there is a distinct concern with deifying Ginsburg. After a certain point it becomes difficult to separate Justice Ruth Bader Ginsburg from the Notorious RBG. As a cause célèbre, she is now beyond the reach of normal commentary on the Court. Criticizing her opinions amounts to criticizing women's rights more broadly. It becomes very dangerous when the law

---

[14] Rebecca Traister, *How Ruth Bader Ginsburg Became the Most Popular Woman on the Internet*, NEW REPUBLIC (Jul. 10, 2014), perma.cc/8RL8-DAEK.

[15] Shana Knizhnik, Notorious R.B.G – Tumblr (Jul. 9, 2014), perma.cc/583V-3KBZ.

[16] Josh Blackman, *David Lat Has Coined Three Words in Black's Law Dictionary (and I got a Slang Tweet from Garner)*, JOSH BLACKMAN'S BLOG (Jan. 27, 2014), perma.cc/X4JT-6XL8. The term "neck doily" is now listed as a slang for *jabot* in the 10th edition of BLACK'S LAW DICTIONARY.

[17] Senior, *supra* note 13.

[18] Amy R. Connolly, *Obama References 'Notorious RBG,' 'Star Wars' at White House Hanukkah Celebration*, UPI (Dec. 10, 2015), perma.cc/Z3VH-9H5V.

[19] Greg Stohr, *Ginsburg Says Court Struck the Right Balance on Gay Marriage*, BLOOMBERG BUS. (Aug. 24, 2013), perma.cc/7R9T-2RCW.

[20] Chris McGonigal, *Here's Every Adorable Obama and Ruth Bader Ginsburg SOTU Embrace Through the Years*, HUFF. POST (Jan. 13, 2016), perma.cc/KB8Z-4JQF.

[21] Kendall Breitman, *Ginsburg: I Wasn't '100 Percent Sober' at SOTU*, POLITICO (Feb. 13, 2015), perma.cc/9A7W-PVZ4.

transcends the judicial opinions and the justices themselves become the locus of the constitutional discourse.[22] This fandom creates a "blind spot" unto itself.

20.4. WHEATON COLLEGE

When *Hobby Lobby* was decided on June 30, 2014 – the last day of the Court's term – the justices' summer vacation could not begin quite yet. Earlier that year, Wheaton College, a Christian liberal arts college in Illinois, challenged the accommodation to the contraception mandate. Like the Little Sisters before them, Wheaton refused to sign EBSA Form 700, claiming that it made them complicit in facilitating abortions. On June 23 – one week before the Supreme Court would rule for Hobby Lobby, and one week before the College would have to comply with the mandate[23] – a federal court in Chicago denied Wheaton's claim. Judge Robert M. Dow, Jr. concluded that Wheaton College's "likelihood of demonstrating that the accommodation process substantially burdens its religious exercise is insufficient to" warrant an injunction.[24] Judge Dow's order did not even mention the Supreme Court's order in favor of the Little Sisters of the Poor, which considered a factually similar situation.

Three days later on June 26, the lawyers for the Becket Fund for Religious Liberty filed an emergency appeal with the Seventh Circuit, which hears appeals from Illinois. "Without immediate relief from this Court," the brief urged, "Wheaton must violate [their] faith or start incurring as much as $34.8 million in fines starting at midnight Monday," July 1. And there was precedent for this relief: "Faced with a materially identical situation just a few months ago, the Supreme Court granted an injunction pending appeal to" the Little Sisters of the Poor.

On June 30, hours after the Supreme Court ruled in favor of Hobby Lobby, a panel of the Seventh Circuit Court ruled against Wheaton College with a two-sentence order. Two of the judges, Richard A. Posner and David F. Hamilton, had previously ruled against Notre Dame, and the third, Ann Claire Williams, agreed. They concluded that Wheaton College "has not shown that it is likely to prevail on the merits." Further, the court quoted

---

[22] Josh Blackman, *Ruth Bader Hubris*, JOSH BLACKMAN'S BLOG (Aug. 3, 2014), perma.cc/ZLK6-2URD.

[23] Due to its modified plan year—like Hobby Lobby—Wheaton College would have to comply with the mandate starting on July 1, 2014. Complaint at 20, ¶ 118, Wheaton College v. Burwell, 50 F. Supp. 3d 939 (N.D. Ill. 2014) (No. 13-cv-08910), bit.ly/21KR1Bt.

[24] Order Denying Temporary Injunction at 9, Wheaton College v. Burwell, 50 F. Supp. 3d 939 (N.D. Ill. 2014) (No. 13-cv-08910), bit.ly/1rBjsFA.

from the hours-old decision in *Hobby Lobby*, which "emphasizes that the accommodation provision (applicable in this case) 'constitutes an alternative that achieves all of the Government's aims while providing greater respect for religious liberty.'" (It is impressive that the panel managed to digest the entire ninety-six-page *Hobby Lobby* decision and issue a ruling so quickly).[25] In short, the Seventh Circuit concluded that the availability of the accommodation to Wheaton College would obviate any religious liberty concerns.

With one day until the mandate would go into effect, Wheaton College filed an emergency appeal with Circuit Justice Elena Kagan, who has supervisory duties for Illinois. Before "midnight tomorrow," Wheaton sought the "same relief from the same government mandate that this Court granted to another religious ministry, the Little Sisters of the Poor." At a minimum, the College "request[ed] a temporary injunction to allow for full briefing and consideration of this Application, without the accumulation of daily fines."

The following evening, at 9:22 P.M., with less than three hours till the mandate would go into effect, at least five justices granted Wheaton College temporary relief.[26] The one-paragraph order stated that the government was "temporarily enjoined from enforcing against applicants the contraceptive coverage requirements." Justices Breyer and Sotomayor dissented, and would not have given Wheaton College any immediate relief. Justices Kagan and Ginsburg, the other two *Hobby Lobby* dissenters, did not voice their disagreement. But this relief was only temporary, and would not last long.

In his brief, the solicitor general told the Court that its two-day-old decision in *Hobby Lobby* "rested on the premise that the accommodation 'achieved all of the Government's aims' underlying the preventive-health services coverage requirement 'while providing greater respect for religious liberty.'" As a result, the accommodation satisfies Wheaton College's conscientious objections. Wheaton responded that "the government merely assumes that *Hobby Lobby* blessed the accommodation. But that is wrong. This Court was clear that it did not 'decide today whether [the accommodation] complies with RFRA for purposes of all religious claims,' and it disclaimed even being 'permitted to address' the accommodation's viability."

---

[25] At 1:50 PM that day – shortly after submitting the *Wheaton College* order – one of the judges on the panel, the prolific Richard A. Posner, managed to write a post on *Slate's Breakfast Table* about the Supreme Court's recent case concerning a buffer zone for abortion protestors. Richard A. Posner, *Supreme Court Breakfast Table*, SLATE (Jun. 30, 2014), bit.ly/2aFmi7x. *See* McCullen v. Coakley, 134 S. Ct. 2518 (2014).

[26] Lyle Denniston, *Opinion Analysis: Does the New Religious Exemption Go Far Enough?*, SCOTUSBLOG (Jun. 30, 2014), perma.cc/94MF-5LXD.

On the afternoon of July 3, as Washington was preparing to celebrate American independence, the justices issued an order halting the mandate. The one-page judgment provided that so long as Wheaton College informs the government that it objects to the mandate, it cannot be forced to self-certify the form. The phrasing of the order was very similar to *Accommodation 3.0*, which was offered by the Court to the Little Sisters six months earlier. Compare the January and July orders side by side.

Little Sisters (January 2014)	*Wheaton College* (July 2014)
• If the employer applicants inform the Secretary of Health and Human Services in writing that they are non-profit organizations that hold themselves out as religious and have religious objections to providing coverage for contraceptive services, the respondents are enjoined from enforcing against the applicants the challenged provisions of the Patient Protection and Affordable Care Act and related regulations pending final disposition of the appeal by the United States Court of Appeals for the Tenth Circuit. • To meet the condition for injunction pending appeal, applicants need not use the form prescribed by the Government and need not send copies to third-party administrators.	• If the applicant informs the Secretary of Health and Human Services in writing that it is a non-profit organization that holds itself out as religious and has religious objections to providing coverage for contraceptive services, the respondents are enjoined from enforcing against the applicant the challenged provisions of the Patient Protection and Affordable Care Act and related regulations pending final disposition of appellate review. • To meet the condition for injunction pending appeal, the applicant need not use the form prescribed by the Government, EBSA Form 700, and need not send copies to health insurance issuers or third-party administrators.

Critically, however, the *Wheaton* order *did not* prevent the government from providing contraceptive coverage to the college's employees, even though Wheaton was not required to actively participate in the process. The Court's order stressed that "nothing in this interim order affects the ability of the applicant's employees and students to obtain, without cost, the full range of FDA approved contraceptives." Since Wheaton College had already objected to certifying the form by filing a lawsuit, the government could "rely on this notice" to "facilitate the provision of full contraceptive coverage under the Act." The government, through this "workaround," could directly contact Wheaton's insurance administrator to coordinate and pay for birth control coverage. For simplicity's sake, I will refer to the order in *Wheaton College* as *Accommodation 4.0*. (In case you were anticipating what comes next, *Accommodation 5.0* would be announced by the Obama administration one month later).

The Court concluded: "In light of the foregoing, this order should not be construed as an expression of the Court's views on the merits." In other words, this would not prejudge the issue of whether Wheaton College, or the Little Sisters for that matter, would win when the case is fully briefed and argued to the Court.

Justice Scalia, who was already abroad teaching in Ireland, "concurred in the result" only, but not the decision itself. Justice Breyer, who had dissented from the temporary injunction two days earlier, was silent. The "fourth feminist" did not express any dissent from the order. However, Justice Sotomayor, joined by Justices Ginsburg and Kagan, issued a sixteen-page dissent. Sotomayor, who had given relief to the Little Sisters of the Poor on New Year's Eve 2014, felt very differently about this issue after *Hobby Lobby*.

20.5. "UNDERMINES CONFIDENCE IN THIS INSTITUTION"

As the most senior member who disagreed with the Court's order in *Wheaton College*, Justice Ginsburg could have written the dissent herself. Instead, she assigned the opinion to Justice Sotomayor. Ginsburg explained in an interview that, "there was enough in my dissent in *Hobby Lobby*. I had said everything I wanted to say on that subject so it was appropriate for somebody else" to write it.

Sotomayor rejected Wheaton College's claim that the accommodation made them complicit in providing abortifacients. Rather, "the provision of contraceptive coverage is triggered not by its completion of the self-certification form, but by federal law." It is "difficult to understand," Sotomayor wrote, "how these arguments make out a viable RFRA claim." While the dissenters did not doubt Wheaton College's sincerely held religious beliefs, they found that "*thinking* one's religious beliefs are substantially burdened – no matter how sincere or genuine that belief may be – does not make it so." Under the regulations, the obligation is "imposed by law, not by the religious non-profit's choice to opt out of it." At bottom, Sotomayor found, "Wheaton objects to the minimally burdensome paperwork necessary for the Government to administer this accommodation." The dissent concluded, "It is not the business of this Court to ensnare itself in the Government's ministerial handling of its affairs in the manner it does here."

While Sotomayor easily dismissed the RFRA claim, the ire of her dissent was focused not on the College, but on her colleagues. She began, "I disagree strongly with what the Court has done." The majority "has no business rewriting administrative regulations" and "stepping into the shoes of HHS ... to craft a new administrative regime." What makes this order even more surprising, Sotomayor wrote, was that just "earlier this week," the *Hobby Lobby* majority – "the very Members of the Court" who ruled for *Wheaton College* – concluded that the accommodation "constitutes an *alternative* that achieves all of the Government's aims while providing greater respect for religious liberty."

How could it be, Sotomayor asks, that only three days later the majority now finds the accommodation inadequate. "Those who are bound by our decisions usually believe they can take us at our word," Sotomayor lamented. "Not so today." After "expressly relying on the availability of the religious-nonprofit accommodation" in *Hobby Lobby*, the majority now "retreats from that position," the dissent charged. The *Wheaton* order "simply does not square with the Court's reasoning in *Hobby Lobby*." This action, Sotomayor concluded, "evinces disregard for even the newest of this Court's precedents and undermines confidence in this institution."

But what about the order for the Little Sisters, to which none of the dissenters openly objected in January? In a footnote, Justice Sotomayor explained that this "case is crucially unlike *Little Sisters of the Poor*." Due to the intricacies of the Little Sisters' "church plan," the January order "did not affect any individual's access to contraceptive coverage," Sotomayor explained. Wheaton College, in contrast, did not have a church plan, so its employees would otherwise be able to receive contraceptive coverage. The Court's July order, however, "risks depriving hundreds of Wheaton's employees and students of their legal entitlement to contraceptive coverage."

The government did not see it that way. Despite the forcefulness of the dissent, which faulted the Court as an institution that did not stand by its own precedents, the Justice Department was not entirely bothered. A senior DOJ official told me of the dissent: "Things go on behind the scenes at the court that we're not privy to." Importantly, however, under the order, the government was not disabled from providing contraceptive coverage, using the work-around of contacting the insurers directly. "So for us," he told me, "it didn't seem like such a terrible outcome. We felt like, 'Okay, fine.'" Because the Court allowed this "work-around, from our perspective, it didn't seem like the end of the world."

Notwithstanding this intricate distinction grounded in the Employee Retirement Income Security Act (ERISA), some found it difficult to reconcile Justice Sotomayor's relief for the Little Sisters of the Poor with her denial of relief for Wheaton College. One of Hobby Lobby's attorneys rejected the characterization that Justice Alito's majority opinion held the accommodation was the least restrictive means to provide cost-free contraceptive coverage. All Alito wrote was that the government "would lose because there were several other ways" to provide contraceptives. But that does not necessarily mean the alternatives are an adequate solution in Wheaton College's case. Another attorney for the Little Sisters told me that the *Hobby Lobby* "majority obviously did not think it had embraced the accommodation as good for everybody, and the dissenters knew the majority did not embrace the accommodation." Recall that Justice Ginsburg said the majority "hedges," and "declines to decide whether the [accommodation] complies with workers for purposes of all religious claims."

In any event, Sotomayor may not have actually agreed with the *Little Sisters* order either. In an interview, Justice Ginsburg suggested that Justice Sotomayor "granted the stay in *Little Sisters of the Poor* [case] because she was the Tenth Circuit justice."[27] The implication was that she did not really think the relief was appropriate, but did so out of her duty as administrator of appeals from Colorado. Ginsburg told Marcia Coyle of *the National Law Journal*, "I think [*Wheaton College*] was another case where [Sotomayor] wanted to make clear what her view was." Ginsburg suggests that Sotomayor's – and presumably her – views were not what she joined in *Little Sisters*.[28] Their true view was reflected in the *Wheaton College* dissent.

20.6. ACCOMMODATION 5.0

Hours after *Hobby Lobby* was released, Senate Democrats called for a legislative response.[29] Two weeks later, Senators Patty Murray (D-WA) and Mark Udall (D-CO) introduced the Protect Women's Health from Corporate

---

[27] Josh Blackman, Little Sisters of the Poor v. Sebelius *(Ginsburg, J., Dissenting From Granting of Stay on Behalf of Sotomayor, J., After the Fact)*, JOSH BLACKMAN'S BLOG (Aug. 22, 2014), perma.cc/S8WA-TDUB. This argument is dubious because Elena Kagan was Circuit justice for the Seventh Circuit, yet she still dissented in the July 2014 order providing an accommodation to Wheaton College.

[28] Ginsburg also added that Justice Sotomayor's dissent in the Michigan Affirmative Action case of Schuette v. BAMN, 134 S.Ct. 1623 (2014), was written so forcefully in light of the fact that she did not dissent in an earlier affirmative action case, Fisher v. University of Texas, Austin, 133 S.Ct. 2411 (2013). Ginsburg explained, "She cared deeply about the issue. She might have been distressed about some of the reports in the [Texas] case where she went along with the court. So if anybody had doubts about her views on affirmative action she wanted to quell them, which she certainly did." *Id.*

[29] Sarah Kliff, *Senate Democrats Plan Hobby Lobby Response*, VOX (Jun. 30, 2014), perma.cc/MD3K-QZLZ.

Interference Act that would have expressly prohibited employers from excluding contraceptive coverage, notwithstanding the religious objections of for-
profit corporations.[30] However, the bill only mustered fifty-six votes in the
Senate and was killed by a filibuster.[31] In any event, it would have been dead
on arrival in the Republican-controlled House of Representatives.[32] With no
congressional fix in sight, in August 2014, HHS put forth yet another administrative modification, which I will refer to as *Accommodation 5.0*.[33] There were
two components to the new policy.

First, religious nonprofits like Wheaton College and the Little Sisters of the
Poor would no longer be required to fill out EBSA Form 700, but would only
need to notify HHS in writing that they object to the mandate.[34] The notice
may be sent by letter or e-mail and must contain (1) the name of the organization; (2) its objection based on sincerely held religious beliefs; (3) the name
and type of the group health plan; and (4) the name and contact information
for any of the insurers.[35] Under the accommodation, the employer would not
be obligated to directly pay for the contraceptives.[36]

After the organization provides HHS with the requisite information, the
government would then contact the employer's insurer, which would then
be responsible for providing employees with access to no-cost contraceptives.
Critically, the coverage would be provided under the auspices of the objecting employer's insurance plan. The regulations made clear that whether the
employer uses EBSA Form 700 or notifies HHS in writing, "the obligations of
insurers regarding providing or arranging separate payments for contraceptive
services are the same."[37] This rule would take effect right away.

Second, closely held religious for-profit corporations would receive *the
same* accommodation that the religious nonprofits would receive. Recall that
during oral arguments, Paul Clement told the justices, "Whatever the answer
is for [the] Little Sisters of the Poor, presumably you can extend the same

[30] Murray, Udall *Introduce Legislative Fix to Protect Women's Health in the Aftermath of Supreme Court Decision* (Jul. 9, 2014), perma.cc/EWZ8-AA4B.
[31] S. 113th Cong., Senate Roll Call Vote (Jul. 16, 2014, 2:09 PM), perma.cc/Z4S6-G6C7.
[32] In hindsight, there were likely never sixty votes to require employers, including for-profit corporations, to pay for contraceptives in violation of their religious beliefs. The sponsors of the
Women's Health Amendment were shrewd in 2009 to assiduously avoid any discussion of how
the provision could give rise to religious liberty conflicts.
[33] Cent. for Consumer Info. & Ins. Oversight, *Women's Preventative Services Coverage
and Non-Profit Religious Organizations*, Cents. Medicare & Medicaid Servs.,
perma.cc/2ALF-W93K.
[34] *Id.* 79 Fed. Reg. 51,092 (Aug. 27, 2014).
[35] Little Sisters of the Poor Home for the Aged v. Burwell, 794 F.3d 1151, 1164 (10th Cir. 2015)
[36] 79 Fed. Reg. 51,094.
[37] CMS, *supra* note 33.

thing to [Hobby Lobby] and there wouldn't be a problem with that." The Obama administration did just that and extended the accommodation to certain closely held for-profit corporations. This rule would not be finalized until July 2015.

However, *Accommodation 5.0* did little to assuage concerns about the mandate violating religious liberty. Shortly after it was announced, the American Center for Law & Justice rejected the notion that replacing the form with an e-mail would make any difference. "Nothing changes," ACLJ wrote, because the contraceptives are still being provided through the employer's policies.[38] In this fashion the employers are still complicit in the provision of birth control they deem sinful.

In September 2014, both the government and the Little Sisters submitted an update to the Tenth Circuit Court of Appeals on the impact of *Accommodation 5.0* on the pending case. The United States claimed that the new accommodation "provides eligible organizations with another means for opting out of contraceptive coverage," and female employees would still be able to receive cost-free access to contraceptives. Since the Supreme Court's January 2014 order, "the women employed by plaintiffs have been and continue to be denied access to contraceptive coverage." This, the government asserts, is "inconsistent" with the Court's subsequent decisions in *Hobby Lobby* and *Wheaton College*, which both "recognized the importance of ensuring that women have access to contraceptive services with minimal obstacles."

The Little Sisters disagreed and told the court that the latest rules "change nothing of substance in this appeal." Instead of the government exempting the Little Sisters as "religious employers," or providing contraceptives directly to female employees, HHS "continues to insist that the only way the United States could possibly distribute contraceptives is with the forced participation of the Little Sisters and their plan." Even though the nuns no longer need to use a specific form, they are still required to "participate by giving information about its plan, which the government uses to offer those entities incentives to take action contrary to the terms of the plan and religious beliefs of the Little Sisters." The Sisters "have never objected to merely identifying themselves so that the government can leave them alone. What they object to is the government's unending attempt to use them and their benefits plan as the vehicle for contraceptive distribution."

---

[38] Matthew Clark, *Despite Supreme Court's Hobby Lobby Ruling Obama Administration Repackages Abortion-Pill Mandate,* Am. Cent. L. & Just. (Sept. 2014), perma.cc/3B5H-KV5J.

Over the next year, the Courts of Appeals would consider whether *Accommodation* 5.0 complies with the Religious Freedom Restoration Act. These cases would wind up at the Supreme Court in March 2016. But first, we return to *Halbig* and *King*, as the Supreme Court would soon consider a far more existential question for Obamacare's survival: whether subsidies are available on the federal exchanges.

PART VI

Nuclear Fallout (July 22, 2014–November 21, 2014)

21

Circuit Split

21.1. "WHAT'S THE LAST WORD?"

July 22, 2014 was a hot, humid day in Washington, D.C., with an expected high of 99 degrees. That morning, around 10:20 AM, Michael Carvin sat at his desk at the Jones Day law firm. His phone rang. The clerk from the D.C. Circuit told him that the opinion in *Halbig v. Burwell* would be released soon. Carvin had only one question: "What's the last word?" It was "reversed." That was all he needed to hear. A reversal meant he won, and the court ruled for the challengers. "I was obviously happy," Carvin told me. "But I wasn't wildly surprised." He added, "I knew of course there would be a dissent."

The call came "literally a minute before" the opinion was publicly released on the D.C. Circuit's website. At 10:21 AM, Howard Bashman published the ruling on his popular *How Appealing* blog. Carvin told his associate, Yaakov Roth, to print out the seventy-two-page opinion. (Even though he had recently upgraded to the twenty-first century with a Blackberry, Carvin still reads opinions the old-fashioned way.)

The majority opinion authored by Judge Griffith, and joined by Judge Randolph, was everything the challengers had hoped for. It began, "On its face, [Section 36B] authorizes tax credits for insurance purchased on an Exchange established by one of the fifty states or the District of Columbia. But the Internal Revenue Service has interpreted Section 36B broadly to authorize the subsidy also for insurance purchased on an Exchange established by the federal government." However, Judge Griffith concluded "that the ACA unambiguously restricts the Section 36B subsidy to insurance purchased on Exchanges 'established by the State,'" because "Section 36B plainly distinguishes Exchanges established by states from those established by the federal government." The Justice Department's broad appeal to the intent of the Affordable Care Act – promoting access to subsidized health insurance nationwide – "d[id] not demonstrate that Congress manifestly meant something other than what Section 36B says." Judge Griffith noted that even if the provision limiting subsidies to state exchanges "may seem odd," it is not "absurd." Therefore, the court concluded, "it is up to Congress rather than the courts to fix it," even if it "may have been an unintentional drafting gap." As the Supreme Court explained during the previous term, "an agency may not rewrite clear statutory terms to suit its own sense of how the statute should operate."

What about the history of the bill, and senators who now insist that subsidies were available on all exchanges? Judge Griffith observed, "The scant legislative history sheds little light on the precise question of the availability of subsidies on federal Exchanges." Specifically, the court found "unilluminating [the] floor statements by Senate sponsors of the ACA touting the availability and benefits of premium tax credits in general, but not addressing the precise issue of whether they would be available on federal Exchanges." Liz Fowler, who worked for Senator Max Baucus and the Obama White House on health care reform, told journalist Steven Brill, "The judges [on the D.C. Circuit] clearly don't care about congressional intent."[1]

In short, Judge Griffith observed, by "asking us to ignore the best evidence of Congress's intent – the text of Section 36B – in favor of assumptions about the risks that Congress would or would not tolerate – assumptions doubtlessly influenced by hindsight – the government and dissent in effect urge us to substitute our judgment for Congress's. We refuse." Judge Griffith closed with a practical assessment of the consequences of his decision, which is worth quoting at length:

> We reach this conclusion, frankly, with reluctance. At least until states wish to set up Exchanges, our ruling will likely have significant consequences both for the millions of individuals receiving tax credits through federal Exchanges and for health insurance markets more broadly. But, high as those stakes are, the principle of legislative supremacy that guides us is higher still. Within constitutional limits, Congress is supreme in matters of policy, and the consequence of that supremacy is that our duty when interpreting a statute is to ascertain the meaning of the words of the statute duly enacted through the formal legislative process. This limited role serves democratic interests by ensuring that policy is made by elected, politically accountable representatives, not by appointed, life-tenured judges. Thus, although our

---

[1] Steven Brill, *The Supreme Court Hears an Obamacare Fairytale*, REUTERS (Mar. 2, 2015), perma.cc/S56C-WFVG.

decision has major consequences, our role is quite limited: deciding whether the IRS Rule is a permissible reading of the ACA.

Judge Griffith was the first federal judge to conclude that the subsidies were unavailable on the federal exchange. His opinion, however, would be met with a swift rebuttal.

Judge Edwards wrote a twenty-eight-page dissent that began as his questions at oral arguments concluded: "This case is about Appellants' not-so-veiled attempt to gut the Patient Protection and Affordable Care Act." He charged that the challenger's position is a "specious argument" and is "nonsense, made out of whole cloth. There is no credible evidence in the record that Congress intended to condition subsidies on whether a State, as opposed to HHS, established the Exchange. Nor is there credible evidence that any State even considered the possibility that its taxpayers would be denied subsidies if the State opted to allow HHS to establish an Exchange on its behalf." More troubling, Judge Edwards observed, this position "would permit States to exempt many people from the individual mandate and thereby thwart a central element of the ACA." The dissent cited a *Wall Street Journal* editorial from Oklahoma Attorney General Scott Pruitt, who wrote that "if subsidies are unavailable to taxpayers in States with HHS-created Exchanges, 'the structure of the ACA will crumble.'"[2] (Two months later, a federal court in Oklahoma would side with the attorney general in *Pruitt v. Burwell*.) Judge Edwards concludes that "[i]t is inconceivable that Congress intended to give States the power to cause the ACA to 'crumble.'"

Judge Griffith responded that the court's ruling should not be viewed as "gutting" the ACA; rather, he argued that the IRS Rule "gives the individual and employer mandates – key provisions of the ACA – broader effect than they would have if credits were limited to state-established Exchanges." First, "by making tax credits available in the 36 states with federal Exchanges, the IRS Rule significantly increases the number of people who must purchase health insurance or face a penalty." Second, "by allowing credits in such states, it exposes employers there to penalties and thereby gives the employer mandate broader reach." In effect, Judge Griffith concluded, the IRS Rule alters the compromises reached by Congress; any crumbling would be a consequence of how the law was designed.

Notably, Judge Edwards rejected the government's lead argument: he did not find that the language in Section 36B clearly provided subsidies on

[2] Scott Pruitt, *Obama Care's Next Legal Challenge*, WALL ST. J. (Dec. 1, 2013), on.wsj.com/1opzaln.

the federal exchange. Rather, he determined that, at best, Section 36B was "ambiguous." The Supreme Court held in its seminal 1984 decision, *Chevron v. Natural Resources Defense Council*, that "if 'the statute is silent or *ambiguous* with respect to the specific issue,' [the courts] defer to the agency's construction of the statute, so long as it is 'permissible.'" In practice, this means that in virtually every instance where Congress drafts an ambiguous statute, the court will defer to the agency's interpretation. This case was no exception for the dissent.

Judge Edwards found that Section 36B was ambiguous, and thus the government's interpretation was "permissible." As a result, the IRS rule "easily survives review under *Chevron*." The dissent faulted the majority opinion for "strain[ing] fruitlessly to show plain meaning when there is none to be found . . . Unfortunately, by imposing the [challenger's] myopic construction on the administering agencies without any regard for the overall statutory scheme, the majority opinion effectively ignores the basic tenets of statutory construction."

It is common practice for a dissenting judge to conclude his opinion, as a mark of collegiality, with "I respectfully dissent." There would be no respect here. "Because the proposed judgment of the majority defies the will of Congress and the permissible interpretations of the agencies to whom Congress has delegated the authority to interpret and enforce the terms of the ACA, I *dissent*."

This ruling should not have come as much of a surprise. Nicholas Bagley, the Michigan law professor, told me, "You kind of knew where the winds are blowing from oral arguments. I think this was not unexpected." The reaction to the decision was swift. Reporter Lyle Denniston wrote at SCOTUSBlog, "Major new blow to health care law."[3] Dylan Scott at TPM made the point more forcefully: "4.7 Million could lose Obamacare subsidies after Huge Court decision."[4] Representative Steny Hoyer (D-MD), who was the whip when the ACA passed the House, rejected the ruling as inconsistent with congressional purpose. "The intent of the Congress, I think, was pretty clear," Hoyer said during a press conference at the Capitol. Whether the exchange "was established by the state or [by] the federal exchange, [then] clearly the subsidies would apply."[5]

Republicans were ebullient. Senator Ted Cruz (R-TX) called the decision a "repudiation of Obamacare and all the lawlessness that has come with

3   Lyle Denniston, *Major New Blow to Health Care Law*, SCOTUSBLOG (Jul. 22, 2014), perma.cc/S8W9-MJZ9.
4   Dylan Scott, 4.7 *Million Could Lose Obamacare Subsidies after Huge Court Decision*, TPM (Jul. 22, 2014), perma.cc/MH8Q-5A5Y.
5   Mike Lillis, *Hoyer: Court Ignores Congress' Intent*, THE HILL (Jul. 22, 2014), perma.cc/U4FA-BVCG.

it. This decision restores power to Congress and to the people and if properly enforced, should shield citizens from Obamacare's insidious penalties, mandates, and subsidies." Cruz added, "This is a significant victory for the American people and the rule of law, but we must not rest."[6] The Senate Republic Conference tweeted, "#ObamaCare is a fundamentally flawed law that continues to *unravel* with each passing day."[7]

At 11:20 AM, White House Press Secretary Josh Earnest held his daily briefing. The first, second, and third questions were all about the D.C. Circuit's hour-old decision.[8] He stressed that "this ruling does not have any practical impact on [customers'] ability to continue to receive tax credits right now. Right now there are millions of Americans all across the country who are receiving tax credits from the federal government." Earnest acknowledged that "while this ruling is interesting to legal theorists, it has no practical impact on their tax credits right now." Before even waiting for an official statement from the Department of Justice – the Press Secretary told the reporters that the government "will ask for a ruling from the full D.C. circuit." He added, "As you know, this was a decision that was issued just by three members of the D.C. Circuit."

Finally, Earnest stressed that "there are four different cases that are making their way through the federal court system," and the others are still "awaiting their rulings." The White House would not have to wait much longer for a victory in one of those other cases.

21.2. "NOW THAT WAS REMARKABLE, WASN'T IT?"

After digesting the seventy-two-page decision, Michael Carvin went to lunch. However, he would not have time to digest his meal before the second bombshell dropped. Barely two hours after *Halbig* was decided, the Fourth Circuit in Richmond released its forty-six-page decision in *King v. Burwell*.

As Carvin had predicted, this decision unanimously went against the challengers. Carvin admitted, "I expected to lose." He stressed, however, that "[i]t could have been a much worse opinion, but not necessarily more persuasive." Fourth Circuit Judge Roger Gregory – like Judge Edwards in D.C. – found that Section 36B was ambiguous as to whether it limited the subsidies to state-established exchanges. Applying the *Chevron* doctrine, the court "uph[e]ld the rule as a permissible exercise of the agency's discretion." Importantly, the

---

[6] Jonathan Topaz, *Cruz: An Obamacare 'Repudiation'*, POLITICO (Jul. 22, 2014), perma.cc/49MA-S5CR.

[7] @Senate_GOP, TWITTER (Jul. 22, 2014, 10:09 a.m.), bit.ly/1T6fdha.

[8] Daily Briefing by the Press Secretary Josh Earnest (Jul. 22, 2014), perma.cc/G6KD-2TKR.

Fourth Circuit concluded that "the Act's legislative history is also not particularly illuminating on the issue of tax credits."[9] The silence on both sides of the debate did not help the government.

Three years earlier, when the Treasury Department attorneys were developing the IRS rule, they had specifically considered how the courts would use *Chevron* deference to save the regulation. Jessica Hauser, deputy tax legislative counsel at the Department of Treasury, e-mailed Cameron Arterton, with the subject line "can you send me ... the two good Chevron cases?"[10] Later that day, Arterton replied, "Here are the two Chevron cases you asked for (plus Chevron for good measure) ... I should also be clear that I don't think these cases are unique in the proposition that tension/conflict between two statutory provisions can create sufficient ambiguity, these are just the two clearest I have found so far." This admission suggests that within the Obama administration there was internal doubt whether the statute was clear enough on its face to survive judicial scrutiny. As a result, the attorneys were trying to identify ambiguities that would lead the courts to apply Chevron deference.

Kim Koch, a career civil service lawyer in the Treasury Department, told the House Oversight Committee that "she could not remember ever working on a previous rule where *Chevron* was discussed prior to the publication of the final rule." Chip Dunham, another career civil service lawyer in the income tax and accounting division at the Office of the Chief Counsel, said "that considering *Chevron* prior to the promulgation of a final rule was very unusual." Tom Christina chuckled when he read how the IRS lawyers were e-mailing each other about *Chevron.* He thought it was "pretty funny" that they had to "place their hope on *Chevron.*" This was from a "moment of panic," as a "subsequent administration might be able to reverse" the position.

Though he lost, Carvin was pleased with the ruling: "I like the fact that even the Fourth Circuit found that [my interpretation] is a perfectly plausible explanation of the statute, but *Chevron* is a tie breaker and will give it to the government." Of the eight federal judges that had considered the question to this point, seven rejected the government's argument that the clearest, most natural reading of Section 36B is that subsidies were also available on federal exchanges. Zero judges concluded that Section 36B was a "drafting error" that the courts could correct. The *Halbig* court found that Section 36B, "[o]n its face," allows subsidies only "for insurance purchased on an Exchange

⁹ King v. Burwell, 759 F.3d 358, 371 (4th Cir. 2014).
¹⁰ *Administration Conducted Inadequate Review of Key Issues Prior to Expanding Health Law's Taxes and Subsidies: Joint Staff Report U.S. House of Representatives*, 113th Cong. at 21 (2014), bit.ly/1TLiH5H.

established by one of the fifty states or the District of Columbia." The *King* court conceded that the "common-sense appeal of [the challengers'] argument" is that "the language says what it says, and that it clearly mentions state-run Exchanges under Section 1311," which it would not have done had Congress actually "meant to include federally-run Exchanges." Only through the deferential *Chevron* doctrine, where courts side with the government's reasonable reading of the law, could the Obama administration's rule prevail.

The lone dissenter on this point was Judge Andre M. Davis. Three years earlier, he upheld the constitutionality of Obamacare's individual mandate, while the other two judges on that panel ruled that the challenge was not yet ripe.[11] For a second time, Judge Davis went further than his colleagues. He determined that Section 36B, when read in the context of the entire ACA, *unambiguously* permits subsidies on the federal exchange.

"A holistic reading of the Act's text and proper attention to its structure lead to only one sensible conclusion: The premium tax credits must be available to consumers who purchase health insurance coverage through their designated Exchange regardless of whether the Exchange is state- or federally-operated." The next federal judge who would agree with Davis would be Chief Justice Roberts. Judge Davis concluded with his own rendition of the gut-the-statute concern: "What [the challengers] may not do is rely on our help to deny to millions of Americans desperately-needed health insurance through a tortured, nonsensical construction of a federal statute whose manifest purpose, as revealed by the wholeness and coherence of its text and structure, could not be more clear."

The federal courts of appeals had diverged on the issue of subsidies on the federal exchange. This sort of schism, known as a "circuit split," usually take months, if not years, to develop. On July 22, 2014, they split within two hours of each other. Everything transpired so quickly that Robert Pear's online report in the *New York Times* was initially titled "Court Rules against Obamacare Exchange Subsidies," but was later changed to "Courts issue conflicting rulings on Health Care Law."[12] By the time the story made it to A1 of the dead-tree version, it became "New Questions on Health Law as Courts Differ on Subsidies."[13] Nina Totenberg's story on NPR's *All Things Considered* summed up the day well: "Obama's Health Care Law Has a Confusing Day in Court."[14] The veteran Supreme Court reporter began, "Another wild legal ride for

[11] Liberty University v. Geithner, 671 F.3d 391, 422 (2011) (Davis, J., dissenting).
[12] Howard J. Bashman, HOW APPEALING (Jul. 22, 2014), perma.cc/LRV3-VHV3.
[13] Robert Pear, *New Questions on Health Law as Rulings on Subsidies Differ*, N.Y. TIMES (Jul. 22, 2014), nyti.ms/20mZjgF.
[14] Nina Totenberg, *Obama's Health Care Law Has a Confusing Day in Court*, NPR (July 22, 2014), n.pr/1PjvScm.

Obamacare on Tuesday: Two U.S. Court of Appeals panels issued conflicting decisions on an issue with the potential to *gut* the health care overhaul."
Mara Liasson added on the same broadcast, "If the Supreme Court upholds
[the D.C. Circuit's ruling], Obamacare will start to *unravel*."[15]

A lawyer for the challengers told me that "the fastest circuit split on record
likely wasn't a coincidence. Isn't it far more likely that the Fourth Circuit had
prepared its ruling and kept it on hold, in anticipation of a likely invalidation
from the D.C. panel? By issuing its ruling right after the D.C. Circuit, the
Fourth Circuit got the last word in the news cycle." I asked a senior Justice
Department how he reacted when the D.C. and Fourth Circuits ruled within
hours of each other. He quipped, "Now that was remarkable, wasn't it?"

Even more remarkable would be the ensuing dogfight between the government and the challengers. Michael Carvin hatched his strategy to get the case
to the Supreme Court right away, as the government steadfastly resisted and
tried to keep the case far away from the justices.

[15] Mara Liasson, *Obamacare's Split Decisions Spell Law's Possible Return to Supreme Court*, NPR (Jul. 22, 2014), n.pr/1Qq5Top.

Dueling Petitions

22.1. "SIMPLE MATH"

Flash back to November 21, 2013. As all eyes were focused on the HealthCare.gov crisis, Senate Majority Leader Harry Reid (D-NV) triggered the "nuclear option." This parliamentary procedure, discussed earlier in Chapter 14, eliminated the filibuster for all presidential nominations except for the Supreme Court. That move paved the way for Senate Democrats to easily confirm three new Obama nominees to the D.C. Circuit Court of Appeals: Patricia Ann Millett, Nina Pillard, and Robert L. Wilkins. Obama's previous nominee to the D.C. Circuit Sri Srinivasan, was confirmed unanimously in May 2013. Ironically enough, the Republicans allowed Srinivasan to come up for a vote to prevent Reid from triggering the nuclear option. This détente was short lived.[1]

Before the confirmation of President Obama's four appointees to the D.C. Circuit in 2013, there were three active judges appointed by President Clinton and four active judges appointed by the Presidents Bush. Afterwards the balance shifted, seven to four. The significance of this realignment would become apparent in the wake of Judge Griffith's decision in *Halbig v. Burwell*.

On the federal courts of appeals, cases are initially heard before a randomly assigned three-judge panel. The party that loses has two options. First, it can appeal directly to the Supreme Court by filing a petition for certiorari. Second, it can ask the *entire* court of appeals to rehear the case by filing a petition for rehearing en banc. En banc translates from French as "in the bench," but is understood "as a group." A majority of the active judges must vote to rehear the case. If en banc review is granted, the

---

[1] Juliet Eilperin, *Sri Srinivasan confirmed to judicial seat in unanimous Senate vote*, WASH. POST (May 23, 2013), perma.cc/FUD3-2NHY.

initial decision from the three-judge panel is vacated – that is, nullified – and the parties are ordered to re-brief and re-argue the case. During en banc proceedings, all of the active judges on the court – including any senior judges from the randomly drawn trio – can rehear the case.

Within hours of the D.C. Circuit's *Halbig* decision, Senator Reid criticized the ruling from "two activist Republican judges" as "absurd."[2] Reid was asked if the imminent en banc vote vindicated his decision to trigger the nuclear option a year earlier, and shift the balance on the court. He replied, "I think if you look at simple math, it does." Senate Majority Whip Richard J. Durbin (D-IL) made Reid's point more explicitly. "There was a strong conservative Republican majority on the D.C. Circuit until we filled the vacancies," Durbin said. "Now it's a *balanced* circuit." Durbin expected a "ruling coming our way, toward the administration."[3] A former administration official told *Politico* that in hindsight, Reid's strategy a year earlier was "pretty brilliant."[4]

Greg Stohr of *Bloomberg* observed that Reid's comments "fueled the perception that the Democratic appointees would tip the balance."[5] Doug Kendall, the founder of the progressive Constitutional Accountability Center, suggested as much. "I would hope President Obama's four extraordinarily qualified nominees [to the D.C. Circuit] would side with the six other judges across the ideological spectrum in rejecting these challenges to affordable health care. One of the most important impacts of filling the four vacancies to this court has been to change dramatically the makeup of the en banc panel."[6] Carrie Severino, Chief Counsel of the conservative Judicial Crisis Network, explained, "I think this is exactly what the president was thinking about when he decided to ram all those judges through." She added, "The president for his whole first term dragged his feet and didn't seem to think judges were really a priority. Then suddenly, out of the blue, he decides he needs to move on what I'd argue is the least busy circuit in the country.... This is the payoff for him."

[2] Humberto Sanchez, *Reid: 'Absurd' Obamacare Decision Vindicates 'Nuclear Option'*, ROLL CALL (Jul. 22, 2014), perma.cc/P76K-U8XR.

[3] *Id.*

[4] Josh Gerstein, *How Obama's Court Strategy May Save Obamacare*, POLITICO (Jul. 22, 2014), perma.cc/DP6D-SGRC.

[5] Greg Stohr, *Obamacare's Latest Threat Nears Turning Point in Court*, BLOOMBERG BUSINESS (Aug. 28, 2014), perma.cc/HB75-W349.

[6] Kendall, who passed away one year later, was an esteemed Supreme Court advocate, and vigorously argued that the original understanding of the Constitution was progressive. Sam Roberts, *Doug Kendall, Liberal Who Challenged Supreme Court's Conservatives, Dies at 51*, N.Y. TIMES (Sept. 29, 2015), nyti.ms/1o3Ztxb.

Mike Carvin and the lawyers at CEI recognized the changed dynamics. "When we filed in D.C. it was the best circuit in the country," Carvin told me. "By the time we got up there, it was not the best circuit in the country." So the goal was simple – appeal the losing *King* case from the Fourth Circuit to the Supreme Court as soon as possible, before the D.C. Circuit could grant rehearing en banc in *Halbig*. But the government had just the opposite strategy. The Justice Department wanted to persuade the D.C. Circuit to grant rehearing en banc as soon as possible, while delaying any appeal to the Supreme Court. If the D.C. Circuit sitting en banc ultimately sided with the government, then there would be no more circuit split, and the Supreme Court was less to even take the case. The race to the Court began.

22.2. "SWORD OF DAMOCLES"

The Fourth Circuit's decision in *King v. Burwell*, rejecting the challenger's reading of Section 36B, was released on July 22, 2014. Under the Supreme Court's Rule 13, parties have ninety days to file a petition for certiorari. Mike Carvin and his associates at Jones Day took nine days. On July 31, 2014, the attorneys for the challengers filed a forty-three-page brief, urging the Supreme Court to take the case right away. The genesis of the petition began well before either court of appeals had ruled. Carvin, and his associate Yaakov Roth, knew that "the minute the Fourth Circuit decision came out, we're going to the Supreme Court." The strategy was to "beat the government going en banc in the D.C. Circuit, and being able to say, 'there's already a case pending in the Supreme Court. Why are you guys going to jump?'" "Yaakov is a really fast writer" and is "just terrific," Carvin relayed. "I told him to have it ready to go and then we will plug in whatever they say." Roth was a summa cum laude graduate of Harvard Law School and clerked for Justice Scalia in 2008.

The petition made a forceful case for why the Court must take the case right away without waiting:

The resulting uncertainty over this major plank of ACA implementation means that millions of people have no idea if they may rely on the IRS's promise to subsidize their health coverage, or if that money will be clawed back. Employers in 36 states have no idea if they will be penalized under the ACA's employer mandate, or are effectively exempt from it. Insurers have no idea if their customers will pay for health coverage in which they enrolled, or if large numbers will default. And the Treasury has no idea if billions of dollars being spent each month were authorized by Congress, or if these expenditures are illegal.

It was this last argument that resonated the strongest with the solicitor general's office. The petition explained that up to $150 billion would be spent each year until the IRS rule is vacated. A senior official in the Justice Department praised this element of Carvin's strategy, saying he is a "superb lawyer and a great tactician. The most powerful part of his cert petition was that as a result of the Fourth Circuit's interpretation of 36B, the government is spending about $2 billion a month in subsidies, that they don't have the authority to spend because the statute doesn't provide for these subsidies. And if you delay the case another a year or two, that's another year or two of the government spending billions of dollars that it doesn't have the authority to spend. Therefore, there's a very important reason to intervene earlier rather than later. I think that was an important argument for the Court granting certiorari."

The petition closed: "It is far better for this Court to resolve this question now, to both preclude further detrimental reliance and to eliminate the Sword of Damocles that will inevitably hang over the IRS Rule otherwise." Carvin told me, "If there's any decent shot that this is going to be overturned, there's a very compelling argument for doing it now rather than waiting for another year. Our entire effort has been to try and get determined to the merits through all the haze of this policy and politics that surround it."

22.3. "DISASTROUS CONSEQUENCES"

Like the lawyers at Jones Day, attorneys in the solicitor general's office had already gamed out how to respond to an anticipated unfavorable ruling. Within an hour of the D.C. Circuit's ruling in *Halbig*, before the Fourth Circuit had even released its decision in *King*, the DOJ announced that it would seek rehearing en banc. "We believe that this decision is incorrect, inconsistent with congressional intent, different from previous rulings, and at odds with the goal of the law: to make health care affordable no matter where people live," a DOJ spokeswoman said.[7] "The government will therefore immediately seek further review of the court's decision."

After the courts of appeals ruled in opposite directions, the solicitor general's office that the case satisfied the criteria for en banc, because there was a circuit split and it was a case of grave importance. The normal practice, though not an iron-clad rule, I was told, is to seek en banc first. Where the

---

[7] *DOJ to appeal D.C. Obamacare ruling*, POLITICO (July 22, 2014), perma.cc/SAG9-8TB5.

"circuit split could be resolved and the criteria of importance is met, it's what we do." This is especially true if the government "plans to later seek certiorari" from the Supreme Court.

The altered composition of the D.C. Circuit certainly made that decision easier. "If such a decision had been made earlier in Obama's tenure," Jeffrey Toobin wrote in the *New Yorker*, "lawyers for his Administration would have been left with a single, risky option: an appeal to the politically polarized, and usually conservative, Supreme Court."[8] After President Obama's "realignment" and "transformation" of the court, Toobin wrote, "the lawyers had another choice."[9] Richard Wolf summed up the issue in *USA Today*: this case "illustrated what liberals have yearned for and conservatives have feared for six years: President Obama's judges are having an impact."[10]

On August 1, 2014, the day after the challengers petitioned for certiorari to the Supreme Court, the Department of Justice filed its petition for rehearing en banc before the D.C. Circuit. The government implored the full court to avoid the "disastrous consequences" that may result from Judge Griffith's decision. The petition stressed that *Halbig* "directly conflicts with a unanimous Fourth Circuit opinion [in *King*] issued the same day." Carvin was not impressed by the Justice Department's brief. He told me that the government wanted to drag this case out so they could "engage in a bait and switch where they get all these people in the exchanges, and then have to say 'Sorry we're going to cut you off midway.'" He paused. "But it's a little tough to say that in court."

In what may be a first, the *New York Times* editorial board wrote in favor of the petition for rehearing en banc.[11] Echoing the political valences of Reid and others, the editorial explained that the Obama administration "would prefer a rehearing" because "[t]hey are confident that the full court, with a majority of judges appointed by Democratic presidents, would overturn the panel's ruling." In contrast, the editorial contended, "The opponents want to fast-track the case to the Supreme Court, hoping that the five conservative justices will uphold the ruling."

On August 18, the lawyers at Jones Day opposed the government's petition for rehearing en banc. The message was simple: "Because the Supreme Court must ultimately resolve the validity of the IRS rule, rehearing would waste both time and effort." Carvin saw "two ways to win." First, the D.C. Circuit

---

[8] Jeffrey Toobin, *The Obama Brief*, New Yorker (Oct. 27, 2014), perma.cc/QDE8-2635.

[9] *Id.*

[10] Richard Wolf, *Obamacare Decision Shows Impact of Obama's Judges*, USA Today (Sept. 4, 2014), perma.cc/A9UK-YVMJ.

[11] *Endless Assault on Health Care Reform*, N.Y. Times (Aug. 30, 2014), nyti.ms/1PpCfdX.

"denies en banc, at which point *Halbig* goes to the Supreme Court." Second, the D.C. Circuit grants en banc, "and we still convince the Supremes to take the case." In either case, the D.C. Circuit would not have the last word.

From a more institutional perspective, the attorneys stressed that the D.C. Circuit has routinely denied en banc review in many "important cases," where "Supreme Court review is otherwise required or likely, [so] rehearing is not only a waste of resources but could actually harm the public." Judge Douglas H. Ginsburg (no relation to Ruth Bader), who served as chief judge of the court from 2001 to 2008, explained this custom in a 1991 law review article. He wrote that that en banc review is not warranted even "[i]f the conflict is important, [but] the Supreme Court is likely to resolve it, and its decision is not likely to be affected by anything that the en banc court could add to the debate."[12]

The Jones Day brief also cited an influential 1987 opinion from Judge Edwards – who dissented on the *Halbig panel* – where he stated, "en banc review should occur 'only in the rarest of circumstances.'"[13] In that decision, the Carter appointee recognized the risk of granting en banc whenever other judges simply disagreed with the panel opinion. This approach would do "substantial violence to the collegiality that *is* indispensable to judicial decision-making.'" Judge Edwards was speaking from experience.

Between 1982 and 1987, President Reagan appointed eight judges to the D.C. Circuit, including Judges Antonin Scalia, Robert Bork, and Kenneth Starr. These appointments tipped the balance, giving the conservatives a majority for en banc votes. As the *Washington Post* reported in 1987, the judges on the second-highest court in the land "have been bickering since the conservatives gained the upper hand last summer after decades of liberal rule ... The rift widened in recent months as Reagan-appointed conservatives, led by Bork, voted to review a series of cases decided by three-judge panels with liberal majorities. In all, the full court had voted since January to hear 11 cases en banc, compared with only three or four such hearings in each of several recent years."[14] In short, the conservatives were using the en banc proceeding to reverse panel decisions from liberal judges. By 1992, the *New York Times* reported that the D.C. Circuit had "reverted to something approaching a state of nature. Some of the judges are feuding openly – even

---

[12] Douglas H. Ginsburg & Donald Falk, *The Court En Banc: 1981–1990*, 59 GEO. WASH. L. REV. 1008, 1025 (1991).

[13] Bartlett ex rel. Neuman v. Bowen, 824 F.2d 1240, 1243–44 (D.C. Cir. 1987) (Edwards, J., concurring in denial of rehearing en banc).

[14] Nancy Lewis, *Factions' Squabbling Rocks U.S. Court of Appeals Here*, WASH. POST (Aug. 1, 1987), perma.cc/58JA-4DGD.

having news releases handed out to reporters in the halls – and publicly questioning each other's integrity."[15]

During this rancorous period, "liberal members of the court accus[ed] their conservative colleagues of deciding cases by majority rule instead of rule of law," while the "conservatives countered that the liberals don't know an important case when they see one."[16] Judge Edwards's dissent was on point: "The implicit view [is] that every time a majority of the judges disagree with a panel decision, they should get rid of it by rehearing the case en banc."

Edwards, who later served as chief judge from 1994 to 2001, was widely praised for bringing collegiality to a court that "had a reputation for being contentious."[17] In a tribute, Ginsburg wrote that Edwards "made it a priority to restore collegiality among the judges, [which] he did with remarkable success." One of Edwards's most significant contributions was to discourage the use of en banc proceedings to reverse panel decisions. Edward's leadership resulted in a sharp decrease in the procedure. Ginsburg explained that in "relatively short order, the number of times the full court sat en banc to rehear a case previously decided by a panel of three judges dropped significantly: The number of rehearings en banc averaged six per year in the 1980s, three in the 1990s, and less than one in the first decade since." Ginsburg added, "In my view, these declining numbers reflect in part the increasing level of mutual trust and respect among the judges."

Conservative lawyer Adam J. White wrote in the *Wall Street Journal* that over the past decade, the D.C. Circuit had only reheard cases en banc nine times, and seven "raised difficult questions of constitutional law, such as the rights of Guantanamo detainees or of terminally ill patients."[18] During that time, Republican-appointed judges outnumbered Democratic-appointed judges. But then the balance flipped in 2013. Robert Weiner, an attorney who served in the Obama administration, rejected this historical practice: "Whatever the validity of those worries when Judge Edwards voiced them, concerns about politicizing the judicial process lack credibility now coming from those who have wielded litigation as an instrument of ideological and political warfare."[19]

---

[15] Neil A. Lewis, *An Ideological Flap Ruffles a Court's Two Wings*, N.Y. Times (Mar. 12, 1992), nyti.ms/1LjMw7Q.

[16] *Id.*

[17] Douglas H. Ginsburg, *The Behavior of Federal Judges, A View from the D.C. Circuit* 109 (Judicature Vol. 97, No. 2, 2013), bit.ly/1ZuSxG8.

[18] Adam J. White, *No Need for a Halbig Rehearing*, Wall St. J. (Aug. 4, 2014), on.wsj.com/1mvxqp5.

[19] Rob Weiner, *En Bunk: A Response to Professor Adler on En Banc Review of the ACA*, Balkinization (Aug. 7, 2014), perma.cc/4XY4-756B.

In 2015, President Obama's first appointment to the D.C. Circuit, Judge Sri Srinivasan, praised the court for not abusing the en banc proceedings as it had in the past when the composition rapidly changed.[20] (Srinivasan was considered on President Obama's "short list" to replace Justice Scalia in 2016.). "On my court, no one had been confirmed to the court for seven years at the time that I was confirmed," said Srinivasan. "In quite rapid succession, four of us who were appointed by President Obama were [confirmed] in the matter of a few months. If we lived in a world where we had the rule of a judge, rather than the rule of law, you would have seen an absolute sea change, an avulsive change in the law as it was interpreted, applied and rendered by our court," the judge explained. Srinivasan noted that after the new confirmations, "we didn't see an immediate sea change in decisions, we didn't see an overruling of prior precedent, we didn't see an immediate call to take en banc any case in which judges make a decision that other judges on the court might disagree with." He noted that "in at least some spheres there was probably some apprehension about [such a radical change] – or glee about that – depending on one's perspective." One such gleeful sphere was Emily Bazelon's column in *Slate*, titled "Obamacare Is Safe." She wrote that Judge Griffith's panel decision will likely be reversed" because the "D.C. Circuit (finally!) has four Obama appointees."[21]

22.4. "A LITTLE BIT ON THE AGGRESSIVE SIDE"

Michael Carvin and his team suspected that a majority of the judges on the D.C. Circuit would grant rehearing, thereby vacating Judge Griffith's panel decision and potentially delaying the Supreme Court's opportunity to hear the case from Virginia. So he rolled the dice once again and took an unorthodox step to prevent further dilatory tactics by the Obama administration.

Under the Supreme Court's rules, the government would have to file its brief in opposition to certiorari thirty days after the challenger's petition for certiorari – that would be on September 3, 2014. However, under the rules, the government could request an extension of up to sixty days. Usually these requests for an extension are granted automatically by the Clerk's office. Carvin worried that the D.C. Circuit may take this additional two-month

---

[20] Josh Gerstein, *Judge: Obama Appointees Bring No Big Shift to D.C. Circuit*, POLITICO (Oct. 30, 2015), perma.cc/3M9Z-LVFU.

[21] Emily Bazelon, *Obamacare Is Safe*, SLATE (Jul. 22, 2014), perma.cc/MZ3P-YNPV. (Emily Bazelon's grandfather, Judge David Bazelon, was appointed by President Truman, and served on the D.C. Circuit from 1950 to 1979).

window to grant rehearing and vacate Judge Griffiths decision. So on August 6, 2014, Carvin sent a letter to the Clerk of the Supreme Court, Scott H. Harris.[22] "I request that any application by [the government] for an extension of that time be submitted to the full Court for consideration." Carvin explained that "this case involves a matter of urgent public importance and petitioners therefore oppose any attempt to delay its resolution." In other words, the letter asked for the full Court – and presumably five justices – to vote before an extension could be granted.

The solicitor general, Carvin mused, "was clearly going to string out the Supreme Court." He told me, "It made no sense to have an extension in these circumstances. They couldn't really make the argument they needed the time. We wanted to stop the informal practice of the clerk giving the Solicitor General the extension, automatically." Ultimately, the sixty days "wasn't huge," because "we were still going to be arguing this term." But the lawyers wanted to give a "heads-ups" to the Justices, and at least the chief justice, to know "it was coming."

A senior official in the Department of Justice was not so keen on Carvin's decision to oppose the extension for the Brief in Opposition. "I thought that was a little," he began, but stopped himself. "It was a little bit on the aggressive side to oppose any extension. I think if I were him what I would have said was I consent to the extension so long as it doesn't preclude the case being heard this term." Indeed, in the government's pleadings, they explained they would only seek one extension to ensure the case wouldn't be kicked over till the start of the next term in October 2015.

As expected, on August 27, 2014 – one week before the deadline – Solicitor General Verrilli filed a letter with the Clerk requesting a thirty-day extension.[23] Verrilli explained that the D.C. Circuit's "disposition of the request [for rehearing en banc] is directly relevant to the [Supreme] Court's consideration of the petition for certiorari." He did not offer a reason why, but the subtext was that if the en banc D.C. Circuit agrees with the Fourth Circuit, there would no longer be a circuit split, obviating the need for the Supreme Court to take the case. The next day, Carvin fired away a final request to the Court, explaining that the solicitor general's arguments for the "last-minute application … are meritless." Specifically, it is *"this Court's* decision whether to hold the certiorari petition until the D.C. Circuit acts," which could take "many months." He concluded, "Given the enormous, urgent implications of the Court's decision for millions of individuals, thousands of employees, the entire insurance

[22] Letter to Clerk from Respondents (Aug. 6, 2014), bit.ly/1QVYGEZ.
[23] Letter to Clerk from Petitioners (Aug. 27, 2014), bit.ly/1rItd4m.

industry, dozens of states, and billions of federal tax dollars, the consequences of that delay should not be understated."

On September 2, 2014, Mike Carvin's phone rang. Scott Harris, the clerk of the Court said he was granting the government's extension after he had talked to the Justices. Harris relayed that it took a while to discuss and figure out what to do, because this issue had seldom arisen. The clerk noted that any future requests for extension by the government would be looked on with "disfavor." The Court's docket was updated with a one-sentence order: "Order extending time to file response to petition to and including October 3, 2014." The solicitor general received his extension.

22.5. "A BUNCH OF OBAMA APPOINTEES"

On September 4 – two days after the Supreme Court granted the thirty-day extension – the D.C. Circuit granted rehearing en banc. Judge Griffith's opinion was vacated and arguments were set for December 17. That meant an opinion would be released, at the earliest, in the spring of 2015. That timeline pushed the calendar too far back for the Supreme Court to resolve *Halbig* by June 2015, meaning that the issue could remain pending until June 2016, if at all. With the vacatur, the circuit split – a key factor the Supreme Court considers when granting certiorari – vanished. The solicitor general's office now saw a shift from a certainty of certiorari being granted to a situation where the government had a much stronger basis to its argument that the Court shouldn't take the case. But even then, Carvin's argument that this was an important case, and billions of dollars are being spent without authority, was "still a good argument." Under the Supreme Court's practices, only four justices must vote to grant certiorari, in order to hear a case.

On Thursday, September 25, Carvin spoke at a Heritage Foundation event previewing the upcoming Supreme Court term. After the event was over, Carvin met with a small group of people, and told them, "I don't know that four justices, who are needed to [take the case] here, are going to give much of a damn about what a bunch of Obama appointees on the D.C. Circuit think. This is a hugely important case."

Sahil Kapur of *Talking Points Memo*, who attended the conference, published these remarks in an article titled "Why This Conservative Lawyer Thinks He Can Still Cripple Obamacare."[24] Carvin was irked by the article, and told me he "thought [the conversation] was off the record." More pressingly, Carvin

---

[24] Sahil Kapur, *Why This Conservative Lawyer Thinks He Can Still Cripple Obamacare*, TALKING POINTS MEMO (Sept. 26, 2014), bit.ly/1Qb2M2g.

insisted that this was a comment he had made "with a number of reporters," but it was – fittingly enough for this statutory interpretation case – "completely rippled out of context." The "context of the conversation" was responding to Harry Reid's "cynical assertion" that the D.C. Circuit would grant rehearing en banc due to the "simple math" of President Obama's four appointments.

Carvin rejected Reid's cynicism, because "the judges are going to judge it by the language of the statute. But if I'm wrong on that," Carvin noted, "and Reid is right, do you think the Supreme Court is going to say, 'Gee, that's cynical, because Obama appointees voted for it because Obama appointed them, there's going to be an influence on the Court.'" In other words, if Reid was correct, there would be no real influence on the Court. "So my entire point about Obama appointees was in reaction to Reid's point that being an Obama appointee was outcome determinative."

22.6. "PUT THESE CHALLENGES TO REST"

On October 3, 2014, as scheduled, Solicitor General Verrilli filed his brief with the Supreme Court opposing the petition for certiorari. The argument was simple: because there is no longer a circuit split, there is no reason for the Supreme Court to get involved. Eleven days later, Michael Carvin and his associates would file one last plea to the Supreme Court, urging the justices to "put these challenges to rest." They charged that the government's attempt to keep the case away from the Court was "irresponsible" and "out of touch with reality." Indeed, three years earlier the government had taken just the *opposite* position, rushing to the Supreme Court to review a decision finding that Obamacare's individual mandate was unconstitutional, without seeking en banc review. (Carvin would know – he was counsel on that case too.) The introduction of the eight-page brief is worth quoting at length.

> In 2011, the Eleventh Circuit became the first Circuit to invalidate the ACA's individual mandate. Although that provision had survived other parallel challenges and was not even scheduled to take effect for more than two years, the Government recognized the imperative to "put these challenges to rest." It therefore eschewed en banc review and asked this Court for definitive resolution. Drawn-out litigation over the legality of a central plank of this landmark legislation, the Government understood, would paralyze the Nation and disserve its citizens.

> So too here. Indeed, the subsidies that the IRS has illegally expanded have already begun to flow, meaning billions of taxpayer dollars are pouring out of the Treasury absent congressional authorization and millions of Americans are ordering their lives around an impugned regulation. Yet the Government

is content to leave the spigots of cash open and the Nation in limbo in the hopes that (i) the en banc D.C. Circuit reverses the *Halbig* panel, and (ii) no other Circuit enforces the Act's plain text. All to avoid this Court's scrutiny....

The question is therefore not *whether* the Court should resolve this issue, but *when*. It can do so now, thus minimizing potential unfairness, providing maximum clarity to those subject to the Act, and preserving the integrity of federal expenditures. Or it can do so in 2016 or 2017, after tens of billions of Treasury funds are irretrievably spent, after the insurance industry restructures to adapt to the new regime, after employers lay off countless workers (or cut their hours) to avoid the employer mandate, and after millions of Americans buy insurance because they believe it will be subsidized (or because they are forced to under an individual mandate from which they are properly exempt).

The Wall Street Journal editorial board called Carvin's brief a "tour de force," a "master class in legal persuasion," and left the "Supreme Court no legal reason to dodge the case."[25] One month later, at least four justices on the Supreme Court would agree.

22.7. "CONGRATS"

On Friday, November 7, Michael Carvin was having lunch at the Hyatt Regency on Capitol Hill, two blocks from his office. He recalled, "Now that I am part of the 21st century, my phone actually rang." (Carvin had only recently learned to carry a Blackberry and use it to read messages, but he still dictated replies to his secretary Dotty.) It was Leonard Leo, Executive Vice President of the Federalist Society. "He said 'Congratulations. Good job.' I was like, 'What?' I looked at my phone, and I saw emails from Yaakov saying that SCOTUSBlog announced that certiorari had been granted. But the Court hadn't posted the file. Then I got like three or four emails in a row saying 'congrats.'" At 12:49 PM, SCOTUSBlog reporter Lyle Denniston wrote that the Court announced they would hear *King v. Burwell* "not long after finishing their closed-door private Conference" earlier that day.[26] The four-month litigation-dogfight with the solicitor general's office was over. Carvin had prevailed. The Supreme Court would hear the case in March, and resolve it by the end of June. A senior DOJ attorney told me, "I wouldn't say that I

---

[25] *Carvin's Obamacare Tour de Force*, WALL ST. J. (Oct. 20, 2014), on.wsj.com/1QaiW5V.
[26] Lyle Denniston, *Court to Rule on Health Care Subsidies*, SCOTUSBLOG (Nov. 7, 2014), perma.cc/X927-9PV9.

thought it was a foregone conclusion that they would grant cert but I wasn't totally surprised."

The D.C. Circuit would no longer need to rehear the case. On November 10, the Jones Day attorneys cheerfully filed a motion with the D.C. Circuit to hold *Halbig v. Burwell* in abeyance pending the resolution of *King v. Burwell*. The motion noted, "The Supreme Court's resolution of *King* will directly control this case." Two days later, the court ordered *Halbig v. Burwell* to be removed from the court's calendar and held in abeyance pending *King v. Burwell*. The eleven judges of the D.C. Circuit would not have another shot at the case. This issue would now be resolved by the justices.

23

"So Sue Me"

23.1. ORIGINATION CLAUSE

Not all of the Obamacare challenges were destined for the Supreme Court. One of the most potentially serious cases concerned another untruth President Obama told to sell the law. During the debates over the Affordable Care Act in the fall of 2009, controversy centered on whether the law's individual mandate imposed a tax on the uninsured. ABC's *This Week* host George Stephanopoulos challenged President Obama on this issue.[1] "Under this mandate the government is forcing people to spend money, fining you if you don't [have insurance]," he said. "How is that not a tax?" The president tried to explain how the mandate would reduce premiums, but Stephanopoulos pushed further. "That may be, but it's still a tax increase," the host said. "No," answered Obama, "That's not true, George … Nobody considers that a tax increase." After some more back-and-forth, Obama faulted the host for reading the definition of "tax" from the dictionary. Stephanopoulos asked point blank: "But you reject that it's a tax increase?" Obama replied, "I absolutely reject that notion." The year prior, candidate Obama pledged not to raise taxes on middle-class Americans. He was shrewd for denying the individual mandate was a tax. It would have been political suicide, as "taxes have never been popular" in America, at least since King George III's Stamp Act.[2]

During the drafting of the ACA, Senate Democrats implicitly recognized the political risk of imposing a tax on the uninsured. The Senate Finance Committee's bill, managed by Chairman Max Baucus of Montana, clearly stated the mandate "imposed a tax" if an individual went uninsured.[3] However,

[1] Chris Good, *Obama in 2009: The Individual Mandate Is Not a Tax*, ABC NEWS (June 28, 2012), abcn.ws/2auyzby.

[2] Nat'l Fed'n of Indep. Bus. v. Sebelius, 132 S. Ct. 2566, 2655 (2012) (joint dissent).

[3] America's Healthy Future Act of 2009, S. 1796, 111th Cong., 1st Sess., § 1301, 1.usa.gov/24Ymfu9.

the bill that emerged from Senator Reid's office, and ultimately became the ACA, struck out the taxation language. "Imposed a *tax*" became "imposed on the taxpayer a *penalty*."[4] In *NFIB v. Sebelius*, Justices Scalia, Kennedy, Thomas, and Alito offered a theory of what transpired. "We have no doubt that Congress knew precisely what it was doing," the joint dissenters wrote, "when it rejected an earlier version of this legislation that imposed a tax instead of a requirement-with-penalty."[5] Senate Democrats were trying to avoid the electoral consequences of raising taxes, in order to ensure the law's passage.

This taxation stigma was so strong that when the ACA was challenged in court in 2010, White House advisers did not even want the Department of Justice to defend the mandate as a tax.[6] They feared this would lead to a political blowback and serve as a repudiation of the president's promise not to raise taxes. Deputy Solicitor General Neal Katyal – who was acting on behalf of a recused Solicitor General Elena Kagan[7] – insisted on keeping this arrow in their litigation quiver.[8]

The White House's decision to acquiesce to this strategy was wise. Two years later, this proved to be the decisive argument that saved Obamacare. Nonetheless, the president's promise on ABC continued to haunt his administration. During oral arguments in *NFIB v. Sebelius*, Justice Scalia asked the solicitor general, "Is it a tax or not a tax? The President didn't think it was." Verrilli could only dodge the question: "The President said it wasn't a tax increase because it ought to be understood as an *incentive* to get people to have insurance."

The linguistic difference between a tax and a penalty is subtle, but the constitutional distinction is decisive. In *NFIB v. Sebelius*, the Chief Justice held that the individual mandate's penalty could not be supported by Congress's power to regulate interstate commerce. Further, the Chief concluded that the law as drafted was a penalty, not a tax, and thus did not fall within Congress's

---

[4]   26 U.S. Code § 5000A(b)(1).

[5]   *NFIB*, 132 S.Ct. at 2655.

[6]   Josh Blackman, Unprecedented: The Constitutional Challenge to Obamacare 286 (2013).

[7]   *Id.* at 73–74. On the evening the ACA passed the House, Associate Attorney General Tom Perrelli organized a meeting to prepare for the imminent litigation. Katyal forwarded the invitation to Kagan and wrote, "This is the first I've heard of this. I think you should go, no? I will, regardless, but feel like this is litigation of singular importance." One minute later, at 6:20 PM, without hesitation, Kagan replied: "What's your phone number?" At 6:22 PM, Katyal replied with his phone number. After this exchange, Kagan would never again discuss this matter of "singular importance," at least not over e-mail. Josh Blackman, *The Question No One Asked at Justice Kagan's Confirmation Hearing: Why Did She Wall Herself Off from the Obamacare Litigation?*, Volokh Conspiracy (Sept. 8, 2013), perma.cc/77V2-4XJF.

[8]   Unprecedented, *supra* note 6 at 286.

power to lay and collect taxes. However, through the application of a "saving construction," Roberts treated the penalty as if it were a tax, and upheld the ACA's mandate. The individual mandate "is therefore constitutional," Roberts wrote, "because it can reasonably be read as a tax."[9]

Although the "saving construction" solved one constitutional quandary for the ACA, it created another. As the joint dissenters pointed out, if indeed the individual mandate was enforced by a tax, rather than a penalty, then the law originated in the wrong house of Congress. Article I of the Constitution provides, "All Bills for raising Revenue shall originate in the House of Representatives; but the Senate may propose or concur with Amendments as on other Bills." The joint dissent explained that a tax that raises revenues "must originate in the legislative body most accountable to the people."[10] In the House of Representatives, "legislators must weigh the need for the tax against the terrible price they might pay at their next election," they observed, "which is never more than two years off." In other words, the political reality of the unpopularity of taxes checks the House of Representative's taxing power. The joint dissenters concluded that the ACA's mandate originated in the Senate as a penalty, to avoid the tax stigma. Or did it?

23.2. SHELL GAME

The Chief Justice's saving construction opened the door for yet another constitutional challenge to Obamacare. In July 2010, Matt Sissel, a public affairs specialist for the National Guard, filed a lawsuit alleging that Congress lacked the power to enact the ACA's individual mandate. Sissel was represented by the Pacific Legal Foundation, a libertarian public-interest law firm. However, the case was put on hold in August 2011 as the other Obamacare challenges raced through the courts of appeals. Oklahoma's challenge to Obamacare, *Pruitt v. Sebelius*, met a similar fate and was also stayed pending the resolution of the further-along ACA challenges. Circumstances changed once the Supreme Court decided *NFIB v. Sebelius* in June 2012. The Pacific Legal Foundation decided to bring a new challenge based on the origination clause.

PLF argued that under the Chief's opinion, the mandate-as-a-tax was unconstitutional, because it originated in the Senate. Indeed, Harry Reid referred to the bill that became the ACA as the "Senate Health Care Bill," to distinguish it from the House's bill, which was moving on a parallel track.[11]

---

[9] *NFIB*, 132 S. Ct. at 2601.
[10] *Id.* at 2655.
[11] Video, *Reid Unveils Senate Health Care Bill*, U.S. SENATOR FOR NEVADA (Nov. 18, 2009), perma.cc/S7XP-846N.

PLF's suit had the potential to invalidate the individual mandate the Court had recently upheld, albeit on different grounds. If the mandate were struck down, then the rest of the ACA would unravel, as the law could not survive without its lynchpin. Yet, the government had another defense at the ready.

The procedural origin of Obamacare is even *more* complicated than we discussed in Chapters 1 and 2. Long before Scott Brown was even a glimmer in Nancy Pelosi's eye, or Ben Nelson had reservations about abortion funding and federal exchanges, the Patient Protection and Affordable Care Act was born as House Resolution 3590. Titled the "Service Members Home Ownership Tax Act of 2009" (SMHOTA), H.R. 3590 unanimously passed the House of Representatives on October 8, 2009.[12] As its name suggests, the six-page bill provided tax credits to servicemembers who purchased homes and increased certain corporate tax prepayment rates.[13] SMHOTA had *absolutely nothing* to do with the pending health care reform debate. Critically, however, SMHOTA was a bill that originated in the House of Representatives that raised revenue.

After it passed the House, SMHOTA crossed Capitol Hill and was placed on the Senate Calendar of Business. However, the Senators would *never* vote on this bill. Instead, Majority Leader Reid offered an "amendment in the nature of a substitute" to H.R. 3590. The "amendment" had the effect of deleting the six pages of text within SMHOTA, replacing it with the 2,700 pages of the Patient Protection and Affordable Care Act. Senate Democrats used SMHOTA as a *shell bill*. With a shell bill, Professor Rebecca M. Kysar writes, the Senate "strikes the language of the bill entirely, and replaces it with its own revenue bill unrelated to the one that began in the House."[14] Kysar refers to "this shell bill game [as] an unconstitutional sleight of hand, obfuscating the bill's true origins in the Senate."

Why did the Senate engage in this parliamentary three-card monte rather than simply introducing a new Senate bill for health care reform? Kate Leone, a Senior Health Counsel for Senator Reid, explained the strategy to Law Professor John Cannan: "[B]asically, we needed a non-controversial House revenue measure to proceed to, so that is why we used the Service Members Home Ownership Tax Act. It wasn't more complicated than that."[15]

---

[12] *Final Vote Results for the Service Members Home Ownership Tax Act*, H.R. 3590, 111th Cong. (2009), 1.usa.gov/25gKTGq.

[13] H.R. 3590, 111th Cong. (2009) (enacted), perma.cc/UA39-AURE.

[14] Rebecca M. Kysar, *The 'Shell Bill' Game: Avoidance and the Origination Clause*, 91 WASH. U. L. REV. 659, 661 (2014).

[15] E-mail from Kate Leone, Senior Health Counsel, Office of Sen. Harry Reid, to John Cannan (Apr. 21, 2011, 3:25 PM), in John Cannan, *A Legislative History of the Affordable Care Act: How*

Internally, Democrats viewed the mandate as a tax in order to comply with the Constitution's origination clause. Publicly, however, President Obama and other leading Democrats obfuscated and misled the electorate on whether the mandate was a tax. Yale Law Professor Jack Balkin, who was a leading defender of the ACA's constitutionality, chided Obama's promise.[16] Balkin explained at a meeting of the progressive American Constitution Society that the president "has not been honest with the American people about the nature of the bill."[17] Much like the promise that people can keep the policies they like, or his "ironclad" executive order for Bart Stupak, the president's assurance that the mandate was not a tax was never genuine. But all three promises were necessary to grease the skids so moderate Democrats could support Obamacare. Without each of these false guarantees the ACA would never have secured enough votes to pass.

Sissel asserted that the "gut-and-amend" procedure "is not 'origination' as the Origination Clause contemplates." However, his challenge did not succeed in court. In June 2013, Judge Beryl A. Howell dismissed the case for two primary reasons. First, even though "the individual mandate raises revenues" and those revenues are "paid into the Treasury," the court found the provision was not designed to raise revenues for the purpose of "support[ing] Government generally."[18] Citing Chief Justice Roberts's opinion in *NFIB*, the district court concluded that the purpose of the individual mandate was "to expand health insurance coverage" even if the payments incidentally "raise[d] considerable revenue." Thus, the provision did not fall within the scope of the origination clause.

Second, even assuming that the individual mandate was a provision for raising revenue, the court concluded that the Senate had the power to amend H.R. 3590, even if the ACA had absolutely nothing to do with providing tax credits to servicemembers. Judge Howell found the origination clause lacked a "germaneness requirement." That is, the shell bill did not need to be related to the final bill. The court concluded that the individual mandate's penalty originated in the House of Representatives, and "was later duly amended by the Senate in a manner consistent with the Origination Clause."[19] One year later in June

---

Legislative Procedure Shapes Legislative History, 105:2 Law Library J., 131, 153 (2013), bit.ly/1slOZfm.

[16]   UNPRECEDENTED, *supra* note 6 at 138.

[17]   W. Gardner Selby, *Supreme Court Upholds Argument That "Penalty" Is a Tax*, POLITIFACT (June 28, 2012), perma.cc/8DWZ-RRA8.

[18]   Sissel v. HHS, 951 F. Supp. 2d 159, 168–69 (D.D.C. 2013).

[19]   *Id.* at 174.

2014, a three-judge panel of the D.C. Circuit Court of Appeals affirmed on similar grounds.[20]

Sissel filed a petition for the entire D.C. Circuit to reconsider the case en banc. Unlike *Halbig v. Burwell*, where the D.C. Circuit jumped at rehearing the case the following month, Sissel's en banc petition lingered for twelve months. Finally, in August 2015, the D.C. Circuit denied rehearing en banc by a vote of seven to four.[21] Judge Brett Kavanaugh wrote a dissent from denial of rehearing en banc – known in the parlance as a "dissental."[22] He vigorously disagreed with the majority about the individual mandate: it did raise revenue. "Lots of revenue," Kavanaugh wrote.[23] He observed that "[i]t is difficult to say with a straight face that a bill raising $473 billion in revenue is not a 'Bill for raising Revenue.'" However, he agreed with the majority that the ACA complied with the origination clause, because "such Senate amendments [of H.R. 3590] are permissible under the Clause's text and precedent." The bottom line was the same: Sissel lost.

PLF appealed the case to the Supreme Court. Would the Chief Justice, who previously held that the ACA was a tax, determine whether in fact the tax originated in the House of Representatives – a question he ignored in *NFIB*? Would the four joint dissenters want another stab at the constitutionality of the individual mandate – it only takes four votes to grant certiorari? No and No. On January 19, 2016, without any dissent, the Court denied certiorari. That was the end of the road for the origination clause challenge.

23.3. "FAITHFULLY EXECUTING THE LAW"

In 2014, three prominent lawsuits were filed stemming from what Chapter 13 referred to as "government by blog post." During the hectic fall of 2013, President Obama took a series of executive actions that modified, delayed, and suspended the ACA's mandates. In January 2014, Senator Ron Johnson (R-WI) struck first with a challenge to the "OPM fix." Under Section 1312 of the ACA, members of Congress and their staff were no longer eligible for participation

---

[20] Sissel v. HHS, 760 F.3d 1, 2 (D.C. Cir. 2014).

[21] The seven judges who voted to deny rehearing en banc were appointed by President Clinton (Merrick Garland, Judith Rogers, David Tatel) and President Obama (Sri Srinivasan, Patricia Millett, Nina Pillard, and Robert Wilkins). The four judges who would have reheard the case en banc were appointed by President George H. W. Bush (Karen Henderson) and President George W. Bush (Janice Rogers Brown, Thomas Griffith, and Brett Kavanaugh).

[22] Alex Kozinski & James Burnham, *I Say Dissental, You Say Concurral*, 121 YALE L.J. ONLINE 601 (2012), bit.ly/1qkZopt.

[23] Sissel v. HHS, 799 F.3d 1035, 1049 (D.C. Cir. 2015) (Kavanaugh, J., dissenting from denial of rehearing en banc).

in the Federal Employees Health Benefits Plan (FEHBP), but had to enroll in a plan "created under" the ACA.[24] For many members of Congress, and their staff, purchasing policies on the Obamacare exchanges would be far more expensive than the heavily subsidized FEHBP.

In response to panic on Capitol Hill, the Office of Personnel Management (OPM) issued a rule that purported to interpret Section 1312. Through the OPM fix, members of Congress and their staff were treated as employees of a "small business," and could purchase subsidized policies on the District of Columbia's Small Business Health Options Program ("SHOP"). Senator Johnson argued that the OPM fix was illegal and contrary to the clear text of the ACA, which required members of Congress and their staff to purchase policies "created under" the ACA. Johnson wrote in the *Wall Street Journal*, "OPM exceeded its statutory jurisdiction and legal authority. In directing OPM to do so, President Obama once again chose political expediency instead of faithfully executing the law – even one of his own making." Article II imposes on the president a duty to "take care that the laws be faithfully executed."[25]

The critical barrier for Johnson's suit, however, was "standing." Unlike the state courts, which have general jurisdiction – that is they can hear any sort of case – federal courts have only specific jurisdiction. Article III of our constitution defines the bounds of the federal courts' limited jurisdiction: they can hear only actual "cases" or "controversies." Courts cannot issue "advisory opinions," where judges opine on abstract issues. Rather, courts can only proceed to analyze questions of law where the plaintiff has what is known as "standing." To have standing, a plaintiff "must have suffered an 'injury in fact' – an invasion of a legally protected interest which is (a) concrete and particularized, and (b) actual or imminent, not conjectural or hypothetical."[26] The Supreme Court has recognized standing as a means to keep purely ideological suits – that is, where no one is injured – out of the federal judiciary. This doctrine serves to preserve the independence of the courts; unless a plaintiff is injured, and the court can provide relief, it is not a matter suitable for judicial review.

In August 2014, Judge William C. Griesbach dismissed the case, finding that Senator Johnson lacked standing.[27] Specifically, the court rejected the notion that members of Congress suffer an injury by participating in conduct that is contrary to law, and thus may injure their reputation. The court relied on the

---

[24] §1312(d)(3)(D).
[25] Zachary Price, *Enforcement Discretion and Executive Duty*, 67 Vand. L. Rev. 671, 676 (2014); Josh Blackman, *The Constitutionality of DAPA Part II: Faithfully Executing the Law*, 19 Texas Rev. Law & Politics 215 (2015).
[26] Lujan v. Defenders of Wildlife, 504 U.S. 555, 560 (1992) (quotations omitted).
[27] Johnson v. OPM, 1:14-CV-009 (E.D. Wisc. 2014), available at goo.gl/GDOvno.

Supreme Court's 1997 decision in *Raines v. Byrd*.[28] In that case, West Virginia Senator Robert Byrd and several other members of Congress challenged the constitutionality of the Line Item Veto Act. They asserted that the law gave the president a legislative prerogative to alter statutes, in violation of the separation of powers. The Supreme Court dismissed the case because none of the plaintiffs were actually injured by the law. Rather, the individual members of Congress could only assert an "abstract dilution of institutional legislative power." In 1998, the Supreme Court would invalidate the Line Item Veto Act in *Clinton v. City of New York*. In the later case, New York City was injured by President Clinton's cancellation of certain budgetary items, and thus had standing.[29]

The Seventh Circuit Court of Appeals affirmed the dismissal of Senator Johnson's case on standing grounds, but did not address the underlying constitutional issue.[30] With that, no court would ever assess the legality of the OPM fix. If a member of Congress could not challenge the executive's rewriting of the ACA, could a state bring such a suit?

23.4. THE ADMINISTRATIVE FIX

The second major lawsuit stemming from the implementation of the ACA, like the origination clause challenge, also arose from one of President Obama's whoppers: "If you like your plan, you can keep your plan." Starting on January 1, 2014, the ACA imposed eight new requirements on health insurers, including a prohibition on discriminating against customers with preexisting conditions and a requirement to provide "minimum essential coverage." Traditionally, states were responsible for regulating their own insurance markets. The federal government could not force, or commandeer, the states to implement Obamacare. As a result, the ACA gave states two choices. First, each state could voluntarily enforce these eight requirements within its borders. Second, if a state declined, HHS must enforce the requirements in its place. The statute provides that if HHS makes a "determination" of nonenforcement by a state, "the Secretary *shall* enforce" the eight requirements. Under the ACA, states were given the first opportunity to enforce the mandates, but if they declined, HHS would do it for them. In West Virginia, neither would happen.

---

[28]   521 U.S. 811 (1997).
[29]   524 U.S. 417 (1998).
[30]   Johnson v. OPM, 783 F.3d 655 (7th Cir. 2015).

During the fall of 2013, millions of plans were cancelled because they did not comply with the eight requirements imposed by the ACA. In response, on November 14, President Obama announced what came to be known as the "administrative fix." Recognizing "how upsetting this can be for a lot of Americans, particularly after assurances they heard from me that if they had a plan that they liked, they could keep it," the president announced that HHS would not enforce the eight requirements against insurers. After all, it was the ACA's mandates that resulted in the cancellation of policies.

However, even if HHS refused to enforce the mandates, the states could still elect to enforce the eight requirements. The president admitted that "state insurance commissioners still have the power to decide what plans can and can't be sold in their states." But that was no longer the problem of the federal government. "What we want to do is to be able to say to folks" with cancelled policies, Obama said, is that "the Affordable Care Act is not going to be the reason why insurers have to cancel your plan." In other words, the fault would lie with the individual insurance companies, and ultimately the states that continued to enforce the statutory mandates HHS disregarded.

As we discussed in Chapter 13, several states, including Washington, continued to enforce the eight requirements. In those states, cancelled plans remained cancelled, and the local elected insurance commissioners took the heat from their constituents. Other states, like West Virginia, had never planned on enforcing the mandates in the first place. But now that HHS would not serve as a backstop, the Mountain State would be confronted with a new choice. Before the administrative fix, the state had no responsibility to enforce the mandates. Now it was up to West Virginia, and West Virginia alone, to decide whether or not the ACA's requirements were enforced. West Virginians who stood to benefit from the mandates would now be out of luck if the state did not step up. Under the president's fix, all conceivable blame would now fall on West Virginia.

On December 26, 2013, the Attorney General of West Virginia wrote a letter on behalf of eleven other state attorneys general, charging that the president's "fixes" to Obamacare were illegal.[31] "We support allowing citizens to keep their health insurance coverage," A.G. Patrick Morrisey wrote, "but the only way to fix this problem-ridden law is to enact changes lawfully: through Congressional action." The statute provides that HHS "shall enforce" the eight requirements – *shall* means *must*. President Obama told HHS not to

---

[31] E-mail from Patrick Morrisey, Att'y Gen., W. Va., to Kathleen Sebelius, Sec'y, HHS (Dec. 26, 2013), bit.ly/25gIziE; Rebecca Shabad, *Eleven Attorneys General Slam Obama Healthcare Fixes as Illegal*, THE HILL (Jan. 2, 2014), perma.cc/5P6X-EQJK.

enforce the requirements, even if a state failed to do so, because it resulted in the cancellation of plans. But it was Congress's plan, as implemented by the Obama administration's own regulations, that resulted in the cancellations. Morrisey concluded that "the illegal actions by this administration must stop."

Seven months later, West Virginia challenged the constitutionality of the fix.[32] (The other signatories to the December letter, I learned, were not willing to join the lawsuit). West Virginia argued that "there is simply no plausible legal defense for the Administrative Fix," citing an academic consensus "from across the political spectrum." One of those scholars was Michigan Law Professor Nicholas Bagley. Though a prominent supporter of the ACA, he wrote in the *New England Journal of Medicine* that the administrative fix was inconsistent with the statute.[33] "The recent delays of ACA provisions," Bagley wrote, "appear to exceed the scope of the executive's traditional enforcement discretion." The "like it, keep it fix," he explained, "reflect[s] the administration's policy-based anxiety over the pace at which the ACA was supposed to go into effect," rather than any sort of "discretionary judgment[s] concerning the allocation of enforcement resources." The latter was perhaps a permissible basis to adjust the implementation of the law, but the former was not legitimate.

Before the court could reach the constitutional questions, however, it had to start with the question of jurisdiction. Judge Amit P. Mehta observed that "the merits of the State's contentions must take a back seat to the threshold issue advanced by" the government, "that West Virginia lacks standing to challenge the Administrative Fix."[34] Like Senator Johnson's suit challenging the OPM fix, the court tossed West Virginia's case due to a lack of standing. "The State's asserted injuries," Judge Mehta wrote, "are not the kind of concrete and particularized injury-in-fact that is actual or imminent – and not conjectural or hypothetical – that is required to establish standing under the standards." A distortion of political accountability in the state, the court found, was not adequate.

Because the state was not injured by the "administrative fix" – indeed, it was not required to undertake any new responsibilities – there was no basis on which the court could assess the legality of the executive action. West Virginia lamented the government's refusal to address the legality of the fix. HHS's brief, the challengers wrote, "is yet another example of this Administration's

[32] In the interest of full disclosure, I reviewed an early draft of West Virginia's complaint.
[33] Professor Nicholas Bagley, *The Legality of Delaying Key Elements of the ACA*, 2014 N. Engl. J. Med. 370 (May 22, 2014), bit.ly/2apytHA.
[34] West Virginia v. HHS, 145 F.Supp.3d 94, 96 (D.D.C. 2015).

continuing effort to avoid answering for the illegality of its repeated failure to faithfully execute politically or ideologically inconvenient federal laws." In April 2016, West Virginia argued its appeal before the D.C. Circuit, which we will visit at the end of this chapter.

23.5. STANDING FOR CONGRESS

Johnson v. OPM reinforced the principle that individual members of Congress lack standing to challenge the president's rewriting of the ACA's mandates. *West Virginia v. HHS* held that states lack standing to challenge the president's suspension of the ACA's mandates, even if it thrusts upon them new political burdens. But could the House of Representatives, as a body, challenge the president's refusal to enforce the law? In a January 2014 editorial in *Politico*, two constitutional lawyers argued that it could.[35] Where the states and individual members of Congress were denied access to federal courts, the House of Representatives could succeed, wrote D.C. attorney David Rivkin and Florida International University law professor Elizabeth Price Foley.

They offered three reasons why the House was an appropriate plaintiff to challenge the president's executive actions. First, with the president's "'benevolent' suspensions" of the law, such as the modification of the employer mandate, "no one person was sufficiently harmed to create standing to sue." In fact, people who would otherwise have their policies cancelled are helped by HHS ignoring Obamacare's mandates. Other than the House, the lawyers explained, "no other plaintiffs possess standing to challenge illegal actions."

Second, because the House of Representatives has a formal mechanism for designating a body to "file lawsuits on their chamber's behalf," the case is brought on behalf of "one of the two chambers of the legislative branch that the institution believes its rights have been violated." This sort of institutional suit would differ from the suit brought by Senator Johnson challenging the OPM Fix, or the individual members of Congress challenging the Line Item Veto Act in *Raines v. Byrd*. As the *Wall Street Journal* would later point out, "the difference between Mr. Johnson's suit and [the House's suit] is that the House is making an institutional challenge to executive abuse."[36]

Third, "a congressional lawsuit would not be about angry losers," the authors noted, "but about Congress defending its legislative power and

[35] David Rivkin and Elizabeth Price Foley, *Can Obama's Legal End-Run Around Congress Be Stopped?*, POLITICO (Jan. 15, 2014), perma.cc/WB9W-YC67.
[36] *So Sue Him*, WALL. ST. J. (July 31, 2014), on.wsj.com/2ohUQNc.

demanding faithful execution of the laws by the president." Without congressional standing, Rivkin and Foley concluded, "there will be no other way to check such presidential usurpation short of impeachment." The Constitution only requires a majority vote to enact a new binding law, but a supermajority vote to remove the president. The president's failure to faithfully execute the law cannot alter that calculus. Over the next six months, the idea of the House of Representatives challenging the legality of President Obama's executive actions started to gain traction. Rumors swirled that Speaker John Boehner supported the plan. The *Wall Street Journal* lauded Rivkin and Foley, who frequently advised the House, as the "architects" of the suit.[37]

The biggest critic of this plan was President Obama. During a speech in Kansas City, Obama mocked the proposed lawsuit. He warned the crowd that Congress planned "to sue me for doing my job."[38] The audience booed. The president continued, "They have announced that they're going to sue me for taking executive actions to help people." He dismissed the litigation as a "political stunt," as this vote is not actually working to "help you." President Obama issued an ultimatum to Republicans: "Middle-class families can't wait for Republicans in Congress to do stuff. So sue me."[39] They did.

On June 25, 2014, Speaker Boehner circulated a memorandum to the House GOP caucus.[40] The Ohioan wrote that "for the integrity of our laws and the sake of our country's future, the House must act now" to stop the president's illegal executive actions. In July, Boehner would bring legislation to the floor to authorize the House General Counsel "to file suit in the coming weeks in an effort to compel the president to follow his oath of office and faithfully execute the laws of our country." On July 30, the House voted along straight party lines – 225 to 201 – to authorize the litigation.[41] (One Republican voted nay.) House Resolution 676 was framed very broadly: the lawsuit could "seek any appropriate relief regarding the failure" of all executive-branch officials – including the president himself – "to act in a manner consistent with that official's duties under the Constitution and laws of the United States with respect to implementation" of the ACA.[42]

---

[37] *Id.*

[38] *Remarks by the President on the Economy*, WHITE HOUSE (July 30, 2014), perma.cc/JSJ2-GJUV.

[39] Dana Davidsen, *Obama to Republicans: 'So Sue Me'*, POLITICAL TICKER (July 1, 2014), perma.cc/6G3M-WX92.

[40] Memorandum from Speaker Boehner to House Members (June 25, 2014), bit.ly/1qDtwg1.

[41] *Final Vote Results for Agreeing on the Resolution*, H.R. RES. 676, 113th Cong. (2014), 1.usa.gov/1YVn3J6.

[42] H.R. Res. 676, 113th Cong. (2014), perma.cc/NAK2-BNMF.

23.6. "TEMPORARY MODIFICATION TO THE HEALTH CARE LAW"

It was widely expected that the House would challenge the legality of the president's delays of the employer mandate. Starting on January 1, 2014, the ACA required most employers to provide their workers with qualifying insurance, or pay a penalty.[43] Section 1513 of the ACA stated that the requirements *"shall apply* to months beginning after December 31, 2013." Six months before the deadline, the president delayed the mandate until 2015. He then pushed it back again until 2016, relaxing the penalties based on the size of a company and percentage of its workforce that is insured. Absolutely none of this is in the statute.

During a congressional hearing, Attorney General Eric Holder was pressed on the government's authority to delay and rewrite the mandate. Representative Steve Chabot (R-OH) asked, "Congress puts effective dates in laws, do we need to further state that the effective date cannot be waived or modified by the executive branch, or is the president required to follow the law, and also follow the dates set by Congress?"[44] Holder demurred. "The president has the duty, obviously, to follow the law," he said, but that "it would depend on the statute." The attorney general added that the Treasury Department reviewed the law "and 'determined there was a legal basis' for the change." During an April 2014 hearing, Deputy Assistant Secretary of Treasury Mark Iwry was asked more than five times if the agency had the authority to delay the individual mandate. Iwry refused to answer the question directly, replying, "If we don't believe it is appropriate to be delaying that provision, if we believe it is fair to individuals to keep that in place because it protects them ... then we don't reach the question whether we have legal authority."[45]

In an interview with the *New York Times*, the president was asked about the legal basis for his delay of the employer mandate.[46] Obama replied, "I will seize any opportunity I can find to work with Congress," but "where Congress is unwilling to act, I will take whatever administrative steps that I can in order to do right by the American people." He added that he would not "sit around and twiddle [his] thumbs for the next 1,200 days" if the "only message from some of these folks is 'no' on everything."

---

[43] *See supra* Chapter 13 for a discussion of the employer mandate.

[44] Jonathan Easley, *GOP Challenges Holder on Legality of Employer Mandate Delay*, THE HILL (Apr. 8, 2014), perma.cc/CM84-7433.

[45] Jonathan Easley, *Treasury Unsure if It Has Authority to Delay Obamacare Individual* Mandate, THE HILL (Apr. 18, 2014), perma.cc/FU9E-CRKT.

[46] Interview by Jackie Calmes & Michael D. Shear with President Barack Obama, N.Y. TIMES (July 24, 2013), nyti.ms/1J9bae3.

The former constitutional law professor lectured Congress about its legal aptitude. "Ultimately, I'm not concerned about their opinions," Obama said. "Very few of them, by the way, are lawyers, much less constitutional lawyers."[47] President Obama may have said more than he intended. He later referred to his rejiggering of the employer mandate as "making a temporary *modification* to the health care law" that Congress said "needed to be *modified*."[48] Presidents cannot "modify" the law, no matter how short-lived the modification is. The very first words of Article I of the Constitution provide that "all legislative Powers" are vested in Congress. The president's duty under Article II is limited to faithfully executing the laws that Congress enacts.[49]

Even ACA supporters questioned the legality of the delay. Michigan law professor Nicholas Bagley worried that the employer mandate delay was not "the result of an agency's failure to hit a deadline," but rather was a "conscious decision to put off the dates" so they would not burdened businesses.[50] This delay, he wrote, could "embody [the] sort of abdication" that runs afoul of the president's duty to take care that the laws are faithfully executed.[51] But Bagley did not believe the House would have standing to challenge this executive action in court.

23.7. CHANGE OF COUNSEL

After the House authorized the suit, David Rivkin and the Baker Hostetler law firm signed a contract to litigate the case, which was capped at $350,000.[52] The reaction from Democrats was swift. The White House called the suit "unfortunate."[53] Minority Leader Nancy Pelosi criticized the case as a waste of "time and taxpayer dollars."[54] Representative Louise M. Slaughter (D-NY) called the

---

[47] *Id.*

[48] Remarks by the President at the Signing of Fair Pay and Safe Workplace Executive Order (July 31, 2014), perma.cc/H68X-5375 (emphasis added).

[49] Brief for the Cato Institute, et al., As Amici Curiae Supporting Respondents, U.S. v. Texas, On Writ of Certiorari to the U.S. Court of Appeals for the Fifth Circuit (Apr. 4, 2016), bit.ly/1TULXqH.

[50] Nicholas Bagley, *Legal Limits and the Implementation of the Affordable Care Act*, 164 U. PA. L. REV. ___ (Forthcoming 2016), bit.ly/1R2il6r.

[51] *Id.*

[52] Contract from Kerry Kircher, General Counsel, House of Representatives, to David Rivkin, Jr. (Aug. 22, 2014), bit.ly/1ZS2MUW.

[53] Justin Sink, *White House: GOP Suit 'Unfortunate'*, THE HILL (Nov. 21, 2014), perma.cc/2UKB-ZS48.

[54] Sebastian Payne, *House Plan to Spend up to $350,000 on Obama Suit*, WASH. POST (Aug. 25, 2014), perma.cc/7TKX-XRB5.

suit a "sorry spectacle of legislative malpractice" and "political theater."[55] Even many conservatives critiqued the decision. Talk radio host Mark Levin, who served in the Reagan administration, called the litigation a "foolish move."[56]

Soon, the law firm was ridiculed on late night television. Jimmy Fallon aired a fake infomercial for Baker Hostetler on the *Tonight Show*.[57] The parody featured an ambulance-chasing lawyer pitching his firm. "At Baker Hostetler, we specialize in one thing," the actor said, "suing the president. For instance, have you ever been forced to pass Obamacare, even though you didn't like it? We can help you waste thousands of dollars in taxpayer money to fight for what you sort of believe in."

The *New York Times* reported that Rivkin was "under pressure after facing criticism" from his colleagues "that he had taken on an overly partisan lawsuit."[58] Partners at his firm, the *Times* wrote, "feared the case against Mr. Obama could drive off potential clients and hurt Baker Hostetler's credibility." I learned from an attorney involved in the matter that when the contract was initially signed, a conflict check was performed, and the firm "backed the case." However, within a week after the contract was announced, partners at the firm started to receive urgent calls from general counsels of clients in the health care industry. Baker Hostetler represents many hospital management firms and insurance companies, particularly at its office in Columbus, Ohio.[59] All of the calls from the general counsels had the "identical" message: they were under pressure, and could not continue to associate with Baker Hostetler if it litigated the House's lawsuit.

The attorney I spoke with said it was "suspicious" that they all gave the "same" message very shortly after the contract was announced. There was a concern – confirmed by at least one general counsel – that the Obama administration was quietly pushing health care companies to drop Baker Hostetler. After these calls came in, Rivkin's colleagues told him, "you can't do this." The contract with the House prohibited partners at Rivkin's firm from any "lobbying or advocacy" concerning the ACA. Many of Rivkin's colleagues lobbied for health care reform. Although the House was willing to amend the contract to strike this provision, all of the parties agreed that this would be a valid basis to cancel the representation.

[55] Ashley Parker, *Republicans Switch Firm Handling Obama Suit*, N.Y. TIMES (Sept. 19, 2014), nyti.ms/25enQfx.
[56] *Id.*
[57] Jimmy Fallon, *Baker Hostetler Suing Obama*, YouTube (Sept. 18, 2014), bit.ly/1TDhM4F.
[58] Ashley Parker, *Republicans Switch Firm Handling Obama Suit*, N.Y. TIMES (Sept. 19, 2014), nyti.ms/25enQfx.
[59] Baker Hostetler: *Healthcare Industry*, bit.ly/1R2js5S.

This withdrawal was particularly bittersweet for Rivkin. In 2010, he was the first attorney to represent Florida in its constitutional challenge to Obamacare. However, after Pam Bondi was elected as attorney general of Florida, she opted to replace Rivkin with SCOTUS-superstar Paul Clement.[60] Bondi wanted to hire someone who would argue at the Supreme Court, though she admitted it was an agonizing decision to switch horses in the middle of the race. In 2013, Rivkin told me that he understood the decision and took it graciously. It was a "typical Washington thing," he said. In 2014, after he had to withdraw from the House's case, Rivkin was angry at this political hardball that was completely beyond his control.

This is also not the first time the House Republicans have been in this sort of predicament. In 2011, the Obama administration announced that it would no longer defend the constitutionality of the Defense of Marriage Act (DOMA). The House of Representatives hired Paul Clement, then of the King & Spalding law firm, to take the case and litigate it all the way to the Supreme Court. Under pressure, the firm asked Clement to drop the case. Rather than resigning from the litigation, Clement announced that he would resign from King & Spalding "out of the firmly held belief that a representation should not be abandoned because the client's legal position is extremely unpopular in certain quarters."[61]

Tony Mauro reported in the *National Law Journal* that "pressure from within King & Spalding – as well as from some of its clients – were said to be factors in Clement's exit."[62] Dahlia Lithwick wrote in *Slate* that "Human Rights Campaign, the gay rights advocacy group that had been agitating against Clement's defense of the law, is happy to claim responsibility for pressuring the firm to abandon its representation."[63] A spokesman for HRC said that the LGBT organization "contact[ed] King & Spalding clients to let them know that the group viewed the firm's defense of DOMA as unacceptable." He added: "We are an advocacy firm that is dedicated to improving the lives of gays and lesbians. It is incumbent on us to launch a full-throated educational campaign so firms know that these kinds of engagements will reflect on the way your clients and law school recruits think of your firm."

In a tradition dating back to John Adams's defense of the Red Coats who opened fire during the Boston Massacre, attorneys are ethically obligated to continue representing a client, even if the cause is unpopular, or if they

---

[60] *Unprecedented, supra* note 6 at 126–128.

[61] Resignation Letter from Paul Clement to King & Spalding (Apr. 25, 2011), bit.ly/1XthpQ5.

[62] Tony Mauro, *Schaerr Leaves Winston to Represent Utah in Marriage* Case, LEGAL TIMES (Jan. 17, 2014), perma.cc/8DEW-CUSZ.

[63] Dahlia Lithwick, *The Best Offense Is a Good Defense*, SLATE (Apr. 26, 2011), bit.ly/2aH6PEj.

may lose other business. Clement wrote in his resignation letter that "when it comes to lawyers, the surest way to be on the wrong side of history is to abandon a client in the face of hostile criticism." Firms should consider those factors *before* accepting a client, not *after* the representation begins. For example, after he retired as attorney general, Eric Holder joined the firm of Covington and Burling. It was reported that the former Obama administration official – no friend of the financial industry – "may have lost a client because the firm hired him back."[64] Holder recalled, "One big bank went to Covington and said, 'If you hire this guy, that is going to put at risk the relationship between this firm and this bank.'"[65] The former attorney general relayed a conversation with the firm's chairman, who said, "I guess we're not going to have a relationship anymore, because he's coming back to Covington." Note that this decision happened *even before* Holder had joined the firm, whereas Clement was forced to resign *after* the firm accepted the case.

Following his resignation, Clement was able to immediately join the Bancroft law firm and continue his representation of the House. Over the next five years, Clement would establish Bancroft PLLC as a preeminent Supreme Court litigation boutique. He personally argued in three Obamacare cases before the justices in five years.

David Rivkin told me that during the summer of 2014, he and his colleagues "spent weeks scrambling to see whether [they] could find a way to continue representing the House." He explained that "this was a very difficult process for all of us as we had to balance our ethical obligations to the House and other Firm clients as well as numerous other considerations," particularly in light of their work over the past year to "develop the legal architecture" of the case. "A number of options were considered," Rivkin said. "Unfortunately, all of them would have required a considerable period of time to implement and the House wanted to file the lawsuit as soon as possible. In the end, withdrawing was the only viable option."

The House, without a lawyer for its case, frantically approached many of the top firms in Washington, D.C. They asked veteran litigator Chuck Cooper, who served in the Reagan administration, to take the case. The founding partner of the Cooper and Kirk law firm declined. The House also asked Michael

[64] Tony Mauro, *Eric Holder: No Apologies for Return to Big* Law, Nat'l Law J. (Apr. 29, 2016), perma.cc/TA6R-R9RB.

[65] Josh Blackman, *Holder: Covington Hired Me Knowing They Would Lose a Big Bank Client. Cf. Paul Clement and King & Spalding*, Josh Blackman's Blog (Apr. 29, 2016), perma.cc/XG25-L9KX.

Carvin and Greg Katsas of Jones Day. Katsas had argued alongside Carvin before the Supreme Court in *NFIB v. Sebelius*. Jones Day also declined the House's case. An attorney at the firm told me they did not think it was a winning argument to challenge the delay of the employer mandate. Specifically, the employer mandate would go into effect in 2016, thus potentially mooting the case before it worked its way up to the Supreme Court. President Obama made a similar point in ridiculing the suit. In his July speech in Kansas City, Obama said, "It's estimated that by the time the thing was done, I would have already left office. So it's not a productive thing to do."

After a harried search, the House selected D.C. lawyer William Burck of Quinn Emanuel Urquhart & Sullivan LLP. I learned that Quinn Emanuel was deemed a better option because it was a litigation firm that did not lobby on behalf of the health care industry.[66] However, three weeks later, without any explanation, Burck withdrew from the case under similar pressure from his firm.[67] An attorney involved in the selection process told me it was "embarrassing." Another attorney said House Republicans were "pissed" and "irritated how everything played out."

After two attorneys dropped out in one month, the House could not afford another miscue. An attorney advised Speaker Boehner that they needed an academic to litigate the case who "would not have any conflicts." They soon chose Jonathan Turley, a law professor at George Washington University. Turley, though a liberal who supported national health care, had been a staunch critic of President Obama's executive actions. Months earlier, he warned that "what the president is doing is effectively amending or negating the federal law to fit his preferred approach. Democrats will rue the day if they remain silent in the face of this shift of power to the executive branch."[68] On November 18, Turley was officially hired.[69] House Democrats still objected to the case. Representative Robert Brady (D-PA) carped that Turley should not allow unpaid law students who have "not passed the bar" to be "exploited" by working on this case.[70]

---

[66] Lauren French, *New Law Firm in GOP Obama Suit*, POLITICO (Sep. 19, 2014), perma.cc/P4MT-UQ9E.

[67] Josh Gerstein & Maggie Haberman, *More Turmoil for House GOP Suit*, POLITICO (Oct. 30, 2014), perma.cc/7VFZ-EYD7.

[68] Robert Pear, *Consumers Allowed to Keep Health Plans for Two More Years*, N.Y. TIMES (Mar. 15, 2014), nyti.ms/1U3SFLa.

[69] Michael Crittenden, *House Republicans Hire Jonathan Turley to Pursue Obama Lawsuit*, WALL ST. J. (Nov. 18, 2014), on.wsj.com/1U4YYew.

[70] Josh Blackman, JOSH BLACKMAN'S BLOG, *Democrat Objects to Jonathan Turley Using GW Law Students on Obamacare Suit* (Nov. 11, 2014), perma.cc/6HE4-BRY6.

On November 21 – nearly four months after the House authorized the suit – Turley filed *House of Representatives v. Burwell*.[71] It would be assigned to Judge Rosemary M. Collyer.

23.8. POWER OF THE PURSE

The ACA used two approaches to reduce the higher premiums caused by the individual mandate. Section 1401 of the ACA directly provides subsidies to consumers to reduce the cost of policies. (In *King v. Burwell*, the Supreme Court would consider the payment of these subsidies on the federal exchange.) Section 1402 reduces certain "cost sharing" fees that insurance companies charge customers, such as deductibles and copays. Congress approached these sections differently. The legislative branch funded Section 1401 through what is known as a permanent appropriation, to ensure that the subsidies will always flow. Congress, however, did not create a separate appropriation for Section 1402 in the ACA. Each year it would require a new line item in the budget. In its fiscal year 2014 budget, the Centers for Medicaid and Medicare Services specifically requested $1.4 billion "for carrying out . . . Section 1402."[72] The Department of Health and Human Services explained in its budget justification for fiscal year 2014 that it required a new "annually appropriated" account for the 1402 program, totaling $1.4 billion.[73]

However, the administration realized there was a problem seeking this funding through an annual appropriation. Due to the sequestration that was in effect for fiscal year 2014, non-defense mandatory programs were cut by 7.2%.[74] (Due to the budget deal reached after the shutdown in the fall of 2013, the sequestration was ultimately rescinded.) As a result, insurers would only receive 93 cents on the dollar for their Section 1402 cost-sharing subsidies. During an April 2013 appropriations subcommittee meeting, Senator Patty Murray (D-WA) noted that the cost-sharing subsidies "appear to be subject to sequestration."[75] She asked, "How will sequestration affect the ability [of insurance companies] to protect lower income people from high out-of-pocket costs

---

[71] Lauren French & Josh Gerstein, *House Files Obamacare Lawsuit* POLITICO (Nov. 21, 2014), perma.cc/XNC4-SBRN.

[72] Office of Mgmt. & Budget, Fiscal Year 2014 Budget of the U.S. Government, App. at 448 (Apr. 10, 2013), bit.ly/22E5dwt.

[73] HHS, Fiscal Year 2014, CMS, Justification of Estimates for Appropriations Committees, at 2, 4, 7, 183-84, bit.ly/1WzOGtH

[74] *Frequently Asked Questions about Sequestration*, HOUSE COMMITTEE ON THE BUDGET, perma.cc/57Q9-L6MK.

[75] Subcommittee of the Committee on Appropriations (Apr. 24, 2013), perma.cc/Q5WZ-EVYY.

at the point of service." The agency representative responded, "We share your concern about the potential adverse impacts of the payment cuts mandated by sequestration." This suggests the government understood, at that point at least, that the appropriation for Section 1402 would be subject to sequestration.

The House of Representative's Ways & Means Committee conducted a deposition of David Fisher, who served as the Internal Revenue Service's Chief Risk Officer.[76] Fisher explained that during the "fall of 2013" he became aware that there was "a little confusion about the funding source for the cost-sharing program, as to whether or not that source was going to be subject to sequester." The IRS's "original understanding," Fisher explained, "was that these funds were going to be appropriated funds and, therefore, subject to the sequester." But there was a "shift" and it became clear that . . . the intent was to use the permanent appropriation to pay the cost-sharing reduction payments." This decision, Fisher said, raised "some confusion and concern . . . from an audit standpoint," because auditors had to be "able to trace these payments all the way back to the source." The chief risk officer explained in his deposition that this decision was personally approved by the attorney general, the secretary of the treasury, and the commissioner of the Internal Revenue Service. Fisher "was in the dissent," because he saw "some risk to making these payments."

In July 2013, the Senate Democrats *denied* the Obama administration's request for an annual appropriation for Section 1402.[77] Note that this is not the usual case of Republicans blocking Obamacare payments to insurance companies. The Committee on Appropriations for the Departments of Health and Human Services, chaired by Senator Tom Harkin (D-IA), rejected the Obama administration's funding request.

This strange decision raised red flags for Senate Republicans. After President Obama nominated Sylvia Matthews Burwell to replace Kathleen Sebelius as HHS Secretary, Senators Ted Cruz and Mike Lee inquired about the government's changed position.[78] The Office of Management and Budget – which Burwell previously headed – had determined in 2013 that the Section 1402 payments were subject to sequestration. However, in

---

[76] *Deposition of David Fisher*, COMMITTEE ON WAYS AND MEANS (May 11, 2016), bit.ly/2oYvELR. Carl Huse, *In a Secret Meeting, Revelations on the Battle over Health Care*, N.Y. TIMES (May 30, 2016), nyti.ms/296raRl. *See* Josh Blackman, *The History of the Section 1402 Payments in House of Representatives v. Burwell*, JOSH BLACKMAN'S BLOG (May 25, 2016), perma.cc/6B9C-KFM4.

[77] Committee on Appropriations Report at 123 (July 11, 2013), bit.ly/1U3Z3n7.

[78] Letter from Sylvia M. Burwell, Dir., OMB, to Senators Ted Cruz and Michael Lee, at p. 4 (May 21, 2014), bit.ly/1UjXcXx.

2014 "OMB changed its position to exempt these cost-sharing subsidies from the sequester." What "legal authority," the senators asked, allowed OMB to "take such action"? Burwell replied that the decision was made "to improve the efficiency in the administration of the subsidy payments." Now the payments would be made "out of the same account" for the Section 1401 premium tax credit portions, which was "not subject to sequestration." This was an admission she was using the permanent appropriation for Section 1401 for the Section 1402 payments.

It appears the Democrats were attempting to solve one problem – ensuring the insurance companies received 100% of the funding they were due. But in the process they created a much more severe problem – spending billions of dollars without an appropriation. The House deemed this spending illegal. Article I of the Constitution provides that "no Money shall be drawn from the Treasury, but in Consequence of Appropriations made by Law." No appropriation, no money.

In Turley's lawsuit filed in November, the House added the allegation that the Obama administration was spending funds that were never appropriated, thereby clipping Congress's power of the purse. This claim was far more potent than the challenge to the employer mandate's delay because (1) it would not become moot in 2016 and (2) the court would not have to *force* the president to implement the mandate. Rather, the remedy here is for the president to stop spending money Congress never gave him. In hindsight, this was a prudent decision, because the employer mandate claim was promptly dismissed by the district court.

Even if the House was correct on the merits – and the president was illegally spending billions of dollars – once again the biggest hurdle was standing. The Justice Department's first line of defense for the Section 1402 funding was the same they employed against Senator Johnson and West Virginia: The House of Representatives was not injured by the payments, so it could not sue. No court had ever before held that the House of Representatives, as a body, could sue the executive branch for alleged violations of the appropriations clause of Article I. These expenditures, the Justice Department argued, did not inflict an injury on the House, so there was no case or controversy for the court to hear. However, Judge Collyer observed that no court had ever held that the House of Representatives *could not* bring suit. "There is no authority that answers the question" on either side of the case, she noted.[79] It was *unprecedented.*

---

[79] United States House of Representatives v. Burwell, 130 F. Supp. 3d 53, 66 (D.D.C. 2015).

The most relevant precedent was *Raines v. Byrd*.[80] The Supreme Court's 1997 decision found that individual members of Congress could not challenge the constitutionality of the Line Item Veto Act. In *Raines*, Justice John Paul Stevens "attach[ed] some importance to the fact that [the members] have not been authorized to represent their respective Houses of Congress in this action, and indeed both Houses actively oppose[d] their suit." That "the plaintiff here is the House of Representatives," Judge Collyer wrote, "distinguishes this case" from *Raines*. The novelty of the case left open the question of whether the House should have standing.

In ruling for the House, Judge Collyer developed what she referred to as a "non-appropriation" theory of standing. For generalized political grievances – such as over the interpretation of a statute – the court found that the House would lack standing. As a result, the House could not raise a challenge to the implementation of the ACA's employer mandate. However, when the House asserts that the executive branch is spending money that the legislative branch had never appropriated, Collyer determined, the president has inflicted a constitutional injury on the power of the purse. In *Federalist* No. 58, James Madison wrote that "this power over the purse may, in fact, be regarded as the most complete and effectual weapon" of Congress to check the executive branch. If Congress "specifically denies funding and the Executive simply finds money elsewhere without consequence," Judge Collyer wrote, then the Legislature "cannot fulfill its constitutional role." Disregarding Congress's spending power, she concluded, "inflict[s] a concrete, particular harm" that gives the House standing to sue. Where Senator Johnson and West Virginia failed to challenge the president's unconstitutional executive actions, the House crossed the standing threshold.

After the court denied the government's motion to dismiss for a lack of standing, the Justice Department requested an interlocutory appeal. Through this procedure, the government wanted to immediately appeal the district court's decision finding that the House had standing. The government did not want the district court to proceed to determine whether in fact the Section 1402 payments were illegal. In a move that surprised many experts, Judge Collyer denied the request for an interlocutory appeal. She announced that she could resolve the entire case "in a matter of months – likely before an interlocutory appeal could even be decided."[81] Collyer reasoned that by moving forward, the parties would be able to appeal both the standing issue and the constitutional

[80] 521 U.S. 811 (1997).
[81] Lisa Schencker, *Obama Loses Another Round in House Republicans' ACA Lawsuit*, MOD. HEALTHCARE (Oct. 20, 2015), perma.cc/T4D9-NTK5.

issue in one case. Of course, the government would much rather win on standing, so they would not have had to defend what by all accounts appeared to be spending money without an appropriation. Judge Collyer's denial of the interlocutory appeal shifted that burden to the Justice Department – a burden they never had to shoulder in Senator Johnson or West Virginia's case.

23.9. "you can't just shake your head and say no"

During an earlier hearing on standing, Judge Collyer expressed her frustration with the government's unwillingness to defend its actions.[82] She chided the Justice Department lawyer, "You can't just shake your head and say no, no, I don't have to answer that question." When he bobbed and weaved, Collyer charged: "This is the problem I have with your brief: It's not direct. It's just not direct. You have to address the argument that [the House] makes and you haven't."

Once the court found standing, the Obama administration was required to defend its spending – and it did not go well. In May 2016, Judge Collyer issued her second decision in the case, ruling that the executive branch had illegally spent billions of dollars under Section 1402, in violation of the Constitution's appropriations clause.[83] The Justice Department offered three primary defenses. First, the government explained that Section 1401's permanent appropriation could be read to also fund Section 1402 – even though there was absolutely no reference to Section 1402. Judge Collyer held that the government's textualist argument "is a most curious and convoluted argument, whose mother was undoubtedly necessity." In other words, the creative lawyers at the Justice Department made a textualist argument because they had to say something in court.

Second, the government argued that the appropriation from Section 1401 can be understood to also cover Section 1402, because the two policies are "economically and programmatically integrated." That is, the two provisions worked in tandem to ensure premiums under the ACA remained affordable. The court disagreed, finding that "an appropriation must be expressly stated; it cannot be inferred or implied." Congress does not "squeeze the elephant of Section 1402 reimbursements into the mousehole of Section 1401." Billions of dollars in spending are not left to implication. Even assuming the two policies are connected, this argument does not work, the court concluded.

---

[82] U.S. House of Rep. v. Burwell, No. CV 14–1967, 2016 WL 2750934 (D.D.C. May 12, 2016).
[83] *Id.*

Third, HHS warned that blocking payments to insurance companies would "yield absurd economic, fiscal, and healthcare-policy results." Judge Collyer dispatched this argument, finding that the "results predicted by the [government] flow not from the ACA," or the court's interpretation of the law, "but from Congress' subsequent refusal to appropriate money." If Congress does not want the government to pay insurance companies for losses suffered because of the ACA, the court concluded, "that is Congress's prerogative; the Court cannot override it by rewriting" the ACA. Judge Collyer ruled that paying the Section 1402 subsidies based on the 1401 appropriation "violates the Constitution. Congress is the only source for such an appropriation, and no public money can be spent without one."

Hours after Judge Collyer's decision, White House press secretary Josh Earnest referred to the case as an "unprecedented ... political fight in the court system." Never before, he said, has Congress "been permitted to sue the executive branch over a disagreement about how to interpret a statute." He noted that Republicans have "been losing this fight for six years. And they'll lose it again." House Speaker Paul Ryan, who had replaced John Boehner in October 2015, praised the decision. "The court ruled that the administration overreached by spending taxpayer money without approval from the people's representatives," he said. "Here, the executive branch is being held accountable to *we the people*." Boehner, enjoying his retirement, felt vindicated: "The president of the United States is not a king or a monarch, with the ability to single-handedly create or change the laws of our country." Jonathan Turley celebrated the decision: "The historic ruling reaffirms the foundational power of the purse that was given to the legislative branch by the Framers." The *Wall Street Journal* predicted that the case would be appealed to the D.C. Circuit, "which Harry Reid and Mr. Obama have packed with liberals precisely to defend his power grabs."[84]

23.10. "BAD BEHAVIOR ALL AROUND"

During oral arguments before the D.C. Circuit in West Virginia's challenge to the administrative fix, Judge Laurence H. Silberman wondered aloud whether the government took the action it did knowing that no court could stop it.[85] He asked the Justice Department attorney, "When the government took the

---

[84] *Vindicating Congress's Power of the Purse*, WALL ST. J. (May 12, 2016), on.wsj.com/1OTPnLQ.

[85] Six year earlier, the Reagan appointee upheld the constitutionality of the individual mandate as a valid exercise of Congress's commerce powers. *See* Seven-Sky v. Holder, 661 F.3d 1 (D.C. Cir. 2011).

action it took, did it think that no one would have standing to challenge it?" The government lawyer responded, "To my knowledge, that inquiry was not undertaken, your honor." Silberman's question was perhaps inspired by the series of dubious executive actions taken by the federal government during the implementation of the ACA. In each instance – the OPM fix, the administrative fix, the employer mandate delay, and the 1402 payments – the government's only meaningful defense was that it could not be sued. Once the standing shield is peeled away, courts can easily dissect the government's shaky case.

In his decision dismissing Senator Johnson's suit for lack of standing, Judge Griesbach expressed deep concern about the legality of the OPM fix. Taking the allegations "as true," he wrote, the "executive branch has rewritten a key provision of the ACA so as to render it essentially meaningless in order to save members of Congress and their staffs from the consequences of a controversial law that will affect millions of citizens." Allowing the administration to rewrite the law and not enforce other requirements, he wrote, "would be a violation of Article I of the Constitution, which reposes the lawmaking power in the legislative branch." Although the scope of the change is minor, Griesbach concluded, "the violation alleged is not a mere technicality." But because there was no standing, the case could not proceed.

During the oral arguments in West Virginia's constitutional challenge, Judge Brett Kavanaugh expressed doubts about the government's case.[86] Under the administrative fix, he said, "certain critical reforms ... were unilaterally suspended by the executive branch." In effect, Kavanaugh explained, the ACA "mandates certain things," and the government said, "we are not going to enforce those, despite the mandatory statute." However, he doubted that anyone was injured. "Who would have standing in this case to challenge the alleged non-enforcement of the statute?" he asked. The Justice Department lawyer responded, "I don't know, your honor. We are not currently aware of any party that could sue." Kavanaugh pushed further and asked, "Who has

---

[86] Judge Kavanaugh has had a healthy diet of Obamacare cases. In 2011, Kavanaugh was on the same panel as Judge Silberman in Seven-Sky v. Holder. Judge Kavanaugh declined to rule on the constitutionality of the ACA, finding that the case was not yet ripe for review because the individual mandate tax had not yet gone into effect. 661 F.3d 1, 21 (D.C. Cir. 2011) (Kavanaugh, J., dissenting); *See* JOSH BLACKMAN, UNPRECEDENTED: THE CONSTITUTIONAL CHALLENGE TO OBAMACARE 152–158 (2013). Kavanaugh also wrote the dissent from the denial of rehearing en banc in Sissel v. HHS, the origination clause case discussed earlier this chapter. 799 F.3d 1035, 1049 (D.C. Cir. 2015) (Kavanaugh, J., dissenting). Finally, Judge Kavanaugh dissented from denial of rehearing en banc of the panel decision in Priests for Life v. HHS, which upheld the accommodation to the ACA's contraception mandate. 808 F.3d 1, 14 (D.C. Cir. 2015) (Kavanaugh, J., dissenting). He would also join the majority opinion in West Virginia v. HHS, 2016 WL 3568089 (D.C. Cir. 2016).

standing among the citizenry to challenge the failure of the government to enforce the statute against private parties?" The government lawyer responded, "We're not currently aware of any citizen who has been harmed in the necessary way, and can bring those allegations." That is exactly the point – when the president fails to enforce onerous mandates, burdens are alleviated, not imposed. When the court dismisses the case on standing grounds, these constitutional doubts will go unanswered. However, once Judge Collyer found standing, the Obama administration's defense of the Section 1402 payments collapsed like a house of cards.

Conservatives have long advocated for a rigorous standing doctrine as a means to prevent "activist" courts from interfering with the democratic process. In 1983, then-Judge Antonin Scalia viewed standing as "a crucial and inseparable element of the separation of powers."[87] He wrote that making it harder for plaintiffs to bring constitutional challenges in federal court would reduce the "overjudicialization of the processes of self-governance." The late Justice's approach to standing is sound in theory, but risky in fact. In recent years, rather than protecting the separation of powers, the standing doctrine has served to insulate presidents who engage in highly questionable executive actions. Cramped standing doctrines allow abuses of presidential power to continue without any scrutiny. Government lawyers can simply walk into court and literally shake their heads "no."

Shortly after Judge Collyer's decision, law professors Jonathan Adler and Nicholas Bagley engaged in a Twitter dialectic about constitutional violations that inflict no injuries.[88] They both agreed that the House lacks standing to sue the executive branch, and both agreed that the payments by the executive branch were illegal. So what should be done when the president is violating the law, without any credible defense, but no one can sue to stop it?

> *@JAdler1969*: If wide agreement on merits, shouldn't admin follow law regardless?
>
> *@Nicholas_Bagley*: I don't mean to cop out, though. Yes, the executive should adhere to the law.
>
> *@Nicholas_Bagley*: But legal compliance is perfect for no president. There are other imperatives, too.

[87] Antonin Scalia, *The Doctrine of Standing as an Essential Element of the Separation of Powers*, 17 SUFFOLK L. REV. 881 (1983).

[88] Jonathan Adler (@jadler1969) & Nicholas Bagley (@nicholas_bagley), TWITTER (May 14, 2016), bit.ly/25amLls. *See* Nicholas Bagley, *Did the Court Get It Right in House v. Burwell?*, NOTICE & COMMENT BLOG (Jun. 2, 2016), perma.cc/EBY8-89EZ.

@*JAdler1969*: "other imperatives"?! Sounds like the Bush Administration.

@ *JAdler1969*: If administration had colorable argument, that would be one thing, but it doesn't

@*Nicholas_Bagley*: Yeah, I'm pretty much with you on all that. Bad behavior all around.

If the president could spend money without an appropriation, Judge Collyer observed, our "constitutional structure would collapse, and the role of the House would be meaningless."[89] Critically, a House lawyer told me, "Congress can't very well use its power of the purse as an alternative to judicial relief in such a case because it's the purse power that's been taken." This long train of abuses warrants a reconsideration of the bounds of the standing doctrine in separation of powers cases.

---

[89] Josh Blackman, *The House Stands Up to Unconstitutional Obamacare Payments*, NAT'L. REV. (May 13, 2016), perma.cc/Q4ZU-DTH9.

PART VII

Subsidizing Obamacare (November 22, 2014–June 26, 2015)

24

#GruberGate

On Thursday, July 24, 2014 – two days after *Halbig* and *King* were decided – Rich Weinstein posted a comment on the *Volokh Conspiracy* blog.[1] It was the sort of all-caps missive about Obamacare that Internet readers had learned to skip over – a fate Weinstein knew all too well. It read:

EVERYONE PLEASE TAKE JUST ONE MINUTE TO WATCH THIS VIDEO.

This is a video of Dr. Jonathan Gruber, MIT. Dr. Gruber was a key part of Romneycare and was brought in byt he [*sic*] Admin to help write the ACA. He's considered an "architect" of the ACA.

Just watch this from 31:30–32:30. Just watch that 1 minute then decide for yourself. Then pass this along to anyone and everyone that cares about this topic.

This was no wording glitch. The law was intentionally written this way.

Weinstein added a link to a YouTube video of MIT economist Jonathan Gruber speaking at the Noblis Innovation Collaboration Center in January 2012.[2] Gruber is asked, "You mentioned the health insurance exchanges for the states, and it is my understanding that if states don't provide them, then the federal government will provide them for the states." His answer rocked the legal world:

---

[1] Ilya Somin, *Why the D.C. Circuit's Interpretation of the ACA in Halbig v. Burwell Is Far from "Absurd,"* WASH. POST (July 24, 2014), perma.cc/8LVE-6HSJ. A copy of the comment thread is available at bit.ly/22FzQ35.

[2] *Jonathan Gruber at Noblis – January 18, 2012,* YOUTUBE (Jan. 20, 2012), bit.ly/1ULteQU.

In the law, it says if the states don't provide them, the federal backstop will. The federal government has been sort of slow in putting out its backstop, I think partly because they want to sort of squeeze the states to do it. *I think what's important to remember politically about this, is if you're a state and you don't set up an Exchange, that means your citizens don't get their tax credits.* But your citizens still pay the taxes that support this bill. So you're essentially saying to your citizens, you're going to pay all the taxes to help all the other states in the country. I hope that's a blatant enough political reality that states will get their act together and realize there are billions of dollars at stake here in setting up these Exchanges, and that they'll do it. But you know, once again, the politics can get ugly around this.

Jonathan Gruber, looking at the camera, had unequivocally articulated the theory of Section 36B that Case Western professor Jonathan Adler and Cato Institute scholar Michael Cannon had been preaching for two years. The evidence the challengers had been searching for was unearthed. This was the face that launched a thousand YouTube clips.

Who the heck is Rich Weinstein? "I'm a nobody," the mustachioed Philadelphian joked. "I'm the guy who lives in his mom's basement wearing a tinfoil hat."[3] (He's actually a hatless investment adviser who moved out a long time ago.) Weinstein's citizen journalism began in late 2013 after his insurance policy was cancelled. "You can understand that when I lost my own plan," he recalled, "and the replacement cost twice as much, I wasn't happy."[4] "When the President said, 'If you like your plan, you can keep your plan,' I believed that just like everybody else."[5] Upset with President Obama for not keeping his promise, Weinstein decided to investigate the "paper trail" of the so-called "architects" of the ACA. This included Dr. Jonathan Gruber, economist at the Massachusetts Institute of Technology and adviser to the Obama administration.

Later in the day on July 24, Ryan Radia of the Competitive Enterprise Institute (CEI) was "perusing the comment section of the *Volokh Conspiracy*," when he noticed a "buried comment with a link by Rich Weinstein."[6] It was fate, as CEI had been coordinating and funding the *Halbig* and *King* litigation since the outset. Radia shared the video at the *CEI* blog. "Obamacare architect admitted in 2012 states without exchanges lose subsidies," the post beamed.

---

3   David Weigel, *Investment Advisor Who's Humiliating the Administration Over Obamacare*, BLOOMBERG POLITICS (Nov. 11, 2014), perma.cc/HN2E-7UVM.
4   *Id.*
5   Sharyl Atkisson, *For the First Time on Camera, Meet the Man Who Exposes the Gruber Videos*, The DAILY SIGNAL (Mar. 2, 2015), perma.cc/2TKM-42P2.
6   WALL ST. J., *ObamaCare's Insider Testimony*, (July 28. 2014), on.wsj.com/1PNHm5N.

Radia added, "Props to *Volokh Conspiracy* commenter Rich Weinstein for bringing this video to my attention."[7] From there, the video went viral and forever altered the debate about Section 36B.

At 4:00 AM on Friday, the Cato Institute's Michael Cannon revealed the discovery of his holy grail. "Gruber doesn't just acknowledge the conditional feature of the ACA's tax credits. He also supplies a plausible purpose for that feature (there were people in Washington who either wanted to 'squeeze the states to do it,' or saw the law as directing them to do so)." Cannon also delighted in the fact that in January 2013, Gruber told the progressive magazine *Mother Jones* that Cannon's ideas were a "screwy interpretation," "nutty," and "stupid."[8] Gruber had also told *MSNBC*'s Chris Matthews that Section 36B was "unambiguously ... a typo."[9] In an amicus brief to the D.C. Circuit in *Halbig*, Gruber called the challengers' argument "implausible."[10] Cannon now firmly believed that his theory could no longer be described as implausible. Agreeing emphatically with Gruber's 2012 statement, Cannon demurred, "I couldn't have said it better myself."

The video continued to reverberate inside the beltway. Robert Pear reported in the *New York Times* that Gruber's "remarks embarrassed the White House."[11] White House Press Secretary Josh Earnest dismissed the relevance of the video. "I think that he described those remarks as a mistake."[12] Kevin Drum explained in *Mother Jones*, "The fact that he bollixed an audience question two years after the law's passage doesn't mean much. It's a nice gotcha moment, but probably not much else."[13]

The next day, Weinstein recalled that he "woke up and turned on [his] iPad," and saw the extensive coverage of the video.[14] "'Holy crap, what is going on?', he exclaimed. It just kept getting bigger and bigger."[15] When he heard

---

7 Ryan Radia, *Obamacare Architect Admitted in 2012 States without Exchanges Lose Subsides*, COMPETITIVE ENTERPRISE INST. (July 24, 2014), perma.cc/6QAL-V93N.

8 Erika Eichelberger, *Conservatives Insist Obamacare Is on Its Death Bed*, MOTHER JONES (Jan. 24, 2013), perma.cc/2XBU-WBVR.

9 Chris Matthews, *'Hardball with Chris Matthews' for Tuesday, July 22nd, 2014*, NBC NEWS (July 22, 2014), perma.cc/JFU4-JBWW.

10 Brief Amici Curiae for Economic Scholars in support of Appellees at 13, Halbig v. Sebelius, No. 14-5018 (D.D.C. 2014), bit.ly/1WjAtkA.

11 Robert Pear and Peter Baker, *Ex-Obama Aide's Statements in 2012 Clash with Health Act Stance*, N.Y. TIMES (July 25, 2014), nyti.ms/1TkkTBT.

12 Press Briefing by Press Secretary Josh Earnest, White House (Jul. 25, 2014), perma.cc/CPH9-Z4SL.

13 Kevin Drum, *Did Congress Actually Intend to Withhold Subsidies from Federal Exchanges?*, MOTHER JONES (July 25, 2014), perma.cc/U9EG-G3Y2.

14 Weigel, *supra* note 3.

15 *Id.*

that the White House press secretary commented, he said, "What do you mean, the White House is responding?"[16] That evening at 9:41 PM, Weinstein wrote a response to Radia at the *Volokh Conspiracy* comment thread. "Holy crap. This is crazy. I've had this video for over 7 months and nobody would take my calls ... I have more." As Weinstein would continue to unearth several more Gruber videos, the exposé evolved into a hashtag: #GruberGate.

24.2. "SPEAK-O"

In Jonathan Gruber's own mind, he is an ACA superhero. So much so that in 2011 the economist published a comic book portraying himself as a cape-less crusader of health care reform.[17] Seriously. The saga begins with a comic-book-styled-Gruber beaming over Governor Mitt Romney. The caption reads, "I was part of the team that came up with the reform that changed the way Massachusetts handles medical coverage for the uninsured." In the next frame, Gruber is standing in the Oval Office, peering over the president sitting at the Resolute desk: "And I worked with both President Obama and the Congress to translate that reform to the national stage." In the next frame, there is a close-up Gruber winking: "So I've got a little experience in this area."

The reality was only slightly less pulpy than Gruber's fiction. A 2012 profile in the *New York Times* feted Gruber as a "numbers wizard at M.I.T." who "spent decades modeling the intricacies of the health care ecosystem."[18] He "had helped Mitt Romney overhaul health insurance when he was the Massachusetts governor." After "Massachusetts, California came calling. So did Connecticut, Delaware, Kansas, Minnesota, Oregon, Wisconsin and Wyoming." But "[t]hen came the call in 2008 from President-elect Obama's transition team, the one that officially turned this stay-at-home economics professor into Mr. Mandate."[19]

The article explained that, "After Mr. Gruber helped the administration put together the basic principles of the proposal, the White House lent him to Capitol Hill to help Congressional staff members draft the specifics of the legislation."[20] In March 2010, Gruber bragged, without qualification, "I helped write the federal bill as well, I was a paid consultant to the Obama

---

[16] *Id.*

[17] JONATHAN GRUBER, HEALTH CARE REFORM: WHAT IT IS, WHY IT'S NECESSARY, HOW IT WORKS (2011).

[18] Catherine Rampell, *Academic Built Case for Mandate in Health Care Law*, N. Y. TIMES (Mar. 28, 2012), nyti.ms/1Q51FOn.

[19] *Id.*

[20] *Id.*

Administration to help develop the technical details of the bill, so I come to you with my biases."[21] "I know more about this law than any other economist," he boasted.

In 2012, Sarah Kliff, then of the *Washington Post*, tweeted "Jon Gruber, the health economist who pretty much wrote Obamacare, owns 8 parrots. That is all."[22] In the *Times* profile, Gruber was photographed with his cockatoo Phoebe perched on his shoulder, both puffing up their feathers.

On Friday morning, after Weinstein's discovery went viral, Jonathan Cohn in the *New Republic* offered a statement from Gruber, whom he called "one of the law's best known advocates and architects."[23]

> I honestly don't remember why I said that. I was speaking off-the-cuff. It was just a mistake. People make mistakes. Congress made a mistake drafting the law and I made a mistake talking about it. But there was never any intention to literally withhold money, to withhold tax credits, from the states that didn't take that step. That's clear in the intent of the law and if you talk to anybody who worked on the law. My subsequent statement was just a *speak-o* – you know, like a *typo*.

Ironically, Gruber described his comment the same way he described Section 36B: a "typo." (If indeed Section 36B was a *typo*, then the courts would be unable to fix it). Cohn praised the "good reporting and sleuthing by Radia and Weinstein," but could not "speak to what Gruber was thinking at the time." The sleuthing had only just started – another video would soon be uncovered.

Later that day, Cohn added an update to his article. "John Sexton of *Breitbart* has an audio recording of Gruber saying the same thing – also in January, 2012, but at a different venue." During a speech at the Jewish Community Center of San Francisco, Gruber said, that "by not setting up an exchange, the politicians of a state are costing state residents hundreds and millions and billions of dollars ... That is really the ultimate threat, [that] people understand that, gee, if your governor doesn't set up an exchange, you're losing hundreds of millions of dollars of tax credits to be delivered to your citizens." Sexton noted, "Gruber can continue to claim he was wrong but it becomes harder to explain this as the equivalent of a typo when he said it more than once."

[21] Health Care Reform, *Gruber: "I Helped Write the Bill,"* C-SPAN (Mar. 11, 2010), cs.pn/1VHwBGe.

[22] @SarahKliff, TWITTER (Mar. 29, 2012), bit.ly/1T6luGw.

[23] Jonathan Cohn, *John Gruber: 'It Was Just a Mistake'*, NEW REPUBLIC (July 25, 2014), perma.cc/LE7T-528B.

24.3. "ONLY IN STATES THAT COMPLIED WITH FEDERAL REQUIREMENTS"

Timothy S. Jost, a Washington and Lee University law professor and longtime supporter of the ACA, defended Gruber. "What I think he meant," Jost told the *Wall Street Journal*, "was that at that point in 2012 it wasn't clear whether the federal exchange would be up and running in 2014, so that if you as a state want to make sure that people in your state get premium tax credits, you'll be safer if you set up a state exchange."[24] But Jost himself wrote about an idea similar to Gruber's *speak-o* in a 2009 article titled "State-Run Programs Are Not a Viable Option for Creating a Public Plan."[25] The thrust of the article was that Congress could not depend on the states to implement health care reform – he was right about that. Jost proposed several approaches for the federal government to leverage or nudge states toward expanding access to health insurance.

Jost's second proposal was for the federal government to "offer income-adjusted subsidies for the purchase of health insurance, but *only* in states that implemented a state public plan option." He added that there are "many precedents for the use of the spending power to secure state compliance with federal requirements, most notably the Medicaid and CHIP programs." Jost's third proposal was that "[t]ax credits could be offered to subsidize the purchase of insurance, but *only* in states that implemented a public program." Again, the author noted that "[t]his was the approach used in implementing the health savings accounts tax subsidies offered by the Medicare Modernization Act."

Jost repeated similar proposals in an article titled "Health Insurance: Legal Issues," published by Georgetown University and the O'Neill Institute.[26] Under a section titled "Federalism Issues," Jost wrote that Congress "could exercise its Constitutional authority to spend money for the public welfare (the 'spending power'), either by offering tax subsidies for insurance *only* in states that complied with federal requirements (as it has done with respect to tax subsidies for health savings accounts) or by offering explicit payments to states that establish exchanges conforming to federal requirements." In their brief to the D.C. Circuit, Michael Carvin and his associates wrote that

---

[24] Louise Radnofsky and Brent Kendall, *Health Law Architect's Taped Remarks Fuel Subsidy Debate*, WALL ST. J. (July 25, 2014), on.wsj.com/2oXytMo.

[25] Timothy S. Jost, *State-Run Programs Are Not a Viable Option for Creating a Public Plan* (June 16, 2009), bit.ly/1QgBRAi.

[26] Timothy S. Jost, *Health Insurance Exchanges: Legal Issues* (O'NEILL INST. GEORGETOWN UNIV. LEGAL CTR., no. 23), (2009), bit.ly/1TyvoxY.

"the Senate Committees working on ACA legislation took up Professor Jost's suggestion."

Jost vigorously rejects this assertion. He refers to the article as an "obscure working paper" in which he "lay[s] out several alternatives through which Congress could encourage the states to establish exchanges, one of which was to limit the availability of tax credits to states that operate exchanges."[27] Jost writes that Congress adopted another one of his suggestions: create a fallback federal exchange if states failed to establish one. However, he notes that there was "no evidence in the voluminous records of debates on the ACA" that any-one adopted his idea of withholding subsidies for states that did not comply with federal requirements. In other words, the professor admitted, no one paid any attention to his ideas.

Michigan law professor Nicholas Bagley agreed and told me that "nobody actually took that idea seriously. Nobody called him up. Nobody said, 'That's how we're going to do it.'" In his dissent in *Halbig*, Judge Edwards referenced Jost's paper and observed, "There is no evidence, however, that anyone in Congress read, cited, or relied on this article." Similarly, in its brief to the Supreme Court, the solicitor general dismissed any reliance on Jost's paper, noting that "there is no indication any Member of Congress saw that paper."

24.4. "HALBIG TRUTHERS"

Sharyl Attkisson, of the conservative *Daily Signal*, interviewed Rich Weinstein. She asked about the media's coverage of the ACA in light of their failure to find the Gruber videos first. "It's pretty disappointing,"[28] he lamented. "The media just has not had any intellectual curiosity. The videos are out there in plain sight. I didn't do anything special to find them. I used, what's that thing called?" He snapped his fingers. "Google." With a smile, the citizen journalist quipped, "My iPad was smoking there for a while."[29]

Weinstein discovered the video in December 2013, but no one was inter-ested. He tried sending messages to *Fox News*, *Forbes*, *National Review*, and Glenn Beck, but nobody called him back. "It was so frustrating," Weinstein recalled.[30] "I tried really hard to give this to the media. I had this and couldn't get it to anybody that knows what to do with it."

---

[27] Michael F. Cannon, *The Halbig Cases: Timothy Jost Responds (Guest Post)*, FORBES (July 14, 2014), onforb.es/276r578.

[28] Atkinson, *supra* note 5.

[29] *Id.*

[30] Howard Kutz, *He Found the Jonathan Gruber Videos – and No Media Outlet Would Call Him Back*, FOX NEWS (Nov. 20, 2014), perma.cc/A4PY-93LN.

Fox News media analyst Howard Kurtz praised his gumption: "Few news organizations could afford to have a reporter spend a long period searching for a needle in an online haystack, especially without a tip that the needle existed at all." But once the needle was found, the conservative and libertarian media embraced the story. Weinstein recalled that after his video went viral, "a friend told me that Rush Limbaugh was talking about this video. I'm at WaWa, and I'm eating a sandwich in the car, and Limbaugh comes back from commercial and says 'There's more on this Gruber video.'" He told me that he was ecstatic.

Weinstein's discovery also reshaped the narrative about the case. Peter Suderman at the libertarian *Reason* concluded, "Either Gruber, a key influence on the legislation who wrote part of the law and who consulted with multiple states on setting up their own exchanges, was correct, and the law explicitly limits subsidies to state-run exchanges. Or he was wrong in a way that perfectly aligns with both the clear text of the legislation and the argument later made by the challengers to the IRS rule allowing subsidies in federal exchanges."[31] Megan McArdle, who writes a libertarianish column at *Bloomberg View*, wrote: "Gruber, one of the law's architects, clearly had an understanding of the provision that liberals now say no one shared."[32] This was "the closest thing we're going to get to a smoking gun." Phillip A. Klein at the conservative *Washington Examiner* stated that "this is nothing short of a bombshell. Liberals have launched a campaign to discredit anybody advancing the idea that subsidies were only available to state-based exchanges as alternately dishonest, ignorant or insane. But now there's video evidence of the left's go-to expert on the law taking the same view."[33]

Brian Beutler, an ACA supporter, took a different tack in the *New Republic*. "What's become incredibly frustrating to me about the *Halbig* brouhaha in the last few days," he wrote, "is watching the conservative health care writers who were in the same trenches watching the same debate unfold – attempting, from a very skeptical vantage point, to explain the bill correctly – suddenly turn around and vouchsafe the *Halbig* Truthers."[34] Beutler had taken to calling those who believed the Adler/Cannon theory "Truthers," as a reference to conspiracy theorists who believe 9/11 was a cover-up; not to be confused

[31] Peter Suderman, *Watch Obamacare Architect Jonathan Gruber Admit in 2013 That Subsidies Were Limited to State-run Exchanges (Updated with Another Admission)*, REASON (July 24, 2014), perma.cc/5EGW-KZ8A.

[32] Megan McArdle, *The Surprise Obamacare Ruling That Wasn't*, BLOOMBERG VIEW (July 25, 2014), perma.cc/L7KS-4C2Q.

[33] Philip Klein, *Obamacare's Architect Took Same View of Subsidies as Legal Challengers He Now Calls 'Nutty'*, WASH. EXAMINER (July 25, 2014), perma.cc/9H4U-4VM6.

[34] Brian Beutler, *Why Are Conservative Health Journalists Covering for Halbig Truthers?*, NEW REPUBLIC (July 29, 2014), perma.cc/AC3T-E62M.

with the "Birthers," who believe that the president was born in Kenya. Beutler faulted the journalists who were endorsing Gruber, as an indictment on the media. It meant that "you and everyone around you failed in the most basic execution of duties as reporters, analysts, government officials and so on." To accept Gruber's statements, Beutler wrote, is to disregard "everyone else" who ridiculed Adler and Cannon. Beutler diminishes Gruber's statement as less a "smoking gun" than a "dribbling water pistol."

Jonathan Chait, also an ACA supporter, added in *New York* magazine, "It is hard to summarize the liberal response to the right's bizarre new revisionism except as the kind of stammering, bug-eyed disbelief that occurs when somebody is forced to defend a factual proposition that everybody knows is true."[35] To believe Gruber's 2012 statement is to disregard reality – as chronicled by their fellow journalists and analysts – and create what Beutler referred to as "an epistemological grey area where none existed." The Trutherism would soon hit much closer to home.

The New Republic's Jonathan Cohn, like Beutler and Chait, has covered the Affordable Care Act thoroughly since its inception, and would identify as a supporter of the law. Two days after Beutler's column, Cohn confessed that he had his own "Obamacare Truther Moment."[36] During a January 12, 2010 appearance on NPR's *Fresh Air*, host Terry Gross asked Cohn what happens if a state "opt[s] out of the exchange?"[37] His answer began, candidly enough. "There is some kind of opt out, and I'll be honest. This is not something I've looked into that closely. Because I don't think it's going to end up in the bill," Cohn continued. Recall that at this point, the Senate bill had passed on Christmas Eve, but Scott Brown had not yet won the special election. Everyone assumed that the Senate bill would be merged with the House bill at conference. More likely than not, the House version – which had a single national exchange – was going to prevail. Therefore, the details of the Senate bill were secondary to securing sixty votes.

Then came Cohn's truther moment, where he suggested that "Ben Nelson" cared about having state-run exchanges. "But you know, basically this I believe was part of the Ben Nelson compromise. Basically, where a state could opt out of the exchanges, I find it hard to believe a state would actually do that." Cohn continued to explain that there is an analogy

---

[35] Jonathan Chait, *The New Secret History of the Obamacare Deniers*, DAILY INTELLIGENCER (July 30, 2014), nym.ag/1QInIhj.

[36] Jonathan Cohn, *My Obamacare Truther Moment*, NEW REPUBLIC (July 31, 2014), bit.ly/2arZx9e.

[37] *Next Up: Turning Two Health Care Bills into One*, 90.9, WBUR (Jan. 12, 2010), perma.cc/9LWC-HA94.

to the strict consequences of states leaving Medicaid. "States can opt out of Medicaid if they want to. They don't because there's a lot of federal money they are entitled to if they participate in Medicaid." In other words, states that do not comply with the federal mandate can lose billions of dollars in funding. Cohn draws the parallel that if a state opts out of the exchange, it would lose that money, and also be "politically responsible" to its citizens for not providing health insurance. "I can't possibly imagine a state opting out of an insurance exchange, given it's a good deal for the state," he said. "And I know a lot of states are nervous about what's going to happen with this, but at the end of the day, I just don't see it happening."

Four years later, Cohn conceded that he "speculate[d] about a mechanism similar to the one that Michael Cannon, Jonathan Adler, and the law's critics have suggested the Senate was trying to create." With admirable candor, he wrote: "I wish I could tell you definitively what I was thinking at the time but, more than four years later, I truly don't know." He added, "I'd be lying if I said that seeing and hearing my own words didn't give me pause. Still, I didn't write the law. I wrote about the law." James Taranto in the *Wall Street Journal* offered an alternate explanation: perhaps the media's lack of inquiry about the challenger's theory was due to motivated reasoning and the in-group bias of Obamacare's press corps: "They and the other journalists they cite are all essentially like-minded on the subject to begin with."[38] Gruber, Jost, and now Cohn shed some light on the "epistemological gray area."

24.5. "THE STUPIDITY OF THE AMERICAN VOTERS"

#GruberGate was not over. In November 2014, another Gruber video surfaced where the professor nonchalantly explained that the "lack of transparency" in enacting the ACA was a "huge political advantage." The "stupidity of the American voters" he said, allowed the law's architects to quietly redistribute wealth from the healthy to the sick.[39]

> This bill was written in a tortured way to make sure [the Congressional Budget Office] did not score the mandate as taxes. If CBO scored the mandate as taxes, the bill dies. Okay? So it's written to do that. In terms of risk-rated subsidies, if you had a law which said healthy people are going to pay in – you made explicit that healthy people pay in and sick people get

---

[38] James Taranto, *Dr. Strangelaw Obamacare Takes Another Darkly Satirical Turn*, WALL ST. J. (July 29, 2014), on.wsj.com/1VHDszq. *See* Miles Hewstone et al., *Intergroup Bias*, 53 ANN. REV. PSYCHOL. 575, 576 (2002).

[39] *AHEC 2013 Conference*, YOUTUBE (Nov. 10, 2014), bit.ly/1rCaNCA.

money – it would not have passed. Okay? Lack of transparency is a huge political advantage.

And basically, you know, call it the stupidity of the American voter or whatever, but basically that was really, really critical to get the thing to pass … Look, I wish Mark was right that we could make it all transparent, but I'd rather have this law than not … Yeah, there are things I wish I could change but I'd rather have this law than not. And I think that involves some trade-offs that we don't prefer as economists but which are realistic.

This statement – far more than the arcane comments about subsidies on the federal exchange – would cause the biggest shockwaves. Gruber, once again, apologized for his remark. On Ronan Farrow's MSNBC show on November 11 (four days after the Supreme Court had granted certiorari in *King*), he confessed: "The comments in the video were made at an academic conference. I was speaking off the cuff, and I basically spoke inappropriately and I regret having made those comments."[40]

Once again, those turned out not to be isolated comments. Gruber made similar remarks in another video that surfaced from a 2013 health care forum at Washington University in St. Louis. He was discussing a proposal by Senator John Kerry (D-MA) to impose a tax on insurance companies rather than taxing Americans directly – knowing full well that the insurance companies would pass the cost onto consumers through higher prices.[41] Gruber explained, "Well that's pretty much the same thing … [but] the American voter is too stupid to understand the difference."

The president quickly moved to distance himself from Gruber. Speaking from the podium at the G20 Conference in Australia, President Obama downplayed the role Gruber played. "I just heard about this. I get well briefed before I come out here. The fact that some adviser who never worked on our staff expressed an opinion that I completely disagree with in terms of the voters is no reflection on the actual process that was run."[42] When Rich Weinstein heard that the president was responding to videos he located, he said it was a "surreal moment. I'm just a regular guy."[43]

The president severely downplayed the role the MIT economist played in his administration. In 2009, HHS contracted with Gruber to provide "technical

[40] Louis Jacobson, *Nancy Pelosi Says She Doesn't Know who Jonathan Gruber Is*, PolitiFact (Nov. 13, 2014), perma.cc/5KKK-Z4MK.
[41] Jerry Diamond, *Obamacare: Voters, Are You Stupid?*, CNN Politics (Nov. 18, 2014), perma.cc/YB3P-FWV7.
[42] *Remarks by President Obama at G20 Press Conference* (Nov. 16, 2014), perma.cc/BD9M-NK8C.
[43] Atkisson, *supra* note 5.

assistance in evaluating options for national healthcare reform."[44] He was chosen as a "sole source" – meaning no one else would be considered – because he "developed a proprietary statistically sophisticated micro-simulation model that has the flexibility to ascertain the distribution of changes in health care spending and public and private health sector costs." Gruber was paid nearly $400,000 for his work.[45]

According to a 2015 report by Stephanie Armour in the *Wall Street Journal*, Gruber "worked [even] more closely than previously known with the White House and top federal officials to shape the law."[46] E-mails released by the House Oversight Committee "show frequent consultations between Mr. Gruber and top Obama administration staffers and advisers in the White House and the Department of Health and Human Services on the Affordable Care Act." Jeanne Lambrew, a top Obama administration health adviser who worked at HHS and the White House, referred to Gruber as "our hero." In 2009, Nancy-Ann DeParle, the director of the White House Office of Health Reform, praised Gruber's work on the White House blog as that of an "MIT economist."[47] She did not reference that he had earned hundreds of thousands of dollars from the federal government.[48] Senator Max Baucus (D-MT), who chaired the Finance Committee, said of Gruber on the Senate floor that "most people think he is one of the best outside experts."[49] Recall that in 2010, Baucus admitted that he didn't actually read the ACA, because "we hire experts" for that.[50] Gruber was one of the experts.

The released e-mails also revealed that Gruber "informed HHS about interviews with reporters and discussions with lawmakers, and he consulted with HHS about how to publicly describe his role." In a November 2009 e-mail, Gruber told a top HHS official that his conversation with Ezra Klein – then of the *Washington Post* and now with *Vox*– went well.[51] Gruber also boasted that Peter Orszag, Director of the Office of Management and Budget, "invited me

---

[44] Clint D. Druk, *Technical Assistance in Evaluating Options for Health Reform*, FEDBIZOPPS (Feb. 25, 2009), perma.cc/V7XU-GAA7.

[45] Glenn Kessler, *Did Jonathan Gruber Earn 'Almost $400,00' from the Obama Administration?*, WASH. POST (Nov. 14, 2014), perma.cc/CPR5-SSHX.

[46] Stephanie Armour, *MIT Economist Jonathan Gruber Had Bigger Role in Health Laws, Emails Show*, WALL ST. J. (June 21, 2015), on.wsj.com/21kmoq7.

[47] Nancy-Ann Deparle, *MIT Economist Confirms Senate Health Reform Bill Reduces Costs and Improves Coverage*, WHITE HOUSE (Nov. 29, 2009), perma.cc/2SAF-FMYZ.

[48] Kessler, *supra* note 45.

[49] Katie Rodriguez, *Sen. Max Baucus: 'Most People' Say Gruber Is One of the 'Best Outside Experts' on Obamacare*, MRCTV (Nov. 14, 2014), bit.ly/1TahFTv.

[50] *Id.*

[51] Klein wrote an account of his interview with Gruber. Ezra Klein, *Does Health-care Reform Do Enough on Cost Control?*, WASH. POST (Nov. 12, 2009), perma.cc/2NAX-AXQ3.

to meet with the head honcho to talk about cost control." White House record logs reveal that Gruber met with the president on July 20, 2009, among a dozen trips to 1600 Pennsylvania Ave. Such a meeting was inconsistent with the president's disavowal of Gruber as "some adviser who never worked on our staff."

Politifact dismissed the president's statement as *mostly false*. "Such a flippant characterization also dismisses Gruber's influence on Obama's positions on health care reform in the lead-up to his presidential bid and during his first year in office"[52] Representative Jason Chaffetz (R-UT), chairman of the House Oversight Committee, rejected the Obama administration's efforts to downplay Gruber's role. "There's no doubt he was a much more integral part of this than they've said. He put up this facade he was an arm's length away. It was a farce."[53]

24.6. "MY OWN INEXCUSABLE ARROGANCE"

On December 9, 2014, Gruber testified before the House Oversight Committee for nearly four hours. Gruber repeatedly apologized for his remarks and insisted he misspoke. "I behaved badly, and I will have to live with that, but my own inexcusable arrogance is not a flaw in the Affordable Care Act."[54] When he was confronted with his past statements, the most he would admit was, "I don't deny it."[55] Ranking member Representative Elijah E. Cummings (D-MD) lambasted Gruber for giving the Republicans such a hot issue: "Man, you did a great job. You wrapped it up with a bow." The *Wall Street Journal* editorialized, "[H]is response to substantive questions suggested that he is mainly sorry for getting caught on tape."[56]

In addition to ignoring the videos, *The Hill* reported that he "repeatedly refused to say how much money he received from the government. He also would not agree to provide documents and data related to his consulting work."[57] When pressed with questions, he replied more than a dozen times, "The committee is welcome to work with my counsel on that." Three days

---

[52] Steve Contorno, *Barack Obama Says MIT Professor Jonathan Gruber Was Just 'Some Adviser,'* POLITIFACT (Nov. 19, 2014), perma.cc/FZC6-Z76M.

[53] Michael Tennet, *E-mails Prove Jonathan Gruber Was Prime Architect of ObamaCare*, NEW AMERICAN (June 25, 2015), perma.cc/9J3P-5AGG.

[54] Tim Howell Jr., *Jonathan Gruber Apologizes for Comments on Obamacare, Says Program Needs More Time*, WASH. TIMES (Dec. 9, 2014), perma.cc/C5NF-ZANE.

[55] John Fund, *Gruber's Pathetic Congressional Testimony*, NAT'L REV. (Dec. 11, 2014), perma.cc/N2DZ-9PC3.

[56] WALL ST. J., *Forrest Gump, Ph.D. Jonathan Gruber Goes to Congress* (Dec. 9, 2014), on.wsj.com/1WM9wSX.

[57] Sarah Ferris, *Gruber Grilled at Marathon Hearing*, THE HILL (Dec. 9, 2014), perma.cc/WX3R-R9CE.

later, Chairman Darrell Issa (R-CA) issued a subpoena asking for an accounting of all of Gruber's state and federal contracts. "This week, Dr. Gruber repeatedly refused to answer several key questions, including the amount of taxpayer funds he received for his work on ObamaCare," Representative Issa said in a statement. Gruber has never responded to the subpoena, nor did Congress seek to enforce it. No doubt his counsel advised him to "say and do nothing," hoping everything would blow over after the Supreme Court decided the case. Today, Gruber is back teaching at MIT, and has never provided the requested documents. He did not respond to my request for comments on this chapter.

24.7. "THANK GOD"

The Gruber videos resonated throughout the political sphere. Their relevance for the courts was a different matter. Nicholas Bagley told me that the Gruber speeches do "cut in favor of Cannon and Adler," and are "hard to explain away." But they are "overwhelmed by contrary evidence." Bagley added that "you can't point to Gruber and ignore the dozens and dozens of people who are reputable, thoughtful people, who are not out there spinning a conspiracy theory. It just doesn't work like that." Rick Hasen, a law professor at the University of California–Irvine, dismissed the relevance of the statement. "Even among those who look to legislative history, a statement of a non-legislator made outside of a hearing should be entitled to very little weight."[58] Politically, however, Hasen recognized the relevance of the video. "I think it provides a nice piece of ammunition and rhetorical points for people who subscribe to this theory, because here you have one of the architects of the law making a statement that appears to support their position."

Michael Carvin's reaction to the Gruber video was at once both ebullient and restrained: "I was like, thank God. I was ecstatic that this ObamaCare architect had confirmed the obvious." But he frankly admitted that what "Gruber thought [in 2012] is a bunch of happy horse shit that has nothing to do with the law." However, Gruber confirmed "what any 3-year-old would have confirmed for me had they read the language."

Yet, the video still found its way to the Supreme Court. In his brief, Michael Carvin drew direct reference to the Jonathan Gruber video. "Tellingly the Government also ignores that Jonathan Gruber – the ACA architect whose work it cited in every brief below but is nowhere mentioned now – articulated

---

[58] Adam Serwer, *Adviser's Past Remarks Could Give Obamacare a Headache*, MSNBC (July 25, 2014), perma.cc/6GHL-2VFH.

the incentive purpose of [the original subsidy language] as early as 2012." Indeed, Gruber's work had been routinely cited by the government in its lower court briefs – that stopped once his videos went viral.[59] An attorney for the challengers compared this disavowal to "how the Soviets would airbrush out disfavored Politburo members from official group photos."

The solicitor general rejected this claim, noting that the challengers "rely heavily on statements made by Jonathan Gruber, an economist, consultant, and supporter of the Act. But those statements were made two years after the Act was passed, and Gruber has clarified that they were taken out of context." The name "Jonathan Gruber" would not be uttered at any point during oral arguments before the Supreme Court.

[59] Lawson Bader, *Where in the World Is Jonathan Gruber?*, HUMAN EVENTS (Oct. 27, 2014), perma.cc/8FRT-6P8A.

King v. Burwell

25.1. "DON'T TAKE MY CARE"

March 4, 2015 was a cold and rainy day in Washington, D.C. Around 5:00 PM the night before, a line started to form along First Street. These spectators waited overnight to secure a ticket to arguments, as small piles of melting snow glistened on the marble palace. By 6:00 AM., crowds began to assemble on the sidewalk in front of the Supreme Court – the only area where demonstrations are permitted. If you attempt to protest on the steps, you will be arrested, for it is unlawful to "parade, stand, or move in processions or assemblages in the Supreme Court Building or grounds."[1] Among the first to arrive were a group of Service Employees International Union (SEIU) organizers, clad in their customary purple T-shirts pulled over heavy winter jackets. The organizers began to distribute different signs to the arriving throngs and told people where to stand. By 8:00 AM – two hours before the hearing was to start – the plaza began to get crowded, and a circus-like atmosphere emerged.

Supporters of the Affordable Care Act (ACA) held up signs, one for each state without an exchange, indicating how many people would lose health insurance if the Court invalidated the IRS rule: 1,565,000 in Texas; 497,000 in Ohio; 438,000 in Illinois. Other signs read "Don't take my care" or "Don't fail our patients." Dozens of doctors in white coats chanted, "Stand up, Fight Back," and held up signs that read "Doctors for Access." Others chanted, "Ho-ho, hey-hey, Obamacare is here to stay." One supporter I saw carried a Notorious RBG tote bag. Eleven people held up twelve placards spelling out the phrase "#SaveHerCare."

---

[1] Robert Barnes, *Protestors Have No Free-Speech Rights on Supreme Court's Front Porch*, WASH. POST (Aug. 28, 2015), perma.cc/UY5Q-UHS7.

A smaller counter protest formed with groups opposed to the Affordable Care Act. Signs read "Choice. $20k under the ACA, or low-cost catastrophic"; "IRS Control Makes Me Sick!"; "Free My Health Care Options." Someone scribbled with a sharpie on top of an umbrella – helpful with the rain – "No Obamacare!" Several people held up a huge banner reading "Keep the IRS out of my Health Care."

Michael Carvin walked to the Court from his offices at Jones Day, half a mile away. Going into argument, he thought the vote was 5-4, with Roberts and Kennedy voting in his favor. The blunt-talking lawyer saw favor in the fact that the Court "took the case when they didn't need to take it." Recall that they could have waited for the D.C. Circuit to hear the case en banc. This signaled they thought it was a "strong case." A senior DOJ official I spoke with did not know how the votes lined up. He speculated that there may have been "five justices who granted cert because it was a big case and there were over $2 billion a month of federal spending, so it's a case that should be heard – even if the justices didn't know how the case should come out."

The gallery of the Supreme Court was filled with top administration officials.[2] HHS Secretary Sylvia Matthews Burwell sat front row center. Reporter Mark Walsh reported that she "look[ed] intently toward the bench."[3] Sitting next to her was Surgeon General Vivek H. Murthy. A few rows back was former HHS Secretary Kathleen Sebelius. From the Republican caucus, Representative Paul Ryan (R-WI) and Senator Orrin Hatch (R-UT) were in attendance. Walsh noted that at 9:45 AM, an officer confiscated Ryan's newspaper, which was prohibited in the chamber. Seated one row away from me were four members of the Democratic caucus: Minority Leader Nancy Pelosi and Senators Patty Murray, Dick Durbin, and Ron Wyden (D-OR). Former-Senator Ben Nelson (D-NE) was nowhere to be seen, though he would pop up during the arguments.

At exactly 10:00 AM, the marshall gavelled the session to order, and announced, "The Honorable, the Chief Justice and the Associate Justices of the Supreme Court of the United States. *Oyez! Oyez! Oyez!* All persons having business before the Honorable, the Supreme Court of the United States, are admonished to draw near and give their attention, for the Court is now sitting. God save the United States and this Honorable Court." Oral arguments would have to wait another nine minutes. First, several Army officers were

---

[2] Mark Walsh, *A View Form the Courtroom: Today's Oral Argument*, SCOTUSBLOG (Mar. 4, 2015), perma.cc/9972-FFPY.

[3] *Id.* I thank Mark Walsh for his excellent "view from the Courtroom" column focused on what transpired during arguments, where cameras could not go.

admitted to the Supreme Court bar. Next, Justice Scalia announced the opinion for the Court in *Alabama Department of Revenue v. CSX Transportation Inc.*, a case involving the Railroad Revitalization and Regulation Reform Act of 1976. There was not much excitement for this opinion.

Then, at 10:09 AM, the Chief Justice began, "We'll hear argument this morning in Case 14–114, King v. Burwell. Mr. Carvin." Carvin approached the lectern. "Mr. Chief Justice, and may it please the Court." This is the customary introduction that begins all arguments before the Supreme Court. "This is a straightforward case of statutory construction where the plain language of the statute dictates the result." Carvin was only able to get out one sentence before the first interruption. Justice Ginsburg inquired if each of the four plaintiffs had "a concrete stake in these questions." She was asking if they were injured by the IRS rule – a prerequisite for standing so the Court can hear the case.

25.2. "IDEOLOGICAL QUESTIONS"

King v. Burwell was filed in federal district court in Richmond, Virginia, on September 16, 2013. There were four plaintiffs in the case, all from the Old Dominion: David King, Douglas Hurst, Brenda Levy, and Rose Luck. The federal courts are not in the business of giving advice on purely legal questions, unless parties are actually injured by the law. They must possess what is known as "standing." The requirement of standing derives from Article III of the Constitution, which creates the bounds of the jurisdiction for the federal courts. So long as at least one of the four plaintiffs suffered an injury, the Supreme Court would be able to hear the case. If none of the plaintiffs suffered an injury, there would not be standing, and the case would have to be dismissed – even if it was already at the steps of the Supreme Court.

Broadly speaking, the standing in *King* was premised on the fact that the availability of subsidized insurance policies on HealthCare.gov made the plaintiffs subject to the individual mandate penalty. The details are somewhat intricate – follow along. Imagine an alternate reality where the IRS never issued the challenged rule. In that scenario, there would not be any subsidized insurance policies available for Virginians on HealthCare.gov. All of the policies would be significantly more expensive. Specifically – as the plaintiffs alleged in their complaint – the "cheapest bronze [health] plan approved for sale to [them] on the federal Exchange in Virginia would cost more than 8% of [their] projected household income for 2014." In other words, without the subsidies, the cheapest available plan would cost nearly 10% of their annual income. Thankfully for the Virginians, the ACA included an exemption from the individual mandate's penalty for anyone who would have to pay more than 8% of his or her annual income on insurance. The insurance is simply too expensive to justify penalizing the uninsured. If the plaintiffs chose to go uninsured, they would be exempted from the individual mandate's penalty. Thus, in this alternate reality without the IRS rule, the plaintiffs, who did not want insurance, could go uninsured without paying the Obamacare penalty.

With the IRS rule in place, however, there are subsidized policies available on HealthCare.gov for the Virginians. Therefore, the cost of the cheapest policy would be *less* than 8% of the plaintiffs' income. Now, if they decided to go uninsured, because affordable insurance is available, they would be hit with the individual mandate's penalty. Herein lies the injury: the plaintiffs would no longer be exempted from the individual mandate, and thus be forced to buy insurance they did not want, or pay the penalty. This additional cost – buying insurance or paying the penalty – is the concrete injury that creates their standing to challenge the IRS rule in federal court. The plaintiffs stated that they do not want insurance. Counterintuitively, the plaintiffs are opposed to the availability of cheaper, subsidized health insurance on the federal exchange because that forces them to pay the penalty. They would much rather go uninsured, and pay no penalty – this is possible only if HealthCare. gov cannot provide subsidies in states without exchanges.

The question of standing came to the forefront in February 2015 following a series of investigative reports published in The *Wall Street Journal* by Louise Radnofsky, Brent Kendall, and Jess Bravin. The articles raised doubts whether each of the four plaintiffs were indeed injured by the IRS rule. The lawyers at Jones Day told me that they had researched each of the questions raised in 2013 when the case was filed, and vigorously dismissed the allegations.

First, the *Journal* wrote that because David King was a veteran, he qualified for "medical coverage with no premiums through the Department of Veterans Affairs."[4] As a result, he would not be subject to the individual mandate's penalty, and thus was not injured. The journalists managed to snag an interview with King at his home. He told them that "he had been to a VA medical center and had a VA identification card, which typically serves as proof of VA-care enrollment." Jones Day associate Yaakov Roth told the reporters, "Even if [King] qualified for VA medical services, [he wasn't] eligible under the legal meaning of the word because [he] hadn't enrolled … and that if Mr. King enrolled, it was after the lawsuit was filed."[5] In a twist of irony, King told the

---

[4] Louise Radnofsky, Jess Bravin & Brent Kendall, *Health-Law Challenger's Standing in Supreme Court Case Is Quartered*, WALL ST. J. (Feb. 6, 2015), on.wsj.com/1LIANQe.

[5] *Id.*

New York Times after the case was argued that if his case were successful, and he were unable to purchase unsubsidized insurance, he would be eligible to access medical care through the Department of Veterans Affairs.[6] But he was not worried, because his lawyers assured him that "things are in play to take care of the problem."[7]

Second, the *Journal* reported that David Hurst's wife described him "on social media as being a Vietnam veteran." During oral arguments, Michael Carvin explained to the Supreme Court: "Mr. Hurst was a veteran for 10 months in 1970. He is not eligible for any veteran's service. You are only disabled from receiving subsidies if you have actually enrolled in a veteran's health services and it's undisputed that Mr. Hurst did not." Carvin later told me, "Even if he was eligible, unless he signed up, it doesn't knock you out for eligibility for the individual mandate."

Third was Brenda Levy. She was sixty-four at the time the case was argued, but would turn sixty-five, and become Medicare eligible, in June – right around the time when the Supreme Court would issue its decision. As a result, she would no longer be subject to future penalties under the individual mandate. However, Carvin explained to the Supreme Court that she was "obviously subject to the individual mandate well in advance of that" date, and therefore suffered an injury.

The biggest riddle was the final plaintiff, Rose Luck. The *Journal* reported that Rose Luck's declared address in the original complaint was the Americas Best Value Inn in Richmond. The receptionist at the motel told the enterprising reporters that Luck did not live there. Her residency was relevant, because insurance premiums are priced based on a person's zip code. If the calculations were wrong because of an incorrect address, the unsubsidized price of insurance may be lower than 8%, and thus she would otherwise be eligible for an exemption from the individual mandate. Nicholas Bagley, the Michigan law professor, observed, "We don't know where Luck now lives and what the price of a bronze plan is in her area. It's thus hard to know whether, absent tax credits, she could reasonably expect to be exempt from the mandate penalty."

Scoffing at the case, Washington & Lee law professor Timothy S. Jost told the *Journal*, "All of these plaintiffs are people they picked off the street for this litigation."[8] Jost was in the ballpark, at least for Luck. Carvin told me that they listed the motel as Luck's address "because she was temporarily out

---

[6] Robert Pear, *Top Plaintiff in Health Subsidies Case Awaits Edict Unperturbed*, N.Y. TIMES (June 17, 2015), nyti.ms/1XPgUoP.

[7] *Id.*

[8] Louis Radnofsky & Brent Kendall, *New Questions Swirl on an Affordable Care Act Challenger*, WALL ST. J. (Feb. 9, 2015), on.wsj.com/1XPgWWF.

of housing" when the case was filed. "I didn't know what else we could do." He added that reporters were camping outside of the other plaintiffs' homes, trying to find out anything they could to upset the case. "We didn't want to tell anybody this because the press was harassing these poor people." In any event, it did not matter for purposes of the case. Luck "lives six blocks away from the motel. So it didn't affect the premiums because she was in the same zip code." Carvin described the *Wall Street Journal's* reporting on the plaintiffs as "really tendentious and stupid. We had thought about all these issues that they raised."

Justice Ginsburg thought otherwise. She asked sixteen consecutive questions to begin the hearing, all about standing. Ginsburg explained that the plaintiffs have to actually be injured. With a not-too-subtle jab at the political nature of the suit, she said, "They can't put [the case] as ideological questions." After Carvin explained that each of the four plaintiffs has standing, Justice Ginsburg finished her questioning: "I don't want to detain you on this any more but I will ask the government what their position is on standing." Later Justice Alito joked, "Should we have a trial here on this issue and find what the facts are?" Appellate courts are not supposed to find new facts, but rather must stick with the record developed in the lower courts.[9] Carvin was happy "they cut me off before I got to say anything," so the justices could put this "standing stuff to bed." He added, "If it's going to come from anybody it might as well come from Ginsburg at the beginning. I didn't want it sprinkled throughout the argument so it continues to distract me. Plus, I never put her in my plus column. And nobody else seemed interested."

Solicitor General Verrilli did not ask the Court to dismiss the case due to a lack of standing. Because Carvin represented that at least one Virginian had standing, Verrilli would "infer that at least one of the [Plaintiffs] has standing." With respect to standing, a senior DOJ official told me the government's position "was very carefully thought through, it wasn't just winging it up there. Unless we have proof that that one person didn't make the requisite income to trigger the obligation to purchase insurance, then we did not have the basis for objecting to standing." More specifically, the solicitor general's office deemed Mike Carvin a "person of integrity who understood the rules. If he wasn't making a representation that anything has changed from the plaintiffs' affidavits, then we have to assume that at least one person has standing." With standing out of the way, the advocates could move on to the merits.

---

9 It would not be unprecedented. Chief Justice John Jay presided over a jury trial the Supreme Court for the 1794 case of Georgia v. Brailsford. 3 U.S. 1 (1794).

25.3. "WHY DID THEY USE THAT LANGUAGE?"

The government's biggest challenge in *King v. Burwell* was to explain how a statute providing that subsidies were available on an exchange "established by the state" were also available on exchanges established by the federal government. Justice Alito's direct question to the solicitor general encapsulated the issue:

> The puzzle that's created by your interpretation is this: If Congress did not want the phrase "established by the State" to mean what that would normally be taken to mean, why did they use that language? Why didn't they use other formulations that appear elsewhere in the Act? Why didn't they say, "established under the Act"? Why didn't they say, "established within the State"? So why would they do that?

Verrilli's answer was meandering, and dodged the question: "We think our position is clearly the better reading of the text." Justice Alito pressed further: "Your answer doesn't explain *why* 'by the State' is in there?" Verrilli parried: "We're talking about specific Exchanges established *in* the specific State." Alito pressed again: "Well, why didn't they say '*in* the State'? That's the phrase you just used, '*in* the State.' Why didn't they say 'in the State'"? Verrilli, in a line that was prepared, responded: "I suppose they could have, but it worked perfectly well this way."

I posed the same question to Michigan law professor Nicholas Bagley. He admitted candidly, "That is absolutely the hardest question for the government, and the government never had a good explanation." But this was not the end of the government's case. Bagley said that the "the plaintiff's brief is really good for two pages, and the government's case is really bad for two pages. But the score switches for the next forty pages."

After failing to answer the *why* question, Verrilli deftly transitioned to his primary two arguments. First, the *best* reading of the statute was that HHS exchanges are, for purposes of this provision, equivalent to state exchanges. Second, if the challenger's reading of the statute prevails, there would be a series of harsh anomalies in how the law works, and potentially coerce the states in an unconstitutionally manner.

25.4. "TERM OF ART"

In its brief to the Supreme Court, the government argued for the first time that "established by the state under Section 1311" was a "*term of art* that includes both an Exchange a State establishes for itself and an Exchange HHS establishes for the State." In law, a *term of art* is defined as "a word or phrase having a specific, precise meaning in a given specialty, apart from its general meaning in ordinary contexts."[10] In other words, Congress used the phrase "established *by* the state" with a special idiosyncratic reference to actually mean "established *in* the state." Tom Christina, who years ago first publicized Section 36B's language, told me that "it wasn't until the briefing of the Supreme Court that the government raised the argument that 'established by the state' was a statutory term of art."

Verrilli's argument was not well received. Bagley told me that the solicitor general's "term of art" position was "an awkward argument but those who criticize the government's brief have never really come up with alternative formulation that I think is more satisfying." Carvin explained that a "term of art" was "mildly more persuasive for an inherently nonsensical argument." The challengers noted in their reply brief: "The Government explains neither why Congress would adopt a 'term of art' contrary to its plain English meaning nor how the Act transforms 'A' into 'B' without ever saying so in text (or even legislative history)."

A senior DOJ attorney with whom I spoke explained that the "term of art" argument was not "some great magic bullet." It was a way of explaining that "you have to figure out the meaning of the phrase by looking at the statute as a whole. Once you look at the statute as a whole, you'll see what the meaning of this phrase is and this phrase works this way." In any event, the government did not think the "term of art" position "was useful for oral argument." Solicitor General Verrilli did not mention it once in Court.

25.5. "SUCH EXCHANGE"

Recognizing the deficiencies of the "term of art" argument, the government sought to shift the focus from four words in Section 36B to one word in Section 1321: "such." Here is the statutory framework – follow along:

- Section 36B provides that subsidies are available for insurance policies "which were enrolled in through an Exchange *established by the State* under Section 1311."
- Section 1311 provides: "An Exchange shall be a governmental agency or nonprofit entity that is *established by a State.*"
- Section 1321 provides: If the Secretary of HHS determines that a state has not established an exchange, then "the Secretary shall (directly or through agreement with a not-for-profit entity) establish and operate *such* Exchange within the State."

[10] BLACK'S LAW DICTIONARY (10th ed. 2014).

The government's argument hinged on the word "such" in Section 1321. Justice Breyer explained the position moments after Justice Ginsburg finished her questions on standing. "If a State does not set up that Exchange," Breyer said, "then the 'Secretary shall establish and operate **such** Exchange.'" Breyer paused to emphasize "such." "So [Section 1321] tells the Secretary, set up *such* Exchange, namely a 1311 State Exchange." That was the argument. What kind of exchange does the federal government establish? *Such* exchange. And what does *such* relate back to? The word "such" in Section 1321 relates back to the exchange established by the state in Section 1311. And Section 36B limits subsidies to an "an Exchange established by the State *under Section 1311*." In effect, the Secretary steps into the shoes of the state, and operates *such* exchange on the state's behalf. A senior DOJ official told me that "'such' provided a textual hook to knit together 36B, 1311, and 1321." It was the only textual hook they had, and it was "very important that we seize on it."

In response to a question from Justice Alito, Solicitor General Verrilli explained that Section 1321 "says to HHS that when a State hasn't elected to meet the Federal requirements, HHS steps in, and what HHS does is set up the required Exchange. It says *such* Exchange." Verrilli paused on the word "such" for emphasis. "Which is referring to . . . the only Exchange required in the Act," which is "an Exchange under Section 1311."

Justice Scalia was skeptical: "Well, you're putting a lot of weight on one word, *such* Exchange." He said, "It seems to me the most unrealistic interpretation of 'such' [is] to mean the Federal government shall establish a State Exchange. Rather, it seems to me 'such' means an Exchange *for* the State rather than an Exchange *of* the State. How can the Federal government establish a State Exchange? That is gobbledygook." Carvin offered a similar rejoinder to the government's position. Section "36B does not say *all* 1311 Exchanges get subsidies, it says Exchanges established by the State under Section 1311" get subsidies. As the challengers explained in their brief, "The word 'such' in § 1321 cannot fill this gaping hole. '[S]uch Exchange' clarifies what HHS is establishing; it does not alter the reality that HHS, not the state, is establishing it. Further, plain text and common sense refute the notion that 'such Exchange' necessarily connotes an Exchange where subsidies are available."

25.6. "RUMP EXCHANGES"

After "such," the government's most potent argument was to point out "anomalies" that would result from adopting the challengers' interpretation of the

ACA. First and foremost, a subsidy-less federal exchange, they argued, would be worthless. The solicitor general explained in his brief, "The point of creating an Exchange is to provide a marketplace where consumers can use credits to obtain affordable coverage, as the overwhelming majority of people buying insurance on Exchanges have done. An Exchange without credits would be a *rump Exchange* bearing little resemblance to its state-run counterpart – if it could operate at all." During oral arguments, Verrilli stressed more explicitly that the challenger's reading of the statute "doesn't work," and "forces HHS to establish rump Exchanges that are doomed to fail." Unsubsidized policies will not sell. Verrilli added, "Under Mr. Carvin's theory of the statute ... you just run into a textual brick wall." A senior DOJ official explained that once Carvin conceded that the "federal exchanges were supposed to be the same exchanges as the state exchanges, then the exchanges have to offer subsidies because otherwise they would be rump exchanges." They couldn't be the same unless there were subsidies available on both.

The justices picked up this line of questioning. Justice Sotomayor asked Carvin, "But no one's going to visit the program if there are no subsidies." Justice Kagan added, "You're essentially setting up a system in which ... there will be no customers." Carvin emphatically disagreed with this line of reasoning. He argued in Court that an exchange could exist without subsidies. Carvin stressed that "many Senators and the President" praised the "valuable benefits to the Exchange" as "one-stop shopping" like "Amazon." Further, even if the challengers win, the federal government would not "empty out" the exchange and shut down HealthCare.gov.

Later, Justice Scalia tried to explain away any anomalies based on the origin of the law. "This is not the most elegantly drafted statute. It was pushed through on expedited procedures and didn't have the kind of consideration by a conference committee that statutes usually do." Why would it be surprising if there were imperfections? Scalia added, "It may not be the statute they intended. The question is whether it's the statute that they wrote." Carvin later told me, "finding anomalies in the ACA is like finding water in Lake Erie."

The solicitor general challenged this assertion: "It was a public hearing. It frankly was covered by C-SPAN." Verrilli sounded annoyed at Scalia's questions. He continued, "The rule is that you read [statutory provisions] in order to ensure that the statute operates as a harmonious whole. You read them so that you don't render the statutory provisions ineffective." Scalia retorted quickly, "If it can only reasonably mean one thing, it will continue to mean that one thing even if it has untoward consequences for the rest of the statute." The longest-serving Justice asked rhetorically, "There are no statutes that make no sense? If that is the case, every statute must make sense and we will twist the words as necessary to make it make sense, that can't be the rule."

Justice Scalia referred to Senator Ben Nelson, but not by name. "There were senators, were there not, who were opposed to having the Federal government run the whole thing, because they thought that would lead to a single-payer system, which some people wanted. And the explanation for this provision is it prevents the federalization of the entire thing. That's certainly a plausible explanation." The solicitor general, even more perturbed, shot back to Scalia. "Mr. Carvin has floated that as an explanation and he suggests that it was Senator Ben Nelson who required it. There is absolutely no contemporaneous evidence, none whatsoever, that anybody thought that way." Referencing a letter the Nebraskan released a few months earlier, Verrilli added that "Senator Nelson has made clear, he has stated that he had no intention of the kind. There's no contemporaneous evidence at all that anyone did."

25.7. "UNCONSTITUTIONALLY COERCIVE"

Ironically enough, the final line of defense for the Affordable Care Act was based on the principle that nearly killed it three years earlier: Federalism. Justice Kennedy asked Michael Carvin a question that altered the course of the entire argument: "Let me say that from the standpoint of the dynamics of Federalism, it does seem to me that there is something very powerful to the point that if your argument is accepted, the States are being told either 'create your own Exchange,' or 'we'll send your insurance market into a death spiral.'" In short, states would be faced with an intractable choice: Establish an exchange, or citizens in your state lose millions of dollars in subsidies as your health insurance market implodes. Could Congress pose such a dire choice to the states without running afoul of the Tenth Amendment?

The federalism argument was advanced by an amicus brief on behalf of Columbia law professors Thomas Merrill and Gillian E. Metzger, along with Abbe R. Gluck from Yale and Nicholas Bagley from Michigan. In *Politico*, Gluck explained: "The case is about federalism – the role of states in our national democracy."[11] She argued that under the challenger's reading of Section 36B, there was no meaningful choice, and that the federal policy would be coercive to states. Gluck highlighted a brief filed by Virginia on behalf of twenty other states, which explained that they had no clue from reading Section 36B that there would be such a drastic penalty if they failed

---

[11] Abbe R. Gluck, *King v. Burwell Isn't about Obamacare*, POLITICO MAGAZINE (Feb. 27, 2015), perma.cc/5KGQ-T788.

to establish an exchange.[12] As the solicitor general relayed during arguments, If the consequences for the state were so severe, the notice "would be in neon lights in this statute. You would want to make absolutely sure that every State got the message."

The argument was targeted directly at Justice Kennedy, who had a soft spot for federalism. "The Supreme Court," Gluck recalled, "led by its conservatives, has spent the past four decades developing a set of legal rules to protect states from federal imposition. If these states' rights rules are real and objective rules of law, they should apply regardless of whose side they happen to serve."

Case Western law professor Jonathan Adler admitted it was a "very powerful brief," but countered that the argument in the brief was still extremely problematic. If this position is "taken seriously, it would cut a wide swath through the U.S. Code," he told me, "particularly in environmental law." Many other federal laws would also be unconstitutional. Adler flagged that in the professors' brief they wrote: "Amici *are not aware* of (and petitioners and their amici do not cite) any program in the U.S. Code in which Congress knowingly set up a federal fallback scheme that was bound to fail." That "gives it all away," Adler explained, "because in fact there are statutes that do those sort of things." For example, under the Clean Air Act, states that do not cooperate "are subject to a series of sanctions, including the loss of federal highway funds and (more relevant here) more stringent regulatory burdens," even though there is a "federal fallback."[13] If too many states opted out, the program would collapse because the federal government cannot manage such a large permitting process. During oral arguments, Michael Carvin noted that all the statute is doing is offering "billions of free Federal dollars. That's hardly invading State sovereignty and it's the kind of routine funding condition that this Court has upheld countless times."

Oklahoma attorney general Scott Pruitt disputed Virginia's claim that states were unaware of the consequences for failing to establish an exchange.[14] He wrote that the Sooner State "knew the consequences of its decision but was not coerced into cooperating with implementation of the Affordable Care Act." Indeed, Oklahoma knew how the statute operated before the state declined to establish an exchange, and before it "sued the Internal Revenue Service." A lawyer in the Oklahoma attorney general's office told me Virginia's argument was "complete B.S., and a blatant attempt to appeal to" Justice Kennedy's views on federalism. How could Virginia not know the statute could be read this way, in light of the fact that numerous objections and lawsuits were lodged

---

[12] Brief of Amici Curiae Former Government Officials in support of Respondents at 25, King v. Burwell, No. 14-114 (S. Ct. Oct., 2014), bit.ly/1OkTQBv.

[13] Jonathan Adler, *Could King v. Burwell Overturn Parts of New York v. United States?*, WASH. POST (Mar. 5, 2015), perma.cc/J225-V3ES.

[14] Scott Pruitt, *A State Reply to Justice Kennedy*, WALL ST. J. (Mar. 4, 2015), on.wsj.com/1QgXXml.

before the Commonwealth had to make its decision. The lawyer also scoffed at Maine, which joined Virginia's amicus brief. This decision was particularly glaring because the Pine Tree State opted not to establish an exchange *after* Michael Cannon convinced its governor that this would deprive the state of subsidies. As Michael Carvin explained to the Supreme Court, the states "had three years to implement this," so it is "a bizarre notion that States were somehow unable to read a statute."

Justice Kennedy continued his questioning of Michael Carvin: "It seems to me that under your argument, perhaps you will prevail in the plain words of the statute, [but] there's a serious constitutional problem if we adopt your argument." Carvin replied that the "government has never made that argument." To laughter, Kennedy interjected, "Sometimes we think of things the government doesn't." The perennial swing Justice continued, "I think the Court and the counsel for both sides should confront the proposition that your argument raises a serious constitutional question." Carvin told me he was surprised with Kennedy's federalism question, and "hadn't anticipated anybody would so robustly make the constitutional argument."

During the solicitor general's argument, Justice Alito asked him the same question. "If we adopt Petitioners' interpretation of this Act, is it unconstitutionally coercive?" Verrilli's answer was, again, murky. "I'm not prepared to say to the Court today that it is unconstitutional. It would be my duty to defend the statute. But I don't think there's any doubt that it's a novel question." Justice Kennedy interjected: "Does novel mean difficult? Because it seems to me that if Petitioners' argument is correct, this is just not a rational choice for the States to make and that they're being coerced." Verrilli offered the pivotal answer. "Justice Kennedy, to the extent the Court believes that this is a serious constitutional question and this does rise to the level of something approaching coercion, then I do think the doctrine of constitutional avoidance becomes another very powerful reason to read the statutory text our way." In other words, the Court should construe Section 36B in a way to avoid the constitutional difficulties, so that subsidies would be available on the federal exchange.[15]

A senior attorney in the Justice Department explained that the "federalism point was valuable, and helped us in a couple ways." First, "it allowed us to talk to Justice Kennedy and the Chief Justice in a way that they might find congenial," and use federalism as an "interpretive tool" to uphold the IRS rule. Second, it

---

[15] This argument was advanced in an amicus brief by Boston University law professor Abigail Moncrieff. Brief of Professors of Health Law and Constitutional Law as Amici Curiae in Support of Respondents, King v. Burwell, No. 14-114 (S. Ct. Oct., 2014), bit.ly/2atacR3.

helped "reinforce the point that the challenger's reading of Section 36B was just alien to the structure and design of the statute because you would expect it to clearly state the consequences of the state's action." None of the federalism arguments would make their way into the final decision in *King v. Burwell*, but it is impossible to know whether they impacted the votes behind the scenes.[16]

25.8. "DID YOU WIN THAT OTHER CASE?"

There was a strong sense of déjà vu between *King v. Burwell* and *NFIB v. Sebelius*, which was argued three years earlier. In both cases, Michael Carvin was arguing opposite of Solicitor General Donald Verrilli. Both cases considered the fate of the Affordable Care Act. With a chuckle, Justice Kagan referred to *King* as part of a "never-ending saga." And in both cases, the outcome would come down to the votes of Chief Justice Roberts and Justice Kennedy.

But there was one significant difference. In *NFIB*, both the chief justice and Justice Kennedy were extremely vocal, and their questions cast serious doubt on the constitutionality of the individual mandate. However, in *King v. Burwell*, while Kennedy was loquacious, Roberts was laconic. During the two-hour hearing on March 27, 2012, Roberts asked twenty questions. But in *King* three years later, Roberts played his cards close to his vest. He let go of his poker face and showed his "tell" only three times. In hindsight, as he often does, he told us exactly what he was thinking – if only anybody was paying attention.[17]

First, Robert's seemed annoyed with the newfound claim that the plaintiffs lacked standing. He asked the solicitor general, "Well, you're *surely* not raising a standing question with us here for the first time at oral argument, are you?" His emphasis on "surely" told us that this case would be decided on the merits and not dismissed on jurisdictional grounds.

Second, the Chief expressed doubts about the IRS rule itself. If the Court deferred to the Obama administration's interpretation of Section 36B, Roberts asked, could "a subsequent administration ... change that interpretation?" In other words, could the winner of the 2016 election promptly undo *King v. Burwell* with a new regulation and unravel Obamacare? Roberts's comment told us that this case would not be decided on the basis of the IRS rule, because

---

[16] Ilya Somin, *The Federalism Dog That Didn't Bark – Court's Ruling in King v. Burwell Avoids Relying on Dubious Federalism Arguments*, WASH. POST (June 25, 2015), perma cc/2WQ4-CZWQ.

[17] For a careful study of how Roberts's comments during his confirmation hearings accurately forecasted how he would behave as a Justice, see Adam J. White, *Judging Roberts The Chief Justice of the United States, Ten Years in*, WEEKLY STANDARD (Nov. 23, 2015), bit.ly/21Qp9vJ.

no matter what the Supreme Court concluded, the next president could unilaterally revoke it. Only the people's representatives – Congress – could change this major plank of the law. As Roberts would note in his majority opinion, "In a democracy, the power to make the law rests with those chosen by the people ... *Congress* passed the Affordable Care Act to improve health insurance markets, not to destroy them." Congress, not the president through executive action, would resolve this issue.

Third, in one of the more light-hearted moments of the day, Roberts recalled that Carvin did not fare so well three years earlier in *NFIB v. Sebelius*. "Mr. Carvin, we've heard talk about this other case. Did you win that other case?" The gallery burst into laughter. The chief added, to more laughter, "So maybe it makes sense that you have a different story today?" History would soon repeat itself for Carvin and Obamacare, albeit with a *different story*.

25.9. ON THE COURTHOUSE STEPS

The arguments ended at 11:34 AM. One minute later, the demonstrators outside danced to the "Electric Slide" to keep warm as they waved signs that read "Don't take my care." C-SPAN slowly panned the camera on First Street to show a man with a shaved head descending the slippery marble steps. Quickly Michael Cannon came into focus. He was the first out of the Court, and the first to speak to the waiting cameras and microphones.[18] Cannon said he hoped this case would bring everyone closer to a "goal that I believe will fix the broken health care system in our country." The Cato Institute scholar, offering the first instant analysis, added: "The government is going to have a hard time winning this case. I think of the two crucial votes, Justice Roberts showed skepticism for the government's position that the Court should defer to the IRS's interpretation." Moments later, his colleague Jonathan Adler approached the microphones and agreed: "What we saw today was that the government's efforts to make this a textual case, did not seem appealing to a majority of the Court." Others, including AEI's Tom Miller, CEI's Sam Kazman, and the Cato Institute's Ilya Shapiro, took their turns at the microphone explaining why the government's case was weak. Afterwards, Elizabeth Wydra of the Constitutional Accountability Center and Neal Katyal of Hogan Lovells provided the opposite perspective and explained why the government had the stronger case.

---

[18] C-SPAN, *Activity and Reaction King v. Burwell Oral Argument*, C-SPAN (Mar. 4, 2015), cs.pn/1ZyTywN.

Back inside the Court, I took my time leaving to soak in the ambience. I overheard Kathleen Sebelius telling an associate that she has a better feeling about this case than *NFIB v. Sebelius* three years earlier. She predicted that both Roberts and Kennedy would vote in favor of the government. Walking out of the chamber, I saw Solicitor General Verrilli, wearing his traditional morning coat, entering the solicitor general's lounge. As he walked in, I heard a thunderous round of applause. Once again, Verrilli had ably defended the president's signature law.

After the arguments, the solicitor general's office thought they "were in the game, but didn't feel like they had it for sure. There was very little to go on with respect to the chief justice. He could have come down either way. For Justice Kennedy, there was a little more to go on, but not a huge amount. With Justice Kennedy's questions, you couldn't tell which way he was going – he could have come down either way." A DOJ official familiar with the solicitor general's thinking recalled that "often in cases the S.G. gets a pretty good sense that they are really against him, but the S.G. didn't feel that way in this case."

Of particular concern for the government was the *chief justice's* silence. The DOJ attorney I spoke with recalled that Roberts was previously silent in *McCullen v. Coakley*, a 2014 case that considered the constitutionality of a "buffer zone" around abortion clinics. In that case, Roberts did not ask a single question, and later fashioned a narrow unanimous opinion that invalidated the buffer zone but suggested that many others would be lawful. The official "read from that history that Roberts thought King was a hard case, because he thought McCullen was a hard case."

Back outside, at 11:49 AM, Michael Carvin finally made his way to the microphone. "I'm Mike Carvin and I argued on behalf of the plaintiffs. I am gratified the Court had a full and candid exchange of viewpoints. I hope the Court will recognize the merits of our argument, and not let the Government rewrite the language of the statute." That morning, a photo of Carvin at the microphone appeared on the front page of the *New York Times*, with a caption that the lawyer now "has a second chance to dismantle a law that conservatives despise."[19]

Carvin later told me that on his way out of the Court, he thought the vote was 5-4 in his favor. As for Kennedy, "I don't think he much likes Obamacare." With respect to the chief justice, adopting the government's "theory of statutory analysis would be so contrary to everything he believes. To endorse the IRS's interpretation is hijacking the statute." Carvin did not think that Roberts has "forever abandoned any fidelity to the rule of law." He added, "I just don't

---

[19] Sheryl Gay Stolberg, *A Lawyer Taking Aim at the Health Care Act Gets a Supreme Court Rematch*, N.Y. TIMES (Mar. 4, 2015), nyti.ms/1OSwkOq. *SCOTUS Health Lawyer*, N.Y. TIMES (Mar. 4, 2015), bit.ly/2aPN4vU.

think I can lose anybody who has not completely abandoned any fidelity in the rule of law." Carvin was half right. The chief justice would not endorse the IRS's interpretation.

After the media scrum wrapped up, Carvin and his associate Yaakov Roth started the walk back to Jones Day. Carvin was smoking a thin cigar, confidently strutting along Constitution Avenue, past the Capitol, to his office half a mile away. They arrived to a celebration of sorts, filled with the *King* plaintiffs, lawyers and staff from CEI, and a buffet of food. Someone joked that they should hold an early birthday party for Brenda Levy, who would soon turn sixty-five, and be freed from Obamacare's mandate.

26

Gridlock

26.1. "ethics of political warfare"

In the run-up to the Supreme Court's decision in *King*, ACA-supporters framed the costs of a loss in terms of human lives. HHS Secretary Burwell said that an adverse decision by the Court could mean that "the number of uninsured would jump dramatically."[1] Further, a "death spiral" could ensue in states that did not establish exchanges, she said, as sicker people kept coverage and healthier ones dropped it. Drew Altman of the *Wall Street Journal* explained that if the Court invalidated the IRS rule, the "vast majority [of people on the federal exchange] would not be able to afford any coverage without financial help and the ranks of the uninsured would become much larger than they would otherwise."[2] As result, "the very sick would be most likely to remain in the insurance markets, rates would spike and insurers would leave the markets, possibly causing the marketplaces in states with federally run exchanges to collapse." This, *The Hill* observed, will "ultimately unravel the law."[3] An amicus brief to the Supreme Court on behalf of the American Public Health Association explained that "a loss of health insurance [subsidies] by [an] estimated 8.2 million persons can be expected to translate into over 9,800 additional deaths annually."[4] The message was clear: if the Supreme Court ruled against the government, nearly 10,000 people would die.

---

[1] Louis Radnofsky and Thomas M. Burton, *HHS's Burwell Sees Spike in Uninsured if Supreme Court Rules Against Health Law*, WALL ST. J. (June 4, 2015), on.wsj.com/1nAvHiM.

[2] Drew Altman, *How 13 Million American Could Lose Insurance Subsidies*, WALL ST. J. (Nov. 19, 2014), on.wsj.com/21l6OoJ.

[3] Sarah Ferris, *Top Policy Group: SCOTUS Move Puts Healthcare at Stake*, THE HILL (Nov. 20, 2014), perma.cc/46JV-4D89.

[4] Brief of Amici Curiae of Public Health Deans, et al., in support of Respondents, King v. Burwell No. 14-114 (S. Ct. Oct., 2014), bit.ly/1VRP8mz.

Other ACA supporters made the attacks personal to the challengers' attorneys. Washington & Lee law professor Timothy S. Jost, a long-time advocate of the ACA, charged that if "the plaintiffs ultimately win, millions of Americans will lose their premium assistance and probably their health insurance. The individual health insurance markets may collapse in several states. This is mean-spirited litigation, intended to deny health insurance to those who Congress intended to help."[5] After the D.C. Circuit decided *Halbig* in favor of the challengers, Northwestern University law professor Andrew Koppelman posed a question: "What's the difference between a Ukrainian rebel with a rocket launcher and a lawyer challenging the Obamacare subsidies?"[6] (The week before, a Ukrainian separatist shot down a Malaysian airliner, killing all 298 aboard.[7]) His answer: "The Ukrainian doesn't intend to hurt innocent people." Koppelman articulated this message in his 2013 book, *The Tough Luck Constitution and the Assault on Health Care Reform*. He viewed Michael Cannon, Jonathan Adler, and their associates as pushing the boundaries of the "ethics of political warfare." He questioned in the *New Republic*, "When is it acceptable to deliberately aim to harm huge numbers of people in order to score a symbolic point? The point here is to discredit Obamacare; the casualties are simply a means to that end."[8]

The challengers, with varying focuses, rejected these attacks. Michael Carvin viewed any potential harm as the result of the IRS's illegal actions, rather than anything he did. "The reason the stakes have become so high is because the IRS completely altered the incentives for states when they were making the original decision." The fact that states do not have exchanges, and thus would lose subsidies, he said, "is directly attributable to the IRS rule." Carvin analogized the Obama administration to "the guy who kills his parents and then goes in front of the judge and pleads for leniency because he's an orphan." Their illegal action is to blame for this crisis, he told me. In the event the Court ruled in his favor, Carvin was open to temporarily assisting people who had relied on the subsidies. Conservatives should say, "Look, ObamaCare has driven these people into this untenable situation so we should give them some help." He always knew from the outset that "any

---

[5] Timothy S. Jost, *The Callous Litigation Aimed at Hobbling Health Care Law*, ACS Blog (July 23, 2014), perma.cc/6Z5C-Y6XR.

[6] Andrew Koppelman, *Halbig and Hurting the Innocent as a Political Tactic*, Balkinization (July 23, 2014), perma.cc/8QG5-VLQC.

[7] Karen DeYoung, *Obama Says Malaysian Plane Shot Down by Missile from Rebel-Held Part of Ukraine*, Wash. Post (July 18, 2014), perma.cc/32SB-SQUM.

[8] Andrew Koppelman, *Obamacare Opponents Are Hurting 4.5 Million Workers to Win a Political War*, New Republic (July 23, 2014), perma.cc/ZP4Z-RS8A.

victory in our case would be thrown back into the political legislative arena."
Along the same lines, in 2012 when this all began, Tom Christina did not think
the suit "would unravel the law because [he] also assumed that Congress
would fix the issue one way or another."

Tom Miller of the American Enterprise Institute, who was one of the early
movers in the litigation, explained that in this case the ends justified the
means. The ACA is unlike anything that was attempted during the New Deal
or Great Society. Obamacare will "fully wrap us up where most of our life is
being run through the administrative state and creating government depen-
dence. That's the fundamental organizing reason why I find it so dangerous
and pernicious." Miller added that the legislative process cannot be the only
approach of ending the law. To destroy it, "you use everything. You don't limit
yourself to one club in the bag."

Professor Jonathan Adler had a slightly different perspective on the litigation. He admitted quite candidly that the prospect of people losing tax credits
and insurance "was something that bothered me." He added, "Prevent[ing]
people from getting tax credits was not the highest thing on my agenda. If
the government is doing something illegal that benefits people, you hope the
government can be stopped in a way that doesn't create victims." Nonetheless,
he stressed, "You don't excuse illegality because some people benefit." His
interest was limited to "forcing the IRS to only do the things Congress gave it
authority to do." The crux of the case was about enforcing the rule of law, not
destroying Obamacare. He hoped that "Congress would address it," though
the legislative branch is "somewhat dysfunctional."

The rampant criticisms from fellow scholars did take a toll on Adler. "When
someone serious accuses you of being wrong, crazy, irresponsible, whatever,
you take it seriously. And so certainly both from a time standpoint and from
an emotional energy standpoint, the case became all-encompassing." At times
the criticisms crossed the line. Adler explained that he received threatening
e-mails and voicemails asking, "What would happen if your family didn't have
health coverage?"

Michael Cannon was willing to accept the potential impact of a ruling in
King halting the subsidies for millions. In an interview with *Vox* he explained,
"Unfortunately, there's going to be a lot of dislocation … [t]here are going to
be a lot of people who lose their subsidies."[9] But he blamed this loss not on the
lawsuit, but on the fact that the president did not "follow the law." He added,
"The reason it will be so painful for them to lose their subsidies … is because

9 Sarah Kliff, *Meet Michael Cannon, the Man Who Could Bring Down Obamacare*, Vox (Feb.
26, 2015), perma.cc/GAU2-HDJ3.

Obamacare increases the cost of the insurance to the point where they can't afford it" without subsidies. Although being unable to affordable insurance will be "painful," he stressed, "they also won't be penalized for not buying it." If "the Supreme Court rules in our favor," Cannon said, "my preference would be that Congress should repeal the whole thing."[10] But short of repeal, the "dislocation" can provide an opportunity for reform. Drew Altman of the *Wall Street Journal* wrote that "The resulting firestorm would likely precipitate a political crisis forcing a negotiation between Democrats and Republicans in Congress to address the problem and potentially opening up discussion of other elements of the ACA in the process."[11]

On June 11, 2015 – two weeks before *King v. Burwell* would be decided – the Competitive Enterprise Institute held its annual gala dinner at the swanky J.W. Marriott in Washington, D.C. (CEI had funded the litigation since the beginning). At the Bourbon & BBQ-themed event, the walls were plastered with Wild-West-styled "Wanted!" posters featuring Sylvia Burwell's picture and the offer of a reward. CEI president Lawson Bader took the stage in front of thousands of attendees, wearing his traditional Scottish kilt. He explained to booming applause that a "victory opens up the potential for real health care reform." In Cannon's words, a ruling in favor of the challengers would "let the political process work."

Senate Majority Leader Mitch McConnell, who called Obamacare "the single worst piece of legislation we've passed in at least the last half century," recognized that the law "bear[ing] the President's name" has a "pretty limited" chance of "full repeal."[12] Who "may ultimately take it down is the Supreme Court of the United States," McConnell explained. "You could have a mulligan here, a major do-over of the whole thing." Republicans could seize on the "opportunity presented to us by the Supreme Court, as opposed to actually getting the president to sign a full repeal, which is not likely to happen." Law professor Nick Bagley replied: "McConnell confirms here that the litigation is politics by other means. It sounds like McConnell is treating the Supreme Court as another political institution."[13]

During our interview two weeks before *King* was decided, Cannon told me that his ultimate motivation is to repeal Obamacare to help the neediest, based on the "potential of markets to make healthcare better and more affordable and more secure, particularly for the poor." He explained, "I am so

---

[10] *Id.*

[11] Altman, *supra* note 2.

[12] *Mitch McConnell and the Republican Plan to Fix the Senate*, WALL ST. J. (Dec. 8, 2014), on.wsj.com/2aHuyD4.

[13] Greg Sargent, *Mitch McConnell: We Can't Repeal Obamacare, but Supreme Court May 'Take It Down' Instead*, WASH. POST (Dec. 2, 2014), perma.cc/E7SQ-2EAP.

adamant about fighting this law and getting rid of this law because I want to make healthcare more affordable for everyone, particularly the poor." A victory, he said, "would free more than 8.3 million residents from being subject to those unlawful taxes, and an additional nearly 57 million from the employer mandate."[14]

I asked him why he decided to fight the IRS rule. With the utmost passion and sincerity, he replied, "Because we won." I was confused: "You didn't win yet." He quickly shot back, "We beat them. We stopped Obamacare." For Cannon, his victory began when thirty-four states "refused to establish exchanges" – in large part based on his barnstorming and advocacy. By rejecting the exchanges the states fought back against the employer and individual mandates. Had the IRS not issued the rule, Cannon told me, states would have seen "the train wreck coming." Insurers would have said, "No subsidies, no mandate, forget it. We are not participating in Obamacare." Then "Congress would have had to repeal it." This would have been far more feasible in 2011 before people began to rely on it. Cannon firmly believed that this would have affected the outcome of the 2012 election. "The President might have lost if Obamacare had been revealed to be as unworkable as it actually is without state buy-in. And more Democrats in 2013 would have had to vote for repeal." He turned to me and said, "We beat them and they stole that victory by rewriting the law. The only reason ObamaCare is still on the books is because the president broke the law, in a massive way." He beamed. "Josh, we won."

26.2. "DEATH KNELL"

During Michael Carvin's impromptu press conference on the steps of the Supreme Court, a reporter asked him if a victory in this case would be a "death knell" to the ACA. He rejected that assertion: "Not at all." Staring directly at the Capitol, which was across First Street, Carvin said, "The leaders in Congress are well prepared to deal with the transition, and if they don't, the states will go ahead to establish exchanges. I'm sure the elected officials will listen to the people." After *King* was argued, Carvin told me that Republicans on Capitol Hill were still "figuring out the policies." He recognized the irony of his own case: "It's genuinely bizarre because I'm trying to implement Obamacare over people who are trying to undo it." He rejected the notion that he is a "politically motivated vindictive crusader." Why? He just "handed a big political problem to the Republican Party." Carvin explained that Republicans at the

---

[14] Michael F. Cannon, *King v. Burwell Would Free More Than 57 Million Americans from the ACA's Individual & Employer Mandates*, FORBES (July 21, 2014), onforb.es/1LUOKQq.

state and federal levels "make it quite clear what I've done to them." If I was "purely political in the sense of electoral chicanery, I wouldn't have done it."

If the Supreme Court ruled that subsidies were restricted to policies on an "exchange established by the state," and that Congress preferred state-run exchanges, the most logical solution would be for each state to establish an exchange. However, this option was problematic for several reasons. First, the states could not swiftly react to the Supreme Court's decision in June 2015. During oral arguments, Justice Alito suggested that the Court could delay the judgment invalidating the IRS rule "until the end of this tax year" – that is, until December 31, 2015 – to avoid "very disruptive consequences."[15] Solicitor General Verrilli admitted the Court would have that power to "reduce the disruption." Internally, the government did not think this option was realistic because it "would be unusual for the Court to agree that the statute prohibits the government from spending $2 billion a month, but that the Court would allow the government to keep spending that money for another six months."

However, "as a practical matter," Verrilli told the justices, "the idea that all of these states" will be able to establish an exchange in six months is "completely unrealistic." At the time, thirty-four states relied on the federal exchange. Building local exchanges was very labor intensive and time consuming. In response to a question from Justice Ginsburg, the solicitor general explained that in order for an exchange to be ready for 2016, it would have to be approved by HHS by May 2015. In other words, a decision to get started in July would already be too late. A senior DOJ attorney told me that "as a practical matter, the delay probably wasn't going to work anyway." The lawyers in the office "would have been very surprised if the justices agreed that they can do that."

Second, most of the thirty-four states that rely on the federal exchange have part-time legislatures that would be out of session by the summer of 2015.[16] Calling a special session is quite difficult and expensive in these states.[17] Even then, the states did not have an incentive to plan for the issue in advance. Most states took a wait-and-see approach. Governor Rick Scott of Florida faced nearly a million Floridians who could lose subsidies. He offered no contingency plan: "I'd wait and see what happens. That's down the road."[18]

Third, and perhaps most potently, in many of the thirty-four states that refused to establish exchanges, Republican opposition to Obamacare was so

[15] N. Pipeline Constr. Co. v. Marathon Pipe Line Co., 102 S. Ct. 2858 (1982).
[16] Nicholas Bagley, David K. Jones & Timothy Stoltzfus Jost, *Predicting the Fallout from* King v. Burwell – *Exchanges and the ACA*, 372 N. ENGL. J. MED. 101, 102 (2015), bit.ly/2agYKGN/.
[17] *Special Sessions*, NAT'L CONF. ST. LEGISLATURES, perma.cc/UHJ3-FC5A.
[18] Marc Caputo, *Supreme Court Challenge to Obamacare Tax Credits Casts Cloud Over Program's Future*, MIAMI HERALD (Nov. 29, 2014), hrld.us/1TPE48V.

fervent that there would be no motivation to do anything to save the law – even if it meant that tens or hundreds of thousands of people in the state would lose their subsidies. Louisiana Governor Bobby Jindal did not even consider the option of establishing an exchange. He explained, "Absolutely not. If the court holds that the law means what it says, that will cause an implosion of the law."[19] An attorney in the Oklahoma attorney general's office explained that in his state, the "politics was that the ACA has to go, and anything to bring it down, we must do." Florida could lose $12 billion in subsidies, Texas $8 billion, and North Carolina $4 billion.

However, not all Republican states were willing to go on record as opposing the IRS rule. Abby Goodnough noted in the *New York Times* that only five other Republican attorneys general joined Oklahoma's amicus brief to the Supreme Court: Alabama, Georgia, Nebraska, South Carolina, and West Virginia.[20] However, the rest of the other thirty-four states without an exchange did not join the brief. Notably absent was Florida attorney general Pam Bondi, who led the constitutional challenge to the individual mandate. Aubrey Jewett, a professor of political science at the University of Central Florida explained, "I do think that there is an emerging schism in the Florida Republican Party on some aspects of Obamacare, and Bondi's more cautious approach may reflect this." Professor Timothy S. Jost told the *Times*, "I suspect what's going on is that Republican states realize what a disaster this would be for their insurance markets."

An attorney from the Oklahoma attorney's general office was "annoyed" with the *Times'* characterization of the states. The amicus brief was only shopped to a group of a dozen states. A lot of the states were "hesitant because of the optics"; they did not want it to look like "they were trying to keep their low-income citizens from getting credits." But every state he talked to was "all for it." They were worried about the "hits they would take in the press" that looked like it was anti-tax credits for poor people.

The brunt of the impact would have fallen primarily on Republican legislators. In the thirty-four states that would have been affected, out of their sixty-seven senators (minus Independent Angus King), forty-nine were Republicans and eighteen were Democrats. That was forty-nine out of the entire GOP caucus of fifty-four. Representative Harry Waxman (D-MI) and the Minority Staff of the House Committee on Energy and Commerce released a district-by-district report explaining the impact of the Supreme Court's decision invalidating

[19] *Id.*
[20] Abby Goodnough, *Health-Law Suit Hints at G.O.P. Divide*, N.Y. TIMES (Jan. 10, 2015), nyti.ms/1WcOOM6.

the tax credits. In total, they estimated $65 billion would be lost.[21] The purpose of this report was to show how people in specific districts, represented by Republicans, would be harmed if the subsidies were eliminated.

I asked Tom Christina at what point he realized this case was going to be a big deal and could put a serious dent into Obamacare. He answered, candidly, "In 2010, I recognized it immediately." The usually demure Christina explained, "That is the only self-aggrandizing thing I will say. It happens to be true." If the states could not establish an exchange quickly enough, the next most logical option would be for Congress to amend Section 36B. That option, however, would be even more problematic.

26.3. "BRIDGE AWAY FROM OBAMACARE"

Congressional Republicans knew that if the Supreme Court ruled against the Obama administration, they would have to pass some sort of legislative fix to restore the subsidies, at least temporarily, to avoid a massive disruption. However, many viewed this window as an opportunity to knock out other portions of the law that the House voted to repeal more than fifty times. One of the first proposals, advanced by Senators Orrin Hatch, Lamar Alexander, and John Barrasso, would "create a bridge away from Obamacare."[22] People with existing plans could keep their subsidies for a "transitional period." Afterwards, states would be given the "the freedom and flexibility to create better, more competitive health insurance markets offering more options and different choices." The proposal was light on details.

Representatives John Kline, Paul Ryan, and Fred Upton proposed an "off-ramp from Obamacare." The central plank was that "[n]o family should pay for this administration's overreach."[23] States would be able to "opt out of ObamaCare's burdensome individual and employer mandates, allowing Americans to purchase the coverage they want." The bill would still protect people with preexisting conditions, prohibit lifetime limits on benefits, and keep twenty-six-year-olds on their parents' plan. Finally, "advanceable" tax credits would be available to help cover the cost of insurance. Ryan announced that the Republicans would have an "immediate response" to

[21] Sarah Ferris, *Dem Report: Justices Could Erase $65 Billion in Obamacare Subsidies*, THE HILL (Dec. 16, 2014), perma.cc/QX5G-9YVR.
[22] Orin Hatch, Lamar Alexander and John Barrasco, *We have a plan for fixing health care*, WASH. POST (Mar. 1, 2015), perma.cc/2GTB-EQME.
[23] John Kline, *Paul Ryan and Fred Upton, An Off-Ramp from ObamaCare*, WALL ST. J. (Mar. 2, 2015), on.wsj.com/1Lf75b2.

King v. Burwell.[24] "We have to be prepared, by the time the ruling comes, to have something," he explained. "Not months later."

Senator Ron Johnson of Wisconsin introduced the most detailed bill, *The Preserving Freedom and Choice in Healthcare Act.*[25] Johnson implored "Republicans [to] come together now, agree on a legislative solution, and take that solution to the American public immediately."[26] Under the proposal, Americans with existing plans would be grandfathered so they could keep their subsidies through August 2017; however, new enrollees would not qualify for subsidies. The bill would also repeal the individual and employer mandates, as well as the minimum essential coverage requirements. "This is a plan Republicans should get behind now," Johnson explained. "If we wait until the ruling in *King v. Burwell* is handed down, it might be too late." Republicans can "give America another 'bite at the apple' – one last chance to repeal ObamaCare and replace it with patient-centered, market-based health-care reforms."

As the end of June drew near, Republicans slowly began to gravitate around the commonalities between these proposal. On June 17, I spoke with a Senate staffer involved in the negotiations, and asked if the Republicans can back a plan if the Court invalidates the IRS rule. He told me, "I think so. The House and Senate leadership are coalescing." But he admitted that there is a question about the "rank and file in the House." They would only vote to repeal the entire ACA.

26.4. "VETO ANYTHING WE SEND HIM"

The most obvious problem with any of these legislative proposals was that there was an absolute certainty President Obama would veto anything that managed to pass both houses. Senator Johnson explained that "President Obama's response will be diabolically simple and highly effective. He will ask Congress to pass a one-sentence bill allowing the subsidies to flow through federal exchanges."[27] The revised provision would be really easy: subsidies are available on an "exchange established by the state under Section 1311 *or by the*

---

[24] Sarah Ferris, *Ryan: GOP Will Have 'Immediate Response' for ObamaCare Court Ruling*, THE HILL (Mar. 27, 2015), perma.cc/3CRK-GYT5.

[25] Preserving freedom and choice in health care act, S. 1016, 114th CONG. (1st Sess. 2015–2016), perma.cc/NQ53-DAWQ.

[26] Ron Johnson, *A Make-or-Break ObamaCare Moment*, WALL. ST. J. (Apr. 13, 2015), on.wsj.com/1pA4FtH.

[27] *Id.*

Secretary under Section 1321." Seven additional words could resolve the entire crisis.

During a hearing, Representative Ryan repeatedly asked HHS secretary Burwell whether the president would veto anything other than a clean bill to restore the subsidies. "The question is what will the administration do: will they stand up with one piece of paper and say 'my way or the highway' or will he work with Congress?" Ryan asked. Burwell declined to comment on "hypothetical" legislation.[28]

Senator Barrasso anticipated that the "president is going to try to force Republicans to pass a one-page fix that says, [take] all that he has done illegal, and make it legal."[29] Barrasso relayed a conversation with the president at the White House that previewed this scenario. "He said, 'There are five million people [who receive subsidies through the federal exchange] – and I know who they are.' He spoke like a community organizer who was going to try to use those people that he has actually caused significant damage to by not applying the law." Senator Johnson added that the president "will also mobilize his massive national political operation. It is easy to imagine the advertising campaign that will promote his simple solutions and viciously attack any opposition. Heart-wrenching examples of Americans who have benefited from ObamaCare – and there are millions who have, through taxpayer subsidies – will flood every TV channel."[30]

Barrasso did think the Republicans had some leverage: "I think if [the President] does want to continue subsidies for some period of time – which will be a limited period of time – that he's going to have to agree to make some significant ... concessions [including] removing more damaging parts of the healthcare law. And that would be eliminating the mandates, giving more freedom and flexibility to those 34 states who haven't set up their own exchanges."[31] But not everyone in his caucus agreed. Senate Majority Leader Mitch McConnell (R-KY) doubted that the president would sign any bill that did not restore the subsidies in full, without preconditions.[32] "What I think he'll probably do is veto anything we send him and put the pressure on the states to cave" and establish exchanges so their residents would be "eligible for

---

[28] Peter Sullivan, *Ryan, Health Chief Clash over ObamaCare Plans*, THE HILL (June 6, 2015), perma.cc/EZ5Q-NLYY.

[29] Philip Klein, *Here Comes the Next Obamacare Showdown*, WASH. EXAMINER (Jan. 26, 2015), perma.cc/638G-6MU8.

[30] Johnson, *supra* note 26.

[31] Klein, *supra* note 29.

[32] Peter Sullivan, *McConnell: Obama Will Veto Any ObamaCare Backup Plan We Pass*, THE HILL (June 5, 2015), perma.cc/X7UF-S4P2.

subsidies." McConnell said. "So we'll have a response to it, depending upon what the Court recommends," he added. "Whether the President will sign it or not is another matter, but we'll let the American people know what we think is appropriate in the wake of the Supreme Court decision."

This triggers a game of chicken. As the subsidies would be cut off, who would be the first to flinch and give in to the other side? Would Republicans be able to resist millions of Americans losing the subsidies and refuse to pass a clean bill? Or would the president be pressured to sign to a bill that would restore the subsidies but eliminate unpopular aspects of the law?

The conventional wisdom was that the Republicans would take the blame. A victory for the Republicans in *King v. Burwell* would be hollow. House Minority Leader Nancy Pelosi said the GOP would "rue the day" if the Court ruled against the government.[33] "They're now going to then go out and say we're going to take subsidies away from people who have health care?" Pelosi told the *Associated Press* in an interview in her office overlooking the Supreme Court. "No, I don't think so." She did not think the Court would rule against the government, but insisted "it would be bad news for [the Republicans], it would be really bad news for them." Senator Harry Reid agreed: "I don't think they will [win the case]. If they do, that's a problem that the Republicans have."[34]

Jeffrey Toobin, writing in the *New Yorker*, took the opposite view and applied the Pottery Barn Rule: "President Obama will have broken health care, so he owns it."[35] He explained, "So if millions lose insurance, they will hold it against Obamacare, and against Obama. Blaming the President in these circumstances may be unfair, but it's the way American politics works." The *Wall Street Journal* echoed this theme: If the president vetoes the proposal from Senator Johnson, "liberals would then need to explain why they're willing to deny health insurance simply because they want more political control over insurance."[36] A House staffer I spoke with in late June admitted candidly that "we don't expect our plans to be signed by the President."

Before oral arguments at the Supreme Court, I bumped into Paul Ryan, the future Speaker of the House. I asked him about the odds of the Republicans passing new legislation, because the president would veto anything they managed to

[33] Joan McCarter, *Pelosi: Republicans Will 'Rue the Day' the Supreme Court Guts Obamacare*, AP (May 15, 2015), perma.cc/EE2G-7WLQ.

[34] Caitlin Owens, *Hill Democrats Aren't Prepping for Potential 'Policy Armageddon'*, ATLANTIC (May 17, 2015), perma.cc/HP3T-8LBJ.

[35] Jeffrey Toobin, *Obama's Game of Chicken with the Supreme Court*, NEW YORKER (May 21, 2015), bit.ly/2aHw5bV.

[36] *In Search of an ObamaCare Breakout*, WALL ST. J. (May 21, 2015), on.wsj.com/1YDd63p.

pass. He told me that they could pass a bill using the budget reconciliation process. Under this parliamentary procedure, certain budgetary matters can be passed in the Senate without meeting the sixty-vote threshold for cloture. Ryan fully expected that this would force the president to veto the bill. But that was part of the plan: shift the blame to the president, who vetoed a bill that would resolve the immediate crisis. If the pressure increased enough, it could lead to further modifications, if not the repeal of Obamacare. Ryan viewed *King v. Burwell* as "the beginning of the end of the Affordable Care Act."[37]

26.5. "NO PLAN B"

During the launch of the ACA in late 2013 and early 2014, the president took a series of executive actions to delay, modify, and suspend the various mandates and deadlines imposed by the law. Some in Capitol Hill believed that the president would pull the same page out of his playbook to maintain the subsidies if the Supreme Court ruled against him in. Senator Johnson speculated that the president could "offer governors a contract to convert their federal exchanges into state exchanges with a simple stroke of a pen."

HHS Secretary Burwell steadfastly denied this charge. She testified before Congress that "we don't have an administrative action that we believe can undo the damage."[38] She refused to explain to Congress whether HHS had any contingency plans: "I'm going to stick with where I am."[39] Representative Joe Pitts (R-PA), chairman of the House Energy, Commerce, and Health Subcommittee, accused HHS of hiding a secret 100-page document explaining the government's contingency plans. "It's hard to fathom that the administration would bury its head in the sand and fail to engage in any contingency planning," Pitts stated. Burwell replied, "This is a document I'm not aware of." Burwell reiterated these comments during a June 3rd *Wall Street Journal* conference. She insisted that "[w]e believe we hold the right position." But "if that's what the courts decide, we can't undo the massive damage."[40] Senator

---

[37] Michael D. Shear, *A Ruling against Obama Would Damage, Not Negate, a Health Care Legacy*, N.Y. TIMES (June 23, 2015), perma.cc/99J3-JKVA.

[38] Sarah Ferris, *Republicans Confront Health Chief on Secret ObamaCare Plan*, THE HILL (Feb. 26, 2015), perma.cc/SR5K-TVKM.

[39] Sarah Ferris, *Defiant Health Chief Says ObamaCare Will Win Day at Supreme Court*, THE HILL (Dec. 23 2014), perma.cc/M7MQ-2HYV.

[40] Louis Radnofsky and Thomas M. Burton, *HHS's Burwell Sees Spike in Uninsured if Supreme Court Rules Against Health Law*, WALL ST. J. (June 4, 2015), on.wsj.com/1nAvHiM.

Barrasso made the charge more explicitly: The president "may try to go around the law again another way by redefining state exchanges to say" states without exchanges "qualify, when in fact they don't qualify."[41]

The allegations that the president could use executive power to "deem" the *federal* exchange as a *state* exchange were not mere speculation. Professors Nicholas Bagley and David K. Jones published an article in the *Yale Law Journal Forum* explaining that "HHS could revise its regulations ... to provide that some states should be *understood* as having established an exchange, even if they never formally elected to do so."[42] In other words, HHS could potentially look to past actions as tacit evidence that states in fact established exchanges, even though they formally chose not to do so. In a paper published with the Federalist Society's *Engage* publication, I concluded that this proposal exceeded the authority that the ACA gave to the president.[43]

White House press secretary Josh Earnest told reporters that "there would be no easy solution for solving that problem because it would likely require an act of Congress in order to address that situation."[44] A senior DOJ official, who was aware of my "blogging on the topic" later told me that there was "no Plan B to deem the federal exchanges as state exchanges."

> I don't think anybody considered anything like that. The law pretty clearly required states to take certain steps in order to establish an exchange. There was some contingency planning to mitigate the downsides, but there was no seamless way to convert a federal exchange into a state exchange so that subsidies would flow uninterrupted. There was no way. Nobody in the government thought we could just wave a magic wand and it could change the federal exchange into a state exchange.

There may have been a different angle to the White House's insistence that the administration had no backup plan. The *New York Times* reported: "Administration officials insist that any steps they could take to prepare for the potential crisis would be politically unworkable and ineffective, and that pursuing them would *send the wrong signal to the justices that reasonable solutions exist*. The do-nothing strategy is meant to reinforce for the court what White House officials believe: that a loss in the health care case would

[41] Klein, *supra* note 29.

[42] Nicholas Bagley & David K. Jones, *No Good Options: Picking up the Pieces after King v. Burwell*, 125 YALE LAW. J. FORUM 13, 19 (2015), bit.ly/1WcVFVC.

[43] Josh Blackman, "The Legality of Executive Action after King v. Burwell," ENGAGE (Jun. 8, 2015), perma.cc/LB28-WPPG.

[44] Fred Lucas, *White House Warns of 'Utter Chaos' if Supreme Court Rules Against Administration in Obamacare Case*, BLAZE (June 3, 2015), perma.cc/4QKB-UKXE.

be unavoidably disastrous for millions of people."[45] There was apparently a concern within the administration that announcing a Plan B could give the justices more confidence that invalidating the IRS rule would not lead to the parade of horribles that supporters feared.

On the flip side, Representative Sandy Levin (D-MI) charged that proposals by Republicans to restore the subsidies "are trying to send a *false message* to the Supreme Court that they could repair the enormous damage that this case could bring to the health care of Americans."[46] He explained that the plan would be "vacuous. The result of an adverse Supreme Court ruling would be hugely dangerous."[47] Peter Suderman summed up the dynamic in *Reason*: "What this messaging tug-of-war leaves us with, then, is an odd dynamic in which the administration insists it has no contingency plan, even though it (likely) does, and Republicans in Congress insist they have a backup, even though they don't."[48]

26.6. "THIS CONGRESS?"

Since 2010, when President Obama lost his filibuster-proof majority in the Senate and the Republicans took the House of Representatives, Washington had become beset by "gridlock."[49] The poster child of this paralysis has been the battle over Obamacare. During oral arguments in *King v. Burwell*, this intransigence seeped into the Supreme Court. Justice Scalia challenged Solicitor General Donald Verrilli about whether the consequences of invalidating the IRS rule would be so dire. "What about Congress?" Scalia charged. "You really think Congress is just going to sit there while all of these disastrous consequences ensue?" House Minority Leader Nancy Pelosi, who was sitting two rows away from me in the Court, perked up with this question. "Congress adjusts, enacts a statute that takes care of the problem," Scalia continued. "It happens all the time. Why is that not going to happen here?"

Verrilli's answer channeled the Obama administration's frustration over the past five years. "Well, *this* Congress, Your Honor?" The clear emphasis was on *this*. Adam Liptak reported in the *New York Times* that the lawyer

---

[45] Michael D. Shear, *White House Plans No Rescue if Court Guts Health Care Law*, N.Y. TIMES (Mar. 3, 2015), nyti.ms/1pbrOlC (emphasis added).

[46] Peter Sullivan, *Top Dem: GOP Sending 'False Message' to Court about ObamaCare Plans*, THE HILL (Mar. 3, 2015), perma.cc/2XZC-G7RC.

[47] *Id.*

[48] Peter Suderman, *Law, Not Policy, Should Guide Supreme Court in Obamacare Subsides Case*, REASON (Mar. 2, 2015), perma.cc/J5XC-2CF6.

[49] Josh Blackman, *The Gridlock Clause*, NAT'L REV. (Nov. 12. 2014), perma.cc/W6R6-Z6RY; Josh Blackman, *Gridlock and Executive Power* (Jul. 15, 2014), bit.ly/1WPL70O. Josh Blackman, *Gridlock*, 130 HARV. L.REV. __ (2016).

"all but rolled his eyes" at Justice Scalia as the "the courtroom erupted in knowing laughter."[50] From my vantage point, Justice Scalia did not appear amused by this comment. Verrilli continued, "You know, I mean, of course, theoretically – of course, theoretically they could." Scalia shot back, "I don't care what Congress you're talking about. If the consequences are as disastrous as *you* say," with the emphasis on *you*, "so many million people without insurance, yes, I think this Congress would act." Verrilli changed the topic and returned to a question from Justice Alito. That exchange resonated long after the hearing was over.

Michael Carvin told me that for the most part, Verrilli "really did a perfectly fine job at the argument. But I thought that line was a huge mistake. I don't think any of the justices liked it. Because it implies two things. One, it implies we're going to have a different rule of deference depending on which party controls Congress. Second, he was asking the Court to short circuit the legislative process because you can't trust these legislators." Carvin did not think the line was ad-libbed. "It's not remotely feasible that he went through moots without being asked that question."

A DOJ official familiar with the solicitor general's strategy joked, "You're allowed to be funny every now and then out there," but added on a serious note that it was an important point to be made. In any statutory interpretation case, "you could always say that if Congress doesn't like how the Court interprets a statute, Congress can change the statute. But that's not really the obligation of the Court. The obligation of the Court is to figure out what the best reading of the statute that Congress already enacted." This approach was especially appropriate because the solicitor general realized that he "couldn't go 'back and forth' with Justice Scalia. This one sentence was a way to get that point across, even if it was perhaps a 'little too flip.'" Carvin seemed to agree: "Well, if you think about it, what other answer was there, other than screw democracy? So, my guess, it's a pure guess, would be he's been thinking about saying something like this thing for a while." Whether or not Verrilli's comment was appropriate for the Court, it was likely accurate.

26.7. "WE HAVE TO ASSUME THAT WE HAVE THREE FULLY FUNCTIONING BRANCHES"

On March 23, 2015 – three weeks after oral argument in *King v. Burwell* – the House Subcommittee on Financial Services & Government hosted Justices

[50] Adam Liptak, *Justices' Words Are Combed for Clues as Major Decisions Loom at Court*, N.Y. TIMES (June 15, 2015), nyti.ms/1QHZ2Td.

Kennedy and Breyer for its annual hearing about the federal judiciary's budget and the Supreme Court's operation. Invariably, the representatives try to pepper the justices with legal questions, which they always avoid. Justice Breyer, who appears every year, has consistently been asked about allowing cameras in the Court. His answer is always the same: "No."[51]

Justice Kennedy's prepared testimony was mundane enough.[52] He thanked the committee for approval of the Court's funding request for fiscal year 2015 and presented the Court's fiscal year 2016 request. "Although our request is small considering the requests you receive from other agencies and departments, we appreciate the funding we receive." He closed, "Although we cannot comment on Court decisions or pending cases, we would be pleased to respond to any budget-related questions that the Members of the Subcommittee may have." However, during the question-and-answer section, he went off script.[53]

Representative Scott Rigell (R-VA) asked the justices how the courts can help deal with the "caustic tone [that] often overtake[s] the public square." Kennedy explained that he often tells students that "the Constitution doesn't belong to a bunch of judges and lawyers and law professors. It's yours ... Some of the great presidents weren't lawyers. They were great guardians of the Constitution. And institutions have to remember this. Institutions have their own visibility, their own reputation, their own duty to inspire others to believe in this system of democracy, these three branches of government we have."

Chairman Ander Crenshaw (R-FL) smiled at Justice Kennedy's remarks, and was reminded of Benjamin Franklin's famous comment at the conclusion of the Constitutional Convention of 1787. When someone asked Franklin what sort of government the delegates had created, he replied, "A republic, if you can keep it." Crenshaw continued, "I've read, Justice Kennedy, from time to time that you had expressed some concern about the increasingly politically charged issues that are now being heard and decided by the Supreme Court. Can you explain what that concern is?"

Kennedy paused for a few, deliberate moments before he responded. "It's not novel or new for justices to be concerned that they are making so many decisions that affect a democracy." But then Justice Kennedy took a sharp turn away from the question. "And we think a responsible, efficient, *responsive* legislative and executive branch in the political system will alleviate some of that pressure." Kennedy emphasized the word *responsive*. "We routinely

---

[51] Tal Kopan, *At Sequestration Hearing, Breyer, Kennedy Say Cameras in the Courtroom Too Risky*, POLITICO (Mar. 14, 2013), perma.cc/L4ZC-M6WY.

[52] Justice Anthony Kennedy, Statement to the House Committee on Apr. 14, 2011, bit.ly/1UQwTgm.

[53] Rep. Ander Crenshaw Holds a Hearing on the Supreme Court of the United States Budget for F.Y. 2016 (Mar. 23, 2015), 2015 WL 1286303.

decide cases involving federal statutes and we say, well, if this is wrong, the Congress will fix it." This was effectively Justice Scalia's question to the solicitor general. "But then we hear that Congress can't pass a bill one way or the other. That there is gridlock. And some people say, well, that should affect the way we interpret the statutes." This was effectively Solicitor General Verrilli's answer to Scalia's question. "That seems to me a wrong proposition," Kennedy said. "We have to assume that we have three fully functioning branches of the government that are committed to proceed in good faith and with good will toward one another to resolve the problems of this republic."

The reaction on Twitter to the otherwise boring budget hearing was quick. *Buzzfeed* reporter Chris Geidner tweeted, "That felt like a direct reference to the Verrilli answer in *King v. Burwell*, didn't it?" Lawrence Hurley at *Reuters* tweeted further, "Kennedy comment that court should not take into account congressional gridlock when interpreting statute not great news for Obama admin." Todd Ruger at *CQ Roll Call* added, "Health care case clearly the example that jumps to mind when considering whether Congress can fix a law."

Georgia State law professor Eric Segall, a vigorous defender of the IRS rule, cringed: "Kennedy just said a dysfunctional Congress is no reason Court shouldn't send laws back to them to 'fix.' Ugggggggggghh." He added, "Justice Kennedy basically just announced how he will vote in *King* and news not good." As a testament to how news is made in the year 2015, *New York Times* reporter Adam Liptak would quote Segall's tweets in an article about combing for clues in major Supreme Court cases.[54] In the hearing, Liptak noted, "Justice Kennedy sounded like Justice Scalia" asking the solicitor general why Congress could not fix the ACA. "If he is right," Liptak concluded, "the fate of the law may rest with Chief Justice Roberts."

[54] Liptak, *supra* note 50.

27

"Unravel What's Now Been Woven into the Fabric of America"

27.1. "RELUCTANCE TO SPEAK OUT"

Over the past six decades, there has been a general convention that presidents do not comment on pending Supreme Court cases. It is during this period – after arguments but before the decision – that statements from the bully pulpit could be viewed as trying to sway the outcome of the case. Harvard Law School Professor Larry Tribe, who taught Barack Obama constitutional law, observed, "Presidents should generally refrain from commenting on pending cases during the process of judicial deliberation. Even if such comments won't affect the justices a bit, they can contribute to an atmosphere of public cynicism."[1] Veteran reporter Lyle Denniston, who has covered the Supreme Court since the Eisenhower administration, agreed. "Often, when Presidents have been asked by reporters to comment on an issue pending before the courts, the response has been a reluctance to speak out while the issue remained in that forum."[2]

The numbers bear out this generalization. According to a study by Professors Matthew Eshbaugh-Soha and Paul M. Collins, Jr., during Denniston's six-decade tenure, presidents have mentioned 850 Supreme Court cases in their public remarks. However, on only 47 occasions the remarks concerned pending cases, and only 13 of which were made after arguments when the case was submitted.[3] The authors concluded that President Obama stands out among his peers. While it is "not unheard of for presidents to take positions

---

[1] Peter Wallsten & Robert Barnes, *Obama's Supreme Court Comments Stir Debate*, WASH. POST (Apr. 4, 2012), perma.cc/4TXF-FSWQ.

[2] Lyle Denniston, *President Lobbying the Court?*, SCOTUSBlog (Apr. 2, 2012), perma.cc/J528-JBE8.

[3] Matthew Eshbaugh-Soha & Paul M. Collins, *Presidential Rhetoric and Supreme Court Decisions* at 34, bit.ly/1T340MD.

on cases before they are decided ... what makes Obama's remarks stand out is that they are bolder and more extensive than what most presidents have said in the past."[4]

Presidents Eisenhower, Kennedy, Nixon, and Reagan were silent about pending cases after they were argued but before they were decided. Presidents Johnson, Ford, and Carter each made one such statement during their respective terms. Of the civil rights case *Hearts of Atlanta Motel v. United States*, Johnson said only that the case "is now in the Supreme Court." Of the private school desegregation case, *Runyon v. McCrary*, President Ford said, "That case is now before the Supreme Court. I think that the individual ought to have a right to send his daughter or his son to a private school if he is willing to pay, whatever the cost might be." (Curiously, Ford's solicitor general, Robert Bork, took the opposite position, and filed a brief with the Supreme Court arguing that the anti-discrimination law was constitutional.) In 1978, President Carter declined to comment about *University of California v. Bakke*, the landmark affirmative action decision that invalidated racial quotas, citing the "separation of powers." "I would say that now that it's in the hands of the Supreme Court," Carter said, "and we have filed our position, that there's nothing additionally that we would do until after the Supreme Court rules."

When several abortion-related cases were pending President George H. W. Bush repeated several times that he favored that *Roe v. Wade* should be overturned. In each instance, however, he refused to comment on the merits of the specific case until after the Supreme Court ruled. In *Webster v. Reproductive Health Services*, the Supreme Court would uphold an Ohio law limiting the use of public employees for performing abortions. On the day the case was argued Bush in appeared at a joint press conference with former president Reagan. A reporter asked, "The Supreme Court today will be considering an abortion case. Would you like to see that be the first step in a move to ban abortion in this country?" Bush replied, "Yes." Reagan answered more diplomatically, "I think we've agreed on that. You know my position on abortion."

Six days before the case would be decided, a reporter asked President Bush about it again: "We may get that decision this week. As I understand your position, you're for a constitutional amendment [overturning *Roe*] regardless of which way the Supreme Court rules. Is that right?" The president replied, "Yes, of course." The reporter pushed back and asked, "Now, if the Supreme Court strikes down

---

[4] Jess Bravin, *President Obama's Supreme Court Remarks Set Him Apart*, WALL ST. J. (June 10, 2015), on.wsj.com/1STrjJ6. I summarize their research at the National Constitution Center's Blog. Josh Blackman, *President Obama, and Arguments About Pending Supreme Court Cases*, CONSTITUTION DAILY (June 17, 2015), perma.cc/8V9T-Z27U.

Roe v. Wade and sends this back to the States, would it not be less divisive to let the States decide this rather than go through the whole long, tortuous process of constitutional amendment?" President Bush avoided the question: "I hate to not respond to your question. But the Court is probably going to make a decision very soon, and I would prefer to address myself to the question after the Court has decided."

Three years later, President George H. W. Bush would re-enter the abortion fray leading up to the Court's landmark decision in *Planned Parenthood v. Casey*. Fourteen days after the case was argued, the president said he supported the "sanctity of life," but "the matter is in the courts, and then we'll see what happens. I don't know how broad the Supreme Court decision will be, but at some point it will go back out to the States again." Two weeks later, and a month before the case was decided, the president repeated that he is committed to the "side of life," but that "that matter is being adjudicated in the courts right now."

In 1995, President Clinton weighed in on the pending *United States v. Lopez*, which considered whether Congress had the power to regulate the possession of guns in school zones. Less than three weeks before the case was decided, President Clinton briefly addressed the case in remarks at the National Education Association School Safety Summit, stressing that his "administration is supporting that law all the way to the Supreme Court." There were no substantive comments about the case. On December 11, 2000, the day *Bush v. Gore* was argued, President Clinton was asked if he had "any comment on the Supreme Court today and what they might do?" The president answered concisely: "No, I think we ought to just wait and see what they do. One way or the other, it will be a historic decision that we'll live with forever."

In January 2003, two months before oral arguments in the University of Michigan affirmative action cases, President George W. Bush noted that "[t]he Supreme Court will soon hear arguments in a case about admissions policies and student diversity in public universities." Echoing the position taken by his solicitor general's brief – which would be filed the very next day – Bush explained that the methods used by the school "to achieve this important goal [of diversity] is fundamentally flawed."

President Bush also made a series of comments after oral arguments in *Hamdan v. Rumsfeld*, which would invalidate the use of military commissions for detainees held at Guantanamo Bay. One month after arguments, the president explained that "[w]e're at war with an enemy, and we've got to protect ourselves," but stressed that "we're waiting for our Supreme Court to give us a decision as to whether the people need to have a fair trial in a civilian court or in a military court." Two months after arguments, and three weeks before the decision would be issued, Bush explained that his administration would "file such court claims once the Supreme Court makes its decision as to ... the proper venue for these trials" for certain detainees. He added, "We're waiting on our Supreme Court to act." Five days later, the president reiterated that the "best way to handle" certain dangerous detainees is "through our military courts. And that's why we're waiting on the Supreme Court to make a decision." Finally, on June 21, eight days before the decision, the president explained once again that "there ought to be a way forward in a court of law, and I'm waiting for the Supreme Court of the United States to determine the proper venue in which these people can be tried."

From Eisenhower to Bush 43, the comments about pending cases were brief, mild, and at worst articulated that the president favored one side over the other. President Obama would set a new precedent.

27.2. "UNPRECEDENTED, EXTRAORDINARY STEP OF OVERTURNING A LAW"

NFIB v. Sebelius was argued on March 26, 27, and 28, 2012, stretching Monday through Wednesday. The justices held their conference on Friday, March 30, to vote on the outcome. The following Monday, April 2, during a press conference, President Obama explained the high stakes of the case. He began by assuring us that he is "confident that the Supreme Court will uphold the law" because "in accordance with precedent out there, it's constitutional." His initial sentiment is consistent with how the forty-first and forty-second presidents addressed questions about submitted cases.

But he went further: "I think it's important – because I watched some of the commentary last week – to remind people that this is not an abstract argument." Putting a face on the case, so it is not viewed as theoretical, the president added, "People's lives are affected by the lack of availability of health care ... The law that's already in place has already given 2.5 million young people health care that wouldn't otherwise have it." He stressed that the "Justices should understand that in the absence of an individual mandate, you cannot have a mechanism to ensure that people with pre-existing conditions can actually get health care." This could be seen as keeping with the forty-third president's remarks, stressing that, "[w]e're at war with an enemy, and we've got to protect ourselves" while the detainee cases were pending.

But then he went even further than his predecessors when he said it would be "unprecedented" for the Court to invalidate the law: "Ultimately, I'm confident that the Supreme Court will not take what would be an *unprecedented*, extraordinary step of overturning a law that was passed by a strong majority of a democratically elected Congress." Obama charged with hypocrisy "conservative commentators that for years" argued that the "biggest problem on the bench was judicial activism or a lack of judicial restraint." The president hoped that "this Court will recognize that and not take that step."

The very next day, on Tuesday, April 3, the president offered extensive comments in response to a question about whether it "would be *unprecedented* for a Supreme Court to overturn laws passed by an elected Congress." He began with what is the normal trope concerning judicial review: "The Supreme Court is the final say on our Constitution and our laws, and all of us have to respect it." Then came the *but*: "[B]ut it's precisely because of that extraordinary power that the Court has traditionally exercised significant restraint and deference to our duly elected legislature, our Congress." To drive the point home, President Obama invoked the jurisprudential bogeyman of *Lochner v. New York*, a case that has come to epitomize an era when a conservative Supreme Court invalidated progressive laws: "We have not seen a Court overturn a law that was passed by Congress on a[n] economic issue ... at least since *Lochner*. Right? So we're going back to the thirties, pre–New Deal."[5]

Next, the president issued a series of admonitions to the Court. He "expect[s] the Supreme Court actually to recognize that and to abide by well-established precedents out there." Further, he has "enormous confidence" that "the Court is going to *exercise its jurisprudence carefully* because of the profound power that our Supreme Court has." He added, "So I don't anticipate the Court striking this down. I think they take their responsibilities very seriously." Toward the end – in a preview of his remarks in 2015 – President Obama explained that "as a consequence" of his prediction of the outcome of the case, "we're not spending a whole bunch of time planning for contingencies." In another foresight of his 2015 comments, the president said that "there is a human element to this that everybody has to remember. This is not an abstract exercise." These are the most pointed and provocative comments identified in Professors Eshbaugh-Soha and Collins's 2014 study.

While President Obama would not offer similar comments during the run-up to *Hobby Lobby*, he shattered his own record in the months and weeks before *King v. Burwell* was decided. On March 2, 2014 – two days before oral arguments – President Obama gave an interview with *Reuters* where he said, "In our view, [there was] *not a plausible legal basis* for striking [the IRS rule]

---

5 For a different perspective of Lochner v. New York, *see* David E. Bernstein, Rehabilitating Lochner: Defending Individual Rights Against Progressive Reform (2011).

down."[6] He added, "Look, this should be a pretty straightforward case of statutory interpretation. If you look at the law, if you look at the testimony of those who are involved in the law, including some of the opponents of the law, the understanding was that people who joined a federal exchange were going to be able to access tax credits just like if they went through a state exchange." *Reuters* asked if the president had a "Plan B" if the Court ruled against him. Obama concluded with a preemptive strike against an unfavorable decision: "If they rule against us, we'll have to take a look at what our options are. But I'm not going to anticipate that. I'm not going to anticipate *bad law.*"

The president made similar remarks during an April 8 interview on CNN with Dr. Sanjay Gupta.[7] "If you read the statute, it's pretty straightforward and it's pretty clear. So I'm not anticipating the Supreme Court would make such a *bad decision.*" Again, a decision against him was pre-emptively labelled *bad*. He added in another interview, "I'm confident in the Supreme Court applying its own rules of interpreting laws [and] will uphold the law. It's pretty clear cut."[8]

The president also targeted the lawyers who brought this case, saying, "I think this is sort of the last gasp of folks who've been fighting against this for ideological reasons."[9] Obama continued, "If the Supreme Court made a ruling that said the folks who have federal exchanges don't get the tax credits, what you would end up seeing is millions of people losing their health insurance." Further, he said, "I don't think the Supreme Court is going to adopt the arguments of those who are arguing" that subsidies are unavailable on the federal exchange.[10] He noted that he receives "letters every day from people who say … the Affordable Care Act saved my life, or saved my kid's life because I got insurance. We hear stories about that all the time and I think that will be factored in when the Supreme Court takes a look at this case."

The president made clear that the Supreme Court would be responsible for people losing their insurance, rather than even entertaining the possibility that the IRS Rule was not authorized by the statute. This philosophy pervaded the Obama administration. A DOJ official familiar with the solicitor general's strategy explained that another purpose of Verrilli's *"this Congress"* remark was

---

[6] Roberta Rampton, *Exclusive: Obama Defends Lack of 'Plan B' for Obamacare Court Case*, REUTERS (Mar. 2, 2015), perma.cc/SQC7-2JSP.

[7] *Transcript Aired April 8, 2015*, CNN (Apr. 8, 2015), perma.cc/5DMX-AJQA.

[8] Jordan Fabian, *President Predicts ObamaCare Victory: Case 'Pretty Clear Cut'*, THE HILL (Apr. 13, 2015), perma.cc/5BWG-9CE5.

[9] Sarah Ferris, *Obama: Healthcare Law Critics Make Their 'Last Gasp' in Supreme Court*, THE HILL (Apr. 8, 2015), perma.cc/5LKF-6FFX.

[10] *Id.*

"to convey that the Court was on the hook for this. It would be the Court's decision that extinguished the subsidies. The 'quip' was a way of conveying the point that the Court has to take responsibility as an institution for the consequence of that reading."

On June 8 – 96 days after oral arguments in *King v. Burwell*, and roughly three weeks before the case would be decided – the president offered more than 600 words about the pending case from the podium of the G7 Summit in Krün, Germany. These remarks are longer and more detailed than any statements identified by Professors Eshbaugh-Soha and Collins's. Mirroring his comments three years earlier, the president said "that under well-established precedent, there is no reason why the existing exchanges should be overturned through a court case." Once again, then came the *but*. "Frankly, [the case] probably shouldn't even have been taken up." In other words, the president's faulted the Court – or at least four justices – for voting to grant certiorari. I could not find any other statement where a president criticized the justices for voting to review a case.

He then turned to the real-world consequences of the Court basing its decision on "a contorted reading of the statute ... It means that millions of people who are obtaining insurance currently with subsidies suddenly aren't getting those subsidies; many of them can't afford it; they pull out." Making the point clearly, he said invalidating the IRS rule is "a *bad* idea. It's not something that should be done based on a *twisted interpretation* of four words" in a 3,000-page statute. Driving the point home after a question of what his "Plan B" is if he loses, the president said, "If somebody does something that *doesn't make any sense*, then it's hard to fix." At this point, the "somebody" referred to the justices voting to invalidate the rule. He concluded that he was "optimistic that the Supreme Court will play it straight when it comes to the interpretation."

The very next day the president spoke at length about the affordable care Act (ACA) in a prepared a speech before the Catholic Health Association Conference. Although he did not mention *King v. Burwell* directly, he alluded to the pending decision: "It seems so cynical to want to take coverage away from millions of people; to take care away from people who need it the most; to punish millions with higher costs of care and *unravel what's now been woven into the fabric of America*. And that kind of cynicism flies in the face of our history."[11]

---

[11] That the president used both the words "unprecedented" and "unraveled" in speeches about the Supreme Court's pending decision in NFIB v. Sebelius and King v. Burwell was entirely propitious; I selected the title of each book before the president used those phrases. Josh Blackman, More on Self-Publishing, JOSH BLACKMAN'S BLOG (Apr. 1, 2012), perma.cc/JY62-RUNQ. ("And what do you think of this for the title of my book? UNPRECEDENTED: THE SUPREME CHALLENGE TO THE AFFORDABLE CARE ACT"). *Constitutional* would later be substituted for *Supreme*.

Russell Berman wrote in the *Atlantic* that the *unraveled* comment "seemed most directed at lawmakers in the Capitol and the justices on the Supreme Court."[12] If the message was directed at Congress, however, "Obama could easily have waited a few weeks to deliver the speech, if he needed to give it at all. But Obama apparently wanted to begin mounting his case now – and, perhaps, sway any justice who might be having last-minute doubts."

"Five years in, what we are talking about it is *no longer just a law*," the president continued. "It's no longer just a theory. This isn't even just about the Affordable Care Act or Obamacare … This is now part of the fabric of how we care for one another." His comments suggest that not even the Supreme Court should mess with the ACA, as it is "no longer just a law" but something greater. Finally, on June 11, the president added one more message to the justices: "One of the things I try to remind people of – what we do here, what the Supreme Court does, what Congress does – these aren't just abstractions. These are things that really matter in people's lives."[13]

Very few presidents have spoken about pending Supreme Court cases after arguments were submitted. Even fewer discussed the merits of the cases. Only a handful could be seen as pre-emptively faulting the justices for ruling against the government. President Obama, however, stands alone in his pointed and directed arguments to the Supreme Court. The forty-fourth president, himself a former constitutional law lecturer, has set a new precedent for *ex parte* arguments to the Supreme Court.

Court watchers questioned the propriety of these statements. Robert Barnes, who serves as the *Washington Post*'s SCOTUS reporter, admitted, "I was a little surprised President Obama weighed in again this week, saying the Court probably should not have taken the case."[14] Tom Goldstein, appellate attorney and publisher of SCOTUSBlog, said the speech "has the real chance to backfire. The justices really don't like being pressured into something. You start jumping up and down at them and the justices get their backs up."[15]

Supporters of the plaintiffs charged the president was trying to intimidate the justices. "Instead of *bullying the Supreme Court*," noted Senator John Barrasso, "the president should spend his time preparing for the reality that

Josh Blackman, SEQUEL TO UNPRECEDENTED: 'UNRAVELED,' JOSH BLACKMAN'S BLOG (Nov. 24, 2013), perma.cc/88H4-8PU7 ("As for a title … what do you think of '*Unraveled.*'").
[12] Russell Berman, *Is Obama Trying to Sway the Supreme Court?*, ATLANTIC (June 10, 2015), perma.cc/QNL3-LQSU.
[13] Sarah Ferris, *TV Anchor Thanks Obama for Saving His Life*, THE HILL (June 12, 2015), perma.cc/JF24-GF23.
[14] James Hohmann, *Q&A with Washington Post Supreme Court Reporter Robert Barnes*, WASH. POST (June 10, 2015), perma.cc/YX8H-3BKQg.
[15] Ferris, *supra* note 13.

the court may soon rule against his decision to illegally issue tax penalties and subsidies on Americans in two-thirds of the country." Michael Cannon wrote, "Today the president delivered a speech designed to cow the Supreme Court Justices into turning a blind eye to the law." Jonathan Adler added, "Presidential reticence about discussing pending cases during judicial deliberations is a sensible convention, and I see no good reason to violate it."[16] The *Wall Street Journal* editorial board exclaimed, "Mr. Obama must know that it does him no good to lacerate the Justices in public if he's trying to influence them to come his way." They closed with idle speculation: "Could it be that legal sources are telling Mr. Obama that he's about to lose, so he is now beginning to prepare the public for an all-out assault on the Court and Republicans?"[17]

Others defended the president's statements. Walter Dellinger, who served as the acting solicitor general under President Clinton, dismissed the relevance of the comments: "The Justices' life tenure secures their independence. There is no reason that issues before the court should be fenced off from public debate."[18] U.C. Irvine law professor Rick Hasen made the point more explicitly – the president *should* opine on these issue: "By speaking about the issues, the President who has the bully pulpit educates the public on the importance of the Supreme Court, the power that they hold and, in appropriate cases, disagreement with what the Court has done or is likely to do."[19] Dana Milbank praised the president's signal to the Court, which he summed up as "You wouldn't dare." Milbank explained that Obama's threat was directed to "five men not in the room: the conservative justices of the Supreme Court, who in the next 21 days will declare whether they are invalidating the most far-reaching legislation in at least a generation because of one vague clause tucked in its 2,000 pages."[20]

It is impossible to know whether Obama's remarks had any impact on the justices. Supreme Court reporter Lyle Denniston observed three years earlier, "Only [the Justices] will know, though, whether they thought it was appropriate for the President to give them a piece of legal and constitutional advice even as they were studying the issues"[21]

[16] Jonathan H. Adler, *Presidential Comments on Pending Supreme Court decisions*, WASH. POST (June 11, 2015), perma.cc/J3P9-D7P8.
[17] Opinion, *ObamaCare Omen? President Obama Goes after the Supreme Court Even before It Rules*, WALL ST. J. (June 9, 2015), on.wsj.com/22l778Q.
[18] Wallsten, *supra* note 1.
[19] Rick Hasen, *The President Should Talk MORE About Pending Cases Before #SCOTUS*, ELECTION LAW BLOG (June 11, 2015), bit.ly/2alg3Ch.
[20] Dana Milbank, *Obama to Supreme Court: You Wouldn't Dare Kill Obamacare*, WASH. POST (June 9, 2015), perma.cc/A5VD-BZL7.
[21] Denniston, *supra* note 2.

27.3. "AFTER MY MESSAGE TO THE CONGRESS"

The solicitor general is often referred to as the tenth justice because of his or her unique position before the Supreme Court.[22] In light of this special communication path, I asked a senior DOJ official how the president's ex parte comments about the justices affect that relationship. He was not bothered in the least by the Obama's remarks. When I asked why, he explained that President Franklin D. Roosevelt frequently spoke directly to the justices. The attorney remarked that he attended a lecture by Jeff Shesol at the Department of Justice in July 2011.[23] Shesol had recently published *Supreme Power: Franklin Roosevelt vs. the Supreme Court*. The book recalled President Roosevelt's proposal in 1937 to shift the balance of the Court to the left by "packing" it with additional justices. Citing Shesol's book, the attorney drew parallels between the present-day tensions in Washington and those between Roosevelt and the Supreme Court.

I was struck by these comparisons, as the Justice Department viewed President Roosevelt's encounters with the Court as a precedent to be followed, rather than a dark period to be avoided. Building on Professors Eshbaugh-Soha and Collins's research – which only goes back to the Eisenhower administration – I searched for all of the speeches where President Roosevelt opined on pending cases. I located ninety instances between 1933 and 1945 where the president used the phrase "Supreme Court."[24] The overwhelming majority of the references criticized the Court's January 1936 decision in *United States v. Butler*, which invalidated the Agricultural Adjustment Act. For years after the case was decided, FDR continued to ridicule the decision, noting how it limited tax revenues to the federal government. However, I could locate only one situation where the president spoke about the Court during a pending case – and it was a monumental one: Roosevelt's most famous clash with the Supreme Court occurred during his "Court Packing Plan."[25]

After his re-election in 1936, Roosevelt proposed the Judicial Procedures Reform Bill of 1937, which would have allowed him to appoint a new justice

---

[22] Seth P. Waxman, *The Solicitor General in Historical Context*, U.S. DEPT. OF JUSTICE (June 1, 1998), perma.cc/7R34-VZEM.

[23] Attorney General's Calendar, July 2011, bit.ly/1YkuUQ8.

[24] President Roosevelt's speeches can be searched on *The American Presidency Project*, bit.ly/1TPOXVe.

[25] According to a study by Professors Bethany Blackstone and Greg Goelzhauser, during 1937, Roosevelt set a record for saying 914 sentences of "negative rhetoric" about the Court. Bethany Blackstone and Greg Goelzhauser, *Presidential Rhetoric toward the Supreme Court.* 97 JUDICATURE 4 (Jan. 2014).

for each justice over the age of seventy. "The purpose of that feature," wrote Professor Richard Friedman, "of course, was very simply to pack the Court, to add enough new members to force it into submission."[26]

What made the timing of this proposal particularly salient is that during this period the Supreme Court was considering *West Coast Hotel v. Parish*. This case raised the question of whether a minimum wage law from Washington State was constitutional. In 1923, the Supreme Court found that the District of Columbia's minimum wage law for women was unconstitutional in *Adkins v. Children's Hospital*. *West Coast* was a challenge to overrule *Adkins*. The case was argued on December 16 and 17, 1936. At that point, Roosevelt had not yet formally announced his "Court Packing Plan," but it was understood that he would propose it soon.

Before the case would be decided on March 29, 1937, the president gave his famous March 9 Fireside Chat, the first of his second term in office. His call was clear: "We have, therefore, reached the point as a Nation where we must take action to save the Constitution from the Court and the Court from itself. We must find a way to take an appeal from the Supreme Court to the Constitution itself. We want a Supreme Court which will do justice under the Constitution – not over it. In our Courts we want a government of laws and not of men."[27]

Although the particulars of *West Coast Hotel* were not mentioned in the Fireside Chat, they did not need to be. Some scholars suggest that President Roosevelt's proposal helped trigger the so-called "switch in time that saved nine." The moderate Justice Owen Roberts changed his vote in *West Coast Hotel*, flipping a 5–4 defeat into a 5–4 victory for the government. Other similar victories would follow. On April 12, 1937, the Court would uphold the National Labor Relations Act on the same 5–4 vote.[28] Finally, on May 24, the Court upheld the Social Security Act, with Justice Roberts in the majority once again.[29] Professor Richard Freidman observed that these three cases in quick succession "gave a definite impression of a politically motivated change in the Court's jurisprudence."[30]

Today the scholarly consensus is that FDR's comments during the pendency of *West Coast Hotel* did not actually affect the justices. But the president certainly took credit for the Court's new direction. During his Constitution Day

---

[26] Richard D. Friedman, *Chief Justice Hughes' Letter on Court-packing.* 22 J. Sup. Ct. Hist. 76–86 (1997).

[27] *Fireside Chat 9: On "Court-Packing,"* Miller Center (Mar. 9, 1937), perma.cc/4K2D-4Z6K.

[28] National Labor Relations Board v. Jones & Laughlin Steel Corporation, 301 U.S. 1 (1937).

[29] Helvering v. Davis, 301 U.S. 619 (1937).

[30] Friedman, *supra* note 26 at 84.

address on September 17, 1937, Roosevelt pejoratively referred to the justices as the "Odd Man on the Supreme Court" and faulted them for frequently ruling against his agenda. But his "message to the Congress" changed that.

> For twenty years the Odd Man on the Supreme Court refused to admit that State minimum wage laws for women were constitutional. A few months ago, *after my message to the Congress on the rejuvenation of the Judiciary*, the Odd Man admitted that the Court had been wrong – for all those twenty years – and overruled himself.

The president was triumphant. His Court-packing plan paved the way for his New Deal, as well as state progressive laws, to continue unimpeded.

The jurisprudential change obviated the need to change the composition of the Court. Yet, Roosevelt's Court-packing scheme stalled in Congress when even Democrats who supported the president's policies viewed the move as constitutionally problematic. One of the most famous Roosevelt supporters who resisted the Court packing was Chief Justice Charles Evan Hughes. After a career in Republican politics, Hughes was nominated to the Court by Presidents Harding, Coolidge, and Hoover (he served as associate justice twice, nonconsecutively, before being elevated to chief). Despite his politics, Hughes would eventually become a defender of Roosevelt's Constitution and write a number of opinions upholding progressive laws, including *West Coast* itself.[31] However, the Court Packing scheme was viewed as too dangerous for Hughes, and he swiftly opposed.

Rather than accepting an invitation to testify before the Senate Judiciary Committee on the proposal, the chief justice opted instead to write a letter. The bulk of the March 22 letter rebutted Roosevelt's claim that the additional justices were needed because the Court was overworked and that it took too long to resolve cases. But at the end of his letter, the chief justice offered a constitutional analysis of Roosevelt's proposal to assign the older justices to different panels. Hughes wrote, "The Constitution does not appear to authorize two or more Supreme Courts or two or more parts of a Supreme Court functioning in effect as separate courts."[32] The *New Republic* called Hughes's analysis an "advisory opinion run riot."[33]

While it is unknown what impact Roosevelt's Fireside Chat had on the Court, the impact of Hughes's letter on Roosevelt was immediate. The

---

[31] West Coast Hotel v. Parish, 300 U.S. 379 (1937); NLRB v. Jones & Laughlin Steel Corp., 301 U.S. 1 (1937).

[32] Letter from Chief Justice Hughes to Senator Charles E. Hughes, Mar. 22, 1937, perma.cc/Q6Q8-KUTK.

[33] *The Chief Justice's Letter*, 90 NEW REPUBLIC (1937), p. 254.

following day the *New York Times* reported that the letter came with "an authority and suddenness which took administration forces by surprise and sent them scurrying to strengthen their defenses."[34] Robert H. Jackson, who would later serve on the Supreme Court, said the letter "turned the tide in the struggle."[35]

Eight decades later, Chief Justice John G. Roberts would praise these actions of his predecessor. During an event at NYU in November 2015, Roberts recounted that "Hughes was pressured," after the Fireside Chat, and that people urged him to respond with a radio address of his own. But that, Hughes realized, would be "fighting the battle on the enemy's turf." Instead, he sent the Senate, in Roberts's words, "a very measured letter."[36] The chief stressed that even though the Court was unpopular, the Constitution and the people prevailed. The Court was "the most unpopular institution in the country," Roberts said, that "as far as anyone knows, has been prolonging the Great Depression by standing up to FDR." The Chief Justice recalled that "it got to the point where FDR said, 'The people are with me.' Well, it certainly wasn't the case that the people were with the Court." The chief paused. "But I think they were with the Constitution and that had a lot to do with how [Hughes] handled the crisis. So there are things to learn from it." *Washington Post* reporter Robert Barnes, who covered the chief's remarks at NYU, observed: "Roberts believes it was Hughes's actions, not Justice Owen Roberts's change of heart on one case – the 'switch in time that saved nine' – that led FDR ultimately to withdraw his plan."[37]

Roberts ranks Hughes among the four greatest chief justices, alongside John Jay, John Marshall, and William Howard Taft. Each of their portraits occupies special "positions of prominence" in the Court's ceremonial conference rooms, Roberts explained.[38] "They all seem to be looking down at me with surprise." And "as they are looking down upon me," he added, "I am looking up to them."[39] In a profile of Roberts, conservative attorney Adam White wrote that Roberts drew lessons from each of the great chiefs. "From Jay, the need for the Court to maintain the public's confidence and respect. From Marshall, the importance of forging the justices' own disparate voices

---

[34] Friedman, *supra* note 26 at 83.
[35] *Id.*
[36] Jess Bravin, *Chief Justice John Roberts on Taking on a Democratic President (FDR)*, WALL ST. J. LAW BLOG (Nov. 21, 2015), on.wsj.com/1UAjhVl.
[37] Josh Blackman, *Chief Justice Roberts on FDR and the New Deal #SCOTUS*, JOSH BLACKMAN BLOG (Nov. 21, 2015), perma.cc/347K-C7KK.
[38] *Role of the Chief Justice*, C-SPAN (Feb. 1, 2007), cs.pn/2alirJ6 (10:00 to 11:15).
[39] Adam J. White, *Judging Roberts*, WEEKLY STANDARD (Nov. 23, 2015), tws.io/1Vdj3nC.

into a truly institutional voice. From Taft, who is responsible for giving the Court a building of its own, the importance of establishing the Court's independence. And from Hughes, the *importance of preserving that independence against FDR's court-packing plan.*"[40] The lessons from these chiefs, Hughes perhaps more than any other, have guided Roberts during his first decade on the Court.

27.4. "IT WOULD BE A DISASTER FOR THE INSTITUTION"

Immediately after the D.C. Circuit's July 22 decision in *Halbig v. Burwell*, all eyes in Washington turned, once again, to Chief Justice Roberts. ACA supporter Ezra Klein set the tone on *Vox* two hours after the decision was released. In an article that was likely prepared in advance, Klein wrote in a register meant to resonate with the chief: "For five unelected, Republican-appointed judges to cause that much disruption and pain would put the Court at the center of national politics in 2015 and beyond. It would be a disaster for the *institution.*"[41] The dog whistle was *institution*.

In a 2007 interview with the *Atlantic's* Jeffrey Rosen, Chief Justice Roberts explained his philosophy and goal. "I think the Court is also ripe for a similar refocus on functioning as an *institution*, because if it doesn't it's going to lose its credibility and legitimacy as an institution." Citing the example of Chief Justice Marshall, Roberts said, "I think that every justice should be worried about the Court acting as a Court and functioning as a Court, and they should all be worried, when they're writing separately, about the effect on the Court as an institution." Roberts told Rosen that "judicial temperament involves a judge's willingness to 'factor in the Court's institutional role,' to suppress his or her ideological agenda in the interest of achieving consensus and stability." After Roberts voted to uphold the ACA in 2012, Rosen praised him, writing that "[t]he fact that Roberts chose to place *institutional* legitimacy front and center is the mark of a successful Chief."[42]

Everyone else, including Ezra Klein, took notice. The *Vox* founder concluded, "All evidence suggests [Chief Justice Roberts] didn't want to rule the mandate unconstitutional. But he thought it would harm the Court to do otherwise. Deciding for the plaintiffs in *Halbig* would do far more damage to the

[40]   *Id.*

[41]   Ezra Klein, No, *The Halbig Case Isn't Going to Destroy Obamacare*, VOX (July 22, 2014), perma.cc/8C79-UZRY.

[42]   Jeffrey Rosen, *Welcome to the Roberts Court: How the Chief Justice Used Obamacare to Reveal His True Identity*, NEW REPUBLIC (June 28, 2012), perma.cc/XM73-AW3L.

law than striking down the mandate and it would do so when the law is actually providing insurance to people. It's not going to happen."[43]

The theme continued with variation. Douglas Kendall of the progressive Constitutional Accountability Center offered the same message: "The *institutional* interests of the Court are stronger at this point [than in 2012] because the law is now in place and providing health coverage for millions of Americans who didn't have it when the first challenge was heard. If Chief Justice Roberts wanted to strike down this law he would have been smarter to do it before it went into effect than he would be in 2015." Jonathan Chait wrote in the *New Yorker*: "Indeed, one thing that both sides agree on about *NFIB v. Sebelius* is that it was a political ruling rather than a legal one: John Roberts ultimately decided that destroying Obamacare would blow up his public credibility in an election year, and decided to let the law stand."[44]

Michael Carvin thought the efforts to pressure the Chief Justice were inappropriate. "They're so clearly directed at Roberts. They're so clearly premised on the notion that they can intimidate him. That confidence is so clearly based on fact that they think they did intimidate him in *NFIB*. My instinct is that, to the extent Chief Justice Roberts pays any attention to it would, completely backfire because it's so insulting to him." One of the attorneys from the Oklahoma attorney general's office explained that after the case was argued, "the left did its usual thing, because it had worked well for them in NFIB v. Sebelius: flood the airwaves and newspapers with messages that people would die if the Court rules for the challengers, in order to influence the outcome of the case. It was a blatant attempt to influence the justices."

Conservatives, however, viewed the case as an opportunity for Roberts to make up for his decision three years earlier. Berkeley law professor John Yoo wrote in *National Review*: "This case will give the Chief Justice the opportunity to atone for his judicial sin of two years ago."[45] The conservative *Breitbart News* questioned, "Will Chief Justice Roberts rewrite ObamaCare to keep it alive again? Or is he irritated by the political pressures that forced him into making that decision last time, and looking to restore his judicial reputation?"[46] University of Texas law professor Lucas A. Powe explained, "He's under the same pressure that he was under in 2012, where his natural allies really want him to gut the statute and be done with it. And as you saw when

---

[43] Klein, *supra* note 41.

[44] Jonathan Chait, *Supreme Court to Hear Newest, Craziest Legal Challenge to Obamacare*, DAILY INTELLIGENCER (Nov. 7, 2014), perma.cc/8BCA-UA8Y.

[45] John Yoo, *Halbig Could be Chief Justice Roberts' Chance to Redeem Himself*, NAT'L REV. (July 22, 2014), perma.cc/BA8V-AB9W.

[46] Josh Blackman, *The Full Court Press of Chief Justice Roberts Has Already Begun*, JOSH BLACKMAN'S BLOG (Nov. 7, 2014), perma.cc/NH5Q-ZXE2.

he voted to sustain Obamacare, the right came fairly close to accusing him of treason."[47]

In addition to the pressures from outside the Court, there are also pressures from within the Court. In July 2012, CBS reporter Jan Crawford stated that the chief's decision to uphold the individual mandate brought out "deep and personal ... discord," as well as "tension and bitterness" from the conservative justices. In an interview with Piers Morgan on CNN a few weeks later, Justice Scalia emphatically rejected that there was any sort of acrimony. "You shouldn't believe what you read about the Court in the newspapers,"[48] Scalia told Morgan. "No, I haven't had a falling out with Justice Roberts," he added. "There are clashes on legal questions but not personally." However, Justice Ginsburg suggested otherwise. In an August 2014 interview with the *National Law Journal's* Marcia Coyle, Ginsburg said the Chief "did distance himself from the court in the health care decision."[49] She added, "He knew he was going to take a lot of criticism from his home crowd for that."

Roberts rejected any assertion that he was affected by pressures from without or within. During a discussion at the University of Nebraska in September 2014, the chief agreed that Congress and the president are "not getting along very well these days. It's a period of real partisan rancor that, I think, impedes their ability to carry out their functions." He stressed, however: "I don't want it to spill over and affect us. That's not the way we do business. We are not Democrats or Republicans. In nine years I have never seen any political issue like that arise between us. We need to keep the partisan divide on the other side of First Street and not let it come over to our sphere."[50] His decision in *King v. Burwell* would make clear that the chief views the four-lane street between the Court and the Capitol as wide as the Grand Canyon. As he would explain on June 25, 2015, "In a democracy, the power to make the law rests with those chosen by the people." Citing Chief Justice Marshall's canonical opinion in *Marbury v. Madison*, Roberts concluded, "Our role is more confined – 'to say what the law is.'"[51]

[47] Sahil Kapur, *Obamacare Returns to SCOTUS: Will John Roberts Crush It This Time?*, TALKING POINTS MEMO (Nov. 26, 2014), perma.cc/9NZU-C9FK.
[48] Bill Mears, *Scalia Dismisses Talk of Internal Court Rancor*, CNN (July 19, 2012), perma.cc/F5FG-HCWR.
[49] Josh Blackman, *RBG: Roberts "Distanced Himself from the Court in the Health Care Decision,"* JOSH BLACKMAN'S BLOG (Aug. 22, 2014), perma.cc/34AC-EL48.
[50] Josh Blackman, *Chief Justice: "Keep the Partisan Divide on the Other Side of First Street,"* JOSH BLACKMAN'S BLOG (Sep. 22, 2014), perma.cc/3TJA-73TM; Brent Martin, *Chief Justice Roberts: Scalia, Ginsburg Wouldn't be Confirmed Today*, NEBRASKA RADIO NETWORK (Sep. 19, 2014), perma.cc/LY8Y-4KSM.
[51] King v. Burwell, 135 S.Ct. 2480, 2495 (2015) (quoting Marbury v. Madison, 1 Cranch 137, 177 (1803)).

28

"Improve Health Care Markets, Not Destroy Them"

28.1. "HEALTHCARE!"

The Court announced that the justices would hand down one or more opinions at 10:00 AM on Thursday, June 25. Michael Carvin was not in the Court that day. He told the *National Law Journal*, "I frankly don't really want to be around a whole lot of other people if we lose."[1] Carvin was also not in the Court when *NFIB* was decided in 2012. I assumed that *King v. Burwell* would be saved for the last day of the term, Monday, June 29, like its Obamacare predecessors *Hobby Lobby* and *NFIB* before it. I was wrong.

At 9:51 AM, Lyle Denniston reported on SCOTUSBlog that there were "Two boxes of opinions." The Court does not announce which or even how many decisions would be handed down on a given day. Reporters have taken to counting the number of boxes that are sitting on the counter of the Public Information Office, which contain the printed opinions. Denniston estimated that two boxes "means 3 or 4 opinions, probably." He would be half right. One of the thousands of people following along on the blog was HHS Secretary Sylvia Matthews Burwell from her office at the Humphrey Building.[2] At 10:00 AM sharp, the justices took the bench.

The chief justice began, "Justice Kennedy has our opinion this morning in Case 13–1371, *The Texas Department of Housing and Community Affairs v. Inclusive Communities Project*." This 5–4 decision allowed plaintiffs to sue the government under the Fair Housing Act, where there is no direct but only statistical evidence of racial discrimination. Kennedy spent about six minutes reading a summary of the case. Mark Walsh noted that "Sherrilyn

---

[1] Marcia Coyle, *As Term Closes, a Waiting Game at the Supreme Court*, NAT'L. LAW J. (June 25, 2015) perma.cc/LLS9-KETR.

[2] Louis Radnofsky, *Burwell Describes 'Emotional' Moment Awaiting Supreme Court Health Ruling*, WALL ST. J. (June 26, 2015), on.wsj.com/1Zhytri.

Ifill, the President of the NAACP Legal Defense and Educational Fund, seated in the second row of the bar section, let[] out a big sigh of relief and bob[bed] her head in relief."[3] That victory was not expected. Kennedy closed, "Justice Thomas has filed a dissenting opinion. Justice Alito has filed a dissenting opinion, in which the Chief Justice and Justices Scalia and Thomas join." As is the usual custom, none of the dissenters would make a statement. Because the justices hand down opinions in the order of seniority, any other opinions would be from Justices Kennedy, Scalia, or the chief justice.

At 10:08 AM, SCOTUSBlog announced, "Here's Lyle again with the next opinion." A moment later, a one-word message announced the decision: "Healthcare!" When Burwell saw the words "Healthcare!" she "knew that this was it." She recalled leaving her office, and "[a]s I was going down the hall, I heard a cheer." Burwell, remembering what had happened in 2012, made her team triple-check the decision. "I'm like, 'Are we sure?'" she said with a laugh, joking about her "anal retentiveness." They confirmed it. Burwell said the experience "was very emotional."[4]

SCOTUSBlog quickly explained that the "Decision of the Fourth Circuit is affirmed in *King v. Burwell*. 6–3. Chief Justice writes for the Court. Holding: Subsidies are available [on the federal exchange]." Amy Howe added to the blog, "Administration wins, to put it another way." Unlike in 2012 when the Supreme Court's website and the opinion were inaccessible, in 2015 the servers held strong. Everyone was able to download the opinion immediately. Those inside the Court would still be in suspense for a few more moments.

28.2. "WE ARE NOT POLITICALLY ACCOUNTABLE TO THEM"

The chief justice announced: "I have the opinion of the Court in case number 14–114 *King v. Burwell*." For the second time in four terms, the chief justice had assigned to himself the opinion in the critical Obamacare case. SCOTUSBlog's Mark Walsh recounted that "everyone in the Courtroom shift[ed] in their seats a bit." Unfortunately for those in attendance, the chief did not show his cards right away. Court reporter Tony Mauro noted, "At first, it was not clear which way Roberts was leaning." However, unlike 2012, where many were misled into thinking he invalidated the ACA, his hand down in 2015 cut to the chase fairly quickly.

---

[3] Mark Walsh, *A "View" from the Courtroom: Barbs and Backslaps in Two Big Cases*, SCOTUSBLOG (June 25, 2012), perma.cc/7DFT-E9CL.

[4] *Id.*

Roberts began by explaining how several states in the 1990s attempted to "expand access to insurance coverage" by "bar[ring] insurers from denying coverage to any person because of his health." The "guaranteed issue requirement" had an "unintended consequence," Roberts said, of "encourag[ing] people to wait until they got sick to buy insurance." The Chief asked rhetorically, "Why buy insurance coverage when you are healthy if you can buy the same coverage for the same price when you become ill?" In such states, "the result was an economic death spiral; premiums rose, the number of people buying insurance declined, that caused premiums to rise further which caused the number of people buying insurance to decline even more and so on, until insurers began to leave the market entirely." Mark Walsh said that "[t]he mention of 'death spirals' appeared promising for supporters of the ACA, though every member of the Court maintains a somewhat grim face throughout the Chief Justice's delivery." The theme of death spirals was a prominent feature in Roberts's 2012 opinion in *NFIB v. Sebelius*, where he wrote that by "requiring that individuals purchase health insurance, the mandate prevents cost-shifting by those who would otherwise go without it."

Citing RomneyCare, Roberts said that the Affordable Care Act "adopts a version of these three key reforms" – known as the three-legged stool. "First, the Act adopts the guaranteed issue requirements. Second, the Act generally requires individuals to maintain health insurance coverage, or if they failed to do so, to make a payment to the IRS." (The chief justice did not refer to the payment as either a *penalty* or a *tax*.) "And third, the Act seeks to make insurance more affordable for a significant number of people by giving tax credits to individuals with household incomes between 100 and 400 percent of the Federal poverty line."

The Chief continued that "the act requires the creation of an exchange *in* each state." His framing gave away the outcome: it is not that the state has to establish the exchange for there to be credits, but the ACA only requires the passive-voice creation of an exchange – *in* the state. "The Act gives each state the opportunity to establish its own exchange, but provides that the Federal Government will establish the exchange if the State does not." This brings us to the crux of the case: "whether the Act's tax credits are available in states that have a Federal Exchange rather than a State Exchange." This becomes an issue, he explained, because Section 36B makes tax credits "available to individuals who buy insurance through an exchange that is 'established by the State under Section 1311 of the Act.'" Roberts paused, ever so briefly, after saying "established by the State."

The Court has "to decide whether a Federal Exchange can be said to be established by the State. At the outset it might seem that a Federal Exchange cannot fulfill this requirement." He paused. "But when *read in context*, the reach of the phrase; established by the State is not so clear.'" *Context* was the magic word the government was waiting for.

The Chief Justice then relied on the solicitor general's two primary positions. First, he adopted the *such exchange* argument. "The Act says that if a State chooses not to establish its own exchange, the Federal Government shall establish *such* exchange within the State," Roberts said, with the slightest accent on *such*. "By using the phrase 'such exchange' the Act tells the Federal Government to establish the same exchange that the State was supposed to establish. In other words, State Exchanges and Federal Exchanges are equivalent; they must meet the same requirements, perform the same functions and serve the same purposes. Although State and Federal Exchanges are established by different sovereigns, the Act does not suggest that they differ in any meaningful way."

This equivalency lead into the second argument the solicitor general advanced – *rump exchanges*. If there were no subsidies, there would be "*no qualified individuals* on Federal Exchanges. But the Act clearly contemplates that there will be qualified individuals on every exchange, state or federal. Again the phrase 'established by the State' may not be as clear as it appears when read out of context." He added that if the plaintiffs' reading prevailed, and no subsidies would be available in states that refused to establish exchanges, "[t]he combination of no tax credits and an ineffective coverage requirement could well push a State's individual insurance market into a death spiral." The Chief concluded, "It is *implausible* that Congress meant the Act to operate in this manner." Although Ben Nelson would not be mentioned, Roberts rejected out of hand that Adler and Cannon's theory could even be plausible.

But then why would the statute use the phrase "established by the state" if Congress "meant to make tax credits available on both State and Federal Exchanges"? Roberts dismissed this concern: "It is true that we generally try to avoid interpreting a statute in a way that makes some language superfluous. But we have said that is not an absolute rule, and it does not seem particularly helpful in interpreting *this* statute." There was a distinct emphasis on the word *this*.

Then Roberts offered a mild criticism of how the law itself was enacted: "The Affordable Care Act contains more than a few examples of inartful drafting." Mark Walsh recalled that "many in the Courtroom snicker[ed]" at this jab, but there were no members of Congress in attendance "to receive this scolding in

person." Roberts explained that "[s]everal features of the Act's passage contributed to the unfortunate reality of its, to be charitable, 'imprecision.'" The
phrases "charitable" and "imprecision" did not make it into Roberts's written
opinion.

"Congress wrote key parts of the Act behind closed doors," the chief said,
"rather than through the traditional legislative process." Further, "Congress
passed much of the Act using a complicated budgetary procedure known as
Reconciliation, which limited opportunities for debate and amendment and
bypassed the Senate's normal 60 vote filibuster requirement." This was a not-
too-subtle reference to the disjointed manner in which the draft Senate bill
became the final bill because of Scott Brown's election.

"As a result, the Act does not reflect the type of care and deliberation
that one might expect of such significant legislation." Roberts referenced
a "cartoon that Justice Frankfurter once quoted in which a senator told
his colleagues that a new bill was too complicated to understand and that
they would just have to pass it to find out what it means." Roberts must
have realized the irony that then-Speaker Nancy Pelosi famously said of
the ACA, "But we have to pass the bill so that you can find out what's in
it."[5] In Roberts's mind, the enactment of the ACA was a caricature of a
cartoon. Yet, "despite all that, we must do our best to understand the Act
as a whole."

The chief said during the hand down in Court, "Petitioner's arguments
are strong. There can be no dispute in that." In the written opinion, Roberts
wrote more specifically that their "[a]rguments about the *plain meaning* of
Section 36B are strong." But then came the *but*. "But we cannot conclude
that the phrase 'established by the state under Section 1311' is so plain in the
context of the act as a whole that we can just stop with those words. Because
the text is properly considered ambiguous, we must look to the broader structure of the Act to determine its correct meaning. And here the rest of the statute compels us to reject the petitioner's interpretation." Tony Mauro noted
that "Roberts read rapidly from his written opinion summary, as if upholding
the health care law was an unpleasant task that he would just as soon wrap
up quickly."[6]

The Chief paused for a few seconds and pivoted to the concluding part of
his opinion, which encapsulated his broader philosophy of the Constitution

---

[5] Jonathan Capehart, *Pelosi Defends Her Infamous Health Care Remark*, WASH. POST (June 20,
    2012), perma.cc/2DSX-PAZ3.
[6] Tony Mauro, *Hugs and Harangues: Inside the Court for the Health Care Ruling*, LAW.COM
    (June 25, 2015), bit.ly/27ckt7r.

and the Court. "In a democracy, the power to make the law rests with those chosen by the people and accountable *to them*." He stressed *to them*, focusing on the object of Democracy: the people, not the courts. "We have not been chosen by the people and we are not politically accountable *to them*." He again stressed *to them*. In the written version of the opinion, Roberts wrote only that "[i]n a democracy, the power to make the law rests with those chosen by the people." In his written statement, he sought to accentuate the notion of political accountability, and that government is ultimately accountable to the people.

Three years earlier, Roberts made a nearly identical point when he upheld the ACA. "The Framers created a Federal Government of limited powers, and assigned to this Court the duty of enforcing those limits. The Court does so today. But the Court does not express any opinion on the wisdom of the Affordable Care Act. Under the Constitution, that judgment is *reserved to the people*." He added, "It is not in any way based on our judgment about whether the Affordable Care Act is good policy. That judgment is for the people acting through their representatives. It is not our job to save the people from the consequences of their political choices."

The chief justice would once again cite the his icon, Chief Justice John Marshall. "Our role is accordingly more limited to say what the law is." In his written opinion, he cited Chief Justice Marshall's iconic statement in *Marbury v. Madison* that "[i]t is emphatically the duty of the Judicial Department to say what the law *is*." Often, lawyers append to the end of the quotation, "not what the law *ought* to be." Roberts made the same point four years earlier in *NFIB v. Sebelius*, stating, "Our decision today is based on our responsibility recognized in *Marbury v. Madison* to say what the law is."

Roberts conceded that saying what the law *is* "is easier in some cases than others." This case, even by Roberts's best lights, was tough. Without skipping a beat, he continued, "[B]ut in every case we must respect the role of the legislature and take care not to undo what it has done." Tony Mauro reported that the Chief was "more somber" when he read this sentence: "A fair reading of legislation demands a fair understanding of the legislative plan."

Roberts closed with reading the penultimate paragraph of his written opinion, verbatim. "Congress passed the Affordable Care Act to improve health insurance markets" – there was a noticeable pause – "not to destroy them. If at all possible, we must interpret the Act in a way that is consistent with the former and avoids the latter. The provisions making tax credits available can fairly be read in a way that is consistent with what we see as Congress's plan and that is the reading we adopt. Tax credits are available for those who qualify for them regardless whether they purchase insurance on a State or Federal

Exchange." Once again, the chief justice ruled in favor of the Obama administration's defense of the Affordable Care Act.

But we were not done yet.

28.3. "SCOTUSCARE"

In an even-toned voice, the chief handed the case off. "Justice Scalia has filed
a dissenting opinion in which Justice Thomas and Justice Alito have joined."
There was a brief moment of silence, and Justice Scalia interjected, "Indeed."
In *NFIB*, Justice Kennedy announced the joint dissent from the bench. Here,
with Kennedy signing onto Roberts's majority opinion, Scalia would read on
behalf of Alito and Thomas. After shuffling his papers, Scalia began his prepared remarks, which would stretch over twelve minutes, more than thirty
seconds longer than the chief's statement.

"The Act provides that an individual may receive tax credits only if he buys
insurance on 'an exchange established by the State.'" Note that he skipped
the final three words in Section 36B, "under Section 1311." Scalia continues,
"You would think the answer would be obvious." In his written opinion, Scalia
added, "so obvious there would hardly be a need for the Supreme Court to
hear a case about it." Then Scalia made what I think may be a Freudian slip:
"The Secretary of Health and Human Services is not a state, so people who
buy insurance through *such* an exchange." He stopped himself, and said, "uh,
uh." He focused on *such exchange*, the crux of the majority's opinion. Scalia
continued, "so an exchange established by the Secretary is not an exchange
established by the State. So people who buy insurance through an exchange
established by the Secretary get no money."

Justice Scalia charged, "Words no longer have any meaning if an exchange
that is not established by a state is 'established by the state.'" He paused deliberately between the first six words. "It's hard to come up with a clearer way to
limit tax credits to state exchanges then to use the words 'established by the
State.' And it's hard to come up with a reason to use those words other than
the purpose of limiting credits to state exchanges." Referencing a question that
Justice Alito had asked Solicitor General Verrilli, Scalia stated that the statute
should have been phrased, "tax credits were available for anyone who purchased insurance 'on an exchange' rather than 'on an exchange established
by the State.'"

"Under all the usual rules of interpretation," Scalia paused, "the government should lose this case." He then omitted one of the most potent lines from
his written opinion. "But normal rules of interpretation seem always to yield to
the overriding principle of the present Court: The Affordable Care Act must

be saved." This was a direct assault on the chief justice, who now twice saved the ACA. Because Scalia was the most senior associate justice, he was seated right next to Roberts. But that would not stop him from ridiculing the chief's opinion in *King*.

Scalia explained that the Court disregarded the fact that the phrase "established by the state" appears seven times in the ACA, and uses the phrase "exchange" by itself elsewhere: "The Court solves that problem, believe it or not, by simply saying that federal exchanges count as state exchanges only, and this is a quotation from the opinion, 'for purposes of tax credits.' How wonderfully convenient and how utterly contrary to normal principles of interpretation!" Again, Scalia charged, the "normal rules" do not apply for the ACA. "The Court turns conventional principles of statutory interpretation upside down by subordinating the express words of the tax credit provision, 'established by the State,' to the supposed implications of other clauses, with only a tangential connection to tax credits."

Next, Scalia turned to the purported purpose of the ACA, which the majority explained as "improving health insurance markets." But purpose matters only Scalia responded, if it "shed[s] light upon an otherwise unclear provision. Could anyone say with a straight face that 'established by the State' is unclear?" The majority ruled it was "ambiguous." Further, Scalia dismissed the "dire economic consequences" of ruling against the government. If the "grim economic forecast is accurate, it would show only that the Affordable Care Act contains a flaw." Here Justice Scalia suggested that the Ben Nelson theory could explain that Congress intended to punish unwilling states, because the law reveals a "congressional preference for state participation." The unavailability of subsidies in states without an exchange would "not show that the law means the opposite of what it says."

Scalia continued, "[T]his Court has no free-floating power to rescue Congress from its drafting mistakes." The Justice asked rhetorically, "What are the odds, do you think, that the same slip of the pen occurred in seven separate places? If there was a mistake here, context suggests it was a substantive mistake in designing this part of the law, not a technical mistake in transcribing it." Section 36B was deliberately written the way it was written.

Whereas Roberts viewed his decision as deferring to the democratic process and those Congress is "politically accountable" to, Scalia viewed the majority opinion's "twistifications"[7] as anti-democratic. "It is Congress'

---

7 Jeffrey Rosen, *John Roberts*, ATLANTIC (Nov. 2012), perma.cc/JTG7-6JDE. Engaging in what Marshall's archrival, Thomas Jefferson, called a 'twistification,' Roberts joined the conservatives in rejecting the mandate's legality according to Congress's power to regulate interstate

responsibility to make laws, and this Court's responsibility only to interpret them," he said. "It is up to our country's elected lawmakers, not its unelected judges, to repair statutes that have unintended consequences, or that do not work out in practice." Roberts thought the role of the Court was to give less weight to text in order to read statutes in a way that reflects the congressional plan. Scalia disagreed: "[W]e have no authority to ignore the law because we believe Congress must have intended something else." Any Congress, including *this Congress*, "should amend the law to conform to its intent."

In the penultimate portion of his opinion, Scalia directed his ire at the Chief Justice. "Today's decision changes the usual rules of statutory interpretation for the sake of the Affordable Care Act. That, alas, is no novelty." Tony Mauro observed that Scalia "ripped into Roberts' opinion, unfazed by the fact that Roberts was sitting right next to him. With a furrowed brow and slight frown, Roberts clearly did not enjoy being lambasted at such a short remove."[8] Scalia described the Chief's 2012 opinion in *NFIB as* "revis[ing]" and "transform[ing]" two "major parts of this law in order to save them from unconstitutionality." With *King v. Burwell*, the "Court today has turned its attention to a third. The Court concludes that this limitation would prevent the rest of the Act from working, as well as hoped, so it rewrites the Act to make tax credits available everywhere." Then came Scalia's pièce de résistance: "We really should start calling this law SCOTUScare." The chamber erupted in laughter. Tony Mauro noted that "even Roberts smiled when Scalia gave the audience his money quote."[9] This was the first time the wire-service-acronym SCOTUS (Supreme Court of the United States) was used by the Court.

Scalia closes with an admonition for the Court:

> But this Court's two decisions concerning the Act will surely be remembered through the years. The interpretive somersaults they have performed will remain as astounding precedent, cited by lawyers to confuse our jurisprudence. And these two cases will publish forever the discouraging truth that the Supreme Court of the United States favors some laws over others, and that it is prepared to sacrifice all the usual interpretive principles, that it is prepared to do whatever it takes to uphold and assist its favorites.

There are special rules for Obamacare.

commerce, but joined the liberals in upholding the mandate as an expression of Congress's power to levy taxes.
8   Mauro, *supra* note 6.
9   Mauro, *supra* note 6.

Usually, a justice concludes a dissent by saying, "I respectfully dissent."[10] However, to signal a more acrimonious feeling toward the majority opinion, a Justice closes with a brusque, "I dissent." For example, Justice Ginsburg disrespectfully dissented in *Bush v. Gore* and *Hobby Lobby*. However, by my count, Justice Scalia led the way with eight disrespectful dissents over the past decade.[11] *King v. Burwell* was no exception. In the written opinion, Scalia finished with "I dissent." However, in his oral hand-down of *King v. Burwell*, he said, "I respectfully dissent." Perhaps his proximity to the Chief deterred him from striking the coup de grâce. Mark Walsh noted that Scalia, who was usually very passionate and engaged with his reading, was "unusually calm and deliberate as he delivers his dissent." It would be the last dissent that Justice Antonin Scalia delivered from the bench.

With that, the hearing was over. The Court would return the following day, when Justice Kennedy announce his decision in *Obergefell v. Hodges*, finding that laws limiting marriage to a man and a woman were unconstitutional. This afforded less than twenty-four hours for *King v. Burwell* to dominate the news cycle.

28.4. 10:10

In 2012, CNN, *Fox News*, and other news outlets botched their coverage of the outcome in *NFIB v. Sebelius*. For about ten minutes they reported that the individual mandate had been invalidated. Even worse, the president watched those reports and thought that he had lost!

In 2015, President Obama would learn about his victory much faster. On decision day, the president was receiving his daily briefing. He sat in a chair between the portrait of President Washington atop the fireplace and the bust of Abraham Lincoln.[12] National Security Adviser Susan Rice was on the couch, along with several other members of the administration. In a picture taken by the White House photographer Pete Souza – who was fortuitously in the Oval Office to capture this moment in history – the grandfather clock over Obama's shoulder shows the time as 10:10. At that moment, Brian Mosteller, director of Oval Office operations, abruptly opened the door and

---

[10] David Auerbach, *R-E-S-P-E-C-T, Find Out What It Means to Scalia*, Slate (June 26, 2015), perma.cc/7NV3-R686.

[11] Josh Blackman, *5 "Disrespectful Dissents" This Term – Scalia Had 4, Sotomayor Had 1*, Josh Blackman's Blog (June 29, 2015), perma.cc/8H4N-2H3H.

[12] The White House, *Behind the Lens: When the President Heard the News of the Supreme Court Decision on the Affordable Care Act*, Medium (June 26, 2015), perma.cc/C5YL-9F5S.

told the president that the Supreme Court ruled for the government by a 6–3 decision.[13]

Souza recalled, "For one split second, the President's face was blank as if he was trying to comprehend the news. He then reacted in jubilation." The photographer shared three photographs taken in rapid fire. In the first, Obama is looking over his shoulder, eyes wide open. In the second, he gazes forward, thinking intently. In the third, his right hand shoots up the air, his eyes closed, with a beaming smile across his face. He gets out of his chair and exchanges smiles with Susan Rice. He exits to the Outer Oval Office, where chief of state Denis McDonough was already waiting for him. Souza writes, "they exchanged hugs and fist-bumps" as they play-boxed, both smiling ear-to-ear. In the background, a TV showed four live news broadcasts from the Supreme Court. Soon Vice President Biden entered the Oval Office. The president stuck out his hand, looking for a high-five. White House counsel Neil Eggleston and Chief of Staff Kristie Canegallo entered to "explain the details of the decision."

"As they were talking," Souza wrote, "I noticed that the clock in the Oval Office still read 10:10 AM. But it was actually almost 10:30 AM." At the moment the president learned of the decision, the clock stopped. "What a coincidence on a historic day," Souza exclaimed.

28.5. "ONE OF OUR GREATEST SOLICITOR GENERALS"

Solicitor General Verrilli, who was in the Court as the opinion was being announced, was likely the last person in the Obama administration who got to celebrate the victory. Around 10:32 AM, Justice Scalia finally finished reading from his lengthy dissent. The session was closed, and the justices quickly retreated behind the red curtains. Mark Walsh reported that Verrilli "smiled broadly. He first hugged his principal political deputy solicitor general, Ian H. Gershengorn. They exchanged backslaps as they embraced. Verrilli then did the same with Edwin S. Kneedler, a career deputy solicitor general who, like Gershengorn, was on the government's brief in *King* with the Solicitor General. That's not something one sees very often just steps from the Supreme Court bench." Tony Mauro added that the hugs and backslaps were "not typical for staid lawyers clad in morning coats."[14] I learned that Verrilli was "not entirely surprised" by the 6–3 vote. "It could have been 5–4 against us, it could have been 5–4 for us." However, he would relish in this victory more than in others. While the United States has had a string of unanimous defeats, with

13 *Id.*
14 Mauro, *supra* note 6.

all of the justices rejecting the government's position, Verrilli has pulled out most of the biggest wins.[15] Supreme Court analyst Ken Jost "hailed [Verrilli] as the Mariano Rivera of Supreme Court advocacy: he closes well in the most important contests."[16]

Verrilli holds a unique place of regard and trust within the Obama administration, and among the justices. He began his service in the Obama administration as an Associate Deputy Attorney General, and later as deputy Counsel to the President. They were not the most glamorous jobs for someone who had argued thirteen cases before the Supreme Court, but they allowed him to get to know the president and to earn his trust. In 2010, when Solicitor General Elena Kagan was elevated to the Supreme Court, Verrilli was asked to interview to become the government's top advocate. Verrilli recalled that "it took me about a nanosecond to say yes."[17] He was selected by the president over then-Principal Deputy Solicitor General Neal Katyal, who ran the office for a year after Kagan's nomination. Katyal submitted his resignation letter the day after Verrilli was sworn into office.

Early during his tenure, Verrilli received criticisms from other progressives for his reserved demeanor. They wanted more fire and brimstone, I learned. But Verrilli made the decision that this was not the right thing to carry out the responsibilities of the office. While in charge, Verrilli has preached that the right way to do the job is to take the temperature down as much as possible, and always operate in a manner that demonstrates profound respect for the members of the Court as an institution and for the legitimacy of process. This is especially true during a time where there is such a stark conflict between the Supreme Court, the executive branch, and Congress. The solicitor general personally tried to do everything he could by word and deed to send the message that this is not a political process, this is a judicial process. And over the previous four years, that message has resonated and calmed down more people on the left. Further, Verrilli communicated to his office that as a pragmatic matter, the fire and brimstone approach was a very poor way to pick up the fifth vote in cases. As a result, the Office believes that it has steadfastly built up some credibility with the Court by following this approach.

A prominent example illustrates this dynamic. During oral arguments in the 2013 case of *Clapper v. Amnesty International*, Verrilli told the Supreme

---

[15] Ilya Shapiro, *Why Obama Keeps Losing at the Supreme Court*, BLOOMBERG VIEW (June 6, 2013), perma.cc/S96X-MYGC.

[16] Kenneth Jost, *Verrilli Scores Well at Supreme Court Despite Questions*, JOST ON JUSTICE (Sep. 29, 2013), perma.cc/EU5V-ENTW.

[17] American Bar Association, *Four Solicitors General Remember Their Time Advocating for the Government and "Playing Traffic Cop"*, ABA (Aug. 3, 2015), perma.cc/MA6J-T6H7.

Court that if government seeks to use information gathered by a 2008 elec-
tronic surveillance program in a criminal prosecution, the government would
have to disclose that information. Verrilli explained, "[A]n aggrieved person,
someone who is a party to a communication, gets notice that the government
intends to introduce information in a proceeding against them."[18] The Court
ruled in favor of the government in a 5–4 decision. Justice Alito's majority
opinion quoted Verrilli's representation almost verbatim. "If the government
intends to use or disclose information obtained or derived from" surveillance
authorized by the 2008 law "in judicial or administrative proceedings, it must
provide advance notice of its intent, and the affected person may challenge
the lawfulness of the acquisition."[19] However, it turned out this was not true.
Adam Liptak reported in the *New York Times*, "Federal prosecutors, apparently unaware of his representations, have refused to make the promised disclosures." Jameel Jaffer of the American Civil Liberties Union referred to this
maneuver as "the government's shell game."[20]

According to journalist Charlie Savage, Verrilli discovered in June 2013
that, contrary to his representation to the Court, the DOJ National Security
Division "did not notify criminal defendants when eavesdropping without a
warrant." After Verrilli became aware of this contradiction, Savage wrote, he
"sought an explanation from the National Security Division." Their "lawyers
had vetted his briefs and helped him practice for his arguments" but apparently did not disclose the full nature of how evidence is withheld. This triggered a "wider debate" between Verrilli and the national security prosecutors
over whether the information could be withheld.

"Ultimately," Savage wrote, Verrilli's "view prevailed and the National
Security Division changed its practice going forward." Verrilli's representation to the Supreme Court was deemed so important that the government's
position was changed to maintain a practice consistent with what he relayed.
This episode speaks to the important bond Verrilli made with the Supreme
Court and the credibility he built there. His experience in the formative years
of the Obama White House made this process of seeking a "unified view of
what the government position ought to be" much easier.[21] At an American
Bar Association discussion with other solicitors general, he noted, "[T]hey've

---

[18] Transcript of Oral Argument at 4, Clapper v. Amnesty International, 133 S. Ct. 1138 (2012), (No.
     11-1025).
[19] Clapper v. Amnesty Int'l USA, 133 S. Ct. 1138 (2013).
[20] Adam Liptak, *A Secret Surveillance Program Proves Challengeable in Theory Only*, N. Y. TIMES
     (July 15, 2015), nyti.ms/1UviAoJ. CHARLIE SAVAGE, POWER WARS 586–93 (2015).
[21] ABA, *supra* note 17.

left me alone, and I've taken advantage of that."[22] He would always, however, identify two or three cases of the term where his position might surprise the administration, so he would call the White House and say, "This is what I'm doing." He was not to asking for permission, but rather giving them a heads-up.

The solicitor general recognized that he arrived at the office at a momentous time. In remarks in his hometown of Wilton, Connecticut, Verrilli acknowledged that he had a higher profile than did his predecessors. "We're in a very unusual place in history," he said. "It is not usual for so many high-profile cases to come before the Supreme Court in a short span of time."[23] He would argue four Obamacare cases in the span of five years. Verrilli added, "We're at a time when a majority of the Supreme Court has a strong ideological perspective different from the president. Aside from the New Deal, this is probably the greatest amount of friction between the executive and judicial branches." He viewed it as his personal "responsibility to lead the representation of the United States in these matters of real historical importance."[24]

On June 11, former Attorney General Eric Holder spoke to the American Constitution Society, a group of progressive legal scholars, at the Capitol Hilton. (Coincidentally that evening, one mile away, the Competitive Enterprise Institute held their annual gala, where they toasted to success in *King v. Burwell*.) During his remarks, Holder praised Verrilli. He said that usually, "Solicitors general are extremely guarded in their independence within the Department [of Justice], but he's not necessarily that guy."[25] Rather, Verrilli was "a very collaborative person" within the Obama administration, and would always share with others, "This is the way I think we want to go with this argument." Holder added that he "bounces things off of people. He is a good friend and a progressive." The former attorney general concluded with a smile, "I think he is going to be seen as an extremely consequential Solicitor General, I think one of our greatest Solicitors General."

28.6. "THIS IS NO LONGER ABOUT A LAW"

Ninety minutes after President Obama learned of the outcome in *King v. Burwell*, he stood alongside Vice President Biden and Secretary Burwell in

---

[22] David Lat, *A Great Legal Job, Or the Greatest Legal Job?*, ABOVE THE LAW (Aug. 3, 2015), perma.cc/5KYD-S888.

[23] Jeanette Ross, *U.S. Solicitor General Donald Verrilli: Telling Tales of Life in the Capital*, WILTON BULL. (June 2, 2014), perma.cc/MVM2-H2U5.

[24] *SCOTUSblog on Camera: Donald B. Verrilli, Jr. (Part Five)*, YOUTUBE (Oct. 29, 2013), bit.ly/1rFnmNC.

[25] Tony Mauro and Katelyn Polantz, *Q&A: Eric Holder Jr. Goes 'Home' to Covington, Reflects on Tenure*, NTL. LAW J. (July 5, 2015), perma.cc/V9ZB-6ERA.

the Rose Garden. "Five years ago, after nearly a century of talk ... we finally declared that in America, health care is not a privilege for a few, but a right for all," the president began. "Over those five years, as we've worked to implement the Affordable Care Act, there have been successes and setbacks. The setbacks I remember clearly." There was laughter. "But as the dust has settled, there can be no doubt that this law is working."[26]

The president stressed that there were always forces pushing against the law – forces that failed. "And today, after more than 50 votes in Congress to repeal or weaken this law; after a presidential election based in part on preserving or repealing this law; after multiple challenges to this law before the Supreme Court – the Affordable Care Act is here to stay." He turned to *King*. "This morning, the Court upheld a critical part of this law that's made it easier for Americans to afford health insurance regardless of where you live." (The case did not uphold any aspect of the law, but merely interpreted it in the same way the government did.) "If the partisan challenge to this law had succeeded, millions of Americans would have had thousands of dollars' worth of tax credits taken from them. For many, insurance would have become unaffordable again. Many would have become uninsured again. Ultimately, everyone's premiums could have gone up. America would have gone backwards. And that's not what we do."

The president reiterated points he had made weeks earlier, in the lead-up to the Court's decision. "The point is, this is *not an abstract thing* anymore ... This is not about the Affordable Care Act as legislation, or Obamacare as a political football." For the first time in a long time, he referred to it as *Obamacare*. "This is health care in America," he stressed, "Five years in, *this is no longer about a law*."

Justice Scalia would no doubt agree with this – indeed, the thrust of his dissent was that the Court applies a special set of rules for the all-important "SCOTUSCare." In his opinion, Scalia questioned, "Perhaps the Patient Protection and Affordable Care Act will attain the enduring status of the Social Security Act... perhaps not." President Obama disagreed – the Affordable Care Act was already on the same plane as the eight-decades-old program. Obama explained, "Three generations ago, we chose to end an era when seniors were left to languish in poverty. We passed Social Security, and slowly it was woven into the fabric of America and made a difference in the lives of millions of people." The Affordable Care Act completed that promise.

---

[26] *Remarks by the President on the Supreme Court's Ruling of the Affordable Care Act*, WHITE HOUSE (June 25, 2015), perma.cc/RET8-2644.

He closed, "What we're not going to do is *unravel* what has now been woven into the fabric of America."

Republicans ripped the Supreme Court's decision. Senator Marco Rubio tweeted, "I disagree with the Court's ruling and believe they have once again erred in trying to correct the mistakes made by President Obama." Senator Ted Cruz exclaimed that "'Today, these robed Houdinis transmogrified a 'federal exchange' into an exchange 'established by the State.' For nakedly political reasons, the Supreme Court willfully ignored the words that Congress wrote, and instead read into the law their preferred policy outcome."

Privately, though, Republicans likely breathed a sigh of relief. Now efforts could turn to repealing and replacing the Affordable Care Act on their own schedule, through the 2016 election. Cruz added, "Every GOP candidate for the Republican nomination should know that this decision makes the 2016 election a referendum on the full repeal of Obamacare." Cruz would make the repeal of the law a cornerstone of his campaign. In a tweet personally signed "-H," former Secretary of State Hillary Clinton exclaimed, "Yes! SCOTUS affirms what we know is true in our hearts & under the law: Health insurance should be affordable & available to all." Clinton would base her campaign on protecting, and improving, the ACA.

A week later, President Obama continued his "victory lap" with a speech in Nashville, Tennessee. "I'm feeling pretty good about how healthcare's going," he said with a smile.[27]

---

[27] Sarah Ferris, *President Takes Victory Lap on Supreme Court ObamaCare Ruling*, THE HILL (July 7, 2015), perma.cc/JVE8-67A5.

PART VIII

The Nuns (June 26, 2015–May 16, 2016)

29

Make Health Care Great Again

29.1. "REPEAL EVERY WORD OF OBAMACARE"

On May 3, 2016, after his decisive victory in the Indiana Republican primary, Donald J. Trump became the presumptive, and ultimate Republican presidential nominee. For years to come, political scientists will study how the New York billionaire prevailed. The scope of this chapter is far more modest: What role did the Affordable Care Act play in the selection process? Six years after its enactment, Obamacare remained the Republican Party's primary target. Each of the seventeen candidates pledged to do what Mitt Romney could not – win the White House and end Obamacare. The twelve GOP debates held between August 2015 and March 2016 offer the clearest windows into this process.[1] During these prime-time confrontations, the candidates articulated their visions of how to repeal Obamacare, and what they would replace it with.

The standard-bearer of this fight was Ted Cruz. At every debate, the Texas Senator promised to "repeal every word of Obamacare." He offered a simple guarantee: "You want to know what I'll do as president? It is real simple. We'll kill the terrorists, we'll repeal Obamacare, and we will defend the Constitution, every single word of it." He bolstered his case for ending Obamacare based on

---

[1] Due to the fact that the candidates repeated themselves, often verbatim, during the several debates, usually in response to the same questions from the moderators and their opponents, throughout this chapter I will quote from the several debates interchangeably: Cleveland, OH (Aug. 6, 2015), perma.cc/JBR6-JWSQ; Simi Valley, CA (Sep. 16, 2015), perma.cc/8RZU-MK2A; Boulder, CO (Oct. 28, 2015), perma.cc/UZ9K-PE8X; Milwaukee, WI (Nov. 10, 2015), perma.cc/X8XE-CP5E; Las Vegas, NV (Dec. 15, 2015), bit.ly/2ajhoiQ; North Charleston, SC (Jan. 14, 2016), perma.cc/F2F4-JBFT; Des Moines, IA (Jan. 28, 2016), perma.cc/WE73-9BDK; Goffstown, NH (Feb. 6, 2016), nyti.ms/1VIsjRJ; Greenville, SC (Feb. 13, 2016), perma.cc/ LZ4Z-493E; Houston, TX (Feb. 25, 2016), perma.cc/G4VY-MMAY; Detroit, MI (Mar. 3, 2016), perma.cc/B6AL-M3LD; Coral Gables, FL (Mar. 10, 2016), nyti.ms/24tZcSy.

his fight against the law in 2013. "Everyone here talks about the need to take on Washington," Cruz said. "The natural next question is, who actually has done so? Who actually has stood up not just to Democrats, but to leaders in our own party? When millions of Americans rose up against Obamacare, I was proud to lead that fight."

Fox News host Brett Baier asked Cruz what he would do about the "millions of people who gained health insurance from Obamacare and now rely on it?" Would he be "fine if millions of those people don't have health insurance?" Cruz responded that the "six years of Obamacare has been a disaster. It is the biggest job-killer in this country. Millions of Americans have lost their jobs, have been forced into part-time work, have lost their health insurance, have lost their doctors, have seen their premiums skyrocket." After its repeal, he said, "we need healthcare reform. It should follow the principles of expanding competition, empowering patients, and keeping government from getting in between us and our doctors."

Cruz articulated "three specific reforms that reflect those principles." First, "we should allow people to purchase health insurance across state lines. That will create a true fifty-state national marketplace which will drive down the cost of low-cost, catastrophic health insurance." Second, "we should expand health savings accounts so people can save in a tax-advantaged way for more routine health care needs." Third, "we should work to de-link health insurance from employment so if you lose your job, your health insurance goes with you and it is personal, portable and affordable." This was a "much more attractive vision for health care," Cruz explained, "than the Washington-driven, top-down Obamacare that is causing so many millions of people to hurt."

Senator Marco Rubio also repeatedly pledged to repeal the ACA: "When I'm president of the United States we are getting rid of Obamacare." The Floridian would "replace it with a system that puts Americans in charge of their health care money again." Rubio's plan allowed employers to continue providing insurance coverage "from any company in America they want to buy it from." Alternatively, employers "can provide [workers with] health care money, tax-free, not treated as income." Workers "can use that money only for health care, but [they] can use it to fund health care any way [they] want." That includes funding health savings accounts. Everyone would also receive "a refundable tax credit that provides [them with] health care money to buy [their] own health care coverage."

Rubio's promise to repeal the ACA contributed to one of the more memorable moments of the campaign. During the debate in Goffstown, New Hampshire, the first-term senator repeated himself, almost verbatim, several times. "And let's dispel once and for all with this fiction that Barrack Obama doesn't know what he's doing," Rubio began. "He knows exactly what he's doing. Barack Obama is undertaking a systematic effort to change this country, to make America more like the rest of the world. That's why he passed Obamacare." Moments later, he repeated, "Let's dispel with this fiction that Barack Obama doesn't know what he's doing. He knows exactly what he's doing."

New Jersey governor Chris Christie went after him: "When you're president of the United States, when you're a governor of a state, the memorized 30-second speech where you talk about how great America is at the end of it doesn't solve one problem for one person." Rubio shot back at Christie, "Here's the bottom line. This notion that Barack Obama doesn't know what he's doing is just not true. He knows exactly what he's doing." Christie gleefully interjected, "There it is. There it is. The memorized 25-second speech. There it is, everybody." Rubio continued along the same line: "We are not facing a president that doesn't know what he's doing. He knows what he is doing. That's why he's done the things he's done. That's why we have a president that passed Obamacare." Later, Rubio repeated, "I think anyone who believes that Barack Obama isn't doing what he's doing on purpose doesn't understand what we're dealing with here, OK ... Obamacare was not an accident." The media dubbed the "glitchy" candidate as MarcoBot.[2]

29.2. "THE PEOPLE HERE IN MY STATE NEED THIS HELP"

After the Supreme Court's 2012 decision in *NFIB v. Sebelius,* states now had a choice of whether to enter into the Affordable Care Act's Medicaid expansion. By 2016, thirty-one states and the District of Columbia had opted in, while nineteen did not.[3] As we discussed in Chapter 8, one of the few Republican governors who bucked the trend was the Buckeye State's John Kasich. But not without controversy. Under the ACA, in order for a state to join the Medicaid expansion, the state's legislature must approve it. The Ohio General Assembly passed a budget that forbade the Medicaid expansion, but Kasich vetoed it.

Taking a page out of President Obama's playbook, Kasich bypassed the legislature. The Controlling Board, a quasi-legislative agency that usually reviews small adjustments to the state budget, voted 5–2 to accept $2.5 billion of federal Medicaid funding. According to the *New York Times,* the move "was

---

[2] Ezra Dulis, *'Marcobot Malfunctions' at GOP Debate,* Huff. Post (Feb. 7, 2016), bit.ly/2aRzebM.

[3] *Status of State Action on the Medicaid Expansion Decision,* Kaiser Family Foundation (Mar. 14, 2016), perma.cc/JQE4-AVU4.

an extraordinary, and possibly illegal ... end run by the governor around the General Assembly."[4] A Democratic member of the legislature praised Kasich, and said turning to the Controlling Board "was a brilliant move."

Kasich justified the decision based on "his sense of Christian compassion."[5] He told a legislator who opposed the expansion, "When you die and get to the meeting with Saint Peter, he's probably not going to ask you what you did about keeping government small. But he is going to ask you what you did for the poor. You better have a good answer."[6] There was also a pragmatic reason for the decision. The billions of dollars in federal funding could be used to help poor and disabled Ohioans. The governor's website noted, "It would make a bad situation far worse if Ohio does not extend Medicaid coverage and reclaim its share of federal taxes."[7]

Kasich was ridiculed for his decision by conservatives. *Fox News* host Laura Ingraham joked, "You guys are practically spooning, you and President Obama. That's amazing."[8] Kasich replied, "I'm the CEO of this state. I have a chance to bring [billions] out of Washington to the people here in my state who need this help." Six Republican members of the General Assembly challenged the legality of the Controlling Board's decision,[9] but the Ohio Supreme Court upheld the expansion.[10]

Two years later, Kasich's decision would prove to be one of his largest liabilities during the presidential campaign. At a town hall meeting in New Hampshire, he was asked about the Obamacare expansion. He replied, "We cannot take health-care coverage from people just for a philosophical reason."[11] During a debate, Kimberly Strassel of *The Wall Street Journal* accused him of abandoning conservative principles of limited government: "In 2013, you pushed through a Medicaid reform, over the objections of many of the Republicans in your state. Total enrollment and overall costs of that program have gone well beyond what anyone had expected, including yourself. How can you argue that this overall growth fits in with conservative ambitions to significantly cut back on the size of federal welfare programs?" Kasich pushed

[4] Trip Gabriel, *Medicaid Expansion Is Set for Ohioans*, N.Y. TIMES (Oct. 21, 2013), nyti.ms/1r4EThm.
[5] *Id.*
[6] Dan Zak, *Spurning the Party Line*, WASH. POST (Jan. 5, 2016), perma.cc/W7KQ-HKNS.
[7] *Id.*
[8] *Id.*
[9] Jason Hart, *Ohio Supreme Court Leaves Kasich's Obamacare Power Grab Unchecked*, MEDIA TRACKERS (Dec. 20, 2013), perma.cc/W6KL-EJNQ.
[10] State ex rel. Cleveland Right to Life v. State of Ohio Controlling Bd., 138 Ohio St. 3d 57, 58 (2013).
[11] Zak, *supra* note 6.

back, noting that "those numbers are incorrect. Our Medicaid programs are coming in below cost estimates, and our Medicaid program in the second year grew at 2.5 percent." But the specifics were far less important than the fact that he voluntarily expanded Obamacare.[12]

Jeb Bush, who opposed the expansion as the former governor of Florida, also faulted Kasich's choice. "Look I admire the fact that Governor Kasich is supporting spending more money on drug treatment and mental health," Bush said. But "Obamacare's expansion, even though the federal government is paying for the great majority of it, is creating further debt on the backs of our children and grandchildren. We should be fighting Obamacare, repealing Obamacare, replacing it with something totally different."

Kasich, with his folksy Midwestern cadence, replied, "Yeah, let me say a couple of things. Now, with Obamacare, I've not only sued the administration, I did not set up an exchange." Ohio was one of the states that stood to lose millions in subsidies if *King v. Burwell* went the other way. "I'm not for Obamacare," Kasich said, "never have been. But here's what's interesting about Medicaid. You know who expanded Medicaid five times to try to help the folks and give them opportunity so that you could rise and get a job? President Ronald Reagan. Now, the fact of the matter is, we expanded to get people on their feet, and once they're on their feet, we are giving them the training and the efforts that they need to be able to get work and pull out of that situation."

Cruz, Rubio, and Kasich finished second, third, and fourth, respectively, in the race for the nomination. The future of the Republicans' effort to stop Obamacare would now be brushed under a red baseball cap that said "Make America Great Again."

29.3. "WE HAVE A DISASTER CALLED THE BIG LIE: OBAMACARE"

On July 16, 2015, the face of the Republican Party was forever altered – and he arrived on a gilded escalator in midtown Manhattan. In his kickoff speech at Trump Tower, New York businessman Donald J. Trump immediately trained his fire on the Affordable Care Act.[13] "We have a disaster called the big lie: Obamacare. And it's going to get worse, because remember, Obamacare really kicks in in 2016. Really big league. It is going to be amazingly destructive.

---

[12] Jessie Balmert, *Fact Check: Kasich's Medicaid Expansion Exceeded Projected Costs*, CINCINNATI ENQ. (Feb. 17, 2016), perma.cc/5CUP-STNS.

[13] *Here's Donald Trump's Presidential Announcement Speech*, TIME (June 16, 2015), perma.cc/X9LM-9VQC.

Doctors are quitting. I have a friend who's a doctor, and he said to me the other day, 'Donald, I never saw anything like it. I have more accountants than I have nurses. It's a disaster. My patients are beside themselves. They had a plan that was good. They have no plan now.'" A Trump presidency would take a different path: "We have to repeal Obamacare, and it can be replaced with something much better for everybody. Let it be for everybody. But much better and much less expensive for people and for the government. And we can do it." During the debates, Trump incorporated Obamacare into his now-famous pledge: "Our country is in serious trouble. We don't win anymore. We have to end Obamacare, and we have to make our country great again, and I will do that."

To the surprise of virtually everyone, over the next year, Trump would secure the Republican nomination for the presidency. However, this decision once again hamstrung the GOP's effort to repeal the ACA. In 2012, the Republican nominee had created the precursor to Obamacare – RomneyCare. As we discussed in Chapter 5, this history made former Massachusetts Governor Mitt Romney utterly ineffective in promising to repeal Obamcare. In 2016, history would repeat itself.

In 2000, Trump considered a run for the White House on the Reform Party ticket. Leading up to this decision, the New Yorker advocated for universal health care. In 1999, Trump told CNN's Larry King, "If you can't take care of your sick in the country, forget it, it's all over .... I believe in universal healthcare."[14] On a 1999 episode of NBC's *Dateline*, he said he was "Liberal on health care. We have to take care of people that are sick ... I love universal."[15]

In his 2000 book *The America We Deserve*, Trump praised single-payer health care systems abroad. "We need, as a nation," he wrote, "to reexamine the single-payer plan, as many individual states are doing." The businessman explained: "We should not hear so many stories of families ruined by health care expenses. We must not allow citizens with medical problems to go untreated because of financial problems or red tape."

Trump even praised Hillary Clinton's "good intentions" for promoting Hillarycare, but wrote that his future opponent was "politically committed to a world view that would have done for modern American medicine what Joseph Stalin did for Ukrainian agriculture." Hillarycare "would likely have created huge bureaucratic nightmares and inefficiencies." Trump stressed that successfully "implementing such a plan is not simple. One major problem is that the

---

[14]   Tom Kertscher, *Donald Trump Wants to Replace Obamacare with a Single-Payer Health Care System, GOP Congressman Says*, POLITIFACT (Sept. 11, 2015), perma.cc/MQ98-MRJP.

[15]   *Trump: I Love Universal Healthcare*, YouTUBE (Sept. 16, 2015), youtu.be/MyFeNEbn2es.

single-payer plan in Canada is in financial difficulty, as is the nationalized plan in the United Kingdom. We have to improve on the prototype." He added that in the long term, America's goal should be to "find an equivalent of the single-payer plan that is affordable, well administered, and provides freedom of choice."

PunditFact concluded that "it's fair to say that in 2000, Trump supported a Canadian-style health care plan."[16] By all accounts, the real estate magnate did not express any views on health care between 2001 and 2011 – including during the ACA debates of 2009 and 2010. When he started to consider a presidential run as a Republican, Trump came out against Obamacare. At the 2011 Conservative Political Action Conference, he announced he would "fight to end Obamacare and replace it with something that makes sense for people in business and not bankrupt the country."[17] He told the *New York Times* that he no longer supported single-payer health insurance. "We had a much different country when I proposed those two things."[18]

Yet, he maintained an affinity for European-style universal health care. On a January 2015 episode of *The Late Show* with David Letterman, Trump praised Scotland's single-payer system.[19] "A friend of mine was in Scotland recently," he recalled. "He got very, very sick. They took him by ambulance and he was there for four days. He was really in trouble, and they released him and he said, 'Where do I pay?' And they said, 'There's no charge.' Not only that, he said it was like great doctors, great care. I mean we could have a great system in this country."

29.4. "THE GOVERNMENT'S GONNA PAY FOR IT"

Throughout 2015, Trump further distanced himself from his prior support of universal health care, but paradoxically still insisted on finding a way to cover all Americans. In July 2015, he explained in a radio interview that he was a "conservative with a heart."[20] Trump told CNN's Dana Bash that he would "repeal and replace [Obamacare] with something terrific." The plan will be "private," Trump insisted. But "at the lower end, where people have no money, I want to

---

[16] Jon Greenberg, *Conservative Columnist: Trump Once Backed Single-payer Health Care*, PunditFact (Jul. 24, 2015), perma.cc/SEN3-MTJM.

[17] Cataline Carnia, *Donald Trump Makes His Case for Presidency*, USA Today (Feb. 10, 2011), perma.cc/6KQG-FFTQ.

[18] Michael Barbaro, *After Roasting, Trump Reacts in Character*, N.Y. Times (May 1, 2011), nyti.ms/1VACiIN.

[19] *Trump Agrees with Bernie Sanders on Health Care*, YouTube (June 16, 2015), youtu.be/DwvikFS1vPA.

[20] *Trump on John Fredericks Show*, SoundCloud (Aug. 2015), bit.ly/1PCHV83.

try and help those people. And I don't think there's anything wrong with that. You have to help people." He admitted, "If I lose votes over that, or if I don't get a nomination over that, that's just fine with me."

On CBS's *60 Minutes*, Trump maintained that "everybody's got to be covered."[21] Host Scott Pelley asked, "Universal health care?" Trump replied, "I am going to take care of everybody .... They're going to be taken care of. I would make a deal with existing hospitals to take care of people." Pelley asked, "Who pays for it?" Trump replied, "The government's gonna pay for it."

The first Republican debate was held on August 6, 2015, at the Quicken Loans Arena in Cleveland – where Trump would accept the nomination at the 2016 Republican National Convention.[22] Early in the debate, *Fox News* moderator Brett Baier said, "Mr. Trump, Obamacare is one of the things you call a disaster." He replied, "A complete disaster, yes." The host continued, "you said 'it needs to be repealed and replaced.'" Trump answered, "correct." Then Baier challenged the businessman: "Fifteen years ago, you called yourself a liberal on health care. You were for a single-payer system, a Canadian-style system."

Trump once again praised universal healthcare: "It works in Canada. It works incredibly well in Scotland. It could have worked in a different age, which is the age you're talking about here." But not for the United States, Trump said. Senator Rand Paul of Kentucky interrupted Trump: "I've got a news flash. The Republican Party's been fighting against a single-payer system for a decade. So I think you're on the wrong side of this [debate] if you're still arguing for a single-payer system." Trump dismissed Paul. "I don't think you heard me. You're having a hard time tonight."

During the GOP debate in Goffstown, New Hampshire, moderator Mary Katherine Ham asked Trump if his vision of health care was closer to Bernie Sanders's single-payer plan or Hillary Clinton's support of Obamacare. He replied, "I think I'm closer to common sense. We are going to repeal Obamacare." But he insisted that "we're going to take care of people that are dying on the street." It is unclear precisely what Trump was referring to. In 1986, President Reagan signed into law the Emergency Medical Treatment and Active Labor Act (EMTALA). The law requires all hospitals receiving Medicare funding – basically all of them – to offer emergency care to anyone who shows up off the street, whether they can pay or not.

Senator Ted Cruz attacked Trump's support for universal health care. "Socialized medicine is a disaster," Cruz said. "It does not work. If you look at

---

[21] Scott Pelley, *Trump Gets Down to Business on 60 Minutes*, CBS NEWS (Sep. 27, 2015), perma.cc/M6Q4-SCBB.

[22] *The Aug. 6 GOP Debate*, WASH. POST (Aug. 6, 2015), perma.cc/VDZ8-MV7U.

the countries that have imposed socialized medicine, that have put the government in charge of providing medicine, what inevitably happens is rationing. Socialized medicine, whether proposed by the Democrats or proposed by a Republican, would hurt the people of this country." Ohio governor John Kasich added that Trump does not think Obamacare went "nearly far enough. And what was amazing" is that "for decades Donald has been advocating socialized medicine. What he's said is government should pay for everyone's health care, and in fact, a couple of debates ago, he said, if you don't support socialized health care, you're heartless. Now, liberal Democrats have been saying that for years."

Trump unequivocally rejected these arguments: "I do not want socialized medicine, just so you understand. [Cruz] goes around saying 'oh, he wants it.' I do not want socialized medicine. I do agree with him that it's going to be a disaster, Obamacare, for the economy." Cruz interrupted Trump: "Donald, true or false, you've said the government should pay for everyone's health care." "That's false," he replied. "You've never said that?" the befuddled Texan asked. "No," Trump answered. (During his *60 Minutes* interview, he said, "I am going to take care of *everybody*" and "the government's gonna pay for it.").

Cruz tried again. "Did you say if you want people to die on the streets, if you don't support socialized health care, you have no heart." Trump answered, "Correct. I will not let people die on the streets if I'm president." Cruz interrupted him, "So does the government pay for everyone's health care? Yes or no. Just answer the question." Trump answered, "Excuse me. We are going to take those people and those people are going to be serviced by doctors and hospitals. We're going to make great deals on it, but we're not going to let them die in the streets." Cruz asked again, "Who pays for it?" Cruz said, "How do we nominate a candidate who agrees with [democratic socialist] Bernie Sanders on health care?"

29.5. "THE LINES AROUND THE STATES"

Donald Trump was far more adept at promising to repeal Obamacare than explaining what he would replace it with. "What I'd like to see is a private system," he said, "without the artificial lines around every state." Under current federal law, health insurance policies can be sold only in a single state. If you "get rid of the artificial lines you will have yourself great plans," the businessman explained. "We're going to take out the artificial boundaries, the artificial lines. We're going to get a plan where people compete, free enterprise. They compete. So much better."

Trump also favored the elimination of Obamacare's individual mandate. CNN's Dana Bash told him, "The insurance companies say [the mandate is] the only way that they can cover people" with preexisting conditions. "Are they wrong?" Trump replied, "I think they're wrong 100 percent. The insurance companies take care of the politicians. The insurance companies get what they want." He fell back on his initial point about selling insurance across states. "We should have gotten rid of the lines around each state so we can have real competition." He continued, "we thought those lines were going to be gone, so something happened at the last moment where Obamacare got approved, and all of that was thrown out the window." Bash asked, "What you're saying is getting rid of the barriers between states, is that going to solve the problem?" Trump answered, "That's going to solve the problem. And, the insurance companies aren't going to say that, they want to keep it. They want to say whatever they have to say to keep it the way it is."

Marco Rubio interjected: "What is your plan? I understand the lines around the state, whatever that means. This is not a game where you draw maps. What is your plan, Mr. Trump?" The two began to talk over each other, and Trump referenced Rubio's exchange with Chris Christie weeks earlier. "You know, I watched him melt down two weeks ago with Chris Christie. I got to tell you, the biggest problem he's got is he really doesn't know about the lines. The biggest thing we've got, and the reason we've got no competition, is because we have lines around the state."

Rubio interrupted him. "So, you're only thing is to get rid of the lines around the states. What else is part of your healthcare plan?" During the crosstalk, Trump repeated something about "the lines around the states." Rubio spoke over him, "That's your only plan." Trump repeated, "You get rid of the lines, it brings in competition. So, instead of having one insurance company taking care of New York, or Texas, you'll have many. They'll compete, and it'll be a beautiful thing." Rubio repeated again, "So, that's the only part of the plan? Just the lines?" Trump answered, "The nice part of the plan – you'll have many different plans. You'll have competition, you'll have so many different plans."

With a grin on his face, Rubio said, "Now he's repeating himself." Trump shot back, "I watched him repeat himself five times four weeks ago." Rubio replied, "I just watched you repeat yourself five times five seconds ago." The irked businessman shot back, "I watched him melt down on the stage like that, I've never seen it in anybody." The freshman senator returned fire, "I see him repeat himself every night, he says five things: everyone's dumb; he's gonna make America great again; we're going to win; he's winning in the polls; and the lines around the state." Same thing "every night."

Bash asked Trump to "talk a little bit more about your plan." He answered, "We're going to have many different plans because of competition." Rubio, who was enjoying himself at this point, interjected, "He's done it again." Trump continued, "There is going to be competition among all of the states. And the insurance companies they're going to have many, many different plans." Bash asked, "Is there anything else you would like to add to that." Trump said, "No, there's nothing to add."

With respect to Obamacare, Trump's most potent attack would focus on a decision Ted Cruz made ten years earlier: supporting John Roberts's confirmation for the Supreme Court.

29.6. "JUSTICE ROBERTS GAVE US OBAMACARE"

During the early days of the 2000 Florida recount, Ted Cruz helped assemble the Bush campaign's legal team. He first called his former mentor, and future Obamacare pugilist, Michael Carvin. Cruz recalled in his autobiography: "[T]here's no one better if you are in a fast-paced, unpredictable litigation. With blazing speed, he can think through all of the difficult tactical decisions likely to occur." The second call went to John Roberts, who also clerked for Chief Justice William Rehnquist. Cruz recalled that "Roberts was not only a brilliant Supreme Court lawyer, but startlingly low-key and self-effacing. Although he was one of the leading Supreme Court litigators in the nation, he had befriended me several years earlier when I was a baby lawyer."

On November 28, 2000 – only two days before the Supreme Court would hear arguments in *Bush v. Palm Beach Canvassing Board* – Cruz saw Roberts leave headquarters with a suitcase. "John, where are you going?" Cruz asked. "I've got to get back to D.C.," he replied. "John, we're in the middle of a battle for the country," Cruz exclaimed. "How can you be leaving?" Roberts replied, "Well, I've got a U.S. Supreme Court argument tomorrow morning." On the morning of November 29, 2000, Roberts argued an intellectual property appeal, *TrafFix Devices Inc. v. Marketing Displays Inc.* He won the case 9–0.[23] Immediately after the argument, Roberts returned to Florida. Cruz called him "the best Supreme Court advocate of [his] generation," due in part to his "exquisite understanding of what makes each of the sitting justices tick."

After President Bush nominated Roberts to fill Rehnquist's vacant seat, Cruz urged the "Senate [to] confirm him swiftly."[24] In *National Review*, the

---

[23] 532 U.S. 23 (2001).
[24] Ted Cruz, *John Roberts Should Be a Quick Confirm*, NAT'L REV. (Jul. 20, 2005), perma.cc/4J3K-P3WU.

then–solicitor general of Texas sought to address concerns that Roberts's "two years on the bench provide insufficient record for [critics] to assess (and attack) his jurisprudence."[25] Cruz assured everyone that notwithstanding his short paper trail, "as a jurist, Judge Roberts's approach will be that of his entire career: carefully, faithfully applying the Constitution and legal precedent."

A decade later, Cruz would recant this praise. In June 2015, after the Court's decision in *King v. Burwell*, Cruz said that Roberts "put on an Obama Jersey."[26] "The chief justice's decisions and opinions in the two Obamacare decision last week and three years ago," Cruz said, "were profound disappointments, and they were disappointments because John Roberts is an incredibly talented lawyer." The fellow Rehnquist clerk added, "[I]f members of the [C]ourt want to write legislation or rewrite it they should resign from the court and run for the Congress."

At Phyllis Schlafly's Eagle Council forum, Cruz lamented President Bush's process of replacing Rehnquist. "In 2005, in one room was John Roberts and in another room was my former boss Mike Luttig, the rock-ribbed conservative on the 4th Circuit Court of Appeals, and George W. Bush picked John Roberts." Cruz said that Bush selected Roberts because he had not "said much of anything." He "didn't have a paper trail," and the administration "wouldn't have a [confirmation] fight" on their hands. Cruz countered, "[I]f you actually nominate a conservative, then you gotta spend some political capital. Then you gotta fight." If Bush had selected Luttig, Cruz explained, Obamacare would be no more.

Donald Trump relished in fabricating Cruz's role in the selection process. During a debate, Trump turned to Jeb Bush, and said, "Ted Cruz told your brother that he wanted John Roberts to be on the United States Supreme Court. They both pushed him, he twice approved Obamacare." Trump called Cruz an "all-talk, no-action politician" who was "the primary supporter of John Roberts, who gave us Obamacare." The implication was clear: Ted Cruz gave us John Roberts, and John Roberts "approved" Obamacare, so this was all Cruz's fault.

Cruz replied, "That's flat-out wrong." Trump charged, "No, it's not. You take a look. He was the primary supporter. He pushed John Roberts, and pushed him, and pushed him, and Bush ultimately appointed him. This is the man that was the primary supporter. There was no stronger supporter of John Roberts than him." Cruz admitted, "I wrote one op-ed supporting

---

25   I have written that a paper trail is a prerequisite for selecting Supreme Court justices. Randy E. Barnett & Josh Blackman, *The Next Justice*, Weekly Standard (Sep. 14, 2015), perma.cc/94V2-MCXS.

26   Andrew Kaczynski, *Ted Cruz: John Roberts "Put on an Obama Jersey,"* BuzzFeed (June 29, 2015), perma.cc/CE49-GXKA.

President Bush's nomination *after* he made it. I would not have made that nomination." Further, there is no evidence that the Texas solicitor general impacted the decision to select Roberts *before* the nomination was made. Notably, President George W. Bush did not give Cruz an influential position in his administration, despite his work on the campaign. Bush admitted, "I just don't like that guy."[27] The notion that Cruz was the "primary supporter" of Roberts, and that President Bush responded to Cruz's urgings, is implausible. Cruz continued, "Donald, please, I know it's hard not to interrupt. But try. Breathe, breathe, breathe." Trump ended the exchange with his nickname for the Texan. "Lyin' Ted."

During the 2012 presidential debates, President Obama scoffed at Governor Romney for his opposition to Obamacare, because Romneycare was "a model for" the national law. Curiously, the Supreme Court's decision in *NFIB v. Sebelius* to uphold the individual mandate, which was only three months old, did not warrant a single mention. In the final chapter of *Unprecedented: The Constitutional Challenge to Obamacare*, I wrote that during the debates, "there were no attacks on the chief justice, and no questions about the Court's legitimacy. It was exactly as John Roberts would have wanted it."[28] My conclusion was premature. Over the next four years, the validity of the chief justice's judicial restraint and "saving construction" would seep into the conservative collective consciousness, and erupt during the GOP debates. I doubt that Roberts, or anyone else for that matter, could have predicted that it would be Donald Trump who brought the simmering conflict to the fore.

29.7. "THE ONLY MAJOR COUNTRY ON EARTH"

While the Republicans debated how to repeal the Affordable Care Act, the Democrats differed over how to build on it. During a surprisingly competitive primary campaign, former secretary of state Hillary Clinton and Vermont senator Bernie Sanders articulated two strikingly different paths forward for health care reform.[29] Sanders insisted that he could achieve

---

[27] Eli Stokols, *George W. Bush Unleashes on Ted Cruz*, POLITICO (Oct. 19, 2015), perma.cc/XT9K-XF8Y.

[28] JOSH BLACKMAN, UNPRECEDENTED: THE CONSTITUTIONAL CHALLENGE TO OBAMACARE, 276 (2013).

[29] In this section I also quote interchangeably from the nine Democrats debates. *See supra* note 1. Las Vegas, NV (Oct. 13, 2015), perma.cc/BCY5-GEE8; Des Moines, IA (Nov. 14, 2015), perma.cc/LL9L-3YFF; Goffstown, NH (Dec. 19, 2015), perma.cc/7TRU-N69H; Charleston, SC (Jan. 17, 2016), perma.cc/4Y7W-QMZ6; Durham, NH (Feb. 4, 2016), perma.cc/8LXV-MVU2; Milwaukee, WI (Feb. 11, 2016), nyti.ms/1tdy52Q; Flint, MI (Mar. 6, 2016),

universal single-payer health insurance. "When you look around the world," the Brooklyn native explained, "you see every other major country providing health care to all people as a right, except the United States." He wondered aloud why the United States is "spending almost three times more than the British, who guarantee health care to all of their people? Fifty percent more than the French, more than the Canadians." He noted, "I live 50 miles away from Canada, you know? It's not some kind of communist authoritarian country. They're doing OK. They got a health care system that guarantees health care to all people. We can do the same."

During a debate in Miami broadcast on Univision, the self-described democratic socialist praised the Cuban health care system. "You may recall way back in 1961 [when] they invaded Cuba, and everybody was totally convinced that Castro was the worst guy in the world," Sanders recalled. "All the Cuban people were going to rise up in rebellion against Fidel Castro. They forgot that he educated their kids, *gave them health care*, totally transformed their society."

Sanders reached back to the progressive pillars of the Democratic Party, Presidents Franklin D. Roosevelt and Harry S. Truman, whose "vision was health care for all people as a right in a cost-effective way." In this "great country of ours," Sanders said, "with so much intelligence, why do we continue to get ripped off by the drug companies who can charge us any prices they want?" Behind Sanders's revolution, "millions of people [stood] up and are prepared to take on the insurance companies and the drug companies," he said. "It will happen, and I will lead that effort. Medicare for all, single-payer system is the way we should go." Hillary Clinton countered that in her experiences, "the revolution never came."

29.8. "BEFORE IT WAS CALLED OBAMACARE, IT WAS CALLED HILLARYCARE"

In 1993, the First Lady proposed a universal health care system that was soundly defeated. During the debates, Clinton insisted that she still does "believe in universal coverage. I fought for it 25 years ago," she reminded millennials who were too young to remember her husband's presidency, but "they beat me." She boasted that she has "the scars to show for it," and that "before it was called Obamacare, it was called Hillarycare."

perma.cc/FV53-H5UK; Miami, FL (Mar. 9, 2016), perma.cc/3AQQ-E3F7; Brooklyn, NY (Apr. 14, 2016), bit.ly/2avAX10.

Launching the fight for single payer in 2017 would be counterproductive, the former secretary of state warned. The "last thing we need is to throw our country into a contentious debate about health care again. And we are not England. We are not France." The United States, she explained, has "a system that was set up during World War II" where "170 million Americans get health insurance right now through their employers." It would be far too disruptive to disturb these relationships.

For that reason, Clinton favored improving the ACA. The former cabinet member was a "staunch supporter of President Obama's principal accomplishment, the Affordable Care Act," in part because she knew "how hard it was to get that done." What "President Obama succeeded in doing was to build on the health care system we have, [and] get us to 90 percent coverage," Clinton observed. "We have to get the other 10 percent of the way to 100. I far prefer that and the chances we have to be successful there than trying to start all over again, gridlocking our system, and trying to get from zero to 100 percent."

Clinton charged that Sanders was naïve. "Between the Republicans trying to repeal the first chance we've ever had to get to universal health care, and Senator Sanders wanting to throw us into a contentious debate over single-payer, I think the smart approach is build on and protect the Affordable Care Act. Make it work. Reduce the cost."

29.9. "THE NUMBERS DON'T ADD UP"

More pressingly, Clinton insisted that Sanders's single-payer plan simply would not work. "There is no doubt by those who have analyzed it," she said, citing "progressive economists," who concluded that "it would pose an incredible burden, not just on the budget, but on individuals." The former proponent of universal health care cited a *Washington Post* article that labeled Sanders's single-payer plan a "train wreck for the poor."[30] Before we go down that road, she said, "we've got to be really thoughtful about how we're going to afford what we proposed, which is why everything that I have proposed I will tell you exactly how I'm going to pay for it." She explained, "I am not going to make promises I can't keep. I am not going to talk about big ideas like single-payer and then not level with people about how much it will cost." Chelsea

---

[30] Max Ehrenfreund, *Study: Bernie Sanders's Health Plan is Actually Kind of a Train Wreck for the Poor*, WASH. POST (Feb. 25, 2016), perma.cc/9WJ2-65JU.

Clinton, the former First Daughter, ratcheted up the conflict. She charged that "Sanders wants to dismantle Obamacare."[31]

Sanders forcefully rejected this charge. "The idea I would dismantle health care in America while we're waiting to pass a Medicare for all is just not accurate." He added, "I don't know what economists Secretary Clinton is talking to." What she "neglected to mention" about the ACA, Sanders pointed out, is that "29 million still have no health insurance" and "even more are underinsured with huge copayments and deductibles." The Vermonter promised, "We're not going to tear up the Affordable Care Act. I helped write it. But we are going to move on top of that to a Medicaid-for-all system."

Clinton pushed back against Sanders's plan, claiming that his "numbers don't add up." But this was not just "about math," she said. "This is about people's lives, and we should level with the American people about what we can do to make sure they get quality affordable healthcare. "I wanna build on and improve the Affordable Care Act," Clinton said, and "we were gonna have to figure out how to get more competition in the insurance market, how to get the cost of prescription drugs down." But Medicaid-for-all was not the way to go.

Clinton warned that Sanders's plan would "increase the federal government dramatically." She paused. "And, you know, my dad used to say, if it sounds too good to be true, it probably is." While both candidates pledged a fidelity to improve the ACA, and promised to address increasing premiums, they both supported a decision that undermined one of the law's few and most significant cost-control mechanisms: The Cadillac tax.

29.10. "TAXING HEALTH BENEFITS FOR THE FIRST TIME EVER"

Since World War II, most Americans have received their health insurance through employer-sponsored plans. Under long-standing federal policy, these benefits are tax-free: Neither the employer nor the employee pays any taxes for the subsidized plans. As a result, employers are able to compensate workers with generous health insurance policies without suffering any adverse tax consequences. Economists have long criticized these so-called "Cadillac" plans, because they encourage wasteful spending and contribute to the increasing cost of health care.

In 2009, the Obama administration vigorously debated whether the ACA should alter this status quo. White House adviser Ezekiel Emanuel recounted

---

[31] Shaquile Brewster, *Chelsea Clinton Takes Aim at Sanders over Health Policy*, NBC NEWS (Jan. 12, 2016), perma.cc/S7N8-HUPZ.

that David Axelrod and the "political team [were] against touching it in any way."[32] In 2008, candidate "Obama had clearly opposed this change," they said. During the presidential campaign, John McCain proposed eliminating the tax exclusion for health insurance. The Obama campaign countered with an advertisement attacking the Republican: "McCain would make you pay income tax on your health insurance benefits," the commercial warned, "taxing health benefits for the first time ever."[33] Beyond reneging on a campaign promise, taxing gold-plated plans also risked alienating a key democratic constituency: unions. Historically, unions have negotiated very generous tax-free health care plans, often with their members contributing little toward the premiums. A tax on these lavish plans, Emanuel recalled, would be viewed as "a direct assault on their core benefits won through collective bargaining."

During a July 2009 meeting, Emanuel made the case to President Obama that eliminating "the tax exclusion was the single-most effective instrument the president possessed to control and reduce private-sector health costs." Obama seemed intrigued by the idea, and his wonks continued to develop different proposals. Ultimately, the ACA included what would become known as the *Cadillac tax*: Starting in 2018, employers would pay a forty percent tax on contributions to insurance premiums above $10,200 for an individual plan, or above $27,500 for a family plan.

The New York Times observed that the tax on "especially generous health plans, set to take effect in 2018, will help pave the way" to control costs "by discouraging companies from offering those plans."[34] By all accounts, the strategy started to work. A 2015 survey by the International Foundation of Employee Benefits Plans revealed that only three percent of the firms that would be hit by the Cadillac tax in 2018 planned to pay it.[35] Rather, more than ninety percent of surveyed large employers had started to take steps to avoid the liability.[36] Nineteen percent were limiting contributions to flexible-spending accounts. Others planned to increase deductibles or downgrade workers to cheaper plans, with less benefits and smaller networks of doctors.[37] Nearly

---

[32] Ezekiel Emanuel, Reinventing Health Care, 179 (2014).

[33] Angie Drobnic Holan, *Health Care Ad Is Right – Until the End*, Politifact (Oct. 3, 2008), perma.cc/LYV9-MQC3.

[34] Rob Mandelbaum, *Why Employers Will Stop Offering Health Insurance*, N.Y. Times (Mar. 26, 2014), nyti.ms/25JFCYi.

[35] Sarah Ferris, *Majority of Businesses Taking Steps to Avoid ObamaCare Tax*, The Hill (May 14, 2015), perma.cc/BP4C-6K9W.

[36] Tevi Troy, *The 'Cadillac Tax' Makes Everyone Sick*, Wall St. J. (Oct. 12, 2015), on.wsj.com/214pQjS.

[37] Reed Abelson, *Health Insurance Deductibles Outpacing Wage Increases, Study Finds*, N.Y. Times (Sept. 22, 2015), nyti.ms/1U57aig.

seventy-one percent of the surveyed firms said they would not increase wages to offset any reduction in health insurance benefits. For the sixteen percent that indicated they would increase wages, the employees would still be worse off: the wages are taxed, whereas the health benefits were not. "At some point," Emanuel predicted, "the Cadillac tax will make it undesirable for employers to continue to offer lavish health insurance."

As a consequence, many firms could simply decide to drop health insurance coverage altogether and allow their workers to buy policies through Obamacare. S&P Capital IQ, a research firm, forecasted that by 2020, ninety percent of American workers who currently receive insurance through their employers would be shifted to the ACA exchanges.[38] This move would save large employers more than $700 billion between 2016 and 2025. By 2025, Emanuel forecasted, fewer than twenty percent of employees will still be on employer-sponsored programs. The five million people whose policies were cancelled in 2013 would pale in comparison to the tens of millions of people who would annually lose their employer-sponsored plans.

29.11. "FIGHT THE FORTY"

For those who have made it through the first twenty-eight chapters of this book, you should already know what happens next: constraints designed to make the ACA sustainable, which burdened important constituencies, were once again eliminated. This time, however, it was not an exercise of *government by blog post*; here Congress took the lead. In April 2015, Democratic members of the House proposed a bill to get rid of the excise.[39] The push to repeal the tax began in earnest after the administration's victory in *King v. Burwell*. *The Hill* reported that the decision "has unfrozen the field for dozens of healthcare groups that have been stymied in their efforts to tweak the law while it was still fighting for survival in the courts."[40] Now "hospitals, doctors, insurers and companies are hoping to finally make headway on Capitol Hill." Mary Grealy, President of the Healthcare Leadership Council, explained, "There was a sense that *King v. Burwell* would be an *unraveling* of the Affordable Care Act." After the decision, "we're no longer talking about dismantling the law, so maybe it's time to move out of that mode and start

---

[38] Neil Irwin, *Envisioning the End of Employer-Provided Health Plans*, N.Y. TIMES (May 1, 2014), nyti.ms/1raJ37r.

[39] Sarah Ferris, *Democrats Take Aim at ObamaCare 'Cadillac' Tax*, THE HILL (Apr. 27, 2015), perma.cc/XEL5-GP7Q.

[40] Sarah Ferris, *ObamaCare Ruling Paves the Way for Lobbying Blitz*, THE HILL (Jul. 1, 2015), perma.cc/XZ5M-5CWK.

talking about improvements." At the top of their wish list was the repeal of the Cadillac tax.

Two weeks after the Court ruled in favor of "SCOTUSCare," a lobbying group launched the "Fight the Forty" campaign. The repeal effort was backed by leading health care firms – including Pfizer and Cigna – joined by labor unions. An official of the AFL-CIO said the Cadillac tax "has become a pretty prominent part of the discussion in many of [their] negotiations."[41] Both Democratic and Republican members of the House opposed the excise, claiming it would harm middle-class workers who had generous health insurance policies.

There were two main problems with repealing the Cadillac tax. First, it eliminated one of the few provisions of the law that controlled costs. The ACA was designed to slow the increase of premiums. Striking the Cadillac tax would remove this leverage for employers to offer less lavish plans. Second, a repeal would extinguish nearly $87 billion of expected revenue over the next decade. The law would no longer be "budget neutral," which is how the Congressional Budget Office (CBO) scored it in 2009.[42] By this point, however, the initial scoring was largely irrelevant. Journalist Steven Brill "counted nearly $100 billion in negative changes by executive fiat since the CBO had scored the law as being deficit neutral." In June 2014, the CBO announced that it could no longer calculate the ACA's impact on the budget: "Isolating the incremental effects of those provisions on previously existing programs and revenues four years after enactment of the Affordable Care Act is not possible."[43]

Many of the wonks who developed the ACA fiercely opposed the repeal movement. More than 100 economists from across the political spectrum – including Jonathan Gruber – implored Congress to maintain the tax.[44] They "united in urging Congress to take no action to weaken, delay, or reduce the Cadillac tax until and unless it enacts an alternative tax change that would more effectively curtail cost growth." Peter Orszag, former director of the Office of Management and Budget, wrote that a repeal reneges on the president's promise of "budget neutrality" and makes "the whole thing ... much

41 Reed Abelson, *Health Care Tax Faces United Opposition from Labor and Employers*, N.Y. TIMES (Jul. 21, 2015), nyti.ms/1PCkXxL.
42 Randy E. Barnett & Josh Blackman, *Dems May Have to Admit Obamacare Tax Increase*, USA TODAY (Oct. 30, 2013), perma.cc/3KKP-T27M.
43 Elise Viebeck, *CBO Throws in the Towel on Scoring ObamaCare*, THE HILL (June 4, 2014), perma.cc/B6ZR-9V6M.
44 Sarah Kliff, *The Coming Fight over Obamacare's Cadillac Tax Is Politicians vs. Wonks*, VOX (Oct. 1, 2015), perma.cc/FT9A-MQ4T.

less sustainable."[45] The economist tweeted that the repeal is "by far the biggest threat to the ACA to date."[46] Professor Timothy S. Jost, a law professor at Washington & Lee, who advised the administration on the health care bill, noted that experts predicted the tax would "never go into effect."[47] Budget neutrality and cost controls were simply selling points to get the law through Congress, and yet more promises that were not meant to be kept.

The *New York Times* editorial page endorsed the tax, because it "makes a start, albeit small, toward reducing the cost of health care by discouraging excessive spending."[48] The *Times* observed that if this excise is eliminated, the sum "would either have to be replaced with other revenues or added to the deficit." The editorial concluded, "The tax should probably be adjusted by Congress to eliminate inequities, but outright repeal would be a mistake that would undermine the viability of the Affordable Care Act." In a rare area of agreement, *National Review* editorialized against the repeal, but for very different reasons.[49] "Eliminating the Cadillac tax is one tax cut that Republicans should resist," Kevin D. Williamson wrote. "The teachers' unions and the AFL-CIO put these clowns in office and inflicted Obamacare on the country, and we should make them pay for it."

By September 2015, support continued to grow among Democrats. Seven prominent Democratic senators, including Bernie Sanders of Vermont and Chuck Schumer of New York, introduced a bill to repeal the Cadillac tax.[50] A few days later, Hillary Clinton "encourage[d] Congress to repeal" it.[51] The presidential candidate told the American Federation of Teachers (AFT), "I worry that it may create an incentive to substantially lower the value of the benefits package and shift more and more costs to consumers."[52] AFT President Randi Weingarten praised Clinton, who "has proven again that she is a champion for working people." *The Hill* reported that the AFT withheld their endorsement of Clinton until she opposed the tax.[53]

---

[45]   Peter Sullivan, *Dem Fault Lines Emerge on 'Cadillac tax'*, THE HILL (Dec. 10, 2015), perma.cc/5ZGP-DLP4.

[46]   Peter Orszag (@porszag), TWITTER (Dec. 8, 2015), bit.ly/1VJc9HD.

[47]   Abelson, *supra* note 41.

[48]   *Keep the Tax on High-End Health Plans*, N.Y. TIMES (Aug. 12, 2015), nyti.ms/1ObfLAK.

[49]   Kevin D. Williamson, *Democrats Asked for Obamacare but Now Try to Duck Out of Paying for It*, NAT'L REV. (Nov. 7, 2015), perma.cc/5D2Q-N4B6.

[50]   Sarah Ferris, *Sanders, Top Dems Urge Repeal of 'Cadillac' Tax*, THE HILL (Sept. 24, 2015), perma.cc/6PVZ-K6KG.

[51]   Brian Faler, *Hillary Clinton: Kill Obama's 'Cadillac Tax'*, POLITICO (Sept. 29, 2015), perma.cc/STV8-8RL9.

[52]   Sarah Ferris, *Clinton Expected to Break with Obama on Healthcare 'Cadillac' Tax*, THE HILL (Sept. 21, 2015), perma.cc/3S4G-TFE6.

[53]   Sarah Ferris, *How Democrats Prevailed over Obama on the 'Cadillac Tax,'* THE HILL (Dec. 21, 2015), perma.cc/CW8J-JCWY.

The Obama administration continued to defend the provision, explaining that there was no way to make up for the $87 billion in tax revenue.[54] The White House's top economic adviser said the excise is "perhaps the single biggest leverage we have on health costs in the private sector."[55] Press Secretary Josh Earnest told reporters, "We certainly strongly oppose the notion of repealing the Cadillac tax."[56] Chief of Staff Denis McDonough warned that the president would veto any repeal bill.[57] In November, House Minority Leader Nancy Pelosi and Senate Minority Leader Harry Reid formally opposed the tax.[58] *The Hill* quoted a Democratic aide who said, "Point is, they both want to get this done."[59] Pelosi and Reid personally met with Obama and expressed their concerns about the Cadillac tax. The president told them the same thing he told Republicans during previous Obamacare negotiations: No deal.[60]

Obama's Capitol Hill generals would soon outflank him. Reid, *The Hill* reported, "forged ahead with secret budget talks with GOP leaders."[61] Buried in Congress's omnibus spending bill was a two-year delay of the Cadillac tax. The tax would not kick in until 2020.[62] Recognizing the delay now enjoyed bipartisan support, the White House acquiesced. After the budget was announced, White House press secretary Josh Earnest now said the impact of the delay was "minimal."[63] Only twenty-four hours earlier, Earnest reiterated the administration's "steadfast opposition to the repeal of the so-called Cadillac tax."[64] Senator Dick Durbin (D-IL) admitted, "I don't think the White House was excited about it, but it was not a deal breaker."[65]

With a temporary delay, the tax is unlikely to ever go into effect as designed. Senator Mark Warner (D-VA) warned, "A two-year delay, I'm concerned, turns into a permanent delay."[66] Further, a delay would do little to reign in

---

[54] Ferris, *supra* note 53.

[55] Sarah Ferris, *Reid, Pelosi Pushing for Repeal of ObamaCare's 'Cadillac Tax,'* THE HILL (Nov. 6, 2015), perma.cc/4ESP-6LAN.

[56] Sarah Ferris, *White House Would 'Strongly Oppose' Cadillac Tax Repeal,* THE HILL (Dec. 9, 2015), perma.cc/6QYF-4FEB.

[57] Ferris, *supra* note 53.

[58] Ferris, *supra* note 56.

[59] Ferris, *supra* note 56.

[60] Ferris, *supra* note 53.

[61] Josh Blackman, *How Pelosi and Reid Beat Obama on the Cadillac Tax,* JOSH BLACKMAN'S BLOG (Dec. 21, 2015), perma.cc/C2WK-VS3E.

[62] Sullivan, *supra* note 45.

[63] *Press Briefing by Press Secretary Josh Earnest,* THE WHITE HOUSE (Dec. 16, 2015), perma.cc/4U9Z-GK8C.

[64] *Press Briefing by Press Secretary Josh Earnest,* THE WHITE HOUSE (Dec. 15, 2015), perma.cc/6AK9-VE5J.

[65] Nancy Cook, *How the White House Lost on the Cadillac Tax,* POLITICO (Dec. 16, 2015), perma.cc/5U7A-QMLZ.

[66] Sullivan, *supra* note 45.

increasing costs. Robert Greenstein, of the left-leaning Center on Budget and Policy Priorities, said that the Cadillac tax's delay "likely means that over the course of time, that health care costs will rise somewhat more rapidly."[67] *Politico* observed, "Increasingly, that argument did not matter to Democrats, even those who long supported the Affordable Care Act."

Conservatives were also disappointed by the decision. "By delaying the Cadillac tax," wrote analyst Avik Roy, "Republicans are making it harder to replace Obamacare with more market-oriented reforms."[68] The two-year delay "is the worst kind of special-interest legislation," Roy said, because "it will enrich labor unions and big business at the expense of taxpayers." Brian Blase of the free-market Mercatus Center added, "Big Business and Big Labor now have very good reason to believe that the Cadillac tax will never take effect."[69]

This episode illustrates how the president has endorsed changes to the ACA – even those that threaten its long-term stability. After delays and modifications to its individual and employer mandate, and a (likely permanent) delay of the Cadillac tax, the administration has undermined several of the key pillars of the law – all to avoid the harmful effects of the ACA's carefully designed constraints.

---

[67] Cook, *supra* note 65.

[68] Avik Roy, *If Republicans Delay the Cadillac Tax, They Will Cost Taxpayers Far More in the Long Run*, FORBES (Dec. 11, 2015), onforb.es/1U5in2f.

[69] Brian Blase, *Delaying and Weakening Obamacare's Cadillac Tax Is a Move in Wrong Direction*, FORBES (Dec. 16, 2015), onforb.es/1Pft3a8.

30

Short-Handed Court

30.1. "IT SEEMS TO ME THE PARK SERVICE DOESN'T HAVE JURISDICTION"

On January 20, 2016 – one year to the date before the forty-fifth president would be sworn in – the Supreme Court heard oral arguments in *Sturgeon v. Frost*. The facts of the case were simple enough. John Sturgeon piloted his hovercraft across a river in an Alaskan park. Alaska law permits the use of the hovercraft. Federal law does not. The National Park Service ordered Sturgeon to remove his hovercraft from the natural preserve. Sturgeon countered that the river was owned by Alaska and, due to the forty-ninth state's unique status, was excluded from federal jurisdiction. Arguing for the federal government was Rachel Kovner, assistant to the solicitor general, who clerked for Justice Scalia nine years earlier.[1] About fifty-three minutes into the hour-long argument, Scalia posed his final question of the day: "And if you read that back into Section 100751, it seems to me the Park Service doesn't have jurisdiction." Kovner replied to her former boss, as she no doubt had said many times before in chambers, "We agree, Your Honor."

Sturgeon would be the last case argued before a month-long break began. During this recess, the justices scattered across the globe.[2] Some stayed local. Justice Sotomayor visited several schools in her hometown of New York City. Justice Thomas traveled to Gainesville to speak to law students at the University of Florida. Chief Justice Roberts visited New England Law School in Boston. Others traveled abroad. Justice Breyer, who is fluent in French, lectured at the Institut Français in Paris. Justice Ginsburg journeyed to the European University Institute in Florence to talk about the "Notorious RBG."

---

[1] David Lat, *More on the Fabulous Rachel Kovner*, ABOVE THE LAW (Sept. 13, 2006), perma.cc/ZU79-ABEN.

[2] SCOTUSMap.com documents all of the justices' speaking engagements, bit.ly/28PN3MK.

During that recess, the Court's greatest globetrotter was the Justice least concerned about international law.[3] Fittingly, Justice Scalia was spreading American law abroad. At the Ninth Circuit Judicial Conference in July 2016, Justice Kennedy recalled that Scalia told him, "Tony, this is my last big trip." On January 24, Scalia traveled to Singapore with his friend and coauthor Bryan A. Garner. A law professor at Southern Methodist University, Garner is the preeminent American lexicographer. On January 28, Scalia gave the Lee Kuan Yew Distinguished Lecture at the University of Singapore on judicial interpretation of legal texts.[4] On February 1, Justice Scalia and Justice Kemal Bokhary of Hong Kong's Court of Final Appeal hosted a dialogue on judges and democracy.[5] The next day, Scalia and Garner discussed their second coauthored book, *Reading Law*, at the Chinese University of Hong Kong.[6]

Garner reminisced that during their busy trip, his colleague was "unbelievably energetic and always on the go," even after working fourteen-hour days.[7] On February 3, their final day in Hong Kong, Garner and his wife Karolyne had their palms read by a soothsayer at a Taoist temple. "Nino, you ought to get your palm read," Garner said. Scalia replied, "No. I don't want to know when I'll die." Garner nudged him, "Come on!" Scalia dissented, "No."

After his worldwide tour, Scalia traveled from the Far East to West Texas. On the afternoon of Friday, February 12, Scalia checked into the "El Presidente" suite at the Cibolo Creek Ranch, a 30,000-acre resort outside of Marfa.[8] That evening, Scalia attended a private dinner with forty other guests.[9] Toward the end of the meal, he retired to bed. The next morning, when he did not arrive for breakfast, an employee of the ranch checked in his room.

[3] Roper v. Simmons, 543 U.S. 551, 622, 627 (2005) (Scalia, J., dissenting) ("Though the views of our own citizens are essentially irrelevant to the Court's decision today, the views of other countries and the so-called international community take center stage."); Sosa v. Alvarez-Machain, 542 U.S. 692, 750 (2004) (Scalia, J., dissenting) ("The Framers would, I am confident, be appalled by the proposition that, for example, the American peoples' democratic adoption of the death penalty, could be judicially nullified because of the disapproving views of foreigners."); Lawrence v. Texas, 539 U.S. 558, 598 (2003) (Scalia, J., dissenting) ("The Court's discussion of these foreign views (ignoring, of course, the many countries that have retained criminal prohibitions on sodomy) is therefore meaningless dicta.").

[4] Lee Kuan Yew Distinguished Visitors List, perma.cc/ME8G-QBQV.

[5] *A Dialogue between the Hon. Justice Scalia and the Hon. Justice Bokhary on Judges and Democracy*, CHINESE UNIVERSITY OF HONG KONG (Feb. 1, 2016), bit.ly/1tvP8gb.

[6] *Justice Antonin Scalia and Professor Bryan A Garner: Reading Law*, CENTRE FOR COMPARATIVE & PUBLIC LAW (Feb. 2, 2016), perma.cc/6QDB-AUUE.

[7] Bryan A. Garner, *Bryan Garner's Tribute to His Friend and Co-author Antonin Scalia*, ABA JOURNAL (Apr. 1, 2016), perma.cc/WBS2-N7EF.

[8] Molly Hennessey-Fiske, *Scalia's Last Moments on a Texas Ranch – Quail Hunting to Being Found in 'Perfect Repose,'* L.A. TIMES (Feb. 14, 2016), perma.cc/4CCR-2NCG.

[9] Guillermo Contreras & Gary Martin, *U.S. Supreme Court Justice Antonin Scalia Found Dead at West Texas Ranch*, MY SAN ANTONIO (Feb. 16, 2016), perma.cc/AGT3-TE72.

Scalia was found dead in his bed. A priest was called to administer last rites. Scalia was seventy-nine years old. He was survived by his wife Maureen, nine children, and thirty-six grandchildren. The justice was seven months short of his third decade on the Supreme Court.

30.2. "WE ARE DIFFERENT, WE ARE ONE"

The justices remembered their late colleague. "He was an extraordinary individual and jurist," John Roberts remembered, "admired and treasured by his colleagues." Anthony Kennedy, now the most senior associate justice, praised Scalia's "jurisprudence, the driving force in all his work, and his powerful personality [that was] shaped by an unyielding commitment to the Constitution of the United States." His closest ally on the Court, Clarence Thomas, said, "In every case, he gave it his all to get the broad principles and the small details right." During his dear friend's funeral mass, Thomas read from *Romans* 5:5–11: "Hope does not disappoint, because the love of God has been poured out into our hearts through the Holy Spirit that has been given to us."

Ruth Bader Ginsburg reminisced, "It was my great good fortune to have known him as a working colleague and treasured friend." Their special bond inspired an opera titled *Scalia/Ginsburg*. "Toward the end of the opera," she recalled, "tenor Scalia and soprano Ginsburg sing a duet: 'We are different, we are one,' different in our interpretation of written texts, one in our reverence for the Constitution and the institution we serve." Their mutual respect was so strong that two decades earlier, Scalia encouraged President Clinton to nominate her to the High Court. In a *National Review* tribute to Nino, as his friends called him, Ginsburg wrote, "[W]hen President Clinton was mulling over his first nomination to the Supreme Court, Justice Scalia was asked, 'If you were stranded on a desert island with a Court colleague, whom would you prefer, Larry Tribe or Mario Cuomo?' Scalia answered quickly and distinctly: 'Ruth Bader Ginsburg.'"[10]

Stephen Breyer praised "Nino Scalia" as "a legal titan. His contribution to the law was a major one." Samuel Alito honored Scalia as "a towering figure who will be remembered as one of the most important figures in the history of the Supreme Court and a scholar who deeply influenced our legal culture." Sonia Sotomayor noted that Scalia "left an indelible mark on our history," and the "dimming of his special light is a great loss for me."

---

[10] Ruth Bader Ginsburg, *Antonin Scalia – A Justice in Full*, NAT'L REV. (Feb. 29, 2016), perma.cc/4H77-EJLV.

Elena Kagan "admired Nino for his brilliance and erudition, his dedication and energy, and his peerless writing." The former Harvard Dean said, "Nino Scalia will go down in history as one of the most transformational Supreme Court Justices of our nation." Nino forged a special relationship with his newest colleague through the most unlikely hobby. "He's made a huntress out of me," Kagan boasted.[11] Before her confirmation, the Upper West Sider met with a number of Republican senators, who asked if she had ever held a gun, or gone hunting. She had not, but promised she would to allay their Second Amendment concerns.[12] True to her word, Kagan asked Scalia if he would help her keep "the only promise I made during my entire confirmation proceedings." He obliged, and she acquired a new pastime. The duo started with bagging quail and pheasant, but soon moved up to big-game hunting. "We went out to Wyoming this past fall to shoot deer and antelope," Kagan recalled.[13] "I shot myself a deer." Kagan would later mourn that, without Scalia, the Court was "little bit duller. It's less fun."

30.3. "YOU HAVE CALLED YOUR SERVANT ANTONIN OUT OF THIS WORLD"

Friday, February 19, was a dreary, cold day at the Supreme Court.[14] At 9:18 AM, the iconic bronze doors opened. Four-score of Justice Scalia's former clerks slowly walked down the forty-four marble steps. The flag was at half-staff. Standing at attention in two parallel lines, the clerks formed a pathway leading into the Court. At 9:27 AM, the honorary pallbearers – including former solicitor general Paul Clement and Sixth Circuit Judge Jeffrey Sutton – walked down that path to meet the arriving hearse. Eight officers of the Supreme Court Police slowly carried Scalia's flag-draped mahogany coffin up the forty-four steps. The clerks stood guard, turning toward the processional as it passed them by. Waiting at the top of the steps was the Scalia family. Father Paul Scalia, one of Antonin's nine sons, ushered the casket into the Court.

The pallbearers carefully walked through the Great Hall, which is lined on both sides with marble busts of the chief justices of the United States. As they walked past the relief of Roger Taney, the face of Sonia Sotomayor came into focus. Standing to her left were Steven Breyer, Clarence Thomas, John

---

[11]   Bruce Vielmetti, *Visiting MU, Justice Kagan Tells of Hunting with Scalia*, J. SENTINEL (Apr. 3, 2012), perma.cc/589G-74DJ.

[12]   Garance Frankie-Ruta, *Justice Kagan and Justice Scalia Are Hunting Buddies – Really*, ATLANTIC (June 30, 2013), perma.cc/93G2-FABR.

[13]   *Id.*

[14]   *Justice Antonin Scalia Lying in Repose*, C-SPAN (Feb. 19, 2016), cs.pn/28VUrMq.

Roberts, Anthony Kennedy, Ruth Bader Ginsburg, Samuel Alito, and Elena Kagan. At 9:36 AM, as the casket proceeded beyond the bust of Chief Justice Edward White, the pallbearers performed an about-face. They lifted the casket up and slowly placed it down on the Lincoln Catafalque, the wooden platform constructed in 1865 to support the body of the slain sixteenth president. By this time, all of the clerks who were waiting on the steps crowded into the Great Hall.

Father Paul began to pray. "In the name of the Father, the son, and of the holy spirit." Justices Alito and Kennedy crossed themselves. The other three Catholic justices – Roberts, Thomas, and Sotomayor – were not in the camera's frame. "God of faithfulness, in your wisdom, you have called your servant Antonin out of this world. Release him from the bonds of sin and welcome him into your presence so that he may enjoy eternal light and peace and be raised up in glory with all your saints."

Father Paul closed his hymnal, made the sign of the cross over the casket, and slowly walked away. For one minute, the eight justices quietly stood at attention – some with their eyes closed, others on the verge of tears. But it felt like an eternity. At 9:43 AM, the justices and their spouses exited the Great Hall. They walked past a portrait of the late justice, which was decorated by a red-white-and-blue floral arrangement donated by Congress. Artist Nelson Shanks included in the portrait a wedding photograph of Antonin and Maureen, Nino's beloved Federalist Papers, and his preferred Webster's second-edition dictionary.[15]

Over the next twelve hours, Scalia's clerks stood vigil – four at a time, two on either side of the casket – as more than 6,000 mourners streamed by.[16] At 3:38 PM, Barack and Michelle Obama entered the great hall to pay their respects.[17] The couple bowed their heads in silence for thirty seconds, as camera shutters flied. Barack nodded, put his arm on his wife's back, and the

[15] Scalia and Garner strongly criticized the follow-up edition, *Webster's Third*, because of "its frequent inclusion of doubtful, slip-shod meanings without adequate usage notes." Antonin Scalia and Bryan A. Garner, *A Note on the Use of Dictionaries*, 16 GREEN BAG 2D 419 (2013). *See also MCI Telecomms. Corp. v. AT&T Co.*, 512 U.S. 218, 228 n.3 (1994) (per Scalia, J.) (noting that "[u]pon its long-awaited appearance in 1961, *Webster's Third* was widely criticized for its portrayal of common error as proper usage," and citing as an instance "its approval (without qualification) of the use of 'infer' to mean 'imply'"). *Merriam-Webster's* editor-in-chief Frederick C. Mish was not troubled. "I regret having to say that Judge Scalia is in error on this matter," Mish said, "but at least he has the satisfaction of knowing that his error is not reversible by a higher court." William Safire, *On Language: Scalia v. Merriam-Webster*, N.Y. TIMES (Nov. 20, 1994), nyti.ms/292OQ9W.

[16] Eric Bradner, Tom LoBianco, & Ariane de Vogue, *Antonin Scalia Lies in Repose at Supreme Court*, CNN (Feb. 20, 2016), perma.cc/L6VZ-TEBD.

[17] *Presidential Respects to Justice Antonin Scalia*, C-SPAN (Feb. 19, 2016), cs.pn/298ogv5.

two walked toward Scalia's portrait. They smiled, pointed, and looked at the life-like representation of Nino with approval. Holding hands, they walked out of the Great Hall into the solicitor general's lounge. There they met the Scalia family and gave their condolences. Chief Justice Roberts welcomed the president on his first official visit to the Supreme Court since Justice Kagan's investiture in 2010.[18]

A makeshift memorial formed outside the Court, with fitting tributes to Scalia's two Obamacare dissents. One mourner brought a crown of broccoli. During oral arguments four years earlier in *NFIB v. Sebelius*, Scalia asked Solicitor General Verrilli: "Everybody has to buy food sooner or later; therefore, can you make people buy broccoli?" Another brought a jar of applesauce. In *King v. Burwell*, Scalia described the majority's reasoning as "pure applesauce." Rounding out the tribute were paper bags and fortune cookies. In his dissent in *Obergefell v. Hodges*, the same-sex marriage case, he ridiculed the justices in the majority: "If, even as the price to be paid for a fifth vote, I ever joined an opinion for the Court that began: 'The Constitution promises liberty to all within its reach, a liberty that includes certain specific rights that allow persons, within a lawful realm, to define and express their identity,' I would hide my head in a bag. The Supreme Court of the United States has descended from the disciplined legal reasoning of John Marshall and Joseph Story to the mystical aphorisms of the fortune cookie."

At 10:08 PM, the last mourner entered the Great Hall.[19] The brunette in a black suit crossed herself, prayed silently for twenty seconds, crossed herself again, and slowly walked away from the casket. Scalia's body would remain at the Court overnight, and would be transported the next day for the funeral service at the Basilica of the National Shrine of the Immaculate Conception.

30.4. "CONSTITUTIONAL DUTY"

Four hours after Justice Scalia's death was announced, President Obama addressed the nation. "For almost thirty years, Justice Antonin 'Nino' Scalia was a larger-than-life presence on the bench – a brilliant legal mind with an energetic style, incisive wit, and colorful opinions," Obama noted. "Today is a time to remember Justice Scalia's legacy." However, he continued, "I plan to fulfill my constitutional responsibilities to nominate a successor in due time."

[18] *Associate Justice Elena Kagan Investiture Ceremony*, SUPREME COURT OF THE UNITED STATES, perma.cc/R2NR-WJ9Y.

[19] *Justice Antonin Scalia Lying in Repose, Part 5*, C-SPAN (Feb. 19, 2016), cs.pn/28XJbQP.

No doubt aware of the rising Republican opposition, the president stressed that the Senate must "fulfill its responsibility to give that person a fair hearing and a timely vote," so the Supreme Court can "continue to function as the beacon of justice that our Founders envisioned." These responsibilities, the president concluded, "are bigger than any one party; they are about our democracy."

Thirty-two days later, in the Rose Garden Obama nominated Merrick B. Garland, the chief judge of the D.C. Circuit Court of Appeals, to fill Scalia's seat.[20] "I've selected a nominee," the President said, "who is widely recognized not only as one of America's sharpest legal minds, but someone who brings to his work a spirit of decency, modesty, integrity, even-handedness, and excellence." Obama explained that this was "a decision that requires me to set aside short-term expediency and narrow politics, so as to maintain faith with our founders and, perhaps more importantly, with future generations." Judge Garland beamed with pride: "Thank you, Mr. President. This is the greatest honor of my life. For me, there could be no higher public service than serving as a member of the United States Supreme Court."

Obama had a simple message for Senate Republicans: "Give him a fair hearing, and then an up or down vote." If they do not, "the reputation of the Supreme Court will inevitably suffer," and "our democracy will ultimately suffer, as well." Under the Constitution, the president has the duty to appoint officials – he "shall nominate ... judges of the Supreme Court." But the executive has this power only "by and with the Advice and Consent of the Senate." Obama concluded, "I have fulfilled my constitutional duty. Now it's time for the Senate to do theirs."

Garland, who was on the short list to replace Justice Souter in 2009, and Justice Stevens in 2010, was widely viewed as more moderate than Obama's previous two appointments to the High Court. The administration calculated that the well-respected jurist – who had been praised by politicians on both sides of the aisle – stood the strongest chance of being confirmed in this hyper-politicized environment. However, long before the nomination was even made, and before Scalia's death was even confirmed, a Republican firewall emerged.

After introducing Garland, President Obama admitted that both parties shared in the blame of the politicization of the nomination process. In this battle, he said, "Republicans will point to Democrats who've made it hard for Republican Presidents to get their nominees confirmed. And they're

---

[20] *Remarks by the President Announcing Judge Merrick Garland as His Nominee to the Supreme Court*, WHITE HOUSE (Mar. 16, 2016), perma.cc/9G96-WG8C.

not wrong about that. There's been politics involved in nominations in the past" on both sides over the past three decades. Obama admitted that many Republicans will "point to the Bork nomination as where this all started." That is exactly where this story begins – and vice president Biden played an oversized role in this thirty-year escalating conflict.

30.5. "BORKED"

On July 1, 1987, President Reagan nominated Robert Bork to replace the retiring Justice Louis Powell. Bork was eminently qualified, having served as a D.C. Circuit judge, solicitor general, and Yale law professor. Democrats, however, rejected the conservative for his legal philosophy and his disagreement with Supreme Court precedents that were inconsistent with the Framers' original intent.[21] During a contentious confirmation hearing, Senator Edward Kennedy (D-MA) charged that "Robert Bork's America is a land in which women would be forced into back-alley abortions" and "blacks would sit at segregated lunch counters."[22]

Chairing that proceeding was Delaware Senator Joe Biden, who told the *Philadelphia Inquirer* in November 1986 that he would support Bork's nomination. "Say the administration sends up Bork and, after our investigation, he looks a lot like (Justice Antonin) Scalia," Biden said. "I'd have to vote for him, and if the (special-interest) groups tear me apart, that's the medicine I'll have to take. I'm not Teddy Kennedy."[23] Biden changed his tune. In August 1987, he formally opposed Judge Bork. "The framers [of the Constitution] clearly intended the Senate to serve as a check on the president and guarantee the independence of the judiciary. The Senate has an undisputed right to consider judicial philosophy."[24] After thirty-two hours of testimony, the Senate Judiciary committee voted against Bork by a vote of 9-5.

Before the full Senate rejected Bork's nomination, Biden charged that President Reagan has "politicized the judicial selection process throughout his Presidency," and that "Judge Bork is the favorite of the ideological right."[25] Nominating Bork was the president's "right," Biden said, but then it "becomes

---

[21] Randy E. Barnett & Josh Blackman, *Restoring the Lost Confirmation*, 83 U. CHI. L. REV. ONLINE 18 (2016), bit.ly/2aLspGk.

[22] James Reston, *Washington; Kennedy and Bork*, N.Y. TIMES (July 5, 1987), nyti.ms/28YfjCn.

[23] Larry Eichel, *Times Change, and That's Bad News for Bork*, PHILLY (July 13, 1987), perma.cc/C5RA-DPYP.

[24] James H. Rubin, *Burger Backs Bork; Biden Disagrees with AM-ABA-Resolution*, ASSOCIATED PRESS (Aug. 11, 1987).

[25] Cong. Rec. – Senate, 100th CONG., Part 21, at 29120 (1st Sess. 1987), perma.cc/ASR4-HSJW.

the Senate's duty to examine that nominee on the terms on which he has been offered to us" by "evaluating whether the ideology of the nomine would be good for the Nation." By a vote of 58–42, the Senate *borked* Bork.[26]

A defeated Reagan announced Douglas H. Ginsburg as his next nominee. But the D.C. Circuit judge abruptly withdrew after Nina Totenberg of NPR reported that the former Harvard professor had smoked marijuana with students.[27] On November 30, 1987, after back-to-back failures, Reagan nominated Judge Anthony Kennedy of the Ninth Circuit. Kennedy, widely viewed as a moderate, sailed through his confirmation hearing.[28] Senator Biden contrasted Kennedy's proceedings with that of Judge Bork: "Today, there is a calmer atmosphere." He added, "The confrontational spirit that characterized the last two nominations has passed as well."[29]

On February 3, 1988, five days before the Iowa caucus, the Senate confirmed Kennedy by a vote of 97–0. During the eight months between Powell's departure and Justice Kennedy's confirmation, the short-handed Supreme Court was unable to decide seven cases. Three cases tied by a vote of 4–4, and four cases were scheduled for reargument the following term.[30] In a preview of swing votes to come, Justice Kennedy broke ties in each of these later 5–4 decisions.

30.6. "STEALTH"

In July 1990, Justice William Brennan, the liberal lion of the Court, retired after nearly thirty-four years on the bench. President George H. W. Bush had the opportunity to alter the direction of the Court. He selected First Circuit Judge David Souter, a relatively unknown jurist who would avoid a brutal confirmation battle. Senator Biden would once again chair the confirmation hearing. With the balance of the Court now divided 4–4, Biden explained, "you, Judge Souter, are the single man in this room who can affect in the near term the outcome of all these issues … You will have the power to determine which direction the Nation will take, which path we will follow, as we reach this critical crossroads."[31] Biden's questioning of Souter was mostly favorable,

---

[26] *Supreme Court Nominations, Present–1789*, U.S. SENATE, perma.cc/XN5C-DXWN.

[27] Linda Greenhouse, *High Court Nominee Admits Using Marijuana and Calls It a Mistake*, N.Y. TIMES (Nov. 6, 1987), nyti.ms/28YkDpb.

[28] Maureen Hoch, *Justice Anthony Kennedy*, PBS (Mar. 9, 2007), perma.cc/NK3K-YKA4.

[29] *S. Comm. On the Judiciary on the Nomination of Anthony M. Kennedy*, 100th CONG., at 22 (1987), bit.ly/28XeKwp.

[30] Josh Blackman & Ilya Shapiro, *Only Eight Justices? So What*, WALL ST. J. (Feb. 23, 2016), on.wsj.com/1UoMSno.

[31] Nomination of David H. Souter to be Associate Justice of the Supreme Court of the United States, 101st CONG. at 3 (1990), bit.ly/28WvuPS.

and his nomination was advanced to the full floor by a vote of 13–1. Only Senator Edward Kennedy voted nay. Souter was confirmed 90–9 on October 2, 1990. The "stealth nominee" strategy failed, however, as Souter would prove to be a reliable member of the Court's liberal wing.

30.7. "BIDEN RULES"

One year later, Biden would chair the contentious hearing for Judge Clarence Thomas's nomination to replace Justice Thurgood Marshall. The early parts of Thomas's hearing focused on the nominee's libertarian views of natural law and property rights. However, Nina Totenberg once again rocked the hearings. She reported that Anita Hill had accused Thomas, her former supervisor at the Equal Employment Opportunity Commission, of sexual harassment.[32] Five days later, Biden allowed Hill to testify before the committee. Thomas denied the allegations, calling the proceeding a "high-tech lynching for uppity blacks who in any way deign to think for themselves." In a decision widely criticized by progressives, Biden concluded the hearing without allowing two witnesses to testify in support of Hill.[33] The Judiciary Committee split 7–7 – with Biden voting nay – on sending Thomas's nomination to the full floor with a favorable recommendation.[34] The committee voted again 13–1 to send the nomination to the floor without a recommendation. On October 15, 1991, Thomas was narrowly confirmed by the full Senate, 52–48, with Biden voting against him.[35]

Eight months later, rumors swirled that there may be another Supreme Court vacancy, which President George H. W. Bush would seek to fill *before* the presidential election. In a June 1992 speech, Senator Biden said that if a vacancy arises, Bush should not make a nomination so close to the election.[36] "It is my view that if a Supreme Court justice resigns tomorrow, or within the next several weeks, or resigns at the end of the summer," Biden said, "President Bush should consider following the practice of a majority of his predecessors and not name a nominee until after the November election is completed."[37]

[32] *Transcript of Nina Totenberg's NPR Report on Anita Hill's Charges of Sexual Harassment by Clarence Thomas*, JEWISH WOMEN'S ARCHIVE (Oct. 6, 1991), perma.cc/E434-CWJY.

[33] Richard Lacayo, *The Unheard Witnesses*, TIME (June 24, 2001), ti.me/292jlNn.

[34] *Judiciary Committee Votes on Recent Supreme Court Nominees*, U.S. SENATE, perma.cc/5LKS-HM2G.

[35] ROLL CALL VOTES ON THE NOMINATION OF CLARENCE THOMAS, 102ND CONG., 1ST SESS. (1991), perma.cc/L4UZ-B3TK.

[36] C. Eugene Emery Jr., *In Context: The 'Biden Rule' on Supreme Court Nominations in an Election Year*, POLITIFACT (Mar. 17, 2016), perma.cc/YL6D-JCSZ.

[37] Ed Whelan, *The Biden Rules*, NAT'L REV. (Feb. 22, 2016), perma.cc/Q5N7-YY3N.

While "the political season is under way … action on a Supreme Court nomination must be put off until after the election campaign is over." Biden explained, "That is what is fair to the nominee and is central to the process." He noted that some may "fret that this approach will leave the Court with only eight members for some time." But having "to re-argue three or four cases that will divide the Justices four to four" is a "minor" cost "compared to the cost" that the "Nation would have to pay for what assuredly would be a bitter fight … if that nomination were to take place in the next several weeks."

Twenty-four years later, Republicans cited the so-called *Biden Rules* to justify not considering Judge Garland's nomination. Now–vice president Biden wrote that his earlier comments did not support the Republicans' "obstructionist position."[38] He said such a "reading distorts the broader meaning of the speech I gave from the Senate floor that year." The longtime chairman of the judiciary committee stated he was talking about a hypothetical vacancy that could have arisen the June before the election. Scalia's vacancy arose four months earlier in February, after both the Iowa Caucus and the New Hampshire primary.

30.8. "CONTRARY TO CORE AMERICAN VALUES"

President Clinton's two nominations to the Supreme Court were largely uneventful. Judge Ruth Bader Ginsburg sailed through her confirmation hearing in July 1993 with an 18–0 committee vote, and was confirmed by the full Senate by a 96–3 vote. Judge Stephen Breyer was also unanimously recommended by the Judiciary Committee, and was confirmed 87–9 in July 1994. Biden chaired both hearings, which did not occasion any substantial Republican opposition. The nonet of Rehnquist, Stevens, O'Connor, Scalia, Kennedy, Souter, Thomas, Ginsburg, and Breyer would stay together for eleven years, the second-longest period without a vacancy in Supreme Court history.[39]

In 2005, President Bush had the opportunity to replace two justices in quick succession. On July 1, Justice Sandra Day O'Connor announced her intent to step down on the confirmation of her successor.[40] The president promptly

[38] Joseph R. Biden, Jr., *The Senate's Duty on a Supreme Court Nominee*, N.Y. TIMES (Mar. 3, 2016), nyti.ms/295598b.

[39] Charlie Savage, *Win May Bring Power to Appoint 4 Justices, Campaigns Urged to Focus on Impact*, BOSTON GLOBE (July 7, 2004), bit.ly/28YPooF. The longest period in American history without a change in the Court's composition was from 1812 to 1823. Michael J. Gerhardt, *Judicial Selection as … Talk Radio*, 39 U. RICH. L. REV. 909 (2005).

[40] Richard W. Stevenson, *O'Connor, First Woman Supreme Court Justice, Resigns after 24 Years*, N.Y. TIMES (July 1, 2005), nyti.ms/28YPzbo.

nominated Judge John Roberts to replace O'Connor. However, two months later Chief Justice Rehnquist passed away. Roberts was now tapped to become the next Chief Justice.

With a Republican Senate majority, this was the first Supreme Court confirmation hearing not chaired by Biden since 1986. Roberts's testified flawlessly, famously promising that "my job is to call balls and strikes and not to pitch or bat."[41] However, as scholar Adam White observed, Roberts hinted during his hearing how he would decide contentious cases, such as *NFIB v. Sebelius*.[42] "If there's another basis on which to evaluate" a constitutional question, Roberts said, and "we don't have to reach these other grounds because of our conclusion, than we should focus on those other alternative grounds and see if we could uphold the act."[43]

Senator Biden voted against Roberts on the Judiciary Committee. On September 29, the full Senate confirmed the new Chief Justice 78–22, with Senator Biden and his freshman colleague Barack Obama voting nay. During the brief period between October 2005 and January 2006, Justice O'Connor served as something of a "lame duck." O'Connor would have cast the tie-breaking vote in three cases, all of which were instead reargued. In all three cases – involving the death penalty, "knock-and-announce" warrants, and the First Amendment rights of public employees – her replacement would cast the decisive vote.[44]

On October 3, Bush nominated his White House counsel Harriet Miers to replace Justice O'Connor. There was a Republican revolt as conservatives attacked the nominee, who had no judicial experience or practice in constitutional law. Senator Biden was similarly perplexed by the selection. "Because so little is known about Ms. Miers," he said, "most Americans – like me – are not sure what type of Supreme Court Justice she will make."[45] After several stormy weeks, the White House announced that Miers had withdrawn her nomination.

Conservatives received a treat on Halloween. Bush announced that Samuel Alito, a well-respected judge on the Third Circuit, would be his new nominee. On January 24, 2006, the Judiciary Committee approved Alito on a straight

[41] *Roberts: 'My Job Is to Call Balls and Strikes and Not to Pitch or Bat,'* CNN (Sept. 12, 2005), perma.cc/VZT3-5DXZ.

[42] Adam J. White, *Judging Roberts: The Chief Justice on the United States, Ten Years In*, WEEKLY STANDARD (Nov. 23, 2015), tws.io/28YoDHU.

[43] *Confirmation Hearing on the Nomination of John G. Roberts, Jr. To be Chief Justice of the United States*, 109th CONG., at 264 (2005), bit.ly/28YzIdP.

[44] Blackman & Shapiro, *supra* note 30.

[45] Joe Biden, Jr., *Statement by U.S. Senator Joe Biden on the Nomination of Harriet Miers to The Supreme Court*, VOTE SMART (Oct. 3, 2005), perma.cc/4W8A-QKN7.

party-line vote, 10–8. Biden cast his fifth vote against GOP Supreme Court nominees. But the battle was not over. Led by Senator John Kerry (D-MA), Democrats announced they would try to filibuster Alito's floor vote, as they had done with Bush's Circuit Court nominees.[46] "People can say all they want that 'elections have consequences,'" the 2004 Democratic presidential nominee said. "But that seems like an awfully convoluted rationale for me to stay silent about Judge Alito's nomination." Senator Obama joined Kerry's filibuster. Judge Alito, he said, "is somebody who is contrary to core American values, not just liberal values."[47] However, Obama conceded the filibuster would fail. "We need to recognize, because Judge Alito will be confirmed, that, if we're going to oppose a nominee that we've got to persuade the American people that, in fact, their values are at stake."

In November, Senator Biden had dismissed talks of filibustering Alito. "My instinct is we should commit" to a vote, the Delawarean said.[48] He changed his tune. On Sunday, January 29, Biden shifted to support the procedural block, though admitted that it "makes sense [only] when you have a prospect of actually succeeding."[49] At the time, there were nowhere near the forty votes needed to stop the nomination. "I will vote one time to say to continue the debate," Biden said, "but the truth of the matter" is that Alito would be confirmed. On January 30, 2016, twenty-five Democrats voted to block cloture on Samuel Alito, including Senators Obama, Biden, Kerry, Clinton, and Reid.[50] Alito was confirmed by a vote of 58–42 – seventeen of the Democrats who supported cloture ultimately voted against him.

30.9. "I HOPE HE SENDS US SOMEONE SMART"

The composition of the Court would remain unchanged until 2009, when Justice David Souter announced his resignation. President Obama's shortlist included Second Circuit Judge Sonia Sotomayor, Solicitor General Elena Kagan, and D.C. Circuit Judge Merrick Garland.[51] On May 26, 2009, Obama

---

[46] David D. Kirkpatrick, *Kerry Gets Cool Response to Call to Filinbuster Alito*, N.Y. TIMES (Jan 27, 2006), nyti.ms/28Ygogm.

[47] Jeff Zeleny, *Obama Joins Filibuster Bid Against Alito*, CHICAGO TRIBUNE (Jan. 30, 2006), perma.cc/76N4-E2JR.

[48] Hope Yen, *Biden: Alito Filibuster Seems Unlikely*, WASH. POST (Nov. 6, 2005), perma.cc/4QNT-4EQ4.

[49] *Sen. Obama Criticizes Filibuster Tactic*, A.P. (Jan. 29, 2006), perma.cc/JDX7-DMJ5.

[50] ROLL CALL VOTES ON THE CLOTURE MOTION ON THE NOMINATION OF SAMUEL A. ALITO, JR., 109 CONG. 2 SESS. (2006), perma.cc/TAM3-RKTP.

[51] Peter Baker & Adam Nagourney, *Sotomayor Pick a Product of Lessons from Past Battles*, N.Y. TIMES (May 27, 2009), nyti.ms/295ggOw.

announced that his first selection to the High Court would be Sotomayor. Conservative groups called for a filibuster of Judge Sotomayor.[52] However, the Republican leadership, including Senator McConnell, opposed a judicial filibuster, which he said was "inappropriate."[53] In any event, a filibuster would be mathematically impossible. Senator Al Franken's contested election in Minnesota would be resolved on July 7, 2009, giving the Democrats their sixtieth vote.[54]

Now serving as president, rather than senator, Obama showed contrition for his filibuster of Alito. "Last-minute efforts using procedural maneuvers inside the Beltway," he said, "have been the wrong way of going about it."[55] Obama added, "what's fair to say is that how judicial nominations have evolved over time is not historically the fault of any single party. This has become just one more extension of politics." White House Press Secretary Josh Earnest referred to Obama's 2006 filibuster as only a "symbolic vote."[56] Earnest sought to distance Obama's rationale for the vote – "making an effective public case about those substantive objections" – from other Democrats who were merely "throwing sand in the gears of the confirmation process." Earnest did not specify which members of the Democratic caucus were trying to "throw sand" in the process. Sotomayor was voted through the Judiciary Committee 13–6, and was confirmed 68–31.

One year later, Justice John Paul Stevens announced his resignation. Justice Scalia personally lobbied for the runner-up from Obama's shortlist, as he did for Ginsburg two decades earlier. At the White House Correspondent's Dinner, the gregarious Justice leaned on White House adviser David Axelrod.[57] "I have no illusions that your man will nominate someone who shares my orientation," he said. "But I hope he sends us someone smart." Axelrod, a little taken aback, replied, "I'm sure he will, Justice Scalia." With his inimitable style, the Sicilian leaned forward. "Let me put a finer point on it. I hope he sends us Elena Kagan." No doubt independent of Scalia's request, President Obama tapped Kagan for the Court.

Senate Republicans, now with forty-one votes, could have filibustered Kagan's nomination. At least in theory. Minority Leader McConnell said "it

[52] Charlie Savage, *Conservatives Ask Republican Senators to Filibuster on Sotomayor*, N.Y. TIMES (June 1, 2009), perma.cc/K7VP-X3D2.
[53] *GOP Lawmakers: Sotomayor Filibuster Unlikely*, CNN (May 31, 2009), bit.ly/2aVwoVd.
[54] Andrew Glass, *Al Franken Sworn In as Minnesota Senator, July 7, 2009*, POLITICO (July 7, 2015), perma.cc/Y8N5-VTQM.
[55] Gregory Korte, *With the Tables Turned, Obama Now 'Regrets' His 2006 Alito Filibuster*, USA TODAY (Feb. 17, 2016), perma.cc/97SK-DATN.
[56] *Id.*
[57] David Axelrod, *A Surprising Request from Justice Scalia*, CNN (Mar. 9, 2016), bit.ly/28YvPqp.

is possible" but would not commit to the strategy.[58] Senator Jeff Sessions of Alabama warned that "If things come out to indicate she's so far outside the mainstream, it's conceivable a filibuster might occur."[59] However, five moderate Republicans announced they would support cloture. Kagan was ultimately confirmed 63–37.[60] Six years later, Merrick Garland, the Susan Lucci of the SCOTUS short list, would finally get his shot.

30.10. "UNTIL WE HAVE A NEW PRESIDENT"

The news of Scalia's passing broke on Saturday, February 13, 2016, at about 4:30 PM.[61] Within minutes, through what Adam Smith would call *the invisible hand*, a Republican strategy spontaneously organized on social media: no confirmation until after the election, regardless of who the nominee is. At 4:56 PM, Conn Carroll, a spokesman for Senator Mike Lee (R-UT), tweeted, "What is less than zero? The chances of Obama successfully appointing a Supreme Court Justice to replace Scalia."[62] Conservative pundits quickly reinforced the message. Sean Davis, who writes at The *Federalist*, posted at 4:52, "If Scalia has actually passed away, the Senate must refuse to confirm any justices in 2016 and leave the nomination to the next president."[63] One hour later, before consulting his caucus, Majority Leader McConnell released a statement: "The American people should have a voice in the selection of their next Supreme Court Justice. Therefore, this vacancy should not be filled until we have a new President." Senator John Cornyn (R-TX) warned that whoever the president nominated had no chance of confirmation, and would "bear some resemblance to a piñata."[64]

Almost immediately all eyes turned to an octogenarian from Iowa. Chuck Grassley, Chairman of the Senate Judiciary Committee, held almost unfettered discretion over whether Obama's nominee would even be considered by the Senate. The *New York Times* reported that Grassley "arguably" has

---

[58] *McConnell: GOP Filibuster of Kagan Supreme Court Nomination Possible*, CNN (June 20, 2010), perma.cc/4QGF-W5V3.

[59] Lauren Seifert, *Sessions: Kagan Filibuster "Conceivable,"* CBS News (June 27, 2010), perma.cc/64UU-XZYU.

[60] Roll Call Votes on the Nomination of Elena Kagan, 111th Cong., 2nd Sess. (2010), perma.cc/2HAQ-5ZCT,

[61] Leon Neyfakh, *How the San Antonio Express-News Got the Scoop on Antonin Scalia's Death*, Slate (Feb. 13, 2016), perma.cc/3Y4A-C2BY.

[62] Conn Carroll (@conncarroll), Twitter (Feb. 13, 2016), bit.ly/28YnDU7.

[63] Sean Davis (@seanmdav), Twitter (Feb. 13, 2016), bit.ly/292Io5I.

[64] Ted Barrett, *Supreme Court Nominee Would Be a 'Pinata,' Cornyn Says*, CNN (Mar. 7, 2016), perma.cc/83WR-58KN.

"more power than any other individual senator in deciding if the process will move forward."[65] Before a nominee was even named, pressure mounted on the folksy Iowan to hold a hearing.

The *Des Moines Register* called on Grassley to proceed with Obama's nominee.[66] "This could have been a 'profile in courage' moment for Senator Grassley. This was an opportunity for our senior senator to be less of a politician and more of a statesman. It was a chance for him to be principled rather than partisan." In the immediate aftermath of Scalia's passing, Grassley was somewhat noncommittal. He told *Radio Iowa*, "I would wait until the nominee is made before I would make any decisions."[67] He called for patience. "One step at a time." The *Times* observed that early on the Iowan "has given off conflicting signals about his intentions."

Republicans defended their opposition to a hearing, citing Democratic filibusters of President Bush's nominees a decade earlier. Democrats countered that they filibustered lower-court nominees, who were at least afforded a hearing, even if they did not receive a vote. Further, the Supreme Court, they argued, was different. Refusing to even hold a hearing was the next level up from blocking a nominee's floor vote. Political commentator Michael Barone's observation is still evergreen: "In politics … all procedural arguments are insincere."[68] In 2010, the Chief Justice lamented the politicization of the confirmation process. "Each political party has found it easy to turn on a dime," Roberts observed, "from decrying to defending the blocking of judicial nominations, depending on their changing political fortunes."[69]

Senator Grassley charged that Roberts had it "exactly backwards."[70] The "confirmation process doesn't make the Justices appear political," the Iowan said. Rather, "the confirmation process has gotten political precisely because the court has drifted from the constitutional text, and rendered decisions based instead on policy preferences." Grassley specifically targeted Roberts's Obamacare decisions. "In fact, many of my constituents believe, with all due

[65] David M. Herszenhorn, *Iowans Urge Senator Charles Grassley to Hold Hearings on Court Nominee*, N.Y. TIMES (Feb. 19, 2016), nyti.ms/29zxYQr.
[66] *Grassley's Supreme Court Stance Is All About Politics*, DES MOINES REGISTER (Feb. 16, 2016), perma.cc/D5B6-5NJD.
[67] O. Kay Henderson, *Grassley Hasn't Decided Whether to Hold Hearing on Obama's Supreme Court Pick*, RADIO IOWA (Feb. 16, 2016), perma.cc/N5DT-7BUQ.
[68] Michael Barone, *Senate Lineup for 2010*, WASH. EXAMINER (May 5, 2009), perma.cc/D87N-V2LX.
[69] Robert Barnes, *Justice Roberts Urges End to Partisan Fights Blocking Action on Federal Judges*, WASH. POST (Dec. 31, 2010), perma.cc/JHX2-4CTR.
[70] *Grassley Floor Statement on the Public Perception of the Supreme Court* (Apr. 5, 2016), perma.cc/V3WQ-F57S.

respect, that the Chief Justice is part of this problem. They believe that a number of his votes have reflected political considerations, not legal ones." To the extent that the Chief's ACA opinions were designed to keep the Court out of the political arena, the plan backfired in ways that were impossible to anticipate.

After some vacillation, the Republican leadership solidified its position. McConnell and Grassley coauthored an editorial in the *Washington Post* expressing their shared strategy.[71] "Given that we are in the midst of the presidential election process," the Kentuckian and Iowan wrote, "we believe that the American people should seize the opportunity to weigh in on whom they trust to nominate the next person for a lifetime appointment to the Supreme Court." As for a question of duty, they wrote that the "Constitution grants the Senate the power to provide, or as the case may be, withhold its consent." The Senate leadership held firm and refused to schedule a hearing for Garland. Many declined to even meet with the nominee.

At the University of Chicago Law School, where Obama had lectured on constitutional law, President Obama ridiculed the Republican strategy. The GOP "simply will not consider the nomination itself," he said, and they are "going to shut down the process," leaving a short-handed Court "for at least two" terms. "That is *unprecedented*." The president, slipping back into professor mode, warned the law students in attendance that if the "process of appointing judges is so broken … then we are going to see the kinds of sharp, partisan polarization that has come to characterize our electoral politics seeping entirely into the judicial system." Obama predicted that "the courts will be just an extension of our legislatures and our elections and our politics," and "that erodes the institutional integrity of the judicial branch."

30.11. "WE HAVE SOME FANTASTIC PEOPLE"

With the Senate Republicans holding firm that the nomination would be filled by the next president, the stakes of the 2016 election grew even higher. And the candidates did not have much time to prepare. Justice Scalia's passing was announced barely four hours before the GOP debate in South Carolina. In politics, virtually every important decision is scripted well in advance after thorough consideration. On February 13, 2016, the candidates had to improvise.

At the time, I was advising Senator Ted Cruz's campaign on legal issues. Within minutes of the announcement, Cruz's policy team kicked into action

---

[71] Chuck Grassley & Mitch McConnell, *Democrats Shouldn't Rob Voters of Chance to Replace Scalia*, WASH. POST (Feb. 18, 2016), perma.cc/368E-624F.

with a series of rapid-fire e-mails. First, the campaign decided to follow the nascent strategy of opposing a hearing, whoever the nominee may be. At 5:27 PM, @TedCruz tweeted, "Justice Scalia was an American hero. We owe it to him, & the Nation, for the Senate to ensure that the next President names his replacement."[72] Moments later, I texted a line for Cruz to use during the debate: "What Reagan was to the Presidency, Scalia was to the Supreme Court." Cruz did not say it that night, but it became part of his stump speech, and he used it during several interviews.[73]

The second major decision was whether Cruz should announce potential candidates to replace Scalia. One of his advisers suggested Mike Luttig, a former judge on the Fourth Circuit Court of Appeals. Luttig, who served as a law clerk for Scalia and had hired Cruz as a law clerk, was a finalist to replace Chief Justice Rehnquist in 2005. However, George W. Bush chose John Roberts instead. Ultimately, the Cruz campaign decided not to name a nominee, as it was too soon, and there was not sufficient time to vet nominees. Donald Trump, as usual, would take a different tack.

The first question of the debate went to the New York real estate magnate. "You've said that the president shouldn't nominate anyone in the rest of his term to replace Justice Scalia," moderator John Dickerson said.[74] "If you were president, and had a chance with 11 months left to go in your term, wouldn't it be an abdication to conservatives in particular, not to name a conservative justice with the rest of your term?" Without hesitation, Trump answered, "If I were president now I would certainly want to try and nominate a justice." But he hoped that "Mitch [McConnell], and the entire group, [are] going to be able to do something about" President Obama's nominee. Then Trump dropped the bombshell of the evening. If he was elected, "we could have a Diane Sykes, or you could have a Bill Pryor, we have some fantastic people."

Almost instantly, my phone lit up with rapid-fire messages from the Cruz campaign. "What do we have on these two? Sykes and Pryor? Are they solid?" Sykes was a Bush appointee to the Seventh Circuit in Wisconsin. Pryor, a Bush appointee to the Eleventh Circuit Court in Alabama, was confirmed after the Gang of Fourteen's compromise broke up the Democratic filibuster. Both had

[72] Ted Cruz (@tedcruz), Twitter (Feb. 13, 2016), bit.ly/295wGVC.
[73] Betsy Klein, *Ted Cruz Will Attend Justice Antonin Scalia Funeral Saturday*, CNN (Feb. 18, 2016), perma.cc/L4K7-QUCA; *'This Week' Transcript*, ABC News (Feb. 14, 2016), bit.ly/291DvaX; *Red Eye*, Fox News (Feb. 13, 2016), bit.ly/28YvMrR; J.D. Durkin, *Did Host Chuck Todd Get Caught Saying 'Oh God' after Cruz Compared Scalia to Reagan?*, Mediaite (Feb. 14, 2016), perma.cc/5RAA-DZSC.
[74] Team Fix, *The CBS News Republican Debate Transcript*, Wash. Post (Feb. 13, 2016), perma.cc/9NK4-SJD3.

ruled against Obamacare's contraceptive mandate. Sykes found that the mandate violated the free exercise of a religious for-profit corporation, and Pryor ruled the accommodation to the mandate infringed the religious liberty of a nonprofit.[75] I texted back that they were both solid. "OK just had to check – DT got good advice then." The move was shrewd. Trump became the first presidential candidate to name the individuals he might appoint to the Supreme Court, and shifted the entire tenor of the debate after Scalia's passing.

The businessman would later claim that he was advised by two prominent conservative legal groups. "I'm getting names," Trump said. "The Federalist people," referring to the Federalist Society for Law & Policy. Both Sykes and Pryor often speak at the Federalist Society's annual convention. Trump added with his usual staccato cadence, "Some very good people. The Heritage Foundation."

In another unprecedented step, three months later, Trump released a list of eleven jurists he would consider for the Supreme Court. (In the interest of full disclosure, I count several of them as colleagues and friends.) In addition to Sykes and Pryor, he named Third Circuit Judge Thomas Hardiman, Sixth Circuit Judge Raymond Kethledge, and Steven Colloton and Raymond Gruender from the Eighth Circuit. Trump also turned to state Supreme Courts, with Justices Allison Eid from Colorado, Joan Larsen from Michigan, Thomas Lee from Utah, David Stras from Minnesota, and Don Willett from Texas.

Willett, whose social media prowess earned him the title of Texas Tweeter Laureate,[76] was perhaps the most surprised by his inclusion. He had repeatedly mocked the New Yorker online.[77] One tweet read, "Can't wait till Trump rips off his face Mission Impossible-style & reveals a laughing Ruth Bader Ginsburg." Willett jabbed at Trump's proposal to make Mexico pay for a border wall with a *Star Wars*–themed meme: "We'll rebuild the Death Star. It'll be amazing, believe me. And the rebels will pay for it. – Darth Trump." Perhaps the most noteworthy tweet was in haiku form:

> Who would the Donald
> Name to #SCOTUS? The mind reels.
> Weeps – can't finish tweet.

[75] Korte v. Sebelius, 735 F.3d 654, 658 (7th Cir. 2013) (per Sykes, J.); Eternal Word Television Network, Inc. v. HHS, 756 F.3d 1339, 1340 (11th Cir. 2014) (Pryor, J., concurring).

[76] Peggy Fikac, *Tweeter Laureate Rocks Social Media from Judicial Post*, SAN ANTONIO EXPRESS NEWS (Dec. 28, 2015), bit.ly/28ZpsAt.

[77] *Possible Trump Supreme Court Pick Has Mocked Him on Twitter*, MOTHER JONES (May 18, 2016), perma.cc/H2NT-UBA2.

Trump announced, "I plan to use this list as a guide to nominate our next" justice, and the list was "representative of the kind of constitutional principles I value." Berkeley law professor John Yoo, who served in President Bush's Justice Department, called it an "all-star list of conservative jurisprudence."[78] Northwestern law professor John McGinnis, who served in the Reagan and Bush administrations, tempered his general opposition to Trump: "We can hardly be confident that his appointments will make America great, but we can be pretty confident that Hillary Clinton's will end the current project of making the Supreme Court a court of law rather than a dynamo of Progressive politics."[79]

Not everyone was convinced by the list. George Mason law professor Ilya Somin warned that "once President Trump discovers that the judges on the list probably won't support his agenda, he might well instead nominate people who will."[80] Orin Kerr, a law professor at George Washington University, called the roster "meaningless" because there was no "commitment to choosing from the list." Trump remained noncommittal during an interview with *Fox News* host Sean Hannity. "We're either going to choose from this list," he said, "or people very close to it." On the campaign trail, SCOTUS would become Trump's trump card. He told Republicans at an event in Iowa, even if you don't like me "you have to vote for me anyway. You know why? Supreme Court judges." He added, "You have no choice." Even with the couched language, this was a particularly important decision for Trump, who had to assuage conservative concerns about his ability to replace Scalia. I was cautiously optimistic about the list, but extremely pessimistic of Trump's constitutional views.[81]

Hillary Clinton's campaign quickly attacked Trump's list, charging that the "terrifying" judges on the list would be hostile in cases involving abortion and the Affordable Care Act.[82] In response, Trump called on Clinton to release her own list. "Because I'd like to see who that list [of justices] consists of," he said. "And you will see it's day and night" with his.[83] The presumptive Democratic candidate would not be goaded into announcing any names. Clinton supported giving Garland a hearing, for the moment at least, but did not promise

---

[78] John Yoo, *Trump's Judicial Appointments List Is Filled with Outstanding Conservatives*, NAT'L REV. (May 18, 2016), perma.cc/WK78-PZWS.

[79] John O. McGinnis, *Trump, Clinton, and the Supreme Court*, LIBRARY OF LAW AND LIBERTY (May 22, 2016), perma.cc/PHZ7-4KU9.

[80] Ilya Somin, *The Big Picture on Trump and the Courts: Why Constitutional Originalists Should be #NeverTrump All the Way*, VOLOKH CONSPIRACY (June 2, 2016), perma.cc/8ATQ-3KA4.

[81] Josh Blackman, *Cautiously Optimistic About Trump's SCOTUS Shortlist*, NAT'L REV. (May 19, 2016), perma.cc/ED43-D89A; Josh Blackman, *Donald Trump's Constitution of One*, NAT'L REV. (May 12, 2016), perma.cc/4TE3-WJ45.

[82] Elizabeth Chan, *President Donald Trump Would Transform the Supreme Court – and Upend Our Most Fundamental Rights*, HILLARYCLINTON.COM (May 19, 2016), perma.cc/4B5R-Q7C5.

[83] Harper Neidig, *Trump: Clinton Should Release List of Judges*, THE HILL (May 20, 2016), perma.cc/3T7T-KW6B.

she would renominate him if elected. Critically, the name "Merrick Garland" was not mentioned at any point during the four-day Democratic National Convention in Philadelphia. Clinton left the door wide open to selecting her own nominee. But first, the eight justices would have to resolve one last Obamacare case – without their beloved Justice Scalia.

30.12. "A BLESSING QUICKLY LOST WHEN FAITH IS BANNED FROM THE PUBLIC SQUARE"

On February 20, 2016, Justice Scalia was remembered at a funeral mass at the Basilica of the National Shrine of the Immaculate Conception. Thousands were in attendance, including Vice President Joe Biden and former VP Dick Cheney. "If you spent a day in a duck blind with Nino," Cheney said, "you got to know the man."[84] In 2004, Scalia refused to step aside from a case involving Cheney, despite their trip to a duck hunt together.[85] Senator Ted Cruz exited the campaign trail on the day of the South Carolina primary to attend the service. President Obama, who had paid his respects to the Scalia family the day before at the Supreme Court, did not attend. He had no events on his public schedule that day.[86] Donald Trump, who also did not attend, tweeted, "I wonder if President Obama would have attended the funeral of Justice Scalia if it were held in a Mosque? Very sad that he did not go!"[87]

As the eight justices walked down the massive nave of the church, they could not get very far from the pending conflict between religious liberty and the state. Presiding over the ceremony was Archbishop Wuerle, who was a plaintiff in *Roman Catholic Archbishop of Washington v. Burwell* – one of the contraceptive mandate cases pending before the Court. Father Paul Scalia delivered a moving homily, and would not let the justices forget about his father's views of religious liberty. Dad "knew well what a close-run thing the founding of our nation was," Father Paul said. "And he saw in that founding, as did the founders themselves, a blessing, a blessing quickly lost when faith is banned from the public square, or when we refuse to bring it there." Justice Scalia, his son remembered, "understood that there is no conflict between loving God and loving one's country, between one's faith and one's public service." That message was not lost on Mother Provincial Lorraine Marie Maguire and two of her fellow Little Sisters of the Poor, who were sitting a few rows behind the justices.

---

[84] Peter Baker & Gardiner Harris, *Washington Pauses for Justice Antonin Scalia's Funeral*, N.Y. TIMES (Feb. 20, 2016), nyti.ms/28WoqTs.

[85] Cheney v. U.S. Dist. Court for D.C., 541 U.S. 913, 914 (2004) (Memorandum of Scalia, J.).

[86] Lynn Sweet, *Obama Guidance, Press Schedule Feb. 20, 21, 2016*, CHICAGO SUN TIMES (Feb. 20, 2016), perma.cc/7BGN-NVRF.

[87] Donald J. Trump (@realDonaldTrump), TWITTER (Feb. 20, 2016), bit.ly/28ZgrbA.

The Little Sisters had been very busy of late. During his visit to Washington, D.C. in September, Pope Francis paid the nuns a surprise visit. "The Holy Father spoke to each of us individually, from the youngest postulant to our centenarian, and then he spoke to all [of] us about the importance of our ministry to the elderly," said Sister Constance Veit, communications director for the Little Sisters.[88] "We were deeply moved by his encouraging words." Though he did not mention the lawsuit, a Vatican spokesman said the meeting was meant as "a sign, obviously, of support for them" in their legal battle.[89] That morning, the Pope had visited the White House to call for stronger protections of religious liberty. One month later, the Little Sisters would have their day in Court.

30.13. "NO WORRY ABOUT SEVEN LAWYERS ELBOWING EACH OTHER AT THE PODIUM"

Throughout 2014 and 2015, five consecutive courts of appeals upheld the validity of the "accommodation" to the ACA's contraceptive mandate.[90] This string of defeats for the religious nonprofits meant that there was no circuit split. Thus, there was no guarantee the Court would even take their case. However, on September 17, 2015, the Eighth Circuit Court of Appeals ruled in favor of Dordt College, a Christian school in Iowa.[91] There was a split, and the government agreed that the justices had to resolve it. One month later, the Supreme Court granted certiorari for seven different plaintiffs: The Most Rev. David A. Zubik of Pittsburgh, Priests for Life, the Roman Catholic Archbishop of Washington, East Texas Baptist University, the Little Sisters of the Poor, Southern Nazarene University, and Geneva College.

The various parties were represented by four different groups: Paul Clement and the Becket Fund for Religious Liberty, Noel Francisco of the Jones Day law firm, Alliance Defending Freedom, and the American Freedom Law Center. Usually, the Supreme Court only gives each side thirty minutes of

---

[88] Sarah Pulliam Bailey & Abby Ohlheiser, *Pope Francis Meets with Little Sisters of the Poor, Nuns Involved in an Obamacare*, WASH. POST (Sept. 23, 2015), perma.cc/V84Q-QTWS.

[89] Matt Hadro, *Pope Francis Made Surprise Stop at Little Sisters of the Poor to Show Support*, CATHOLIC NEWS AGENCY (Sept. 23, 2015), perma.cc/Q6A3-VFN4.

[90] Geneva Coll. v. HHS, 778 F.3d 422 (3rd Cir. 2015); E. Texas Baptist Univ. v. Burwell, 793 F.3d 449 (5th Cir. 2015); Univ. of Notre Dame v. Burwell, 786 F.3d 606 (7th Cir. 2015); Little Sisters of the Poor Home for the Aged v. Burwell, 794 F.3d 1151 (10th Cir. 2015); Priests for Life v. HHS, 772 F.3d 229 (D.C. Cir. 2014).

[91] Dordt Coll. v. Burwell, 801 F.3d 946 (8th Cir. 2015).

argument time. Due to the diversity of the plaintiffs with different insurance plans, the parties requested an enlargement of time. The Court granted that motion and gave the challengers a total of forty-five minutes.

Clement and Francisco split that time, without any conflicts. "Paul and I are very good friends," Francisco told me. "I think we all understood that it was really to our style and strategic advantage to have two advocates up there, but then it was a pretty straightforward split at the time." At a reception after the case was argued, Clement recalled "there was no worry about seven lawyers elbowing each other at the podium. We were able to cooperate and reach an early agreement about argument division."

Clement would argue in his third Obamacare case. Francisco, who works at the same law firm as Michael Carvin, would make his Obamacare debut. The former Scalia clerk told me that when the contraceptive mandate was first announced, he knew that the Dioceses "were in need of assistance and so we reached to the U.S. Conference of Catholic Bishops." Francisco said there was a "real sense of gratitude" that "there was a law firm that was willing to join with them to figure a way out of the woods." The Conference agreed to work with Jones Day, and "file seventeen lawsuits across the country." The purpose of having "a really diverse group of organizations" was to "demonstrate the broad impact" the mandate was having on the "well-being of the people within the Diocese."

When certiorari was first granted with nine justices on the bench, Francisco told me, "we thought that we had a fighting shot at winning." As usual, Justice Kennedy's vote "was in play but we thought we had a pretty good shot of convincing him to our side." In light of his "open-ended" concurring opinion in *Hobby Lobby*, Francisco explained, "his mind was open on the issue, and it was up to us to convince him."

But after Scalia's death in February, the lawyer noted, we "instantly lost what I regarded as one of our potential five." He added, "I thought pretty strongly we're looking at a real possibility of an equally divided court as our best case scenario." That would have been a loss, because it would have affirmed the judgments of the lower courts that had ruled for the government. The changed bench "didn't affect our strategy," he said, but "it did make it so that our path to victory seemed a lot steeper." The hope was now to persuade Justice Kennedy to vote to "hold it over for re-argument next term," when a newly appointed ninth justice could rule for the challengers.

The government, on the other hand, did not think Justice Scalia's passing would have much effect on the outcome of *Zubik*. There were already "four solid votes to flat out reverse," a DOJ official told me, "and it would have been up to Justice Kennedy to decide what to do." Justice Kennedy's position was really tough to predict because "he seems to find this to be a really hard case." He sees a "real burden on religious organizations, but also thinks that the employees' rights should be protected." The difficulty is that "he can't make the two things add up." Even with Scalia's absence, the government's strategy to "win five votes was more or less the same."

31

"Hijacked"

31.1. "I'LL HAVE NUN OF IT"

The Supreme Court would hear the Little Sisters' prayer for relief on March 23, 2016 in the consolidated cases of *Zubik v. Burwell*. Coincidentally, this was the sixth anniversary of President Obama signing the Affordable Care Act. As has become tradition, the sidewalk outside the Supreme Court was packed with demonstrators supporting both sides of the cases. There were scattered signs stating "I ❤ birth control access, and so do most Americans," "Get my Boss out of my Bedroom," and "#HandsOffMyBC." However, unlike the scene outside arguments in *Hobby Lobby* two years earlier, the mandate's opponents now dwarfed its supporters. First Street was flooded with nuns, priests, and Catholic school students, clad in their uniforms, cheering on the Little Sisters of the Poor. One nun held up a pink sign that said, "Women for Religious Liberty." Another sign said, "Let them serve." A third read, "Help a sister out." My favorite: "HHS Mandate: I'll have nun of it." A woman, standing off to the side, held up a white banner that said "ABORTION," with a picture of a bloodied and dismembered 21-week-old fetus. At 8:40 AM, as I made my way into the Court, dozens of nuns held their hands over their hearts and recited the Pledge of Allegiance, followed by a rousing rendition of "God Bless America." The scene resembled a casting call for *The Sound of Music*. Alas, there was no performance of "How do you solve a problem like Scalia?"[1]

Eight of the Little Sisters managed to secure coveted tickets to the arguments: Mother Provincial Loraine Maguire, and Sisters Marie, Mary Bernard, Georgia, Joseph, Marie Christine, Roberts, and Constance. Sister Constance, director of vocations for the group, wrote an editorial in *The New York Times* on

---

[1] *Maria, The Sound of Music*, perma.cc/DJ25-2EVS. *Capitol Steps: How Do You Solve a Problem Like Scalia?*, LYRICWIKIA, perma.cc/YBL5-UPUE.

the eve of arguments. She explained that the mandate "force[s] us to change
our religious health plan and start offering benefits that violate our religious
beliefs."[2] A native New Yorker, Sister Constance told me that that it was her
"lifelong dream" to publish in the *Times*.

Joining the Sisters in the Court were several leaders from the Catholic
Church. The Most Rev. David Zubik, the bishop of the Diocese of Pittsburgh,
and the namesake of the case, was joined by the Most Rev. Lawrence Persico,
the bishop of the Diocese of Erie. Cardinal Donald Wuerle, the archbishop of
the Archdiocese of Washington, also attended. One month earlier, Cardinal
Wuerle presided over Justice Scalia's funeral mass at the Basilica of the
Shrine of the Immaculate Conception. Absent, however, were any members of the Obama administration. The year before in *King v. Burwell*, the
past and present HHS Secretaries – Sylvia Matthew Burwell and Kathleen
Sebelius – attended.

At 9:39 AM, Solicitor General Donald Verrilli entered the Court for what
would be his last Obamacare argument. He shook hands with opposing advocates, Paul Clement and Noel Francisco.[3] Also sitting at counsels' table were
Erin Murphy, David Raimer, and Mark Rienzi.

31.2. "necessary qualifications"

For one month after Justice Scalia's passing, the Court itself was in a state of
mourning. Justice Scalia's empty chair and the section of the bench directly
in front of it were draped with a black wool crepe in remembrance.[4] A black
drape also hung over the entrance to the chamber.[5] This tradition dates back
to the passing of Chief Justice Salmon P. Chase in 1873. St. John's law professor John Q. Barrett observed that the ritual is meant to "signify the existence
of the office," even though it is temporarily unfilled.[6] The period of mourning
ended two days before *Zubik* was argued. The crepes, drapes, and empty chair
were removed.

---

[2] Constance Veit, *Obamacare's Birth-Control 'Exemption' Still Tramples on Rights*, N.Y. TIMES
      (Mar. 18, 2016), nyti.ms/1samgK2.
[3] During oral arguments, both Chief Justice Roberts and Solicitor General Donald Verrilli pro-
      nounced Francisco's name as "Franchesca." Noel told me that he pronounces it like San
      Francisco. Verrilli, I was told, said "that is how you would pronounce it in proper Italian."
[4] SUPREME COURT OF THE UNITED STATES, For Immediate Release (Feb. 16, 2016),
      perma.cc/M498-6D42.
[5] Mark Walsh, *Courtroom Draping for Justice Scalia*, SCOTUSBLOG (Feb. 17, 2016),
      perma.cc/H6FR-FL7D.
[6] Tony Mauro, *Scalia's Empty Chair Is Draped Black, Marking His Death*, NAT'L. LAW J. (Feb.
      16, 2016), perma.cc/C6TJ-CULQ.

At exactly 10:00 AM, eight justices emerged from behind the vermillion curtains and sat in the eight chairs behind the bench. The justices always sit in order of seniority, with the chief justice in the middle; the most senior associate justice sits to the right of the chief, the next most senior justice sits to the left of the chief, and it continues to alternate across the bench. During the period between October 2010 and January 2016, the justices sat in the same order (from left to right): Sotomayor, Breyer, Thomas, Scalia, Roberts, Kennedy, Ginsburg, Alito, and Kagan. Now, with only eight justices, everyone moved one seat up: Kagan, Alito, Ginsburg, Kennedy, Roberts, Thomas, Breyer, and Sotomayor. Though Justice Thomas is notoriously silent – speaking only once during arguments between 2006 and 2016[7] – he can often be seen joking with his seatmate Justice Breyer. Fortunately, even after the shift, the two can continue ribbing each other.

Before arguments began, motions were heard for admission to the bar of the Supreme Court. Scott S. Harris, the clerk of the Court, called out: "Ilya Shapiro." Chief Justice Roberts repeated, "Mr. Shapiro." Shapiro, a senior fellow at the Cato Institute, approached the wooden rostrum and spoke into the delicately positioned microphones. "Mr. Chief Justice and may it please the Court," he began. "I move the admission of Joshua Michael Blackman of the Bar of the Commonwealth of Virginia. I am satisfied he possesses the necessary qualifications." Chief Justice Roberts announced, "Your motion is granted. Mr. Blackman will be admitted."[8] A few moments later, the chief justice said, "If all the applicants would stand." Sitting in the front row of the Court, a few feet from counsel table, I proudly stood up. "The clerk will administer the oath. But before he does so, I would like to extend to you a warm welcome as a member of the bar of this Court and as officers of this Court." Wearing the traditional morning coat, with his left hand on the bible, Mr. Harris announced, "Please raise your right hand. Do you solemnly swear as an attorney and counsel of this court you'll conduct yourself according to the law and support the Constitution of the United States, so help you God?" Without any hesitation, whatsoever, I replied, "I do." I had a perfect view of

---

[7] Laura Wagner, *Clarence Thomas Asks 1st Question from Supreme Court Bench in 10 Years*, NPR (Feb. 29, 2016), n.pr/22pjmgZ.

[8] Journal of the Supreme Court – October 2015 at 649 (Mar. 23, 2010), bit.ly/2aGc50s. My propitiously-timed admission to the Supreme Court Bar was featured in SCOTUSBLOG's *View from the Court* column. Mark Walsh, *A "View" from the Courtroom: Sister Act*, SCOTUSBLOG (Mar. 23, 2016), perma.cc/EXY4-KMFR. ("Also being sworn into the Supreme Court Bar today is Josh Blackman, an associate law professor at South Texas College of Law in Houston, and a frequent commentator on the work of the Court, particularly on the Affordable Care Act cases.").

arguments, and the back of my head made it into Art Lien's sketch of the hearing.[9]

For the third time in five years, Paul Clement appeared before the Supreme Court to challenge provisions of the Affordable Care Act. But this time, rather than representing a group of states trying to dismantle Obamacare, or a for-profit corporation asserting a religious identity, Clement now defended a sympathetic group of nuns who were fighting for their rights of conscience. Under the Obama administration's latest accommodation (version 5.0 if you are still counting), houses of worship were exempted from the mandate altogether.[10] However, religious nonprofits, such as the Little Sisters, were treated differently. These groups were not required to pay for the coverage; instead, the insurer would pay for the contraceptives directly after the employer notified the government of its faith-based objection. Under this proposal, female employees would receive contraceptive coverage through their preexisting health insurance plan, and receive treatment through their regular doctors.

The Little Sisters, and other nonprofits, objected to submitting the notification because they believed that it triggered the provision of contraceptive coverage – even if they were not paying for it – and made them complicit in sin. The government countered that providing the notice did not create the obligation for the insurer to provide contraceptive coverage, and that this proposal was the least-burdensome means to provide female employees with "seamless" coverage.

31.3. "CHURCHES ARE SPECIAL"

"We'll hear argument this morning in *Zubik v. Burwell,*" the chief justice announced. "Mr. Chief Justice, and may it please the Court," Paul Clement began. "The Little Sisters of the Poor face a dilemma that the Religious Freedom Restoration Act does not allow." During the opening statement, Justice Kennedy gazed forward, with his chin resting on his hand. "They can adhere to their religious beliefs and pay millions of dollars in penalties," Clement explained, "or they can take steps that they believe to be religiously and morally objectionable." To stress the point, Clement noted that the obviously religious Little Sisters of the Poor are subject to the mandate, while "345,000 churches, their integrated auxiliaries, and religious orders" are exempt. If the Little Sisters received the same treatment as the churches, he

---

[9] Art Lien, *Little Sisters and the Supremes*, COURTARTIST.COM (Mar. 24, 2016), perma.cc/9Q6L-YT8P.

[10] For a refresher of the various accommodations, *see supra* Chapters 4, 6, 15, and 20.

said, "we'd fill out any form" the government provided. "But the problem is we have to fill out a form, and the consequence of us filling out that form is we will be treated very differently from those other religious employers."

Both Justices Kagan and Ginsburg asked questions suggesting that it was unremarkable to treat churches differently. There is a "very strong tradition in this country," Kagan said, "which is that when it comes to religious exercises, churches are special." Why couldn't the government "treat the church as special," Ginsburg asked, "and give it an exemption that it doesn't give to religious-oriented organizations?" She pushed further. "Can the government say we are going to treat the church itself [as] ultra protected," while, "religious-oriented organizations are protected, but not at that same level?" During arguments, the solicitor general suggested that not all religious nonprofits were equally religious. Even if groups like the Little Sisters may "appear very close to entities that have an exemption," Verrilli offered, "there are also going to be lots of other entities whose connection to that core religious mission is much more attenuated." The solicitor general stressed that the government has "constrained ourselves," and has "tried to be especially careful with houses of worship."

The advocates for the Little Sisters steadfastly resisted this schism. "If my clients would have just stuck to their knitting," Clement joked, and "not helped the elderly poor, they could qualify" for the exemption. But because the nuns went out to help the elderly of all faiths, suddenly the government downgraded the Sisters' religiosity. During his argument, Noel Francisco added, "I don't think the government can take the position that the Little Sisters of the Poor are any less at the core [like a] 'church' than a house of worship."

This answer concerned Justice Kennedy. "It's going to be very difficult for this Court to write an opinion," he said, "which says that once you [exempt] a church organization, you have to treat a religious university the same." A senior Justice Department official told me that Justice Kennedy's concern might have been animated by the fact that many universities were "huge employers with thousands of workers and students who are not co-religionists." Justice Kennedy observed, "I just find that very difficult to write." When the Court's perennial fifth vote explains that it will be hard to write an opinion, that means it is not a winning argument.

31.4. "WHERE DO WE DRAW THE LINE?"

A few minutes into the argument, Justice Breyer asked Paul Clement, "Are you finished?" Clement, who knew what was about to hit him, replied, "Yeah, I am." The former law professor has a reputation for making long, winding statements that do not end with an actual question. Rather, Justice Breyer

uses these asides to share his wide-ranging thoughts about the case. I have
referred to these ponderings as *Breyer Pages*, because his remarks will often fill
up an entire page in the transcript. During her remarks to the Second Circuit
Judicial Conference in May 2016, Justice Ginsburg cited my discussion her
colleague's loquaciousness.[11] "According to a law professor who keeps tabs on
these things," Ginsburg said, "then blogs about them, Justice Breyer asked the
longest question at oral argument." According to my informal record-keep-
ing, Justice Breyer shattered his own record in *Zubik*, with an uninterrupted
statement that spanned 2 minute and 45 seconds – nearly 10 percent of Paul
Clement's allotted time at the rostrum.[12]

Breyer's soliloquy was deeply pensive. He wondered aloud where the government could draw a line between a burden that should and should not
require an accommodation. He observed that religious people, who are not
"hermits or monks," have to "accept all kinds of things" in society "that are just
horrible for [them]." Breyer offered the example of "Christian Scientists who
know when they report [a car] accident, [their] child will go to the hospital
and receive medical care that is against their religion." (Christian Scientists
have a religious objection to medical treatment). But they are still required to
report car accidents. Quakers "who objected to Vietnam," Breyer said, still had
to pay taxes that funded the war. Yet, Sabbatarians (such as Jews or Seventh
Day Adventists) were excused from working on Saturday if the government
also excused Christians from working on Sunday.

"What is the line?" Breyer asked. Clement responded that the Court does
not need to answer that question, and can "weed out some claims," by asking
if "there is a substantial burden on religious exercise." Breyer interrupted him,
"No, the Quaker, the Quaker. You think that wasn't a substantial burden?"
Later during the argument, Breyer asked Noel Francisco the same question.
"I'm trying to find the basis for the distinction between those things that we
do require people to do despite their religious objection and those things that
we don't." Francisco admitted it was a "tough line." The usually docile Breyer,
somewhat excited, interjected: "What – what is the right line?" Francisco
replied, "I don't think there's a clear line." Breyer smiled and leaned back in

---

[11] Ruth Bader Ginsburg, *Remarks for the Second Circuit Judicial Conference* (May 26, 2016),
bit.ly/1OQtZle.

[12] Josh Blackman, *We Have a New #SCOTUS Record! 49-Line #BreyerPage in Zubik*, JOSH
BLACKMAN'S BLOG (Mar. 23, 2016), perma.cc/FPN8-JSDJ. Coincidentally, Breyer would
shatter his *Zubik* record barely three weeks later during oral arguments in U.S. v. Texas, with
a question that stretched 3 minutes and 10 seconds. Some have speculated that without Justice
Scalia's jocular interjections, Justice Breyer can more easily continue his musings unabated.

his chair: "Give me a hint what the direction is." He was genuinely struggling with this question.

During the government's case, Justice Sotomayor asked the solicitor general to "go back to the substantial burden question," because "Justice Breyer has been talking about how to draw this line." We "live in a pluralistic society," she said, and "government has to function." If every imposition became a substantial burden that the government had to accommodate, Sotomayor suggested, our polity could not exist.

The solicitor general agreed: "A sensible balance is essential in a pluralistic society like ours in which people of every faith on earth live and work side by side." In our country, Verrilli said, "the government has got to administer rules that are fair to everyone." He conceded, "no line is perfect, and I'm sure this line isn't perfect, but the line is a valid line." Breyer asked again where the line should be drawn. Verrilli answered, "We are not urging you to state a comprehensive standard here." Breyer interrupted, lifted his palms up in frustration, and said, "Well, then what do I do?" A senior Justice Department attorney related to me that the government's "best strategy was to admit it was not a perfect line, but you can't draw a perfect line in this area."

Justice Sotomayor tried to offer her colleague a life raft. "Every believer that has ever come before the Court," she said, "is saying that my soul will be damned in some way." She was careful to stress that she was not "naysaying" their beliefs, but stated that the substantial burdens may only be "*perceived*." If that is the rule, and people can object to the laws based on any alleged burden, Sotomayor asked, "how will we ever have a government that functions?" She suggested that the government should draw the line where one's "religious belief is asking the government to change its behavior with respect to others" – that is, when accommodating a person's faith harms a third party that does not share that faith. Justice Breyer seemed to be persuaded by this line of reasoning. He referenced the amicus brief authored by NYU law professor Burt Neuborne. Justice Breyer asked rhetorically whether the Court should draw the line where "we have a program that affects third parties in a big way." He responded to his own question: "That might be the answer."

During his rebuttal, Paul Clement tried to respond to Justice Breyer's angst over line-drawing. "Now, my friend on the other side says the line doesn't have to be perfect. Well, under [the Religious Freedom Restoration Act], it at least has to be pretty good. And the line that they have drawn here is absurd." He later referred to the line as "terrible." Clement added, "All of these exemptions have to be treated the same, Justice Breyer. There is no excuse. There is no other way than to do the hard work of looking at the exemptions and seeing whether they make sense."

31.5. "COMPLICIT IN THE MORAL WRONG"

"General Verrilli." The chief justice invited the Solicitor General to make his sixth, and final, defense of Obamacare in five years. "Mr. Chief Justice, and may it please the Court," he began. "The accommodation that Petitioners challenge in this case strikes precisely the sensible balance between religious liberty and compelling governmental interests that Congress sought when it enacted RFRA." Verrilli sought to persuade the Court that "the accommodation seeks to respect" *both* "the religious liberty of Petitioners by exempting them from the contraceptive requirement" and "the interest of Petitioners' employees." The accommodation, he said, "comes as close as we can to ensuring that the employees who may not share the [Little Sisters'] religious beliefs get what the law entitles them to while at the same time ensuring that the employer does not have any legal obligation to pay for the coverage."

Thirty seconds into Verrilli's argument, Justice Kennedy interrupted him, and immediately changed the tenor of the entire case. "Is it fair for me to infer from the way you open your remarks that you concede that there is a substantial burden here?" A hushed silence fell over the Court. The solicitor general vigorously pushed back against the question. The government "concede[s] that the religious belief is sincere," but does not "concede there's a substantial burden."

Verrilli insisted that through the accommodation, "from the perspective of the employer, that [contraception coverage] is provided through a separate program," so there is no burden. Justice Kennedy interjected, "But you're saying, 'don't worry, religions, you're not complicit.' That's what you're saying?" Verrilli countered that "there is an objective limit that RFRA recognizes on the scope of what is a cognizable burden." Not every imposition on free exercise rises to the level of a substantial burden, the solicitor general implored the Court.

Justice Kennedy interrupted Verrilli again: "Do you question their belief that they're complicit in the moral wrong?" Verrilli answered, as he had to: "No we do not." Kennedy replied, "Then it seems to me that that's a substantial burden." With his index finger pointing at the solicitor general, the swing Justice explained that it was enough that the Little Sisters felt that they were "complicit in the moral wrong," whether or not the government agreed. That was adequate to demonstrate a substantial burden for purposes of RFRA. Justice Kennedy did not, in the least, seem troubled by the theological dilemma that confounded Justice Breyer. Noel Francisco told me he took these questions as a "hopeful sign" of which way "Justice Kennedy was leaning."

Recognizing that he had to cut short his losses, Verrilli decided to change directions. A senior DOJ attorney told me that the government understood that "it was going to be very hard to win the case" by proving that the accommodation did not impose a substantial burden on the free exercise of the Little Sisters. The government "needed to argue vigorously that there was no substantial burden." But "there was very little prospect for getting a fifth vote" on that point. Specifically, "it was going to be difficult for Justice Kennedy to come to the conclusion that there was no substantial burden." The government's "best strategy to win" was to argue that the accommodation satisfied RFRA, "even assuming for the sake of argument that there was a substantial burden." Verrilli quickly pivoted to the question of whether other alternatives would achieve the same compelling interest.

31.6. "SEAMLESS"

Under the Religious Freedom Restoration Act, if the government imposes a "substantial burden" on the free exercise of religion, the courts must assess whether the approach the government chose to achieve its goals was the "least restrictive" means – that is, whether the government could accomplish the same goal with a smaller infringement on religious liberty. If the answer is "yes," then the government's preferred, more burdensome approach would violate RFRA.

Justice Kennedy instructed the solicitor general how the case should be decided: "It seems to me then the analysis has to be whether this the least restrictive alternative?" Verrilli replied, "We would be content if the Court were to assume a substantial burden, but [conclude] that the government has satisfied its burden under RFRA to show that this is the least restrictive means of achieving" its "compelling interest." Justice Ginsburg interjected. "Now, you aren't giving up on the substantial burden?" RBG asked. A senior Justice Department attorney later told me that RBG "did not like hearing that at all." "No, we are not giving up on it," Verrilli countered, "but we do think the discussion this morning [has suggested] that this is a hard question, and it is important to us. And that's why we're fighting on it and not giving up on it."

Every "single" alternative proposed by the Little Sisters to deliver contraceptive coverage, Verrilli explained, "defeats the very purpose for which Congress imposed the preventive services requirement." The mandate was designed to ensure female employees received coverage "as part of their regular care from their regular doctor with no barriers." The solicitor general's brief explained that the accommodation "secur[es] for women the ability to

receive the coverage the Affordable Care Act guarantees them 'in a seamless manner' from the same insurers … that administer coverage for their
other medical care."[13] The phrase *seamless* was repeated nine times during
arguments – including by both Clement and Francisco, plus Justices Roberts,
Kagan, and Sotomayor – although never by Verrilli himself.

However, the government understood that the seamlessness argument
was a "double-edged sword." A senior DOJ official told me that seamlessness
"sounds like we are saying we are riding on the back of their plans." But the
solicitor general, I learned, "was not optimistic there were five votes" in their
favor on the substantial burden question. Instead, seamlessness was a way to
articulate that the government's interest of providing barrier-less contraceptive
coverage could not be achieved with separate plans. In other words, seamless
coverage could only be provided *through* the plans of the non-profits. The government was willing to sacrifice the substantial-burden element of the RFRA
analysis to bolster the least-restrictive-means component.

The chief justice promptly illustrated the downside of this strategy: "Your
compelling interest," Roberts said, "is that women obtain the contraceptive
services through the insurance plan of the Little Sisters." All barriers are eliminated by utilizing the Little Sisters' plan. Roberts noted that the Little Sisters
"used the phrase 'hijacking,' and it seems that is an accurate description of
what the government wants to do. They want to use the mechanism that the
Little Sisters have set up to provide services because they want the coverage
to be seamless." Roberts repeated that the petitioners object that "the government is hijacking their process." Justice Kennedy agreed that the accommodation makes it "necessary to hijack the plans." Noel Francisco told me that once
he heard Justice Kennedy asking about hijacking plans, he sensed that they
had their "four votes locked down."

Justice Sotomayor tossed the solicitor general a softball: "Can you explain
why you don't see this as a 'hijacking'?" Under the accommodation, Verrilli
answered, the coverage is provided "as separate means through separate funds
without [the plaintiffs'] involvement, and therefore, it's not 'hijacking'." The
solicitor general drew a distinction, noting that the government strikes an
"independent arrangement with third parties," the insurers. He continued,
"It isn't *through* that plan, it's in parallel to that plan." The chief shot right
back: "They are not third parties. They are the insurance company that

---

[13]   The solicitor general's brief cited Judge Nina Pillard's decision in Priests for Life v. HHS,
       which first utilized this phrase. 772 F.3d 229, 267 (D.C. Cir. 2014) ("The accommodation is the
       least restrictive method of ensuring that women continue to receive contraceptive coverage *in
       a seamless manner* while simultaneously relieving the eligible organizations of any obligation
       to provide such coverage.") (emphasis added).

the [Little Sisters] have hired." There was an inherent tension in the government's argument. If indeed their compelling interest was in providing "seamless coverage" so that the female employees are not even aware of the accommodation, then by necessity the accommodation operates *through* the employer's plan. Paul Clement pointed out that it is "little rich for the government" to simultaneously argue that the nuns are not burdened and insist that their employees receive "seamless coverage" through the Little Sisters' plan.

If this approach did not work, what would? Justice Kagan asked Noel Francisco whether there was "any kind of notification that would be acceptable" that would result "in women employees of your clients ... getting contraceptive coverage" as "part of an employer-based plan." Francisco answered that his clients sought the same treatment as houses of worship. But the female employees of churches, Kagan said, "do not get contraceptive coverage through the employer-based plan." She asked the question again: Is there "any accommodation that would result in the women employees getting contraceptive coverage seamlessly through an employer-based plan that you would find acceptable?" After several back-and-forths, Francisco explained that this accommodation would only work if there were a separate plan that would not operate through the plan created by the Little Sisters. Similarly, Paul Clement urged the Court, "My clients would love to be a conscientious objector, but the government insists that they be a conscientious collaborator. There is no such thing."

So "it has to be some other plan," Justice Ginsburg observed. This point proved to the government that there was no way to accommodate the religious nonprofits, short of a flat-out exemption. During my conversation with a senior DOJ attorney, he wondered aloud about the policy judgment made by the Obama administration. "Was the benefit of extending the coverage to these categories of employees worth the cost of having this big culture war fight over religious liberty?" That answer could go either way. But once that judgment was made, from a legal perspective, "nothing could have been done to avoid this fight" unless the employers had no involvement whatsoever. And that's precisely what the Little Sisters wanted.

31.7. "ONE-OFF JERRY-RIGGED SEPARATE CHANNEL"

In a pre-Obamacare world, perhaps the only way to provide contraceptive coverage to workers was *through* their employers' group health insurance plan. But what about with the ACA exchanges, Justice Alito inquired. Why couldn't a female employee of a religious nonprofit "obtain a contraceptive-only policy free of charge on one of the Exchanges," he asked. "Why would that not be a less restrictive alternative" than using the Little Sisters' plan? Solicitor General Verrilli rejected this alternative, because it "creates the very problem that Congress was trying to solve in this provision." It "would require setting up a one-off jerry-rigged separate channel to get contraceptive coverage." Female employees would have to "go out and get a separate policy."

A contraceptive-only policy, Verrilli explained, would not be "equally effective at achieving the government's interest, because the whole point of this provision is that you get this care from your regular doctor as part of your regular health care without any barriers." These "small barriers," Verrilli said, "work as a sufficient disincentive that many fewer people would use contraception than would otherwise."

Alito pushed back, and asked why that was such a big deal. "So she'll have two insurance cards instead of one," Alito offered. She will have "one from the employer, and she'll have one from this plan, just as a lot of people have one insurance card for medical services and one for prescription drugs." He continued, "What type of burden does that impose?" With his tongue in his cheek, Alito asked: Is it because "these exchanges are so unworkable, even with the help of a navigator?" The audience in the Court chuckled at the subtle dig at HealthCare.gov. Chief Justice Roberts took a similar shot at the ill-fated website: "It's a hassle to go to the exchange? You know, I've heard about how easy it is" to use.

Justice Sotomayor interjected: "They're not on the Exchanges. That's a falsehood." The ACA exchanges, she said, only allow "full-service health insurance policies with minimum coverages." A senior DOJ official told me that it would be "clearly unlawful" under the ACA to offer a contraceptive-only plan on the exchanges. The chief justice asked Verrilli, "Is that true with respect to every policy sold on the Exchanges" that they must provide a wide range of benefits? He began to answer, "Yes, every policy sold on the Exchanges—" Roberts interrupted him: "What about pediatric dentistry?" The ACA authorizes standalone pediatric dental care plans to be sold on the exchanges, because it is deemed "essential coverage." Verrilli replied, "Well, except for that one." Sarcastically, the Chief replied, "Oh, except for pediatric dentistry. So you could have a separate health coverage product sold on the Exchanges. You, in fact, do it already."

The solicitor general countered, "You couldn't do it under current law, Your Honor." Roberts replied, somewhat agitated, "Well, the way constitutional objections work is you might have to change current law." A lawyer familiar with the Solicitor General's thinking told me that he "dropped the ball" there, because the government "had a pretty strong answer" ready for that question. It was true that under the First Amendment, the government had to change laws that violated free speech. But, the Supreme Court's First Amendment free exercise cases did not involve changing *the law*, but rather granting a free pass to conscientious objectors. Further, RFRA was a statute, not a constitutional provision, and Congress was not required to rewrite laws in the same fashion. There was no precedent to support the chief's suggestion.

31.8. "FROM THE PERSPECTIVE OF THE WOMAN EMPLOYEE"

Since the introduction of Senator Barbara Mikulski's amendment in 2009, the "preventive care" mandate has been, at bottom, about a simple fact: women have different health care needs than men do. During oral arguments, a concerted effort was made to shine a light on how an exemption affects female employees that do not share their boss's faith.

With a series of questions, Justice Sotomayor shifted the discourse from the faith of the nuns to the health care needs of their female employees. "Why are we worried about this case at all," she asked Noel Francisco, if "the majority [of the employees] are part of the religion" and "are not going to buy contraceptives? That's their religious tenet." Francisco began to reply, but this rhetorical question was not meant to be answered. "We are worried," Sotomayor said, "because we perceive the government has determined [women] have a real need for contraceptives." (Recall that Congress was silent about what constituted "preventive care.") The issue of the importance of contraception for women as an end unto itself was not directly before the court, but Justice Sotomayor raised it. Noel Francisco briefly answered that there is an "utter absence of evidence" to support that judgment. "What is the utter absence" she asked. "There is plenty of evidence that was relied upon to show that when contraceptives are provided to women in a seamless way, that the number of unintended pregnancies dramatically falls, as does the number of abortions. And so that health risk to women who want contraceptives who can't get it is proven, scientifically and otherwise."

The solicitor general made a similar entreaty. A senior DOJ attorney told me that he thought that "it came naturally to many of the Justices to put themselves in the shoes of the Little Sisters," but he wanted them to "think of themselves as the employee who does not get what everyone else gets because the employer has a religious belief." Verrilli's strategy was to get the point across "bluntly."

"Consider this, please, from the perspective of the woman employee," Verrilli implored the Court. Imagine if a female employee, who "has a health plan from her employer goes to her regular doctor. She may have a medical condition that makes pregnancy a danger for her. She may be one of the women who needs contraception to treat a medical condition, or maybe she just wants the contraception that's appropriate for her." Under the Little Sisters' proposal, "her regular doctor has to say to her, 'Sorry, I can't help you.'" The doctor cannot write her a prescription, "counsel or educate the patient." Chief Justice Roberts countered that the Little Sisters "do not object to the fact that the people who work for them will have these services provided. They object to having them provided through the mechanism that they have set up because they think that complicity is sinful."

With his time running out, the solicitor general wound down his defense of Obamacare. "If I could, just in closing," Verrilli asked, "what I'd ask this Court to do is to weigh the alternatives that have been put before you." Verrilli looked at each justice one after the other, oscillating his head from left to right. "On the one side, you've got a serious, thoughtful effort to respect Petitioners' religious beliefs by creating a system that allows them to exempt themselves from the requirement in a straightforward manner and that protects the fundamental rights and liberties and dignity of their employees, many of whom may not share their religious beliefs about contraception. On the other side of the scale, what you've got is a demand that the rights of those employees who may not share Petitioners' beliefs be extinguished until such time as Congress creates and enacts a different program." The government's position achieves a "sensible balance," but the Petitioners' "position is very, very far from that balance and, therefore, the court of appeals should be affirmed."

The chief justice closed the proceedings. "Thank you, counsel. The case is submitted."

31.9. "LET THEM SERVE"

In 1929, former president and then–Chief Justice William Howard Taft charged architect Cass Gilbert with the task of designing a "building of dignity and importance suitable for its use as the permanent home of the Supreme Court of the United States."[14] Since 1801, the justices were transients, meeting in a half-dozen different places throughout the Capitol. Finally, in 1935, the justices had a home of their own. Among the most distinctive features of Gilbert's design are the forty-four marble steps leading up to the monumental bronze doors and into the chamber.

[14] SUPREME COURT OF THE UNITED STATES, *The Supreme Court Building*, perma.cc/S944-PNKX.

In 2010, the Supreme Court sealed the front doors to the public as a security measure, requiring visitors to use a side entrance.[15] Justice Breyer, joined by Justice Ginsburg, released a statement to "regret ... the closing of the Court's front entrance."[16] Breyer wrote that the "Court's forty-four marble steps ... does its part to encourage contemplation of the Court's central purpose, the administration of justice to all who seek it." Cass Gilbert's plan, Breyer observed, "leads visitors along a carefully choreographed, climbing path that ultimately ends at the courtroom itself." The justice – also a juror for the Pritzker Prize, architecture's greatest honor[17] – recalled that "the steps appear in countless photographs commemorating famous arguments," and are "not only a means to, but also a metaphor for ... dignified openness and meaningful access to equal justice under law." The steps have formed an important part of the Court's heritage. It is customary that the chief justice accompanies each new associate justice down the steps after his or her investiture. In an iconic photograph taken the day after *Brown v. Board of Education* was decided, an African American mother and her daughter sat on the steps, holding a newspaper that read "High Court Bans Segregation in Public Schools." Only one month earlier, eighty of Justice Scalia's clerks lined the steps as his casket was carried into the Court.

Though the doors are closed upon entering the Court, as Breyer noted, "visitors will remain able to leave via the front entrance." On the morning of March 23, 2016, Gilbert's steps witnessed one of the most dramatic departures in the Court's history.[18] On the street below, hundreds of nuns, priests, and Catholic students in full regalia cheered and chanted: "Let them serve! Let them serve!"[19] Shortly after the arguments concluded, the Little Sisters of the Poor emerged from behind the now-ajar bronze doors. Led by Mother Provincial Loraine, eight sisters proudly walked down the steps, smiling and waving to the rapt onlookers. As the nuns made the slow, deliberate walk down the forty-four steps, the majesty of Gilbert's plan became crystal clear.

---

[15] Robert Barnes, *Supreme Court Closes Its Front Doors to the Public*, Wash. Post (May 4, 2010), perma.cc/LD2C-S9TF.

[16] *Journal of the Supreme Court – October 2009* at 831 (May 3, 2010), (Statement concerning the Supreme Court's Front Entrance), (Breyer, J., dissenting from denial of reentry), bit.ly/244XiHK.

[17] Robin Pogrebin, *Breyer Invited to Make a Case for Architecture*, N.Y. Times (Oct. 6, 2011), nyti.ms/1saqdyl.

[18] *Crowd Goes Wild for Little Sisters of the Poor at the Supreme Court*, YouTube (Mar. 29, 2016), youtu.be/zdSx9lNEYDI.

[19] *Id.*

The star of the day, Sister Loraine, approached the waiting bank of microphones, flanked by her colleagues. Her remarks were memorized, and delivered flawlessly:

> Hello. My name is Sister Loraine Marie Claire. The lord has given me a beautiful calling, and that is being a Little Sister of the Poor. We Little Sisters of the Poor are a group of women who make religious vows to God, and we dedicate ourselves to serve the elderly poor, caring for them regardless of race or religion, offering them a home where they're welcomed as Christ. They're cared for as our own family and we accompany them until God calls them home to himself. We've done this work for over 175 years. Now we find ourselves in a situation where the government is requiring us to make changes in our religious health care plan to include services that really violate our deepest held religious beliefs as Little Sisters. It's hard for us to understand why the government is doing this. The government is threatening us with fines of over $70 million a year. It's such a privilege for us to care for the most vulnerable members of our society, serving them, comforting them, just being a loving and healing presence in their everyday lives, just being their Little Sister every day is our joy. And really that's all we want to continue to do. Our motive is to continue our work as we've always done it. After today's hearing, we are hopeful for a positive outcome. Our Mother Foundress taught us and said, 'The work is God's. He will help us.' So we put our trust in Him. He'll be there for us as he's always been for 175 years. Thank you very much. God bless you.

Mark Rienzi, the Becket Fund lawyer who represented the Little Sisters, told the media, "If the government wants to provide these services, the government is free to provide them. The Little Sisters are asking the government to use all of its services," including the ACA exchanges, "to provide the services it wants. It is very easy to provide these services without nuns. Let them serve." (The #LetThemServe hashtag was trending on Twitter that morning). The Becket Fund's staff then escorted the Little Sisters off the Supreme Court's plaza. There would be no need for a bus full of nuns, as the Sisters did not have to travel far.

A few moments later, Louise Melling of the ACLU approached the microphones to discuss the case. An onlooker asked why the employees could not get coverage from the ACA exchanges. She rejected that approach. "That's like saying women have to go through the back door in order to get the care we want. It's offering an alternative that's fostering discrimination in response to something that is meant to address discrimination." Melling referenced Justice Breyer's angst: "Justice Breyer was asking over and over, how do we think about the line, the line between religion and its intersection in secular society? The line is to say that religious liberty doesn't mean the right to impose your views on others or the right to discriminate."

Father Frank Pavone, director of Priests for Life, addressed the media with a more direct message. He warned that "we will not obey this mandate, no matter how this Court rules." Pavone closed with a forecast: "We predict this will be a split 4–4 decision." Noel Francisco told me after leaving the Court he was hopeful the Court would deadlock internally, and "set it for reargument the next term in the hopes that a ninth Justice would be appointed." Another lawyer for the challengers told me they worried about "holding it over for reargument because of the uncertainty of the political landscape." The challengers had "no idea what the Court is going to look like" when it is reargued. It could be a "Court that looks quite bad for us."

The government predicted the case was "up in the air." There was not much of a chance the United States thought it would lose five-to-three or six-to-two, but it was very far from certain that the government would win five-to-three or six-to-two. A four-to-four lockup was conceivable but unlikely. In theory, at least, the justices could "roll it over" and reargue it the next term, a DOJ official told me. But in light of Scalia's contested seat, there may "have been considerable uncertainty about holding it over," because it may not be filled until 2017.

Solicitor General Verrilli would not return to the Court for the next round of Obamacare litigation. After his final argument in *United States v. Texas*, a challenge by the Lone Star State to President Obama's executive action on immigration, Verrilli announced that he would step down. President Obama hailed Verrilli as "a dedicated public servant who has helped our nation live up to its promise of liberty and justice for all."[20] Attorney General Loretta Lynch praised Verrilli, who "successfully defended the constitutionality of the Affordable Care Act, preserving a law that has helped millions to obtain health insurance." During a series of interviews before his departure, the outgoing solicitor general reflected on the confrontational relationship between the Court and the president during his tenure. "I can't think of a time since the 1930s," he said, "when the role of the court in the life of the nation and in the unfolding of the political process has been as central as it's been in the last five years."[21] The Obama administration sought to "use the power that we believe the Constitution gives the federal government to address the great

---

[20] Statement by President Obama on the Departure of Solicitor General Don Verrilli, THE WHITE HOUSE (Jun. 2, 2016), perma.cc/44HU-MNLQ.

[21] Richard Wolf, *Obama's Supreme Court Lawyer Ends 'Intense' Tenure*, USA TODAY (Jun. 21, 2016), perma.cc/HSA2-WRFN.

problems confronting the nation." The Court greeted those actions with "a degree of skepticism."

Verrilli singled out his victories in *NFIB v. Sebelius* and *King v. Burwell* as the most important of his tenure. "Those were cases, from the perspective of the administration," he said, that involved "one of its most important policy, where virtually everything was on the line."[22] Verrilli praised Chief Justice Roberts as a "fair-minded jurist" who "cares about the place of the institution in our constitutional structure." He was asked about future legal challenges to the ACA. Citing the six votes in favor of the government in *King v. Burwell*, Verrilli said, "I think the debate is effectively over."

31.10. "CLIENTS ARE HEROES"

As the last person walked away from the bank of microphones after oral arguments, a voice off camera announced, "I think we're done. We would've hoped Paul Clement would be here." Another observed, "I saw him walk away. He left." A third said, "I've not seen that happen before." Clement, who usually addresses the media following a big argument, would soon deliver his closing statement one block away.[23]

In what has become a tradition, lunches are scheduled after high-profile Supreme Court arguments. These gatherings serve to celebrate all of the hard work that goes into litigating a case before the High Court, and also allows everyone involved to relax after an otherwise stressful day. At 12:00 PM, roughly thirty minutes after arguments concluded in *Zubik v. Burwell*, the Becket Fund for Religious Liberty and Alliance Defending Freedom hosted a lunch at the Top of the Hill Center. For the first course, a room full of priests, nuns, and attorneys enjoyed Manchego cheese and pears, followed by an herb-grilled airline breast of chicken.

Before the dessert of a bright berry tart was served, Paul Clement addressed the crowd. "I thank the Little Sisters, and any clients who are present," he said in front of a podium, draped with a "Let them serve" banner. "There are no lawyers who are heroes," Clement explained. "Clients are heroes. I can't thank them enough to have the courage to stick out their neck for the cause of religious liberty." The attorney offered a cautious prediction: "We are in the game, but not at the point where we are done needing your prayers. The

---

[22] Ari Melber, *Top Obama Lawyer: Obamacare Fight Over*, MSNBC (Jun. 17, 2016), perma.cc/A42Y-V65R.

[23] *Religious Leader Reaction to Zubik vs. Burwell Oral Argument (Full Event)*, C-SPAN (Mar. 23, 2016), cs.pn/1saqJfF.

Court is very divided." Clement, who clerked for the late Justice, confided that he "very much wished" that Justice Scalia was there. "If he was here today, I would have a lightness to my step." He urged everyone to "continue praying for the Court to find a way to protect religious liberty."

Next, Sister Loraine addressed the captivated room. She spoke of this case as a calling. This is "what God wanted for us at this time. We are all united. He wants the best for us. He has to help us out of this." She noted that the entire process was "a bit overwhelming," but was "edified by your dedication. You all dedicate your lives to a higher calling."

Before she sat down, Sister Loraine told everyone to "keep praying, I don't know when this will be over." Usually after the briefs are written, and the case is argued, the parties can only wait for a decision – usually at the end of June. This case, however, was *far* from over.

32

"Accommodation"

32.1. "THE COURT FELT THE NEED TO FASHION SOME SOLUTION"

In the wake of Justice Scalia's passing, Chief Justice Roberts downplayed the impact of his absence on the Court's decision-making process. "It's a great loss, the loss of Justice Scalia. But the process is pretty much what it has been."[1] He stressed, "Sometimes we talk about cases longer to see if we can reach some type of agreement. But that's it." His colleagues largely agreed. Justice Alito, when asked about the short-handed Court, simply said, "We will deal with it."[2] Justice Breyer duly noted, "We'll miss [Justice Scalia], but we'll do our work. For the most part, it will not change."[3]

The newest justice offered more expansive thoughts on the Court's altered dynamics. Justice Kagan commented that down to eight, the justices "are working hard to reach agreement."[4] This was true with a full bench, she explained, but "we're especially concerned about that now." The former law school dean quipped, "There is a reason why courts do not typically have an even number of members." Kagan praised Roberts for his leadership during these tough times. "I give great credit to the Chief Justice, who I think in general is a person who is concerned about consensus building, and I think all the more so now," Justice Kagan said. "He's conveyed that in both his words and his deeds."

---

[1] Robert Barnes, *Roberts Refuses to Be Drawn into Controversy about Filling Supreme Court Vacancy*, WASH. POST (May 4, 2016), perma.cc/R985-WXET.

[2] Ariane de Vogue, *Samuel Alito on Supreme Court Vacancy: 'We Will Deal with It'*, CNN (Feb. 23, 2016), perma.cc/XUA6-R3NP.

[3] John Gerstein, *Breyer on 8-Member Supreme Court: 'We'll Do Our Work'*, POLITICO (Feb. 25, 2016), perma.cc/PE5R-YVS2.

[4] Adam Liptak, *Supreme Court Is Working Hard to Avoid Deadlocks, Kagan Says*, N.Y. TIMES (Apr. 4, 2016), nyti.ms/22nGgW2.

After oral arguments concluded in *Zubik*, the eight-member Court appeared deadlocked. Justices Ginsburg, Kagan, and Sotomayor seemed firmly convinced that the accommodation was a sensible approach to balancing religious liberty and expanding contraceptive coverage. Justice Breyer was conflicted over where to draw the line, but was troubled that exempting the Little Sisters could burden their female employees. On the other side, Chief Justice Roberts and Justices Alito and Kennedy viewed the accommodation as *hijacking* the Little Sisters' plan. Justice Thomas, who did not ask any questions, was unlikely to side with the government. With a short-handed Court, the vote was seemingly tied.

Traditionally, when a justice does not participate in a case, and the eight-member court is evenly divided, the judgment of the lower court is affirmed, without setting any precedent.[5] Since Justice Scalia's passing, the Court had already twice affirmed other judgments by an equally divided margin.[6] However, this option was not feasible for the Obamacare cases, because the lower courts did not agree. The Third, Fifth, Tenth, and D.C. Circuit Courts of Appeals ruled for the federal government. The Eighth Circuit Court of Appeals ruled for the challengers. Had the Court simply divided 4 to 4, the circuit split would persist. The accommodation to the contraception mandate would have been valid in some states but not in others. A senior Justice Department official told me that the "Court would be reluctant to have different rules apply in different parts of the country," especially where employers operate across state lines. Following arguments in *Zubik*, Paul Clement told the audience at the Top of the Hill Center that the Court "felt the need to fashion some solution." And that is precisely what the justices attempted to do.

32.2. "THE PARTIES ARE DIRECTED TO FILE SUPPLEMENTAL BRIEFS"

On Friday, March 25, the justices held their conference to discuss *Zubik*. It is impossible to know exactly what transpires at the private conference; only the justices are allowed to attend. One of the few things we know for certain is that the most recently appointed justice has a very important task: answering the door when someone knocks. Justice Tom C. Clark referred to the position as "the most highly paid doorman in the country."[7] Justice John Paul Stevens

---

[5] Josh Blackman & Ilya Shapiro, *Only Eight Justices? So What*, WALL ST. J. (Feb. 23, 2016), on.wsj.com/1UoMSno.

[6] Friedrichs v. Cal. Teachers Ass'n, 136 S. Ct. 1083 (2016); Hawkins v. Cmty. Bank of Raymore, 136 S. Ct. 1072 (2016).

[7] JOHN PAUL STEVENS, FIVE CHIEFS: A SUPREME COURT MEMOIR 141 (2011).

recalled when he committed an "unforgivable error" early in his career. During "my first or second conference," the Ford appointee said, "I was so absorbed in the discussion that I did not realize that someone had knocked until Bill Brennan on my left and Bill Rehnquist on my right pushed back their chairs and got up to answer the door. That humiliating lesson taught me to keep track of priorities."[8] Elena Kagan, who has been the junior justice since 2010, recalled that when there is a knock, "I have to immediately jump up and get the door," she said. "And literally, if I don't jump up to get the door, nobody gets the door."[9] For the *Zubik* conference, however, the surprise would come from inside the room.

Three days later, the justices assigned some unexpected homework: "The parties are directed to file supplemental briefs that address whether and how contraceptive coverage may be obtained by petitioners' employees through petitioners' insurance companies, but in a way that does not require any involvement of petitioners beyond their own decision to provide health insurance without contraceptive coverage to their employees."[10] In English, the Court asked the parties to discuss whether there was some way for the nonprofit's insurer to pay for their employees' contraceptives *without* the nonprofit formally objecting. Critically, the Court suggested, "such coverage is not paid for by petitioners and is not provided *through* petitioners' health plan." But the Court was not committed to this approach. "The parties may address other proposals along similar lines," the order stated, "avoiding repetition of discussion in prior briefing."

Requests for additional briefing by the Supreme Court are extremely rare. Over the last three decades, the Court has ordered supplemental briefing in only twenty-eight cases: eight cases were rescheduled for argument the following term,[11] in nine cases additional briefing was requested *before* the case was argued,[12] and in eleven cases additional briefing was requested *after*

---

[8] *Id.* at 140.

[9] Liptak, *supra* note 4.

[10] Zubik v. Burwell, 2016 WL 1203818 (mem.) (Mar. 29, 2016).

[11] Kungys v. United States, 483 U.S. 1017 (1987); Reno v. Bossier Par. Sch. Bd., 527 U.S. 1033, (1999); Price v. Bossier Par. Sch. Bd., 527 U.S. 1033 (1999); Slack v. McDaniel, 528 U.S. 949 (1999); Vermont Agency of Nat. Res. v. United States, 528 U.S. 1015 (1999); Citizens United v. Fed. Election Comm'n, 557 U.S. 932 (2009); Kiobel v. Royal Dutch Petrol. Co., 132 S. Ct. 1738 (2012); Johnson v. United States, 135 S. Ct. 939 (2015).

[12] Hartigan v. Zbaraz, 481 U.S. 1008 (1987); Swint v. Chambers Cty. Comm'n, 513 U.S. 958 (1994); Ford Motor Co. v. McCauley, 536 U.S. 987 (2002); Abdur'Rahman v. Bell, 537 U.S. 996 (2002); Norfolk S. Ry. Co. v. James N. Kirby, Pty Ltd., 542 U.S. 963 (2004); Panetti v. Quarterman, 549 U.S. 1320 (2007); Christeson v. Roper, 135 S. Ct. 14 (2014); Wittman v. Personhuballah, 136 S. Ct. 25 (2015); Kingdomware Techs., Inc. v. United States, 136 S. Ct. 444 (2015).

the case was argued.[13] The 354-word order in *Zubik*, however, was *unprecedented*. Rather than responding to changed facts, or questions that arose from the briefs or arguments, the *Zubik* order was a product of the justices' own agitation. Or maybe one justice's conciliation. Professors Richard C. Schragger and Micah Schwartzman of the University of Virginia Law School and Professor Nelson Tebbe of Brooklyn Law School speculated that perhaps Justice Breyer, the "pragmatist and problem solver" of the Court, was behind the unexpected order.[14] A lawyer for the Little Sisters agreed, and told me that the long, winding order sounded like a question Justice Breyer would ask during arguments – especially the sentence at the end that invited the parties to "address other proposals along similar lines." The Court was looking for something – anything – to resolve the case without fracturing on the difficult religious-liberty questions.

Solicitor General Verrilli's initial reaction to the order, I learned, was "Oh geez." After the order was issued, the Obama administration assembled all of the agency lawyers and all the attorneys in the Justice Department to systematically go through all every possible option and determine what could and could not be done. Though feasible, the administration was not optimistic about the Court's request. A senior DOJ official told me that "it was unrealistic to think this was going to achieve any resolution of the case." But he understood "why the Court was trying to achieve a resolution."

Noel Francisco viewed the Court's order as a "hopeful sign." Coming out of arguments it looked like a "four-to-four logjam," he said, and the justices "were trying to figure out whether there could be a fifth vote for" the Little Sisters. Francisco noted that "it was hard to see how the questions" the justices asked could "hurt us." But it was "easy to see how it would help us."

In drafting their reply, Francisco told me that the "entire issue has to be driven by the clients, because it's their religious views that were at stake." He noted that the Court's question was "fairly open-ended" so the lawyers had to "explain to our clients what the Court is asking, and what the potential ranges of possibilities are." Then, the lawyers have to "follow their lead." Because

13 W. Air Lines, Inc. v. Bd. of Equalization of S. Dakota, 479 U.S. 958 (1986); Whitman v. Dep't of Transp., 547 U.S. 1124 (2006); United States v. Resendiz-Ponce, 549 U.S. 974 (2006); Hall St. Associates, L.L.C. v. Mattel, Inc., 552 U.S. 1035 (2007); Dada v. Mukasey, 552 U.S. 1138 (2008); Kennedy v. Plan Adm'r for DuPont Sav. & Inv. Plan, 555 U.S. 990 (2008); Montejo v. Louisiana, 556 U.S. 1150 (2009); Coeur Alaska, Inc. v. Se. Alaska Conservation Council, 556 U.S. 1219 (2009); New Process Steel, L.P. v. N.L.R.B., 559 U.S. 1059 (2010); Douglas v. Indep. Living Ctr. of S. California, 132 S. Ct. 546 (2011); Zubik v. Burwell, No. 14-1418, 2016 WL 1203818, at *2 (U.S. Mar. 29, 2016).
14 Richard Schragger, Micah Schwatzman, & Nelson Tebbe, *The Contraceptive Compromise*, SLATE (Apr. 14, 2016), perma.cc/WLP5-MSLD.

many of the clients were Catholic, and the Catholic Church is "somewhat hierarchical," the lawyers could "look to certain leaders and have them frame their initial views." That helped "achieve consensus fairly quickly." Once all of the briefs were submitted, the parties could only wait.

32.3. "PER CURIAM"

On Monday, May 16, Solicitor General Verrilli was slated to give the commencement address at Wayne State University Law School in Detroit.[15] That morning at 10:00 AM, as the Court began its session to hand down opinions, Verrilli followed along over the in-flight Internet access.

Justice Kagan had the first opinion of the day in *Merrill Lynch v. Manning*, a securities case. "This is not going to be very helpful to most of you," Kagan quipped to laughter in the Court, "that is, to the non-lawyers here"[16] The longtime law professor added that the complicated language in the case should convince the non-lawyers in attendance that they "made the right decision by not going to law school." The second opinion was from Justice Sotomayor in *Husky International Electronics v. Ritz*, which involved fraudulent conveyances under the federal bankruptcy code. Third, Justice Alito announced the Court's decision in *Spokeo v. Robins*, which considered whether a search engine could be sued because it posted inaccurate information about a person. The fourth case from Justice Ginsburg, *Sheriff v. Gillie*, involved a federal debt collection case. This quartet, none of which were particularly earthshattering, seemed part of the Court's practice of "bringing down" the number of pending cases as the term wound to a close. But then the Court quickly changed course.

At 10:14 AM, Amy Howe posted on SCOTUSBlog, "It's a busy day at the Court today." Three minutes later she exclaimed, "*Zubik v. Burwell* is here. Holy cow!" Mark Walsh, also of SCOTUSBlog, reported that at that moment, "a hush [fell] over the Courtroom" as the chief justice began to speak. Traditionally, the Court holds its blockbuster decisions until the last week of June. Beyond the theatrics of saving the best for last, there is a pragmatic reason: divisive opinions take longer to write. Majority opinions have to respond to dissents, and this process takes time. By all accounts, *Zubik* was one of the most evenly divided cases of the term – so difficult that the Court had to

---

[15] *U.S. Solicitor General to Speak May 16 at Wayne Law Commencement*, WAYNE LAW (Apr. 20, 2016), perma.cc/4NAH-44GM.

[16] Mark Walsh, *A "View" from the Courtroom: Something We Can Live with*, SCOTUSBLOG (May 16, 2016), perma.cc/9DMR-AVQ9.

ask for additional briefing. As a result, this May announcement took virtually everyone, your author included, by complete surprise.

Chief Justice Roberts, who had announced the judgments of the Court in *NFIB v. Sebelius* and *King v. Burwell*, immediately made clear that the opinion was not his alone. Rather, he said, "the Court today is issuing a *per curiam* decision, which I will read." A *per curiam* opinion – translated from Latin as "by the court as a whole" – does not have a single author. Rather, all of the justices sign onto the opinion. This is a common practice for uncontroversial cases, where the justices summarily reverse a lower court without even hearing arguments.

As soon as the chief began to announce the judgment, the Court's website posted a PDF of the opinion. Solicitor General Verrilli received an e-mail on board the plane with the decision attached. I learned that he was "scrambling like mad trying to figure out what's what." At first he couldn't make "heads or tails" of it. Noel Francisco was also "surprised" by the Court's per curiam decision, because he had "not seen anything quite like that before."

Initial headlines from the media also disagreed about what the unanimous Court actually did. *Reuters* wrote, "U.S. top court sidesteps major ruling on Obamacare contraception coverage."[17] The *Washington Times* declared, "Supreme Court rejects Obama's birth control plan, sends case to lower courts."[18] The *L.A. Times* explained, "Supreme Court clears the way to free birth control for women with religious employers."[19] The *New York Times* reported, "Justices, Seeking Compromise, Return Contraception Case to Lower Courts."[20] All four outlets offered slightly different accounts; all four were correct.

32.4. "PUNTED"

The chief justice proceeded to read the three-page decision, verbatim, omitting only the citations. This would not be a case where the announcing justice improvised and blurted out something his colleagues did not

[17] Lawrence Hurley, *Supreme Court Dodges Major Decision on Obamacare Birth Control*, REUTERS (May 17, 2016), perma.cc/X6G3-B8TU.

[18] Tom Howell Jr., *Supreme Court Rejects Obama's Birth Control Plan, Send Case to Lower Courts*, WASH. TIMES (May 16, 2015), perma.cc/G6QR-RLFV.

[19] David Savage, *Supreme Court Ruling Should Clear the Way to Free Birth Control for Women with Religious Employers*, L.A. TIMES (May 16, 2016), perma.cc/Q4L6-SDTB.

[20] Adam Liptak, *Justices, Seeking Compromise, Return Contraception Case to Lower Courts*, N.Y. TIMES (May 16, 2016), nyti.ms/1TT0B2d.

sign onto. The chief stuck to the script. "Following oral argument," Roberts began, "the Court requested supplemental briefing from the parties addressing 'whether contraceptive coverage could be provided to petitioners' employees, through petitioners' insurance companies, without any such notice from petitioners.'"[21] Both parties "now confirm that such an option is feasible." The nonprofits, Roberts relayed, "have clarified that their religious exercise is not infringed where they 'need to do nothing more than contract for a plan that does not include coverage for some or all forms of contraception,' even if their employees receive cost-free contraceptive coverage from the same insurance company." (Notice how Roberts said the same insurance "company," not the same insurance "plan.") Additionally, the United States "has confirmed that the challenged procedures 'for employers with insured plans could be modified to operate in the manner posited in the Court's order while still ensuring that the affected women receive contraceptive coverage seamlessly, together with the rest of their health coverage.'" By all accounts, the chief suggested both the plaintiffs and the government agreed a compromise could be worked out. For those still keeping track, this would be *Accommodation 6.0*. (As we will see later, this is hardly a compromise, because there remains a sizeable gap between their positions, which the Court did not acknowledge.)

"In light of the positions asserted by the parties in their supplemental briefs," Roberts said, "the Court vacates the judgments below and remands" to the courts of appeals. The *vacate and remand*, as it is known, had the effect of nullifying all of the lower-court decisions ruling against the challengers. The justices chose to remand, Roberts explained, because it is "more suitable than addressing the significantly clarified views of the parties in the first instance." Recognizing the "gravity of the dispute and the substantial clarification and refinement in the positions of the parties," the chief continued, the lower courts should give the parties "an opportunity to arrive at an approach going forward that accommodates petitioners' religious exercise while at the same time ensuring that women covered by petitioners' health plans 'receive full and equal health coverage, including contraceptive coverage.'"

The chief justice noted, "We anticipate that the Courts of Appeals will allow the parties sufficient time to resolve any outstanding issues between them." Reporter Mark Walsh offered a translation: "Please go away and don't come back until we have a full complement of Justices." Or, if you prefer it in haiku form: "This case is too hard / Let the appeals courts deal with / Birth control mandate."[22] The *Zubik* opinion was an effort to chart some sort of middle

---

[21]   Zubik v. Burwell, No. 14–1418, 2016 WL 2842449, at *2 (U.S. May 16, 2016).
[22]   Houston lawyer Keith Jassma reduces every Supreme Court decision to a haiku, perma.cc/KX7D-ZJNY.

ground that would obviate the need for the Court to draw the figurative line between conscience and compliance – at least for now.

In closing, Roberts noted, the "Court expresses no view on the merits of the cases. In particular, the Court does not decide whether petitioners' religious exercise has been substantially burdened, whether the Government has a compelling interest, or whether the current regulations are the least restrictive means of serving that interest." On this point, Justice Sotomayor wrote a concurring opinion, joined by Justice Ginsburg. She warned other judges not to construe the opinion as a "signal of where this Court stands." Indeed, Sotomayor scolded lower courts that have ignored "similarly explicit disclaimers in previous orders." On remand, she insisted, "the Courts of Appeals should not make the same mistake." Harvard law professor Adrian Vermeule tweeted a pithy rejoinder to Sotomayor's warning: "Rule of thumb: whoever writes separately to interpret the Per Curiam is afraid of a more obvious interpretation."[23] Noel Francisco relayed that, at least "implicitly," the justices "recognized the importance of the petitioners' arguments" in a way that the lower courts "did not."

The order was not a complete loss for the government. The last paragraph of the per curiam decision was the most critical for the Obama administration. Consistent with the Court's 2014 order in *Wheaton College*, the Court stated that nothing in *Zubik* "affects the ability of the Government to ensure that women covered by petitioners' health plans 'obtain, without cost, the full range of FDA approved contraceptives.'" The government could rely on the fact that the plaintiffs challenged the mandate as the requisite "notice" to "facilitate the provision of full contraceptive coverage going forward." Further, "because the Government may rely on this notice, the Government may not impose taxes or penalties on petitioners for failure to provide the relevant notice." In other words, because the plaintiffs have already given the government information about their insurers through the course of the litigation, the government can then work directly with those insurers to provide payments for contraceptives.

A senior DOJ official told me that "everything that matters is in the last paragraph," which gave "each side something." The religious organizations could not be subjected to penalties, because the act of filing the lawsuit itself qualifies as notice. For the government, "nothing is blocking us from providing

---

[23] Adrian Vermeule (@avermeule), Twitter (May 16, 2016), bit.ly/1XaoG5C. For a discussion of Supreme Court signaling, *see* Richard Re, *Justice Sotomayor on Signaling in the Contraception Cases*, Re's Judicata (May 17, 2016), perma.cc/3K7X-8E82; Richard Re, *Narrowing Supreme Court Precedent from Below*, 104 Geo. L.J. 921, 970 (2016); Josh Blackman & Howard M. Wasserman, *The Process of Marriage Equality*, 43 Hastings Const. L.Q. 243, 245 (2016).

the contraceptive coverage" since we already have the notice of most of the parties. Noel Francisco was "frankly thankful for" the order, because it was "far better than a loss." Given the short-handed Court, Francisco said, "it was about as good an outcome as we could have hoped for." No matter how you look at it, he told me, "it takes us from a four-to-four affirm, which is a loss, to something that is not a loss."

A few hours after the decision, President Obama sat down for an interview in the Roosevelt Room with *Buzzfeed* reporter Chris Geidner. He explained that the "practical effect" of *Zubik* is that "right now women will still continue to be able to get contraception."[24] White House Press Secretary Josh Earnest offered a similar message. "We obviously were pleased with the announcement from the Supreme Court today," he said. "It will allow millions of women across the country to continue to get the health care coverage that they need. So this obviously is an outcome that we are pleased to see."[25] Critically, the Court did not strike down the accommodation. This ruling, Earnest explained, "preserved women's access to health care and it's preserved the protections for religious liberty that this administration has prioritized."

32.5. "AN INTRICATE, NOT AT ALL EASY, ERISA CASE"

The aftermath of *Zubik* is far more complicated than the per curiam decision suggested. To understand this Obamacare compromise, perhaps regrettably, you will have to learn something about ERISA. The Employee Retirement Income Security Act of 1974 is considered a perennial tormentor on the Supreme Court's docket. Every year, the justices accept a handful of cases involving ERISA-based pensions or health insurance claims. Court watchers speculate that the chief justice will usually assign the tedious ERISA cases, known as the proverbial "dogs" of the docket, to the most junior justices, to spare more senior colleagues.[26] Justice Ginsburg recalled that in 1993, she "anxiously awaited [her] first opinion assignment, expecting – in keeping with tradition – that the brand-new justice would be slated for an uncontroversial,

---

[24] Mark Sherman, *8-Justice Supreme Court Dodges Decision on Birth Control*, ASSOCIATED PRESS (May 16, 2016), perma.cc/G59A-CB7Z.
[25] Daily Press Briefing by Press Secretary Josh Earnest, THE WHITE HOUSE (May 16, 2016), perma.cc/F7CQ-XWR2.
[26] Richard J. Lazarus, *Back to "Business" at the Supreme Court: The "Administrative Side" of Chief Justice Roberts*, 129 HARV. L. REV. 33, 47 (2015) (Chief Justice Roberts's "assignment patterns also suggest a possible practice of assigning the 'dogs' (that is, the less interesting cases) of the docket disproportionately to other, less favored Justices.")

unanimous opinion."[27] Chief Justice Rehnquist had other plans. "When the list came around," she wrote, "I was dismayed. The chief justice gave me an intricate, not at all easy, ERISA case." Justice O'Connor agreed the case was "tedious," but urged Ginsburg to write the opinion quickly and "get the job done," so she does not receive another awful assignment.[28]

In *Zubik*, the various religious nonprofits utilized three different types of insurance plans that are treated differently for purposes of ERISA: (1) insured plans, (2) self-insured plans, and (3) church plans. The differences between these plans are extremely important, and essential to understanding how the Court purported to mediate this conflict and what will happen going forward.

32.5.1. *Insured Plans*

Several of the plaintiffs use *insured plans*. With an insured plan, the employer purchases a group plan from a health insurer, such as Aetna. Aetna then manages all aspects of the group plan. The Affordable Care Act and its implementing regulations *require* Aetna to make payments for contraception coverage. If a religious employer notifies the government that it objects to the mandate and wants the accommodation, Aetna must provide contraceptive payments separately from the employer's insured plan.

In their order, the justices proposed that employers with insured plans would no longer need to object in the manner specified by the regulations. Instead, they might simply "inform their insurance company that they do not want their health plan to include contraceptive coverage of the type to which they object on religious grounds." Once the insurance company is "aware that petitioners are not providing certain contraceptive coverage on religious grounds," the same insurer can provide contraceptive payments directly to the employees.

How would this work in practice? A religious university with an insured plan tells its insurer that it would like to contract for a group plan that excludes contraceptives. The insurance company can put two and two together and realize that this request is premised on a faith-based objection. As a result, the insurer would then provide the contraceptive payments without *any* involvement whatsoever by the employer. Critically, female employees or students

---

[27] Justice Ruth Bader Ginsburg, *'A Woman's Voice May Do Some Good,'* POLITICO (Sept. 25, 2013), perma.cc/FZ6J-4TM9.

[28] *Id.*

could still use their same insurance plan, with their regular doctors, without having to apply for any additional plans.

In its supplemental brief, the solicitor general wrote that this modified accommodation would work "for employers with *insured plans* ... while still ensuring that the affected women receive contraceptive coverage seamlessly, together with the rest of their health coverage." (It will not work for self-insured plans; we will get there shortly). A senior DOJ attorney told me that the administration concluded that the Court's proposed solution would "probably work" for insured plans. It "will not be perfect," and there would probably be "leakage" where some women would not receive contraceptive coverage. But it was feasible.

The challengers *mostly* agreed that with respect to insured plans, their religious exercise is not infringed where they "need to do nothing more than contract for a plan that does not include coverage for some or all forms of contraception." But there was a critical distinction. This approach would be acceptable for the nonprofits so long as contraceptive payments were made pursuant to a totally "separate plan," and only if the women were required to opt in to such a new insurance policy before seeking any reimbursements. Noel Francisco told me that the Court's order was a "fairly general statement," and what the challengers offered in their supplemental brief was a "specific alternative that was consistent with what the Court suggested, and was also consistent with his client's religious beliefs." There is a significant gap between the parties about whether the same or separate plan is necessary. The Supreme Court's order entirely glossed over that critical difference. On remand, the lower courts will have to decide in the first instance whether providing the payments without a "separate plan" violates RFRA. More pressingly, the justices' *Zubik* decision *only* discussed insured plans.

32.5.2. *Self-Insured Plans*

Rather than purchasing a policy from an insurer, employers can choose to *self-insure*. Through a *self-insured plan*, the employer acts as its own insurer and assumes financial responsibility for its employees' health care claims. To reduce the administrative burdens, these employers will contract with a third-party administrator, who will manage the administration of the plan.

Under the Obama administration's accommodation, when a self-insured employer notifies the government that it objects to the mandate, the government then requires the third-party administrator to pay for the contraceptive coverage. The employer would not have any involvement with the payments. However, because of the technicalities of ERISA, the third-party administrator would *still* be offering the coverage under the auspices of the religious non-profit's plan. This prompted the "hijacking" metaphor that was discussed during oral arguments. If the nonprofit does not provide this notification, the third-party administrator would *still* work for the nonprofit. As the government conceded in its supplemental brief, the Court's alternative approach "would not work" for a self-insured plan, because ERISA does not authorize the government to require the third-party administrator to provide payments *independent* of the employer's plan.

A senior DOJ official told me that though the government was able to work out a solution for insured plans, they "could not really think of anything they could do differently for self-insured plans." Under ERISA, he said, "the only way to create the obligation for the insurer is to make them a plan administrator." In order for that to happen, the religious employer has to be "un-designated as the administrator." Without this initial notification from the self-insured plan, it will not work. The government "tried to brainstorm like crazy to see if there was some way to get around this," and they simply could not make it work. The solicitor general suggested a workaround: self-insured employers "could avoid any objectionable features of the regulations applicable to such plans by switching to insured plans."

An attorney for the challengers said it would be extremely problematic for a religious nonprofit to switch from a self-insured plan to an insured plan. For example, California requires insured plans to cover surgical abortions, but exempts self-insured plans. Switching is a huge burden. "It's not even close," he told me. The challengers offered their own workaround: exempt self-insured plans from the mandate altogether.

The Supreme Court's decision to remand *all* of the cases means that the lower courts will now have to grapple with whether the accommodation violates RFRA with respect to self-insured plans. Further, many of the religiously organized *for-profit* corporations use self-insured plans – as a means to avoid state law mandates – so this issue will linger even after the religious nonprofit cases are sorted out.

32.5.3. *Church Plans*

Certain nonprofit employers who are affiliated with a house of worship can use a *church plan* for their employees' insurance. These special plans, also managed by third-party administrators, are exempted from ERISA altogether. As a result, the government cannot require the third-party administrators for church plans to provide contraceptive payments. Instead, the government can only offer to *voluntarily* compensate the third-party administrator to provide this coverage – which, in this case (as with insured plans), would be entirely outside the auspices of the nonprofits' plan. As the solicitor general noted in his brief, an employer with a church plan is "relieved of its obligations," regardless of what the third-party administrator does.

The Little Sisters of the Poor utilize a church plan. Ironically enough, of the dozens of plaintiffs challenging the accommodation, the Little Sisters had the least to fear. Toward the tail end of oral arguments, Justice Alito interrupted the solicitor general. "Before you sit down, General Verrilli," he asked, "could I just ask you this informational question about this *particular* situation of the Little Sisters?" The Little Sisters hired the Christian Brothers Employee Benefit Trust as their third-party administrator. Because Christian Brothers also objected to the contraceptive mandate, Alito noted, they "will not provide the coverage." As a result, he asked, is there any way for the government to provide "contraceptive coverage for their employees" so long as the Little Sisters contract with Christian Brothers? In other words, "would the Little Sisters still be subject to fines for failing to comply?" Verrilli answered, "No, we don't think so." In five words, the solicitor general admitted that the Little Sisters would not be subject to any fines if they refused to provide the notification to the government, or if their third-party administrator declined to offer payments. In her dissent in *Wheaton College v. Burwell*, Justice Sotomayor explained that the Little Sister's "third-party administrator was [under] a 'church plan' that had no legal obligation or intention to provide contraceptive coverage."[29] Because the Little Sisters' "church plan" contracts with Christian Brothers, the government was never able to penalize the nuns for failing to comply.[30] The Court's *Zubik* order in no way impacted religious organizations with church plans.

Going forward, church plans will remain exempt from fines, but the lower courts will have to figure out what to do with *insured* plans and *self-insured plans*. The unanimous per curiam decision solved little. The parties are no closer on these issues than they were before the case was argued.

White House press secretary Josh Earnest expressed some optimism that a deal could be reached. He told reporters that in light of the remand to the

---

[29] Wheaton Coll. v. Burwell, 134 S. Ct. 2806, 2814 (2014) (Sotomayor, J., dissenting); *see* Little Sisters of the Poor Home for the Aged v. Burwell, 794 F.3d 1151, 1189 (10th Cir. 2015) ("The lack of substantial burden is especially evident when the group health plan is administered by a TPA that has made clear it will not provide contraceptive coverage….").

[30] Marty Lederman, *What to Expect from the Zubik Remand*, Balkinization (May 17, 2016), perma.cc/U62R-PSLA ("The government does not have the legal authority to require the third-party administrators (TPAs) of church plans to provide payments for contraceptive services once the employers opt out – it can only request the TPAs to do so voluntarily.")

lower courts, "there may be another process that plays out," and the administration will "continue to engage in the process."[31] Noel Francisco told me it was possible the challengers could "win it through negotiation if we can come up with a compromise with the government that everyone can live with." At the end of the day, he said, "we are not ideologues, we're just here to solve our clients' problems." One Justice Department official told me he was "hoping there is some possibility of a settlement, because it would be good for everyone." The likelihood of a settlement, he noted, may improve "after election day if it appears that there will be a ninth member of the Court, appointed by a Democratic president."

Not everyone was so sanguine about the opportunities for a settlement. One of the lawyers for the challengers said "there will be some round of negotiations with the government," but he was "not all that hopeful we will reach an arrangement. If we do, great! Problem solved. If not, then we may find ourselves back in court." Linda Greenhouse of the *New York* TIMES was far more pessimistic about the supreme mediation: "I think the court is engaged in an exercise of understandable but fruitless wishful thinking."[32]

32.6. "UNPRECEDENTED"

Stanford law professor Michael McConnell described the "resolution of the case" as "peculiar and seemingly unprecedented."[33] McConnell, who served as a federal appeals court judge from 2002 to 2009, said he had "never heard of an appellate court saying, in effect, 'No, we'd prefer not to decide the case. Go back to the lower courts and work it out.'" When parties choose not to settle the case themselves, McConnell explained, "and the courts have jurisdiction, the courts decide the legal merits." The per curiam decision scrounged together three cases to demonstrate that "this Court has taken similar action in other cases in the past."[34] But in each precedent, the justices sent the case

---

[31] *See Press Briefing, supra* note 25.

[32] Linda Greenhouse, *The Supreme Court's Wishful Thinking about Compromise*, N.Y. TIMES (May 26, 2016), nyti.ms/2axmced.

[33] Eugene Volokh, *Prof. Michael McConnell on Zubik v. Burwell (Yesterday's Supreme Court RFRA/Contraceptive Decision)*, THE VOLOKH CONSPIRACY (May 17, 2016), perma.cc/7RN9-5ZAC.

[34] Madison County v. Oneida Indian Nation of N. Y., 562 U. S. 42, 43 (2011) (per curiam) (remanding case to "address, in the first instance, whether to revisit its ruling on sovereign immunity in light of this new factual development, and – if necessary – proceed to address other questions in the case consistent with its sovereign immunity ruling."); Kiyemba v. Obama, 559 U. S. 131, 132 (2010) (per curiam) (remanding case to "determine, in the first instance, what further proceedings in that court or in the District Court are necessary and appropriate for the full

back to the lower court due to circumstanced changed by the parties. Here, the remand was caused by the justice's own instigation.

Cornell law professor Michael Dorf wrote that the order looked "very much like an attempt to perform a function that federal district judges routinely play: facilitating settlement."[35] Dorf explained that "parties and their lawyers can, through creative negotiating, craft a resolution that is better accepted than one imposed by the court." This order was, in effect, an effort by the court to encourage a rapprochement. The *New York Times* editorial page was far less charitable to the short-handed, "crippled" Court: "The court's job is not to propose complicated compromises for individual litigants; it is to provide the final word in interpreting the Constitution and the nation's laws."[36] Michael Carvin – the attorney who represented the challengers in *King v. Burwell* – joked that the justices were emulating mediation maestro Ken Feinberg. (Feinberg was appointed as the special master for the September 11th Victim Compensation Fund and the Troubled Asset Relief Program.) By all accounts, Carvin was right. David Savage, who reported on *Zubik* for the *L.A. Times*, observed that "Chief Justice John G. Roberts Jr. read a three-page statement in the court Monday, announcing what sounded like a settlement."[37]

In his interview with *Buzzfeed*, President Obama would not "speculate as to why they punted." But his "suspicion" was that "if we had nine Supreme Court justices instead of eight, we might have had a different outcome."[38] His press secretary wondered aloud if the nine would "have been able to cobble together a different agreement if Justice Scalia were still alive and serving on the bench, or if Chief Judge Garland had been confirmed as he should be to the Supreme Court?"[39] Justice Breyer rejected this speculation. He said the Court was not diminished with only eight members. "We may divide 4–4 in four or five cases," he said, or "we may not."[40] *Zubik* was a case where the Court did not divide 4–4, publicly at least.

---

and prompt disposition of the case in light of the new developments."); Villarreal v. United States, 134 S. Ct. 1939 (2014) (remanding case "for further consideration in light of the position asserted by the Solicitor General in his brief for the United States filed on March 21, 2014").

[35] Michael C. Dorf, *Supreme Court Convenes a Settlement Conference*, VERDICT (Apr. 6, 2016), perma.cc/Q7C6-8SHH.

[36] *The Crippled Supreme Court*, N.Y. TIMES (May 16, 2016), nyti.ms/20QSfKc.

[37] Savage, *supra* note 19.

[38] Ariane de Vogue, *Supreme Court Sends Obamacare Case Back to Lower Court*, CNN (May 16, 2016), perma.cc/FL2Z-J6F8.

[39] *Press briefing, supra* note 25.

[40] Sam Hananel, *Breyer Says Supreme Court Not Diminished with Only 8 Members*, ASSOCIATED PRESS (May 23, 2016), perma.cc/2KPV-7DAU.

Had the Little Sisters' case been argued and decided months earlier, Justice Scalia would have likely casted the deciding vote. While it is impossible to know how he would have voted, Justice Scalia's past dissents in *NFIB v. Sebelius* and *King v. Burwell* allow us to conclude this saga with a thought experiment: how would he have viewed the Court's unprecedented decision, because, once again, "the Affordable Care Act must be saved."[41]

32.7. (SCALIA, J., DISSENTING)

ZUBIK, ET AL V. BURWELL, ET AL

JUSTICE SCALIA, dissenting.

Dozens of religious nonprofits asked the federal courts to determine whether the contraceptive mandate's "accommodation" violated the Religious Freedom Restoration Act (RFRA). Five circuit courts of appeals addressed this question: Four ruled for the government, one ruled for the plaintiffs. This Court was asked, and agreed, to determine whether the accommodation – a regulation that had been litigated for three years – violated RFRA. That question has a *yes* or *no* answer. Alas, today's decision does not decide. Not because the Court lacks jurisdiction or because the parties have voluntarily settled the case. Rather, the majority has proposed a different accommodation altogether – one the parties never asked for, nor want.

We only have the authority to resolve the "cases" or "controversies" brought to us – we cannot create new ones. There is simply no precedent for this appellate bait-and-switch. Perhaps the majority views its decision as Solomonic. Hardly. Confronted with two parents, each laying claim to the same child, this indecisive Court would instead urge them to consider adoption.

On remand, the courts of appeals are saddled with the unenviable task of addressing this SCOTUScare fiction in the first instance. The majority insists that it "expresses no view on the merits of the cases." The concurring opinion even warns the lower courts "not to construe" the opinion as a "signal of where this Court stands." Article III judges do not need a weatherman to know which way the wind blows. The fact that the Court issued the opinion it did speaks volumes about the RFRA analysis.

First, if the government's accommodation did not impose a substantial burden on the petitioners' free exercise, then the government should

---

[41] King v. Burwell, 135 S.Ct. 2480, 2497 (2015) (Scalia, J., dissenting).

have won. Full stop. Four courts of appeals so held. That did not happen here, which can only mean that there was likely a substantial burden.

Second, if the government's accommodation was the "least restrictive means" – that is, the least burdensome approach – then the government should have won. Full stop. The D.C. Circuit so held. Again, that did not happen here. Instead, the court floated an alternative approach, which neither party completely embraced.

Third, this so-called "compromise" suggests that the government's actual accommodation violates RFRA. If a less restrictive approach exists, the government must abandon the old burdensome accommodation. The mere fact that the Court instructed the lower courts to analyze this new alternative does not relieve them of the responsibility of deciding whether the government's actual regulation violates RFRA. That is the only real "case" or "controversy" to resolve. That accommodation cannot indefinitely linger in jurisprudential purgatory.

In the end, rather than decide the difficult question, the Court punts. The lower courts, serving as our special masters, must do the dirty work of nudging the parties toward a settlement. Once again, the normal rules yield to the overriding principle of the present Court: The Affordable Care Act must be saved. Instead of confronting reality, the majority chose to hop through the looking glass to a judicial wonderland.

I dissent.

Epilogue

After nearly eight years of attacks from every conceivable direction, the Affordable Care Act is still standing, and more than twenty million Americans now rely on its expanded coverage. Though the law itself has survived, Obamacare has unraveled our political, cultural, and legal landscape. To assess Obamacare's impact, and forecast its future, we must be frank about both its significant benefits as well as the lingering costs. The former, which ACA supporters readily extoll, are far easier to quantify than the latter, which are largely unseen but ever-present.[1] This parting chapter endeavors to provide a thorough assessment of Obamacare's transformation of our gridlocked political state, divided cultural crossroads, and fragmented legal order. We conclude with a cautious look toward the future, premised on how the ACA's great expectations were altered by its unexpected implementation.

E.1. OBAMACARE AND GRIDLOCK

President Obama's proposal for health care reform began as a noble compromise. Much to the dismay of his caucus, he did not advocate for a HillaryCare-style universal healthcare system. Instead, he adapted a plan from the conservative Heritage Foundation, which was implemented by Massachusetts Governor Mitt Romney.[2] However, when it became clear the GOP would not accept any reform, the tenor of the debate changed. With a filibuster-proof sixty-vote majority in the Senate, the president decided to push forward without any Republicans votes.[3] On Christmas Eve 2009, the ACA passed

---

[1] Frédéric Bastiat, *What Is Seen and What Is Not Seen* (1848), bit.ly/29hA9S8.
[2] JOSH BLACKMAN, UNPRECEDENTED: THE CONSTITUTIONAL CHALLENGE TO OBAMACARE 8–11 (2013).
[3] Robert Farley, *Obama Says Health Plan Incorporates the Ideas of Democrats and Republicans – Mostly False*, POLITIFACT (Sep. 9, 2009), perma.cc/4GT5-P3CV.

the Senate by a vote of sixty to thirty-nine. Shortly before the vote, Minority Leader Mitch McConnell warned that "this fight is long from over." Citing the "party-line votes," he promised, "My colleagues and I will work to stop this bill from becoming law." His caucus would do just that, even after the bill was signed by the president.

This lack of bipartisanship was unprecedented. All of the landmark social welfare and civil rights laws enacted in the twentieth century were passed with bipartisan support, often through messy political compromises and bargaining. The Social Security Act of 1935 was supported by 77 Republicans in the House, joined by 288 Democrats. In the Senate, 15 Republicans joined 60 Democrats. The Civil Rights Act of 1964 passed the Senate because of a coalition of 27 Republicans and 44 Democrats united to break a segregationist-led filibuster. The Social Security Amendments of 1965, which created Medicaid and Medicare, passed the House by a vote of 307–116, with 70 Republicans voting in favor. This monumental health care legislation cleared the Senate by a vote of 70–24; 13 Republicans crossed the aisle. The Voting Rights Act of 1965 was passed with broad bipartisan support, as was the Civil Rights Act of 1968. In 1990, the Americans with Disabilities Act passed with 90% agreement in the House and Senate.

In one respect, the president's decision to proceed only with Democratic support can be viewed as a legitimate countermeasure to the steadfast GOP opposition. "When I first came into office," President Obama recalled, "the head of the Senate Republicans said, 'my number one priority is making sure President Obama's a one-term president.'"[4] But this defense only goes so far. It is true that the Republicans, as a bloc, refused to support the ACA. But the fact of the matter is that the 2008 election did not provide a mandate to enact far-reaching healthcare reform. A January 2009 *Pew* survey found that the "top priority" issues for voters were (1) the economy; (2) jobs; (3), terrorism; (4) social security; (5) education; (6) energy; and finally, at (7) and (8), Medicare and health care.[5] Chuck Schumer of New York, the second-highest-ranking Democrat in the Senate, lamented that his party squandered their electoral majority in 2009 by focusing on health care.[6] "Unfortunately, Democrats blew the opportunity the American people gave them" in 2009, Schumer said. "We took their mandate and put all our focus on the wrong

---

[4] Glenn Kessler, *When Did McConnell Say He Wanted to Make Obama a 'One-Term President'?*, Wash. Post (Sep. 25, 2012), perma.cc/37HA-KS3X.
[5] *Economy, Jobs Trump All Other Policy Priorities in 2009*, Pew Research Center (Jan. 22, 2009), perma.cc/9QTN-9MES.
[6] Kathleen Hunter, *Democrats Erred by Acting on Health Care in 2010, Schumer Says*, Bloomberg Politics (Nov. 24, 2014), perma.cc/DX5H-E832.

problem – health care reform." He admitted that "the plight of uninsured Americans and the hardships created by unfair insurance company practices certainly needed to be addressed. But it wasn't the change we were hired to make" in the 2008.

Beyond forgoing opportunities to advance other legislative agendas – such as immigration or environmental reform – the decision to force the ACA on a party-line vote was a contributing factor to the stultifying gridlock during the final six years of the Obama presidency. The "one-term president" comment was indeed made by Senator Mitch McConnell, but not in early 2009. Rather, he said it on the eve of the midterm elections in October 2010, six months *after* the ACA passed. McConnell linked his opposition to Obama's re-election with the GOP's goal of eliminating Obamacare. "If our primary legislative goals are to repeal and replace the health [care] bill," he said, "the only way to do all these things it is to put someone in the White House who won't veto any of these things."

In July 2016, President Obama lamented the "hyperpartisanship" surrounding healthcare reform. He wrote that "through inadequate funding, opposition to routine technical corrections, excessive oversight, and relentless litigation, Republicans undermined ACA implementation efforts."[7] The president's criticism is well founded, but ignores his own role in institutionalizing this gridlock. It was hubristic to think that after enacting a monumental law, without any bipartisan buy-in, opponents would simply fall in line. As history played out, Republicans had no problem undermining a law they had no part in enacting and felt no attachment to. Senator Max Baucus, chairman of the Finance Committee that drafted the healthcare bill, "fret[ted]" about the ACA's origin. "It is my belief," he said in December 2013, "that for major legislation to be durable, sustainable, it has to be bipartisan. I mean, one party can't jam legislation down the other party's throat. It leaves a bitter taste."[8]

King v. Burwell, perhaps more than any other case, illustrates this "bitter taste." Let's assume for a moment that members of both parties originally intended for subsidies to be made available on state *and* federal exchanges. In the process of compiling a 3,000-page bill, a draftsman inadvertently wrote that subsidies were limited to an "exchange established by the state." Once that "glitch" was discovered after the bill was signed into law, the same majority of Congress could easily enact a one-sentence amendment, making clear

[7] Barack Obama, *United States Health Care Reform Progress to Date and Next Steps*, JAMA (Jul. 11, 2016), bit.ly/29Riqia.
[8] Sheryl Gay Stolberg, *Baucus, Conflicted Architect of Health Overhaul, Is Obama's Pick for China*, N.Y. TIMES (Dec. 18, 2013), nyti.ms/29rGdYI.

that subsidies are available on either exchange. Now, back to reality. The Senate bill, which contained the "established by the state" provision, was never meant to be the final version of the bill, and was supposed to be cleaned up in conference. But because of Scott Brown's election, Democrats were forced to rely on the draft version of the bill. Republicans, who had opposed the process from the outset, had no incentive to pass a one-sentence bill to provide the subsidies. Instead, they saw *King* as a chance for a mulligan on ending Obamacare. As a result, the Court was confronted with resolving a question that would decide the fate of the health care exchanges.

The ACA's polarized history complicates its future. Going forward, public health discussions will be inextricably interwoven with partisan rancor. University of Chicago health law professor Harold Pollack lamented that "so many promising [health care] delivery reforms are tinged by their association with President Obama's signature domestic policy achievement."[9] In 2017, and beyond, any effort to unravel health care and politics will prove unavailing. Future reforms of the ACA will be permanently entrenched along Obamacare's battle lines.

E.2. CONSCIENCE AND ACCOUNTABILITY

During oral arguments in *Hobby Lobby*, Justice Kennedy was perplexed that the Department of Health and Human Services had exempted certain corporations from the contraceptive mandate – totally apart from any religious objection – but refused to excuse the religiously-inspired craft store. "What kind of constitutional structure do we have," Kennedy asked, "if the Congress can give an agency the power to grant or not grant a religious exemption based on what the agency determined?" With a "First Amendment issue of this consequence," he continued, "shouldn't we indicate that it's for the Congress, not the agency, to determine" who receives religious exemptions?

One of the most remarkable aspects of the contraceptive mandate is that Congress did not create *any* religious exemptions. In contrast, Congress carved out a specific "religious conscience exemption" to excuse people from the individual mandate.[10] Members of certain "religious sect[s] or divisions" or "health care sharing ministr[ies]" did not have to pay the penalty. However, with the law Congress voted on, *no* religious groups are excused. Not houses

---

[9] Harold Pollack, *The Politicization of Everything after Health Reform*, THE INCIDENTAL ECONOMIST (Aug. 9, 2014), perma.cc/N26M-YXYM.

[10] 26 U.S.C. § 5000A(d)(2).

of worship, not religious charities like the Little Sisters of the Poor, and not religious for-profit corporations like Hobby Lobby. Only after the first round of regulations were houses of worship exempted. But initially, religious nonprofits were still required to pay for the emergency birth control. After more outrage, the various accommodations were proposed. But in the first iteration, the Obama administration was content to force an order of nuns to pay for Plan B.

As we discussed in Chapter 3, Senator Mikulski was deliberately obtuse when introducing the Women's Health Amendment, focusing exclusively on treatments such as mammograms and cancer screenings – services that no employer would object to. During the floor debates, Mikulski insisted that the bill would not cover "abortion services," but resisted any effort to define what services would be covered. Vague, scattered mentions of "family planning" in the legislative history meticulously avoided any specifics. Instead, Senator Mikulski was content to write a blank check to the administrative state, knowing full well how the agencies would implement the mandate.

Had Senator Mikulski made clear what *all* employers would be mandated to pay for – including emergency contraceptives – and that there would be *no* statutory religious exemptions for any group, pro-life Democrats would not have supported it. Certainly, Congress would have thought that requiring religious organizations to pay for contraceptives would warrant an exemption. The contraceptive mandate, and how it has been implemented, bears no resemblance to the debate held over the Women's Health Amendment in 2009. Once again, the public was misdirected during the debate over the ACA, and the administration then took executive action to implement its own policy agenda.[11]

While it is always impossible to prove a counterfactual, we do have one data point. In March 2012, shortly after the contraceptive-mandate controversy arose, Senator Roy Blunt (R-MO) proposed a bill that would have let employers refuse to pay for contraceptives based on their "religious belief and moral conviction."[12] It was voted down 51–48 – far short of the 61-vote bloc that approved the Women's Health Amendment. However, joining the

---

[11] For the lawyers reading this, my argument is not premised on whether courts should defer to executive branch agencies when interpreting the phrase "preventive care." Rather, the question is whether HHS has the authority, in the words of Justice Kennedy, "to grant or not grant a religious exemption based on" its own judgments. This is a question that only Congress can decide. That Congress was silent, and expressed no awareness of potential free-exercise issues, strongly suggests that HHS lacked the power to pick and choose which groups would be burdened. *See* Josh Blackman, *Gridlock*, 130 Harv. L.Rev. __ (2016); Brief for the Cato Institute et al., Zubik v. Burwell (Jan. 11, 2016), bit.ly/29eaJEc.

[12] Matt Negrin, *Senate Blocks Blunt's Repeal of Contraception Mandate*, ABC NEWS (MAR. 1, 2012), abcn.ws/1Ol7zdA.

Republicans in support of the bill were two pro-life Democratic Senators: Bob Casey and Joe Manchin. Had those two understood the import of the Mikulski Amendment in 2009, it could have never been added to the ACA.

In an interview given shortly before his retirement, Solicitor General Verrilli expressed surprise at the contraceptive mandate litigation.[13] "There's a lot of ferment out there," he said. "More than I had anticipated." Verrilli observed that the "accommodation the government is trying to work out to provide contraceptive coverage to employees of religious nonprofits seems like it's a big effort to respect religion and to respect the employee's health." That it has "drawn such sharp criticism," he said, "personally surprises me." From Verrilli's perspective, the executive branch was "working very hard in these circumstances to try and find a way that protects religious exercise, religious liberty, and protects the rights of employees." The White House's efforts were well-intentioned, but misguided. This was a sensitive judgment that could only be made by the diverse legislative branch, and not the cloistered unitary executive.

E.3. POTUS AND SCOTUS

From its birth, Obamacare was mired in lawfare. Moments after President Obama signed the ACA into law, twenty-six states challenging its constitution-altiy. More than fifty religious for-profit corporations sought to invalidate the contraceptive mandate. More than one hundred religious universities, chari-ties, and dioceses contested the accommodation to the contraceptive mandate. The Competitive Enterprise Institute (CEI) litigated two separate challenges to halt the subsidies on the federal exchange. The House of Representatives challenged the delay of the employer mandate and payments made to insur-ance companies without an appropriation. Over the past six years, nearly every controversial aspect of Obamacare found its way before a federal judge, with four appeals making it to the Supreme Court.

It is impossible to untangle the political and legal valences of these cases. During oral arguments in *NFIB v. Sebelius*, Justice Scalia asked attorney Paul Clement if all "twenty-six states opposing [the ACA] have Republican governors and all of the states supporting it have Democratic governors?" His former law clerk cagily replied, "There's a correlation." Michael Greve, who helped initiate CEI's litigation against the IRS rule, promised that the "bastard," Obamacare, "has to be killed as a matter of political hygiene,"

---

[13]   Tony Mauro & Marcia Coyle, *Cases and Controversies: Verrilli on Privacy, Voting Rights and Doing Penance*, NAT'L. LAW J. (June 27, 2016), perma.cc/7D4T-EZ9E.

and he did not care whether it was done by a "court some place or the United States Congress." The bulk of the contraceptive-mandate cases were filed by socially conservative groups. The House of Representative's suit against the Obama administration was authorized without a single Democratic vote.

Yet, ACA supporters have been far too quick to dismiss these challenges as purely partisan attacks. This book, which paid careful attention to the arguments developed by scholars and attorneys, demonstrates that there is legal merit to each of these cases, regardless of which way the Court ultimately ruled (or will rule). When the challenge to the individual mandate was filed, the professoriate scoffed at the notion that Congress lacked the power to require individuals to engage in commerce. The ensuing battle of ideas over the next two years proved that the precedents did not cut one way or the other. The chief justice, though he saved the law by rewriting a penalty into a tax, agreed that Congress's commerce power could not compel economic activity.

ACA advocates insisted that the phrase "established by the state" unambiguously provided subsidies on the federal exchange. Though the Court ultimately ruled for the government, all of the justices agreed that the challengers' "arguments about the plain meaning of [the provision] are *strong*." With respect to the contraceptive mandate, critics ridiculed the idea that a corporation could exercise religion. Ultimately, only two justices would dissent from this position. Later, the administration was convinced that its accommodation to the contraception mandate imposed no burden on free exercise. This position could not prevail with a majority of the justices, as their *Zubik* order implicitly recognized that there had to be a better way for the government to achieve its interests.

There is a distinct risk in tarring any challenge to the ACA as a policy dispute masquerading as a legal controversy. President Obama, through his statements made while the ACA cases were pending, injected a new degree of politics into already highly charged cases. (See our discussion in Chapter 27.) On April 2, 2012, days after *NFIB v. Sebelius* was argued, Obama said, "Ultimately, I'm confident that the Supreme Court will not take what would be an *unprecedented*, extraordinary step of overturning a law that was passed by a strong majority of a democratically elected Congress." The next day, Obama repeated that it "would be *unprecedented* for a Supreme Court to overturn laws passed by an elected Congress." The president added that he had "enormous confidence" that "that the Court is going to *exercise its jurisprudence carefully* because of the profound power that our Supreme Court has."

While many critics accused the president of intimidating the Court, and the chief justice in particular,[14] I think his remarks had a very different effect. He prejudged any decision against ACA as being motivated only by nonlegal considerations: invalidating the mandate would be *reckless*, rather than *careful* jurisprudence. That is, there can be no sound, neutral principle on which the individual mandate was unconstitutional. Reasonable minds can and do differ on difficult constitutional questions, but the president's remarks discredit that debate.

Fast-forward to 2015 and *King v. Burwell*. The president said there was "*not a plausible legal basis*" for striking [the IRS rule] down," and he was "not going to anticipate *bad law*." He continued, "If the Supreme Court made a ruling that said the folks who [use] federal exchanges don't get the tax credits, what you would end up seeing is millions of people losing their health insurance." If the justices determined that the plain text of the statute did not permit subsidies on the federal exchange, according to the president, they would now bear the blame of people losing their health insurance. In later remarks, after the case was argued, Obama said he was "optimistic that the Supreme Court will play it *straight* when it comes to the interpretation." The implication is that a ruling against the government would not be straight – that is, *crooked*, or to borrow a favorite catchphrase from the vernacular of Donald J. Trump, *rigged*.[15] The president's decision to target the court, personalize it against the justices, and preemptively polarize their decision delegitimizes this independent branch of government.

Outgoing Solicitor General Donald Verrilli reflected on the confrontational relationship between President Obama and the Supreme Court.[16] Citing the "dysfunction in the legislative process," Verrilli said, "the executive branch has had to decide how it's going to use executive power in order to try to protect and advance the country's interests. That's created conflict." The actions taken by a "progressive administration," he noted, were "being evaluated by a court whose majority probably started out with a degree of skepticism." The

---

[14] *See* Randy E. Barnett, Foreword to UNPRECEDENTED: THE CONSTITUTIONAL CHALLENGE TO OBAMACARE at xi (2013) ("After this case was submitted to the Supreme Court, many on the left – from President Obama to Patrick Leahy, the chairman of the Senate Judiciary Committee … vociferously waged what I called a 'campaign of disdain' against the conservative justices in general, and Chief Justice Roberts in particular, in an effort to influence and even intimidate one or more of the justices to capitulate.").

[15] Josh Blackman, *Donald Trump's Dangerous Attack on U.S. District Judge Gonzalo Curiel and the "Rigged" Federal Judiciary*, JOSH BLACKMAN'S BLOG (May 27, 2016), perma.cc/F238-T5M4.

[16] Richard Wolf, *Obama's Supreme Court Lawyer Ends 'Intense' Tenure*, USA TODAY (Jun 21, 2016), perma.cc/G3PX-PADC.

president's remarks about pending cases, whether aimed at that skepticism or serving ulterior purposes, had the inevitable effect of creating more conflicts. Verrilli recalled that this tension harkened back to an era very familiar to students of constitutional law. "It's been a remarkable stretch," he said. "I can't think of a time since the 1930s when the role of the [Supreme] Court in the life of the nation and in the unfolding of the political process has been as central as it's been in the last five years." President Obama, like President Roosevelt before him, shares in the blame in ratcheting up the politicization of the judiciary. But one way or the other, his efforts were successful. After the Chief's decision in *King v. Burwell*, Verrilli concluded, "the debate [over Obamacare] is effectively over."[17] He's right.

E.4. GREAT EXPECTATIONS

Since its enactment, more than 20 million Americans have gained coverage through the Affordable Care Act.[18] The uninsured rate of Americans has dropped from 48.6 million in 2010 to 28.6 million in 2016.[19] On the federal and state exchanges, there were 8 million enrollments in 2014,[20] 11.7 million in 2015,[21] and 12.7 million in 2016.[22] Beyond the exchanges, enrollments for Medicaid and the Child Health Insurance (CHIP) have increased significantly.[23] Before the ACA went into effect, there were 57.8 million monthly enrollments. The ranks increased to 64.2 million in 2014, 71.4 million in 2015, and 72.5 million in 2016.

A complete measure of the ACA's success, however, cannot be limited to its results in the abstract. Like any other public policy, the actual outcomes must be compared to its predicted outcomes. In 2015, President Obama boasted that the ACA "is working not just as intended, but better than intended."[24] Despite

---

[17] Ari Melber, *Top Obama Lawyer: Obamacare Fight Over, Muslim Ban Unlikely*, NBC NEWS (Jun. 17, 2016), perma.cc/ND3J-P87Z.

[18] Peter Sullivan, *Obamacare Enrollment Drops to 11.1M*, THE HILL (Jun. 30, 2016), perma.cc/D9D6-47ND.

[19] *Early Release of 2015 National Health Interview Survey* at 2-3, CDC (May 2016), bit.ly/29Filft.

[20] *Health Insurance Marketplace: Summary Enrollment Report (10/1/2013-3/31/2014)*, HHS (May 1, 2014), bit.ly/29rHSxC.

[21] *Health Insurance Marketplace 2015 Open Enrollment Period (11/15/2014-2/15/15)*, HHS (Mar. 10, 2015), bit.ly/29iJ3xM.

[22] *Health Insurance Marketplace 2016 Open Enrollment Period (11/1/15-2/1/16)*, HHS (Mar. 11, 2016), bit.ly/29hu35a.

[23] *Total Monthly Medicaid and CHIP Enrollment*, KAISER FAMILY FOUNDATION (1/2014-3/2016), perma.cc/4MYF-QXDD.

[24] Robert Pear, *House G.O.P. Again Votes to Repeal Health Care Law*, N.Y. TIMES (Feb. 3, 2015), nyti.ms/29i1sts.

these important expansions of coverage, the ACA is *far* underperforming its original expectations.

a. The Incomplete Medicaid Expansion

The Affordable Care Act's planners expected the Medicaid expansion to take effect in all fifty states. Because the federal government could not force a state to enter the expansion, the ACA threatened to withhold *all* of a refusenik state's Medicaid budget. This cudgel, its drafters thought, would be a sufficient incentive for all states to participate. Seven justices thought otherwise. While Justices Scalia, Kennedy, Thomas, and Alito voted to invalidate the entire Medicaid expansion, finding it unconstitutionally coercive, Chief Justice Roberts – joined by Justices Breyer and Kagan – rewrote the expansion. Now states had a choice of whether to enter the expansion.

Thirty-one states and the District of Columbia agreed to participate. Nineteen states did not. As a result, Medicaid and CHIP enrollments have lagged far behind initial estimates. An April 2010 report from the Centers for Medicare and Medicaid Services (CMS) Chief Actuary predicted that the expansion would add 23 million new enrollees.[25] A March 2010 report from the Congressional Budget Office offered a more conservative estimate of 17 million new enrollees.[26] As of March 2016, with nineteen states staying out, the number is only 14 million.[27] (The 14 million Medicaid enrolees represent the overwhelming majority of the 20 million people who gained coverage through the ACA.)

Millions of low-income citizens who otherwise would be eligible for the Medicaid expansion cannot benefit in non-participating states. For example, between January 2014 and March 2016, New York's Medicaid enrollment increased from 5.6 million to 6.4 million. During the same time in Texas, which did not enter the expansion, the Medicaid enrollment ticked upward slightly from 4.4 million to 4.7 million. The ACA does not provide subsidized insurance for people who would be eligible for the *new* Medicaid, because Congress anticipated that people in that income bracket would be eligible for the gratis government health care. As a result, perversely, if a citizen in one of the non-expansion states did not qualify for the *old* threshold for Medicaid, but did qualify for the *new* threshold, she cannot receive any subsidies on

[25] *Estimated Financial Effects of the "Patient Protection and Affordable Care Act,"* at Table 2, CMS Chief Actuary (Apr. 22, 2010), bit.ly/29bWBvm.
[26] Letter to House Speaker Nancy Pelosi from Douglas W. Elmendorf, director of the Congressional Budget Office at Table 4 (Mar. 20, 2010), bit.ly/299LsX9.
[27] *Medicaid Enrollment, supra* note 32.

HealthCare.gov. Yet, that citizen's federal tax dollars are being used to subsidize the Medicaid expansion in other states. For example, a person who qualified for the expanded Medicaid in Texarkana, Arkansas would receive neither Medicaid nor subsidies on HealthCare.gov if she moved across the border to Texarkana, Texas.[28]

This fragmented result – entirely contrary to the ACA's design – is another unintended but entirely foreseeable consequence of the Supreme Court's decision to rewrite the expansion. The joint dissent in *NFIB v. Sebelius* presciently observed, "If that destabilizing political dynamic, so antagonistic to a harmonious Union, is to be introduced at all, it should be by Congress, not by the Judiciary."[29]

b. Enrollments on the ACA Exchanges

Chapters 14 and 18 recounted the stunning turnaround of HealthCare.gov, as 8 million customers enrolled by April 2014. In light of the botched launch of the website six months earlier, this result was nothing short of miraculous. However, the enrollments on the exchanges lag far, far behind government estimates. To assess these gaps, Table E.1 provides forecasts from the Centers for Medicare and Medicaid Services (CMS) in 2010 – before the ACA passed the House – and from the Congressional Budget Office (CBO) in 2010, 2012, 2013, 2014, 2015, and 2016.[30] These predictions are contrasted with the actual number of enrollees, and the number of enrollees who continued to pay their premiums throughout the year.

In 2014, Obamacare met the CBO's original goal from 2010, as well as the average forecast, with 8 million enrollments. This was truly a red-letter year for the ACA, demonstrating that there was strong demand for the exchange policies. After 2014, however, the demand has leveled off. In 2015, there were 11.7 million enrollments, far fewer than the CBO's average forecast of 13.25 million. From 2010 through 2015, CBO consistently predicted that enrollments would spike up in 2016, with 20–24 million enrollments. For example, in its February 2014 report, CBO wrote that "more people are expected to respond to the new coverage options, so enrollment is projected to increase *sharply* in 2015 and 2016."

---

[28] Annie Lowrey, *In Texarkana, Uninsured and on the Wrong Side of a State Line*, N.Y. Times (Jun. 8, 2014), nyti.ms/29tNOmK.

[29] Nat'l Fed'n of Indep. Bus. v. Sebelius, 132 S. Ct. 2566, 2676 (2012).

[30] *Chief Actuary, supra* note 34. *Elmendorf Letter, supra* note 35. *Estimates for the Insurance Coverage Provisions of the Affordable Care Act Updated for the Recent Supreme Court Decision*

TABLE E.1. *Forecasts of enrollment of nonelderly people on exchanges (in millions)*

	2014	2015	2016
Estimates			
CMS (4/2010)	16.9	18.6	24.8
CBO (3/2010)	8.0	13.0	21.0
CBO (7/2012)	9.0	14.0	23.0
CBO (5/2013)	7.0	13.0	22.0
CBO (2/2014)	6.0	13.0	22.0
CBO (6/2015)	–	–	20.0
CBO (3/2016)	–	–	10.0
CBO Average	7.5	13.25	19.7
Actual			
Confirmed Enrollees	8.0	11.7	12.7
Confirmed and Paid Enrollees	6.7	9.3	10.0 (estimate)

The surge never happened. In March 2016, CBO drastically downgraded its forecast by half to 10 million enrollees. As of July 2016, there have been 12.7 million confirmed enrollees on the exchange – beating the revised 10 million figure, but falling significantly short of the expected 20 million. Brian Blase, of the free-market Mercatus Center, observed that the "magnitude of how wrong the initial predictions appear to be should cause legislators and the public to approach future estimates of the impact of major legislation cautiously."[31] Contrary to the forecasts, he wrote, "people [found] exchange plans so much less attractive than experts assumed when the law was passed," and even after two years of the marketplace being open. The ACA's expansion of coverage to 20 million Americans is still far short of even its most conservative estimate of more than 30 million Americans gaining coverage.

As weak as these enrollment numbers are, the actual numbers of customers who continued to pay their policies for nine consecutive months is *even lower*. In 2014, only 6.7 million out of 8 million enrollees paid their premiums

at Table 3, CBO (Jul. 2012), bit.ly/29cNCq1. *Estimate of the Effects of the Affordable Care Act on Health Insurance Coverage* at Table 1, CBO (May 2013), bit.ly/29jA4LU. *Updated Estimates of the Insurance Coverage Provisions of the Affordable Care Act* at Table B-2, CBO (Feb. 2014), bit.ly/29rayUo. *Budgetary and Economic Effects of Repealing the Affordable Care Act* at Table 3, CBO (Jun. 2015), bit.ly/29hBchG. *Federal Subsidies for Health Insurance Coverage for People Under Age 65* at Table 1, CBO (Mar. 2016), bit.ly/29mASAk. These forecasts will be cited throughout the Epilogue.

[31] Brian Blase, *Examining Plummeting Obamacare Enrollment, Part I*, FORBES (Oct. 19, 2015), perma.cc/7PNW-Y63Q.

through September.[32] This 19% drop-off puts the 2014 figures *well below* the CBO forecasts. In 2015, only 9.3 million out of the 11.7 million paid their premiums through September.[33] More than 25% of enrollees failed to consistently pay their bills. In 2016, only 11.1 million out of 12.7 million paid their premiums through March, with an expected 10 million to continue paying through September.[34] Factoring in customers who actually continue to pay for coverage, the state and federal risk pools are barely at 50% of their anticipated size.

The underpayment problem is even more severe because savvy shoppers have learned to game the system: they sign up, receive treatment, and cancel coverage. The ACA was designed to only allow people to sign up at specific times to frustrate this opportunism. In 2009, CBO wrote that in addition to the individual mandate, the ACA's "annual open enrollment period" would tend to mitigate ... adverse selection."[35] In his brief to the Supreme Court, the solicitor general explained that restricting enrollment to a fixed period "would reduce opportunities for healthy people to wait until illness struck before enrolling."[36]

However, in order to boost raw enrollment numbers, the Obama administration consistently delayed signup deadlines.[37] According to the *New York Times*, HHS created more than thirty "special enrollment" windows, many of which were only mentioned in "informal 'guidance documents.'"[38] For example, customers were allowed to sign up late due to unspecified "exceptional circumstances," "serious medical condition[s]," and – the most capacious standard – "other situations determined appropriate" by HHS.

The first special enrollment period came shortly after the pivotal March 31, 2014 deadline. Customers were allowed to continue signing up in April. In addition, the Johnny-come-latelies were excused from the individual mandate's penalty.[39] *The Hill* reported that the "move essentially nullifies the

---

[32] Charles Gaba, *2014 Graphs*, ACASIGNUPS.NET (Nov. 14, 2014), perma.cc/7BC2-A4C8.

[33] *September 30, 2015 Effectuated Enrollment Snapshot*, CMS (Dec. 22, 2015), perma.cc/Q75U-PC3C.

[34] Sullivan, *supra* note 26.

[35] Letter to Senator Evan Bayh from Douglas W. Elmendorf, Director of the Congressional Budget Office (Nov. 30, 2009), bit.ly/23j3lcX.

[36] Reply Brief for the Respondents (Severability) at 12, *NFIB v. Sebelius* (Mar. 2012), bit.ly/1UVeQUn.

[37] Robert Pear, *Insurers Say Costs Are Climbing as More Enroll Past Health Act Deadline*, N.Y. TIMES (Jan. 9, 2016), nyti.ms/29rJkzI.

[38] *Id.* Robert Pear, *Proof Needed to Enroll in Health Plan Post-Deadline*, N.Y. TIMES (Feb. 24, 2016), nyti.ms/29koSKK.

[39] Elisa Viebeck, *HHS Widens O-Care Penalty Exemptions*, THE HILL (May 2, 2014), perma.cc/9UT7-7N8F.

month of April for the purposes of enforcing the mandate."[40] Until the very end, the goalposts kept moving to ensure as many people as possible were able to get covered.

In February 2015 – after the regular enrollment period concluded – the Obama administration created another special enrollment period. To qualify, customers had to demonstrate that they were subject to the penalty in 2014 and "first became aware of, or understood the implications of" it when preparing their 2014 return. In other words, people who went uninsured in 2014, and missed the enrollment period in 2015, were able to sign up late because they were unaware that they had to pay a penalty until they did their taxes.

The National Association of Insurance Commissioners complained that "consumers are not required to provide documentation to substantiate their eligibility for a special enrollment period."[41] Kaiser Permanent, a large health insurer, said that the potential for abuse "poses a significant threat to the affordability of coverage, and to the viability" of the exchanges. In 2016, the Government Accountability Office (GAO) concluded that HHS "has assumed a passive approach to identifying and preventing fraud."[42] The agency's *honor system* policy "allowed an unknown number of applicants to retain coverage, including subsidies, they might otherwise have lost, thus producing higher costs for the federal government."

Leading insurance companies submitted regulatory comments to HHS, warning that the extra signup windows risked destabilizing the insurance markets.[43] Blue Cross Blue Shield explained that "individuals enrolled through special enrollment periods are utilizing up to 55 percent more services than their open enrollment counterparts." Aetna added that "many individuals have no incentive to enroll in coverage during open enrollment, but can wait until they are sick or need services before enrolling and drop coverage immediately after receiving services … less than four months" later. United Healthcare, which will exit from most of the Obamacare exchanges in 2017, explained that more than 20% of its customers signed up during a special enrollment period, and they used 20% more health care than those who enrolled during the regular enrollment period.[44] Anthem told the government that these modifications of the deadlines were "harming the stability of the exchange markets

[40] *Id.*
[41] Pear, *supra* note 46.
[42] *CMS Should Act to Strengthen Enrollment Controls and Manage Fraud Risk*, GAO (Feb. 2016), bit.ly/1QdQEOv
[43] Pear, *supra* note 46.
[44] Phil Galewtiz, *Why United Healthcare's Exit from Obamacare Matters*, Money (Apr. 20, 2016), perma.cc/5NJU-P8JW.

and resulting in higher premiums." The Obama administration's sign-up-as-many-people-as-possible approach has eliminated one of the key constraints embedded in the ACA and reduced the force of the individual mandate.

c. Suspending the Individual Mandate

Because insurers could no longer discriminate against customers with pre-existing conditions – due to the guaranteed-issue and community-rating provisions – customers could free-ride and "wait to purchase health insurance until they needed care."[45] As the United States explained to the Supreme Court, this free-riding "would drive up premiums and threaten the viability of the individual insurance market."[46] The individual mandate was designed to solve this problem. President Obama explained the simple economics behind the mandate during a February 2014 radio appearance: "If you can afford [insurance], and you don't get it, you're going to pay a fee. So you might as well just go ahead and get health insurance instead of paying a penalty with nothing to show for it."[47]

Solicitor General Verrilli warned the Supreme Court that the ACA operating without an individual mandate would "create an adverse selection cascade," the dreaded death spiral, "because healthy individuals would defer obtaining insurance until they needed health care, leaving an insurance pool skewed toward the unhealthy." Without the mandate, Verrilli wrote, "premiums would increase significantly" and "the availability of insurance would decline." This implosion, the government explained, was "exactly the opposite of what Congress intended in enacting the Affordable Care Act." The mandate was essential for nudging the uninsured into the health care market. Yet, the mandate would never go into effect as designed. The government's numerous exemptions from the mandate's penalty risked the very parade of horribles the government warned about.

In addition, the revenue generated from the penalties was designed to offset the cost of expanding coverage. In 2015, the penalty for an adult was $325, and $975 for a household.[48] Table E.2 provides CBO's projections of penalty payments (in billions) that the individual mandate was expected to generate.

[45] 42 U.S.C.A. 18091(a)(2)(I).
[46] Brief for Respondents (Severability) at 7, NFIB v. Sebelius (Jan. 2012), bit.ly/1YzOcDs.
[47] Michael D. Shear, *Stiffer Tax Penalties Used to Spur Insurance Enrollment*, N.Y. TIMES (Feb. 13, 2015), nyti.ms/29fiAxD.
[48] Matthew Rae, *The Cost of the Individual Mandate Penalty for the Remaining Uninsured*, KAISER FAMILY FOUNDATION (Dec. 9, 2015), perma.cc/YEZ3-3S6U.

TABLE E.2. *Forecasts of Penalty Payments by Uninsured Individuals (in billions)*

	2015	2016	2017	Three-Year Total	Eleven-Year Total
CBO (7/2012)	3.0	6.0	7.0	16.0	55.0
CBO (5/2013)	2.0	4.0	5.0	11.0	45.0
CBO (2/2014)	2.0	4.0	5.0	11.0	52.0
CBO (6/2015)	1.5	4.0	4.0	9.5	43.0
CBO (3/2016)	1.5	3.0	3.0	7.5	38.0

Like the exchange enrollment numbers, the collected penalty revenue has lagged far behind original estimates. But there is an incongruence to these forecasts. The number of people who have gained covered on the ACA exchange is far *fewer* than originally forecasted: 10 million instead of 20 million. As a result, more people who otherwise would have obtained coverage, should now be subject to the mandate's penalty. The revenue should be far *greater* than originally predicted. But the exact opposite happened. As time progressed, and it became clear that the ACA would fall far short of its projected enrollment numbers, CBO downgraded its forecast for the penalty payments. For example, shortly after the Supreme Court upheld the ACA in *NFIB v. Sebelius*, CBO expected the individual mandate would generate $3 billion in 2015, $6 billion in 2016, and $7 billion in 2017. In February 2014, CBO revised its forecast for that year to $2 billion. Ultimately, it was even less than that. John A. Koskinen, the Commissioner of the Internal Revenue Service, reported to Congress that 7.5 million taxpayers paid an average of $200 in penalties, totaling $1.5 billion in penalties for 2014.[49] CBO's most recent forecast further lowered its expectations. The budget office predicted a flat $3 billion in revenue in 2016 and 2017, and shrank the eleven-year total to $38 billion. These numbers do not add up.

Some of this discrepancy is due to fact that fewer business than expected have not cancelled employer-provided plans. "Employers have not 'dumped' employees to the extent that some people feared and predicted," said Ceci Connolly of the Alliance of Community Health Plans. But that explains only part of the gap.[50] A more complete explanation for this incongruence considers the effect of the executive's actions, which have unexpectedly excused millions of taxpayers from the penalty. In June 2014, CBO

---

[49] Letter from John A. Koskinen, Commissioner of Internal Revenue Service to Members of Congress (Jul. 17, 2015), bit.ly/29gU2pE.

[50] Paul Demko, *Obamacare's Sinking Safety Net*, POLITICO (Jul. 13, 2016), perma.cc/G9PF-C7CW.

wrote that its downward forecast for penalty payments was due "in part to regulations issued since September 2012 by the Departments of Health and Human Services and the Treasury."[51] As a result, there is "an increase in [its] projection of the number of people who will be exempt from the penalty."[52]

According to the IRS commissioner, 12.4 million taxpayers claimed an exemption from the mandate for 2014.[53] Koskinen explained that many taxpayers claimed an exemption because "health care coverage [was] considered unaffordable." This is not one of the exemptions carved out by Congress in the ACA.[54] Rather, this was a consequence of the president's executive action in December 2013, which waived the individual mandate's penalty for taxpayers who told the government that a new policy was too expensive. Recall from our discussion in Chapter 13 that applicants were on the honor system, and their request was not subject to any verification.

At the time, ACA supporters downplayed any impact the waivers would have on the markets. MIT Economist Jonathan Gruber said it was "not an imminent threat to the individual mandate" because it would only be used for "extreme hardships."[55] This was originally viewed as only a temporary measure. However, four months later, it was extended. In a brief footnote in a seven-page technical bulletin, the government quietly noted that the fix would be extended for *two more years* until October 1, 2016.[56] Once again, applicants were on the honor system, and only had to tell the government they "find other options to be more expensive."

The *Wall Street Journal* warned that the never-ending hardship exemption was a "regulatory loophole" that "sets a mandate non-enforcement precedent." It becomes more and more difficult to eliminate the exemptions for people who cannot afford policies. "The longer it is not enforced," the *Journal* noted, "the less likely any President will enforce it."[57] Kathleen Sebelius defended the waiver to the House Ways & Means Committee. "The hardship exemption was part of the law from the outset," she said. "There was a specific rationale

[51] *Payments of Penalties for Being Uninsured Under the Affordable Care Act: 2014 Update*, CBO (Jun. 2014), bit.ly/29d6DbK.
[52] *Id.*
[53] Letter from John A. Koskinen, commissioner of Internal Revenue Service to Members of Congress at 5 (Jan. 8, 2016), bit.ly/29a2STG.
[54] 26 U.S.C. § 5000A(e).
[55] Jacqueline Klimas, *Few Will Use Obamacare Hardship Exemption, Analysts Say*, WASH. TIMES (Mar. 23, 2014), bit.ly/29lLK13.
[56] *Insurance Standards Bulletin Series – Extension of Transitional Policy through October 1, 2016*, CMS (Mar. 5, 2014), bit.ly/1ZZgO7O.
[57] *Obamacare's Secret Mandate Exemption*, WALL ST. J. (Mar. 12, 2014), on.wsj.com/29hvOzi.

there, and it starts with the notion that if you can't afford coverage you are not obligated to buy coverage."[58] But as we discussed in Chapter 13, the ACA carved out specific income requirements to qualify a hardship exemption. It does not count if Obamacare's mandates made insurance too expensive. Obamacare itself cannot be the hardship.

The shortfall in individuals paying the penalty can also be attributed to the president's "if you like your plan, you can keep your plan" *administrative fix*. Through this November 2013 policy, the federal government allowed insurance companies to continue offering plans that did not comply with the ACA's strict coverage requirements. Individuals who remained on these grandfathered plans, which did not provide "minimum essential coverage," would be excused from the individual mandate's penalty. There were risks to allowing people to remain on old plans. Jim Donelon, president of the National Association of Insurance Commissioners, warned that the administration's decision "threatens to undermine the new market, and may lead to higher premiums and market disruptions in 2014 and beyond."[59] *Moody's Investor Service* forecasted that the administrative exemption would result in "exposure to adverse selection" and was "likely to negatively affect earnings in 2014."[60] Harvard economist David Cutler was more cautious. "If it turns out to be a delay of a year, then we can work through that," he told Megyn Kelly on *Fox News*.[61] "If it becomes a permanent situation that people who are healthier stay away and people who are sicker go into the exchanges, that becomes a very big problem. That could be the beginning of a death spiral. That is, you could have a situation where people in the exchanges are very unhealthy people with high premiums."

The fix was originally slated to provide temporary relief for one year. However, that would have resulted in millions of plans being cancelled in the fall of 2014, on the eve of the midterm elections. The president would not let that happen. HHS announced that noncompliant plans could be grandfathered through the end of 2016.[62] Insurers were now able to renew noncompliant policies as late as October 1, 2016, so coverage could continue past the next presidential election into 2017. The *New York Times* observed this action

---

[58] *Sebelius vs. Accuracy*, WALL ST. J. (Mar. 12, 2014), on.wsj.com/29ISYua.

[59] Brett, LoGuirato, *Insurance Commissioners Have No Idea How Obama's Obamacare 'Fix' Is Going to Work*, BUSINESS INSIDER (Nov. 14, 2013), perma.cc/5E78-JS8A.

[60] *US Insurers See Low Enrollment in Affordable Care Act, a Credit Negative*, ADVISOR MAGAZINE (Nov. 19, 2013), perma.cc/QBN7-ZFYA.

[61] Avik Roy, *Obama to Nation: If You Like Your Plan, You Can Keep Your Plan (At Least Until The Next Election)*, FORBES (Nov. 15, 2013), bit.ly/29tVwoj.

[62] Elisa Viebeck, *New O-Care Delay to Help Midterm Dems*, THE HILL (Mar. 3, 2014), perma. cc/8T9Y-RRNF.

"essentially stall[s] for two more years one of the central tenets of the much-debated law, which was supposed to eliminate what White House officials called substandard insurance and junk policies."[63]

The Hill reported that the delays would avert the "firestorm for Democratic candidates in the last, crucial weeks before Election Day" 2014.[64] Former-House Majority leader Eric Cantor charged that the president "is once again trying to hide the effects of Obamacare. It is not fair to pick and choose which parts of an unpopular law should be enforced."[65] Senate Republican leader Mitch McConnell said the delay was "a desperate move to protect vulnerable Democrats in national elections later this year."[66] Indeed, in announcing the policy, HHS said it was crafted "in close consultation" with three Senate Democrats in vulnerable seats: Mary L. Landrieu of Louisiana, Mark Udall of Colorado, and Jeanne Shaheen of New Hampshire.[67] Only Shaheen was reelected.

Extending the grandfathering of noncompliant plans, health care industry consultant Robert Laszewski observed, "tends to undermine the sustainability of Obamacare" because it reduces incentives for customers to purchase policies on the exchanges.[68] And more likely than not, these grandfathered customers are younger and healthier, because they were able to obtain insurance even before the ACA's guaranteed-issue requirement kicked in. The "administrative fix" has inhibited the exchanges from attracting the young and healthy members who were essential to stabilizing the risk pools. Alan Murray of CareConnect, a New York healthcare plan, observed that after two years, "everybody who's in the individual market on average is not as healthy as we were led to believe."[69]

The government has not announced how many people benefited from the administrative fix, but we can hazard a guess. A McKinsey report estimated that 3.7 million Americans were still using noncompliant plans that otherwise would have been cancelled under the ACA.[70] An October 2013 Gallup poll found that "[n]early two in three uninsured Americans say they will get insurance by Jan. 1, 2014, rather than pay a fine as mandated by the Affordable Care

[63] Robert Pear, Consumers Allowed to Keep Health Plans for Two More Years, N.Y. Times (Mar. 5, 2014), nyti.ms/29fjJFk.

[64] Viebeck, supra note 73.

[65] Pear, supra note 74.

[66] Id.

[67] HHS 2015 Policy Standards Fact Sheet, CMS (Mar. 5, 2104), perma.cc/C3LE-45E4.

[68] Pear, supra note 74.

[69] Id.

[70] Demko, supra note 61.

Act (ACA), while one in four say they will pay the fine."[71] If we assume that
2/3 of the 3.7 million people whose plans were grandfathered, would have
otherwise purchase insurance the exchange, the ranks would have increased
by another 2.5 million customers. Assuming the other one-fourth chose to pay
the penalty – which averaged $200 in 2014 – it would have generated nearly
$200,000,000 in revenue.

These were only two in a series of ad hoc, unpublicized waivers the Obama
administration issued. The *New York Times* reported that the White House
"has already granted … 30 types of exemptions."[72] The myriad exemptions
have skewed the risk pools with older, and sicker, customers, which further
drives up premiums, making future policies even less attractive.[73] By exempting millions of Americans from the individual mandate, the Obama administration disturbed the fragile balance Congress designed to prevent an adverse
selection death spiral.

E.4. Delaying the Employer Mandate and the Cadillac Tax

The ACA's employer mandate requires businesses with more than 50 workers
to pay a fine of $2,160 for each uninsured employee. In July 2013, the Obama
administration announced that the employer mandate would not be enforced
in 2014. Seven months later, the administration further postponed the mandate for 2015. Businesses with between 50 and 100 employees were excused
from the mandate entirely. Businesses with more than 100 employees would
be excused from the penalty so long as 70% of their employees were covered.
Starting in 2016, businesses that cover 95% of its workforce will not have to
make the payments. (Chapter 13 discussed how none of these requirements
were consistent with the statute.) Additionally an unknown number of waivers
were granted to favored employers.

The Congressional Budget Office's downward-sloping forecasts, represented in Table E.3 reflect this tinkering with the employer mandate. Initially,
the mandate was expected to generate $24 billion by 2016. After the president's
executive actions, it generated $0 through 2016. Additionally, the expected
revenue from 2014 through 2019 dropped from $65 billion to $45 billion.

---

[71] Frank Newport, *Two in Three Uninsured Americans Plan to Buy Insurance*, GALLUP (Sep. 30, 2013), bit.ly/29i3gTl.

[72] Robert Pear, *White House Seeks to Limit Health Law's Tax Troubles*, N.Y. TIMES (Jan. 31, 2015), nyti.ms/29pjY46.

[73] Kate Pickert, *Obama Offers Partial 'Fix' To 'You Can Keep It' Health Care Promise*, TIME (Nov. 14, 2013), perma.cc/X7LB-T5AZ. Henry J. Aaron, *Obamacare Policy Jiu-Jitsu*, BROOKINGS INSTITUTION (Nov. 14, 2013), perma.cc/38QQ-WPNU.

TABLE E.3. *Forecasts of Penalty Payments by Employers (in billions)*

	2014	2015	2016	2017	2018	2019	Five-Year Total
CBO (7/2012)	4	9	11	12	14	15	65
CBO (5/2013)	0	10	11	14	15	16	66
CBO (2/2014)	0	0	11	14	15	16	56
CBO (6/2015)	0	0	9	13	15	16	53
CBO (3/2016)	0	0	0	9	16	20	45

TABLE E.4. *Forecasts of "Cadillac" Tax Payments (in billion)*

	2018	2019	2020	2021	2022	Five-Year Total
CBO (7/2012)	11	18	22	27	32	110
CBO (5/2013)	5	9	11	14	18	57
CBO (2/2014)	5	9	11	14	18	57
CBO (6/2015)	3	6	7	9	11	36
CBO (3/2016)	0	0	3	7	9	19

Far fewer employers will be hit with the penalty and have an incentive to provide their workers with insurance.

The ACA's Cadillac tax imposes a 40% excise tax on generous health insurance plans starting in 2018. Popular among economists, the provision would have created an incentive for firms to reduce health care costs. Unpopular among workers – particularly labor unions with gold-plated insurance plans – the excise tax did not stand a chance. Despite President Obama's initial objection, in December 2015 he approved of Congress's two-year delay of the Cadillac tax. As a result, the excise is not scheduled to go into effect until 2020. As we discussed in Chapter 29, it is unlikely this unpopular provision will ever go into effect. This delay has greatly altered the revenue the Cadillac tax was expected to generate, as illustrated by Table E.4.

Under the CBO's initial estimate, employers were expected to pay $110 billion in taxes for Cadillac plans between 2018 and 2022. This payment was a pivotal offset in order for the ACA to achieve a budget-neutral scoring. Now, with the delay of the Cadillac Tax, CBO only projects the excise will generate $19 billion through 2022. This number could very likely drop to $0 if the Cadillac Tax is perpetually delayed.

When assessing a law that transformed nearly 20% of the U.S. economy, it is not enough to focus only on how many people gained coverage; we must also consider the costs of achieving this goal. The Affordable Care Act has fallen far short of its great expectations.

E.5. THE ONCE AND FUTURE HEALTH CARE REFORM

To paraphrase Mark Twain, reports of Obamacare's death spiral have been greatly exaggerated. Indeed, there is not one "Obamacare," but fifty-one separate markets. Some states are thriving under the ACA. According to a 2016 *McKinsey* study, the individual marketplaces in Washington, California, and Vermont posted positive profit margins above 5%.[74] However, insurers in forty-one states lost money. Leading the pack were Montana, Nebraska, and Utah, where insurers on the individual market had negative profit margins below 20%. Blue Cross Blue Shield of North Carolina lost $400 million in 2014 and 2015.[75] UnitedHealth lost nearly $1 billion in two years, and announced that it would leave most of the ACA exchanges it operates in 2017.[76] As more insurers drop out, there is less competition, and premiums increase. Other companies that plan to remain in the markets are concerned. "We continue to have serious concerns about the sustainability of the public exchanges," Mark Bertolini, the CEO of Aetna, said. He pointed out that the risk pool was older and sicker than expected.[77]

Perhaps no state drew closer to the death spiral's event horizon than Alaska. All insurers, except for Blue Cross Blue Shield, decided to exit Alaska's individual market for 2017. However, state regulators rejected Blue Cross's significant rate increase, which the insurer insisted was necessary to cover its costs. If a compromise could not be reached, 23,000 Alaskans were at risk of suddenly losing their insurance. To avert catastrophe, the conservative state created a $55 million emergency fund – through an excise tax on group insurance providers – to further subsidize enrollments on the individual market.[78] Calamity was averted, temporarily at least.

Alaska is the canary in the coal mine for the ACA. In 2017, Alabama, and rural counties in Kentucky, Tennessee, Arizona, and Oklahoma, will have

---

[74] *2014 Individual Market Post-3R Financial Performance*, McKinsey on HealthCare (Feb. 2016), perma.cc/EW2E-YX7E.

[75] Demko, *supra* note 61.

[76] Paul R. La Monica, *UnitedHealthcare to Exit Most Obamacare Exchanges*, CNN Money (Apr. 19, 2016), bit.ly/29kiRkk.

[77] Peter Sullivan, *Aetna Voices 'Serious Concerns' on Obamacare Sustainability*, The Hill (Feb. 1, 2016), perma.cc/9V7L-TRPJ.

[78] Rachan Pradhan, *Alaska Scrambles to Prevent Obamacare Collapse*, Politico (Jun. 10, 2016), perma.cc/4NS5-J8TV.

only insurer.[79] As a result, costs will continue increase. The Kaiser Family Foundation (KFF) forecasted that in 2017, premiums will rise on average 10%, double last year's rate hike of 5%.[80] The ACA's difficulties become more severe in 2017 when the *reinsurance* and *risk corridor* programs expire.[81] Reinsurance reimburses insurers that enroll sicker customers. Risk corridors limit how much insurers can lose and gain on the marketplace. Both of these temporary measures designed to cushion the ACA during its infancy go away. "Something has to give," explained Larry Levitt of KFF. "Either insurers will drop out or insurers will raise premiums."[82]

In July 2016, President Obama recognized that some areas have "struggled" with "only 1 or 2 issuers," which leads to higher premiums.[83] To solve this lack of competition, he urged Congress to "revisit a public plan to compete alongside private insurers." A few days earlier, candidate Hillary Clinton also endorsed the public option "to reduce costs and broaden the choices of insurance coverage for every American."[84]

One of the most critical debates over the enactment of the ACA concerned the public option. The House of Representative's health care bill would have allowed customers to purchase a Medicare-like plan on the exchanges. Republicans charged that "forcing free market plans to compete with these government-run programs would create an un-level playing field and inevitably doom true competition." They argued that a public option was only a pit stop on the road to "a single government-run program controlling all of the market."[85] The insurance companies – whose support was essential to enact reform – also opposed the public option. Ron Williams, the then-chief executive of Aetna, said that with a public option, "you have in essence a player in the industry who is a participant in the market, but also is a regulator and a referee in the game."[86] Senator Joe Lieberman – an Independent

[79] Anna Wilde Mathrews & Stephanie Armour, *Insurance Options Dwindle in Some Rural Regions*, WALL ST. J. (May 15, 2016), on.wsj.com/29z5Eqp.

[80] Phil Galewtiz, *Study Projects Sharper Increases in Obamacare Premiums for 2017*, KAISER HEALTH NEWS (Jun. 15, 2016), perma.cc/H24D-CJBC.

[81] Eric Pianin, *Obamacare Insurers Received More than $15 Billion in Taxpayer 'Bailouts,'* FISCAL TIMES (May 25, 2016), perma.cc/CVW2-FL36.

[82] Peter Sullivan, *Insurers Warn Losses from Obamacare Are Unsustainable*, THE HILL (Apr. 15, 2016), perma.cc/KT4M-6FCY.

[83] Obama, *supra* note 10.

[84] Hillary Clinton, *Health Care: Affordable Health Care Basic Human Right*, HILLARYCLINTON. COM, perma.cc/93W2-L99R.

[85] Timothy Noah, *Obama: Soft on Health Insurance?*, SLATE (Mar. 6, 2009), perma.cc/KY22-MMQA.

[86] *Aetna CEO: Public Insurance Option 'Wrong Way to Go,'* PBS NEWSHOUR (Aug. 18, 2009), perma.cc/UK9D-CJGW.

from Connecticut who caucused with the Democrats – announced he would filibuster the bill unless it eliminated the public option.[87] "To put this government-created insurance company on top of everything else," he said, "is just asking for trouble." Needing Lieberman's support to clear the sixty-vote threshold, the public option, was ultimately cut from the Senate bill.

With economic calamities on the horizon the public option is now part of the game plan to bail out Obamacare. After only three years, the ACA's intricate planning – designed to ensure the viability of the health markets – has already proven unsustainable. Economist Herbert Stein's rule applies forcefully to the ACA: "If something cannot go on forever, it will stop."

On June 28, 2012, Chief Justice Roberts announced that "the Court does not express any opinion on the wisdom of the Affordable Care Act. Under the Constitution, that judgment is reserved to the people." Later that day, President Obama confidently predicted that "twenty years from now, the nation will be better off because of having the courage to pass this law and persevere." Ultimately, it will be the American people – those who supported the law *and* those who didn't – who will decide if Obamacare is *unbreakable* or if it will be *undone*. For now, the fate of the ACA is simply *unwritten*.

After joining me on this journey, I must leave you with a cliff-hanger. The final installment in this Obamacare trilogy will chronicle what happens to the ACA in 2017 and beyond.

---

[87] Manu Raju, *Lieberman: I'll Block Vote on Reid Plan*, POLITICO (Oct. 27, 2009), https://perma. cc/8CJL-VJXC.

Acknowledgments

This book would not have been possible without the help of many dear friends and colleagues.

First, I profited greatly from interviews with virtually all of the participants in the *King* litigation, including Jonathan H. Adler, Michael Cannon, Michael A. Carvin, Thomas M. Christina, Gregory Conko, Michael S. Greve, Sam Kazman, Thomas P. Miller, and Yaakov Roth. Second, I gained unique insights into the contraceptive mandate litigation through interviews with Mark Rienzi, Noel J. Francisco, and others attorneys with the Becket Fund for Religious Liberty and Alliance Defending Freedom. From Bancroft PLLC, I thank Erin E. Murphy. This book also profited immensely from off-the-record interviews with current and former administration officials, lawyers for the state attorneys general, and attorneys on Capitol Hill.

Third, I am grateful to several health policy experts, namely Nicholas Bagley, Seth J. Chandler, Mark Hall, and Timothy S. Jost, for providing me with an education of the ins and outs of Obamacare. Fourth, I am indebted to the kind souls who took the time to provide comments on this probably-too-long manuscript: Brian Blase, Matt Bowman, Simon Lazarus, Greg Lipper, Adam Liptak, Jordan Lorence, Andrew M. Grossman, Charlie Savage, Julie Silverbrook, Elizabeth Slattery, David B. Rivkin, Jr., and Yaakov Wolbe.

Fifth, I am very grateful to the South Texas College of Law and my colleagues on the faculty for their support and confidence in me during the process of writing this book. I thank Jonathon Austin, Catherine Diktaban, and Rebecca Marshall for providing excellent research assistance. Sixth, I feel fortunate to be an adjunct scholar at the Cato Institute, and am thankful for the support from David Boaz, Roger Pilon, John Samples, and my dear friend Ilya Shapiro.

Seventh, I am indebted to the excellent representation of Don Fehr of Trident Media Group and the insightful editing of Matt Gallaway and his colleagues at Cambridge University Press. This book would not have come together without their experience and support.

Eighth, I am very grateful to the followers of JoshBlackman.com and @JoshMBlackman. When I launched my blog and twitter account in September 2009, I had no idea what I was doing. Seven years, ten thousand blog posts, and thirty thousand tweets later, these forums have allowed me to exchange ideas, develop thoughts, and hone my writing. Without these online channels, I could have not have written *Unprecedented* or *Unraveled*.

Finally, and most importantly, I owe a debt that I can never repay to my amazing family, Mom, Dad, and Alix, I am only where I am today because of what you have done for me. To Militza, thank you so much for your support, patience, and insights throughout this entire process. I love you all.

Index